ENVIRONMENTAL POLICY AND POLITICS

Covering global threats such as climate change, population growth, and loss of biodiversity, as well as national, state, and local problems of environmental pollution, energy use, and natural resource use and conservation, *Environmental Policy and Politics* provides a comprehensive overview of U.S. policymaking processes, the legislative and administrative settings for policy decisions, the role of interest groups and public opinion in environmental politics, and the public policies that result. It helps readers understand modern environmental policy and its implications, including the need for a comprehensive and integrated approach to problem-solving.

New to the Seventh Edition

- Each chapter includes the latest information about environmental challenges and governmental responses to them, with extensive citation of sources and websites that allow students to find the most recent studies and reports.
- Each chapter covers key political and policy decisions through early 2017, including presidential appointments, budgetary decisions, major legislative initiatives, and congressional actions.
- Each chapter introduction includes new statements about learning objectives to facilitate student understanding of key concepts and their applications, arguments advanced over environmental challenges and policies, and the goals and methods of environmental policy analysis.
- Chapters compare decisions about major environmental, energy, and natural resource policies among the presidential administrations of George W. Bush, Barack Obama, and Donald Trump, to the extent possible.
- Each chapter's case studies have been changed or updated to include the latest developments and examples that should improve their appeal to students. These include controversies over the Keystone XL and Dakota Access pipelines, the EPA's Clean Power Plan and new fuel economy standards, new policies on toxic chemicals, the role of environmental and energy policies in the 2016 elections, changes in the nation's reliance on energy resources, standards for evaluating environmental and resource policies, and the Paris Agreement on climate change.
- Summaries of scientific studies, government reports, and policy analyses have been updated throughout the text to reflect the most current research and information in the field.
- All chapters include revised discussion questions and new suggested readings.
- The writing and flow of material have been improved throughout to make the chapters more accessible and useful to students.

Michael E. Kraft is Professor of Political Science and Public Affairs Emeritus and Herbert Fisk Johnson Professor of Environmental Studies Emeritus a̶ ̶ ̶ ̶ ̶ ̶ ̶ ̶ ̶ ̶ Green Bay.

Environmental Policy and Politics

SEVENTH EDITION

MICHAEL E. KRAFT

University of Wisconsin–Green Bay

Routledge
Taylor & Francis Group

NEW YORK AND LONDON

Published 2018
by Routledge
711 Third Avenue, New York, NY 10017

and by Routledge
2 Park Square, Milton Park, Abingdon, Oxon, OX14 4RN

Routledge is an imprint of the Taylor & Francis Group, an informa business

First edition published by Pearson Education, Inc. 1996
Sixth edition published by Pearson Education, Inc. 2014, and Routledge 2016

Library of Congress Cataloging-in-Publication Data
Names: Kraft, Michael E., author.
Title: Environmental policy and politics / Michael E. Kraft, University of
Wisconsin-Green Bay.
Description: Seventh edition. | New York : Routledge, 2018.
Identifiers: LCCN 2017005813| ISBN 9781138218789 (hardback) | ISBN
9781138218796 (pbk.) | ISBN 9781315437057 (ebook)
Subjects: LCSH: Environmental policy--United States. | United States--Politics
and government--2001-2009. | Pollution--Government policy--United States.
Classification: LCC GE180 .K73 2018 | DDC 363.700973--dc23
LC record available at https://lccn.loc.gov/2017005813

ISBN: 978-1-138-21878-9 (hbk)
ISBN: 978-1-138-21879-6 (pbk)
ISBN: 978-1-315-43705-7 (ebk)

Typeset in Sabon and Univers
by Saxon Graphics Ltd, Derby

MIX
Paper from
responsible sources
FSC   FSC™ C013985
www.fsc.org

Printed in the United Kingdom
by Henry Ling Limited

BRIEF CONTENTS

CONTENTS

PREFACE

The 2016 election put Republican Donald Trump in the White House and promised to bring about significant and possibly radical changes in U.S. environmental policy. We will know what those changes are over the next several years after the Trump administration and the new Congress put their stamp on public policies and the agencies that administer them. There is no question, however, that the direction of environmental policy will change greatly from what we have seen in the eight years of the Obama administration. At this writing, we do not know whether the Trump administration will resemble Ronald Reagan's from the 1980s or that of George W. Bush of the 2000s, or whether it will differ from each of these earlier Republican administrations. Certainly, with both the House and Senate in Republican hands, there will be fewer checks on what the new president will be able to do.

President Barack Obama's first term yielded a mixed record on the environment as he struggled with a lagging economy, bitterly contested health care reform, and ongoing wars in Iraq and Afghanistan. His second term was far more productive, but he was forced to rely largely on administrative actions because he faced a divided Congress that was not very supportive on most issues. In his last two years, both houses of Congress were held by Republicans, providing even less support for the president's environmental and energy agenda.

Despite these political obstacles and policy disappointments, the Obama administration pursued a strikingly different environmental policy from that of President George W. Bush's administration. Environmentalists strongly criticized the Bush White House for its reluctance to tackle global climate change, for its misuse or disregard of science, and for environmental protection and natural resource policies that strongly favored economic development over public health and resource conservation. President Obama charted a new path of action. It was evident in his appointees to important administrative posts, such as Environmental Protection Agency (EPA) administrator, energy secretary, interior secretary, and science adviser in both his first and second terms; his budgetary proposals; and dozens of major regulatory actions on energy, environmental protection, and natural resource use.

Although the president failed to gain congressional approval for climate change policy, he did negotiate an historic agreement with the auto industry to raise vehicle fuel efficiency standards to 54.5 miles per gallon by 2025. By 2016, he did much the same for heavy-duty trucks, vans, and buses. In addition, his EPA mounted major regulatory actions on air pollution and greenhouse gas emissions (the Clean Power Plan), and the Interior and Energy Departments sought to reverse the Bush priorities by emphasizing use of renewable energy resources and pursuing a more balanced approach to management of public lands. His major policy actions and those of previous administrations are discussed throughout the text.

Most of this was good news for environmentalists, who generally cheered the administration's new policy directions even as they criticized those presidential initiatives with which they disagreed, such as expanded offshore oil and gas development and an initially equivocal position on the contested Keystone XL pipeline that was to bring Canadian tar sands oil to the United States; eventually the president vetoed a congressional measure to approve the pipeline. Yet environmental economists and policy analysts of all persuasions would add that the time is ripe for even more significant changes in U.S. environmental policies despite the 2016 election results.

Many of these policies, including the Clean Air Act, Clean Water Act, and Endangered Species Act, are nearly 50 years old, and have remained substantially unchanged since their initial approval despite questions about their effectiveness, efficiency, and equity that date back to the late 1970s. Dozens of major studies have offered trenchant criticisms of the policies and have identified promising new approaches and methods. Indeed, many policy changes already have been adopted at the state and local level, where innovation and experimentation, often through community sustainability action, are far easier than they are at the national level of government, and through an array of administrative and judicial actions that required no approval by Congress. Nonetheless, more substantial policy changes are needed to deal effectively with twenty-first-century environmental challenges.

Future achievements depend on securing essential public and political support at a time of competing policy priorities, designing policies that best fit the problems faced, and implementing them effectively. This would be true even if the federal and state governments were flush with funds. But addressing these needs is even more critical in light of continuing federal budgetary deficits.

If anything, environmental challenges at the global level are even more daunting. The world must learn how to respond creatively and effectively to the risks of global climate change and many other equally complex and difficult issues such as the destruction of forests and soils, the loss of biological diversity, and a surging human population that will likely rise to nearly 9.9 billion by 2050. No responsibility of government and society will be more difficult over the next generation than accommodating the level of economic development needed to meet human needs and aspirations while simultaneously averting devastating effects on the environmental systems that sustain life.

In industrialized nations such as the United States, this new environmental policy agenda makes clear the imperative of integrating environmental protection with other social and economic activities, from energy use and transportation to agriculture and urban planning. We can no longer afford to think of environmental policy as an isolated and largely remedial activity of cleaning up the residue of society's careless and wasteful habits. Emphasis must be placed on prevention of future harm through redesign of economic activities around the concept of sustainability and sustainable development.

Achieving such goals requires that governments work closely with the private sector in partnerships that can spur technological innovations while avoiding the protracted conflicts that have constrained environmental policy in the past. This does not mean that tough regulation should be abandoned when it is necessary to achieve environmental goals. It does signal, however, the need to supplement regulation with other strategies and policy tools such as information disclosure, market-based incentives, and collaborative decision making that promise to speed the realization of those goals or significantly lower the costs of getting there.

Whether governments and other organizations will succeed in resolving environmental problems of the twenty-first century ultimately will depend on public understanding, support, and actions. A new generation of environmental policies will require significant social and behavioral changes. This is evident if one merely thinks of energy use in homes and our choices in transportation and food. But demands on individuals and businesses will go far beyond these concerns. Meeting these needs is possible only if people educate themselves about the issues, and work cooperatively for environmental sustainability. To be effective over the next several decades, environmentalists will need to hone their political skills and forge broader alliances with new constituencies around common interests in sustainability.

New to This Edition

This seventh edition of *Environmental Policy and Politics* has been updated and revised throughout.

- Each chapter includes the latest information about environmental challenges and governmental responses to them, with extensive citation of sources and websites that allow students to find the most recent studies and reports.
- Each chapter covers key political and policy decisions through early 2017, including presidential appointments, budgetary decisions, major legislative initiatives, and congressional actions.
- Each chapter introduction includes new statements about learning objectives to facilitate student understanding of key concepts and their applications, arguments advanced over environmental challenges and policies, and the goals and methods of environmental policy analysis.
- Chapters compare decisions about major environmental, energy, and natural resource policies among the presidential administrations of

George W. Bush, Barack Obama, and Donald Trump, to the extent possible.

- Each chapter's case studies have been changed or updated to include the latest developments and examples. These include controversies over the Keystone XL and Dakota Access pipelines, the EPA's Clean Power Plan and new fuel economy standards, new policies on toxic chemicals, the role of environmental and energy policies in the 2016 elections, changes in the nation's reliance on energy resources, standards for evaluating environmental and resource policies, and the Paris Agreement on climate change.
- Summaries of scientific studies, government reports, and policy analyses have been updated throughout the text to reflect the most current research and information in the field.
- All chapters include revised discussion questions and new suggested readings.
- The writing and flow of material have been improved throughout to make the chapters more accessible and useful to students.

Like the previous editions, the seventh edition offers a succinct overview and assessment of U.S. environmental policy and politics. It differs from other texts in several respects. It encourages students to judge environmental problems for themselves, by reviewing evidence of the risk they present to human health and well-being as well as to ecological processes. It summarizes an extensive collection of scientific studies, government reports, and policy analyses to convey the nature of environmental problems, progress in dealing with them, and the implications of keeping or revising present policies. It covers global threats such as climate change and loss of biodiversity as well as national, state, and local problems of environmental pollution, energy use, and natural resource use and conservation.

The book offers what most readers would want in any text of this kind. It describes major U.S. environmental and natural resource policies, their origins, the key policy actors who have shaped them, their achievements and deficiencies, and proposals for policy change. It offers a thorough yet concise coverage of the U.S. policymaking process, the legislative and administrative settings for policy decisions, and the role of interest groups and public opinion in environmental politics. Rather than offering separate chapters on each environmental problem (air, water, land, toxics, endangered species, energy use, and the like), it organizes the substantive policy material into two related clusters of issues dealing with environmental protection and natural resources, the latter including energy resources.

Chapter 1 introduces the subject of environmental policy and places it within the political and economic trends of the early twenty-first century that affect that policy. It also sets out a modest analytic framework drawn from policy analysis and environmental science that helps connect environmental policy to the political process. Chapter 2 follows up on this introduction by reviewing scientific evidence that speaks to the nature of various environmental problems, the risk they present to the public, and the policy implications.

Chapter 3 helps set the scene for the rest of the book by describing the U.S. policymaking process in broad terms, with a focus on agenda-setting and policy change, and the role of policy entrepreneurs in these processes. The chapter also identifies the main features of U.S. government and politics at federal, state, and local levels. Chapter 4 uses the concepts introduced in Chapter 3 to trace the evolution of environmental policy and politics from the earliest days of the nation through the emergence of the modern environmental movement and political reactions to it.

The core of the book, Chapters 5 and 6, turns to the basic character of U.S. environmental, energy, and natural resource policies. Chapter 5 discusses the leading environmental protection statutes administered by the U.S. EPA and their continuing evolution. It also describes and assesses the EPA's work in implementing these policies, from its staffing and budgetary resources to its relationship with the states to the legal and procedural intricacies of standard-setting, rule-making, and enforcement actions.

Chapter 6 offers comparable coverage of energy and natural resource policies. The chapter outlines the history of efforts to design national energy policies in the last several presidential administrations, the adoption of new national energy policies in 2005 and 2007, and continuing efforts through early 2017, particularly as these decisions affect climate change. It also describes the evolution of natural resource policies and the many continuing conflicts between natural resource protection and economic development.

Chapter 7 revisits the major critiques of environmental protection and natural resource policies discussed in Chapters 5 and 6, and outlines new directions for policy change in the twenty-first century.

Finally, Chapter 8 looks to the future and to the need for global policy action as well as efforts at the state and local levels and within the business community to foster sustainability. It describes the remaining policy agenda for the early twenty-first century, including the goal of sustainable development, and describes the leading international environmental policy actors and institutions as well as limitations on their policymaking capacity.

A book like this has to cover a great deal of technical material on environmental problems and public policies. I have tried to make it all as current as possible, faithful to the scientific literature, and also understandable. If in some instances the text has fallen short of these goals, I hope readers will alert me to important omissions, misinterpretations, and other deficiencies. I can be reached at kraftm@uwgb.edu.

ACKNOWLEDGMENTS

In preparing a book manuscript one incurs many debts. The University of Wisconsin–Green Bay and its Department of Public and Environmental Affairs supplied me with essential support for the early editions of this text. The organization of the book and its content owe much to my teaching there. I am grateful to my undergraduate and graduate students over the years, whose interest in environmental policy and politics gave me the opportunity to discuss these issues at length with concerned and attentive people as well as the chance to learn from them. I also have benefited immeasurably from the individuals whose analyses of environmental politics and policy, and U.S. government and politics, make a book like this possible. I hope the extensive references in the text adequately convey my reliance on their scholarship and my gratitude to them.

Reviewers of previous editions of the text, including Craig Allin of Cornell College, Robert Duffy of Colorado State University, Larry Elowitz of Georgia College and State University, Daniel Fiorino of American University, Robert E. Forbis Jr. of Texas Tech University, Lilias Jones Jarding of Oglala Lakota College, Daniel Lipson of SUNY New Paltz, Leigh Raymond of Purdue University, and D. G. Webster of Dartmouth College, offered thoughtful suggestions for revision, and I greatly appreciate their assistance. Naturally, I assume responsibility for any errors in the text that remain.

This book is dedicated to the memory of my parents, Louis and Pearl Kraft. Their compassion, generosity, and caring for their fellow human beings embodied the social concerns that today are reflected in an environmental ethic. They also provided me and my brothers with the opportunity to grow up in a stunning environment in southern California and experience the wonders of the desert, mountains, and ocean that exist in such close proximity in that part of the country.

CHAPTER 1

Environmental Problems and Politics

Between 2008 and 2013, gasoline prices in the United States periodically spiked to a record high of over $4 a gallon, reflecting economic growth around the world that consumes vast quantities of oil and other fossil fuels. Politicians responded to public outcries over the high prices by searching for ways to ease the pain. Many sought to increase domestic oil supplies (which they argued would reduce prices) by greatly expanding oil and gas exploration and drilling on public lands, in offshore areas, and in the Arctic. Others argued for construction of the Keystone XL pipeline to bring Canadian tar sands oil to the United States, and thereby both add to oil supplies and reduce dependency on oil imported from less friendly nations. At the same time, U.S. natural gas supplies soared and prices plummeted, relieving at least some concern about rising energy costs and their impact on the nation's economic competitiveness. Indeed, the now abundant natural gas supplies have sparked a renaissance in U.S. manufacturing, and helped to hasten the transition from dirty coal-fired power plants as a source of electricity to cleaner natural gas and renewable energy sources such as wind and solar.

After reaching such new heights, however, gasoline prices fell sharply in 2015 and 2016 as a global surplus of oil flooded the market. A gallon of regular gas dropped below $2 a gallon in many regions before rising to about $2.30 a gallon by early 2017. One consequence of dramatically falling prices was a rebound in public demand for gas-guzzling large SUVs and light trucks, a shift that jeopardizes the goal of reaching a new-car fleet average fuel economy of 54.5 miles per gallon by 2025.[1] Yet even the low price of fuel was not enough to persuade lawmakers to increase the federal gas tax, last raised in 1993 by 4.3 cents a gallon. Doing so could help to reduce consumer demand and encourage the shift to a more efficient vehicle fleet.

The new visibility of energy issues in the mid-2010s came with plenty of political controversy and policy debates. As always the case, some participants, particularly conservatives, emphasized the need to increase energy supplies, primarily from fossil fuels, while others, notably environmentalists, argued for reducing energy demand through conservation and efficiency, or shifting

1

to less polluting, renewable resources. Not surprisingly, intense battles erupted over construction of the Keystone pipeline, the Obama administration's Clean Power Plan to reduce greenhouse gas emissions from coal-fired power plants, oil and gas drilling on public lands, natural gas fracturing ("fracking") because of its potential for contamination of groundwater sources and nearby lands, and plans to site large-scale wind and solar power facilities on public lands in the West (Weber, Bernell, and Boudet 2016).

The new attention to these and other energy issues is an encouraging development even if the conflict over them is not. Too often over the past 50 years, Americans and citizens of other developed nations have taken abundant energy supplies and low prices as a given. These conditions have fueled a growing appetite for energy to power our cars, heat and cool our homes and businesses, and keep our cell phones, computers, tablets, printers, televisions, and the many other electronic gadgets of modern life ready for use. Increasingly, however, we are now forced to confront the environmental and economic impacts of our energy use, including the consequences for climate change.

The new salience of energy issues means that citizens, policymakers, and business leaders now tend to think more seriously about energy use and alternative ways to meet the rising national and global demand. As one consequence, governments in the United States have fostered new standards for energy efficiency and environmental quality, and have invested tens of billions of dollars in cutting-edge energy research and development. These actions have helped to spur a revolution in energy technology that is already visible in the rapidly rising fuel efficiency of new cars, reduced energy consumption in commercial and residential buildings, new designs for solar and wind power generation, and promising breakthroughs in energy storage technologies and production of biofuels.

This chapter seeks to:

- improve understanding of environmental, energy, and natural resource problems faced today, both in the United States and globally;
- build a capacity for analyzing diverse causes of environmental problems and possible solutions through the use of scientific, economic, ethical, and political perspectives;
- aid readers in understanding the role of government and politics, reasons for relying on democratic political processes, and the breadth of modern environmental policy; and
- improve analysis of environmental policy and politics through introduction of a framework that should help readers think critically and creatively about diverse environmental risks and alternative ways for public policy to address them.

Environmental Challenges and Public Responses

The exciting developments in energy research and technology as well as the continuing political battles over what kinds of energy sources, regulations, and investments best serve the national interest tell us much about environmental policy and politics in the twenty-first century. The problems often are hard to identify, and taking action on them is rarely easy because it requires policymakers to resolve sometimes deep conflicts over what government ought to do and what should be left to individual and corporate choices in the marketplace. For example, should government provide generous subsidies for oil and gas companies to encourage greater energy production, as it has for years? Should it impose mandatory energy efficiency requirements to reduce demand, as Congress did in 2007—and the Obama administration in 2009 and 2012—by raising the federal fuel economy standards for vehicles, or should it provide an economic incentive to achieve the same end, for example, through a hike in the gasoline tax or imposition of a carbon fee or tax? Should it fund scientific and technological research that could help develop new sources of energy, as President Obama did both in the economic stimulus measures that Congress approved in February 2009 and in his first presidential budget recommendations? Or should such energy investments be left to the private marketplace, as many Republicans have favored? Each strategy has its backers among scientists, policy analysts, interest groups, and policymakers, and each group is convinced that its approach is the best way to address the problem.

These kinds of policy disagreements might suggest that no consensus at all exists about environmental problems or their solutions today. Yet nearly all serious students of environmental policy recognize the many reasons for concern, and that environmental threats, if anything, are more pervasive and ominous today than they were when the modern environmental movement began in the late 1960s (Kamieniecki and Kraft 2013; Vig and Kraft 2016).

The problems are familiar to most people, if not always easy to understand. They include air and water pollution, public exposure to toxic chemicals and hazardous wastes, the production of large quantities of solid wastes (including new electronic waste, such as discarded cell phones) that wind up in landfills or need reprocessing, heavy reliance worldwide on use of fossil fuels that contribute to the risks of climate change, and the destruction of critical lands and forests, which in turn hastens the loss of biological diversity and threatens ecosystem stability. To these problems we can add continuing growth of the human population and high levels of consumption of energy and natural resources; these two patterns can exacerbate all other environmental problems (Tobin 2016). Many also would put on the list the worsening quality of life and threats to public health in increasingly congested cities around the world.

Reports on these and related issues fill the airwaves and newspapers nearly every day, and are covered and debated intensely on tens of thousands of websites, with social media sites such as Facebook, Twitter, and YouTube used increasingly in this ongoing societal conversation. Not surprisingly, the studies and reports may provoke public apprehension over apparently unceasing environmental degradation. Individuals can see the evidence in their own neighborhoods, communities, and regions, and often they understand how a deteriorating environment can affect them.

Not only in the United States but worldwide, people have long believed that the environment is in serious decline, and have strongly supported efforts to reverse the trend even when environmental and energy issues have not been as salient as many other issues, such as the economy (Dunlap and York 2008; Global Strategy Group 2004; Guber and Bosso 2013a; Leiserowitz, Maibach, and Roser-Renouf 2009). Their fears have been shared by many of the world's policymakers, who helped set the agenda for the historic Earth Summit, the United Nations Conference on Environment and Development, held in 1992 in Rio de Janeiro, Brazil, and the follow-up World Summit on Sustainable Development held in Johannesburg, South Africa, in 2002 as well as the Rio+20 Conference on Sustainable Development held once again in Rio in 2012, and many other international conferences.

The 1992 Earth Summit was the largest international diplomatic conference ever held, attracting representatives from 179 nations (including 118 heads of state). More than 8,000 journalists covered the event. In addition, representatives from more than 7,000 nongovernmental organizations (NGOs) attended a concurrent Global Forum at a nearby site in Rio. The follow-up summits received much less media attention, but also attracted a large number of official delegates, NGO representatives, and members of the press. These kinds of meetings have been instrumental in setting the global environmental agenda and building political consensus for action despite many disagreements among nations about the proper course of action (Najam 2015; O'Neill 2009, 2013).

For example, in the planning sessions for the 1992 Earth Summit and at the conference itself, one could detect a palpable sense of urgency over worsening environmental problems and their implications for economic development, especially in poor nations. Yet there was also much evidence of public determination to deal with the problems. In a post-summit UN publication containing that conference's Agenda 21 action program, the meeting's organizer, Maurice Strong, spoke optimistically about what he termed "a wildfire of interest and support" that the Earth Summit had ignited throughout the world and that he hoped would stimulate a global movement toward sustainable paths of development (United Nations 1993, 1). Five years earlier, the report of the World Commission on Environment and Development (the Brundtland Commission), *Our Common Future* (1987), had similar effects. It sold 1 million copies in 30 languages and spurred extensive policy changes in both the government and private sectors.

Sadly, neither the Brundtland Commission report nor the 1992 Earth Summit and the two follow-up conferences fundamentally altered political priorities around the world. But they did provide some clarity to the inherently vague concept of sustainable development. The Brundtland Commission defined it as "development that meets the needs of the present without compromising the ability of future generations to meet their own needs" (World Commission on Environment and Development 1987, 43). What does this mean? Scholars and policymakers have argued that needs can be defined and met in many ways, and there have been proposals for "strong" and "weak" versions of sustainability, with differing expectations for societal responses, whether the actions take place in international agencies, local governments, or on college and university campuses (Hempel 2009, 2013; Portney 2009, 2013, 2015; Mazmanian and Kraft 2009). Yet at a practical level, the implications are clear enough: that many societal activities, such as use of fossil fuels or reliance on current food production methods, cannot continue in their present form because they are not sustainable on a finite planet. Consider this summary and appraisal from one prominent report released a year before the 1992 summit that underscored astonishing world trends in population and economic growth in the twentieth century:

> Since 1900, the world's population has multiplied more than three times. Its economy has grown twentyfold. The consumption of fossil fuels has grown by a factor of 30, and industrial production by a factor of 50. Most of that growth, about four-fifths of it, has occurred since 1950. Much of it is unsustainable. Earth's basic life-supporting capital of forests, species, and soils is being depleted and its fresh waters and oceans are being degraded at an accelerating rate.
> (MacNeill, Winsemius, and Yakushiji 1991, 3)

At the time the authors were looking back to social, economic, and environmental changes earlier in the twentieth century. What lies ahead in the rest of the twenty-first century is equally striking and worrisome. For example, the United Nations estimates that the world's 2016 population of 7.3 billion people will grow to nearly 9.9 billion by 2050, with virtually all of that growth occurring in the developing nations. To feed, house, clothe, and otherwise provide for people's needs and aspirations will greatly tax natural resources and ecological systems throughout the world (Population Reference Bureau 2016; Smil 2013). This is particularly so given the high level of economic growth that is also expected over the next half century. The U.S. National Intelligence Council reported in late 2012, for example, that because of rapid industrialization in the developing world, "the volume of urban construction for housing, office space and transport services over the next 40 years could roughly equal the entire volume of such construction to date in world history" (U.S. National Intelligence Council 2012, 26). The council pointed to the economic opportunities such growth would create, but the impacts on resource use and the environment are equally profound.

One can see the implications in China for energy development and transport. China has long expected its economic output to quadruple over the next 15 years, although global economic troubles from 2008 to 2016 clearly slowed its growth rate somewhat. By the late 2000s, every week China was opening a coal-fired power plant large enough to serve the energy needs of every household in Dallas or San Diego. India also was rapidly increasing use of coal for similar purposes, and was expected to add almost 50 more plants within four years.[2] By 2016, however, partly in response to worsening air quality in its major cities and its new commitment to reduce release of greenhouse gases, China announced it would slow the rate of growth somewhat.[3] It was ahead of the United States in the transition to cleaner coal-fired plants, and was rapidly advancing in solar and wind power technology (Gallagher and Lewis 2016).[4] Yet automobile sales in China have been soaring even as the nation continues to build mass transit lines to handle increasing demand for transportation. By 2016 it was the world's largest car market, with record sales for both small SUVs and electric vehicles. China easily surpassed the United States in sales of electric vehicles, with strong government backing of them.[5]

This kind of economic growth is important for increasing opportunities for billions of people around the world and advancing social justice (B. Friedman 2005), yet it must also be compatible with the limits of natural systems. It is difficult for most of us to understand these historic trends and their effects. As biologist Jane Lubchenco noted in a 1997 presidential address to the American Association for the Advancement of Science (AAAS), over the last several decades "humans have emerged as a new force of nature." We are, she argued, "modifying physical, chemical, and biological systems in new ways, at faster rates, and over larger spatial scales than ever recorded on Earth." The result of these modifications is that humans have "unwittingly embarked upon a grand experiment with our planet," with "profound implications for all of life on Earth" (Lubchenco 1998, 492).[6] Some commentators characterize this new human impact on the environment as constituting an "anthropocene era" to distinguish it from previous historical periods.[7]

These remarkable transformations raise fundamental issues for the study of environmental policy and politics. Will the Earth be able to accommodate the kind of growth widely anticipated over the next century? If so, what will be the likely human and ecological cost? How well equipped are the world's nations to respond to the many needs created by such social, economic, and ecological trends? Will political systems around the world prove able and willing to tackle these problems, and will they act soon enough? For example, will they be able to design, adopt, and implement effective policies to protect public health, and to do so before millions of people face dire consequences? Will they be able to do the same to promote sustainable use of natural resources before ecological systems are pushed to the breaking point?

This book tries to address these questions, although it can only scratch the surface. For that reason I provide extensive references to key studies and reports, and point throughout to the most useful websites to encourage readers to explore many topics in more detail. In the chapters that follow, I review and appraise major policy actions and proposals for policy change, whether at the U.S. federal level or the state and local level, where much of the most innovative environmental policy actions take place today. As space allows, I also discuss some of the most important environmental policies and proposals at the international level.

Environmental Policy and Politics

Put most simply, politics is about the collective choices we make as a society. It concerns policy goals and the means we use to achieve them as well as the way we organize and govern ourselves, for example, through the governmental institutions on which we rely and the political processes we use to make decisions. Over the next several decades, the United States and other nations face important choices. They can maintain current policies and practices, or they can envision a better future and design the institutions and policies necessary to help bring the needed change. They can rely on an unregulated marketplace where individual choice reigns, or they can try to accelerate and consciously direct a transition to that future in other ways. Such decisions are at least as important in the United States as they are in other nations, and the ecological consequences are probably greater here than in any other nation in the world. The National Commission on the Environment captured the choices well in a report from the early 1990s:

> If America continues down its current path, primarily reacting to environmental injuries and trying to repair them, the quality of our environment will continue to deteriorate, and eventually our economy will decline as well. If, however, our country pioneers new technologies, shifts its policies, makes bold economic changes, and embraces a new ethic of environmentally responsible behavior, it is far more likely that the coming years will bring a higher quality of life, a healthier environment, and a more vibrant economy for all Americans.
>
> (1993, xi)

The commission concluded that "natural processes that support life on Earth are increasingly at risk," and as a solution it endorsed sustainable development. Such development could serve, the commission said, as a "central guiding principle for national environmental and economic policy making," which it saw as inextricably linked, and thereby restore environmental quality, create broad-based economic progress, and brighten prospects for future generations. Consistent with its bipartisan composition, the commission observed that such a strategy would involve a combination of market forces, government regulations, and private and individual initiatives. These comments were made more than two decades ago, and yet they are equally, if not more, appropriate today, as evident in many of the proposals put forth by the Obama administration and Congress to act on energy and climate change, and comparable proposals at the state and local level (Rabe 2010, 2016; Bryner and Duffy 2012).

The nearly universal embrace of the idea of "sustainable development" is an important signpost for the early twenty-first century, even if it remains a somewhat vague term that can mask serious economic and political conflicts, particularly between rich and poor nations. It was evident in the name given to the 2002 Johannesburg and 2012 Rio conferences, and in a major, but largely neglected, report by the Clinton administration's President's Council on Sustainable Development (1996). Such widespread endorsement of the principle of sustainability would have been inconceivable forty or fifty years ago. In the early 1970s, books describing the "environmental crisis" and proposing ways to deal with "limits to growth" and "ecological scarcity" may have won over some college audiences and urged on nascent environmental organizations, but they had little discernible effect on the higher reaches of government and corporate officialdom in the United States and most other nations. In the 2010s, however, the language of sustainability is not only common at that level but has also kindled promising grassroots activity and corporate commitment both across the nation and around the world, including on many college and university campuses that now have a sustainability director or coordinator (Axelrod and VanDeveer 2015; Mazmanian and Kraft 2009; Starke 2008, 2012). Moreover, best-selling authors such as Thomas Friedman (2006, 2008) and Jeffrey Sachs (2015) have done much to popularize both the need for and the difficulty of achieving sustainable development in a world that increasingly is, in Friedman's terms, "hot, flat, and crowded"— where climate change, rapidly growing populations, and an expanding middle class brought on in part by globalization threaten the planet.

These developments signal fundamental changes that have occurred in both U.S. and global environmental policy and politics over the past five decades. The initial environmental agenda of the 1960s and 1970s focused on air and water pollution control and the preservation of natural resources such as parks, wilderness, and wildlife. This is often called the first generation of environmental policy. In this period, the problems were thought to be simple and the solutions both obvious and relatively easy to put into effect. Public and congressional enthusiasm for environmental protection policy supported the adoption of innovative and stringent federal programs that would force offending industries to clean up. That was true even where policy goals appeared to exceed both available technical knowledge and the capacity of administrative agencies to take on the new responsibilities mandated by law (Jones 1975). In such a supportive political climate, the costs of achieving new environmental standards were rarely a major consideration.

Yet, as the new policies were implemented, their ambitious goals proved to be far more difficult to achieve than anticipated and much more costly. By the late 1970s and early 1980s, policymakers and environmentalists became increasingly frustrated with the slow pace of progress, and complaints from regulated industry and state and local governments mounted steadily (Durant 1992; Vig and Kraft 1984). These concerns, particularly on the part of business groups, economists, and conservatives, led to a second generation of environmental policy efforts that began in the early 1980s in Ronald Reagan's administration, with an emphasis on more efficient regulation and promotion of alternatives to regulation, such as use of market incentives, voluntary pollution control initiatives, public–private partnerships, and collaboration among various stakeholders (Fiorino 2006; Mazmanian and Kraft 2009).

Almost all of the initial environmental laws remain in force today despite nearly five decades of criticism and experimentation with such alternatives at both national and state levels. The reasons are largely political. There has been no agreement on how to reform the core environmental statutes, despite some limited success with modification of the Clean Air Act in 1990, the Safe Drinking Water Act in 1996, and pesticide control policy in 1996 through the Food Quality Protection Act. Democrats and Republicans— and environmentalists and business groups—have fought for much of this time, with some of the fiercest battles taking place during the Clinton administration in the 1990s, the Bush administration in the 2000s, and the Obama administration (Eisner 2007; Klyza and Sousa 2013; Vig and Kraft 2016). As we will see in the chapters that follow, the challenges today involve not only how best to modernize U.S. environmental policy, but how to grapple with a new and complex array of third-generation problems and policy actions that have emerged, from dealing with global climate change to local sustainability initiatives. In this sense, we can detect continuities with the old environmental politics even as a new era is unfolding that is rich in hope and possibilities.

Perspectives on Environmental Problems

Even a casual review of commentary on the environment over the past decade reveals widely disparate views of ecological problems and what ought to be done about them (Huber 2000; Layzer 2012; Lomborg 2001; Kamieniecki and Kraft 2013). That should not be surprising. Definitions and understanding of any public problem are affected by political ideologies and values, education and professional training, and work or community experience. They vary greatly across society and among scientists, policymakers, and the public.

This book is about the role of politics and government in identifying, understanding, and responding to the world's environmental problems. It argues that policy choices are inescapably political in the sense that they seek to resolve conflicts inherent in the balancing of environmental protection and other social and economic goals. That is, such a process involves a struggle over whose definition of the public interest should prevail and precisely how we should reconcile environmental goals with other competing values such as economic well-being, individual rights, a desire for limited governmental regulation, and social justice. It also serves as a reminder of the important role that government plays in dealing with environmental problems. Before turning directly to that role, however, several other leading perspectives on environmental problems, their causes, and their solution should be noted. These are (1) science and technology; (2) economics and incentive structures; and (3) values and ethics. These differing perspectives are usually discussed to some extent at various points in the policymaking process, but it is nonetheless worth highlighting the differences in the way environmental problems are seen and acted on.

Scientific Knowledge and Its Use

Many scientists (and business leaders as well) believe that environmental problems can be traced chiefly to a lack of scientific knowledge about the dynamics of natural systems or the use of technology, or the failure to adopt a systems view that highlights the interrelationships among components of complex environmental and economic systems (Meadows 2008; Meadows, Randers, and Meadows 2004). They may also point to a failure to put such knowledge to good use in both the government and the private sector. That is, they have a great deal of confidence in science and engineering for solving environmental problems. For example, ecologists believe that improving our knowledge of biological diversity will highlight existing and anticipated threats; thus such knowledge may contribute to the strengthening of public policy to protect endangered species and their habitats. Better knowledge of the risks to human health posed by toxic chemicals could facilitate formulation of improved pollution control strategies. Knowledge of new production technologies likewise could lead industry to adopt so-called green business practices, as many have done. Or businesses may choose to market greener products, such as plug-in hybrid or fully electric automobiles, because advances in battery technology allow them to do so in a highly competitive marketplace (Press and Mazmanian 2016).

Not surprisingly, scientists and engineers urge increased research on environmental and energy issues, more extensive and reliable monitoring of environmental conditions and trends over time, better use of science (and scientists) in policymaking, and the development of new technologies that have fewer negative environmental impacts. Government policymakers also may share this view, which helps to explain why the federal government has invested billions of dollars a year in research on energy technologies, climate change, and other kinds of environmental research. There has been no shortage of recommendations for additional spending or for scientists playing a more active role in communicating scientific knowledge to the public and policymakers, as Jane Lubchenco (1998) urged in her AAAS address mentioned earlier.[8]

The Obama administration's willingness to invest billions of dollars in energy research speaks to the power of these kinds of recommendations. Obama's selection of John Holdren, a Harvard physicist and noted environmental policy scholar, as his science adviser, and of Steven Chu, a Nobel laureate and strong advocate for action on climate change, as his first secretary of energy, suggested his commitment to such ideas. Indeed, early in his presidency a speech he made at the National Academy of Sciences confirming his support for scientific research was exceptionally well received; said one academy member: "the days of science taking a back seat to ideology are over."[9] The reference was clearly to a number of decisions in the Bush administration that scientists inside and outside of government thought were made without sufficient regard for scientific evidence. The disputes ranged from the appropriate standards for mercury emissions from power plants to issues of climate change and protection of biological diversity (Andrews 2006b, 2016; Ascher, Steelman, and Healy 2010; Lubell and Segee 2013; Rosenbaum 2013a). It should be noted that Obama and his appointees also were criticized for ignoring the advice of scientists and other experts in the Environmental Protection Agency (EPA) and other agencies, even if not to the extent of the Bush administration. The Trump presidency seems likely to resemble the Bush administration's outlook on the role of science more than that of Obama, to judge from Trump's stance on climate change and other scientific issues, but the scientific community argues that continued support for scientific research and use of science in decision making will help to ensure that economic progress continues.[10]

In recent years, many environmental scientists also have argued for a novel approach to setting research priorities by emphasizing the need for an interdisciplinary "sustainability science" that "seeks to understand the fundamental character of interactions between nature and society" (Kates et al. 2001, 641). Other scientists have called for a new federal body, an independent Earth Systems Science Agency, which might transcend bureaucratic boundaries and promote innovative solutions to environmental problems (Schaefer et al. 2008). Advocates of these kinds of scientific research and agency realignment believe that a much closer affiliation between environmental science and the world of public policy is needed. At least one of the reasons they take this position is their concern that scientific work may not be properly appreciated or understood by the public and policymakers, in part because science always contains an element of uncertainty, which can be substantial for highly complex problems. There are good reasons for such concern. As we will see in Chapter 4, the public's understanding of environmental issues is quite limited, and many people continue to hold views directly at odds with current scientific evidence, for example, on climate change. Such findings have led scientists to call for programs to improve the public's scientific and environmental literacy.[11] A further benefit of any financial investment in environmental science and technology might be to make the nation more competitive in a global economy heavily dependent on scientific and technological advances.

Economics and Incentives

Another group of commentators, particularly economists, finds the major causes of environmental ills to be less a deficiency of scientific knowledge or available technologies than an unfortunate imbalance of incentives. We misuse natural resources, especially common-pool resources such as the atmosphere, surface waters, and public lands, or we fail to adopt promising new technologies such as solar and wind power because we think we gain economically from current practices or we do not suffer an economic loss (Ostrom 1990, 1999). In his classic essay on the "tragedy of the commons," Garrett Hardin (1968) illustrated how individuals may be led to exploit to the point of depletion those resources they hold in common. Sometimes natural resource policies have the perverse effect of encouraging the very degradation they are designed to prevent by setting artificially low market prices (e.g., for irrigation water or use of public lands for timber harvesting, mining, oil and gas drilling, or grazing) through government subsidies to resource users (Burger and Gochfeld 1998; Myers and Kent 2001; Roodman 1997).

We can see evidence of this general phenomenon of short-sighted action in nearly every economic sector, but solutions are available, and some of them draw from the kind of insights found in Elinor Ostrom's Nobel Prize-winning work (1990, 1999). For example, in 1994, faced with a fishery on the verge of collapse due to both ecosystem changes and unrestrained fishing, an industry-dominated fishery management council in New England recommended a drastic cutback in allowable fishing in the Georges Bank area off Cape Cod. Previous limitations on fishing proved insufficient to prevent the exhaustion of the principal species that had supported commercial fishing in the area for generations. Facing a similar set of circumstances, Maine's lobster industry was saved in part through new self-imposed limits on harvesting lobsters, and the agreement on lobster sustainability is widely cited as a model for using public–private partnerships to protect resources of this kind.[12]

Another common example of perverse economic incentives can be found in urban areas. Individuals tend to resist using mass transit and insist on driving their automobiles to work even though the highways are heavily congested and thus cost them valuable time, and the cities in which they live become polluted with their collective vehicle exhaust. Why do they behave this way?

Although they can plainly see the environmental degradation that their behavior causes, they lack sufficient incentives to change their driving habits.

Because of such behavioral patterns, economists, planners, and policy analysts propose that we redesign the economic and behavioral incentives that current unrealistic market prices create (Freeman 2006; Keohane and Olmstead 2007; Ostrom 2008). These prices send inaccurate and inappropriate price signals to consumers and businesses and thus encourage behavior that may be environmentally destructive. We need, such analysts say, to internalize the external costs of individual and collective decision making and establish something closer to full social cost accounting that reflects real environmental gains and losses. It might be done, for example, with public tax policies. As we saw at the chapter's beginning, a tax on the use of gasoline and other fossil fuels could discourage their use and build demand for energy-efficient technologies; in 2009, Congress seriously considered imposing such a tax as one element in a proposed climate change policy.

Similarly, many European cities have imposed various forms of a congestion tax to limit vehicle traffic in central cities. Another example is a tax credit for use of energy-efficient appliances such as refrigerators and air conditioners or for hybrid, electric, or other fuel-efficient vehicles, which encourages individuals to make such purchases; doing so saves them money and reduces the use of fossil fuels to generate electricity. Such a credit could also give manufacturers more reason to make products of this kind. The popularity of such action could also be seen in legislation approved by Congress in 2009 to offer federally funded vouchers in return for trading in and scraping older cars with poor fuel efficiency (often termed "cash for clunkers"); the vouchers (as high as $4,500) could be used to reduce the cost of buying new, more efficient vehicles. Half a dozen states have tried similar, though less generous, programs. The Car Allowance Rebate System became so popular with auto dealers and buyers that the $1 billion that Congress had set aside for it was exhausted within one week and had to be supplemented with $2 billion in additional funds to extend the program for a few additional weeks.[13]

This argument extends to reform of the usual measures of economic accounting, such as the gross national product (GNP). Critics, such as the organization Redefining Progress (www.rprogress.org), complain that such measures fail to consider the value of environmental damage, such as loss of forest or wetland habitats. Some even call for a new paradigm of ecological economics and a fair valuing of "nature's services" to humans (Cobb, Halstead, and Rowe 1995; Costanza 1991; Daily 1997). For example, one widely discussed report in 1997 estimated the economic value of the services of all global ecological systems and the natural capital stocks that produce them at an astonishing $33 trillion a year. In comparison, the global GNP at the time was $18 trillion a year (Costanza et al. 1997). On a more concrete level, in 1997 New York City decided to spend $660 million to preserve a watershed in the Catskill Mountains north of the city because the water supply could be purified by microorganisms as it percolated through the soil. The city's alternative was to construct a water treatment plant that could have cost $6 billion or more.[14] Many other cases of this kind could be cited. With increased attention to climate change, for example, environmental and other organizations, and some businesses, are beginning to calculate the carbon footprints of foods and many other products. It seems evident that only with accurate price signals and revised accounting mechanisms can individual and market choices steer the nation and the world in the direction of environmental sustainability.

Environmental Values and Ethics

Philosophers and environmentalists offer a third perspective. The environmental crisis, they believe, is at heart a consequence of our belief systems and values, which they see as seriously deficient in the face of contemporary ecological threats, whatever their other virtues may be. For example, William Catton and Riley Dunlap (1980) have defined a dominant social paradigm (DSP), or worldview, of Western industrial societies that includes a number of core beliefs: Humans are fundamentally different from all other species on Earth over which they have dominion, the world is vast and provides unlimited opportunities for humans, and human history is one of progress in which all major problems can be solved. Other premises and values follow from these beliefs: the primacy of economic well-being; the acceptability of risks associated with technologies that produce wealth; a low valuation of nature; and the absence of any real limits to economic growth (summarized in Milbrath 1989, 189).

Environmentalists argue that the values represented by the DSP strongly affect our personal behavior and institutional priorities, and thus constitute one of the most fundamental causes of natural resource depletion and environmental degradation (Kempton, Boster, and Hartley 1996; Milbrath 1984, 1989; Paehlke 1989), and also a major limitation on what any public policies realistically can achieve when they need the public's support to succeed. Environmentalists therefore contend that the DSP and the values related to it must change if human behavior is to be made more consonant with sustainable use of the biosphere, and if appropriate public policies are to be adopted and implemented.

Such ideas are not new, even if they are more prominent today than in earlier periods. For example, Aldo Leopold, one of the most celebrated advocates of an environmental ethic, wrote in his prophetic *A Sand County Almanac* (originally published in 1949) that society would gain from adoption of an environmental ethic, which he termed a "land ethic." It stated: "A thing is right when it tends to preserve the integrity, stability, and beauty of the biotic community. It is wrong when it tends otherwise" (Leopold 1970, 262).

Contemporary accounts reflect Leopold's view. Robert Paehlke, for example, derived a list of 13 values that constitute the "essential core of an environmental perspective." He further distilled these into three key goals: (1) protection of ecological systems, wilderness, and biodiversity; (2) minimization of negative impacts on human health; and (3) establishment of sustainable patterns of resource use (Paehlke 2000). Much environmental writing espouses similar values to achieve these broad ends, and environmental organizations often urge their members to change their behavior in these ways, such as reducing their use of energy and water and seeking food grown and distributed with minimal environmental impact (e.g., Durning 1992; Leiserowitz and Fernandez 2008; Princen, Maniates, and Conca 2002; Starke 2008).

The implication is that merely reforming environmental policies to improve short-term governmental actions without any change in society's core values will not be enough to achieve long-term goals of sustainability. Instead, changes in political, social, cultural, and economic institutions may be needed as well. Pope Francis made this kind of argument in 2015 in his widely discussed encyclical letter on climate change, *Laudato Si': On Care for our Common Home*, where he framed the challenge in moral as well as scientific terms (Heald 2016). This is true even if environmental writers continue to debate precisely what kinds of societal changes are necessary. For example, political scientists disagree about key political values and institutions, including such fundamental issues as the structure and authority of government and the role of the public in decision making (Baber and Bartlett 2013; Dryzek and Lester 1995; Lewis 1994; Ophuls 2011; Ophuls and Boyan 1992; Whitford and Wong 2009).

Such an emphasis on ethics and values suggests that public policies must be evaluated in part on this basis, and not solely on widely used standards such as effectiveness in solving a problem or efficiency in the use of public and private resources. Many public policy texts acknowledge that a range of public values ought to be considered in determining whether policy proposals merit serious consideration and adoption, and these include such ethical concerns as promotion of equity, or social and environmental justice (Kraft and Furlong 2018; Patton, Sawicki, and Clark 2016). Some of the most important consequences of climate change, for example, will be on those nations or states without sufficient resources to adapt to new climatic conditions. Moreover, ethical questions of intergenerational equity, or what is fair to future generations, surround nearly all major environmental challenges today, and particularly those such as climate change, disposal of nuclear waste, or loss of biological diversity, where the detrimental effects may be greatest for generations yet to be born.

The Role of Government and Politics

Each of these three perspectives offers distinctive insights into environmental problems and their solutions. All make sense, although none alone offers a complete understanding or a sufficient agenda for action. Few would question that society needs better scientific knowledge, a shift to environmentally benign and more productive technologies, or more comprehensive and integrated policy analysis and planning. Nor would many deny the need for greater economic and personal incentives to conserve energy, water, and other resources, or a stronger and more widely shared commitment to environmental values in our personal lives.

Moreover, few would disagree that diverse actions by individuals and institutions at all levels of society, in the public as well as the private sector, will be essential to the long-term goals of environmental protection and sustainable development. People may choose to live close to where they work and walk or commute on bicycles or use mass transit rather than private automobiles, or they may at least use highly fuel-efficient vehicles. They may also seek durable, energy-efficient, and environmentally safe consumer goods and use fewer of them, recycle or compost wastes, and adjust their air-conditioning and heating systems to conserve energy. Similarly, businesses can do much to improve energy efficiency, prevent pollution, and promote other sustainable practices, and many are trying to do so today (Esty and Winston 2006; Press and Mazmanian 2016).

Government nonetheless has an essential role to play in resolving environmental problems. Public policies shape the kind of scientific research that is supported, and thus the pace and character of many scientific and technological developments. Governmental policies also affect the design and use of economic incentives (think gasoline taxes), changes in society's environmental values (e.g., through educational programs in public schools), and the use of energy and resources by government agencies themselves, such as the Defense Department. We look to government for such policies because environmental threats represent public or collective goods problems that *cannot* be solved through private action alone. The costs may simply be too great for private initiatives, and certain activities may require the legal authority or political legitimacy that only governments possess. Examples include setting aside large areas of public lands for national parks, wilderness, and wildlife preserves, and establishment of a range of international environmental, development, and population assistance programs.

Much the same is true of national or state regulatory and taxation policies. Such policies are adopted largely because society concludes that market forces by themselves do not produce the desired outcomes—a message strongly reinforced by the deep recession that began in 2008 that many attributed to decisions not to regulate highly speculative financial activities on Wall Street. Even free-market enthusiasts admit that "imperfections" in markets (such as inadequate information, lack of competitiveness, and externalities such as pollution) may justify government regulation. In all these cases, private-sector activity may well contribute to desired social ends. Yet, the scope and magnitude of environmental problems, the level of resources needed to address them, and urgent public pressures for action may push the issues onto governmental agendas.

In these ways, the resultant public policies help fill the gaps created when millions of individuals and thousands of corporations make independent choices in a market economy (Ostrom 1990; Ostrom et al. 2002). However rational such choices are from the individual or corporate viewpoint, they are almost always guided by greater concern for personal gain and short-term corporate profits than for the long-term social goals of a clean and safe environment or for sustainable development. Hence, there is a need for establishing some limits on those choices or providing incentives to help ensure that individuals and organizations make them in a socially responsible manner. Those are the preeminent purposes of environmental policy.

The goals of environmental policies and the means chosen to achieve them are set by a variety of political processes, from the local to the international level. They are also a product of the interaction of the many individuals and groups that participate actively in those processes. Environmentalists are well represented in decision making at most levels of government today, if not quite on a par with business and industry groups (Bosso 2005; Duffy 2003; Kraft and Kamieniecki 2007). The presence of a multiplicity of interest groups and the visibility of environmental policies usually guarantees that policy goals and instruments are subject to intense political debate, with particular scrutiny given to their costs and effectiveness today.

Democracy, Politics, and Environmental Policy

Most of this text presents an overview of U.S. environmental policies and their evolution over nearly five decades. But there is an overall perspective imbedded in this description as well. It is that democratic decision making and public support are crucial to successful environmental politics. They are especially important if environmental policy is to be socially acceptable as well as technically sound. Democratic politics is rarely easy, and it is made especially difficult when individuals, interest groups, and political parties hold sharply divergent perspectives on the issues and are reluctant or unable to compromise on their views. Conflict over environmental policy has been common since the beginning of the modern environmental movement, and it continues today, as evident in disputes over energy policy and climate change, among many other issues. At the same time, there are prominent examples at all levels of government that demonstrate how conflicts can be resolved through collaborative processes and how broadly supported environmental policies can be adopted and put into effect (Gerlak, Heikkila, and Lubell 2013; Layzer 2008, 2013; Lubell, Leach, and Sabatier 2009; Mazmanian and Kraft 2009; Sabatier et al. 2005).

Not all appraisals of environmental politics are so positive about the potential for democratic solutions. Critics have argued that public involvement or civic environmentalism (John 1994, 2004) can be problematic when citizens lack the capacity to understand often-complex environmental issues, or are adamantly opposed to actions that they believe may threaten their way of life. As the next generation of environmental policies does indeed begin to take on questions of lifestyle (e.g., consumption of energy), such critics wonder if democratic processes might not make it very difficult for governments to take essential action and to do so expeditiously (Ophuls 2011; Ophuls and Boyan 1992).

On the other side of this argument, scholars have found that public concern about the environment and support for environmental protection efforts have been relatively high and persistent over time even if most people are not well informed on the issues (Dunlap 1995; Guber and Bosso 2013a). Others maintain that the public can deal reasonably well with difficult technical issues if given the opportunity to learn about and discuss them. It is also possible to design public policies to make it easier for people to participate in decision making and thus increase the responsiveness of government to citizen needs (Baber and Bartlett 2005; Daley 2007, 2013; Ingram and Smith 1993; Kraft 2000). Whatever one's appraisal of governmental capabilities and the potential for democratic politics, environmental policies adopted since the 1960s will have real and important effects within the United States and globally. Some may be positive and some negative. It makes sense to try to understand their origins, current forms, achievements, and deficiencies. I try to do that throughout the text.

Defining Environmental Policy

Public policy can be defined as a course of government action in response to social problems; it is what governments choose to do about those problems. Environmental policy refers to governmental actions that affect or attempt to affect environmental quality or the use of natural resources. It represents society's collective decision to pursue certain environmental goals and objectives and to use particular tools to achieve them. Environmental policy is not found in any single statute or administrative decision. Rather, it is set by a diverse collection of statutes, regulations, and court precedents that govern the nation, and it is affected by the attitudes and behavior of the officials who are responsible for implementing and enforcing the law. Environmental policy includes not only what governments choose to do to protect environmental quality and natural resources but what they decide *not* to do; a decision not to act means that governments allow other forces to shape the environment. For example, by choosing not to have a comprehensive energy policy in the last several decades, the nation in effect left the decisions about how much and what kind of energy we use to individuals and corporations. That choice is now being seriously reconsidered as we come to appreciate the consequences of the nation's heavy reliance on fossil fuels.

Public-policy scholars also remind us that policies may be tangible, with real consequences, or largely symbolic (Anderson 2015). That is, not all environmental policies are intended to solve problems. Some are mainly expressive in nature. They articulate environmental values and goals that are intensely important to the public and especially to key interest groups, such as environmentalists. Such statements may have little direct relationship to legally specified policy goals and objectives, although they may nevertheless bring about important environmental changes over time by influencing public beliefs and organizational values and decision making (Bartlett 1994; Cantrill and Oravec 1996). A good example at the international level is the Kyoto Protocol on climate change. Signing or not signing the protocol sent an important message during the 1990s and 2000s about a nation's position on the issue, and adoption of the protocol itself signaled that nations around the world took climate change seriously. Yet agreeing to the protocol said little about what nations actually did regarding their policies and practices that contributed to emissions of greenhouse gases (Harrison and Sundstrom 2010; Selin and VanDeveer 2016).

Policy Typologies

Political scientists have found it useful to distinguish among several basic types of policy actions, such as regulatory, distributive, and redistributive policies. Each is associated with different patterns of policymaking (Anderson 2015; Lowi 1979). Most environmental policies fall into one category or the other, although, as is the case with most typologies, the fit is imperfect.

Regulatory policies attempt to reduce or expand the choices available to citizens and corporations to achieve a social goal. They may raise the cost of, prohibit, or compel certain actions through provision of sanctions and incentives. The most common approach is the setting and enforcement of standards such as the amount of pollutants that a factory or utility may emit into the air or water. Most environmental protection policies such as the Clean Air Act and the Clean Water Act are regulatory. The politics associated with regulatory policy tend to pit environmental and public health groups against industry. The former seeks benefits for the general population (such as reduced exposure to toxic chemicals), whereas the latter tries to minimize the costs and burdens imposed by government regulators. When the issues are highly visible and the public is supportive, government may impose a tough policy. If the issues are not very prominent or the public is less united, however, industry does better in getting its way (Kraft and Kamieniecki 2007; J. Wilson 1980).

In contrast to environmental protection efforts like this, most natural resources, energy, and conservation policies historically have been distributive. They have allocated or distributed public resources, often in the form of financial subsidies or comparable specific benefits to clientele groups. The purpose has been to achieve social goals such as providing access to public lands for mining, grazing, forestry, or recreation; protecting biological diversity; or fostering the development of energy resources such as oil, coal, or nuclear power (Clarke and McCool 1996; Duffy 1997; McConnell 1966). The U.S. Congress traditionally has favored such distributive (critics call them "pork-barrel") policies, which convey highly visible benefits to politically important constituencies for whom the issues are highly salient. The general public usually has little interest in the issues, so its political influence is often minimal. Not surprisingly, such policies often are criticized for fostering inequitable and inefficient uses of public resources and often environmentally destructive practices (Lowry 2006; Lubell and Segee 2013; Myers and Kent 2001).

The Breadth of Environmental Policy

As might be expected, environmental policy choices are affected by social, political, and economic forces that vary from year to year and from one locality to another. As a result, the United States has a disparate and uncoordinated collection of environmental policies that were enacted in different historical periods and for quite different purposes. For example, policies regulating gold mining on public lands that were first approved in the nineteenth century were still in effect in 2016, and are at odds with more contemporary views on what kinds of mining serve the public interest. President Obama's first secretary of the interior, Ken Salazar, promised to try to reform the policy, and in recent years the Senate considered such changes, with support from groups such as the Pew Campaign for Responsible Mining. Generous subsidies for nuclear power development approved in the 1950s and 1960s also continue today, despite public skepticism about the acceptability of nuclear power. Much the same is true for subsidies for oil and gas development, despite record oil company profits in the 2010s.

Taken together, this collection of environmental, energy, and resource policies seems to defy common sense. Certainly it falls short of an integrated approach to solving environmental problems. As Dean Mann put it long ago, U.S. environmental policy "is rather a jerry-built structure in which innumerable individuals, private groups, bureaucrats, politicians, agencies, courts, political parties, and circumstances have laid down the planks, hammered the nails, plastered over the cracks, made sometimes unsightly additions and deletions, and generally defied 'holistic' or 'ecological' principles of policy design" (1986, 4). Political commitments like these initiated decades ago make it difficult for policymakers to start over. Thus normally they consider incremental adjustments to the present mix of policies rather than wholesale or radical policy change.

Environmental policy today also has an exceedingly broad scope. Traditionally, it was considered to involve the conservation or protection of natural resources such as public lands and waters, wilderness, and wildlife, and thus was concerned with recreational opportunities and aesthetic values in addition to ecological preservation. Since the late 1960s, the term has been more often used to refer to environmental protection efforts of government, such as air and water pollution control, which are grounded in a concern for human health. In industrialized nations, these policies have sought to reverse trends of environmental degradation affecting the land, air, and water, and to work toward achievement of acceptable levels of environmental quality (Desai 2002; Steinberg and VanDeveer 2012).

However, environmental policy extends well beyond environmental protection and natural resource conservation. It includes, more often implicitly than explicitly, governmental actions affecting human health and safety; energy use; transportation; urban design and building standards; agriculture and food production; human population growth; national and international security; and the protection of vital global ecological, chemical, and geophysical systems (Deudney and Matthew 1999; Matthew 2013; Mazmanian and Kraft 2009; O'Neill 2009; Starke 2008, 2012). Hence, environmental policy cuts an exceptionally wide swath and has a pervasive and growing effect on modern human affairs. It embraces long-term and global as well as short-term and local actions.

Environmental Problems and Public Policy

As the preceding discussion suggests, identifying the nature of environmental problems and the solutions that may be needed to address them is rarely an easy task. Since the late 1960s, we have been bombarded with news about a multitude of threats to public health and the environment, with varying hints about the degree of scientific consensus or the extent of disagreement between environmentalists and their opponents. Sometimes the dangers are highly visible, as they are to residents of neighborhoods near heavily polluting industries. Usually, however, they are not, and citizens are left puzzled about the severity of the problems, whom to believe, and what they ought to do.

Increasingly, it seems, environmental problems of the third generation, such as global climate change and loss of biodiversity, are even more difficult to recognize and solve than the more familiar issues of the first generation of environmental concerns of the early 1970s (e.g., air and water pollution). Solutions may be very costly, and the benefits to society are long term and may be difficult to recognize and measure even as the short-term costs are easily identifiable and affect specific industries or practices (Daily 1997). Thus third-generation environmental problems tend to be more politically controversial and more difficult to address than the environmental problems of earlier eras.

For all these reasons, students of environmental policy need to develop a robust capacity to sort through the partial and often biased information they encounter in the nation's media, from ideological talk radio programs and narrowly focused social media sites to the best newspaper and journal coverage. Policymakers and the public need the same skills, particularly in the highly polarized and partisan political atmosphere of the 2010s where objective evidence often seems to be elusive.

Despite these challenging conditions today, there is no great puzzle about the pertinent questions to ask about any public policy controversy, including those associated with the environment. They concern the nature and causes of the problems that are faced (including who or what is affected by them and in what ways), what might be done about them, and if government intervention is called for, what kind of policy tools (such as regulation, public education, or use of market incentives) are most appropriate. These are the same kinds of questions posed in any discussion of government and public policy, whether the issues are health care, education, the economy, or foreign affairs (Anderson 2015; Kraft and Furlong 2018).

Defining the Problems: The Nature of Environmental Risks

One set of concerns focuses on the nature of environmental problems, their causes, and their consequences. An enormous amount of information is available on the state of the environment, and new research findings appear continually. Much of that information is easily available on the Internet, particularly at government agency websites and at sites maintained by environmental, health, business, and other organizations, many of which are discussed throughout the text. Whatever the source of data, critical evaluation is essential because some sites and their reports reflect more credible scientific and professional analysis than do others.

Forecasting Environmental Conditions Some of the most difficult estimates about environmental problems involve forecasts of future conditions. What will the human population be in 2050 or how much energy will the United States use in 2025, and how much of it will likely come from fossil fuel sources, and how much from wind or solar energy? All such forecasts involve making assumptions about economic, social, and technological change, which may not be fully understood. The best studies carefully set out the assumptions that underlie their projections and describe the forecasting methods they use. Even so, uncertainty and controversy are common, and some of it centers on what critics may charge are unwarranted assumptions and faulty methods.

One illustration of the kind of challenge involved with forecasting is climate change. The Intergovernmental Panel on Climate Change (IPCC), a UN-sponsored body, has reflected overwhelming scientific consensus in its projections of anticipated climate change in the twenty-first century. Such changes could significantly raise global mean temperatures over the next 100 years as well as lead to a variety of potentially devastating environmental and economic effects (IPCC 2007, 2013). Yet, scientific and political debate continues over the validity of particular projections and their policy implications. Part of the reason is that questions remain about the precise relationship between greenhouse gas concentration in the atmosphere and temperature increases, the probability that temperatures will rise by a certain amount, and the location and timing of climate disturbances such as increased rainfall and the severity of storms. The complex computer models that scientists use to make these projections cannot provide all the answers, and even where the forecasts agree on environmental effects, economists and policymakers may reach very different conclusions about the costs and benefits of possible policy actions (DiMento and Doughman 2014; Nordhaus 2008; Selin and VanDeveer 2009, 2016; Stern 2007).

Contemporary politics, of course, has created a demand for simple ideas expressed in news conference or talk radio soundbites, or prominently featured on popular websites, and this is true for both environmentalists and their opponents. Those who contribute to or turn to these sources of information often are disinclined to work through complex scientific issues and their inevitable uncertainty, and to consider tough policy choices. These tendencies are especially great when an environmental problem first becomes visible and is judged quickly and superficially. With experience, debate, and learning, ideology may give way to more thoughtful appraisals of problems and solutions.

Assessing Risks: Social and Technical Issues As the climate change example indicates, we always need to ask some critical questions about the nature of the environmental problems at issue. A common way to do that is to use the language of risk assessment or risk analysis. Analysts try to estimate the magnitude of risks that are posed to public health or to the environment, say from toxic chemicals or a warming planet. The information from such analysis often becomes central to public policy debates (Kraft 2017b).

Yet, risk assessment involves use of a relatively new and evolving set of methods for estimating both human health and ecosystem risks, and there is considerable disagreement over how to apply these methods and what to do with the information they produce. Environmentalists often have been opposed to its use for fear that it will diminish the urgency of the problems (Andrews 2006b). Industry representatives and many political conservatives have their own doubts about how the EPA and other agencies use risk assessment, but they are supportive of the methods because they see them as one way to avoid excessive regulation of small risks that can drive up costs (Huber 2000; Lichter and Rothman 1999).

Supporters of risk assessment argue that it can be a useful, if imperfect, tool for systematic evaluation of many, though not all, environmental problems. It also can help establish a formal process that brings into the open for public debate many of the otherwise hidden biases and assumptions that shape environmental policy (Davies 1996; National Research Council 1996; Presidential/Congressional Commission on Risk Assessment and Risk Management 1997). But they also note that risks are seen very differently by professionals than they are seen by the general public.

The technical community (e.g., scientists, engineers, and EPA professional staff) tends to define risk as a product of the probability of an event or exposure and the consequences that may follow, such as health and environmental effects. This is expressed in the formula $R = PC$, where R is the risk level, P is the probability, and C is a measure of the consequences. For risk assessors, the task is to identify and measure a risk (such as the health effects of fine particulates or mercury released to the air by coal-fired power plants) and then to evaluate the level or magnitude of the risk to judge how acceptable it is. Those risks that are viewed as unacceptably high are obvious candidates for regulation.

In comparison, the general public tends to see risks in a very different way. Ordinary citizens give a greater weight to qualities such as the degree to which risks are uncertain, uncontrollable, inequitable, involuntary, dreaded, or potentially fatal or catastrophic (Slovic 1987). On those bases, the public perceptions of risk may differ dramatically from those of government scientists, as they do most notably in the case of nuclear power and nuclear waste disposal. In these examples, experts believe the risks are small and the public thinks they are large. Hence people tend to oppose nuclear waste repositories that are located nearby (Dunlap, Kraft, and Rosa 1993; U.S. EPA 1990b).[15]

Scholars describe these differences in terms of two conflicting concepts of rationality, and they argue that both are valid. Susan Hadden captures the differences well in saying that "technical rationality" refers to a "mindset that trusts evidence and the scientific method, appeals to expertise for justification, values universality and consistency, and considers unspecifiable impacts to be irrelevant to present decision-making." In contrast, she says, "cultural rationality" appeals not to experts so much as to "traditional and peer groups." In addition, it tends to focus on personal and family risks as opposed to statistical approaches that experts use. Moreover, it tends to trust process rather than to appeal to evidence. That is, people look to qualities such as openness, transparency, and public involvement in a decision-making process (Hadden 1991, 49).[16]

These differences in understanding environmental and health risks can greatly complicate the conduct, communication, and use of risk assessments in environmental policy decisions. That is particularly so when government agencies lose public trust, a recurring problem, for example, in hazardous waste and nuclear waste policy actions (Kraft 2000; Munton 1996; Slovic 1993). Yet such different perspectives on risk do not eliminate the genuine need to provide credible risk assessments to try to get a useful fix on the severity of various environmental problems (such as air pollution, drinking water contamination, or risk of exposure to toxic chemicals) and to decide what might be done about them—that is, how best to reduce the risks.

In 2016, for example, parents in a wealthy Malibu, California high school became highly concerned about PCBs in the caulking of the school's windows. The school district and the EPA said the classrooms were safe with routine cleaning and ventilation. The PCBs posed no health risks, they said, and in any event, all of the caulking would be removed over several years under the school's planned renovations at far less cost. Yet many parents and teachers were concerned nonetheless, and they sued the district to remove all of the contaminated caulking immediately.[17] The overreaction in Malibu can be contrasted with the justifiable concern of parents in Flint, Michigan in 2015 when the city's drinking water supply was found to be contaminated with lead at dangerous levels, and with officials initially belittling citizen complaints. The city had switched water supplies to save $1 million to $2 million a year, but neglected to treat the new water with an anti-corrosive chemical that could have prevented the leaching of lead from old piping.[18]

Even without such disparities in risk perception between technical experts and the public, assessing the severity of environmental problems must take place amid much uncertainty. Consider the challenge of dealing with indoor air pollutants such as radon, a naturally occurring, short-lived radioactive gas formed by the decay of uranium found in small quantities in soil and rocks. Colorless and odorless, it enters homes through walls and foundations (and sometimes in drinking water), and its decay products may be inhaled along with dust particles in the air to which they become attached, posing a risk of lung damage and cancer. In 1987 the EPA declared that radon was "the most deadly environmental hazard in the U.S.," and in recent years the agency's webpage described it as the second leading cause of lung cancer in the United States, second only to smoking, and the leading cause among nonsmokers. The EPA says that radon is responsible for some 21,000 lung cancer deaths a year, of which 2,900 are among people who have never smoked. Not surprisingly, the agency urges people to test their homes for radon.[19]

The best evidence of radon's effects on human health is based on high-dose exposure of uranium miners. Yet extrapolation from mines to homes is difficult. Moreover, although radon experts agree that the gas is a substantial risk at levels that are two to four times the EPA's "action level" for home exposure, it is more difficult to confirm a significant cause-and-effect relationship at the lower levels found in the typical home. EPA and other scientists believe that the indirect evidence is strong enough to take action to reduce exposure to radon in individuals' homes. But critics question how aggressively the nation should attempt to reduce radon levels, in part because they think that doing so could be quite costly (Cole 1993).

Coping with Environmental Risks

As the radon example shows, another set of important questions concerns what, if anything, to do about environmental problems once we recognize them. Are they serious enough to require action? If so, is governmental intervention necessary, or might we address the problem better through alternative approaches, such as private or voluntary action? Such decisions are affected by judgments about public needs and the effects on society and the economy. For example, in the 1990s the Clinton administration tended to favor mandatory government regulation of many environmental risks, whereas George W. Bush's administration in the 2000s favored voluntary action and market incentives. President Obama's administration was closer to Clinton's in these kinds of judgments, but the balance shifts depending on the particular issue. Donald Trump's administration is likely to resemble that of President Bush in these regards; he campaigned against excessive federal regulation and vowed to reverse course.

What Is an Acceptable Risk? For the public and its political representatives, two difficult issues are how to determine a so-called acceptable level of risk and how to set environmental policy priorities. For environmental policy, the question is often phrased as "How clean is clean enough?" or "How safe is safe enough?" in light of available technology or the costs involved in reducing or eliminating such risks and competing demands in other sectors of society (e.g., education and health care) for the resources involved. Should drinking water standards be set at a level that ensures essentially no risk of cancer from contaminants, as the Safe Drinking Water Act required prior to 1996? Or should the EPA be permitted to weigh health risks and the costs of reducing those risks within reasonable limits? In 1996 Congress adopted the latter position. Equally important are the questions of who should make such judgments and on what basis judgments should be made. Countless decisions of this kind are made every year in the process of implementing environmental policies. Over the last few years, for example, the EPA has struggled with standards on arsenic and other chemicals in drinking water, mercury and particulate emissions from power plants, greenhouse gas emissions from industry, and pesticide residues allowed in food (Andrews 2006b, 2016; Rosenbaum 2013a).

These judgments about acceptable risk involve chiefly policy (some would say political), not technical, decisions. That is, they call for a judgment about what is acceptable to society or what might survive a legal challenge to the agency making the decision. Even when the science is firm, such decisions are difficult to make in the adversarial context in which they are debated. Moreover, the seemingly straightforward task of setting priorities will naturally pit one community or set of interests against another. That so much is at stake is another reason to rely on the democratic political process to make these choices, or at a minimum to provide for sufficient accountability when decisions are delegated to bureaucratic officials.

Remediation of hazardous waste sites illustrates the dilemma of making risk decisions. Estimates of the costs for cleaning up the tens of thousands of sites in the United States, including heavily contaminated federal facilities such as the Hanford Nuclear Reservation in the state of Washington, have ranged from $500 billion to more than $1 trillion, depending on the cleanup standard used (Russell, Colglazier, and Tonn 1992). In 2009, the U.S. Department of Energy (DOE) estimated the costs just for its own former nuclear weapons production facilities at $265 to $305 billion over the next 30 years, and it characterized the task as one of the most technically challenging and complex cleanup efforts in the world (National Research Council 2009). At the 570-square-mile Hanford site, among the worst in the nation, the DOE and its predecessor agencies allowed 127 million gallons of toxic liquid waste to leak into the ground. Between 750,000 and 1 million gallons of high-level nuclear waste have leaked from single-shell storage tanks, and they have contaminated more than 200 square miles of groundwater. Cleanup of the Hanford site alone could cost $45 billion and take many decades to complete.

Yet, are all these sites equally important for public health and environmental quality? Should all be cleaned up to the same standard regardless of their future use, cleanup costs, and disputed estimates of the benefits that will result? How do we consider the needs of future generations in making such judgments so that the present society does not simply pass along hidden risks to them? Is the nation prepared to commit massive societal resources to such a cleanup program? We've done a poor job historically of answering these difficult questions, but Congress did address many of them throughout the past several decades as it considered renewal of the Superfund toxic waste program. That Congress could not agree on a course of action indicates the extent of the controversy.

Comparing Risks and Setting Priorities Governments have limited budgetary resources, a situation made much worse by the recession that began in 2008, the federal government's massive economic stimulus spending that followed, and the highly partisan debates over federal budget deficits and the cumulative national debt. The public also has little appetite for tax increases. These conditions force policymakers and the public to face real choices. If we cannot do everything, which programs and activities merit spending and which do not?

The federal EPA has issued several reports ranking environmental problems according to their estimated seriousness. They include a 1987 report, *Unfinished Business*, and a 1990 report, *Reducing Risk*. Little has changed since that time. One striking finding is that the American public worries a great deal about some environmental problems, such as hazardous waste sites and groundwater contamination, which the EPA accords a relatively low rating of severity. The public also exhibits much less concern about other problems, such as the loss of natural habitats and biodiversity, ozone depletion, climate change, and indoor air pollution (including radon), which are given high ratings by EPA staff and the agency's Science Advisory Board. Historically, the U.S. Congress has tended to reflect the public's views, and has set EPA priorities and budgets in a way that conflicts with the ostensible risks posed to the nation (Andrews 2006b; U.S. EPA 1987, 1990b).

Critics charge, with good justification, that such legislative decisions promote costly and inefficient environmental policies. Thus they suggest that we need to find ways to compare environmental and health risks and to distinguish the more serious risks from the less important. Such efforts will likely play an increasingly important role in the future to help frame environmental policy issues, promote public involvement and debate over them, and assist both the public and policymakers in making critical policy choices.

Public Policy Responses

Finally, if governmental intervention is thought to be essential, what public policies are most appropriate, and at which level of government (international, national, state, or local) should they be put into effect? Governments have a diversified set of tools in their policy repertoires. Among others they include regulation, taxation, use of subsidies and market incentives, funding for research, provision of information, education, and purchase of goods and services. Policy analysts ask which approaches are most suitable in a given situation, either alone or in combination with others (Kraft and Furlong 2018; Patton, Sawicki, and Clark 2016; Weimer and Vining 2016).

A lively debate has arisen in recent years over the relative advantages and disadvantages of the widely used regulatory approach ("command and control") as well as such competing or supplementary devices as market-based incentives, information disclosure, and public–private partnerships (Bennear and Coglianese 2013; Eisner 2007; Fiorino 2006; Press and Mazmanian 2016). Such newer approaches have been incorporated into both federal and state environmental policies, from the Clean Air Act to measures for reducing the use of toxic chemicals. Both the federal and state governments also have helped spur technological developments through their power in the marketplace. Governments buy large quantities of certain products such as computers and other office equipment and motor vehicles. Even without regulation, they can alter production processes by buying only those products that meet, say, stringent energy efficiency or fuel economy standards. Analysts typically weigh such policy alternatives (e.g., use of regulation or reliance on public education via disclosure of information) according to various criteria. These include the policy's likely effectiveness, technical feasibility, economic efficiency, and political and social acceptability. None of this is easy to calculate or consider, and yet the exercise brings useful information to the table to be debated (Patton, Sawicki, and Clark 2016).

As noted earlier, to address questions of equity or social justice, analysts and policymakers also need to ask about the distribution of environmental costs, benefits, and risks across society, as well as internationally and across generations. Numerous studies suggest that many environmental risks, such as those posed by industrial facilities, disproportionately affect poor and minority citizens, who are more likely than others to live in heavily industrialized areas with oil refineries, chemical plants, and similar facilities or in inner cities with high levels of air pollutants (Konisky 2015; Ringquist 2006). Similarly, risks associated with anticipated climate changes are far more likely to affect poor nations than affluent, industrialized nations that can better afford to adapt to a new climate regime, even at the low to middle range of climate change scenarios (IPCC 2007; Selin and VanDeveer 2016).

For programs already in existence, we need to ask many of the same questions. Which policy approaches are now used, and how successful have they been? Would other approaches work better? Would they be more effective? Would they cost less? Would their costs and benefits be more equitably distributed than they now are (Kraft and Furlong 2018; Morgenstern and Portney 2004)? Some programs might be made more effective through higher funding levels, better implementation, institutional reforms, and similar adjustments. But some programs may be so poorly designed or so badly implemented that they should be ended.

Conclusions

A simple idea lies behind all these questions about the nature of environmental problems and strategies for dealing with them. Improving society's response to these problems, particularly in the form of environmental policy, requires a careful appraisal and a serious effort to determine what kinds of solutions hold the greatest promise. We will never have enough information to be certain of all the risks posed, the effects that present policies may have, and the likely effectiveness of proposed courses of action. As citizens, however, we can deal better with the welter of data and arguments by focusing on the core issues outlined in the preceding sections and acknowledging that disagreements are at least as much about different political values and policy goals as they are about how to interpret limited and ambiguous scientific information (Stone 2012). If citizens demand that policymakers do the same, we can move a lot closer to a defensible set of environmental policies that offer genuine promise for addressing the many challenges that the nation faces.

Chapter 2 focuses on an overview of contemporary environmental problems, from pollution control and energy use to loss of biological diversity and the consequences of human population growth. The intention is to ask the kinds of questions posed in the previous sections related to each of the major areas of environmental concern, and thus to lay out a diverse range of contemporary environmental problems, the progress being made to date in dealing with them, and the challenges that lie ahead.

Discussion Questions

1   How clear is the concept of sustainable development? Can it be used effectively to describe the long-term goal of environmental policy? Does doing so help to build public understanding and support for environmental policy actions or not?

2   What is the current relationship between environmental science and environmental policy? What should the relationship be? Should scientists do more to help inform the public and policymakers on environmental issues? If so, what would be the best way to do that?

3   How do economic incentives affect individuals' behavior with respect to the environment, such as decisions to buy a car, home, or appliance? How might such incentives be altered to help promote more environmentally positive outcomes?

4   How would a broader societal commitment to an environmental ethic affect environmental policy decisions? What might be done to improve the public's understanding of environmental issues? What might be done to increase the saliency of those issues in people's daily lives?

5   Is it useful to think about environmental problems in terms of the risks they pose to human and ecological health? Given the controversies over risk assessment, to what extent do you think that public policy decisions should be based on scientific assessments of risk? How might the public's understanding of risk be improved?

Suggested Readings

Brown, Lester R. 2009. *Plan B 4.0: Mobilizing to Save Civilization*. New York: W. W. Norton.

Fiorino, Daniel J. 2006. *The New Environmental Regulation*. Cambridge, MA: MIT Press.

Friedman, Thomas L. 2008. *Hot, Flat, and Crowded: Why We Need a Green Revolution and How It Can Renew America*. New York: Farrar, Straus, and Giroux.

O'Neill, Kate. 2009. *The Environment and International Relations*. New York: Cambridge University Press.

Meadowcroft, James, and Daniel J. Fiorino, eds. 2017. *Conceptual Innovations in Environmental Policy*. Cambridge, MA: MIT Press.

Starke, Linda, ed. 2013. *State of the World: Is Sustainability Still Possible?* Washington, DC: Island Press.

Vig, Norman J., and Michael E. Kraft, eds. 2016. *Environmental Policy: New Directions for the Twenty-First Century*, 9th edn. Washington, DC: CQ Press.

Notes

1 Matt Richtel, "American Drivers Regain Appetite for Gas Guzzlers," *New York Times*, June 24, 2016; and Daniel F. Becker and James Gerstenzang, "Stalling on Fuel Efficiency," *New York Times*, March 10, 2016. Despite battles over passenger vehicle standards, the EPA and the trucking industry reached agreement in August 2016 on new fuel economy standards for 18-wheelers, buses, delivery trucks, and similar heavy-duty vehicles which account for about one-fifth of carbon dioxide releases in the transportation sector.

2 Peter Galuszka, "China Leads the Way as Demand for Coal Surges Worldwide," *New York Times*, November 12, 2012.

3 Michael Forsythe, "China Curbs Plans for More Coal-Fired Power Plants," *New York Times*, April 25, 2016.

4 Keith Bradsher, "China Far Outpaces U.S. in Building Cleaner Coal-Fired Plants," *New York Times*, May 11, 2009; and Michael Forsythe, "China Aims to Spend at Least $360 Billion on Renewable Energy by 2020," *New York Times*, January 5, 2017. China also was poised to pass the United States as the largest market in the world for wind power equipment, and it is building more nuclear power plants than all other nations in the world combined. For an overview of China's movement toward green energy sources, see Gallagher and Lewis (2016).

5 Bloomberg News, "China Auto Sales Growth Accelerates on Rising SUV Demand," July 7, 2016.

6 Lubchenco, a leading marine ecologist, was named by President Obama to head the National Oceanic and Atmospheric Administration, and took office in early 2009.

7 See, for example, Michael Balter, "Archaeologists Say the 'Anthropocene' Is Here But It Began Long Ago," *Science* 340 (April 19, 2013): 261–262.

8 For an overview of issues related to the intersection of science and environmental policy, particularly efforts by scientists in recent decades to play a more central role in policymaking, see Keller (2009) and Ascher, Steelman, and Healy (2010).

9 Jeffrey Mervis, "Obama Courts a Smitten Audience at the National Academy," *Science* 324 (May 1, 2009): 576–577. For Holdren's views on the role of environmental science in public policy, see his AAAS presidential address, "Science and Technology for Sustainable Well-Being," *Science* 319 (January 25, 2008): 424–434.

10 Jeffrey Mervis, "Scientists Start to Parse a Trump Presidency," *Science* 354 (November 18, 2016): 811–812; and Rush Holt, "What Now for Science?" *Science* 354 (November 25, 2016): 947.

11 For example, see Leon M. Lederman and Shirley M. Malcolm, "The Next Campaign," *Science* 323 (March 6, 2009): 1265. Editorials in *Science* frequently call for improvements in the public's scientific literacy, and often advocate

increased involvement by scientists in public policy processes. Conflicts between the public's view of climate change and that of scientists can be seen in recent polls summarized in "An Inside/Outside View of U.S. Science," *Science* 325 (July 10, 2008): 132–133.

12 See Pam Belluck, "New England's Fishermen Fret for Industry's Future," *New York Times*, August 19, 2002.

13 David M. Herszenhorn and Clifford Krauss, "Enthusiasm Builds for Helping a Shift to Fuel-Efficient Cars," *New York Times*, March 30, 2009; and Matthew L. Wald, "Cash Deal for 'Clunkers' So Popular That It's Broke," *New York Times*, July 31, 2009.

14 See Kirk Johnson, "City's Water-Quality Plan Working So Far, U.S. Finds," *New York Times*, June 1, 2002.

15 For instance, a book published in 2002, a year after the terrorist attacks of September 11, 2001, highlighted public anxiety over unfamiliar, and highly publicized, risks; see David Ropeik and George Gray, *Risk: A Practical Guide for Deciding What's Really Safe and What's Really Dangerous in the World Around You* (Boston, MA: Houghton Mifflin, 2002). The book sold briskly at the online sites for Amazon.com and Barnes and Noble.

16 One of the most thorough reviews of the disputes over the meaning of "rationality" in risk assessment and management and the implications for citizen participation in environmental policy is by the philosopher K. S. Shrader-Frechette (1991, 1993). See also Kraft (1994b, 1996), and Slovic (1993).

17 Ian Lovett, "Health Scare at Malibu School Sets Off Media War," *New York Times*, April 4, 2016.

18 Julie Bosman, Monica Davey, and Mitch Smith, "As Water Problems Grew, Officials Belittled Complaints from Flint," *New York Times*, January 21, 2016.

19 See the EPA's webpage on the subject: www.epa.gov/radon/.

CHAPTER 2

Judging the State of the Environment

Hardly a week passes without a federal or state agency taking some significant action on environmental problems, and those decisions invariably involve a judgment about the risk to human health or ecosystems and what degree of protection is needed. For example, what level of pesticide residue should be allowed in the food we eat? What should be done to reduce our exposure to toxic and hazardous chemicals in the air we breathe and the water we drink? Should the government impose a carbon tax to reduce the nation's reliance on fossil fuels, and thereby to lower the risk of climate change and prevent its many consequences for human health and well-being? Should it subsidize the development of renewable energy sources for the same reasons? What can cities do to limit urban sprawl and help establish more sustainable and livable communities?

The rest of the book deals with U.S. environmental policy and politics, and thus focuses on decisions like this. It describes government institutions and the various policy actors, formal and informal, who influence the adoption and implementation of environmental policies, including approval of the often complicated rules and regulations that put them into effect. It concentrates on the major federal policies, their goals and objectives, their strengths and weaknesses, and proposals for improving them, and also notes important state and local actions. All of this can best be understood by turning first to the problems themselves and the challenges they present to society and government. After all, policymaking starts with a given problem and its effects on us, and what might be done about it.

Which problems should be covered in such a survey? Although everyone would agree that long-standing issues like air and water pollution should be included, other topics, such as energy use and population growth, might be thought to be less central. But environmental quality also is closely tied to many other aspects of society, such as agricultural practices and other land use decisions; where we choose to live and how we design our cities and buildings; and the transportation choices that we make, such as reliance on automobiles or mass transit. I focus here on selected problems that are commonly addressed in reports by government agencies and other

33

organizations. Of necessity, I cannot cover some important topics such as the state of oceans and natural resource use (mining, grazing, forestry, parks), but many of these topics will be addressed later in the book as we take up questions of public policy. Despite this limitation, most readers will agree that among the most important problems to cover are air and water pollution, toxic chemicals, hazardous wastes, consumer and solid wastes, energy use and climate change, loss of biodiversity, and population growth.

All of these problems have become important concerns in recent years, and even a brief assessment of them illustrates how the scope of environmental policy extends well beyond the traditional topics of pollution control and land conservation. Such a review also shows how these problems are interrelated; that is, transportation choices affect energy use, but also air quality and climate change, and population growth affects land use decisions and biodiversity loss as well as consumption of resources. So ideally we would analyze and act on all of these problems in a comprehensive and integrated manner that is linked to the long-term goal of sustainable development. However appealing and sensible, this approach is difficult to put into practice and is rarely found today in public policy decision making. Nonetheless, it is increasingly recognized as imperative for the future, particularly at the local and regional levels where citizens and policymakers confront real and consequential decisions about transportation, housing, urban redevelopment, access to reliable water supplies, improvement of local air quality, and related issues (Bartlett 1990; Mazmanian and Kraft 2009; Portney 2013, 2015).

As noted in Chapter 1, it is not always easy to understand all of the causes of these diverse problems and the effects they have on human health, the environment, or the economy. Nor is it any easier to determine exactly what policy actions are needed to deal with them. Sometimes science can provide only partial and incomplete information, for example, about climate change or biodiversity loss. Sometimes the science is clear, but there are disagreements over what to do because of the economic implications or conflicts over the role for government in acting on the problems. Sometimes all of these conflicts can be resolved, but government still finds it difficult to act because different departments and agencies, or different levels of government (federal, state, local), cannot come to an agreement. These challenges are particularly difficult in the fragmented U.S. political system, but also can be found in other nations with a more unified governmental structure (Steinberg and VanDeveer 2012). Similarly, there simply may not be enough money to fully support environmental programs in light of the ever-present competition for funds with other policies and programs, from national defense to health and education. Hence policymakers cannot do all that they would like to do.

The chapter seeks to:

- improve understanding of selected environmental problems, their causes, and their effects on society;

- build a capacity to locate, synthesize, and interpret available scientific and technical information on the problems; and
- aid readers in analyzing how well public policies are addressing these problems and the promise of proposed solutions to them.

Extensive references are provided throughout the chapter and in the endnotes to enable readers to find the most up-to-date information about both science and policy developments in future years.

Air Quality

Air pollution is one of the most pervasive and easily recognizable environmental problems both in the United States and in other nations. Its effects range from impairment of visibility to serious impacts on human health. U.S. policies on air quality date back to the late nineteenth century, when cities such as Chicago, New York, and Pittsburgh began to regulate smoke emissions. Contemporary efforts, however, largely began with the federal Clean Air Act Amendments of 1970, with its focus on human health and national standards for protecting it. Since then, scientific understanding of the effects of air pollutants on public health has improved greatly. Yet, controversies continue over what to do and how much to spend to improve air quality.

Air pollution results from myriad and complex causes, many of which have proven difficult to address, particularly with a rising population and strong economic growth. In large part, however, air pollution may be traced to the combustion of fossil fuels to generate power for manufacturing, and heating and cooling of homes and offices; industrial and other processes (metal smelters, chemical plants, petroleum refineries, and manufacturing facilities, and solvent utilization); and mobile sources of transportation (trucks, buses, trains, aircraft, marine vessels, and automobiles). Urban smog develops when nitrogen oxides from the burning of fuel and volatile organic compounds (VOCs) interact with sunlight to form ground-level ozone (to be distinguished from the protective stratospheric ozone layer) and other chemicals. The use of motor vehicles powered by internal combustion engines is the major source of urban air pollution in most industrialized nations. The U.S. EPA puts these various contributions to air pollution into four categories: stationary sources (e.g., factories, power plants, and smelters), area sources (e.g., smaller stationary sources such as dry cleaners and degreasing operations), mobile sources (e.g., cars, buses, planes, trucks, and trains), and natural sources (e.g., windblown dust and volcanic eruptions).

Aside from problems of reduced visibility and mild irritation, outdoor air pollution exacts a heavy toll on public health, causing thousands of premature deaths each year in the United States and perhaps as many as 3 million worldwide, with another 3.5 million deaths attributed to household air pollution, primarily in developing nations. About 300 million children, or one in seven globally, live in areas that have what the U.N. Children's Fund calls "toxic" levels of air pollution. Outdoor air pollution contributed to about 1.6 million premature deaths annually in China alone in recent years (Chivian et al. 1993; International Energy Agency 2016; U.S. EPA 2016).[1] Largely because of these concerns, the Clean Air Act requires the EPA to set national air quality standards for six principal pollutants, referred to as "criteria" pollutants: carbon monoxide (CO), lead (Pb), nitrogen dioxide (NO_2), ozone (O_3), particulate matter (PM), and sulfur dioxide (SO_2). The standards set the maximum level of human exposure to the pollutants that is to be allowed. The Act and its later amendments provide the basic framework for efforts to improve air quality, which is discussed in depth in Chapter 5. Prior to passage of the Act, the United States witnessed massive increases in air emissions of these chemicals. For example, between 1900 and 1970, the EPA estimates that emissions of VOCs increased some 260 percent, sulfur dioxide about 210 percent, and nitrogen oxides nearly 700 percent. The trends since adoption of the Act have been encouraging, and illustrate how much public policy can accomplish over time.

Gains in Air Quality and Remaining Problems

By most measures, air quality in the United States has improved significantly since Congress approved the Clean Air Act Amendments in 1970. For example, as shown in Figure 2.1, between 1980 and 2015, total emissions of the six principal air pollutants decreased by 63 percent while the nation's gross domestic product (GDP) increased by 153 percent, the vehicle miles traveled increased by 106 percent, energy consumption increased 25 percent, and the U.S. population grew by 41 percent.[2] Total release of toxic air pollutants dropped by about 60 percent between 1990 and 2011. However, the nation continues to release about 89 million tons of the six criteria pollutants to the air each year (down from 267 million tons in 1980), in addition to 740 million pounds of toxic chemicals reported via the annual Toxics Release Inventory (U.S. EPA 2016).

As indicated in Table 2.1, national monitoring data also show substantial improvement over the past thirty-five years in atmospheric concentrations of the six criteria pollutants as well as in emissions. Some of these declines in air pollution might have occurred even without the push of public policy. Yet there is little question that the Clean Air Act itself has produced major improvements in air quality and thus in public health. Similarly, the EPA monitors a number of the toxic air pollutants regulated by the Clean Air Act, and found that the majority of monitoring sites in the nation show a decrease in concentrations, including for those chemical of greatest concern for public health (U.S. EPA 2016).

Despite such welcome news, in 2015, 121 million people lived in counties where the air is unhealthy at times because of high levels of one of the six

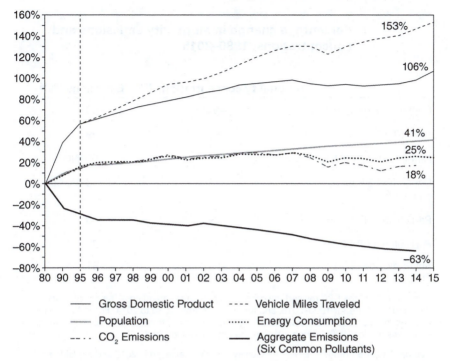

FIGURE 2.1 Comparison of growth areas and emissions, 1980–2015

Source: U.S. EPA, "Air Quality: National Summary," www.epa.gov/air-trends/air-quality-national-summary. Retrieved September 12, 2016.

major pollutants covered by the act, principally ozone or particulates. Air quality remains unacceptable in many of the large urban clusters in which most Americans live. In recent years, many of those urban areas experienced a large number of "unhealthy" days, defined as when the air quality index exceeds 100. Yet most cities continue to see progress, with fewer unhealthy air days each year than occurred a decade earlier (U.S. EPA 2016). As the number of cars on the road and the miles driven increase, and as the population grows, many areas may well find it difficult to meet new federal air quality standards without taking action affecting the use of motor vehicles.

Ground-level ozone in particular is a major public health risk. It is capable of causing respiratory difficulties in sensitive individuals, reduced lung function, and eye irritation. It can also inflict damage on vegetation and ecosystems, reducing forest and agricultural productivity by making plants more susceptible to disease, pests, and other environmental stressors. Other major air pollutants are associated with a range of health and environmental effects, from eye and throat irritation and respiratory illness to cardiovascular and nervous-system damage.

TABLE 2.1 Percentage change in air quality emissions and concentrations, 1980–2015

	Air quality concentrations (%)	Emissions (%)[b]
Carbon monoxide (CO)	−84	−69
Lead (Pb)	−99	−99
Nitrogen dioxide (NO$_2$)	−60	−55 (NO$_x$)
Ozone (O$_3$) 8-hours standard[a]	−32	−53 (VOCs)
Particulates (PM-10)[a]	−39	−58
Particulates (PM-2.5)[a]	−37	−25
Sulfur dioxide (SO$_2$)	−84	−81

Notes: [a] In 1997 the EPA revised the ozone and particulate standards. The concentration data for PM-10 are for 1990–2015, and for emission from 1980 to 2014. For PM-2.5, data for concentration are for 2000–2015 only, and for emission, from 1990 to 2014. [b] Data for emissions are for 1980 through 2014 unless otherwise indicated.

Source: Adapted from U.S. EPA, "Air Quality Trends," released in 2016 and available at: www.epa.gov/air-trends/air-quality-national-summary.

According to the EPA, fine particulate matter in air pollution from fuel combustion in motor vehicles, power generation, and industrial facilities could be responsible for perhaps 20,000 deaths a year in the United States, and other studies put the number considerably higher; these occur mostly among the elderly, individuals with cardiopulmonary disease such as asthma, and children. Air pollution also contributes to hundreds of thousands of acute asthma attacks annually.[3]

Indoor Air Quality

The quality of indoor air poses as high a risk for many people as does the air outside, although for years indoor air pollution was ignored by the public and government agencies alike. Indoor air quality is particularly a concern in those areas of the world that rely on primitive household cooking fires that burn wood, crop residues, charcoal, or coal. The World Health Organization considers such indoor pollution to be the leading environmental cause of death worldwide.[4]

Recently, the EPA has expressed concern about indoor pollutants, ranking them as one of the top risks to public health, a finding confirmed by independent studies.[5] Radon (discussed in Chapter 1) and environmental tobacco smoke (ETS) are especially worrisome. In January 1993, after years of extensive investigation, two public reviews, and recommendations from its Science Advisory Board (SAB), the EPA classified ETS as a known human (group A) carcinogen and a "serious and substantial public health threat" (Browner 1993).[6]

The EPA report was instrumental in later actions by the federal government, state and local governments, and the private sector to restrict or ban smoking in the workplace, in college and university buildings, in public housing, and in many public places.[7] As often the case, California took the most aggressive action, eventually banning smoking in all restaurants and bars as well. Most states and many cities have since done the same. Studies strongly suggest that ETS is a factor in heart disease in addition to cancer, potentially doubling the risk and contributing to as many as 30,000 to 60,000 deaths a year in the United States (Kawachi et al. 1997). Smokers themselves assume the greatest risk. The federal Centers for Disease Control and Prevention (CDC) reports that smoking is the single most preventable cause of premature death in the United States, accounting for more than 440,000 deaths a year, with an additional 42,000 deaths attributable to secondhand smoke exposure.[8]

For several reasons, indoor air quality has worsened over the past several decades, quite aside from ETS. Modern homes, schools, and office buildings that are tightly sealed to improve their energy efficiency have the distinct drawback of allowing a multitude of pollutants to build up indoors if the building is not properly ventilated. Use of synthetic chemicals in building materials and furnishings (such as particleboard, insulating foam, and carpeting) also contributes to the problem, as does the use of many household cleaning and personal care products. Important indoor pollutants in addition to tobacco smoke and radon include vinyl chloride, formaldehyde, asbestos, benzene, fine particulates, lead (from lead-based paint), combustion products such as carbon monoxide from gas stoves and inadequately vented furnaces, and biological agents such as molds, the last of which are suspected as a major factor in allergic symptoms and sinus infections (Ott and Roberts 1998; Samet and Spengler 1991).

Based on recent studies, the EPA has estimated that indoor levels of many air pollutants may be two to five times, and occasionally 100 times, higher than they are outdoors. Those studies are particularly troublesome because Americans now spend an estimated 90 percent of their time indoors. Ironically, as the air outdoors has improved, the quality of indoor air has been declining. Moreover, because most modern office buildings come equipped with permanently sealed windows, the quality of indoor air that many people breathe all day depends on the workings of finely tuned ventilating systems that sometimes fail.[9]

Acid Precipitation

Two of the major air pollutants, sulfur dioxide and nitrogen dioxide, react with water, oxygen, and oxidants to form acidic compounds. These compounds fall to the ground in either a dry or wet form and are commonly called "acid rain." They can be carried for hundreds of miles by the wind, crossing both state and national boundaries. In the United States, a major source of these emissions is coal-fired power plants, and the problem is particularly acute for older utilities that operate with fewer environmental controls.

Comprehensive federal studies have found that acid precipitation adversely affects aquatic ecosystems, forests, crops, and buildings. It may also threaten the health of individuals with respiratory problems and degrade visibility (National Acid Precipitation Assessment Program 1990; U.S. EPA 2016). As a result of such concerns, the 1990 Clean Air Act Amendments created an Acid Rain Program to sharply reduce emissions of both sulfur dioxide and nitrogen dioxide. The Act established an innovative program of economic incentives through emissions trading to help meet those goals (Bryner 1995; Portney and Stavins 2000). The U.S. EPA (2016) subsequently has pointed to significant reductions in acid precipitation. Yet much remains to be accomplished, with serious and continuing effects noticeable in the Adirondacks region of New York State and elsewhere in the northeast (Smardon and Nordenstam 1998). These and similar findings of continuing damage in Colorado's Front Range, in the Appalachians, and elsewhere have led to calls for strengthening acid rain policies.

CFCs and the Stratospheric Ozone Layer

Some air emissions are more important for global atmospheric conditions than for urban air quality. With several other chemicals, chlorofluorocarbons (CFCs) have been linked to depletion of the stratospheric ozone layer, located between 6 and 30 miles above Earth, which shields life on the surface from dangerous ultraviolet radiation. Chemically stable and unreactive, CFCs rise to the stratosphere, where they are broken down by intense ultraviolet light. The freed chlorine atoms can destroy as many as 100,000 ozone molecules before being inactivated. In this way, CFCs reduce the capacity of the ozone layer to block ultraviolet radiation from penetrating to the surface of Earth. CFCs are also a major greenhouse gas, and thus they contribute to climate change.

Evidence of the depletion of the ozone layer became more compelling by the 1980s, with the loss particularly notable above the North and South Poles. As the stratospheric ozone concentration decreases, there is an increase in ultraviolet B (UVB) radiation reaching the surface of Earth, and hence a likely increase in adverse health effects. These include an increase in nonmalignant skin cancer as well as malignant skin cancer, or melanoma. Other possible health effects include depression of immune systems, which would allow otherwise minor infections to worsen, and increased incidence of cataracts—clouding of the eye's lens that has long been the leading cause of blindness in the world. An increase in ultraviolet radiation also could adversely affect animal and plant life, and therefore agricultural productivity. Scientists have expressed concern that higher UVB radiation could severely harm oceanic phytoplankton and thus affect the food chain as well as the capacity of oceans to regulate climate.[10]

Scientific consensus on the risks of CFC use was great enough for the industrialized nations to agree on the phaseout of CFCs, halons, and other ozone-destroying chemicals on a fairly aggressive schedule. That agreement was embodied in the Montreal Protocol, approved in 1987 after several years of international meetings. When evidence suggested ozone depletion was more extensive than had been believed, policymakers strengthened the agreement with a series of amendments. Because of the way it integrates continuous assessment of environmental trends with policy action, the Montreal Protocol is often cited as a model for global environmental governance (Axelrod and VanDeveer 2015; Benedick 1991). The U.S. Congress also included a supplement to the Montreal Protocol in the 1990 Clean Air Act Amendments. The United States committed itself to a more rapid phaseout of the production and use of ozone-depleting chemicals and other measures such as recycling and disposal of such chemicals from discarded appliances. By January 1996, U.S. production of CFCs and several other ozone-depleting chemicals such as halons almost completely stopped. The same is true for most other developed nations. The chemical industry, well aware of the burgeoning new market for non-CFC refrigerants and other uses, has developed substitutes for CFCs, and it continues to search for better products, in part because the replacements have had unintended consequences, contributing to greenhouse gas emissions.[11] Taken together, these actions seem to have been effective, although it will take decades for the ozone layer to recover.

Water Quality

The availability of water resources and the quality of that water are vital to life and to the nation's economy. Water resources support agriculture, industry, electric power, recreation, navigation, and fisheries, and they are distributed around the nation (and world) unevenly; that is, some areas have an abundance of water while others suffer from water scarcity; climate change is expected to worsen water scarcity in many areas. Natural hydrologic conditions and cycles (particularly the amount of rain and snow) determine the amount of water in any given location, although human uses of that water can make a substantial difference in its availability. For example, some 80 percent of water used nationwide goes to farm irrigation, which can deplete groundwater supplies, as it has in many parts of the country.[12] Water quality is also affected by human uses, including point discharges from industry and municipalities and nonpoint sources such as agriculture and runoff from urban areas.

The state of the nation's water quality is more difficult to measure than its air quality, in part because of the very large number of bodies of water and great variability nationwide in their condition. Hence, evidence of progress since the 1970s is more limited and mixed. Most assessments deal separately with surface water quality (streams, rivers, lakes, and ponds), groundwater, drinking water quality, and the quantity of water resources available for human uses such as drinking and agriculture. Both human and ecosystem health effects of water quality have been objects of concern. Only a few key indicators of conditions and trends are reviewed here.

Pollution of Surface Waters

The state of the nation's water quality is improving only slowly despite expenditures of hundreds of billions of dollars since adoption of the Clean Water Act of 1972, mostly on "end-of-pipe" controls on municipal and industrial discharges. Lack of reliable data makes firm conclusions about the pace of progress difficult, but many studies and monitoring programs are now under way that will eventually provide a fuller accounting. In the meantime, some trends are fairly clear.

Perhaps most important is a major reduction in the raw pollution of surface waters. The percentage of the U.S. population served by wastewater treatment plants rose from 42 percent in 1970 to 74 percent as early as 1985, with a resulting estimated decline in annual releases of organic wastes of about 46 percent. Striking declines have also been noted since 1972 in discharge of priority toxic organic pollutants and toxic metals as regulation of point sources of pollution (such as factories) took effect. This kind of control of point sources is largely responsible for the gains in water quality evident around the nation. A notable case is the Cuyahoga River, which runs through Cleveland, Ohio. The river burst into flames in 1969 as oily pollutants caught fire, one of the more spectacular images of 1960s-era environmental pollution. The fish may be returning to such rivers, but warnings against eating them (based on contamination with mercury and other toxins) and also bans on swimming and boating have continued across the nation.

Information on water quality is collected biennially by the states and submitted to the EPA, which prepares a report to Congress as well as making the state data available on its webpage.[13] Unfortunately, what we have falls well short of a complete inventory of U.S. waters. In the most recent national summary of the data, the states and tribes evaluated only 32 percent of rivers and streams, and 44 percent of the nation's lakes, ponds, and reservoirs. Worse still, few states assess the state of bays and estuaries. In addition, the EPA reports great variation in the methods used by the states to measure their water quality as well as in the frequency of their reports. Thus the picture provided by the EPA data is incomplete, if nevertheless indicative of remaining problems.

The states reported that 45 percent of the surveyed river and stream miles fully supported all uses set by the states and tribes, with 55 percent found to be impaired to some extent. Some 29 percent of lakes, ponds, and reservoirs supported all uses, while 71 percent were impaired. A classification as impaired means that water bodies were not meeting or fully meeting the national minimum water quality criteria for "designated beneficial uses" such as swimming, fishing, drinking water supply, and support of aquatic life. These figures generally indicate some improvement over previous years, but they also show that the nation's water quality continues to be unsatisfactory. Prevention of further degradation of water quality in the face of a growing population and strong economic growth could be considered an important achievement. At the same time, water quality clearly falls short of the goals of federal clean water acts. Further evidence can be found in the large number of fish consumption advisories issued because of contamination by toxic chemicals such as mercury, polychlorinated biphenyls (PCBs), chlordane, and dioxins, and the number of beach closings and swimming advisories related to pollution. Table 2.2 summarizes some of the key findings on water quality.

TABLE 2.2 National surface water quality

	Amount assessed (%)	Fully supporting all uses (%)	Impaired for one or more uses (%)	Leading sources of impairment
Rivers and streams (miles)	32.0	44.7	54.8	Agricultural activities, unknown sources, air deposition, hydrological modifications, habitat alterations, urban runoff, municipal discharge
Lakes, ponds, reservoirs (acres)	44.3	28.7	71.1	Air deposition, unknown sources, agricultural activities, natural/wildlife, nonpoint source pollution
Bays and estuaries (square miles)	*	*	*	Air deposition, unknown sources, municipal discharge, industrial sources, nonpoint sources

Note: *Assessments of wetlands, bays, and estuaries by the states are very limited, and criteria for meeting all uses are not well established. Thus the data are not included in this table.

Source: U.S. EPA, "National Summary of State Information, Assessed Waters of the United States," http://ofmpub.epa.gov/waters10/attains_nation_cy.control (accessed September 12, 2016).

According to the EPA database, by far the biggest source of water quality problems in rivers and streams comes from agriculture in the form of nutrients (farm fertilizers and animal wastes), pesticides, and suspended solids. Large animal feedlots favored by agribusiness have been a particular target of environmentalists, forcing the EPA and the Agriculture Department to issue new rules in 2002 to reduce that source of water pollution, although the rules will likely have only a modest effect.[14] Other major sources of impairment are atmospheric deposition of chemicals, hydrologic modification (e.g., loss of wetlands), urban runoff and storm water, municipal sewage treatment plants, habitat modification, and resource extraction. Most of these sources account for pollution of lakes and ponds as well. Urban runoff from rain and melting snow carries a wide assortment of chemicals, many of them toxic, into local rivers, bays, and lakes or into the groundwater. For instance, a National Academy of Science report in 2002 estimated that thousands of tiny releases of oil from cars, lawn mowers, and other dispersed sources on land equaled an Exxon *Valdez* spill (10.9 million gallons) every eight months.[15]

Continued loss of wetlands is particularly important because of the role they play in maintaining water quality. Twenty-two states have lost more than half of the wetlands they had in the nation's early years, and seven of those—California, Indiana, Ohio, Missouri, Kentucky, Illinois, and Iowa—have lost more than 80 percent. Nationally, between the mid-1950s and the mid-1970s, an estimated 458,000 acres a year of marshes, swamps, and other ecologically important wetlands were lost to development, highways, and mining. The rate slowed to about 290,000 acres a year lost by the mid-1980s, and the Interior and Agriculture departments maintain that the net rate has slowed further in recent years and that there even may be a net gain in wetlands.[16] However, the states are collecting so little information about wetlands that the numbers are unreliable. Other estimates of continued wetland loss are higher than the EPA's (Gaddie and Regens 2000). One consequence of the loss of wetlands was seen when Hurricane Katrina struck New Orleans in 2005. The effects were more devastating because the damaged wetlands could no longer offer protection against storm surges. Beyond these long-standing concerns, there is also accumulating evidence of oxygen-starved "dead zones" in many coastal areas as human activity has worsened water quality and depleted these areas of marine life.[17]

Regulatory water quality programs have concentrated on conventional sources of pollution such as biological waste products that can be assimilated and eventually cleaned by well-oxygenated water. Regulators are only beginning to deal with the more challenging problem of toxic chemicals that enter the nation's waters and their ecological effects. In some areas of the country, the effect of both conventional pollution and toxic contaminants on aquatic ecosystems has been severe.

Drinking Water Quality

Drinking water quality across the nation remains a problem, even though the EPA has long said that the nation has "one of the safest water supplies in the world." The agency also reminds citizens that "national statistics don't tell you specifically about the quality and safety of the water coming out of your tap." This is because drinking water quality varies substantially from one location to another, "depending on the condition of the source water from which it is drawn and the treatment it receives" (U.S. EPA 2006). Nationwide there are about 155,000 public drinking water systems, providing drinking water to 90 percent of Americans; the EPA does not regulate individual or private wells used for drinking water. Most of the large public systems are doing a good job of keeping the water clean, but problems have arisen with small, rural, and poorer systems, which often cannot afford to treat their water appropriately or test for water quality.[18] Information about each city's drinking water quality is now available, thanks to a "right-to-know" provision of the Safe Drinking Water Act Amendments of 1996. Consumer Confidence Reports are mailed once a year with water utility bills.

What is in drinking water that may be harmful? This varies across the nation, but studies find a variety of dangerous compounds, including disease-causing microorganisms, lead, chloroform (from the chlorine used to disinfect water supplies), and increasingly an array of pharmaceuticals that have been disposed of improperly.[19] In part because of lax enforcement, violation of federal health standards is not as rare as it should be. An example of the effects could be seen in Milwaukee, Wisconsin, in 1993. A waterborne parasite, *Cryptosporidium*, entered the city water supply and created an epidemic of intestinal disease, affecting more than 400,000 people and contributing to the deaths of more than 100 of them. According to the local press, thousands of residents lost their confidence in the safety of the local water supply, and a year later were still boiling their tap water or buying bottled water. The outbreak cost an estimated $54 million in health care expenses and lost productivity, and generated more than 1,400 lawsuits against the city.

As discussed in Chapter 1, in 2015 residents of Flint, Michigan discovered that their water supply was contaminated with lead, sometimes at dangerous levels, because improperly treated city water drawn from the Flint River leached lead from old pipes. As the city struggled to respond to the public health crisis, it blamed the state for the situation, while state officials said the fault lay with the city and its failure to treat the new water source with anti-corrosives that would have minimized the leaching.[20] Others criticized the federal EPA for lax supervision of city and state decisions, despite sharp cuts to its budget in recent years that have restricted its capacity to oversee the states (see Chapter 5).[21] Many other cities and school districts have suffered from comparable water quality problems, sometimes including leakage of industrial chemicals into well water.[22]

Several studies indicate that problems with city (and private) water supplies are not uncommon, particularly when groundwater is used as the source. The EPA's water quality inventory in the early 2000s indicated that leaking underground storage tanks were the highest priority of state water officials, with over 100,000 confirmed releases. Landfills and septic systems were identified as the next most important concerns, along with agricultural practices, such as the use of pesticides, herbicides, and fertilizers (U.S. EPA 2002).[23] The agency also stated that groundwater was of good overall quality, but that many problems of contamination were reported throughout the country. Information is often too incomplete, because of limited monitoring, to draw firm conclusions about water quality, and this includes groundwater that may be affected by chemicals used in natural gas fracturing or fracking. Groundwater supplies nearly 50 percent of the nation's population with drinking water.[24]

In a major 2016 study, the EPA concluded that under some circumstances natural gas fracking could harm drinking water quality when using water from sources that are already limited; by injecting water, chemicals, and sand into groundwater resources; through leakage of that mix into groundwater; by failing to treat wastewater appropriately before it is disposed of; or by dumping wastewater into pits where it can leak out.[25]

The U.S. Geological Survey (USGS) also examines water quality, and based on testing of wells around the country, it found one or more VOCs in a large percentage of urban wells as well as in some rural wells. Easily searchable data for each state can be found on the USGS website.[26] Leading environmental organizations also study drinking water quality, and they find a range of problems, from deteriorating waterworks to dated treatment technology. Among those that have issued such reports in recent years are the Natural Resources Defense Council (NRDC) and the Environmental Working Group (EWG). The EWG frequently issues reports on the quality of the nation's tap water and it has raised concerns about contaminants found in local water supplies across the nation.[27] The overall quality of U.S. drinking water is very high, but as these reports suggest, consumers ought to be alert to possible contamination of local supplies and make use of the various databases noted to check on local drinking water quality.

Public doubts about the safety of municipal drinking water help explain the surge in popularity of bottled water. Yet environmentalists have campaigned strongly against its use in part because of the vast amount of energy required to produce and transport the water.[28] Generally, they recommend the use of filtered tap water, and some of them, such as the EWG, have released test data on the quality of bottled water. Both the EWG and NRDC have provided some comparisons of the cost of bottled water and tap water; the bottled water may be from 240 to 10,000 times as expensive as ordinary tap water.

One analysis estimated that U.S. bottled water consumption required 32 to 54 million barrels of oil, depending on the distance the water was shipped.[29] Disposal is a problem as well. According to the Beverage Marketing Corporation, in 2015, Americans consumed an average of 37 gallons a year of bottled water, almost two-thirds of which was sold in single-serve plastic bottles. Such usage translates into more than 30 billion bottles a year, and only about 39 percent of them are recycled. However, experts see no advantage in most communities in using bottled water instead of tap water in terms of comparative quality; if anything, at least tap water is tested by public water systems under EPA requirements whereas bottled water is not. It falls under Food and Drug Administration regulation, which means less frequent and much less transparent testing; the results also are not available to consumers. Of course, in those areas of the world where tap water is unsafe, use of bottled water makes a lot more sense.

Toxic Chemicals and Hazardous Wastes

Modern industrial societies such as the United States depend heavily on the use of chemicals that pose risks to public health and the environment, and they continue to produce vast quantities of them. The scope of the problem is captured in part in the quantities of chemicals produced and emitted into the environment each year, the amount of hazardous wastes produced as by-products of industrial production and other processes, and the number of contaminated sites in the nation in need of cleanup or restoration.

Toxic Chemicals and Health Effects

The United States uses tens of thousands of different chemical compounds in commercial quantities, and industry develops perhaps a thousand or more new chemicals each year. U.S. production of synthetic chemicals burgeoned after World War II, increasing by a factor of 15 between 1945 and 1985. Similarly, agricultural demand for chemical pesticides such as dichlorodiphenyltrichloroethane (DDT) soared in the same period because of their low cost, persistence in the soil, and toxicity to a broad spectrum of insects. Use of pesticides nearly tripled between 1965 and 1985, with more than 6 pounds applied per hectare (2.47 acres) in the United States by 1985 (Postel 1988); according to EPA the national total for use of all herbicides, insecticides, and fungicides is more than 5 billion pounds a year. Although the effects are disputed, consumer groups argue that U.S. fruits and vegetables contain unacceptably high levels of pesticide residues, and urge citizens to inform themselves on the risks and choose foods with low levels of residues (Wargo 1998).

The Risk of Toxic Chemicals The overwhelming majority of all these widely used chemicals—exceeding 90 percent—are considered safe even though most have never been fully tested for toxicity. Toxic chemicals are usually defined as a subset of hazardous substances that produce adverse effects in living organisms. To measure such toxicity in humans, we usually look to epidemiological data on the effects of human exposures (which may occur through pesticide residues on food, contaminated water supplies, or polluted air). Researchers compare health statistics such as death rates with prevailing environmental conditions in areas around the nation. Such data, however, are often incomplete or inconclusive, making health effects difficult to establish.

Only cancer has been studied extensively, and it may be too soon to detect effects from exposures over the past several decades. Researchers have estimated that 2 to 8 percent of avoidable cancer deaths (i.e., those attributable to lifestyle or environmental factors that can be modified) can be associated with occupation, 1 to 5 percent to pollution, and less than 1 to 2 percent to industrial products (Shapiro 1990). As Michael Shapiro noted, even these low percentages, if correct, would translate into thousands of chemically related cancer deaths annually in the U.S. population. A 2010 report by the President's Cancer Panel reaffirmed a long-standing estimate that the number of cancer cases attributable to environmental chemicals was about 34,000 a year in the United States, or about 6 percent of cancer cases (4 percent from occupational exposure and 2 percent from community or other settings); the panel stated that these numbers, if anything, underestimate the link between environmental exposure and cancer.[30]

Other less well-documented chronic health effects add to the problem. For example, reports on so-called endocrine disrupters, or hormonally active agents such as DDT, dioxin, PCBs, and some chemicals found in plastics, suggest that in addition to cancer they may affect development of the brain and the reproductive system. These other effects may occur at very low exposure levels that are unlikely to lead to cancer.[31] Other health effects associated with toxic chemicals may include birth defects, neurotoxic disorders, respiratory and sensory irritation, dermatitis, immune-system dysfunction, and chronic organ toxicity such as liver disease. Scientists are paying more attention to possible synergistic or interactive effects, even at low levels of exposure, of diverse chemicals, including pesticides and herbicides, heavy metals such as lead and mercury, and the ubiquitous PCBs and other chlorinated organic chemicals (Shapiro 1990). An EPA rule that took effect in 2000 established or strengthened reporting requirements for 27 "persistent bioaccumulative toxics," including dioxin, PCBs, and mercury. In addition, the agency has tried to improve the transparency of chemical usage in the nation, and it provides multiple links to chemical information sources on its website.[32]

The Toxics Release Inventory Under the 1986 Emergency Planning and Community Right to Know Act, Title III of the Superfund law, manufacturers falling under the law report annually to the EPA and to the states in which they have facilities the quantities of nearly 700 different toxic chemicals they release to the air, water, and land. The information covers what the EPA calls a "significant portion" of toxic chemical releases to the environment, but not all releases by all sectors of the economy. The EPA records these data in its Toxics Release Inventory (TRI), which is posted on the EPA website and elsewhere; citizens can easily locate information for their areas and communities (see Box 2.1).

In its report for the year 2014 (released in January 2016), the EPA said that about 22,000 industrial facilities released or disposed of some 3.9 billion pounds of toxic chemicals on-site and off-site. Approximately 740 million pounds of those chemicals went into the air; 220 million pounds were discharged into the nation's rivers, lakes, bays, and other bodies of water; and 2.5 billion pounds were disposed of on land. Most of the off-site releases reflect transfer of chemicals to disposal facilities such as landfills and underground injection sites. None of these numbers can be easily converted into a public health risk, but the EPA has developed some methods that will make it easier for people to translate TRI data into such risk information for specific localities, and the future should bring better ways to understand what all this chemical information means within specific communities.[33]

Aside from mining, most of these environmental releases and wastes are associated with coal-burning power plants, chemical manufacturing, and production of primary metals, petroleum and coal products, paper, rubber, plastics, and transportation equipment. The release of such data since the late 1980s had led many companies, such as Dow Chemical and Monsanto, to commit to a significant reduction of their emissions of toxic chemicals. These decreases are documented in the annual TRI reports, which show much progress since the program began in the late 1980s. Based on the chemicals that have been reported on consistently, total on-site and off-site releases decreased by about 60 percent between 1988 and 2014. Releases of TRI chemicals to the air alone declined by 55 percent just between 2003 and 2014; in addition, carcinogens released to the air declined by about 48 percent in the same period.

Interpretation of progress in dealing with toxic chemicals, however, is somewhat difficult. This is because of changing definitions of what constitutes toxicity, certain exclusions from the TRI database, and noncompliance by some of the facilities that are required to report. Environmental groups also complain that the TRI data significantly understate the problem of toxic chemicals in the nation, even with expansion of the list of covered chemicals. More importantly, the decline in releases over time does not apply to all facilities because their environmental performance varies widely. Some have moved strongly to a greener operation while others have lagged significantly (Kraft, Stephan, and Abel 2011).

State and local governments have made considerable use of the TRI data to target certain areas of concern and measure environmental achievements. In addition, the public as well as environmental organizations have been able to use the data to understand local environmental conditions better and to bring pressure to bear on industry. Box 2.1 indicates where TRI data are available and how the data can be used to provide information about local toxic chemical emissions.

■■■■ BOX 2.1 USING THE TOXICS RELEASE INVENTORY ■■■■

The TRI database contains extensive information about the release of toxic chemicals in the United States. It can be accessed directly from a dedicated TRI EPA webpage (www.epa.gov/toxics-release-inventory-tri-program/tri-for-communities) as TRI Explorer, or the agency's broader Envirofacts page (www3.epa.gov/enviro/), which includes information about air, water, land, waste, radiation, and other subjects as well.

In addition, the group Chemical Right to Know provides TRI data to the public (www.chemicalright2know.org), and the EPA provides a new mobile application for use on cell phones or personal computers called My-Right-to-KnowTRI(www.epa.gov/toxics-release-inventory-tri-program/my-right-know-application).

All of these sources are easy to use, as they list all major polluting industries in a community and what chemicals they release, but they do require some care to evaluate just what chemicals are being released to the environment and the risk they pose.

Hazardous Wastes

The United States produces large quantities of hazardous waste each year, including household waste (batteries, oil, paints and solvents, and the like) and a diversity of commercial and industrial wastes. Hazardous wastes are a subset of solid and liquid wastes disposed of on land that may pose a threat to human health or the environment with improper handling, storage, or disposal.

It is difficult to describe precisely the severity of the threat of hazardous waste, but it is not a small problem. In the late 1980s, the volume of hazardous waste generated each year was estimated at 250 million metric tons, and that material came from more than 650,000 different sources (Dower 1990; Halley 1994).[34] This volume and the large number of sources make it extraordinarily hard to track where it all went, particularly before Congress enacted the Resource Conservation and Recovery Act (RCRA) in 1976 (Dower 1990); RCRA is the nation's major hazardous waste control policy (see Chapter 5). The EPA collects current data from the states on hazardous waste generation, management, and final disposal for wastes covered by RCRA, and the agency publishes it in a National Biennial RCRA Hazardous Waste Report available at the EPA website. In recent years the total amount produced each year in the United States counted under the program has been about 34 million tons from some 16,000 generators. The numbers vary widely by state, with Texas alone accounting for nearly half of the national total of hazardous waste being generated annually. Today companies store these wastes at the point of generation and carefully track the materials sent elsewhere for disposal or some form of treatment. Industry is also more likely today to recycle and otherwise reduce the production of hazardous wastes through pollution prevention initiatives (Sigman 2000).

Much less is known about previous production and disposal of these chemicals. It is no secret that much of the waste historically was disposed of carelessly. Since 1950, for example, more than 6 billion tons of hazardous waste was disposed of on the land, usually with no treatment and with little regard for the environmental consequences (Postel 1988). More than 50,000 sites have been used for hazardous waste disposal at some point, and thousands of these sites are thought to pose a serious risk to the environment and possibly to public health.

The chief concern for hazardous chemicals is that they can leak from corroded containers or unlined landfills, ponds, and lagoons, and then they can contaminate groundwater. This is one reason why in 1984 Congress added underground storage tanks (USTs) to RCRA; well over a million USTs are thought to exist in the United States, and the EPA has estimated that 15 to 20 percent of tanks covered by the law are leaking or are expected to leak; if they do, they could pose a significant risk to both groundwater and human health (Cohen, Kamieniecki, and Cahn 2005).

The chemical soup found in hazardous waste sites contains a variety of dangerous compounds such as trichloroethylene, lead, toluene, benzene, PCBs, and chloroform. It is impossible to generalize about health risks at each site because of variations in waste types and exposure. Moreover, as Roger Dower (1990) observed, although the potential health risks of exposure may be substantial, "little is known about the *actual* risks to the public from past and current disposal practices" (p. 159). In 1986 Congress required the EPA to assess the risks to human health posed by each of the Superfund National Priorities List (NPL) sites. The EPA and other federal agencies continue to study the risks, and at some potential Superfund sites they conduct elaborate risk assessments to provide such information to the public. The absence of such data in many cases, however, has fueled debate over the benefits that would accrue from the most inclusive and demanding cleanup policies.

Progress in cleaning up hazardous waste sites has been slow. The most frequently cited example is the federal Superfund program, which Congress created in 1980 following the highly publicized Love Canal chemical waste scandal near Niagara Falls, New York. The Superfund legislation required the EPA to identify and clean up the worst of the nation's abandoned hazardous waste sites. By 2016 the EPA reported that 1,439 sites on the NPL had been cleaned up, but the pace in future years may well slow because of scarce federal funds for the program. In addition, some of the most challenging and costly cleanups, including chemical containments in rivers and bays, lie ahead.[35]

There are thousands of other highly contaminated lands across the country, such as abandoned mines that often are located on Departments of Agriculture, Interior, Defense, and Energy lands in the West. In one notable case in 2015, workers, including EPA contractors, were engaged in maintenance work on the abandoned Gold King Mine near Silverton, Colorado when they accidentally triggered a massive wastewater spill that contaminated rivers in the area with heavy metals. The local jurisdictions had previously declined to have such sites included under Superfund because they feared loss of tourism. After the spill, they were eager to have Superfund money be used to clean up the site, and Gold King and 47 other sites in the region were added to the Superfund list. The effort will likely take decades and will be very expensive. The battle over whether mining companies should pay for cleaning up such abandoned mines continues.[36]

The Government Accountability Office reported in 2015 that the Agriculture Department had identified nearly 1,500 contaminated sites and many others that might be affected, and the Forest Service estimated that there were some 27,000 to 39,000 abandoned mines on its lands, 20 percent of which might poses a threat to human health. The Interior Department found nearly 5,000 such sites, and the Bureau of Land Management about 30,000 abandoned mines that were not yet assessed to see if they posed a threat. The Department of Defense had nearly 40,000 such sites with some degree of contamination.[37]

Contaminated Federal Facilities

One of the most demanding tasks facing the nation is the cleanup of some of the worst federal government facilities such as military bases and former nuclear weapons production plants. Those sites, although fewer in number than Superfund sites and the other contaminated sites mentioned just above, are generally larger and present a more complex cleanup challenge, in part because of the mix of chemical and radioactive wastes (U.S. Office of Technology Assessment 1991). Russell, Colglazier, and Tonn (1992) estimated that over the next several decades, remediation activities by the Department of Defense (DOD) and the Department of Energy (DOE) could cost hundreds of billions of dollars. Some 11,000 DOD sites may be in need of cleanup, as well as more than 4,000 that are managed by the DOE.

The cost of cleaning up the DOE's 17 principal weapons plants and laboratories alone, as noted in Chapter 1, is likely to be $265 to $305 billion over the next 30 years (National Research Council 2009). Much of that spending has been directed at five sites: Hanford Reservation in Washington state, Savannah River in Georgia, Rocky Flats in Colorado, Oak Ridge in Tennessee, and the Idaho National Engineering and Environmental Laboratory; cleanup at Rocky Flats was completed in 2005 at a total cost of about $10 billion. At a current spending level of $6 to $8 billion per year for environmental management, cleanup of federal facilities easily dwarfs the EPA's operating budget (less than $4 billion a year), and greatly exceeds annual Superfund cleanup costs. At many of the sites, large volumes of soil and groundwater have been contaminated with hazardous chemicals and radioactive wastes, and significant quantities of waste have leaked from damaged storage containers. The job of cleaning up these facilities is enormous, with more than 100 sites in 30 states around the nation. Even with extensive cleanup, hazards are likely to remain at many of the sites, thus requiring long-term stewardship (Probst and McGovern 1998).[38]

Radioactive Wastes

The disposal of high-level radioactive wastes from commercial nuclear power plants represents a comparable problem and has proved to be equally, if not more, difficult to resolve. The United States had over 70,000 metric tons by 2016, most of it consisting of spent fuel rods from nuclear power plants; about 20 metric tons of such wastes are generated annually from each of the 100 nuclear power reactors in the United States. The spent fuel rods remain dangerous for tens of thousands of years, and thus must be isolated from the biosphere. The DOE has estimated that the nation will have over 100,000 metric tons of spent fuel by the year 2040, and more if nuclear power enjoys a resurgence of interest.

Although planning and construction began on two new reactors at one site in Georgia in 2012 (the first in three decades) and another two in South Carolina in 2013, four reactors at other plants were taken out of service in 2013, and another ended its operation in late 2014. So the number of reactors has remained about the same. There seems to be no strong interest on the part of U.S. electric utilities to build costly new plants, and the relatively low price of natural gas today is likely a factor in these decisions; the two new Georgia reactors, for example, will cost about $14 billion, and nuclear power proponents are watching the construction for signs of the industry's future.[39] Elsewhere in the world, however, and particularly in Asia, nuclear power is enjoying rapid growth despite the catastrophic accident at the Fukushima Daiichi plant in Japan in 2011.

The U.S. high-level wastes have been stored since the 1950s in water-filled basins within the reactor buildings. More recently they have been stored in concrete and steel casks located on the reactor property but outside of the buildings; in recent years, the wastes were stored at 122 sites in 39 states. As storage space runs out, the future of the nuclear industry depends on finding more permanent locations for the wastes. After the terrorist attacks of September 2001, new concerns were expressed about the vulnerability of these sites. The federal government and the nuclear industry had been eager to see the proposed waste repository at Yucca Mountain, Nevada, completed, but both technical and political challenges arose, complicating its future. By 2008 the federal government had spent more than $11 billion on its assessment of the site's suitability over the previous 23 years. If opened and operated for about 100 years, the DOE estimated that the total Yucca Mountain cost would have risen to about $90 billion (Dunlap, Kraft, and Rosa 1993; Kraft 2013b).

In 2002, following a recommendation from the DOE and President George W. Bush, Congress approved establishment of a repository at Yucca Mountain. The next step would have been for the Nuclear Regulatory Commission to approve the facility if it were to be opened. However, the proposed repository faced numerous political, regulatory, and legal hurdles that could have delayed its opening, including anticipated public controversy over transportation of the waste to site, located about 100 miles northwest of Las Vegas, and continued opposition by the state of Nevada. President Obama had expressed opposition to the repository as well, and in 2009 he effectively ended consideration of the Yucca Mountain site.

In early 2010, the president appointed a Blue Ribbon Commission on America's Nuclear Future, which issued its report in early 2012. It called for a new national nuclear waste policy that emphasized a "consent-based approach" to siting of future nuclear waste storage and disposal facilities, but the future of U.S. nuclear waste policy remains uncertain.[40]

Solid Waste and Consumer Waste

An early concern of the environmental movement dealt with the by-products of the consumer society that clogged municipal landfills. The problem continues to this day. Recycling and reusing materials help, but reducing use of consumer goods would help even more. As noted in Chapter 1, that is the message from environmentalists on "green consumption," and many organizations and websites offer advice to citizens on how to change their purchasing habits to help conserve natural resources and promote sustainability.[41]

The size of the solid waste problem can be seen in figures compiled annually by the U.S. EPA. The agency estimated that in 2013, U.S. households, institutions, and businesses produced about 254 million tons of municipal solid waste (before recycling), nearly three times the 88 million tons produced in 1960, and considerably higher than the 151 million tons in 1980. For 2013 this figure represented 4.4 pounds per person per day, or more than 1,600 pounds a year for each of us; this is about twice the waste per capita generated in western European nations or Japan. Household, institutional, and commercial wastes, however, are only the tip of the solid waste mountain. The vast majority of solid waste comes from industrial processes, including agriculture and mining, raising the total to over 13 billion tons per year.[42]

Added increasingly to conventional wastes are millions of discarded computers, monitors, printers, cell phones, tablets, and other electronic devices or "e-wastes" that contain lead, mercury, and other toxic substances. The Consumer Electronics Association estimates that the average U.S. household owns some 24 electronic gadgets, and the EPA estimates that 438 million electronic products were sold in the most recent year for which data are available. By an EPA count in 2011, there were more than 400 million computers at the end of their useful life, an equal number of computer displays, about 350 million televisions, and nearly 800 million mobile devices (chiefly cell phones). Much of this electronic waste is not recycled properly; often it finds its way to developing nations, where it presents a health hazard to local people who attempt to recycle it.[43]

Recycling can make a big difference in this picture, and the percentage of waste that is recycled has been rising steadily to the current rate of about 34 percent. Recycling rates vary considerably, however, with over 99 percent for car batteries, 71 percent for steel cans, 67 percent for paper, 55 percent for aluminum beer and soda cans, and 31 percent for plastic soft drink and water bottles. Rates for consumer electronics have risen significantly and now stand at about 40 percent.[44] Many states have comprehensive recycling laws, and some innovative programs have been adopted at the municipal level to increase recycling. One example is the city of Seattle, which has become a model for effective curbside recycling. It uses economic incentives to promote reduction in waste and citizen cooperation. Such programs are called "volume-based recycling," "unit pricing," or "pay as you throw," with the fee reflecting the volume of waste to be collected. These programs are increasingly popular. Many cities recently have moved to a single container recycling (with papers, cans, and bottles combined) in an effort to boost recycling rates. Other actions, including enactment of the federal Pollution Prevention Act of 1990, the creation of new markets for recycled goods, and tightening restrictions on disposal of hazardous waste, should reduce industrial waste quantities as well.

Energy Use and Climate Change

Energy use has a major effect on most of the environmental problems already discussed, especially air pollution, acid precipitation, and the production of greenhouse gases. These effects flow primarily from a reliance on fossil fuels—oil, natural gas, and coal. Energy use also affects both the health of the economy and national security because, despite a shift to domestically produced energy in the last several years, the United States still relies on imported oil for about 25 percent of its needs. That oil comes to the nation at a high cost and from politically unstable regions of the world. Despite these consequences, the United States has never found it easy to address energy problems and policy proposals (see Chapter 6).

The Nature of Energy Problems

Energy problems may be defined, in part, by the total amount of energy used, the efficiency of use, the mix of energy sources relied on, and the reserves of nonrenewable sources (e.g., oil and natural gas) that remain available. Among the most important considerations are the environmental costs associated with the life cycle of energy use: extraction, refining, transport, use, and disposal. For example, when oil is transported by ship, on rail, or through pipelines, accidents may occur, sometimes spectacular ones like the spilling of 10.9 million gallons of crude oil from the Exxon *Valdez* supertanker in Prince William Sound off Alaska in 1989. The process of extraction itself can be risky as well, as the BP *Deepwater Horizon* oil spill in the Gulf of Mexico in 2010 demonstrated vividly (Freudenburg and Gramling 2010). Even without accidents, extraction of oil and natural gas can come at a high environmental cost, as opponents of Canada's vast tar sands oil industry have argued for years, and as early exploration of oil deposits in the Arctic has made clear. In the aftermath of the terrorist attacks of September 11, 2001, there is also increasing concern that large oil tankers are vulnerable to acts of terrorism.

There are other concerns as well. The by-products of energy generation sometimes present difficult tasks of disposal. For example, as noted earlier, when the fuel rods that power nuclear plants are "spent," this highly radioactive waste needs to be isolated from the biosphere for thousands of years. But the effect that most concerns students of energy policy is global climate change because of the buildup of greenhouse gases, discussed briefly in Chapter 1. The most consequential greenhouse gas is carbon dioxide (CO_2), produced in the burning of all fossil fuels even if some are cleaner than others; use of natural gas, for example, releases half the greenhouse gases of burning coal, but production of natural gas can release methane, a powerful greenhouse gas. Despite declines in emissions in recent years, the United States releases more greenhouse gases per capita than any other large developed nation, and it is the second largest emitter of those gases in the world after China.[45] The vast majority of these emissions come from fossil fuels that power automobiles, make electricity, run industrial processes, and heat and cool homes.

An overview of selected data on energy use conveys a simple message. It would be hard to overstate the importance of the world's choice of energy paths for the future. At the same time, energy use is so closely tied to vital industrial processes and highly valued public conveniences, such as air conditioning, home heating, and automobile use, that it is also easy to understand the difficulty nations have in trying to alter that path in the short term. Even as developed nations reduce energy use for manufacturing processes, energy demand is soaring to power Internet servers at the nation's data centers that serve Google, Facebook, Amazon, and other digital companies. U.S. data centers alone used about 70 billion kilowatt hours of electricity in 2014, equal to about 6 million average homes, although these operations are becoming more efficient in energy use. Global demand, of course, is much higher.[46]

As might be expected in light of rapid economic development around the world, demand for energy is likely to increase substantially in the future. The U.S. DOE's *International Energy Outlook 2016* forecasts an increase of more than 48 percent over the next three decades, with about half of the increase coming from developing nations in Asia. Total energy use is projected to rise from 549 quads (quadrillion British thermal units or Btus) in 2010 to more than 815 quads in 2040, a 48 percent increase. Renewables are expected to be the world's fastest-growing energy source, with coal, natural gas, and renewable energy sources providing about the same shares of global electricity by 2040. Nonetheless, fossil fuels will continue to constitute more than three-fourths of total global energy use under this scenario.

As shown in Figure 2.2, in 2015 the United States derived about 81 percent of its energy from fossil fuels (oil, coal, and natural gas) and 19 percent from other sources: nuclear (9 percent) and renewables (10 percent).[47] Global reliance on fuel sources has been similar in recent years.

Another problem the nation has faced has been its reliance on imported oil to meet growing demand. In 2007, the United States imported about 58 percent of the oil that it consumed, about twice the level that prevailed in 1973 at the time of the first major energy crisis. This heavy reliance on imported oil was much debated during the 2008 presidential campaign, in part because the nation has only about 3 percent of the world's known oil reserves while it has been using about 20 percent of world oil production. Since 2007, however, a combination of increased domestic oil drilling and improved vehicle fuel efficiency reduced reliance on imported oil to about 25 percent by 2016. Most of the oil we use is for transportation, and continued reduction in its use depends on further improvements in transportation efficiency, for example, with more fuel-efficient vehicles or greater reliance on mass transit. In fact, transit use reached a five-decade high in 2008, when gasoline prices spiked.[48]

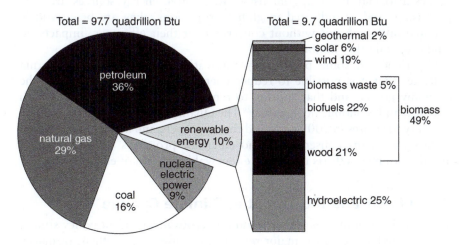

FIGURE 2.2 U.S. energy consumption by energy source, 2015

Note: Sum of components may not equal 100% because of independent rounding.
Source: U.S. Energy Information Administration, Monthly Energy Review, tables 1.3 and 10.1 (April 2016), preliminary data.

As noted in Chapter 1, gasoline prices in the United States have fluctuated in recent years, although gas remains inexpensive compared to its cost in European nations. Such low prices over the past several decades have discouraged conservation and investments in efficiency and alternative energy sources, but the picture is changing. One example is that auto manufcturers are producing far more fuel-efficient vehicles, partly in reaction to consumer demand and also in response to new federal fuel economy standards discussed in Chapter 1.

Projection of future energy use is difficult because so much depends on developments in energy efficiency (e.g., in cars, appliances, and homes), new technologies, market prices, government policies, and changing consumer and corporate behavior. For example, the nuclear power industry has sought a major expansion in plants around the world, including in the United States. It is optimistic about new reactor designs that promise cheaper and safer nuclear energy. Yet public opposition in the United States and in other nations remains strong, costs are uncertain, and controversies over nuclear waste continue to hamper expansion of the industry. Of course, as noted earlier, the Fukushima Daiichi nuclear accident in 2011 strengthened public opposition in many nations. One major advantage of nuclear power, however, is that it produces few greenhouse gases during its operation, and some environmentalists are beginning to support it as one way to mitigate climate change. Yet uranium used in the plants needs to be mined and refined; this is very energy-intensive, and will be more so if less rich deposits of uranium are used. The plants also contain enormous quantities of concrete and steel that generate carbon dioxide in manufacturing. Storing radioactive wastes also may be energy-intensive. Renewable energy sources are very promising, and as indicated in global projections, they are being widely adopted, although not without concerns over their efficiency, impacts on land use, and other limitations.

Experience in some particularly innovative states such as California indicates that it is possible to reduce energy use substantially even as the economy grows, and that shifting to renewable sources of energy is both practical and economically feasible.[49] The Obama administration's economic recovery measures in 2009 endorsed this approach, and allocated billions of dollars for energy conservation and efficiency programs and for research and development efforts to promote renewable sources of energy.

Fossil Fuels and the Threat of Climate Change

The world's scientific community and numerous independent policy studies support the basic case for major reductions in use of fossil fuels, primarily because of their contribution to climate change. Reports from the UN-sponsored Intergovernmental Panel on Climate Change (IPCC 2007, 2013) have confirmed the seriousness of climate change and the considerable risk of inaction (see also Stern 2007). Other reports, including those from the National Research Council (2011) and the National Climate Assessment (2014), are consistent with the IPCC findings, and typically refer to climate change as a problem that needs urgent attention and action. That action has been slow to come, however, in part because citizens in the United States and in other nations have not viewed climate change as either important or urgent. In addition, fossil fuel companies have strongly resisted policies that would threaten their operations, and they have been assisted by intense opposition to climate change policies by political conservatives in what has become a widening partisan divide on the issue (Dunlap and McCright 2015; Dunlap, McCright, and Yarosh 2016).

In what the *New York Times* called a "grim and powerful assessment," the 2007 IPCC report said that global warming was "unequivocal" and that human activity was the main driver, "very likely" causing most of the gain in temperatures observed since 1950. In the 2013 assessment, the IPCC expressed even more confidence in this conclusion, saying that it is "extremely likely that human influence has been the dominant cause of the observed warming since the mid-20th century."

The fundamental causes are the use of fossil fuels and deforestation. The recent IPCC reports indicate that the buildup of greenhouse gases in the atmosphere likely means that the world will face rising temperatures, rising sea levels, and abrupt and unpredictable shifts in weather patterns in the years to come, with devastating consequences.[50] The warming range projected by the IPCC studies is about 2.7 to 8.6 degrees Fahrenheit by the end of the twenty-first century if, as anticipated, carbon dioxide concentration in the atmosphere rises to about twice the level that prevailed in 1750— before industrialization. Most experts worry about the effects on agriculture, and thus the food supply, and major risks to ecosystem integrity and biodiversity as well as to human health. These effects are likely to be worse in poor nations that lack the capacity to deal with the changes. Additional concerns include the likely impacts on ocean temperatures as much of the heat is absorbed by the world's oceans, acidification from update of atmospheric carbon dioxide, and impacts on fisheries and thus food supplies. At least some climate experts are convinced that the IPCC reports have been too conservative, that is, that climate change could be far worse than the panel is projecting; this was one conclusion in the International Energy Agency's *World Energy Outlook 2016*.[51] Despite the severity of the warnings, the world's nations have been slow to act, although the 2015 Paris Agreement on climate change constitutes a major step forward. It took effect in November 2016 (DiMento and Doughman 2014; Selin and VanDeveer 2016).[52]

Under the UN Convention on Climate Change approved at the 1992 Earth Summit, the United States and other developed countries that agreed to the treaty were to cut carbon dioxide and other greenhouse gas emissions significantly. However, both the U.S. Congress and the Bush administration were cool to the international climate change agreement, the Kyoto Protocol, and President Bush in early 2001 rejected it as "fatally flawed" based on its economic impact as well as perceptions of inequity in the lesser demands made on developing nations under the agreement. His administration preferred voluntary efforts to reduce greenhouse gas emissions and an expanded research program in climate change. The Paris Agreement and its likely effects are addressed in Chapter 8.

Political stalemate on climate change at the national level in the last few years has stimulated innovative policies and agreements on the need to act in more than half of the states and over 1,000 cities across the nation. Taken together, they may be a better sign of the country's response to the threat of climate change (Betsill and Rabe 2009; Rabe 2010, 2016; Selin and VanDeveer 2016). California and states in the Northeast have been among the most creative in stepping up with new energy policies, including carbon pricing and so-called cap-and-trade markets, and the Citizens Climate Lobby has pressed nationally for a carbon fee and dividend approach that would return all revenues from a new carbon "tax" to citizens, thereby making such an approach a "revenue-neutral" way to stimulate changes away from use of fossil fuels.

Biological Diversity and Habitat Loss

Biological diversity, or biodiversity, refers to the variety and variability among living organisms and the ecological complexes in which they occur. Scientists generally examine three types of biodiversity: genetic, species, and ecosystem diversity. The diversity of species and the habitats that support them derive from the ecological and evolutionary processes that have shaped them over geological time spans and will continue to do so in the future.

People have long taken biodiversity for granted and have enjoyed the free services it has provided. Yet human activity, both intentional and inadvertent, has had a devastating effect on biodiversity over the past 10,000 years. People have always cleared land and have overhunted some species and caused the extinction of others. The present is distinguished from the past primarily by the magnitude of destruction and rates of change. The principal causes of the new threats to biodiversity are habitat loss and modification (including fragmentation), pollution and contamination, overexploitation of species and habitats, introduction of exotic and competitive species, and the interactive effects of these activities. There is also good reason to believe that a warming climate could rival the destruction of habitat as a cause of biodiversity loss.

Put bluntly, human beings are using an ever greater portion of the planet's natural capital and leaving less for other species. Some recent estimates suggest that human activity has transformed a third to a half of Earth's surface and that today we consume or directly use 40 to 50 percent of the land's biological production and more than half of all available fresh water. As the human population continues to grow and as the world's economy expands, these trends are likely to continue. As a result, many conservationists are growing more pessimistic about how much can be done to preserve natural areas and biodiversity. They hope to slow the human impact and to protect as many "biological hot spots" as they can, both within the United States and internationally, over the next few decades.[53]

In the broadest terms, biologists, environmentalists, and others who argue for biodiversity conservation seek to ensure the continuation, or restoration, of the full range of biological entities on Earth. From an ecological perspective, preservation of biodiversity in turn will help ensure ecosystem stability and productivity, on which human and other life depends. Ecologists also argue that it is essential to maintain the capabilities of all species to reproduce successfully, to regenerate after population losses, and to adapt in a period of significant environmental change (Daily 1997).

Biodiversity Loss and Implications

Between 1600 and 1900, human activities led to the extinction of perhaps 75 species of birds and mammals, or about one species every four years. A comparable number was lost in the first half of the twentieth century. Biologists estimate that in the mid-1970s, anthropogenic, or human-caused, extinctions rose to about 100 species per year (Tobin 1990). Edward O. Wilson, one of the nation's leading authorities on biodiversity, has argued that the extinction rate in the mid-1980s was accelerating rapidly and was at least 400 times the natural rate (Wilson 1990, 54). Others suggest that the rate is probably 36 to 78 times the background or historic rate—lower but still disturbingly high (Gibbs 2001).[54] Even the congressional Office of Technology Assessment reported in a major 1987 study that the loss of biological diversity was of "crisis proportions."

The effect of such species loss is particularly acute in tropical rainforests. Although the number of species in existence is uncertain, biologists have estimated that more than half of all identified species live in moist tropical forests. Such forests cover only about 6 percent of land area but are biologically rich, especially with insects and flowering plants. The forests are vulnerable ecosystems, however, and they illustrate the larger threat to biodiversity of human interventions.

From the dawn of agriculture approximately 12,000 years ago to the present, humans have eliminated about a third of the world's forest cover (Myers 1997). The loss has been especially great in tropical forests in Amazonia, Central America, and Indonesia, where more than half of the original forest cover has been lost. During the late 1990s, the continuing loss was put at an estimated 1 percent of the total rain forests annually, or nearly 25 million acres a year; more recent estimates are similar, from 5 to 10 percent per decade (Reid 1997). The United States also has experienced extensive deforestation. For example, about 90 percent of old-growth forests in the Pacific Northwest have been lost to development. According to a comprehensive

UN report in 2005, an estimated 50,000 square miles of forests worldwide, an area about the size of New York State, are cleared or logged annually. Moreover, about half of this activity occurs in areas where no significant human use took place previously. The current rate of deforestation would be higher if China were not engaged in extensive tree planting.[55]

The reasons for this loss of ecologically critical forestland are not in much dispute. Among the major factors are the clearing and burning of rainforests to make room for rapidly growing and poor populations, conversion of forests for planting of cash crops and cattle pastureland, commercial logging, overharvesting of fuel wood, and dam construction. Short-sighted government policies have encouraged many of these and similar activities (Miller, Reid, and Barber 1991; Reid 1997; Smil 2013; Tobin 2016).

As the forest habitat is destroyed, species are lost. The Global Biodiversity Assessment (GBA), an independent analysis of the state of scientific knowledge about biodiversity commissioned by the UN Environment Programme and released in 1995, provides some useful data on these rates. If the current rate of loss in tropical forests continues for another 30 years, the GBA concluded that the number of species would decline by 5 to 10 percent from present levels. Some scientists have suggested a much higher rate of decline.

GBA analysts also estimated that more than 5,400 species of animals and 26,000 species of plants are threatened globally. Several studies suggest that "at least 11 percent of all bird species are threatened, along with 25 percent of mammal species, 34 percent of fish species, 25 percent of amphibian species, and 11 percent of plant species."[56] One study released in 2009 estimated that nearly a third of the 800 U.S. bird species are endangered, threatened, or in serious decline.[57] Yet it is easier to describe the status of well-known species than for others. For the vast majority of the 1.8 to 1.9 million known species (mostly insects) and the many millions of those not yet discovered (estimated to be between 13 and 14 million), information for reliable assessments is lacking.

In many respects, the exact rate of species or other biodiversity loss matters less than understanding the implications of such trends for human well-being as well as for ecosystem functioning. There are many reasons to worry about biodiversity loss. Forests provide human beings with opportunities for recreation and for aesthetic enjoyment. They also are a treasure trove of medicinal drugs, oils, waxes, natural insecticides, and cosmetics, and they could contain future sources of food (World Commission on Environment and Development 1987). Of the 80,000 edible plants, humans have used an estimated 7,000 for food, but we actively cultivate only about 200 and rely heavily on only about 20, such as wheat, rye, corn, soybeans, millet, and rice (Wilson 1990).

Yet as important as those ecological and agricultural values are from an anthropocentric perspective, they are not as compelling as arguments advanced from an ecocentric or ecology-centered viewpoint. Biodiversity, whether in tropical forests or elsewhere, is important because it provides irreplaceable ecological values, including the genetic heritage of millions of years of evolution. We risk damage to the functioning of ecosystems with species loss and the permanent disappearance of diverse genetic codes that could prove invaluable for species adaptation in what may be a rapidly changing environment in the future.

Ecologists have debated the precise relationship between biodiversity and ecosystem health or productivity, that is, how the loss of species affects ecosystem functions (Myers 1997; Tilman 1997). Yet no one disagrees that the functions put at risk with loss of biodiversity are critical. These roles include the cycling of nutrients, partial stabilization of climate, purification of air and water, mitigation of floods and droughts, decomposition of wastes, generation and renewal of soil and soil fertility, pollination of crops and natural vegetation, and control of agricultural pests (Daily 1997). One recent estimate puts the economic value of pollination by insects worldwide alone at some $200 billion a year, and the value of other ecosystem services is almost certainly in the tens of trillions of dollars a year.[58] The issue is not, as journalists often put it, whether a single species is lost. Rather, it is that we risk the destruction of critical habitats and ecosystems, as well as the biogeochemical cycles, on which life depends.

A Millennium Ecosystem Assessment that involved more than 1,300 ecologists and other researchers from 95 countries was released by the World Health Organization in 2005, and concluded that 60 percent of critical ecosystem functions that support life are being degraded by various human activities. The exhaustive study contains detailed information about the effects of economic development on ecosystem health.[59] In addition, reports from the IPCC suggest that 20 to 30 percent of plant and animal species assessed to date might be at an increased risk of extinction if global temperatures increase by more than 1.5 to 2.5 degrees Celsius.[60]

Policy Actions and Effects

Protection of biodiversity was one of the most controversial issues at the 1992 Earth Summit, which also produced an accord on protection of the world's forests. The Convention on Biological Diversity (CBD) took effect in late 1993, with the United States among the nations supporting it, although the U.S. Senate did not ratify the agreement. The CBD is largely a framework convention that encourages governments to develop conservation strategies and action plans. See Chapter 8 for a fuller discussion.

Solutions to biodiversity challenges are not scarce even if the political will to adopt and enforce them is. Policymakers and environmental organizations have proposed a wide range of actions. These strategies include swapping international debt for preservation of natural areas, land reform that gives a local population more access to and control of the land, gaining the support of local people for conservation strategies, finding ways to derive local economic benefits from conservation, practicing conservation at the bioregional level, ending or reducing governmental subsidies (e.g., for agriculture or timber production) that encourage deforestation, and increasing investment in biodiversity research (Reid 1997; Tobin 2016). None of these actions is easy to take because the public and policymakers are not committed enough to conservation to overcome opposition from powerful economic and political forces. In his *Requiem for Nature*, biologist John Terborgh (1999) argues that the competitive nature of the global economy and "our collective obsession" with maximizing economic growth make sustainable development of this kind "currently unattainable."

In the United States, protection of biodiversity is tied closely to enforcement of the 1973 Endangered Species Act (ESA) (discussed in Chapter 6). Although the act has a broad mandate for ecosystem conservation, emphasis to date has been on protection of individual species. Even here, the act has achieved only modest success after more than 40 years. As of 2016, more than 1,594 U.S. plant and animal species have been listed as threatened or endangered, and many others are candidates for listing. The Fish and Wildlife Service (FWS), which implements the act for terrestrial and some aquatic species, has designated over 700 critical habitats and has developed more than 1,000 habitat conservation plans and over 1,150 active recovery plans. The FWS reported in 2008 that 33 percent of listed species were stable, 8 percent were improving, and 34 percent were declining. The status of another 23 percent was uncertain, and the remaining 2 percent were assumed to be extinct or living only in captivity; no summary statistics were provided in more recent reports (U.S. Fish and Wildlife Service 2012). Unfortunately, relatively few endangered species have fully recovered and been removed from the list, and significant progress on recovery for many species could well take decades. The recovered and delisted species include the peregrine falcon, brown pelican, much of the gray whale population and the gray wolf population, the American bald eagle, and the American alligator.[61]

Population Growth

An increasing human population affects every environmental and resource challenge discussed in this chapter, from air and water pollution and the generation of waste to the loss of biodiversity. Yet the environmental community has not always been attentive to these issues. Some of the mainstream environmental organizations such as the National Audubon Society, the National Wildlife Federation, and the Sierra Club, which had long ignored population growth, rediscovered it in the 1990s. Many environmental organizations actively promoted the urgency of action on population growth in conjunction with the UN International Conference on Population and Development held in September 1994 in Cairo. They did so again in October 1999 when the world population surpassed the symbolically important level of 6 billion people, more than twice the 1950 population of 2.5 billion (Crosette 1999). Nonetheless, other environmental groups, the news media, and government policymakers often give population issues remarkably little attention. Partly for these reasons, population growth is rarely a salient issue for the public, even if it is arguably one of the most important determinants of environmental quality and human well-being.

Population and Sustainable Development

Despite wide variability in definitions of sustainability, the concept must include the enduring capacity of a given ecosystem to support the demands that its human population imposes on it. A high rate of population growth can significantly affect the environment because it requires the provision of additional food, clean water, shelter, energy, and other resources to meet the demands of additional people. The rate of growth may also affect the depletion of critical resources and threaten ecosystem integrity (Daily 1997; Smil 2013).

Estimates vary widely, but the world's present agricultural production probably can support only about 2.3 billion people if they have a diet similar to Americans (heavy on consumption of meat), 6 billion with a Japanese diet, and perhaps as many as 15 billion if people live on a subsistence diet. Such assessments remind us that population numbers are not the only important factor to consider. They also suggest that it is inappropriate to think of the land's population "carrying capacity" in static terms. Lifestyles and the technologies that we use are equally significant (Tobin 2016). They are captured in the concept of our "ecological footprint," or the effect we have on the environment as a consequence of trying to meet our needs through use of natural resources (Wackernagel and Rees 1996). Still, it is becoming evident that the human population is currently close to many estimates of the upper range of sustainability, particularly because a Western diet, with a heavy consumption of meat, is increasingly common as nations industrialize and become more affluent (J. Cohen 1995). A number of websites allow simple calculations of ecological footprints (e.g., www.footprintnetwork.org and www.rprogress.org).

The cost in human lives attributable to population growth (and the poverty that often results) is also great. The United Nations Food and Agriculture Organization estimates that nearly 800 million people in the world, or one of every nine people, are chronically malnourished. Perhaps as many as 8 million people die each year from hunger or hunger-related diseases, primarily in developing countries, with millions more harmed for life. These numbers could easily rise in the future if food supplies shrink for any reason, such as prolonged drought from climate change. Beyond the impact of malnutrition, more than 130,000 children under the age of five die *each week* (about 7 million a year) in poor nations from treatable diseases such as malaria, diarrhea, measles, tetanus, and acute respiratory infections that rarely kill Americans (Tobin 2016).[62] In addition, high population growth rates may affect political stability within nations as well as conflict among them over access to scarce natural resources such as water and arable land. Sustained economic growth, national security, social peace, and human justice all depend on limiting and eventually halting human population growth. They depend as well on improving scientific knowledge and technological systems, and on reallocating critical resources such as land and water to more efficient and equitable uses.

Birthrates have declined since the 1960s, but they remain well above the replacement level (slightly more than two births per woman of childbearing age) that eventually produces a stable or nongrowing population. Projections of future population, both globally and in the United States, provide little basis for complacency, either for economic development in poor nations or for protection of critical environmental resources worldwide. The impact on habitats and biodiversity, air and water quality, energy and water use, and other aspects of environmental quality is likely to be enormous but also geographically quite varied. Some nations and regions of the world will be affected far more than others by food and water shortages, poor health, environmental degradation, and economic dislocations, including widespread unemployment. A large percentage of the world's population lives on less than $2 a day, and well over a billion people live in severe poverty, with particularly high rates of poverty in south Asia and sub-Saharan Africa (Tobin 2016).

We can hardly place all the blame on the poor nations, where nearly all of the future growth in human numbers will occur. The industrialized nations consume a far greater proportion of the world's resources and have a much higher per capita effect on the environment. For example, the richest quarter of the world's nations controls about 75 percent of the global income; consumes a large share of the world's meat and fish; and uses most of its energy, paper, chemicals, iron, and steel (Tobin 2016). The United States, with only 4.4 percent of the world's population, consumes about one-fifth of its commercial energy and has among the world's highest level of greenhouse gas emissions per capita. By some estimates, those of us who live in developed nations consume about thirty-two times more resources as do those who live in developing nations.[63] Residents of rich countries have a very large ecological footprint.

These numbers suggest what the future might hold if high global population growth rates are combined with intensive economic development based on the technologies currently in use in the developed nations. They also indicate a moral imperative for developed nations to lower energy and materials consumption and to assist the developing nations as they attempt to improve their lot.

Growth Rates and Projected Population Increases

According to United Nations data, in early 2017 the world's human population was growing at 1.2 percent annually, adding more than 88 million people every year to its base of 7.4 billion. This is a net increase in the world's population (not the number born) of about 240,000 people per day. Although fertility rates continue to decline slowly, the United Nations' most likely projection for the year 2030 is 8.5 billion people, and for 2050 it is about 9.9 billion (Population Reference Bureau 2016; United Nations 2015).[64] Table 2.3 summarizes some of the most notable figures and trends for the United States and the world.

These kinds of projections depend critically on assumptions about economic and social development, the availability of family planning programs, and the extent of contraceptive use. Social developments such as improved education, a higher status for women and improved gender equity, better reproductive health care and nutrition, adoption of old-age security programs, and economic reform are all as important as provision of family planning services. The United Nations has recognized both the continuing need for family planning and the imperative of social and economic

TABLE 2.3 U.S. and world estimated populations and growth rates, 2016

Estimated population (millions)

Region or country	2016	2030	2050	Rate of increase (2016) (%)
World total	7,418	8,539	9,869	1.2
More developed nations	1,254	1,298	1,322	0.1
Less developed nations	6,164	7,241	8,548	1.5[a]
United States	324	359	398	0.7

Notes: The United States has a "natural rate of increase" listed in this and similar databases of 0.4%. The estimated rate included in the table, 0.7%, reflects the addition of substantial legal immigration (about 1 million per year) that does not exist for most other nations. Current estimates of U.S. and world population can be found at the Census Bureau's population clock display at www.census.gov, and also at the Population Reference Bureau website noted here.
[a] The rate for developing nations if China is not counted in this category is higher: 1.7%. China's rate of population growth is 0.5% a year.

Source: Population Reference Bureau, 2016 World Population Data Sheet (Washington, DC: Population Reference Bureau, August 2016), at www.prb.org.

development. These kinds of measures were strongly endorsed at the 1994 UN International Conference on Population and Development held in Cairo, Egypt, at the Johannesburg Summit on Sustainable Development in 2002, and at the Rio+20 conference in 2012.

The combination of such efforts has produced striking declines in fertility levels in some nations, including Bangladesh, Kenya, Mexico, South Korea, Thailand, Tunisia, and China. Many nations have made much less progress toward lower growth rates. An added factor for developing nations is rapid urbanization of the population, often leading to overcrowded and severely polluted megacities.

In contrast to the world average of 1.2 percent, the population of developed nations is growing by an average of only 0.1 percent per year, creating a demographically divided world. The U.S. rate, however, is more than five times the average for developed nations. The U.S. population (324 million in 2016) increases by about 2.3 million people a year. Moreover, growth is likely to continue throughout the twenty-first century even if the fertility rate remains below the replacement level. About half of this anticipated growth is attributable to the nation's high level of immigration, which might change in the future. The U.S. Census Bureau projects that the nation is likely to reach nearly 400 million by 2050 and perhaps 478 million by 2100. These estimates are the middle-level projections; the actual results could be lower or higher.[65]

The effect of such changes in selected areas of the nation, such as Florida, Arizona, Colorado, Nevada, and California, or in rapidly growing cities elsewhere is often dramatic. During the 1990s, for example, Florida was gaining more than 6,000 residents every week. The Raleigh–Durham–Cary, North Carolina area, with a population of just over 1 million, grew by 40 percent between 2000 and 2009. Phoenix, with a population of over 4 million and once the fastest-growing of America's large cities, surged by more than 30 percent between 2000 and 2009; the Austin, Texas metro area, with a population of over 2 million, grew by 35 percent between 2000 and 2009, and the city itself soared from 790,000 in 2010 to 932,000 in 2015, or more than 20 percent in five years. The Las Vegas metropolitan area, which has experienced explosive growth in recent years, is now home to over 2 million people; throughout the 2000s it was often adding about 8,000 residents each month, and in recent years over 3,000 per month, putting enormous demands on area water supplies.

Such growth also exacts a toll on farmland and tree and forest cover in urban areas, especially as cities spread out to distant suburbs. In recent decades, urban sprawl and development in the form of housing, shopping malls, and roadways have consumed about 3 million acres a year of forest, cropland, and other open space, with some modest reversals in loss of cropland lately.[66]

Going forward, cities and states will have to plan carefully to minimize adverse impacts on land, water supplies and water quality, air quality, critical habitats, urban infrastructures, and the overall quality of life as population grows and congestion increases. Given these trends, rising public support for growth management and the preservation of green spaces and increasing local efforts to build sustainable communities are both welcome news (Portney 2013, 2016; Press 2002).

Conclusions

This selective overview of U.S. and global environmental problems provides at least some indication of the scope and severity of current threats to public and ecosystem health as well as to the quality of our lives. As always, debate continues on how to interpret available data, leaving plenty of room for environmentalists and their opponents to disagree. Government agencies and both domestic and international environmental organizations recognize the inadequacy of present monitoring of environmental trends and the need to improve data collection, its integration, and its assessment. Progress on these fronts is evident across the board compared with past decades. Yet, even the best scientific information cannot eliminate disagreements over environmental policies that are rooted more in politics, economics, and cultural values than in science.

The rate of environmental change threatens to outstrip our capacity to assess and respond to it. Thus we need more accurate modeling of environmental trends and improved forecasts of what may lie ahead. Just as important, however, is providing adequate opportunities for citizens to discuss the information and participate in any decisions on what actions to take, from individual communities to state, national, and international levels. The movement toward creating sustainable communities in many areas of the nation indicates a strong potential for such integrated assessment of local and regional environmental data as well as for citizen involvement in decision making (Mazmanian and Kraft 2009; Paehlke 2013a; Portney 2013, 2016).

Partly because of the paucity of reliable scientific information, disputes continue over the extent of progress being made in dealing with air and water quality, toxic chemicals and hazardous wastes, and most of the other environmental and other challenges summarized in this chapter. As will be made clear in later chapters, there are also frequent conflicts over what role government should play in dealing with these problems, in part because policymakers and other policy actors have sharply conflicting views of just how severe the problems are. Disagreement is particularly intense over how much more should be done, with what policy instruments (regulation, market incentives, public education), and at what cost.

There is another message for all students of environmental policy. We need to improve our individual and collective capacities to review and judge the scientific facts and the various political assertions tied to them. This is increasingly difficult to do because partisan and ideological debates over environmental policy sometimes brings diametrically opposed analyses of the problems as each side "frames" the issues to suit its case (Guber and Bosso 2007, 2013b; Layzer 2007). Citizens can jump into these battles at any time, but they will do better if they understand the issues and learn how to sort out reasonable from unreasonable claims.

Discussion Questions

1 For any of the environmental problems reviewed in the chapter, how severe is the risk to public health or the environment? What is the basis for your conclusions? For example, how severe is air pollution, or contaminated drinking water? How serious is global climate change? The loss of biological diversity? For any of these issues, what do you see as the implications for public policy?

2 Based on improvements in air quality since its adoption, how would you evaluate the federal Clean Air Act? Has it been successful? What changes might make it more effective in the future? What about the Clean Water Act? The Endangered Species Act?

3 What kind of government policies might help address environmental risks such as indoor air quality for which a conventional regulatory approach would not work? What about the similar challenge of dealing with nonpoint source water pollution? Public education? Economic incentives? Something else?

4 The Toxics Release Inventory (TRI) provides an enormous amount of information about toxic chemicals released to the local environment, yet the public is not well informed about community risks. What changes might make TRI information more visible and more useful to the public?

5 What might be done to make community and state recycling programs more effective? To increase the national recycling rate for solid waste and consumer electronic goods?

6 Why has the United States not been more effective in reducing its energy use, particularly the use of fossil fuels? What actions might increase energy conservation and efficiency?

Suggested Readings

Alexander, David E., and Rhodes W. Fairbridge, eds. 1999. *Encyclopedia of Environmental Science*. Boston, MA: Kluwer Academic.

Brown, Lester R. 2010. *Plan B 4.0: Mobilizing to Save Civilization*. New York: W. W. Norton.

Daily, Gretchen C., ed. 1997. *Nature's Services: Societal Dependence on Natural Ecosystems*. Washington, DC: Island Press.

DiMento, Joseph F. C., and Pamela Doughman, eds. 2014. *Climate Change: What It Means for Us, Our Children, and Our Grandchildren*, 2nd edn. Cambridge, MA: MIT Press.

Kamieniecki, Sheldon, and Michael E. Kraft, eds. 2013. *The Oxford Handbook of U.S. Environmental Policy*. New York: Oxford University Press.

Portney, Paul R. and Robert N. Stavins, eds. 2000. *Public Policy for Environmental Protection*, 2nd edn. Washington, DC: Resources for the Future.

Starke, Linda, ed. 2012. *State of the World 2012: Moving Toward Sustainable Prosperity*. Washington, DC: Island Press.

Notes

1   The estimate for China is recounted in Dan Levin, "Study Links Polluted Air in China to 1.6 Million Deaths a Year," *New York Times*, August 13, 2015. For a fuller account of this kind of data, see the World Health Organization's report "The Global Burden of Diseases, Injuries, and Risk Factors Study" (released in December 2010), available at the WHO website: www.who.int. See also Brady Dennis, "1 in 7 Children Globally Lives with 'Toxic' Air, Study Finds," *Washington Post*, October 31, 2016.

2   The data can be found on the EPA website: www.epa.gov/air-trends. Summary accounts are provided for more recent periods in the full EPA report that is issued every year or two (U.S. EPA 2016).

3   A National Academy of Sciences study released in 2009 estimated that nearly 20,000 people a year in the United States die prematurely from criteria air pollutants emitted by power plants and vehicles. See Matthew L. Wald, "Fossil Fuels' Hidden Cost Is in Billions, Study Says," *New York Times*, October 20, 2009. For higher estimates, see Jennifer Chu, "Study: Air Pollution Causes 200,000 Early Deaths Each Year in the U.S.," *MIT News*, August 29, 2013.

4   William J. Martin II, Roger I. Glass, John Balbus, and Francis S. Collins, "A Major Environmental Cause of Death," *Science* 334 (October 11, 2011): 180–181.

5   See Peter Audrey Smith, "The Kitchen as a Pollution Hazard," *New York Times*, July 22, 2013; and Jennifer M. Logue, Phillip N. Price, Max H. Sherman, and Brett C. Singer, "A Method to Estimate Chronic Health Impact of Air Pollutants in U.S. Residences," *Environmental Health Perspectives* 120 (2011): 216–222.

6   The EPA report is titled *Respiratory Health Effects of Passive Smoking: Lung Cancer and Other Disorders*. The EPA's staff strongly defended its 530-page health risk assessment against tobacco industry charges of inadequate science.

7   See, for example, Mireya Navarro, "U.S. Will Ban Smoking in Public Housing Nationwide," *New York Times*, November 30, 2016.

8   The data can be found on the CDC web page. Retrieved September 12, 2016 at: www.cdc.gov/tobacco/data_statistics/fact_sheets/fast_facts/index).htm#toll.

9   See the EPA's indoor air quality webpage for a review of these issues: www.epa.gov/indoor-air-quality-iaq.

10 The EPA maintains a webpage on all of these health and environmental effects of ozone layer depletion: www.epa.gov/ozone-layer-protection.

11 Brent Harris, "A Coolant That Threatens to Heat Up the Climate," *New York Times*, July 22, 2016.

12 For a basic fact sheet on irrigation water use and its effects, see the U.S. Geological Survey site: http://ga.water.usgs.gov/edu/wuir.html. See also Michael Wines, "Wells Dry, Fertile Plains Turn to Dust," *New York Times*, May 19, 2013.

13 The state data are available at: http://ofmpub.epa.gov/waters10/attains_nation_cy.control, and the same page provides a national summary of data in the individual state reports.

14 Elizabeth Becker, "U.S. Sets New Farm-Animal Pollution Curbs," *New York Times*, December 17, 2002. Becker reports that the new rules are expected to reduce the major pollutants from animal feedlots by approximately 25 percent.

15 See Andrew C. Revkin, "Offshore Oil Pollution Comes Mostly as Runoff, Study Says," *New York Times*, May 24, 2002. A 2016 U.S. Geological Services survey found that polycyclic aromatic hydrocarbons or PAHs from coal tar sealants on parking lots and driveways were a major source of contamination of local waterways and a threat to aquatic life. The chemicals are washed into stormwater drains and then into those waterways.

16 Felicity Barringer, "Officials Report the First Net Gain in Wetlands," *New York Times*, March 31, 2006.

17 See Bina Venkataraman, "Rapid Growth Found in Oxygen-Starved Ocean 'Dead Zones,'" *New York Times*, August 15, 2008.

18 See the EPA website: http://water.epa.gov/infrastructure/drinkingwater/pws/factoids.cfm. A link on this page provides access to data on local drinking water systems across the nation. On the smaller systems, see Laura Ungar and Mark Nichols, "4 Million Americans Could Be Drinking Toxic Water and Would Never Know," *USA Today*, December 13, 2016.

19 Jeff Donn, Martha Mendoza, and Justin Pritchard, "AP Probe Finds Drugs in Drinking Water," Associated Press, March 10, 2008. See also an extensive investigation by the *New York Times* that includes an online and interactive database for water quality problems nationwide: Charles Duhigg, "Millions in U.S. Drink Dirty Water, Records Say," *New York Times*, December 6, 2009; and Charles Duhigg, "Tap Water Is Legal But May Be Unhealthy," *New York Times*, December 17, 2009. Small water systems may be particularly vulnerable to these lapses in ensuring drinking water quality.

20 Julie Bosman, Monica Davey, and Mitch Smith, "As Water Problems Grew, Officials Belittled Complaints from Flint," *New York Times*, January 20, 2016; and Monica Davey and Mitch Smith, "2 Flint Ex-Emergency Managers Charged Over Tainted Water," *New York Times*, December 20, 2016.

21 Mitch Smith, "Flint Wants Safe Water, and Someone to Answer for Its Crisis," *New York Times*, January 10, 2016; Lisa Riordan Seville and Phil Helsel, "EPA Administrator Quits Amid Flint Water Crisis," NBC News, January 21, 2016; and Dana Milbank, "The Poisonous Conservative Thinking That Caused the Flint Crisis," *Washington Post*, March 18, 2016.

22 Michael Wines and John Schwartz, "Unsafe Lead Levels in Tap Water Not Limited to Flint," *New York Times*, February 8, 2016. On community water supplies contaminated with industrial chemicals, see Nathanial Rich, "The Lawyer Who Became DuPont's Worst Nightmare," *New York Times Magazine*, January 6, 2016.

23 One particular concern is small quantities of the weed killer atrazine in drinking water, from its use on crops, golf courses, and lawns. See also Charles Duhigg,

"Debating Just How Much Weed Killer Is Safe in Your Water Glass," *New York Times*, August 23, 2009.

24 The EPA no longer includes groundwater and drinking water in these national inventory reports, but it now has a separate webpage for reporting on these subjects: http://water.epa.gov/drink/index.cfm.

25 Chelsea Harvey, "EPA Changes Its Stand on Fracking, Says It Can Harm Drinking Water in 'Some Circumstances,'" *Washington Post*, December 13, 2016.

26 The USGS National Water Information System is designed to describe the status and trends in the quality of the nation's groundwater and surface water resources. Its webpage contains a wealth of data on the nation's water quality: http://waterdata.usgs.gov/nwis.

27 These reports can be found at www.ewg.org/, and also at the NRDC website: www.nrdc.org.

28 P. H. Gleick and H. S. Cooley, "Energy Implications of Bottled Water," *Environmental Research Letters* 4(1) (February 19, 2009), available at: http://iopscience.iop.org/article/10.1088/1748-9326/4/1/014009/meta.

29 The estimate was reported in *Science* 323 (March 6, 2009): 1271.

30 See Marla Cone, "President's Cancer Panel: Environmentally Caused Cancers Are 'Grossly Underestimated' and 'Needlessly Devastate American Lives,'" *Environmental Health News*, May 6, 2010.

31 A general overview of the problem can be found in Colborn, Dumanoski, and Myers (1996).

32 See the EPA site at: www.epa.gov/learn-issues/learn-about-chemicals-and-toxics.

33 This is the agency's Risk-Screening Environmental Indicators (RSEI) model. For a history of the TRI program and its effects, see Hamilton (2005) and Kraft, Stephan, and Abel (2011).

34 In recent years, the number of generators covered by RCRA has increased enormously, largely because of the reduced threshold for waste quantities for inclusion in this category. Historically and currently, the vast majority of hazardous waste comes from a small percentage of generators; 2 percent of them generate 95 percent of the waste. But many of the small generators are still important for their local environment.

35 The EPA reports current achievements and challenges at its website for the Superfund program: www.epa.gov/superfund. On cleanup of rivers, see Anthony DePalma, "Superfund Cleanup Stirs Troubled Waters," *New York Times*, August 13, 2012.

36 Christopher Dean Hopkins, "More Than a Year after Spill, Colorado's Gold King Mine Named Superfund Site," National Public Radio, September 8, 2016; and Bruce Finley, "Gold King One Year Later: Colorado's Mustard-Yellow Disaster Spurs Plans for Leaking Mine," *Denver Post*, August 5, 2016.

37 See Government Accountability Office, "Numbers of Contaminated Federal Sites, Estimated Costs, and EPA's Oversight Role" (Washington, DC: GAO, GAO-15-830T, 2015).

38 The GAO has found repeatedly that the DOE cleanup projects have been poorly managed, contributing to the high cost. See, for example, "Nuclear Waste: Action Needed to Improve Accountability and Management of DOE's Major Cleanup Projects" (Washington, DC: GAO, GAO-08-1081, September 2008).

39 See Matthew L. Wald, "Nuclear Power's Future May Hinge on Georgia Project," *New York Times*, June 11, 2013; and Wald, "Nuclear Plants, Old and Uncompetitive, Are Closing Earlier than Expected," *New York Times*, June 14, 2013.

40 See Blue Ribbon Commission on America's Nuclear Future, "Report to the Secretary of Energy" (Washington, DC: Blue Ribbon Commission, January 26, 2012), available at: http://cybercemetery.unt.edu/archive/brc/20120620211605/http:/brc.gov//.

41 See Durning (1992). John C. Ryan and Alan Thein Durning's *Stuff: The Secret Lives of Everyday Things* (Seattle, WA: Northwest Environment Watch, 1997) offers a sobering view of the environmental effects of the daily consumer products we use, from coffee to automobiles.

42 The EPA compiles such data. See: www.epa.gov/learn-issues/learn-about-waste.

43 U.S. EPA, "Electronics Waste Management in the United States through 2009" (Washington, DC: EPA, Office of Resource Conservation and Recovery, May 2011). For a recent account of how electronic waste is shipped to other nations, see Michael Smith and Isabella Cota, "We Found Your Last Smartphone, Next to Your Old VCR," *Bloomberg Businessweek*, November 14, 2016.

44 EPA data on municipal solid waste and recycling rates can be found at: https://archive.epa.gov/epawaste/nonhaz/municipal/web/html/index.html. One concern is that some of the most hazardous of these wastes, such as car batteries and electronics, find their way to developing nations, where their treatment often is not well regulated and thus exposes workers and local residents to an assortment of chemicals.

45 Some small nations, such as Qatar and Kuwait, emit more greenhouse gases per capita than does the U.S., largely because of their high level of oil and gas production.

46 See James Glanz, "Power, Pollution, and the Internet," *New York Times*, September 22, 2012; and Katie Fehrenbacher, "Data Centers Are No Longer the Energy Hogs They Once Were," *Fortune*, June 27, 2016.

47 The Energy Information Administration in the Department of Energy publishes a comprehensive *Annual Energy Review* that surveys the nation's production and consumption of all major energy sources. It is available online: www.eia.doe.gov/. A comparable international survey is the annual *World Energy Outlook*, published by the International Energy Agency.

48 Michael Cooper, "Transit Use Hit Five-Decade High in 2008 as Gas Prices Rose," *New York Times*, March 9, 2009.

49 Coral Davenport, "Signs Are Promising That Economies Can Rise as Carbon Emissions Decline," *New York Times*, April 5, 2016. See the webpage for the California Energy Commission for ongoing coverage of the state's efforts and results: www.energy.ca.gov/. See also the websites for nonprofit organizations that regularly cover developments of this kind: the Alliance to Save Energy (www.ase.org/), the Natural Resources Defense Council (www.nrdc.org), and the American Council for an Energy Efficiency Economy (www.aceee.org/).

50 For a summary, see Elisabeth Rosenthal and Andrew C. Revkin, "Science Panel Says Global Warming Is 'Unequivocal,'" *New York Times*, February 3, 2007. The full reports and what the panel calls "summaries for policymakers" are available at the website: www.ipcc.ch. See also "Scientific Assessment of the Effects of Global Climate Change on the United States," a report from the

president's National Science and Technology Council, May 2008, available at the council's website: www.ostp.gov/cs/nstc; and National Academy of Sciences, "America's Climate Choices" (Washington, DC: National Academy of Sciences, 2011). See also the U.S. EPA's climate change page for regular updates on these forecasts: www3.epa.gov/climatechange/; and the EPA's Climate Change Indicators page for the latest data on climate change impacts: www.epa.gov/climate-indicators#explore.

51 International Energy Agency, *World Energy Outlook 2016*, available at the IEA website: www.worldenergyoutlook.org/publications/weo-2016/.

52 Andrew C. Revkin, "Nobel Halo Fades Fast for Panel on Climate," *New York Times*, August 4, 2009. The less conservative projections are discussed in Eli Kintisch, "Projections of Climate Change Go from Bad to Worse, Scientists Report," *Science* 323, March 20, 2009: 1546–1547.

53 See Bruce A. Stein, "A Fragile Cornucopia: Assessing the Status of U.S. Biodiversity," *Environment* 43 (September 2001): 11–22; and Richard Pearson, "Protecting Many Species to Help Our Own," *New York Times*, June 2, 2012.

54 A 2015 study puts the rate of loss of mammal species at 20 to 100 times the rate that prevailed in the past. See Sarah Kaplan's report on the study: "Earth Is on Brink of a Sixth Mass Extinction, Scientists Say, and It's Humans' Fault," *Washington Post*, June 22, 2015.

55 The UN report is available at: www.fao.org/forestry. The webpage for the UN Convention on Biological Diversity provides a wealth of information on scientific assessments and policy actions related to biodiversity loss: www.biodiv.org.

56 See Walter V. Reid, "Strategies for Conserving Biodiversity," *Environment*, 39(7) (September 1997): 16–20, 39–43; and reports released by the International Union for Conservation of Nature, available at its webpage: www.iucn.org. For other estimates of species loss, see Gerardo Ceballos et al., "Accelerated Modern Human-Induced Species Losses: Entering the Sixth Mass Extinction," *Science Advances* 1(5) (June 19, 2015).

57 North American Bird Conservation Initiative, U.S. Committee, *The State of the Birds, United States of America, 2009*. Washington, DC: U.S. Department of the Interior, 2009.

58 See, for example, Richard Pearson, "Protecting Many Species to Help Our Own," *New York Times*, June 1, 2012. For the value of global ecosystem services, see Costanza et al. (1997).

59 The reports are available at: www.millenniumassessment.org/en/index.aspx. See also a special report, "Despite Progress, Biodiversity Declines," *Science* 329 (September 2010): 1272–1280. Another valuable compilation of such ecosystem changes within the U.S. was released by the H. John Heinz III Center for Science, Economics and the Environment (2008). For an intriguing analysis of how humans are "harvesting the biosphere" to meet their ever-increasing needs, and harming it in the process, see Smil (2013).

60 Carl Zimmer, "Predicting Oblivion: Are Existing Models Up to the Task?" *Science* 317 (August 2007): 892–893.

61 The Fish and Wildlife Service website provides extensive data on threatened and endangered species and habitat recovery plans: www.fws.gov/.

62 UNICEF, the United Nations Children Fund, provides a biennial report on children's welfare, the latest of which is *The State of the World's Children 2016: A Fair Chance for Every Child*, available at: www.unicef.org. Estimates on

deaths from hunger are taken from the Food and Agriculture Organization (FAO). This figure is down sharply from a decade earlier, when as many as 40 million died each year from hunger. See *The State of Food Insecurity in the World 2015*, available at: www.fao.org/.

63 Jared Diamond, "What's Your Consumption Factor?" *New York Times*, January 2, 2008.

64 There is much uncertainty in these kinds of projections, and the longer the timeframe, the more uncertainty there is. See the UN website, www.unfpa.org/ and www.un.org/popin, for updates on population projections and reports. The Population Reference Bureau (www.prb.org) also has a wealth of population data in easily readable form. Its World Population Data Sheet is updated annually based on UN data. Readers can find a continuously updated population clock with current world and U.S. populations at: www.census.gov/popclock/.

65 In addition to the UN website, see the U.S. Census Bureau site for reports on U.S. population trends: www.census.gov/. See also Kent and Mather (2002).

66 The data are reported in the National Resources Inventory released in August 2015 (for the year 2012) by the U.S. Department of Agriculture's Natural Resources Conservation Service.

CHAPTER 3

Making Environmental Policy

In a rare instance of bipartisan cooperation on environmental policy, in June 2016, Congress passed and the president signed legislation to modernize the Toxic Substances Control Act (TSCA). For the forty years after its initial approval in 1976, TSCA was widely faulted as one of the weakest of the major environmental laws adopted during the environmental decade of the 1970s (see Chapter 5). EPA had made little progress in implementing the Act, and the chemical industry blocked stronger national action even as the states independently began requiring tougher measures to protect the public from toxic chemicals. With passage of the Frank R. Lautenberg Chemical Safety for the 21st Century Act, Congress finally came to terms with the need to do more to protect the American public from harmful exposure to chemicals while also assuring industry that it would be treated fairly. The law was named after former Senator Frank Lautenberg, who was long involved in the fight to reform TSCA.

Serious attempts to revise and update most of the major environmental laws of the 1970s had become nearly impossible because the two major parties disagreed so fundamentally about the issues, the power of the EPA, and the economic impact of environmental regulations (Kraft 2013a, 2016). At first, the rewrite of TSCA was thought to be equally improbable, but several senators, including Tom Udall (D-NM) and Edward Markey (D-Mass.), forged an ideologically diverse coalition of senators willing to work together for passage of the Act. Markey summed up the result this way: "it could be one of the most historic moments in environmental law in our country."[1]

The final version of the bill won the backing of industry groups, trial lawyers, public health advocates, and some, but not all, environmental groups. A senior scientist at one of those groups, the Environmental Defense Fund (EDF), described the new policy as "an overhaul of a badly broken and outdated law that has allowed toxic chemicals into our homes, schools and workplaces."[2] How well the EPA will handle implementation of the new Act, how much opposition from the chemical industry and others will arise during this process, and what the ultimate impact of the policy change will be on the public's exposure to toxic chemicals remain to be seen.

U.S. environmental policy was not always so divisive, nor was it as visible an area of public policy. Prior to the 1960s, environmental issues were barely mentioned in the national media, and most policymakers at both the federal and state and local levels took little interest in them. That pattern of minimal attention to the challenges continued even as evidence of both national and global environmental degradation mounted during the 1960s. By the late 1960s and early 1970s, however, the political climate changed dramatically as the environment rose abruptly as an important concern for government. The two major parties differed on their assessment of the issues, and yet there was frequent bipartisan cooperation in enacting most of the major environmental policies of the 1970s and 1980s (Andrews 2006a; Eisner 2007; Kamieniecki and Kraft 2013). Since that time, the salience of environmental issues has ebbed and flowed in response to shifts in the economy and the political climate and to changing perceptions of environmental, natural resource, and energy problems.

More importantly, today those issues exhibit far more conflict than consensus. In the 2010s, it is common to see sharp ideological and partisan polarization over the environment, energy, and natural resources, particularly at the national level. Most analysts attribute this important change chiefly to a strong rightward move on the part of the Republican Party—a divide that is especially evident on environmental, energy, and climate change issues (Below 2013; Dunlap, McCright, and Yarosh 2016; Daniels et al. 2013; Guber and Bosso 2013a; Shipan and Lowry 2001). Indeed, as measured in roll call votes in the U.S. Congress, the two major parties are more divided today than they have been in over 100 years (Persily 2015; Poole and Rosenthal 2007).[3] This development has contributed greatly to what many scholars and pundits see as an increasingly dysfunctional national government that is unable to reach agreement on a wide range of contemporary challenges, from tax reform and health care to energy and climate change (Mann and Ornstein 2012).

These fluctuations speak to an important aspect of environmental policymaking. The mere existence of detrimental environmental conditions and dire warnings about the future provide no guarantee that the public will pay attention, that elected officials will cooperate in a search for solutions, or that governments will act on the problems. Public concern and government action require that the problems achieve a sufficient level of visibility and make it onto the policy agenda (Baumgartner and Jones 1993; Kingdon 1995). Even after reaching the agenda, the problems may return to obscurity or at least to a lower level of attention if prominent events push them off, as occurred following the terrorist attacks of September 11, 2001. For six months after the attacks, major environmental policy actions by the Bush administration received negligible coverage in most national news outlets (Bosso and Guber 2006).

When governments choose to take action, the policies considered and chosen may or may not be the best way to address the problem. Much depends on available scientific information and how policymakers appraise the situation, including the anticipated cost of action and its impacts on society. Politics has a great deal to do with such policy choices. Among the most central factors in the politics of the environment are the extent of public concern and involvement; the activities of major environmental, business, and other interest groups; and the beliefs, attitudes, and values of public officials. The striking difference between environmental policy decisions of the Bush administration in the early to mid-2000s and the Obama administration that took office in 2009 makes clear that the views of the president and his top advisers matter a great deal (Vig 2013, 2016; Vig and Kraft 2016).

This chapter focuses on the policymaking process and the general features of U.S. government that influence environmental politics and policy. In Chapter 4, the concepts developed here are used to assess the evolution of natural resource and environmental policy. Special emphasis is given there to the rise of the modern environmental movement, the diversity of interest groups that are active on the issues, and public support for environmental policy actions.

Taken together, these two chapters speak to the capacity of the U.S. political system to deal effectively with environmental problems. It is important to ask how well governments at all levels in the United States have responded to the challenges to date, and how well they are likely to deal with a new generation of more complex and politically challenging problems, such as climate change.

This chapter seeks to:

- improve understanding of both the formal and informal aspects of U.S. policymaking processes, the structure and operation of governmental institutions, and the constitutional and legal characteristics that shape how they work;
- develop a capacity to critically appraise the performance of governmental institutions and processes that affect environmental decision making; and
- alert readers to opportunities for citizens, nonprofit organizations, and businesses to engage in and influence policymaking and implementation decisions, and enhance their ability to do so effectively.

Understanding Environmental Politics

As the chemical safety policy example illustrates well, the U.S. policymaking process is often highly complex, frequently contentious, and sometimes utterly mystifying in the bargains that must be struck to make progress. Policy decisions also may focus on narrow and highly technical issues understood only by those who are intimately involved with the specific policy or program. Fortunately, the overall character of policymaking and the stages through which most environmental policies move are more comprehensible.

Political scientists use several different models and theories that help explain how the policymaking process works and how it results in the policies on which we rely. A few of these bear mentioning. Some, such as elite theory, emphasize the role of economic or governing elites (such as corporate leaders), who may hold values and policy preferences that differ substantially from those of the public at large (Gonzalez 2001). Such ideas may help to explain the success of oil companies, refineries, and utilities in climate change negotiations, as well as the power of large manufacturing interests. Other closely related theories, particularly group theory, see public policy as the product of a continuous struggle among organized interest groups, such as business and environmental groups (Duffy 2013; Kamieniecki 2006; Kraft and Kamieniecki 2007). Compromises reached on pesticide policy, for example, may reflect a balance between preferences of agricultural chemical companies and environmental and health groups. Where elite theory emphasizes the frequent success of elites, group theory suggests that who wins and who loses is a function of how well different interests are organized and how effectively they press their case. The many compromises made on the 2009 House climate change bill clearly reflected the persistent efforts of diverse interest groups.[4]

A third perspective, institutional theory, emphasizes the formal and legal aspects of government institutions—for example, the way they are structured or arranged, their legal powers, and procedural rules that they follow in making decisions. Among these are how much public or stakeholder involvement is allowed in government decisions, to what extent such involvement and collaborative forms of decision making are actually facilitated, and how much authority is given to state governments to act on their own under the principle of federalism (Daley 2013; Gerlak, Heikkila, and Lubell 2013; Ostrom 2007; Rabe 2016).

Finally, a fourth view, rational choice theory, draws heavily from economics. It assumes that in making decisions individuals try to maximize their self-interest. Thus it seeks to explain public policy in terms of the actions of individual policy actors who are motivated in this way, whether they are voters, interest group leaders, legislators, or agency officials (Anderson 2015; Moe 1980; Rothenberg 2002). In the climate change debates of 2009, for example, it is easy to understand that oil- and gas-producing companies, the coal industry, and oil refiners would seek to minimize adverse economic impacts that would affect their business. It is equally clear why members of Congress from Midwestern states with heavy industry would be leery about imposing added costs on those businesses, especially during a severe recession.[5]

Each one of these perspectives is helpful for explaining some aspects of environmental politics and policy. That is, each can identify some element of policymaking that is important, such as the role that elites, interest groups, or governmental rules and procedures may play. Each can help as well in explaining why policymaking in the U.S. political system is often difficult. Yet no one theory or model by itself is completely satisfactory because it tends to miss other factors that also are important. Another approach, however—the policy process or policy cycle model—incorporates most of the valuable elements from each of these approaches. It also has the distinct advantages of clarity and flexibility. For these reasons, this chapter and the rest of the book make extensive use of the policy process model.

The Policy Process Model

The policy process model proposes a logical sequence of activities that affect the development of public policies. It depicts the policymaking process and the broad relationships among policy actors within each stage. The model can also be helpful in understanding the flow of events and decisions within different cultures and institutional settings (Sabatier 2007). The discussion that follows focuses on the national level of government, but similar activities are just as evident at state and local levels (Lowry 1992; Rabe 2016; Scheberle 2004, 2013) or at the international level (O'Neill 2009). As indicated in Table 3.1, the model distinguishes six distinct, if not entirely separate, stages in policymaking.

Agenda Setting

Agenda setting is one of the most critical stages for environmental policymaking. It includes how environmental problems are perceived and defined, the development of public opinion on them, and the organization of public concerns and new policy ideas to demand action by government. Agenda setting comprises all those activities that bring environmental problems to the attention of both the public and political leaders and also shape the ideas and policy alternatives that get serious consideration in government (Anderson 2015; Baumgartner and Jones 1993; Guber and Bosso 2013b; Pralle 2006; Stone 2012). This includes scientific research and government studies and reports of the kind discussed in Chapter 2, prominent environmental accidents, media coverage of environmental events, and the promotional activities of environmental advocacy groups and their adversaries.

In one effort to explain the rise and fall of issues on both the larger societal agenda and what is usually called the institutional or governmental agenda, John Kingdon (1995) proposed an intriguing model. It is useful for understanding how environmental problems come to be objects of public concern or not, how they gain or fail to gain the attention of public officials,

TABLE 3.1 The policymaking process

Stage of the process	What it entails	Illustrations
Agenda setting	How problems are perceived and defined; command attention in the media; and are framed and discussed by interest groups, the general public, and policymakers.	Energy problems rose to prominence in 2001, and again in 2008 and 2009. Yet Republicans and Democrats defined them differently, emphasizing a need to increase energy supplies, reduce demand through conservation and efficiency, or altering subsidies for competing energy sources.
Policy formulation	The design and drafting of policy goals and strategies for achieving them. Usually involves the use of environmental science, economics, and policy analysis.	Attempts to develop a U.S. policy on global climate change have floundered because of conflicts over the meaning of scientific data and concern about economic effects. More agreement existed by 2009, when the issue was high on the congressional agenda.
Policy legitimation	Justifying and authorizing government action. Involves mobilization of support by the public, interest groups, and elected officials.	Approval of the Clean Air Act Amendments of 1990, including new provisions for control of acid rain and stronger actions on urban air pollution. Had broad political support.
Policy implementation	Provision of institutional resources for putting the programs into effect within a bureaucracy.	Implementation of the federal Endangered Species Act by the Interior Department. Shortages of budgetary resources and shifting administrative priorities have reduced its effectiveness.
Policy and program evaluation	Measurement and assessment of policy and program effects, including success or failure.	The Clean Air Act of 1970 is widely viewed as a success because urban air quality has improved significantly. Many policies have been less successful.
Policy change	Modification of policy goals and means in light of new information or a shifting political environment.	Pesticide regulation, largely unchanged for decades, was finally modified by adoption of the Food Quality Protection Act of 1996.

Sources: Adapted from Kraft and Furlong (2018). Similar models can be found in Jones (1984) and Anderson (2015). The original policy process model can be traced to Harold Lasswell's early work on the policy sciences.

and how environmental policy takes the form it does. It can also serve as a guide to developing political strategies for influencing the future development of environmental policy. In addition, it provides some concepts that are helpful for reviewing, if only briefly, the history of environmentalism and environmental policy in the United States, the subject of Chapter 4.

Problems, Policies, and Politics Kingdon argues that three separate but interdependent "streams" of activities (related to problems, policies, and politics) flow continuously through the political system. They sometimes converge, with the assistance of policy entrepreneurs, such as political leaders, and create windows of opportunities for policy development. Much of this activity occurs within policy communities of specialists and interested parties, such as the environmental and industry groups that focus on air and water pollution, pesticide use, natural gas fracking, or climate change.

Kingdon defines the agenda as "the list of subjects or problems to which government officials, and people outside of government closely associated with those officials, are paying some serious attention at any given time" (1995, 3). The governmental agenda may be influenced by the larger societal agenda, the problems that most concern people, as would be expected in a democracy when the public is mobilized around salient issues. It may also be shaped by the diffusion of ideas among policy communities (or policy elites) or by a change in the political climate. Good examples of the latter include the election of President Ronald Reagan in 1980, which inaugurated an unprecedented period of anti-environmental rhetoric and action and the Republican capture of the House of Representatives in the 1994 and 2010 elections, both of which resulted in sharp challenges to environmental policy from the House (Kraft 2016). President Obama's victory in the 2008 election, following on the heels of strong Democratic gains in Congress in 2006, paved the way for a new environmental policy agenda that differed sharply from that of the Bush administration in the preceding eight years (Vig and Kraft 2016). The way in which the government's agenda is set depends on the flow of those problem, policy, and political streams.

The *problem stream* influences the agenda by providing data about the state of environmental conditions and trends, as reviewed in Chapter 2. The information may come from government reports and program evaluations such as EPA studies of air or water quality; assessments by the National Academy of Sciences and other scientific bodies; reports by presidential commissions and task forces; and studies sponsored by environmental groups, industry, and others. The data and assessments circulate among policy specialists, affecting their perceptions and understanding of the problems regardless of whether or not they produce any immediate effects on policy decisions.

The problem stream is also affected by other variables such as environmental crises or disasters, technological developments, and ecological changes. Accidents such as the chemical plant explosion at Bhopal, India, in

1984, the Exxon *Valdez* oil spill off Alaska in 1989, the BP *Deepwater Horizon* oil spill in the Gulf of Mexico in 2010, and the disastrous Fukushima Daiichi nuclear accident in Japan in 2011 often receive extensive media coverage. Such reporting may prompt people to pay greater attention to the problems of storing and using highly toxic chemicals, transporting or drilling for oil in highly vulnerable areas, and operating nuclear power plants without sufficient safeguards. Catalytic or focusing events like these accidents increase the credibility of studies and reports that document the environmental or health risks at issue, and they help ensure they will be read and debated and thus influence policy decisions (Birkland 1997).

The *policy stream* concerns what might be done about environmental problems. Proposals are developed by analysts, academics, legislators, staffers, and other policy actors, as noted earlier. These proposals are floated as trial balloons and become the objects of political speeches, legislative hearings, and task forces. They get tested by the policy community for technical acceptability and political and economic feasibility. They are endorsed or rejected, revised, and combined in new ways. As Kingdon suggests, this is somewhat like a process of biological natural selection; the fittest ideas survive and may flourish, and ultimately they may become the basis for public policy action.

Ideas that are inconsistent with the current political mood may be dropped from consideration and relegated to the policy back burner for warming or incubation until the climate improves. Such was the fate in the early 1990s of proposed stiff carbon taxes to discourage consumption of fossil fuels; yet by 2009, a close cousin of carbon taxes, the "cap-and-trade" proposal taken up by Congress, was far more appealing, if not quite enough to gain congressional approval. These ideas, however, were received much more favorably at the state level and in Canadian provinces (Rabe and Borick 2012). Conventional policy alternatives such as "command and control" regulation may drop from favor, as they did during the 1990s, the early 2000s, and the 2010s, while other ideas, such as market-based incentives, public–private partnerships, and collaborative decision making, are viewed more positively. In this way, a shortlist of acceptable policy alternatives emerges at any given time, reflecting the prevailing sense of what kinds of government activity are deemed to be socially and politically legitimate.

The language used and symbols evoked in these debates can make a big difference between acceptance and rejection (Cantrill and Oravec 1996; Guber and Bosso 2013b; Edelman 1964). This is sometimes called the *framing* of issues. For instance, coal companies facing more stringent EPA regulations for their contribution to air pollution and climate change fought back by asserting that the Obama administration declared a "war on coal," thus hoping such a framing of the issues might attract public and media support; in 2012, the House actually passed a largely partisan Stop the War on Coal Act, which, as expected, died in the Senate.[6] For the same reasons, in 2011 and 2012, President Obama's critics often accused him of backing "job-killing" regulations proposed by the U.S. EPA, which they opposed for their alleged adverse economic impacts.

These kinds of verbal games are evident in every area of public policy, and environmental policy is no exception. Language matters a great deal for the way citizens and policymakers think about the problems and acceptable solutions. So the public and some policymakers may reject the idea of higher fuel efficiency standards for automobiles because they think about them as an extension of government regulation, which they dislike. They might be more sympathetic if such standards are linked with a goal they support, such as reduced reliance on imported oil, a stronger economy, or improved national security (Nisbet 2009, 2016). Or they might prefer setting a renewable energy target instead of imposition of a carbon tax as one component of a climate change policy, because the latter leaves them open to the charge that they are raising taxes (Rabe and Borick 2012).

Some of the harshest criticism of such issue framing has been directed at large coal and oil companies, such as ExxonMobil. Along with other climate change deniers, for many years they attempted to convince the public and policymakers that global climate change was not really a problem and no government action was needed (DiMento and Doughman 2014; Dunlap 2013; Dunlap and McCright 2015). They were so successful that their actions prompted environmentalists and their supporters to search for their own way to frame the issues to counter such efforts (Layzer 2007; Skocpol 2013).

Finally, the *political stream* refers to the political climate or national mood as revealed in public opinion surveys, election results (particularly a change in presidential administrations), and the activities and strength of competing interest groups. The political mood is never easy to decipher, and sometimes judgments are well off the mark, as was the case with the reputed Reagan election mandate in 1980. Many Reagan supporters and political analysts assumed that the public became more conservative on environmental issues during the 1980s. The evidence suggests that this assessment was seriously in error (Dunlap 1987; Kraft 1984). The same kinds of conflicting interpretations of electoral mandates were evident following the 2012 elections that gave President Obama a second term of office while simultaneously keeping control of the House in Republican hands.[7] The election of Donald Trump in 2016 may signal another shift, as Republicans kept control of both house of Congress as well, creating a unified federal government for the first time in years. Most elected officials develop a well-honed ability to detect important shifts in public attitudes, at least in their own constituencies. Thus environmentalists and other advocacy groups try to mobilize the public around their issues by stimulating a sense of public outrage over existing problems or actions by policymakers with which they disagree. It has often been a highly effective political strategy.

Policy Entrepreneurs and Policy Change Environmental policy entrepreneurs—leaders inside and outside of government who devote themselves to the issues and their advancement—often help bring these three streams (problems, policy ideas, and politics) together. By doing so, they facilitate the process of policy change, discussed later in the chapter. Normally the three streams of activities flow through the political system independently; that is, each is affected differently and unrelated to the others. But sometimes these activities come together, or, to use the water metaphor, the streams combine into a river of action; at that time public policy breakthroughs can occur.

Often this is no accident. The entrepreneurs act when they see windows of opportunity open, as they do when a major accident or crisis occurs or at the beginning of a new presidential administration. For example, after more than ten years of congressional inaction on oil spill legislation, the Exxon *Valdez* spill prompted Congress to enact the Oil Pollution Act of 1990 (Birkland 1997).[8] It required companies to submit oil spill contingency plans to the Coast Guard and the EPA, and to train their employees in oil spill response. Similarly, enactment of the Superfund Amendments and Reauthorization Act (SARA) of 1986 and its section creating the public's right to know about toxic chemicals in their communities was a direct result of the disastrous chemical plant accident in Bhopal, India. The accident raised fears of the possibility that similar accidents and loss of life might occur in the United States (Hadden 1989; Kraft, Stephan, and Abel 2011). The experience with Bhopal and the subsequent enactment of "right-to-know" policies such as SARA stimulated many related efforts to adopt information disclosure policies, including the 1996 revision of the Safe Drinking Water Act discussed in Chapter 2.

Policy entrepreneurs are prepared to take advantage of the opportunities created by such accidents and other focusing events. In the meantime, they continue to stimulate interest in the problems, educate both the public and policymakers, circulate new studies, and otherwise "incubate" the issues; that is, they keep them warm until they are ready to be hatched, when the political climate is favorable. Entrepreneurs are not equal in their ability to perform these essential tasks. Environmental and other public interest groups have greatly increased their political clout since the 1960s. Nonetheless, according to several recent studies, they still lack the financial and other resources that business and industry groups typically possess (Bosso 2005; Duffy 2013; Furlong 1997; Kraft and Kamieniecki 2007; Schlozman and Tierney 1986).

This kind of convergence of the three streams helps explain some peculiar patterns of environmental attention and inattention. Energy issues, for example, were at the top of the political agenda in the late 1970s as President Jimmy Carter sought (but largely failed) to enact a comprehensive national energy policy. Carter did much to promote energy conservation and efficiency, symbolized by placing solar panels on the roof of the White House. Energy issues, however, disappeared from sight in the 1980s as the White House and members of Congress lost interest in the subject when energy prices fell and public concern dissipated. The Reagan administration had the Carter solar panels removed, a fitting indicator of the administration's view that energy problems required no government intervention in the marketplace beyond the conventional subsidies for nuclear energy and fossil fuels that had existed for years (see Chapter 6).

Attention to energy issues increased again in 1988 as a hot, dry summer stirred fears of global warming. That concern was aided by the activism of scientists such as James E. Hansen, former director of Goddard Institute for Space Studies of the National Aeronautics and Space Administration (NASA), and the late noted climatologist Stephen Schneider. They spoke out frequently (unusual for scientists) about the risks of climate change and the need for governmental action. By 2001 national concern over a short-term energy crisis in California and weaknesses in the electric power grid in the East led to a Bush administration proposal for a national energy policy that focused heavily on increasing energy supplies. After four years of intense debate and negotiation in Congress, parts of that proposal were finally approved in 2005 amid concern about high energy costs. The case of reforming toxic chemical regulation discussed at the chapter's beginning is yet another example of congressional policy entrepreneurs and many outside of Congress working for years to develop legislation that would attract political support at the right time (Kraft 2013a, 2016; Selin and VanDeveer 2016).

Policy Formulation

The formulation of environmental policy refers to the development of proposed courses of action to resolve the problem identified. It often involves the use of scientific research on the causes and consequences of environmental problems, including projections of future trends, such as rising energy use, population growth, or anticipated water scarcity due to climate change. Typically, formulation includes analysis of the goals of public policy (such as improved energy efficiency) and various policy options to reach them (e.g., regulation or use of market incentives). Ordinarily, such assessment of policy options includes consideration of economic, technical, political, administrative, social, ethical, and other issues.

Increasingly, scholars have underscored the importance of policy design in selecting a course of action that is likely to be successful. That means careful assessment of the characteristics of target populations (i.e., the groups at which policy actions are directed, such as chemical manufacturers, automobile companies, or the general public) as well as trying to figure out what policy tools or mechanisms will likely bring about the intended behavior. For example, if a state wanted to encourage energy conservation among the public, it would want to know whether that goal can best be achieved through public education campaigns or provision of financial incentives (Schneider and Ingram 1990, 1997). In 2001, California found that financial incentives worked remarkably well, as substantial energy conservation by the public helped avert an energy crisis.[9]

Many policy actors play a role in policy formulation. They include environmental and business groups, think tank policy analysts, and policymakers and their staffs in legislatures and executive offices (of the president, governors, county executives, mayors, and city managers). Even the courts get involved as they attempt to resolve environmental disputes by issuing legally binding policy decisions (Vig and Kraft 2016). Given the technical nature of policy action on climate change, protection of biodiversity, or pollution control, it is not surprising that the scientific community (both within and outside of government agencies) is often important as well, even if not as active as many scientists would like to see (Ascher, Steelman, and Healy 2010; Keller 2009; Lubchenco 1998). As noted in Chapter 1, scientists also sometimes protest that politicians give their views insufficient weight. This complaint was common during the George W. Bush administration when national scientific groups, including many Nobel Prize winners, complained that the president was ignoring or distorting science on many environmental issues (Andrews 2006a; Rosenbaum 2013a; Shulman 2006).[10]

International policy actors are also important in U.S. environmental policy decisions (Chasek, Downie, and Brown 2014; DeSombre 2000; O'Neill 2009). U.S. policymakers are pressured by their European allies on issues ranging from climate change to population assistance policies. International NGOs, which number in the tens of thousands, similarly try to influence press coverage of environmental issues such as energy use, biodiversity protection, and agricultural subsidies, and thereby alter American public opinion. Especially in formulating international environmental policy positions, U.S. policymakers are likely to hear from a diversity of multinational corporations, environmentalists, scientific organizations, and officials at the leading international organizations, such as the World Bank and the United Nations Development Programme (Axelrod and VanDeveer 2015; Harrison and Sundstrom 2010; O'Neill 2013).

Even under the best of circumstances, the various policy actors involved in environmental policymaking are rarely equal in their political resources or influence, as noted earlier. The business community, for example, has far more resources for lobbying legislators and administrative agencies than do environmental groups. Indeed, some theorists worry that policymaking can be dominated by one set of interests or another (the business community or environmentalists) and thus distort the nation's ability to devise effective and equitable environmental policies (Dryzek 2005; Kraft and Kamieniecki 2007).

A related issue is the extent of influence by technical experts such as environmental scientists and engineers in policy formulation. Some theorists worry that such specialists may dominate the policymaking process, creating a kind of technocratic decision making that can drive out democracy (Fischer 1990; Sclove 1995). Such concerns are widely shared, sparking interest in the various ways in which the public might participate in environmental decisions, from the local to the international level (Baber and Bartlett 2005; Beierle and Cayford 2002; Daley 2013; Ingram and Smith 1993; Press

1994). On the other side of this dispute, at least some environmental theorists have warned of the risks of democracy when the public is not well informed on the issues or stoutly resists policy actions that arguably are in its own interests. These theorists tend to prefer an even greater role for scientists and experts in the belief that they can devise technically superior public policies (Ophuls 2011; Ophuls and Boyan 1992).

Policy analysts and other experts both within the government and outside clearly do play a significant role in policy formulation, and especially on routine and noncontroversial issues. Indeed, ad hoc policy task forces or commissions, as well as career bureaucrats, may do much of the work before a proposal is modified and formally endorsed by elected officials (Keller 2009). Yet unlike western European nations, in the U.S. system elected officials and their appointed top-level assistants, rather than permanent professional staff in the agencies, make the final policy decisions. The National Energy Strategy that President George H. W. Bush proposed to Congress in early 1991, for example, followed 18 months of study by a policy task force in the DOE. The task force held extensive public hearings, consulted closely with other federal agencies, and ultimately endorsed strong energy conservation initiatives as a core element in its recommendations. In this case, the Bush White House significantly modified the energy strategy before sending it to Capitol Hill. In particular, Bush's top economic and political advisers persuaded the president to eliminate virtually all the important energy conservation proposals.

Similarly, in 2001 President George W. Bush established an energy task force, the National Energy Policy Development Group, under the direction of Vice President Dick Cheney. The group took its cue primarily from energy industry leaders, and distinctly not from environmental organizations.[11] The task force report and the president's recommendations to Congress were highly favorable to the energy industry, even though the Bush White House maintained that the report, *Reliable, Affordable, and Environmentally Sound Energy for America's Future*, was the product of a balanced process that solicited advice from a diversity of interests.

Comprehensive environmental policy analysis would seem a prerequisite for policy formulation. Yet, as is common in the U.S. policymaking process and illustrated by the work of the Bush energy task force, such analysis faces substantial intellectual, institutional, and political barriers (Bartlett 1990). It is hard to engage in comprehensive analysis when the requisite information is not always available, the process may be hindered by competition among different government agencies and offices, and political pressures from affected interest groups may push the process toward a more narrow examination of the issues than might be desirable. The result is that policy formulation typically proceeds incrementally, slowly, and in small steps (Bryner and Duffy 2012; Lindblom and Woodhouse 1993). That said, on occasion the political system surprises with decidedly non-incremental changes, which Baumgartner and Jones (1993, 2002) have called punctuated equilibrium. Examples include adoption of the Clean Air Act in 1970 and other national environmental policies in that decade and since (Repetto 2006).

Policy Legitimation

Policy legitimation is usually defined as giving legal force to decisions, or authorizing or justifying policy action, such as through a majority vote in a legislature or a formal bureaucratic or judicial decision (Anderson 2015; Jones 1984). It also includes the legitimacy of action taken (i.e., whether it is viewed as a proper exercise of governmental authority) and its broad acceptability to certain publics, and the extent to which the public views governmental institutions and policymakers as legitimate and trustworthy. Public trust and confidence in government have fallen substantially since the 1960s, which greatly complicates the task of legitimation. Legitimacy or acceptability also can flow from several other conditions. The action being proposed may be viewed as consistent with constitutional or statutory specifications, or it is seen as compatible with U.S. political culture and values, and seems to have demonstrable popular support. It may also be approved through an open and transparent decision-making process where relevant publics and policy officials interact extensively. For example, they may have the opportunity to debate the issues at length and to try to reconcile differences of opinion. Of course, there is always a chance that some legitimate interests (e.g., the poor or minority groups) may be excluded from the decision-making process, either intentionally or because they lack the time, expertise, knowledge of the opportunities, or adequate finances to participate. In addition, the political process today can be heavily influenced by well-organized and ideologically motivated groups that can easily polarize rather than unite the electorate.

Public participation, or sometimes opinion polls indicating the public's views on the issues, is a significant part of policymaking, and particularly important for the policy legitimation stage. From the national to the local levels, such participation often means that environmental interest groups, and those who oppose them, try to speak for the public, or at least for their members, within legislative and bureaucratic settings. Such action might involve lobbying for the passage of new laws or trying to affect their implementation by influencing decisions within agencies such as the EPA or the Interior Department, a state environmental protection agency, or a local land use planning agency (Kraft and Kamieniecki 2007).

At local and regional levels, public involvement may be far more direct and extensive, with citizens taking part in public meetings and hearings, sitting on task forces and planning groups, and working directly with policymakers to ensure that decisions reflect their concerns (Daley 2007, 2013; John 2004; Meadowcroft 2004; Sabatier et al. 2005; Weber 2003). The growth of the sustainable-community movement is a case in point. It has provided citizens in hundreds of communities nationwide the opportunity to affect significant local decisions on transportation, energy use, land use, urban sprawl, and the quality of life (John and Mlay 1999; Mazmanian and Kraft 2009; Paehlke 2013a; Portney 2013).

The process of legitimation often is interconnected with formulation of the policy proposal, and we can see multiple cycles or feedback loops over time. As policy ideas and formal proposals are discussed and criticized, they can change. Certain ideas, such as a carbon tax, may be viewed as unacceptable and put aside, at least temporarily. Administrative proposals, such as the Clean Power Plan formulated by the Obama administration, can be harshly criticized by affected interests such as the coal industry and utilities, and by political conservatives, and then reworked to some extent to enhance the proposal's political acceptability, for example, by giving the states great flexibility in how they can comply with the plan's requirements.

The mere passage of legislation or adoption of a regulation at any level of government is no guarantee that policy legitimation has occurred. In some cases, such as the National Environmental Policy Act (NEPA), legislation may be enacted with little serious consideration of the likely effects. NEPA sailed through the House and Senate in 1969 with virtually no opposition and few members asking what difference the new law actually would make; this is remarkable in light of how controversial the Act later became. Much the same was true of the demanding Clean Air Act Amendments of 1970 (Jones 1975). Concern over costs and other impacts of environmental policies has been so great in recent years, however, that such oversight is far less likely to occur today; yet it still happens on occasion. For instance, rapid action by Congress in 1995 on the Contract with America provided few opportunities to consider its effects on the environment and public well-being (Kraft 2013a). Critics of the Obama administration's $787 billion economic renewal package, formulated and approved quickly in early 2009 as the nation faced an unprecedented economic crisis, raised many of the same concerns about whether the money, about $80 billion of which was directed at energy projects, would be spent wisely.

Much like policies that are carelessly formulated (e.g., using poor data, unreasonable assumptions, or questionable forecasting), policies adopted or changed without sufficient legitimation run some important risks. They may fail because of technical misjudgments or inaccurate appraisals of public acceptability. Such was the fate of the Nuclear Waste Policy Act of 1982. Congressional proponents of the Act seriously misjudged the public's willingness to accept nuclear waste repositories and its trust and confidence in the DOE, the bureaucracy in charge of the program (Flynn et al. 1995; Kraft 2000, 2013b). Risks of policy failure or ineffectiveness of this kind may be minimized by ensuring participation by all key interest groups and citizens ("stakeholders" in government reports), opportunities for careful review of policy proposals, and maintenance of political accountability for decision makers. This is, however, not easy to pull off.

If not handled well, stakeholder engagement, for example, can heighten political and policy disagreements and adversely affect a policy's implementation (Daley 2007, 2013).

Policy Implementation

Policy implementation refers to activities directed toward putting programs into effect. These include interpretation of statutory language; organization of bureaucratic offices and efforts; provision of sufficient resources (e.g., money, staff, and expertise); and the details of administration such as provision of benefits, enforcement of environmental regulations, and monitoring of compliance. Those activities occur at all levels in the United States—federal, state, and local—as well as internationally. Most federal environmental protection policies are implemented at both the federal and levels. The federal government approves environmental standards and rules, but the day-to-day enforcement typically is handled at the state level, and as might be expected, conflicts often arise between the federal government and the states over program goals and priorities (Rabe 2016; Ringquist 1993; Scheberle 2004, 2013).

Implementation is rarely automatic, however, and involves more than a series of technical and legal decisions by bureaucratic officials. It is deeply affected by political judgments about statutory obligations, priorities for action, provision of resources, and selection of implementation tools, such as the imposition of fines and other penalties. For example, the Bush administration, like the Reagan administration, focused heavily on quietly rewriting administrative rules and regulations to achieve environmental policy goals that would have been unattainable had it sought congressional approval; debate in Congress would have been more visible and aroused far more opposition (Vig 2013, 2016).[12] Implementation is also influenced by the responses or expected responses of target groups and other publics. Variables such as the commitment and administrative skills of public officials in charge of the program make a difference as well (Mazmanian and Sabatier 1983). Later chapters explore these issues in detail as they apply to the major environmental protection and natural resource policies and their implementation by both federal and state bureaucracies.

Policy and Program Evaluation

Once implemented, analysts and policymakers need to ask whether environmental policies and programs are working well or not. This is usually taken to mean the extent to which they are achieving their goals and objectives. Policies also may be judged against other standards, such as the extent of public involvement, fairness or equity in environmental enforcement actions, or efficiency in the use of resources. Despite extensive criticism directed at environmental programs over the past four decades, formal evaluation of this kind is surprisingly rare. It is also not easy to do. Yet there is little question that we will see more evaluations in the future. The costs and effects of environmental policies are creating new demands for better appraisal of how well the policies are working and whether alternative approaches might work better (Bennear and Coglianese 2013; Coglianese and Bennear 2005; Morgenstern and Portney 2004; Susskind and Schulman 2013).

Environmental policies may be evaluated in several different ways, but the most common is to ask whether they produce the expected outcomes. For example, does the Clean Air Act result in cleaner air? Does the Endangered Species Act save threatened and endangered species and habitats? Evaluations may be rigorous attempts to measure and analyze specific program outcomes and other effects. As is the case with other public policies, however, they may also be far less systematic assessments by congressional committees, internal agency review bodies, or environmental and industry interest groups (Anderson 2015; Kraft and Furlong 2018). As is true of all stages in the policy cycle, political pressures and judgments affect whether, and to what extent, policymakers consider such information when they decide to continue or alter environmental policies and programs. We turn to the details of policy evaluation in Chapter 7.

Policy Change

The last stage in the cycle is policy change. Particularly if the results of public policies are not satisfactory, they may be revised in an attempt to make them more successful, or they may be terminated or canceled. Revision may involve establishing new policy goals, granting different authority to an agency, spending more money on the program, using new approaches (such as market-based incentives or information disclosure), or setting new priorities for implementation. Termination itself is a rare form of policy change, but environmentalists and many others have suggested taking exactly this action for some natural resource policies that they view as wasteful and harmful to the environment. Examples include some Western land and water use policies, agricultural subsidies that flow chiefly to wealthy farmers, and continued subsidies for oil production even in the face of record oil company profits. Of course, such policies are nonetheless stoutly defended by politically powerful constituencies that benefit from their continuation; these include ranchers, farmers, miners, and logging interests (Lowry 2006; Lubell and Segee 2013). By the same token, many business organizations have argued that some environmental protection policies do more harm than good (Superfund is often mentioned, as are some sections of the Clean Air Act) and should be terminated. As the case with policy evaluation, we will explore policy change in detail in Chapters 5 and 6 when we turn to the substance of U.S. environmental, energy, and natural resource policies.

Although analytically distinct and logically arranged, this sequence of activities in the policy process may follow a different order, the stages may overlap one another, and the actions may take place in more than one institutional setting—for example, at the state level. As is discussed later, state governments are intimately involved in implementing federal environmental protection policies. They also are often well ahead of the federal government in policy developments. A notable example is California's adoption in 2002 of state regulations on greenhouse gas emissions by automobiles, the first such effort in the nation, and its later adoption of other significant climate change policies (Rabe 2016).

As should be clear from the preceding discussion, the overall policy process is also highly dynamic. It can change greatly over time as specific policy actors come and go, new data and arguments are advanced, problems are defined and redefined, and new policy solutions, such as market incentives and public education, are put forth and judged. That should be good news to environmental activists as well as to their opponents. The process of policymaking never really ends. Defeat in one venue or at one time (e.g., in Congress in the early 2010s) may mean that the battle is fought again at a later time or that it shifts to a different location, such as the states or even local governments (Klyza and Sousa 2013; Rabe 2016).

Box 3.1 highlights key sources of information about institutions and policy actors that are influential in environmental policy processes. These include website references for the most significant departments and agencies of the federal government, the 50 states, and policy think tanks that are often active on environmental policy issues.

BOX 3.1 FINDING INFORMATION ABOUT ENVIRONMENTAL POLICYMAKING ON THE WEB

Government websites provide a vast quantity of environmental data, such as EPA reports on air and water quality and toxic substances and Fish and Wildlife Service accounts of threatened and endangered species. Similarly, both government and nongovernmental websites are essential sources for information about current environmental policies and programs, proposed policies and evaluations of them, and the process of policy development and implementation. These sites are cited throughout the text as major policies and their implementing agencies are discussed. Some of the most general and useful portals to those sites are listed here.

Federal Executive Agencies and the Legislative Branch

The best web portal for access to the range of federal environmental agencies and programs and Congress is USA.gov (www.usa.gov). Either programs or agencies are easily located. Among the leading federal government sites are the following:

- www3.epa.gov/ (U.S. Environmental Protection Agency)
- www.doi.gov (U.S. Department of the Interior)
- www.energy.gov (U.S. Department of Energy)
- www.usda.gov (U.S. Department of Agriculture)
- www.nrc.gov (U.S. Nuclear Regulatory Commission)
- www.whitehouse.gov/ administration/eop/ceq (Council on Environmental Quality)
- www.congress.gov (the official portal for the U.S. Congress)
- www.gao.gov (U.S. Government Accountability Office)

Federal Courts

Information about the courts can be found at www.uscourts.gov. The site has links to the Supreme Court, the courts of appeals, and the district courts as well as to the administrative offices that help run the court system. The Supreme Court page (www. supremecourtus.gov) offers access to details about the Court's docket, or cases up for review, the current schedule of cases being heard, oral arguments made before the Court and briefs submitted, Supreme Court rulings, and the full text of opinions.

State and Local Governments

The website for the Council of State Governments (www.csg.org) provides links to all 50 state government home pages, which in turn have links to the major policy areas, including environmental protection and natural resources. The Council also has extensive news reports on policy activities within the states, such as environmental policy innovation. Another top site is the Environmental Council of the States (www.ecos.org), a national and nonprofit organization of state and territorial environmental administrators that collects invaluable state data on policy actions, including environmental innovations, delegation of national authority to the states, spending and regulatory enforcement actions, and state agency organization. See also the National Governors Association (www. nga.org), the National Conference of State Legislatures (www.ncsl.org), the Pew Charitable Trusts' site for State and Consumer Initiatives (www.pewtrusts. org/en/topics/state-policy), and the Initiative and Referendum Institute (www.iandrinstitute.org) for analysis of state environmental ballot propositions.

Interest Groups

Major interest groups provide a variety of pertinent policy information, from news accounts of policy developments to studies and reports on environmental issues. A comprehensive list of both environmental groups and their adversaries is provided in Table 4.3.

Policy Research Groups

Among the leading sites for policy analysis groups (think tanks) active on environmental policy are the following:

- www.rff.org (Resources for the Future)

- www.brookings.edu (Brookings Institution)
- www.ucsusa.org (Union of Concerned Scientists)
- www.wri.org (World Resources Institute)
- www.worldwatch.org (Worldwatch Institute)
- www.aei.org (American Enterprise Institute)
- www.heritage.org (Heritage Foundation)
- www.cato.org (Cato Institute)
- www.cei.org (Competitive Enterprise Institute)

Characteristics of U.S. Government and Politics

Some unique characteristics of the U.S. political system shape the policy process outlined here and the environmental policies that emerge from it (Durant, Fiorino, and O'Leary 2017; Kamieniecki and Kraft 2013; Klyza and Sousa 2013).[13] Formal institutional structures, rules, and procedures are never neutral in their effects. Some groups gain advantages from certain institutional arrangements while others may lose. One of the most persistent concerns, identified long ago by the political scientist E. E. Schattschneider (1960), is that some ideas and some groups may be excluded from the decision-making process as a result. For example, poor and minority groups may have little say about the location of polluting factories that can affect their health (Konisky 2015; Ringquist 2006). Another example is that efforts to limit uncontrolled urban growth or sprawl could gain no footing for years; they were kept off the agenda in many cities (Portney 2013). Generalizing about such phenomena, Schattschneider said that all organizations "have a bias in favor of the exploitation of some kinds of conflict and the suppression of others because *organization is the mobilization of bias*. Some issues are organized into politics and others are organized out" (1960, 71; emphasis in original). We study the details of government institutions in part because they channel political conflict and thus affect the policy process and its results.

Constitutional and Political Features

The U.S. Constitution sets out the basic governmental structure and establishes an array of individual rights that have been largely unchanged for over 225 years. Government authority is divided among the three branches of the federal government and shared with the 50 states and some 80,000 local units of government (cities, counties, and a host of special districts, such as those dealing with water resources). The logic of the tripartite arrangement of the federal government was to limit its authority through creation of separate and countervailing powers in each branch and to protect individual rights.

Additional guarantees of freedom for individuals (and corporations) were provided in various sections of the Constitution. Most notable is the due process clause of the Fifth Amendment, which puts a premium on the protection of property rights and thereby creates significant barriers to governmental action.[14] Decentralization of authority to the states likewise reflected public distrust of the national government in the late eighteenth century and a preference for local autonomy. At that time, the nation's small population of 4 million lived largely in small towns and rural areas, and the activities of the federal government were minuscule compared with its present size and scope of responsibilities. Yet the constraints placed on the government's authority to act, on decision making by majority rule, and on prompt policy development continue today (Anderson 2015; Kraft and Furlong 2018).

Other constitutional dictates and political influences also have important implications for environmental policy. They include staggered terms of office for the president, senators, and representatives, which tend to make members of Congress independent of the White House, and the House and Senate independent of one another. That motivation is reinforced by the geographic basis of representation and an electoral process that induces members to pay more attention to local and regional interests directly related to their reelection than to the national concerns that preoccupy presidents and executive branch officials. To this inherent legislative parochialism, we can add a preoccupation with individual political goals. Members of Congress assumed almost complete responsibility for their own political fund-raising and reelection campaigns as the number and political influence of narrowly focused interest groups surged. The interest group "explosion" from the 1970s to the present has severely eroded the broader and more integrative forces of political parties and the presidency (Berry and Wilcox 2009).

Competition between the two parties and their increasingly polarized positions on the issues also inhibit coalition-building and the development of comprehensive and coordinated environmental policies. As noted earlier, an extensive scholarly literature confirms a strong association between partisanship and environmental policy support among elected officials, and the gap has grown markedly since the 1970s. Democrats are far more supportive of environmental protection policy than are Republicans (Below 2013; Calvert 1989; Guber and Bosso 2013a; Kamieniecki 1995). The differences are clearly evident in congressional voting scores compiled by the League of Conservation Voters (LCV) and are also seen in national party platforms. In recent years, Senate Democrats averaged about 85 percent support for the positions endorsed by the LCV and the environmental community. Senate Republicans averaged about 8 percent. A similar division is found in the House, where Democrats averaged about 86 percent and Republicans 10 percent.

Analysis of LCV scores over more than 40 years indicates that the two parties show increasing divergence from the early 1970s through the 2010s

(Below 2013; Dunlap, McCright, and Yarosh 2016; Kraft 2016; Shipan and Lowry 2001).[15] This trend also can be seen in the general electorate, which helps to explain the congressional voting patterns. Recent surveys by the Pew Research Center for the People and the Press showed that environmental issues exhibited the second largest partisan division among the electorate; only social safety-net issues divided the two parties more. These differences were negligible in a comparable 1987 survey.[16]

Institutional Fragmentation and Policy Stalemate

These formal constitutional and informal political forces have led some scholars to question whether the U.S. government is capable of responding in a timely and coherent way to environmental challenges (Ophuls and Boyan 1992). There is good reason to be concerned. Constitutionally created checks and balances may constrain abuses of authority by either Congress or the president, but they also can lead to policy stalemate or gridlock, where environmental problems cannot be addressed quickly or adequately. Sometimes the reason is a lack of public consensus on the issue. Sometimes it can be found in the intense competition among organized interest groups, and sometimes in the inability of the two major parties to reach agreement. But the structure of government, such as fragmentation of authority within Congress and the executive branch, is also a contributing cause of policy inaction, even when solid scientific evidence is available about the severity of the problem (Kraft 2016).

Dispersal of Power in Congress The congressional committee system is a good example of the tendency to fragment authority in the U.S. political system and to make policymaking difficult. Most of the policymaking in Congress takes place in the committees rather than on the floor of the House or Senate. But no single committee on the environment exists in either the House or Senate. Rather, seven major committees in the House and five in the Senate are responsible for different aspects of environmental policy, as shown in Table 3.2. Sometimes the committees work cooperatively, especially in the House when the party leadership favors action (Davidson et al. 2016). Yet sometimes they disagree on what course of action is best, as has been the case on energy and climate change in recent years. There also can be conflicts between the authorizing committees of the House and Senate and the appropriations committees. That is, a committee may create a new program or agency, as was done for the Advanced Research Projects Agency-Energy (ARPA-E) in the DOE in 2007, only to find that the appropriations committees do not fund it or supply far less money than needed for effective implementation because they do not value the agency's work or accord it a high priority in a competitive budgetary process. In this case, Obama's first secretary of energy, Steven Chu, got ARPA-E funded in 2009 as part of the administration's economic stimulus package.[17]

TABLE 3.2 Major congressional committees with environmental responsibilities

Committee	Environmental policy jurisdiction
House of Representatives	
Agriculture	Agriculture, forestry, pesticides and food safety, soil conservation.
Appropriations[a]	Appropriations for all programs.
Energy and Commerce	All energy sources, the Department of Energy and the Federal Energy Regulatory Commission, nuclear energy industry and nuclear waste, air pollution, safe drinking water, pesticide control, Superfund and hazardous waste disposal, toxic substances control.
Natural Resources	Public lands and natural resources; mineral resources on public lands; national parks, forests, and wilderness areas; fisheries and wildlife; coastal zone management; Geological Survey.
Science, Space, and Technology	Environmental research and development; energy research and development; research in national laboratories; NASA, National Weather Service, and National Science Foundation. Subcommittee on environment oversees EPA, NOAA, and NASA research.
Transportation and Infrastructure	Transportation, including civil aviation, railroads, water transportation, and transportation infrastructure; water resources and the environment; bridges and dams.
Senate	
Agriculture, Nutrition and Forestry	Agriculture, soil conservation and groundwater, forestry, nutrition, pesticides, food safety.
Appropriations[a]	Appropriations for all programs.
Commerce, Science, and Transportation	Interstate commerce and transportation; coastal zone management; marine fisheries; oceans, weather, and atmospheric activities; surface transportation.
Energy and Natural Resources	Energy policy; mines, mining, and minerals; national parks and recreation areas; wilderness areas; wild and scenic rivers; public lands and forests.
Environment and Public Works	Environmental policy in general; air, water, and noise pollution; safe drinking water; fisheries and wildlife; Superfund and hazardous wastes, solid waste disposal and recycling; public works, bridges, and dams.

Note: [a] Both the House and Senate Appropriations Committees have Interior and Environment subcommittees that handle all Interior Department agencies as well as the Forest Service and the EPA. Other environmental agencies fall under different subcommittees.

Source: Adapted and updated from a similar table prepared for Vig and Kraft (2016). All descriptions of committee jurisdictions are taken from the individual committee websites. The names and jurisdictions of subcommittees can change from one Congress to another.

In some respects, the dispersal of power in Congress is even greater than suggested by looking only at the activities of the major environmental committees. Dozens of committees and subcommittees have some jurisdiction over environmental issues, and some 20 of them in the Senate and 28 in the House have jurisdiction over at least some EPA activities (Rosenbaum 2013a; National Academy of Public Administration 1995). Different committees also have quite varied agendas, and some are more supportive of the EPA's activities than others. Much depends on the party in control of Congress (and therefore in control of the committees) and the individuals who chair the committees and subcommittees. As one striking example, in 2016, Rep. Lamar Smith of Texas chaired the House Science, Space, and Technology Committee, and he used that platform to sharply criticize the Obama administration's climate change policies and to launch multiple investigations into what he viewed as the flawed science of climate change and the activities of scientists speaking out on the subject.[18] One consequence of this fragmentation of authority is that agencies can be subject to unclear and inconsistent instruction from Congress about the preferred direction of environmental policy (Durant, Fiorino, and O'Leary 2017; Fiorino 2013; Kraft 2016; Rosenbaum 2013a).

One other effect of this kind of dispersion of power within Congress is important. Building a consensus on policy goals and means is often unattainable because of the diverse policy actors and the multiplicity of committees involved. Action may be blocked even when public concern about the environment is high and consensus exists on broad policy directions. The reason is that it is much easier for opponents to stop legislative proposals from going forward than it is for those favoring action to build broad coalitions in support of them. One of the best examples is that the Clean Air Act could not be reauthorized between 1977 and 1990 because of persistent controversies over acid rain and other issues. Much the same has been true in recent years on energy and climate change, as discussed in Chapter 6.

Still, one message is that, as Barbara Sinclair (2017) has argued, lawmaking in Congress is often "unorthodox" or unusual today. It is not as straightforward as civics books suggest, and party and committee leaders sometimes find creative ways to get around the many obstacles to taking action on environmental and other policy issues. This capacity helps to explain how a fragmented and politically polarized Congress nonetheless can approve significant changes in environmental policy from time to time. Approval of legislation on toxic chemical regulation discussed at the chapter's beginning is one example. Others include major energy policies in 2005 and 2007 and enactment of the Omnibus Public Lands Act of 2009, which set aside large parcels of federal lands for wilderness protection. In addition, dozens of less visible environmental, resource, and energy measures are approved every year, as is funding for existing programs (Kraft 2016).

Divided Authority in the Executive Branch A similar division of authority characterizes the executive branch, where it is often difficult to act quickly, coherently, and effectively on environmental problems. Figure 3.1 indicates the large number of executive branch agencies with environmental responsibilities. The EPA has authority for the major environmental protection statutes, but for much of what it does, it shares responsibility with other agencies and departments (Durant, Fiorino, and O'Leary 2017; Rosenbaum 2013a).

In addition to the EPA, 12 cabinet departments have significant roles in environmental policy. Four departments have major responsibilities for either environmental protection or natural resources: Interior, Agriculture, Energy, and State (the last for international policies). Others, such as Commerce and Transportation, arguably have a comparable effect on the environment through their implementation of research and management programs dealing with mass transit, highways, oil pollution, and coastal zones. Independent agencies such as the Nuclear Regulatory Commission and selected offices in the executive office of the president (the Council on Environmental Quality, Office of Management and Budget, Council of Economic Advisers, and Office of Science and Technology Policy) are also regular participants in formulating and implementing environmental policies. As might be expected, the various agencies and departments sometimes find it difficult to work cooperatively; for example, the EPA and the DOE have clashed frequently on a range of issues because the former emphasizes environmental quality and the latter the production of energy, as have the EPA and the president's economic advisers over the cost of environmental regulation. These conflicts may be one reason for President Obama's decision in his first term to create a new White House position as coordinator of energy and climate policy; he named Carol Browner, EPA administrator during the Clinton presidency, as the new "climate czar." Although such an innovative approach was much applauded by students of environmental policy (e.g., Bryner and Duffy 2012, 34), after several years, Browner left the White House and the duties of the new office were subsumed under the Domestic Policy Council.

Under the conditions prevailing in both Congress and the executive branch, policymaking depends on bargaining among power-wielders to frame compromises that are acceptable to most policy actors. In turn, as discussed earlier, the process of bargaining and compromise means that environmental policies ordinarily change incrementally rather than dramatically or quickly, although exceptions do occur. Successful policymaking in the U.S. political system also requires skillful and determined political leadership. Policy entrepreneurs and other leaders must be capable of assembling coalitions of stakeholders, fashioning legislative and executive compromises, and shepherding the resultant measures through Congress or an executive agency. Former Senate majority leader George Mitchell's (D-Maine) leadership on the Clean Air Act of 1990 exemplified those qualities, as made clear in Richard Cohen's (1995) insider account of the Act's passage. So too do the efforts of Representatives Henry Waxman and Edward Markey in support of climate change legislation in 2009.

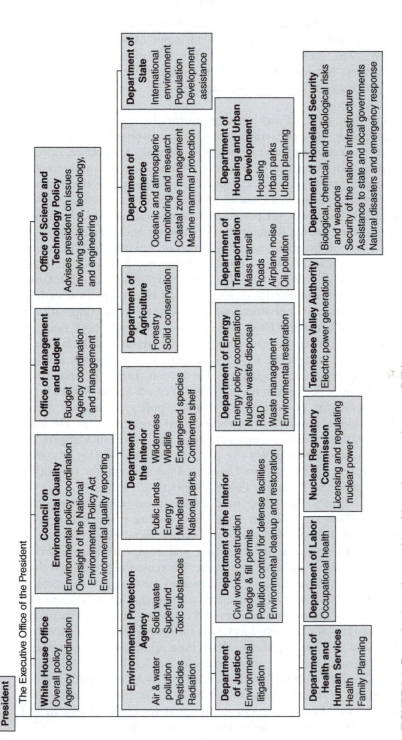

FIGURE 3.1 Executive branch agencies with environmental responsibilities

Sources: Council on Environmental Quality, *Environmental Quality: Sixteenth Annual Report of the Council on Environmental Quality* (Washington, DC: Government Printing Office, 1987); *United States Government Manual 2008–2009* (Washington, DC: Government Printing Office, 2008); and author. A similar figure is used in Norman J. Vig and Michael E. Kraft, eds., *Environmental Policy New Directions for the Twenty-First Century*, 9th edn. (Washington, DC: CQ Press, 2016).

The Benefits of Dispersed Power

Would more centralized or integrated political institutions produce a better outcome than the decentralized and loose policymaking apparatus we now have? The answer is not entirely clear (Mazmanian and Nijaki 2013; Rosenbaum 2013b). Despite criticism of the present institutional arrangements in government, a decentralized and competitive political process has some attractive and often overlooked qualities. Among them are the many opportunities created for interest groups and policy entrepreneurs, including environmentalists, to promote issues of concern to them. There are also innumerable points of access in the highly permeable U.S. system for those who wish to oppose the policies promoted by the president, members of Congress, or others.

Congressional Committees The decentralization of the congressional committee system, for example, virtually guarantees that environmental advocacy groups (and their opponents) can find a friendly audience somewhere to publicize and promote their cause. Environmentalists discovered the attractiveness of this strategy during Ronald Reagan's presidency (1981–1989), when they became highly adept at stimulating public and congressional opposition to the president's efforts to weaken environmental policies. During the Republican Congress of the mid- to late 1990s, the tables were turned. The more ideologically committed House conservatives became aggressive in their use of Congress's oversight powers to keep the Clinton environmental bureaucracies from taking actions they opposed. With the House in Republican hands in the 112th through the 114th Congresses (January 2011- January 2017), much the same pattern was evident, with congressional ire directed particularly at the Obama White House and the EPA (Kraft 2016).[19]

More positively, the existence of some 200 congressional committees and subcommittees means that almost any organized group can find a member of Congress who is willing to introduce legislation and perhaps to move the issue to a committee hearing or investigation. In this way, members of Congress can help set the agenda by providing a forum for raising an issue's visibility. Historically, for instance, some members of Congress have been willing to promote environmental and resource issues that were of little interest to either the president or party leaders within Congress, such as population growth and its effect on the environment, or climate change. Congress is nearly a perfect setting for such entrepreneurial behavior because of the freedom and flexibility that members have to define their jobs and set their priorities, and their continuing search for activities that will bring them some attention and political credit (Kraft 1995, 2013b, 2016).

The Role of the Courts Similarly, the federal courts offer a rich opportunity for groups that seek to influence environmental policy, particularly when they wish to challenge the prevailing sentiment in Congress or in the executive agencies. Even before President Reagan assumed office, for example, environmentalists had come to rely heavily on using the federal courts to pressure reluctant executive agencies to implement the tough new statutes adopted during the 1970s. Much of the bitter fight over protection of old-growth forests in the Pacific Northwest took place in the federal courts, with either environmentalists or the logging industry challenging administrative plans that sought to balance competing interests (Yaffee 1994). Environmental groups have become adept at playing a kind of watchdog or oversight role, keeping a close eye on administrative decision making that is often obscure to the general public. Industry groups are likely to do the same to guard against what they see as burdensome and costly actions by the EPA, the Interior Department, or other agencies. Both groups make their case in the courts when they cannot succeed in Congress or in executive agency proceedings (Kraft and Kamieniecki 2007; O'Leary 1993, 2016).

Courts shape environmental policy in many ways. One is that they serve a kind of gatekeeper function by deciding who has standing to sue, or the right to appeal to the federal courts, and whether a dispute is ready for review. Environmentalists won an important victory in early 2000 when the U.S. Supreme Court voted 7–2 in the case of *Friends of the Earth v. Laidlaw* to uphold "citizen suit" provisions of environmental laws such as the Clean Air Act and Clean Water Act that business and conservative interest groups had long opposed. By permitting such a "standing to sue," the Court kept the door open for citizen groups trying to pressure federal agencies into more aggressive enforcement of environmental laws. Such a lawsuit filed by environmental groups in 1989 to force the development of water pollution standards for large animal feedlots (increasingly important in rural areas) met a degree of success when new rules were announced in 2002 to reduce such pollution.[20]

The courts also set standards for review, including whether they will defer to the expert judgment of administrative agencies or instead review an agency's decisions more critically. The EPA, for instance, sets environmental quality standards that are one of the first steps in regulating pollution (see Chapter 5). The agency is frequently sued over the standards that it chooses, putting the decision into the federal courts. Where a statute is silent or ambiguous on a given issue, the courts usually defer to the expert judgment of an agency as long as it is reasonable and not arbitrary or capricious.

One important example of this process concerns the EPA's decision in 1997 to tighten standards for fine particulates and ozone (supported by the Clinton White House). The decision was contested by the American Trucking Association, which represented a coalition of industry groups opposed to the new standards. The group argued that the EPA did not consider the costs of the new standards nor did it conduct a cost–benefit analysis to support them. It also argued that the decision by Congress to delegate such broad rule-making authority to the EPA was unconstitutional.

In February 2001, in one of the most important environmental law rulings in years, the Supreme Court unanimously upheld the EPA's action. It said that the Clean Air Act required only the consideration of public health and safety, and that it "unambiguously bars cost considerations" from the standard-setting process. The Court also defended the congressional delegation of authority to the agency as a legitimate exercise of congressional lawmaking power, rejecting a ruling by a federal appeals court to the contrary. The decision constituted a major victory for environmental groups and for the EPA.[21]

Frequently the courts must interpret the Constitution, statutory language, administrative rules, regulations, executive orders, treaties, and prior court decisions that may serve as a precedent or standing judicial policy. The policy language in these various documents may be ambiguous or vague, or new situations arise that the architects of that language failed to anticipate. For example, in 1995, in a major victory for supporters of the Endangered Species Act, the Supreme Court upheld (in a 6–3 decision) a Clinton administration interpretation of the Act's prohibition on the "taking" of a species. Secretary of the Interior Bruce Babbitt promulgated a regulation that defined the Act's prohibition of such taking as including "significant habitat modification or degradation where it actually kills or injures wildlife." A group called the Sweet Home Chapter of Communities for a Great Oregon (representing small landowners, logging companies, and families who depend on the forest products industry) filed suit. They asserted that the secretary of the interior exceeded his authority under the Act in issuing such an interpretation. A series of judicial rulings turned on how to interpret the word "harm" in the ESA, culminating in the Supreme Court ruling (O'Leary 2016).[22]

As this example illustrates, the courts have the final say on what the law means, although Congress always has the right to revise the law to make its meaning clearer if it disagrees with court rulings. Court decisions on "regulatory taking" of property (when government regulations deprive property owners of some rights to use their property), for instance, have led conservative property rights groups to press state legislatures and Congress to change the law to make it more difficult for regulatory agencies to affect property rights in this way (see Chapter 6).

State and Local Governments Environmentalists also look increasingly to state and local governments when they are stymied in Congress or executive agencies. In many ways state and local policy action is easier, in part because there is much less of the ideological and partisan wars that so often are found at the national level of government. Moreover, state officials may be able to play the role of policy entrepreneur discussed earlier. That is, they can follow an issue closely, build coalitions of support, and take advantage of windows of opportunity to advance their policy initiatives (Rabe 2004). For these reasons, some of the most innovative environmental policies recently can be found at the state level, the "laboratories of democracy"; this includes the use of "green taxes" and other economic incentives, public disclosure of information on toxic chemicals, pollution prevention programs, and even climate change policies (John 1994, 2004; Klyza and Sousa 2013). For example, by 2012, 29 states with 60 percent of the U.S. population had adopted renewable energy portfolios, 23 states were developing carbon cap-and-trade systems, and California in 2006 adopted a Global Warming Solutions Act that affected nearly every sector of the economy that generated greenhouse gases (Rabe 2016). By 2009, California once again was leading the nation in the push to expand the use of solar power; it had twice the solar capacity of all other states combined.[23]

States were also frequently in conflict with the federal government during the Bush administration over clean air standards, mercury emissions, and failure to regulate greenhouse gas emissions, among other issues; in many of those cases the states went to court to challenge the administration, often successfully (O'Leary 2016; Rabe 2007, 2016). Much the same pattern is likely in the Trump administration. By late 2016, a number of states, and most notably California, indicated that even if the federal government pulled back from the Obama administration's energy and climate change policies, they would maintain or expand their own commitment to reducing greenhouse gas emissions, expanding mass transit, and relying more on renewable energy sources. Similarly, many cities pledge to continue their efforts on climate change despite reduced federal interest and support.[24]

Some states—including California, Michigan, Minnesota, Wisconsin, New Jersey, Oregon, Washington, and New York—historically have ranked consistently among the most innovative and committed to environmental protection goals (Konisky and Woods 2012, 2016). Yet a state's willingness to innovate or take strong enforcement action depends on a number of factors that can change over time. Among them are the partisan alignments at the state level, the strength of the state's economy, public support, and the relative influence of environmental and industry interest groups. In Wisconsin, for example, in 2010, voters elected a Republican governor and Republican majorities in both houses of the state legislature, and as a result, many of the state's historical commitments to strong environmental policies were weakened.[25]

The importance of the states' role in environmental policy is easily demonstrated. The Environmental Council of the States estimates that the states operate 96 percent of all federal environmental programs that may be delegated to them. The states also issue more than 90 percent of all environmental permits, are responsible for most of the environmental enforcement actions in the nation (90 percent), and collect nearly 95 percent of the environmental data that the federal government uses. Of course, increasingly most states have faced severe budgetary constraints in recent years that may well limit what they are able to do (Rabe 2016; Scheberle 2004, 2013).

Something of the same pattern can be found in local and regional environmental policy developments. For example, states in the Great Lakes Basin have cooperated in developing regional initiatives to promote environmental sustainability, particularly as it affects water quality (Rabe and Gaden 2009). Across the nation, but particularly in the Pacific Northwest, local and regional watershed councils and similar grassroots organizations have demonstrated the promise of collaborative and participatory decision making that brings together citizens, key stakeholder groups, and government agencies in a search for acceptable solutions to long-standing conflicts over environmental protection and economic development. These ad hoc and voluntary processes have helped foster consensus on habitat conservation plans for protecting endangered species, restoration efforts for degraded ecosystems, smart growth strategies for suburban communities, and redevelopment of contaminated lands (Layzer 2008, 2013; Paehlke 2013a; Portney 2013; Sabatier et al. 2005; Weber 2003).

Many local governments, particularly in progressive communities and university towns, such as San Francisco; Portland, Oregon; Seattle, Washington; Boulder, Colorado; and Davis, California, have adopted their own distinctive policies on issues as diverse as recycling programs, land conservation, water conservation, energy conservation and efficiency, transportation, building designs to promote efficient energy use, and use of alternative energy sources. Along with the newly expanded state actions on the environment, these local activities have created a richness and diversity in environmental policy that would not be possible in a more centralized and unified system (Mazmanian and Kraft 2009; Press and Nakagawa 2009; Portney 2009, 2013).

Conclusions

This chapter has reviewed some of the key features of the policymaking process. It also has highlighted certain characteristics of U.S. government and politics that shape the way environmental issues are defined and acted on by policymakers. Critics are correct to say that the U.S. political system suffers from serious institutional deficiencies when weighed against the imperatives of contemporary environmental policy needs (Ophuls and Boyan 1992). The U.S. system, however, also has significant strengths that environmentalists and other political activists know well. There are some reasons to be optimistic about the potential for policy development, particularly at the state and local levels of government, where policy gridlock is less a problem than it is in Washington. Yet formulating and adopting effective environmental policies that can be broadly supported is not easy at any level of government.

Chapters 5 through 7 discuss the way U.S. government and politics affect environmental decisions. Another way to judge governmental performance is to take a brief retrospective look at the development of environmental policy since the 1960s, which is the focus of Chapter 4. Such an examination offers persuasive evidence that government has been responsive to changing public concerns about the environment, which is particularly the case when the issues are politically salient, thus giving policymakers a reason to take seriously the public's environmental views. It is no exaggeration to say that public opinion has been the driving force in modern environmental policy.

What is less evident is whether such influence will continue at a time when many environmental policy decisions are increasingly technical, when they are made largely in administrative agencies and the courts rather than in legislatures, and when few who are not active participants in issue networks can easily understand them. Whether at the national level or at community, regional, and state levels, the message should be clear to environmentalists and to their opponents. Whatever the broad preferences of the public—which remains sympathetic to the goals of the environmental movement—political influence depends on building a strong understanding of the issues, organizing supportive publics or constituencies, and persistently advocating one's case when opportunities present themselves.

Discussion Questions

1   Should environmental scientists and other experts play a greater role in the policymaking process, as some suggest? What might the consequences be if they did so? Would it improve public and policymaker understanding of the issues? Would it facilitate the adoption of more effective policies?

2   Many analysts and policymakers call for further devolution of environmental responsibilities to state and local governments, although the record of these governments has been mixed. What are the major advantages of such a devolution of authority for environmental protection? What are the most important disadvantages?

3   Environmental policy gridlock in Congress has become common in recent years, and reached something of a new high in recent years. What are the major causes of such a policy stalemate? What might be done to overcome it?

4   Environmental policy responsibilities are widely distributed in government, particularly in the federal executive branch and between the federal government and the states. What are the major disadvantages of such fragmentation of authority? What are the major advantages of it?

5   Would the quality of environmental policy decisions be improved with greater public participation, particularly at the state and local levels of government? Why do you think so? What actions or events might encourage the public to take a greater interest in and to participate more in the policy process?

Suggested Readings

Anderson, James. 2015. *Public Policymaking: An Introduction*, 8th edn. Stamford, CT: Cengage.

Kingdon, John. 1995. *Agendas, Alternatives, and Public Policy*, 2nd edn. New York: Longman.

Klyza, Christopher McGrory, and David Sousa. 2013. *American Environmental Policy, 1990–2006: Beyond Gridlock*, revised and updated edn. Cambridge, MA: MIT Press.

Kraft, Michael E., and Scott R. Furlong. 2018. *Public Policy: Politics, Analysis, and Alternatives*, 6th edn. Washington, DC: CQ Press.

Layzer, Judith A. 2016. *The Environmental Case: Translating Values into Policy*, 4th edn. Washington, DC: CQ Press.

Lazarus, Richard J. 2004. *The Making of Environmental Law*. Chicago: University of Chicago Press.

Vig, Norman J., and Michael E. Kraft, eds. 2016. *Environmental Policy: New Directions for the Twenty-First Century*, 9th edn. Washington, DC: CQ Press.

Notes

1 Quoted in Juliet Eilperin and Darryl Fears, "Congress Is Overhauling an Outdated Law that Affects Nearly Every Product You Own," *Washington Post*, May 19, 2016.

2 Carl Hulse, "Obama Set to Sign Bipartisan Update of 1976 Toxic Substance Law," *New York Times*, June 22, 2016. EDF provides its assessment of the law and a summary of its provisions on its website: www.edf.org/health/policy/chemicals-policy-reform.

3 See, for example, Ronald Brownstein, "Pulling Apart," *National Journal*, February 26, 2011, updated on May 29, 2013; and Frank James, "Political Scientist: Republicans Most Conservative They've Been In 100 Years," National Public Radio, April 13, 2012.

4 John M. Broder, "With Something for Everyone, Climate Bill Passed," *New York Times*, July 1, 2009.

5 The various models and theories are reviewed briefly in Kraft and Furlong (2018) and Anderson (2015).

6 See, for example, Bryan Walsh, "The War on Coal Is Being Won in the U.S., but the Real Battle Is Overseas," *Time*, November 21, 2012; and Robert B. Semple Jr., "'Stop the War on Coal' Act," *New York Times*, September 20, 2012.

7 Jonathan Weisman, "Republican Act with Air, if Not a Vote, of Confidence," *New York Times*, March 17, 2013.

8 The full title of the Act is the Oil Pollution Prevention, Response, Liability, and Compensation Act. Birkland (1997) offers a history of how federal oil spill policy was altered by the Exxon *Valdez* accident.

9 See Timothy Egan, "Once Braced for a Power Shortage, California Now Finds Itself with a Surplus," *New York Times*, November 4, 2001.

10 The Union of Concerned Scientists was especially active in documenting concerns about the lack of scientific integrity; its reports are available at its website: www.ucsusa.org.

11 See Don Van Natta Jr. and Neela Banerjee, "Documents Show Energy Official Met Only with Industry Leaders," *New York Times*, March 27, 2002.

12 For an account of such efforts, see Bruce Barcott, "Changing All the Rules," *New York Times Magazine*, April 4, 2004: 39–44, 66, 73, 76–77.

13 For a detailed analysis of U.S. government institutions and environmental policy, see the edited collection by Lester (1995) and the volume by Kamieniecki and Kraft (2013). In both books, leading environmental policy scholars assess the characteristics and performance of Congress, the bureaucracy, the courts, and state government as well as public opinion, interest groups, and political parties, among other topics. Chapters in Vig and Kraft (2016) also offer appraisals of how Congress, the presidency, the courts, the EPA, and the states have dealt with environmental policy challenges in recent years.

14 The Fifth Amendment states, among other provisions, that no person shall "be deprived of life, liberty, or property, without due process of law; nor shall private property be taken for public use, without just compensation."

15 League of Conservation Voters (LCV), "National Environmental Scorecard" (published annually, Washington, DC: LCV), available at: http://scorecard.lcv. org/scorecard. The LCV used to report party averages in its annual scorecard, but it no longer does so. The difference between the parties remains evident, however, within most state delegations, between the two parties' leadership on the key environmental committees, and between the House and Senate leaders of each party. For the 2015 report, for example, House Democratic leaders averaged 92 percent and Republicans 0 percent. In the Senate, Democratic leaders averaged 99 percent in comparison to Republican leaders at 2 percent.

16 See Pew Research Center, "Trends in American Values: 1987–2012: Partisan Polarization Surges in Bush, Obama Years" (Washington, DC: Pew Research Center for the People and the Press), June 4, 2012.

17 Elise Craig, "A Sparkplug for Energy Innovation," *Business Week*, August 3, 2009: 34.

18 Lisa Rein, "Meet the House Science Chairman Who's Trying to Put Global Warming Research on Ice," *Washington Post*, December 22, 2015; and David Hasemyer, "Lamar Smith Hearing Attempts to Bolster Legal Argument for Subpoenas," *Inside Climate News*, September 14, 2016, available at: www. insideclimatenews.org.

19 See, for example, Leslie Kaufman, "Republicans Seek Big Cuts in Environmental Rules," *New York Times*, July 27, 2011; John M. Broder, "Bashing E.P.A. Is New Theme in G.O.P. Race," *New York Times*, August 17, 2011; Paul Kane, "House GOP Revs Up a Repeal, Reduce and Rein-in Agenda for the Fall," *Washington Post*, August 28, 2011; Coral Davenport, "Republicans Vow to Fight E.P.A. and Approve Keystone Pipeline," *New York Times*, November 10, 2014; New York Times Editorial Board, "G.O.P. Assault on Environmental Laws," *New York Times*, June 8, 2015.

20 Elizabeth Becker, "U.S. Sets New Farm-Animal Pollution Curbs," *New York Times*, December 17, 2002.

21 The case is *Whitman v. American Trucking Association*, 531 U.S. 457 (2001); it was previously called *Browner v. American Trucking Association*. See Linda Greenhouse, "E.P.A.'s Authority on Air Rules Wins Supreme Court's Backing," *New York Times*, February 28, 2001.

22 The case is *Babbitt v. Sweet Home Chapter for a Great Oregon*, 515 U.S. 687 (1995).

23 Felicity Barringer, "With Push Toward Renewable Energy, California Sets Pace for Solar Power," *New York Times*, July 16, 2009.

24 Tatiana Schlossberg, "As Trump Signals Climate Action Pullback, Local Leaders Push Forward," *New York Times*, December 16, 2016; John Metcalfe and Laura Bliss, "How Cities Plan to Fight Climate Change in the Trump Years," Atlantic *CityLab*, November 22, 2016, available at: www.citylab.com; and Adam Nagourney and Henry Fountain, "California, at Forefront of Climate Fight, Won't Back Down to Trump," *New York Times*, December 26, 2016.

25 Siri Carpenter, "How Scott Walker Dismantled Wisconsin's Environmental Legacy," *Scientific American*, June 17, 2015; and Steven Verburg, "Scott Walker, Legislature Altering Wisconsin's Way of Protecting Natural Resources," *Wisconsin State Journal*, October 4, 2015.

CHAPTER 4

The Evolution of Environmental Policy and Politics

In the short history of modern U.S. environmental politics, the 2008 presidential campaign stands out in several respects. It was the first in which energy and environmental issues emerged as leading concerns, and it was the only one in which both major party candidates, Barack Obama and John McCain, agreed on the imperative of fighting global climate change—even if they differed significantly in their proposed solutions.[1] Yet, voters were more preoccupied with other issues than they were with the environment, including the dire state of the economy, the rising cost and availability of health care, challenges facing public education, and national security.

By 2016, the major parties diverged sharply on climate change as well as on most other environmental, energy, and resource issues. The Republican nominee, Donald Trump, consistently sided with the climate change denial community in maintaining that climate change was a hoax. He pledged to dismantle the Obama administration's initiatives on that front, including the EPA's Clean Power Plan, and to withdraw the United States from the historic Paris Agreement on climate change signed in December 2015 and ratified in November 2016; the threat to exit from the accord drew a sharp rebuke from the nation's most eminent scientists.[2] Trump initially said he would abolish the EPA, and then moderated his stance to "refocus the EPA on its core mission of ensuring clean air, and clean, safe drinking water for all Americans." During the campaign he also said he favored turning most key EPA regulatory functions over to the states. The Democratic nominee, Hillary Clinton, called climate change an "urgent threat and a defining challenge of our time." She promised not only to maintain Obama's environmental policies but to strengthen them, and she called for "taking on the threat of climate change and making America the world's clean energy superpower." The contrast between the candidates and their party's positions could hardly have been greater.[3]

The Libertarian party, which attracted considerable interest and support in 2016, was much closer to the Republican views on the environment because of its strong antigovernment and antiregulatory positions. The Green Party platform, as might be expected, was strong on environmental and sustainability issues, even though its presidential nominee, Jill Stein, drew relatively little political support.[4]

Climate change also emerged as a significant issue on the campaign trail and in the polls, thanks in part to President Obama's decision to make environmental protection, resource conservation, and climate change central elements of his presidential legacy.[5] Hillary Clinton made climate change a significant issue in her campaign, with the press reporting it was "taking on a prominence it has never before had in a presidential election campaign."[6] The shift in emphasis likely reflected new global temperature records set in 2016, unprecedented rainstorms in Texas, Louisiana, and North Carolina that drew intense media coverage, and rising public concern.[7] Gallup polls reported that in 2016 more Americans worried a "great deal" or a "fair amount" about climate change than previously—about 64 percent, the highest number reached since 2008. Nearly the same percentage said they believed that rising temperatures were caused by human activities, such as the burning of fossil fuels, suggesting a growing public consensus on the issue even as it remained fairly low in salience, particularly in comparison to concerns about the economy.[8]

These developments and notable shifts in political strategy in the 2016 election campaigns speak to the striking change in environmental politics over the last four decades. In the late 1960s and 1970s, environmental policy was embraced by both political parties, if not with the same degree of enthusiasm. The American public was strongly supportive of policy action, and elected officials competed with one another to claim political credit for their environmental actions. The policies adopted at that time remain in force today, but the political mood of the nation has changed substantially, as evident in the starkly different positions staked out on environmental and energy issues by the two major parties—both in the presidential race and in contests for congressional seats across the country.

The concepts of policymaking introduced in Chapter 3 are helpful for understanding the history of U.S. environmental policy and the evolution of the issues and political stances on them since the late 1960s, when the modern environmental movement grew to prominence. It is equally important to understand the role and effect of environmental and other interest groups today and the influence of public values and attitudes on environmental policy.

This chapter seeks to:

- build an understanding of the history of environmental policy, including the forces that shaped policymaking in the first decades of the modern environmental movement and patterns of presidential actions on policy choices since that time;

- assist readers in understanding and evaluating the role of interest groups in shaping environmental policy, major differences among them, and the strategies they use to affect governmental decisions; and
- aid in analyzing public opinion on the environment, the influence it has had on policymaking, and the role of environmental issues in recent election campaigns.

Natural Resources and Environmental Policies in Historical Perspective

Modern environmental policy emerged in the 1960s and became firmly established on the political agenda during the so-called environmental decade of the 1970s, when Congress enacted most of the major environmental statutes that form the bedrock of contemporary U.S. environmental policy. Actions at state and local levels paralleled these developments. Senator Gaylord Nelson of Wisconsin organized the first Earth Day, held on April 22, 1970, which was widely celebrated across the nation and signaled the arrival of a mass political movement dedicated to ending environmental degradation (Nelson 2002). Politicians responded eagerly to what many at the time considered to be a motherhood issue that posed little political risk and offered many electoral dividends.

Yet concern about the environment and the value of natural resources arose early in the nation's history and periodically sparked the adoption of preservation, conservation, economic development, and public health policies that continue to shape the environmental agenda today (Andrews 2006a, 2013). Most of those policy actions coincided with three periods of progressive government in which other social and economic issues also advanced: the Progressive Era from about 1890 to 1915, the New Deal of the 1930s, and the era of social regulation of the 1960s and 1970s. Within each period, perceived environmental or health crises, catalytic or focusing events, and the leadership of policy entrepreneurs heightened public concern and kindled policy innovation. Broader social, economic, and technological changes also contributed to recognition of looming environmental and resource problems and created the political will to deal with them. As suggested in the model of agenda-setting introduced in Chapter 3, these developments helped set the intellectual, scientific, aesthetic, moral, and political foundations of contemporary environmentalism (Shabecoff 1993).[9]

The Settlement and "Conquest" of Nature

In the early seventeenth century, in one of the first conservation actions in the new nation, New England colonists adopted local ordinances protecting forestland and regulating timber harvesting. Such actions did not prevent the colonists from attempting to subdue what they saw as wilderness and to fundamentally alter the landscape and ecology of New England as the population grew and the land was cleared for agriculture and settlements (Cronon 1983). As the colonists expanded from their small coastal settlements, they expropriated land from Native American communities that had managed the resources for thousands of years, initiating a long pattern of displacement and injustice. Moreover, European settlers generally did not follow the sustainable land and resource use of the small Native American populations (Berkes 1999). The colonists' behavior was an early indication of the limits of policy intervention in the face of profound pressures for expansion and a culture that favored exploitation of the nation's rich natural resources they considered to be virtually without limits (Andrews 2006a).

By the mid-nineteenth century, new trends were emerging. The study of natural systems was gaining stature within the scientific community, and in 1864 George Perkins Marsh published his influential treatise, *Man and Nature*. The book documented the destructive effects on nature from human activity. Literary figures contributed as well to the sense that industrialism and technology were not entirely beneficent in their effects. Henry David Thoreau's *Walden*, a poignant account of his two years in the wilderness at Walden Pond, reflected many of the same concerns as today's "deep ecology" writing.

The late nineteenth century brought significant advances in conservation policy as the consequences of human activities began to attract more attention, although by present standards the effects of the policies were modest. Discoveries of vast areas of unsurpassed beauty in the newly explored West led to the establishment of Yosemite Valley, California, as first a state park (1864) and later as a national park (1891). In 1872 Congress set aside 2 million acres in Wyoming, Montana, and Idaho to create Yellowstone National Park as a "pleasuring ground for the benefit and enjoyment of the people," the first of a series of national parks.

During this same period, however, the federal government sought to encourage rapid development of its vast holdings in the West. It adopted public policies toward that end that reflected prevailing beliefs in Congress and elsewhere that the West was an immense frontier promising "limitless opportunities" for resource exploitation and creation of wealth. Chief among those actions were classic distributive policies: the generous distribution of public lands (free or at token prices) to private parties, such as railroad companies and homestead settlers.

For example, the Homestead Act of 1862 allowed individuals to acquire 160 acres of public land by living on it and working it as a farm. More than 250 million acres were converted to farms through this Act. The federal government transferred over 94 million acres to railroad corporations and an additional 800 million acres to the states, veterans, and other groups under various programs. Over 1 billion acres of the 1.8 billion in the original public domain were privatized in these ways between 1781 and 1977, leaving about 740 million acres of public land, of which 330 million acres are in Alaska (Wengert 1994).[10] A number of government actions also gave large subsidies to ranchers, farmers, and mining companies, all with the same objective of encouraging development of the West by providing access to public lands and waters. For example, the 1872 General Mining Law gave miners virtually free access to rich mineral deposits on public land with no obligation to pay royalties on the minerals extracted. The Reclamation Act of 1902 provided for public construction of dams and other projects to make cultivation of desert lands possible. The federal government also established a U.S. Fish Commission to investigate and seek to reverse decreases in commercial fisheries in both coastal and inland waters, and to promote restoration of the resources; the commission was yet another reflection of intense conflict over natural resources amid exploitation by powerful economic interests (Allard 1978). The West did indeed gain population and the economy prospered, but at a high cost to the environment.

Another important effect was more political. Those who received the subsidies came to believe they were entitled to them indefinitely. The legacy affects natural resource policy even today. For years, powerful Western constituencies (e.g., the mining industry, ranchers, large farming operations, and timber companies) dominated these natural resource policies; they did so by forming protectionist subgovernments in association with members of key congressional committees and executive agencies. Such alliances operate autonomously with little political visibility, and conflict over policy goals typically is minimal. Disputes that do arise are resolved through logrolling, or mutually beneficial bargaining, in which each party may gain its goals (McCool 1990). The existence of these political arrangements allowed the natural resource subgovernments to ward off significant policy changes sought by conservationists and others until the mid-twentieth century. Some of them, such as the mining industry, have continued to fight successfully against reform of the old laws (Foss 1960; Lowi 1979; McConnell 1966). We return to the importance of these kinds of natural resource subsidies in Chapters 6 and 7.

The Conservation Movement and Advances in Public Health

By the late nineteenth century, winds of change began to blow as the Progressive Era unfolded. Reflecting the growth of concern about preservation of natural resources and public lands in response to reckless exploitation in earlier decades, John Muir founded the Sierra Club, the first broad-based environmental organization, in 1892. Muir led the preservationist wing of the incipient environmental movement, with a philosophy of protecting wilderness areas, like his beloved Yosemite Valley, from economic development. Such areas, Muir argued, should be preserved for their own sake and used exclusively for recreational and educational purposes.

A countervailing conservationist philosophy took hold under Gifford Pinchot, a Yale graduate trained in forestry in Germany who became the first professional forester in the United States. In 1898 Pinchot, who emphasized efficient use (or "wise management") of natural resources for economic development, became chief of the Division of Forestry, the forerunner of the modern U.S. Forest Service. Pinchot's approach to conservation soon became the dominant force in twentieth-century natural-resource policy in part through his close association with President Theodore Roosevelt. In 1908 Pinchot chaired a White House Conference on Resource Management that firmly established his brand of conservation as the nation's approach to natural resources. The heritage can be seen in key doctrines of what historian Samuel P. Hays (1959) called the "progressive conservation movement," among them "multiple use" and "sustained yield" of the nation's resources.

Despite the differences between Muir and Pinchot, the conservation movement achieved early successes in the creation of national parks and forest reserves, national monuments such as the Grand Canyon (1908), and government agencies such as the Forest Service (1905), National Park Service (1916), and Bureau of Reclamation (1902 under its first name, the Reclamation Service). Many of the prominent national conservation groups also emerged at this time or shortly thereafter. In addition to the Sierra Club in 1892, the National Audubon Society was founded in 1905 and the National Parks Conservation Association in 1919. Other environmental organizations emerged between the world wars, including the Izaak Walton League in 1922, the Wilderness Society in 1935, and the National Wildlife Federation in 1936.

Environmental protection efforts focusing on public health did not appear for the most part until the 1960s. There was, however, a Progressive Era parallel to the conservation movement in the establishment of urban services (such as wastewater treatment, waste management, and provision of clean water supplies) and improvements in nutrition, hygiene, and medical services. Such gains were spurred by concerns that developed in the late nineteenth century over the excesses of the Industrial Revolution and a system of private property rights that operated with virtually none of the restraints common today.

Consistent with the new emphasis on urban public health, the first air pollution statutes in the United States were designed to control heavy smoke and soot from furnaces and locomotives. They were approved in Chicago and Cincinnati in the 1880s, and by 1920 some 40 cities had adopted air pollution control laws. Although a few states such as Ohio took action as early as the 1890s, no comprehensive state air pollution policies existed until 1952, when Oregon adopted such legislation (P. Portney 1990; Ringquist 1993). Similarly, in the 1880s, many cities established policies to ensure safe drinking water following adoption of the 1893 Interstate Quarantine Act, which was designed to reduce the spread of diseases caused by contaminated water. The federal Public Health Service set the first drinking water standards for interstate commerce under that Act in 1914; the standards served as guidelines to community water systems across the nation, but not formal regulations.

From the New Deal to the Environmental Movement

The environmental agenda during President Franklin Roosevelt's 12-year tenure emphasized the mitigation of natural resource problems, particularly flood control and soil conservation, in response to a series of natural disasters. The most memorable of these was prolonged drought and erosion in the Dust Bowl. Activities such as the creation in 1933 of the Tennessee Valley Authority (TVA) were intended to stimulate economic development and employment to pull the nation out of the Depression. Yet the TVA also was important for demonstrating that government land use planning could be used to benefit the broad public in a region. Other actions—for example, the establishment of the Civilian Conservation Corps and the Soil Conservation Service—were directed at repairing environmental damage and preventing its recurrence. Notable among the many New Deal policies was the Taylor Grazing Act of 1934, which was intended to end the abuse from overgrazing of valuable rangelands and watersheds in the West by authorizing the Department of the Interior to issue grazing permits and regulate rangeland use. Congress created the Bureau of Land Management in 1946 and ended the massive privatization of public lands (Wengert 1994).

During the 1950s and 1960s, a third wave of conservation focused on preservation of areas of natural beauty and wilderness, stimulated in part by increased public interest in recreation and the efforts to stem the tide of economic development threatening key areas. The Wilderness Act of 1964 was intended to preserve some public lands in their natural condition through a National Wilderness Preservation System. The Land and Water Conservation Fund Act, enacted in 1964, facilitated local, state, and federal acquisition and development of lands for parks and open spaces. In addition, Congress created the National Wild and Scenic Rivers System in 1968. Its purpose was to preserve certain rivers with "outstandingly remarkable" scenic, recreational, ecological, historical, and cultural values. At the request of President Lyndon B. Johnson, Lady Bird Johnson, and the President's Commission on Natural Beauty, Congress approved legislation to "beautify" federal highways by, among other actions, reducing the number of unsightly billboards to promote aesthetic values (Gould 1999). Stewart Udall, secretary of the interior under both Presidents John F. Kennedy and Johnson, was a forceful advocate of conservation policies.

This latest "wilderness movement" eventually evolved into the modern environmental movement, with a much broader policy agenda. Congress adopted the first federal water and air pollution control laws in 1948 and 1955, respectively, and gradually expanded and strengthened them. The federal government gingerly approved its first international population policies in the early 1960s several years after congressional policy leaders held hearings and incubated the controversial measures. In his 1965 State of the Union address, President Johnson called for federal programs to deal with "the explosion in world population and the growing scarcity in world resources." The following year Congress authorized the first funds for family planning programs abroad (Kraft 1994b).

The successes of conservation efforts and the nascent environmental movement also depended fundamentally on long-term changes in social values that began after World War II. These value changes accelerated as the nation developed economically and the production and consumption of consumer goods escalated dramatically in the 1950s and 1960s. The United States slowly shifted from an industrial to a postindustrial society. An increasingly affluent, comfortable, and well-educated public placed new emphasis on the quality of life (Hays 1987; Inglehart 1990). Concern for natural resource amenities and environmental protection issues was an integral part of this change. By the 1970s it was evident across all groups in the population, if not to the same degree. Similar factors help account for the growth of the global environmental movement at the same time (McCormick 1989).

Scientific discoveries brought new attention to the effects of pesticides and other synthetic chemicals on human health and the natural environment. These were documented in Rachel Carson's influential *Silent Spring* (1962), Murray Bookchin's *Our Synthetic Environment* (published about six months before Carson's book under the pseudonym Lewis Herber), and Barry Commoner's *The Closing Circle* (1971), a trenchant analysis of ecological risks inflicted by use of inappropriate technologies. Paul Ehrlich's *The Population Bomb* (1968) underscored the role of human population growth in resource use and environmental degradation. Rapid growth in the capacity of the nation's media to alert the public to such dangers heightened public concern, and policy entrepreneurs like consumer activist Ralph Nader helped tie environmental quality to prominent health and safety issues.

The effect of these developments was a broadly based public demand for more forceful and comprehensive governmental action to protect valued natural resources and to prevent environmental degradation. New environmental organizations quickly arose and adopted the tactics of other 1960s social movements, using well-publicized protests and university-based teach-ins to mobilize the public to press for policy change (Nelson 2002). A variety of political reforms, including congressional redistricting and easier access by public interest groups to the courts and legislatures, and changes in the mass media facilitated their success.

The Modern Environmental Movement and Policy Achievements

The environmental movement of the late 1960s and 1970s represented one of those unusual periods in U.S. political history when the problem, policy, and political streams discussed in Chapter 3 converged. The nation's media confirmed the problems in the public's mind, reporting new evidence of the effects of pesticides and toxic chemicals and rising concern over threats to marine mammals, and then showing vividly Cleveland's Cuyahoga River catching fire and the impacts of a major oil well blowout off the coast of Santa Barbara, California.

This convergence set the stage for a dramatic shift in environmental policies. In an unprecedented fashion, a new environmental agenda rapidly emerged. It sought to expand and strengthen early conservation programs and to institute new public policies organized around the integrative and holistic concept of environmental quality. Environmental quality could bring together such otherwise distinct concerns as protection of public health, control of industrial pollution, conservation of natural resources, energy use and its effects, population growth and its impacts, urbanization, consumer protection, and recreation (Caldwell 1970). That agenda drew from new studies of health and environmental risks and from widespread dissatisfaction with the modest achievements of early federal air and water pollution control policies and equally limited state efforts (Davies and Davies 1975; Jones 1975). The legacy of this period includes the major federal environmental protection statutes, a host of important natural resource measures, and countless state and local initiatives that established environmental concerns firmly on the governmental agenda.

Contributing to the building of this new environmental policy agenda was an extraordinary bipartisan group of policy entrepreneurs on Capitol Hill. They and their staffs had been patiently incubating these issues for years before public demand had crystallized and the media (and the White House) discovered the environment. They included such influential environmental lawmakers as Henry Jackson, Edmund Muskie, and Gaylord Nelson in the Senate and Paul Rogers, John Saylor, Paul McCloskey, Morris Udall, and John Dingell, among many others, in the House (Kraft 1995, 2013a).

By early 1970 there was abundant evidence of the problem stream changing quickly and influencing members of Congress who dealt with environmental policy. Indeed, the 92nd Congress (1971–1972) was the most productive in history for environmental protection and natural resources policy. It enacted measures on water pollution control, restrictions on ocean dumping, protection of sea mammals and coastal zones, and regulation of pesticides. Within a few years, other legislation followed on endangered species, drinking water quality, disposal of hazardous waste, control of toxic substances, and management of federal lands and forests. Table 4.1 lists most of these federal laws.

With a rapid rise in public concern about the environment, extensive coverage of the issues in the media, and lobbying by new environmental groups with growing membership, it is not surprising that the key statutes received strong bipartisan congressional support. For example, Congress approved the Clean Air Act Amendments of 1970 by overwhelming margins. The vote was unanimous in the Senate, and in the House it was 375 to 1. Even by 1990, when the Act was strengthened during the presidency of Republican George H. W. Bush, the Senate voted was 89 to 10 in favor and

TABLE 4.1 Major federal environment laws, 1964–2016

1964	Wilderness Act, PL 88-577
1968	Wild and Scenic Rivers Act, PL 90-542
1969	National Environmental Policy Act, PL 91-190
1970	Clean Air Act Amendments, PL 91-604
1972	Federal Water Pollution Control Act Amendments (Clean Water Act), PL 92-500 Federal Environmental Pesticide Control Act of 1972 (amended the Federal Insecticide, Fungicide and Rodenticide Act [FIFRA] of 1947), PL 92-516 Marine Protection, Research and Sanctuaries Act of 1972, PL 92-532 Marine Mammal Protection Act, PL 92-522 Coastal Zone Management Act, PL 92-583 Noise Control Act, PL 92-574
1973	Endangered Species Act, PL 93-205
1974	Safe Drinking Water Act, PL 93-523
1976	Resource Conservation and Recovery Act (RCRA), PL 94-580 Toxic Substances Control Act, PL 94-469 Federal Land Policy and Management Act, PL 94-579 National Forest Management Act, PL 94-588
1977	Clean Air Act Amendments, PL 95-95 Clean Water Act (CWA), PL 95-217 Surface Mining Control and Reclamation Act, PL 95-87
1980	Comprehensive Environmental Response, Compensation, and Liability Act (CERCLA or Superfund), PL 96-510
1982	Nuclear Waste Policy Act of 1982, PL 97-425 (amended in 1987 by the Nuclear Waste Policy Amendments Act of 1987, PL 100-203)
1984	Hazardous and Solid Waste Amendments (RCRA amendments), PL 98-616
1986	Safe Drinking Water Act Amendments, PL 99-339 Superfund Amendments and Reauthorization Act (SARA), PL 99-499
1987	Water Quality Act (CWA amendments), PL 100-4
1988	Ocean Dumping Act of 1988, PL 100-688
1990	Clean Air Act Amendments of 1990, PL 101-549 Oil Pollution Act, PL 101-380 Pollution Prevention Act, PL 101-508
1992	Energy Policy Act, PL 102-486 The Omnibus Water Act, PL 102-575

TABLE 4.1 (continued)

1996	Food Quality Protection Act (amended FIFRA), PL 104-120 Safe Drinking Water Act Amendments, PL 104-182
2002	Small Business Liability Relief and Brownfields Revitalization Act, PL 107-118
2005	Energy Policy Act of 2005, PL 109-58
2007	Energy Independence and Security Act of 2007, PL 110-140
2009	The American Recovery and Reinvestment Act of 2009, PL 111-5 (for its energy components)
2009	Omnibus Public Lands Management Act of 2009, PL 111-11
2016	Frank R. Lautenberg Chemical Safety for the 21st Century Act, PL 114-182

Note: The list is current as of January 2017. A fuller list with a description of the key features of each act can be found in Vig and Kraft (2016: appendix 1).

the House 401 to 25.[11] In comparison, by 2016, nearly every environmental policy proposal sharply divided the Congress.

The key features of environmental and natural resource policies are discussed in Chapters 5 and 6. It is worth noting here, however, that the major federal environmental protection statutes adopted in the 1970s departed sharply from previous efforts, and reflected the punctuated equilibrium model discussed in Chapter 3. Environmental policy was "nationalized" by adopting federal standards for the regulation of environmental pollutants, action-forcing provisions to compel the use of particular technologies by specified deadlines, and tough sanctions for noncompliance. Congress would no longer tolerate the cumbersome and ineffective pollution control procedures used by state and local governments (especially evident in water pollution control). Nor was it prepared to allow the states to compete economically by seeking the lowest environmental standards possible.

To some critics, these distinctly nonincremental (some might even say radical) changes in environmental policy were risky. The new policies attempted to hasten technological developments and went beyond the government's short-term capabilities. They invited administrative delays and imposed heavy burdens on industry and state and local governments that were ill-prepared to respond to the new demands (Jones 1975). The political attractiveness of these new policies in the warm glow of the early 1970s, however, was obvious to all who followed their formulation and approval not only in Congress but among the 50 states.

These policy developments coincided with a massive third wave of broader social regulation in the 1970s. It focused on health and safety issues as well as environmental quality, and resulted in the formation of new federal agencies, including the Occupational Safety and Health Administration, the Consumer Product Safety Commission, and the EPA itself. The EPA was established not by a law of Congress, but through an executive order issued by President Richard Nixon that consolidated into one agency programs dealing with environmental protection or pollution control that previously were scattered among a dozen federal offices.

The new social regulation differed from the old in several important respects. It reflected a deep distrust of establishment organizations (especially the business community) and a determination to open the administrative process to public scrutiny. It led to a more activist or reformist orientation within the agencies, depending on the administration in power, and to extensive participation by new public interest groups such as consumer organizations and environmentalists (Berry 1977; Eisner, Worsham, and Ringquist 2006; Harris and Milkis 1996). By the 1980s these very qualities contributed to efforts in the Reagan presidency to reverse policy advances of the 1970s, particularly in response to complaints of excessive and needlessly expensive regulation. Environmental regulations were prime targets of this criticism and retrenchment, much as they are today when similar concerns are raised (Vig and Kraft 1984, 2016).

The new environmental movement that was so critical to bringing about the innovative policy changes of the 1970s drew much of its political strength and moral force from the American public itself, which has continued to be one of the most important determinants of U.S. environmental politics and policy. Anthony Downs (1972) captured the new power of environmental public opinion in comments about the "issue-attention cycle," referring to the cyclical nature of the rise and fall of attention to environmental issues. Downs postulated that prior to the upsurge in public concern in the late 1960s, the nation was in a "pre-problem stage" on the environment. Such a stage exists when highly undesirable social conditions may exist but attract little public attention, even if a few experts, public officials, or interest groups are alarmed by them. As a result of a series of catalytic events and the publicity they receive, the public "suddenly becomes both aware of and alarmed about" the problem.

The dramatic rise in public concern over environmental quality in the late 1960s was confirmed by survey research, as was its slow decline during the 1970s to a lower but still substantial level and its striking resurrection in the 1980s during the Reagan administration (Dunlap 1992). Hazel Erskine (1972, 120) described the initial rise as a "miracle of public opinion" because of the "unprecedented speed and urgency with which ecological issues have burst into American consciousness. Alarm about the environment sprang from nowhere to major proportions in a few short years." Coverage of the environment by both print and electronic media followed a similar pattern, as did congressional agenda-setting activity such as hearings held on the subject (Baumgartner and Jones 1993). Despite a decline in their salience by the mid-1970s, environmental issues had become part of mainstream American values and were viewed almost universally as a positive symbol, with few negative images attached to it (Dunlap 1992, 1995; Mitchell 1984, 1990).

Environmental Interest Groups

Both the older and the newer environmental groups found such a supportive public opinion to be an invaluable political resource in their lobbying campaigns in Washington and in state capitals. Many of the established conservation groups saw their membership soar between 1960 and 1970. For example, the Sierra Club grew from 15,000 members in 1960 to 113,000 in 1970, more than a sevenfold increase. The newer environmental organizations grew rapidly as well (Mitchell, Mertig, and Dunlap 1992). The trend continued through the 1970s and then accelerated in the 1980s as environmental groups mounted highly successful membership recruitment campaigns in response to the anti-environmental agenda of Ronald Reagan's presidency. The groups' budgets and staffs grew in parallel with membership rolls (Baumgartner and Jones 1993, 189; Bosso 2005). The results can be seen in Table 4.2, which reports memberships over time and recent budgets for selected national environmental groups.

One other set of figures on the groups' financial strength bears mentioning. The National Center for Charitable Statistics reported that in 1999, thanks to a surging stock market, individuals, corporations, and foundations together contributed an astonishing $3.5 billion to environmental groups, double the level of 1992. That was nearly $9.6 million per day. The Nature Conservancy, easily the donors' favorite, netted $402 million that year (Duffy 2003). Such donations declined in the aftermath of a stock market crash and the rise of new concerns about global terrorism. Yet the success of environmental groups in attracting this kind of money speaks to the continuing appeal of their message—particularly if it is framed in the right way (Guber and Bosso 2007, 2013b; Skocpol 2013).

Despite their many shared values and political goals, by the 1980s environmentalists began to splinter visibly into factions with often sharply conflicting styles and political strategies. The differences became so great that some analysts wondered whether the groups could be subsumed under the same label at all. For example, writing in the late 1980s, Robert Mitchell noted that the unity of environmental groups was "tempered by a diversity of heritage, organizational structure, issue agendas, constituency, and tactics" (Mitchell 1989, 83). Moreover, they competed with one another for both funding and publicity, which they all need to survive. Some of these divisions were noticeable even in the 1970s, but they became far more evident by the early twenty-first century (Bosso 2005).

TABLE 4.2 Membership, supporters, and budgets of selected national environmental organizations, 1960–2010

Membership or supporters

Organization	Year founded	1960	1970	1980	1990	2004	2010[a]	2010 revenue ($ million)
Sierra Club	1892	15,000	113,000	181,000	630,000	736,000	1,400,000	97.0
National Audubon Society	1905	32,000	148,000	400,000	600,000	550,000	600,000	80.0
National Parks Conservation Association	1919	15,000	45,000	31,000	100,000	375,000	325,000	38.9
Wilderness Society	1935	10,000	54,000	45,000	350,000	225,000	500,000	23.0
National Wildlife Federation	1936	NA	540,000	818,000	997,000	650,000[b]	4,000,000	98.4
Environmental Defense Fund	1967	c	11,000	46,000	200,000	350,000	500,000	54.9
Natural Resources Defense Council	1970	c	c	40,000	150,000	450,000	1,300,000	96.9

Notes: [a] For 2010, the membership figures refer to what groups call their "supporters," which includes dues-paying members as well as donors and other backers. [b] The NWF used to distinguish between regular and affiliated members, but it consolidated the two in the mid-1990s and now reports only the combined figure. For 2000 this figure was 4 million. Bosso and Guber (2006), however, estimate that in 2004 regular, dues-paying members constituted 650,000. [c] In 1960, neither Environmental Defense Fund nor the Natural Resources Defense Council existed, and in 1970 NRDC was not a membership organization.

Sources: Membership data are taken from Bosso and Guber (2006) and Bosso (1994). Membership in most of the groups in 2010 was likely close to what is reported for 2004, and most report current membership on their websites. Membership figures, however, are notoriously hard to pin down because of conflicting data and varying definitions of what constitutes membership. All figures reported here should be considered estimates and used only to illustrate growth over time. It is for this reason that the broader term "supporters" is used for 2010, and this is taken from Guber and Bosso (2013a). Much more extensive information on the groups' sources of revenue and spending can be found in Bosso (2005). The 2010 revenue figures are taken from Guber and Bosso (2013a).

At least three major categories of environmental groups should be distinguished: mainstream, greens, and grassroots. The mainstream organizations, such as the Natural Resources Defense Council (NRDC), Sierra Club, National Audubon Society, and the National Wildlife Federation (NWF), have evolved into highly professional and chiefly Washington-based organizations that focus on public policy issues. In the 1990s the NWF, for example, had 35 people in its Washington office assigned to tracking legislation; in 2000 it had a total staff of nearly 700 (Bosso 2005).

Most of these organizations engage in the full range of activities common to nearly all interest groups active in the policy process. They collect and disseminate information on environmental problems and policy proposals, lobby members of Congress and their staffs, mobilize their members to contact public officials through grassroots lobbying campaigns, participate in the often-detailed administrative processes of executive agencies such as rule-making, and defend or challenge environmental decisions of those agencies through the judicial process (Duffy 2013; Kraft and Kamieniecki 2007). Environmental advocacy groups, much like other groups and political parties, have long made extensive use of social networking sites—especially Facebook, Twitter, and YouTube—and e-mail alerts for distributing information and mobilizing supporters (Bosso and Collins 2002; Duffy 2003).

Yet using online resources cuts both ways. Mainstream environmental groups are finding new competition in the rise of groups such as MoveOn (www.moveon.org) and Bill McKibben's 350.org (https://350.org/), which can raise money via online appeals and mobilize supporters without having to build and staff conventional organizations (Nisbet 2016). The Obama and Clinton presidential campaigns and other modern election campaigns have used similar tactics, and indeed have advanced them significantly with sophisticated data mining that facilitates sending highly targeted messages and fundraising appeals.[12] So in some respects, the established environmental groups now have much more competition.

Of course, groups that tend to oppose environmentalists, such as business organizations, the fossil fuel industry, conservative activist groups, and the climate denial community, use much the same kinds of appeals to rapidly spread their own messages to supporters. Such actions foster greater division and polarization among the public than seen in prior decades (Dunlap, McCright, and Yarosh 2016). One effect of that political polarization is the often uncivil online commentary found in newspapers across the nation, where anonymity puts few limits on what people say on any environmental question. Similarly, ideologically driven talk-radio hosts and commentators in what has become an increasingly partisan mass media often contribute to the contentious debates, potentially drowning out the voices of average citizens and scientifically informed commentary. Essential public dialogue on the issues can become more difficult as citizens must contend with biased and misleading reports, including so-called fake news, which are frequently circulated by partisan media outlets (Jamieson and Cappella 2010; Persily 2015).

Beyond the activities of mainstream environmental groups, the more radical greens (including groups like Greenpeace) face different kinds of challenges over the next few years. They tend to emphasize public education, social change, and direct action more than lobbying or administrative intervention. The greens are distinguished from the mainstream groups chiefly by their dedication to more ecocentric philosophies and a conviction that basic changes in human values and behavior are required to deal with environmental problems. However, they have found it increasingly hard to raise money and may no longer be in tune with the prevailing political culture today.

At least some of the radical groups go well beyond the mainstream and even the other green groups in advocating eco-sabotage to highlight destructive industrial practices and gain visibility for their cause. For example, in March 2008, activists affiliated with the Earth Liberation Front (ELF) claimed responsibility for burning down five newly built luxury homes in a wooded subdivision near Seattle, Washington, where they opposed such developments; the Federal Bureau of Investigation described the actions as acts of "domestic terrorism."[13] Most mainstream groups strongly reject ELF's approach and believe that these kinds of actions are counterproductive and create a negative image for all environmentalists.

Finally, grassroots groups have sprung up in great numbers around the nation at local and regional levels. They deal chiefly with local environmental issues such as threats from hazardous waste sites, urban sprawl, or loss of ecologically or esthetically important lands. Such groups sometimes are affiliated with state chapters of the major national organizations such as the LCV, National Audubon Society, the Nature Conservancy, or the National Wildlife Federation. Often, however, the grassroots groups are independent and reflect the concerns of local citizens who organize on their own to deal with community and regional environmental challenges. These may be restoration of lakes and rivers, preservation of important lands and waters, or improvements in urban land use, energy efficiency, and public transportation (Mazmanian and Kraft 2009; K. Portney 2009, 2013; Press 2002; Press and Nakagawa 2009). Many of the independent grassroots groups also maintain their own webpages and often are well positioned to circulate environmental studies and reports and other information to concerned citizens in the area. While they gain little national media coverage, they can be very influential at the local and regional level.

These categories of mainstream, greens, and grassroots groups are intended to highlight some fundamental differences among groups that use a common "environmental" or "conservation" language, but often have unique goals and strategies for building public and political support. That they sometimes are thrown together under the broad umbrella of "environmentalists" should not disguise these important distinctions. Table 4.3 lists some of the most prominent national environmental organizations and their websites, along with their leading adversaries in the business community and among conservative policy research groups.

TABLE 4.3 Websites for leading environmental organizations and their adversaries

Organization	Major issues or orientation	Web address
Sierra Club	Broad environmental education and policy action	www.sierraclub.org
National Audubon Society	Diversified conservation of resources	www.aubudon.org
Wilderness Society	Wilderness protection	www.tws.org
National Wildlife Federation	Wildlife and land conservation	www.nwf.org
Environmental Defense Fund	Diversified environmental education, policy, law	www.edf.org
Natural Resources Defense Council	Diversified environmental education, policy, law	www.nrdc.org
League of Conservation Voters	Congressional voting and elections	www.lcv.org
Union of Concerned Scientists	Science and environmental protection	www.ucsusa.org
Greenpeace USA	International environmental action	www.greenpeace.org/usa
Izaak Walton League of America	Land and water conservation	www.iwla.org
Nature Conservancy	Land conservation	www.nature.org
World Wildlife Fund	Wildlife conservation and global environment	www.worldwildlife.org
Ocean Conservancy	Protection of ocean resources	www.oceanconservancy.org
American Cetacean Society	Protection of cetaceans: whales, dolphins, porpoises	www.acsonline.org
Rainforest Action Network	Rain forest protection	www.ran.org
American Farmland Trust	Farmland conservation	www.farmland.org
Population Connection	Population growth	www.populationconnection.org

TABLE 4.3 (*continued*)

Groups and Policy Research Institutes Often in Opposition to Environmentalists

U.S. Chamber of Commerce	Represents business interests	www.uschamber.com
National Association of Manufacturers	Represents manufacturing interests	www.nam.org
National Federation of Independent Businesses	Represents interests of small businesses	www.nfib.com
American Chemistry Council	Represents chemical manufacturers	www.americanchemistry.com
Competitive Enterprise Institute	Conservative research institute focusing on regulation	www.cei.org
Cato Institute	Libertarian policy institute	www.cato.org
Heritage Foundation	Conservative think tank	www.heritage.org
Heartland Institute	Conservative, free-market think tank	www.heartland.org

Note: For a broader list of groups, see www.webdirectory.com (organized by subject area, such as pollution and sustainable development).

Other prominent environmental organizations are quite different from all of these groups. They emphasize not activism, but rather independent and nonpartisan education, policy analysis, and scientific research. By doing so, they play a vital but quite different role in environmental policymaking. Among the most visible of these organizations are Resources for the Future (a highly regarded research organization specializing in economic analysis), the Union of Concerned Scientists, the Center for Climate and Energy Solutions, the Worldwatch Institute, and the World Resources Institute. This category also includes hundreds of other scientific and professional organizations that study and report on environmental conditions and policy alternatives, and whose work is often relied upon in the policymaking process.

One other development is recent and somewhat unexpected. Increasingly environmental groups are building new coalitions with those who have not historically been among their supporters, including conservative religious organizations and unions. In 2006, for example, 86 evangelical Christian leaders announced their support for an Evangelical Climate Initiative to combat global warming, out of concern for its likely effect on impoverished people around the world.[14] For largely economic reasons, unions have found common cause with environmentalist campaigns on energy use and climate change in part because such initiatives are likely to create what are usually termed "green jobs" in renewable energy development, rebuilding public transportation systems, and creating a more sustainable domestic manufacturing base. Particularly in his first term, President Obama frequently invoked the promise of such jobs. Formation of the group BlueGreen Alliance is one of the most visible signs of how organizations can integrate the environment and economic development (www.bluegreenalliance.org).

These intriguing developments notwithstanding, the environmental movement today is in the throes of change, leading some critics a decade ago to speak of the "death of environmentalism."[15] Environmental groups do face a daunting array of new challenges and dilemmas that flow from their very success since the 1960s, but they are far from dead. The mainstream groups, for instance, are now a political fixture in Washington and in many state capitals; as noted, many of them have substantial memberships and budgets to facilitate their work. Yet in some respects these groups, such as the Sierra Club, are losing ideological fervor and the capacity to attract and hold public support to the greens and especially to emerging grassroots and regional environmental groups. Their activities in Washington and in state capitals may be important for achieving the environmentalist policy agenda, but increasingly that agenda is too narrowly defined to capture the public's attention and mobilize its energies. The green groups and grassroots organizations seem to have a greater capacity to appeal to the public's identification with local and regional environmental issues—such as local land use and pollution disputes, transportation choices, environmental justice concerns, and community sustainability—even if they often lack the funding and technical expertise to succeed entirely on their own. The success of these groups suggests a substantial potential for a robust and broadly supported civic environmentalism organized around such issues, especially when groups can effectively blend environmental, social, and economic concerns in urban settings (Mazmanian and Kraft 2009; Paehlke 2013b; K. Portney 2013, 2016).

All the leading environmental groups face difficult choices as well over organizational priorities and strategies if they are to continue to thrive and represent their positions well in the political process at all levels of government. Disagreements over goals, strategies, and political styles—as well as competition for members and funds—have divided the environmental community for well over a decade (Bosso 2005; Shaiko 1999). In addition, during the early to mid-1990s, most of the national groups struggled to stem declining memberships and dwindling financial contributions. The Nature Conservancy, a group devoted to private land conservation efforts, was one major exception. In 1995 its membership reached 800,000, its highest level ever, and its fundraising rose to an all-time high. It has done even better since that time, with a membership total in 2016 of more than 1 million; it also had enough resources to hire a staff of over 3,000 people, including over 600 scientists, and it works in all 50 states and 69 countries. Some other groups, such as NRDC, have recovered as well; NRDC membership rose from 185,000 in 1995 to 450,000 by 2004. In 2016, NRDC reported that it had over 2 million members and online activists and a staff of more than 500 lawyers, scientists, and other professionals. It also quotes a favorable *New York Times* assessment that refers to NRDC as "one of the nation's most powerful environmental groups."

As has been evident over the past two decades, environmentalists have been confronted at local, state, and national levels by a newly energized opposition in the business community (Kraft and Kamieniecki 2007; Layzer 2012) and among property rights movements; conservative organizations; and groups representing extractive industries such as timber, mining, ranching, oil and gas development, and other land development interests (Bosso and Guber 2006; Brick and Cawley 1996; Cawley 1993; Switzer 1997). Depending on the way the issues are framed and on the strength of the opposition, they may enjoy victory or suffer defeat in public debates, ballot propositions, elections, or policymaking actions. Many of these groups strongly backed Donald Trump's campaign for the presidency.

Despite widespread acknowledgement of the risks of climate change, there also are activist groups reflecting what is usually termed the "climate change denial" or "climate skeptic" movement. Many of the groups have been funded for years by the fossil fuel industry and conservative foundations and they maintain websites, including Committee for a Constructive Tomorrow (www.cfact.org) and Climate Depot (www.climatedepot.com), where they aggressively critique mainstream science and news reports (Dunlap and McCright 2015; Oreskes and Conway 2010). These skeptical views of climate science, and often of environmental science itself, also are well represented at the leading conservative think tanks, such as the Heartland Institute and the Competitive Enterprise Institute. The fossil fuel industry and many of these supportive organizations are likely to be influential actors in the Trump administration.[16]

Environmental groups' access to policymakers and their success in shaping legislative and regulatory battles turn in part on election results. They found their access to the White House and Congress significantly diminished for much of the 2000s during the Bush administration and when the Republican Party dominated Congress.[17] It improved markedly after Democrats regained their majorities in the 2006 election and added to their margins in 2008 (Kraft 2013a). More significantly, with the election of Barack Obama, environmentalists gained more support in the White House and executive agencies. One of their greatest challenges for the future is to reframe their goals and policy proposals in a way that will help to communicate with and mobilize their supporters among the American public, and to respond effectively to frequent challenges by business and conservative groups (Duffy 2013; Guber and Bosso 2013a, 2013b; Nisbet 2011, 2016).

Public Opinion and the Environment

The American public has long expressed concern about the environment, and for decades it has strongly supported public policy actions for environmental protection and resource conservation. Public opinion surveys from the 1970s to the present offer abundant evidence of that concern and support, particularly as it applies to public-health threats (Daniels et al. 2013; Dunlap 1995; Guber 2003). At the same time, these surveys tell us that the public is not well informed on environmental, energy, and natural resource issues, and that these issues are much lower in salience than many other concerns. For example, in May 2015, the economy and jobs easily topped the list of public concerns, followed by the federal budget deficit and federal debt, all much in the news at the time. Among noneconomic issues, the public mentioned most often dissatisfaction with government, terrorism, and immigration. Where was "the environment" on this list? Near the bottom, with only about 2 percent of the public reporting that it was the "most important problem" facing the nation at the time. Mention of energy issues was even rarer. Sadly, these were typical findings for the Gallup Poll measure of environmental issue saliency.[18]

Even if environmental problems are not front and center for most citizens most of the time, we have pretty good evidence that in recent years, Americans tend to rate the quality of the environment as unacceptable (42 percent said "poor or very poor"), they believe it is not getting better, and they believe it will get worse in the future. Not surprisingly, strong majorities say they want Congress, the president, and business to help improve the situation "a great deal or a lot" (Daniels et al. 2013). These results are consistent with surveys on the environment going back several decades. Between 50 and 60 percent of the public have said they are either active in or sympathetic to the environmental movement.

More interesting, however, is that both older and newer surveys have found only a very small percentage of the public (2 to 5 percent) who say they are *un*sympathetic to the environmental cause (Bosso and Guber 2006; CEQ 1980). This is well below what one might assume from the deep and widening partisan divide seen on the issue in recent years, among both party leaders and the general population (Dunlap and McCright 2008; Dunlap, McCright, and Yarosh 2016; Guber and Bosso 2013a; Ladd and Bowman 1995).[19] Why does the opposition seem to be so much larger than these numbers suggest? At least part of the explanation lies in media coverage of the issues, which has given environmental opponents, and especially climate change deniers, considerable attention and has increased public uncertainty over the nature of the threats. Other factors may include the intensity of opponents' views and the relative quiet of the majority who side with environmentalists (Dunlap 2013; Dunlap and Jacques 2013).

As this brief summary suggests, surveys also have found that support for environmental protection has become something of a consensual issue that ordinarily generates little overt opposition among the general public. As one major study in the 1990s concluded, "most Americans share a common set of environmental beliefs and values" (Kempton, Boster, and Hartley 1996, 211). Findings about the public's support or opposition to particular proposals will vary, of course, and readers should consult the latest survey findings where available. Many of the best survey organizations make their findings available online, and they are easily located. One good example has been a series of surveys on public attitudes toward climate change and energy policy conducted by a team at Yale and George Mason Universities and available at the Yale Project on Climate Change Communication. One set of findings released in June 2010, for example, found large majorities of Americans favoring specific proposals for energy and climate change actions, including funding for renewable energy research, providing tax rebates for fuel-efficient cars and solar panels, and even for regulation of greenhouse gas emissions—even though at that time political conflict in Congress suggested a contrary view.[20]

Surveys of the kind summarized here are informative but also misleading. They almost never ask about the depth of public concern or how well informed the public is about environmental problems, and they rarely point to inconsistencies in the public's beliefs and attitudes or document the saliency of these issues for the average person. Yet these characteristics are all important for understanding public opinion on the environment and its implications for policy action (Daniels et al. 2013; Guber 2003; Heberlein 2012).

Consistency of Opinions and Depth of Concern   On many policy issues the public's views are inconsistent and sometimes contradictory. Environmental opinions are no different. For example, people say that they favor greater environmental protection in the abstract, but over the past decade they have also indicated they prefer less government, less regulation, and lower taxes, again in the abstract. Similarly, people say that they support energy conservation, but they are unwilling to pay even modest sums in increased gasoline taxes to further that goal. Politicians are so convinced of the public's hostility to increased fuel taxes or carbon taxes that such proposals have rarely been given serious consideration in the United States. The public's general preference for environmental protection also may weaken when people face real and intense local or regional conflicts in which environmental measures are believed to affect employment or economic well-being adversely. Thus, the level of public support for environmental protection depends heavily on the way issues are framed in any given controversy.

One way to judge public preferences is to ask whether people act on their pro-environmental opinions. As a journalist once put it, "tree talk" is cheap, but it creates a "lip-service gap" when the public is unwilling to make the necessary personal sacrifices to clean up the environment. Survey data speak to this point and tend to confirm Everett Ladd and Karlyn Bowman's 1995 description of the American public as "Lite Greens"; they are generally favorable toward environmental protection activities but exhibit little depth or personal commitment (see also Guber 2003). Recent surveys indicate that many Americans say they are willing to pay a little more for environmentally friendly products, such as automobiles, furniture made from "green" wood, and greener printer paper, and a majority say it is important to them to purchase such products. But will they, in fact, do so?[21]

Moreover, people tend not to be politically active. Fewer than 5 percent claim they regularly contribute money to environmental groups, write to public officials about environmental issues, or write to specific companies about their environmental concerns. This is closer to the finding in many surveys that peg the hardcore environmental activists among the public at between 1 and 5 percent, and the attentive public (those who are interested and relatively well informed) at perhaps 5 to 10 percent. Of course, even 1 percent of the population is a lot of people, and they may influence many others.

Environmental Knowledge and Opinion Saliency As noted earlier, there are reasons to question the public's knowledge about environmental issues and about environmental policy actions. Annual surveys commissioned by the National Environmental Education Foundation and conducted by the Roper Starch Worldwide survey firm have found consistently that relatively few people are knowledgeable about environmental problems. In a September 2005 summary of 10 years of such "environmental literacy" surveys, the organization said there had been "a persistent pattern of environmental ignorance even among the most educated and influential members of society" (Coyle 2005). Just 12 percent of Americans, it said, could pass a basic quiz on energy topics (see also Smith 2002), and only a third could pass a comparable test of environmental knowledge. These results led the organization to conclude that Americans are "unprepared to respond to the major environmental challenges we face in the 21st century." Similarly, a 2010 survey on Americans' knowledge of climate change found "important gaps in public knowledge and common misconceptions about climate change." The authors concluded that "only 8 percent of Americans have knowledge equivalent to an A or B, 40 percent would receive a C or D, and 52 percent would get an F" (Leiserowitz, Smith, and Marlon 2010).

More recent scholarship, however, finds that the public is much better informed on energy and climate change, more pragmatic than ideological, more in agreement than they are divided about their concerns, but also more attuned to local than global environmental impacts. At the local level, the public demonstrates an ability to sort out relative costs and environmental harms associated with different energy alternatives. At heart they want energy to be both cheap and clean, which suggests that actions targeting the local impacts of coal, natural gas, or renewable resources such as wind and solar power, could engage the public more than abstract national and global debates about energy and climate change (Ansolabehere and Konisky 2014).

Most of the findings summarized above are consistent with what may be the most important attribute of public opinion on the environment. Environmental issues, especially in the abstract, are rarely considered to be important by the American public except for major catastrophes. This is especially so in the face of other problems considered to be more pressing or closer to home, such as the economy, health care, or terrorism.

Surveys do suggest, however, that environmental issues rise to the top of the list of issues that people think will be most important some 25 years from now. For example, a Gallup poll conducted in 2007, asking an open-ended question about the most important problem that the country will face in 25 years, found that 14 percent of the sample named environmental troubles. This was nearly twice the percentage than any other issue, including health care, social security, terrorism, or energy, garnered.[22] A similar Gallup survey in 2010 found the environment ranked third after the federal budget and the economy, still an impressive showing. Similarly, a 2007 survey conducted for the Yale Project on Climate Change found that nearly two-thirds of the public agreed that the country "is in as much danger from environmental hazards such as air pollution and global warming as it is from terrorists," and the same percentage thought that the environment in the United States was getting worse—an increase of 10 percent since a comparable question was asked in 2005 (Leiserowitz, Maibach, and Roser-Renouf 2009).

As noted just above, surveys have long found that Americans are most concerned about environmental problems that are more local and more visible and that seem to threaten their health, such as water pollution, pollution of drinking water, contamination by toxic waste, and air pollution. Historically, they have been far less concerned about what they see as abstract and distant issues such as acid rain and climate change, although as shown earlier, expressed concern about climate change has increased substantially in recent years (Leiserowitz et al. 2015).

Given the generally low salience of the environment, people usually are not motivated to invest the time and energy needed to keep up with the issues and to become informed about them. Nonetheless, the importance of environmental issues can change abruptly if a local problem—such as contaminated drinking water—becomes unusually visible or controversial, or if environmental groups or their opponents successfully mobilize the public. As noted in Chapter 2, this happened in Flint, Michigan in 2015 when local water supplies were found to have high levels of lead, and then in many other cities across the nation and in public schools when testing also revealed unsafe levels of lead in drinking water.[23] Opponents of environmental protection have sometimes fallen into the "salience trap" of believing that the low salience of these issues necessarily implies a low level of public concern (Bosso 2000). Little evidence, however, suggests that public concern for the environment is likely to wane anytime soon either within the United States or globally (Dalton 2005; Dunlap and York 2008, 2012).

An intriguing question remains. How readily would people change their behavior if given the necessary information, encouragement, and incentives? It is not fair to fault people for failing to act on their views if there are too many barriers to doing so. Similarly, it is easy to disparage the public's low level of civic involvement, but this may be a consequence of limited opportunities for getting involved. A high level of cynicism and distrust toward government, politics, and politicians further diminishes the likelihood of public participation in the political process and in community affairs, and polls in the 2010s provide abundant evidence of such distrust (Putnam 2000; Skocpol and Fiorina 1999).[24]

The success of many local environmental initiatives, however, indicates that considerable potential may exist to improve public knowledge and to foster involvement in community and regional decision making. People in the United States and elsewhere may be ready to respond to political and community leaders who learn how to appeal to their concerns, fears, and hopes for the future, especially when the issues can be linked with the public's concern with the economy, health, national security, and well-being. This is precisely what a focus on sustainability could do, and the popularity of new urban sustainability initiatives linking the environment, economy, and social concerns is one indication of that potential (Mazmanian and Kraft 2009; Paehlke 2013a; K. Portney 2013).

Beyond U.S. borders, most of the same issues arise. International surveys have found an equivalent level of concern for environmental quality around the world in both developed and developing nations. In 1992, the Gallup Health of the Planet (HOP) survey covered two dozen nations, from low income to high income, and found "little difference in reported levels of environmental concern between people of poor, less economically developed nations and those of the richer, highly industrialized nations." Majorities in 21 of the 24 nations surveyed reported either a "great deal" or a "fair amount" of concern. Subsequent HOP and other world surveys reinforce these early findings (Dalton 2005; Dunlap, Gallup, and Gallup 1993, 11; Dunlap and York 2008, 2012). They showed clearly that citizen concern for the environment was not dependent on a nation's affluence. As is true in the United States, however, the pursuit of the worldwide sustainable development goals, endorsed at the 1992 Earth Summit and the two later UN meetings in 2002 and 2012, requires a generally sympathetic and concerned public that is better informed than it has been to date, and one that can be encouraged to play an active role in environmental and development decisions at local, regional, and community levels.

Environmental Issues in Election Campaigns

One way that environmental organizations reach new constituencies and broaden public support is to promote environmental issues in election campaigns. Environmental issues only rarely have been a decisive factor in elections, even though they have long been prominent in selected contests in Oregon, Washington, California, New Jersey, Colorado, and other states. Moreover, there is little evidence to date of the existence of a reliable "green" vote in most areas of the United States.

The Green Party itself has attracted sustained support only within a few regions of the country, unlike in Europe. Yet the U.S. electoral system is strongly biased against third or minor parties, which accounts for the challenges the party faces in national elections. When Green Party candidate Ralph Nader ran in the 2000 presidential election, he managed to win 2.8 million votes, or 2.7 percent of votes cast (3.8 percent in California). Gore won the popular vote, but Nader drew enough votes in the exceedingly close campaign between Bush and Gore to cost Gore the Electoral College votes in several states, including the hotly contested election in Florida. Nader received over 97,000 votes in Florida, far more than the thin margin that separated Gore and Bush in the state. The election results were both good news and bad news for the Green Party. Nader demonstrated his nationwide appeal (and the frustration of many voters with the two major parties). Yet his very success demonized him within the Democratic Party, which had otherwise become the nominal home for environmentalists. That history may help to explain the relatively low ranking of the Green Party presidential candidate, Jill Stein, in 2016. She won 1 percent of the national vote (1.9 percent in California), and Libertarian candidate Gary Johnson won about 3 percent.

Several environmental groups have tried to influence elections through candidate endorsements, financial support for candidates, and voter mobilization. The League of Conservation Voters has engaged in such electioneering actions since the 1970s, and the Sierra Club has long had a political action committee for this purpose. Both have done well in these efforts, but they face obstacles discussed earlier, especially the low salience of environmental issues in most campaigns.

In 2016, the billionaire environmentalist Thomas Steyer and his political advocacy organization NextGen Climate pledged to spend at least $25 million on a get-out-the-vote campaign targeting young voters in competitive states. They tend to be supportive of climate change action, but also have far lower turnout rates than other demographic groups. Steyer spent $74 million during the 2014 elections, including some $67 million to support candidates who emphasized climate change as a major issue. On the other side of the debate, it was unclear how much Charles G. Koch, a frequent supporter of conservative, anti-regulatory groups on the environment and climate change, would spend in 2016. In that election, Koch and other wealthy donors were reluctant to embrace and fund Republican nominee Donald Trump, but there is little doubt about the enormous influence the Koch network has had on the Republican Party and Congress.[25] Exit polls in 2016, as expected, indicated that environmental issues had relatively little impact on voters' decisions.[26]

The environment certainly could play a role in future elections. When voters are asked whether a candidate's position on the environment will be important in their voting decision, large majorities have long said yes. In one survey in 2004, for example, 84 percent of Americans said a candidate's stance on the environment would be a factor in how they voted (Global Strategy Group 2004). Whether people really do think about the environment during election campaigns is likely to depend on the efforts made by groups such as the LCV and the Sierra Club to inform and mobilize the public, the extent of media coverage of environmental issues in campaigns, and the willingness of candidates to speak out on their environmental records or positions. Similarly, when opponents of environmental policy actions assert that they will use climate change or regulation of coal against those officials who support such initiatives, the outcome will depend greatly on what they actually try to do to make these issues salient in the next campaign.

Campaigns do matter, as do statements candidates make during them. In one fascinating study, political scientists Evan Ringquist and Carl Dasse (2004) found that statements made by candidates for the House of Representatives are usually an accurate guide to what they try to do in office; that is, campaign promises are meaningful. So if voters pay attention to the differences, they can learn a lot. Yet in the 2004 study and in a later one (Ringquist, Neshkova, and Aamidor 2013), one finding stands out. The likelihood of "defecting" from a campaign promise is affected by partisanship. Defections from pro-environmental campaign promises are twice as common as are those from anti-environmental promises. Republicans are more likely to defect from their pro-environmental campaign promises, while Democrats move in the other direction; they are more likely to defect from anti-environmental campaign promises.

Further positive news about the electoral potential for environmental issues can be found in voting on ballot measures for land conservation and other environmental actions. In the November 2014 elections, for example, voters in 19 states approved more than $29 billion in funding on measures dealing with open space, water quality, parks, and coastlines. These measures did well even in conservative states and counties.[27] According to the Trust for Public Land, in November 2016, voters approved local and state ballot measures that provided more than $6 billion for land conservation, parks, and restoration, even though many measures called for tax increases or new bonding authority. There were 86 land conservation measures on the ballot in November, and 68 of them were approved. Earlier in the year, 14 of 17 park and land conservation measures were approved, with some $3.3 billion committed, bringing the total for 2016 to $9.6 billion, the most since 2008.[28]

In a comparable action, in Colorado in 2004, voters approved a state referendum mandating that 10 percent of the state's electricity must come from renewable sources by 2015. This was after the state legislature refused three times to pass a bill requiring utilities to take similar action. Colorado was the 18th state to set such standards, but the first to do by a direct citizen action (Rabe and Mundo 2007). The result was particularly striking in light of the generally conservative voting record in the state and intense opposition to the ballot measure by most energy companies there.[29]

In a similar defeat for energy companies, in 2010, California voters firmly rejected an attempt to overturn the state's landmark Global Warming Solutions Act via a referendum, Proposition 23. The referendum effort was supported in large part by two out-of-state oil refining companies that sought to delay implementation of the Act for years. The "No on 23" campaign won support from a diverse coalition of environmental groups, clean technology companies, Silicon Valley venture capitalists, and financial managers, all of whom had a direct stake in seeing the climate policy move toward implementation in 2012.[30]

Political Reaction to Environmentalism

So far in the chapter we have examined the evolution of environmental policy through the 1970s, and have focused on the rise of a powerful environmental movement and a supportive public opinion that together helped establish and maintain a remarkable array of national and state environmental policies. As indicated in the preceding discussion, however, environmental issues have divided the U.S. public despite the generally positive attitudes toward a strong government role. Before turning in the next two chapters to the details of environmental policies and the politics associated with them, we should pay at least some attention to this political reaction to environmentalism that began in the late 1970s, was vividly apparent during Ronald Reagan's presidency, and emerged again both in U.S. Congress in the mid- to late 1990s, in the administration of George W. Bush in the early 2000s, and in Congress during President Obama's tenure in office.

If the 1970s reflected the nation's initial commitment to environmental policy, by the early 1980s there was at least some ambivalence about how far to go in pursuit of policy goals and at what price. Such concerns had surfaced in both the Nixon and Ford administrations and again in the late 1970s in the Carter administration, partly because of the effect of the Arab oil embargo of 1973 and other energy and economic shocks of the decade (Vig 1994; Whitaker 1976). Industry had complained about the financial burdens of environmental regulation, and some labor unions joined in the chorus when jobs appeared to be threatened.

Environmental Policy in the Reagan and Bush Administrations

These criticisms reached full force in Ronald Reagan's presidency (1981–1989) and returned in the 104th Congress (1995–1996), when a Republican majority governed. Reagan and his advisers brought with them a dramatically different view of environmental issues and their relationship to the economy than had prevailed, with bipartisan support, for the previous decade. Virtually all environmental policies were to be reevaluated, and reversed or weakened, as part of Reagan's larger political agenda. That agenda included reducing the scope of government regulation, cutting back on the role of the federal government, shifting responsibilities where possible to the states, and relying more on the private sector.

Set largely by the right wing of the Republican Party and Western ranchers and others associated with the Sagebrush Rebellion, Reagan's agenda was the most radical in half a century (Kraft 1984). The major problem he faced was that Congress and the American public continued to favor the programs he was so anxious to curtail. Reagan tried as much as he could to bypass Congress in pushing his agenda through an administrative strategy of deregulation, defunding of regulatory agencies, and appointment of high-level personnel more in tune with his own conservative ideology. That strategy was only moderately effective and soon backfired.

Although initially successful in gaining congressional support for deep budgetary cuts that he justified largely on economic grounds, Reagan soon found his deregulatory actions sharply criticized and blocked by Congress. EPA administrator Anne Burford was forced to resign after less than two years in office. Reagan replaced her in March 1983 with William D. Ruckelshaus, who had served as the first EPA administrator between 1970 and 1973. Secretary of the Interior James G. Watt, the administration's controversial point person on environmental policy, lasted only a little longer before resigning in October 1983. He was replaced by William P. Clark, who, like Ruckelshaus, was more moderate and sought to repair some of the political damage Watt had caused (Vig and Kraft 1984).

Congress went on to renew and strengthen every major environmental statute that came up for renewal in the 1980s (Kraft 2016). These statutes included the Resource Conservation and Recovery Act (RCRA) in 1984, Superfund amendments and the Safe Drinking Water Act in 1986, and the Clean Water Act in 1987. By 1990 even the Clean Air Act, the nation's most important environmental law, was expanded and enhanced with the support of Reagan's vice president and successor, George H. W. Bush. The reasons could be found in public opinion and the capacity of environmental leaders to capitalize on the public's favorable stance toward environmental policy and its distrust of both industry and government. Early in 1990, for example, public opinion surveys indicated that more than 70 percent of the U.S. public favored making the Clean Air Act stricter, over 20 percent favored keeping it about the same, and only 2 percent wanted it less strict.[31]

The message was not lost on Bush's political advisers. During his run for the presidency in 1988, he broke openly with the Reagan environmental agenda. He promised to be a Republican president in the Teddy Roosevelt tradition: a "conservationist" and an "environmental president" (Vig 2016). Bush's record on the environment was decidedly mixed, although it clearly was different from Reagan's.

Clinton and Gore Reform Environmental Policy and Battle Congress

During the Clinton administration, many of the same conflicts became evident, only this time it was the Republican Congress that sought to pull back from the environmental commitments of the 1970s and 1980s. The Democratic White House assumed the role of defender of the status quo in environmental policy. The administration also pushed strongly for "reinventing environmental regulation" that would help address some of the most persistent criticisms of environmental policy, such as its high cost, burdens on industry and state and local governments, inflexibility, and inefficiency—criticisms to which we return in Chapter 7 (Kraft and Scheberle 1998; Vig 2016). Clinton was generally praised by environmentalists for his appointments, most notably Carol Browner as EPA administrator and Bruce Babbitt as secretary of the interior. The president sharply increased spending on environmental programs, and earned praise from environmental groups for speaking out forcefully against the attempts within Congress to weaken environmental protection legislation (Kraft 2016). More significantly, the administration took important steps toward shifting the environmental agenda in the direction of sustainable development and more integrative policy action. Clinton ended his term as president with numerous measures to protect public lands, including executive orders that established 19 new national monuments and enlarged three others (Vig 2016).

George W. Bush and the Transition to Barack Obama

The administration of George W. Bush took a dramatically different stance on most environmental and resource issues. Bush entered office with the weakest of mandates, having lost the popular vote in the 2000 election to Al Gore. Yet it was clear from the election campaign and from Bush's record as governor of Texas that he would depart significantly from the Clinton administration's environmental, energy, and resource policies.

Bush appointed the moderate former governor of New Jersey, Christine Todd Whitman, as EPA administrator, and he named conservative Gale Norton, a protégée of James Watt, as secretary of the interior. After frequent disagreements with the White House, Whitman resigned in 2003 and was replaced first by Michael Leavitt, former governor of Utah, and then in May 2005 by Stephen Johnson, a career EPA employee. Almost all the other high-level executive appointees in offices dealing with the environment and natural resources were pro-business advocates who came to the administration from corporate posts or from positions with conservative ideological groups.[32]

In short order, President Bush charted a new direction in environmental policy, both domestic and international. He withdrew the United States from the Kyoto Protocol and exhibited far less concern with climate change than the Clinton administration had. He proposed a national energy policy grounded in increased oil and gas drilling, including in the Arctic National Wildlife Refuge, much of which Congress approved in 2005. And in numerous decisions on water quality standards, clean-air rules, energy efficiency standards, protection of national forests and parks, and mining regulations, the administration sided with industry and economic development over environmental protection (Vig and Kraft 2016). Many of those decisions are discussed throughout the remainder of the text.

Unlike the Reagan administration, with which the president's environmental policy actions were widely compared, Bush kept a low profile on controversial decisions of this kind and defended them as balanced and in the public interest. Even where the polls indicated public disapproval of his environmental policies, the president did not appear to suffer politically from them. His popularity, which soared in the aftermath of the terrorist attacks of September 11, 2001, and the global war on terrorism, helped minimize criticism from environmental groups and the media (Bosso and Guber 2006).

President Barack Obama brought a far more supportive stance on environmental issues when he took office in January 2009, and yet was reluctant to push too aggressively on many environmental and energy issues for fear of harming the economy or facing the wrath of the business community; this was particularly the case as the nation slowly recovered from a deep recession that began late in the Bush administration (Vig and Kraft 2016). In his second term, the president continued to face a Republican House that was strongly opposed to many of his proposed environmental and energy actions, and a sharply divided Senate with only a slim Democratic majority (Kraft 2016). Nonetheless, Obama, much like Clinton, generally backed strong environmental and energy positions even if he did not speak out on the issues as often as many environmentalists preferred. Climate change is a major example. Yet by 2016 the president began an energetic push for expansive executive actions to combat climate change as an alternative to seeking unlikely support from Congress (see Chapter 6).[33] The chapters that follow cover Obama's key initiatives. Of course, some of them are likely to be targeted by the Trump administration for reversal or at least significant changes. Yet even the Obama administration's outgoing EPA administrator, Gina McCarthy, argued that environmental policy in the Trump administration may reflect more continuity with the past than many observers were forecasting in late 2016. The reasons, she noted, include the American public's continued support for the goals of environmental policy and the momentum of market forces, such as the commitment of leading corporations to those same goals.[34]

Conclusions

In at least one respect, the Reagan administration's efforts during the 1980s to curtail environmental policy actions and the controversies that reappeared in the Congress in the mid- to late 1990s, in the administration of George

W. Bush, and again in Congress in the 2010s, left an important legacy. Environmental policy must be judged by many of the same standards applied to other public policies today, such as effectiveness, efficiency, and equity. Good intentions are not enough, and agencies must offer demonstrable evidence of success. When programs fail to measure up, alternatives should be examined. If environmental standards are to be set at high levels, some indication of positive benefits needs to be offered to justify the costs and burdens imposed on society.

All these considerations lie at the heart of current efforts to appraise and change environmental policy, to integrate it well with related policy actions, and to set it on a more defensible and enduring path for the future. The next two chapters turn to the goals and chosen instruments of U.S. environmental protection policy and natural resource and energy policy, and to debate over issues of this kind. Chapter 7 then offers an even more direct assessment of the more than four decades of U.S. environmental policy and the promise of policy alternatives such as market incentives, flexible regulation, privatization, information disclosure, and other approaches. Regrettably, however, environmental policy has become so politically polarized in the 2010s that even the best science and policy analysis often is insufficient to bring the two parties and their supporters to agreement on needed action (Dunlap, McCright, and Yarosh 2016; McCright, Xiao, and Dunlap 2014).

The record of policy evolution reviewed in this chapter also points to an important paradox of U.S. environmental policy and politics. Policy achievements of the 1960s and 1970s withstood a severe challenge during the 1980s and at several other critical points from the 1990s to the 2010s in large part because the American public favored prevention of further environmental degradation and protection from environmental and health threats. In this sense, the U.S. political system proved to be fairly responsive to public demands despite its institutional fragmentation and other barriers to majority rule. The paradox is that government may be too responsive to short-term public *demands* and insufficiently attentive to, and capable of acting on, long-term public *needs*.

In response to public concern over environmental threats from air and water pollution to hazardous waste sites, Congress has mandated that the EPA and other agencies take on many more tasks than they can handle with their budgets and staffs. Environmental interest groups have lobbied effectively for adoption of those policies and their strengthening over time. Understandably, they also resist the many recent efforts taken in Congress and the states to alter them in a way they distrust. Yet in many respects the policies are very much in need of reform to bring them into the twenty-first century and to help launch a more sustainable era of environmental policy both domestically and internationally (Bryner and Duffy 2012; Eisner 2007; Fiorino 2006; Kamieniecki and Kraft 2013; Mazmanian and Kraft 2009).

As discussed in Chapter 1, this tendency to reflect public fears about the environment and to overload and underfund administrative agencies translates into significant inefficiencies in U.S. environmental policy. As a nation we spend a great deal of money and time dealing with some problems that pose relatively little risk to public and ecological health, but not nearly enough on problems such as climate change, loss of biological diversity, and indoor air quality of far greater consequence (U.S. EPA 1990b). So democratic political processes have worked fairly well in representing public concerns, but they are failing the public in protecting its health as well as ensuring ecological health and sustainable development. An important question is how environmental politics and policy can better serve the public's long-term needs by building a sustainable and just society both within the United States and in the rest of the world.

Discussion Questions

1   What best explains the rise of the environmental movement in the 1960s and 1970s? Similarly, what accounts for the outpouring of federal and state environmental policies during the 1960s and 1970s? Why was there an increase in political opposition to environmentalism from the 1980s to the 2010s?

2   The environmental movement today is much less cohesive than often supposed. Why do environmental organizations find it so hard to cooperate in pursuit of common goals? What difference does that make for achieving environmental policy goals?

3   Most survey research finds the U.S. public both concerned about environmental problems and supportive of strong public policies. Yet the public is not well informed on the issues, and they are not usually salient to the average person. Why is that? What actions might raise the public's awareness of environmental issues and their salience?

4   Only a few national environmental groups, such as the League of Conservation Voters and the Sierra Club, have been active in the electoral process. Why have other groups chosen not to participate in the electoral process? If more environmental organizations were active in campaigns and elections, what effects do you think that would have on environmental politics and policy?

5   The adversaries of environmental groups, or the "environmental opposition," have become far more active and influential than they were in the 1970s and 1980s. Given broad public support for environmental policy, why are these groups so influential today?

Suggested Readings

Andrews, Richard N. L. 2006. *Managing the Environment, Managing Ourselves: A History of American Environmental Policy*, 2nd edn. New Haven, CT: Yale University Press.

Duffy, Robert J. 2003. *The Green Agenda in American Politics: New Strategies for the Twenty-First Century*. Lawrence: University of Kansas Press.

Guber, Deborah Lynn. 2003. *The Grassroots of a Green Revolution: Polling America on the Environment*. Cambridge, MA: MIT Press.

Klyza, Christopher McGrory, and David Sousa. 2013. *American Environmental Policy, 1990–2012: Beyond Gridlock*, revised and expanded edn. Cambridge, MA: MIT Press.

Kraft, Michael E., and Sheldon Kamieniecki, eds. 2007. *Business and Environmental Policy: Corporate Interests in the American Political System*. Cambridge, MA: MIT Press.

Layzer, Judith A. 2012. *Open for Business: Conservatives' Opposition to Environmental Regulation*. Cambridge, MA: MIT Press.

Notes

1 Margaret Kriz, "Shades of Green," *National Journal*, June 21, 2008, 34–38; Margaret Kriz, "Energy and the Environment," *National Journal*, October 4, 2008, 40–42; and Andrew C. Revkin, "McCain and Obama Agree on Real Need to Address Issue of Global Warming," *New York Times*, October 19, 2008.

2 375 members of the National Academy of Sciences, including 30 Nobel Prize winners, signed a letter to Trump criticizing his threat to withdraw from the Paris Agreement. The letter and the signatories can be found at: responsiblescientists.org/. In addition, after the election, more than 800 earth scientists and energy experts sent a letter to the president-elect urging him to take six critical steps that would address the looming threat of climate changes. See Michael D. Lemonick "An Open Letter from Scientists to President-Elect Trump on Climate Change," *Scientific American*, December 6, 2016. The letter was accompanied by an online petition that sought additional support from the nation's scientific community.

3 See Phil McKenna, "GOP and Democratic Platforms Highlight Stark Differences on Energy and Climate," *Inside Climate News*, July 26, 2016, and Clinton's positions on her website: www.hillaryclinton.com/issues/climate/. See also Ben Adler, "11 Ways the Republican Platform Attacks the Environment," *Grist*, July 19, 2016. The complete party platforms for 2016 as well as earlier years can be found at: www.presidency.ucsb.edu/platforms.php.

4 The media did not cover the Libertarian platform much in 2016, but it can be found at the party's website: www.lp.org/platform. The Green Party platform can be found at: www.gp.org/platform.

5 Coral Davenport, "Obama Builds Environmental Legacy with 1970 Law," *New York Times*, November 26, 2014; and Julie Hirschfeld Davis, "Obama Creates Atlantic Ocean's First Marine Monument," *New York Times*, September 15, 2016.

6 Coral Davenport, "Climate Change Divide Bursts to Forefront of Presidential Campaign," *New York Times*, August 1, 2016. Even so, the subject of climate change was nearly absent in the three presidential debates of 2016. No debate moderator asked a question about it.

7 Karen Workman, "August Ties July for Hottest Month on Record," *New York Times*, September 12, 2016; and Justin Gillis, "Flooding of Coast, Caused by Global Warming, Has Already Begun," *New York Times*, September 3, 2016.

8 Chris Mooney, "Why This Could Finally Be the Election Where Climate Change Matters," *Washington Post*, May 9, 2016. See also Christopher Borick, Sarah Mills, and Barry Rabe, "American Views on Climate Change at the Dawn of the Trump Presidency," Brookings Institution, December 15, 2016.

9 In addition to Philip Shabecoff's history of the environmental movement, many recent volumes on U.S. conservation history provide a full account of what can only be summarized briefly here. See Lacey (1989), Nash (1990), Hays (1959, 1987, 2000), Brooks (2009), and especially Andrews (2006a).

10 These public lands are managed chiefly by the National Park Service, now responsible for about 83 million acres; the U.S. Forest Service, about 190 million acres; and the Bureau of Land Management, about 264 million acres (CEQ 1998). The balance of land outside of Alaska consists of desert, rangeland, and mountain land.

11 See U.S. Senate, Committee on Environment and Public Works, Majority Staff Report, "A Strong EPA Protects Our Health and Promotes Economic Growth," October 6, 2001.

12 See Jim Rutenberg and Jeff Zeleny, "Obama Mines for Votes with High-Tech Tools," *New York Times*, March 8, 2012.

13 William Yardley, "Ecoterrorism Suspected in House Fires in Seattle Suburb," *New York Times*, March 4, 2008.

14 Laurie Goodstein, "86 Evangelical Leaders Join to Fight Global Warming," *New York Times*, February 8, 2006. See also Blaine Harden, "What Would Jesus Do about Global Warming?" *Washington Post* National Weekly Edition, February 14–20, 2005.

15 The phrase comes from a provocative essay with that title by Michael Shellenberger and Ted Nordhaus that was circulated via the Internet in October 2004, stimulating widespread reaction, pro and con.

16 See Juliet Eilperin, Steven Mufson, and Philip Rucker, "The Oil and Gas Industry Is Quickly Amassing Power in Trump's Washington," *Washington Post*, December 14, 2016.

17 Margaret Kriz, "Out of the Loop," *National Journal*, February 5, 2005: 344–349.

18 The percentages are taken from the Gallup Poll's "most important problem" measure for May 2016, available at: www.gallup.com/poll/1675/most-important-problem.aspx.

19 A 2007 Gallup survey used this range, and is reported in *National Journal*, April 28, 2007, 82. For some of the most striking findings on partisan differences on climate change, see Anthony Leiserowitz et al., "Politics and Global Warming: Democrats, Republicans, Independents, and the Tea Party," released in September 2011 by the Yale Project on Climate Change Communication: www.climatechangecommunication.org/.

20 See Anthony Leiserowitz et al., "Climate Change in the American Mind: Public Support for Climate and Energy Policies in June 2010," available at the Yale Project on Climate Change Communication: www.climatechangecommunication.org/. More recent surveys are included on the site as well.

21 The results are from a July 2008 Roper-Yale School of Forestry and Environmental Studies survey, and the findings are available at: http://environment.yale.edu/Roper.

22 Reported in *National Journal*, March 31, 2007: 72.

23 Michael Wines and John Schwartz, "Unsafe Lead Levels in Tap Water Not Limited to Flint," *New York Times*, February 8, 2016.

24 See the Gallup Poll's findings on declining trust in government at: www.gallup.com/poll/5392/trust-government.aspx. The Pew Research Center finds much the same trend: www.people-press.org/2015/11/23/1-trust-in-government-1958-2015.

25 Coral Davenport, "Billionaire Environmentalist to Spend $25 Million to Turn Out Young Voters," *New York Times*, April 25, 2016. On the Koch network, see Theda Skocpol and Alexander Hertel-Fernandez, "The Koch Network and Republican Party Extremism," *Perspectives on Politics*, 14(3) (September 2016): 681–699.

26 Nives Dolsak and Aseem Prakash, "The US Environmental Movement Needs a New Message," *The Conversation*, December 12, 2016, available at: www.theconversation.com.

27 Reported in the April/May 2015 issue of *Nature Conservancy*, p. 18.

28 For the Trust for Public Land's assessment, see "Voters Approve Billions for Local Parks and Natural Areas," November 10, 2016, available at: www.tpl.org.

29 Kirk Johnson, "Coloradans Vote to Embrace Alternative Sources of Energy," *New York Times*, November 24, 2004.

30 See Colin Sullivan and Debra Kahn, "Voters Reject 2-Sided Assault on Climate Law," *New York Times*, November 3, 2010.

31 National Journal, "Opinion Outlook: Views on the American Scene," *National Journal*, April 28, 1990: 1052.

32 Katharine Q. Seelye, "Bush Picks Industry Insiders to Fill Environmental Posts," *New York Times*, May 12, 2001.

33 Justin Gillis, "Obama Puts Legacy at Stake with Clean Air Act" and Andrew C. Revkin, "Obama's Ambitious Global Warming Action Plan," *New York Times*, June 25, 2013.

34 Mark Trumbull and Zack Colman, "EPA Chief Voices Cautious Hope as Trump Inauguration Nears," *Christian Science Monitor*, December 5, 2016.

CHAPTER 5

Environmental Protection Policy

Controlling Pollution

In June 2014, the U.S. EPA proposed a long-term plan to cut greenhouse gas emissions from existing power plants. The agency described its Clean Power Plan (CPP) as a "commonsense" way to reduce risks to public health and the economy posed by climate change. EPA administrator Gina McCarthy also said she was committed to working closely with the states to achieve the CPP's goals at minimal cost to the economy. To that end, each state was to have 15 years to make adjustments consistent with its unique situation, and each could choose from many options to reach the plan's goals. These included cleaning up the worst of its coal-fired power plants, relying more on renewable sources such as wind or solar power, using cleaner natural gas or nuclear power, investing in energy efficiency and conservation, or joining with other states in regional cap-and-trade market-based programs.

As expected, critics from the fossil fuel industry and its supporters argued not only that the EPA exceeded its legal authority under the Clean Air Act, but that its plan would harm the economy and cost jobs. The EPA addressed the economic argument in some detail. It estimated that the climate and public health benefits of its proposed rule were worth from $55 billion to $93 billion per year by 2030, an amount that greatly exceeded the estimated compliance costs of $7.3 billion to $8.8 billion a year. From the EPA's perspective, the rule would create an annual net benefit to the economy of between $49 billion to $84 billion by the year 2030, and also create tens of thousands of new jobs, especially in the renewable energy sector.[1] In short, the EPA said we could reduce carbon pollution, clean up urban air pollution, and still enjoy strong economic growth. Of course, costs and benefits, and job gains and losses, are not uniform across the nation; some states and regions will be affected more than others. This is one reason that the agency plan gave the fifty states exceptional flexibility and encouraged them to find the most economical ways to reach their goals.

When the EPA issued its revised and final rule in August of 2015, it called it an "historic and important step in reducing carbon pollution from power plants that takes real action on climate change." It noted as well that the rule was shaped by "years of unprecedented outreach and public engagement," including more than 4.3 million comments that the agency received on the draft rule. The agency said that in its view the final plan was "fair, flexible and designed to strengthen the fast-growing trend toward cleaner and lower-polluting American energy."[2]

The plan's goal is to reduce carbon pollution from power generators, chiefly older coal-fired plants, by 32 percent from 2005 levels, to be achieved by 2030 when the plan is fully in place. Such plants are the largest source of greenhouse gas emissions and they are being phased out already because of their age and inefficiency. More than 30 states already were on track to be half way toward their emissions targets in five years. The plan's critics, however, including 28 states, remained unhappy with the final EPA plan, and they filed suit in federal court to block it.[3]

Why did the EPA pursue what was certain to be a highly contentious regulatory action on climate change? It had little choice. The Obama administration had long indicated that it preferred that Congress draft a national climate change policy rather than rely on a regulatory approach. Congress came close to doing that in 2009. Yet, after the 2010 election, there was little chance that a Republican-controlled Congress would take any action at all because of widening partisan differences on the issue (Dunlap and McCright 2015; Kraft 2016). Thus the administration concluded that an EPA rule was the only option that it had as the threat of climate change grew and international negotiations on a climate change agreement neared completion; that agreement was reached in December 2015. The CPP, along with new fuel economy standards, was the heart of the nation's climate change policy.

The fractious struggle over the EPA rule illustrates well how difficult environmental protection actions had become by 2016, and how much the two major parties were divided on the issues. For example, the Republican presidential nominee in 2016, Donald Trump, made clear that if elected he would repeal the CPP and other Obama environmental rules, withdraw from the Paris climate accord, and weaken the EPA by turning over more of its functions to the states.[4] Most Republican members of Congress had argued for much the same agenda. Given Trump's success in the election, the next several years are likely to be time of significant contention over the direction of environmental policies.

As shown in Chapter 4, over the past four decades the American public has made clear its desire for clean air, clean water, and a healthy environment free of toxic chemicals and hazardous wastes. Yet for most of this period it also has been ambivalent about its willingness to pay higher taxes and product costs or to tolerate regulatory activities at the federal and state levels to achieve these environmental quality goals. Congress has responded to public opinion by enacting and, over time, strengthening seven major environmental protection, or pollution control, statutes: the Clean Air Act; Clean Water Act; Safe Drinking Water Act; Toxic Substances Control Act; Federal Insecticide, Fungicide, and Rodenticide Act; Resource Conservation and Recovery Act; and Comprehensive Environmental Response, Compensation, and Liability Act (Superfund). The first six statutes look primarily to the future. The EPA develops regulations that affect the current and future generation, transportation, use, and disposal of chemicals and pollutants that pose a significant risk to public health or the environment. The last statute is largely, although not exclusively, remedial. It aims to repair damage from careless disposal of hazardous chemicals in the past. The Superfund act also affects present and future pollution control efforts.[5]

Separately and collectively, these acts mandate an exceedingly wide array of regulatory actions that touch virtually every industrial and commercial enterprise in the nation and increasingly affect the lives of ordinary citizens, as made clear by the EPA's action on climate change. Routine implementation decisions as well as the periodic renewal of the acts by Congress invariably involve sharp debates over the extent of the risks faced, the appropriate standards to protect public and ecological health, and the policy strategies used to achieve those standards. As illustrated by the CPP rule of 2016, policymakers and interest groups argue as well over the degree to which environmental and health benefits should be weighed against the costs of compliance and other social and economic values.

As shown in Chapter 2, these policies have produced substantial and well-documented gains, particularly in urban air quality and in control of point sources of water pollution. It is equally true, however, that the policies have fallen short of expectations, and in some cases distressingly so, as actions on toxic chemicals, pesticides, and hazardous wastes clearly illustrate. Existing policy barely touches some major risks, such as indoor air quality; and others, such as surface water, groundwater, and drinking water quality, have proved far more difficult to control than originally expected. As welcome as they are, the achievements to date also have not been cheap. The U.S. General Accounting Office (now the Government Accountability Office [GAO]) estimated that between 1972 and 1992 the cumulative expenditures for pollution control exceeded $1 trillion; to put that number into perspective, the U.S. gross domestic product in 1992 was $6.5 trillion, or $9.4 trillion in 2016 dollars (U.S. GAO 1992). By the 2000s, the continuing cost to government and the private sector of these same policies was probably about $200 billion per year.[6]

The nation remains committed to the broad policy goals of controlling pollution and minimizing public health risks. Yet implementation and compliance costs and the intrusiveness of environmental regulation will test its resolve over the next several decades. Tight budgets at all levels of government, as well as growing impatience with ineffective and inefficient public policies, are creating new demands that programs either produce demonstrable success or be changed. In particular, the federally driven command-and-control approach to pollution control adopted during the 1970s is increasingly viewed as only one component in a larger policy arsenal that may be directed at environmental problems in the twenty-first century (Eisner 2007; Fiorino 2006; Kamieniecki and Kraft 2013; Mazmanian and Kraft 2009).

This chapter seeks to:

- build an understanding of the goals of major U.S. environmental protection policies, the way the policies are implemented by the EPA and the states, and key revisions made to the core statutes over time;
- develop a capacity for critical analysis of the policies and for appraisal of conflicting assessments of how well they have worked and the need for policy change; and
- describe and help readers analyze the EPA's organization, staffing, budgeting, and decision-making processes; the political and administrative forces that affect the agency's rule-making and enforcement; and the legal challenges made to its development of rules and regulations.

The Contours of Environmental Protection Policy

The first part of the chapter reviews the configuration of current environmental protection policy to provide some perspective on the developments just cited and on contemporary debates about the future of pollution control efforts. The second part turns to the EPA to assess its role as a government agency charged with implementing the policies through setting and enforcing environmental quality and emission standards, among other activities.

Each of the seven policies reviewed here has different goals, uses distinctive means to achieve them, and sets out its own standards for balancing environmental quality and other social goals. Yet these policies may also be grouped together for present purposes. All focus on environmental protection or pollution control, and all seek primarily to protect public health even when ecological objectives are included as well. All of these policies also rely on national environmental quality standards and regulatory mechanisms, and all are implemented primarily by the EPA, in cooperation with the states. Table 5.1 provides an overview of these seven policies and their key provisions.

TABLE 5.1 Major federal environmental protection policies

Statute	Key provisions and features
Clean Air Act Amendments of 1970, PL 91-604, revised in 1977 and 1990	Requires the EPA to set primary and secondary national ambient air quality standards and emission limits, and the states to develop implementation plans. Regulates motor vehicle emissions and fuels. The 1990 amendments sought to limit acid deposition, to phase out CFCs, and to regulate major sources of toxic and hazardous air pollutants.
Federal Water Pollution Control Act (Clean Water Act) Amendments of 1972, PL 92-500, amended in 1977 and 1987	Sets national water quality goals, establishes a pollution discharge permit system for dischargers of waste into U.S. waters. The 1987 amendments established a state revolving loan fund to help build wastewater treatment plants, and urged states to develop nonpoint source pollution management plans.
Safe Drinking Water Act of 1974, PL 93-523, amended in 1986 and 1996	Sets standards to safeguard the quality of public drinking water supplies and to regulate state programs for protecting groundwater sources. Provides loans and grants to assist localities with meeting standards. The 1996 amendments require local water systems to distribute annual reports on drinking water safety.
Resource Conservation and Recovery Act of 1976, PL 94-580, amended in 1984	Sets federal regulations for hazardous waste treatment, storage, transportation, and disposal and provides assistance for state programs. The 1984 amendments prohibited land disposal of certain hazardous liquid wastes and mandated state consideration of recycling programs.
Toxic Substances Control Act of 1976, PL 94-469, amended in 2016	Authorizes premarket testing of chemical substances and allows the EPA to ban or regulate the manufacture, sale, or use of chemicals presenting an "unreasonable risk of injury" to health or the environment.
Federal Insecticide, Fungicide, and Rodenticide Act of 1972, PL 92-516, amended in 1996 as the Food Quality Protection Act, PL 104-170	Requires registration of all pesticides in U.S. commerce and allows the EPA to cancel or suspend registration when needed to protect public health or the environment. Amendments of 1996 created a new "reasonable risk" approach for raw and processed foods, and required the EPA to adopt a tenfold margin of safety to protect children.

TABLE 5.1 *(continued)*

Comprehensive Environmental Response, Compensation, and Liability Act (Superfund) of 1980, PL 96-510, revised in 1986.	Authorizes the federal government to respond to hazardous waste emergencies and to clean up chemical dump sites through use of a fund of money supported by taxes on the chemical and petroleum industries. Also sets liability for cleanup costs. The 1986 amendments (SARA) added the Emergency Planning and Community Right-to-Know Act, which established the Toxics Release Inventory program.

The Clean Air Act

The Clean Air Act (CAA) is one of the most comprehensive and complex statutes ever approved by the U.S. government. It is the premier example of contemporary environmental regulation. Unsurprisingly, since the early 1970s the Act has been a frequent target of critics even while environmentalists and public health specialists have sought to strengthen and expand it. The battles continued throughout the 1990s, 2000s, and 2010s. Congress approved the 1990 amendments to the CAA with President George H. W. Bush's active support. Yet Bush's own White House Council on Competitiveness tried repeatedly to weaken EPA regulations for implementing the Act in an effort to reduce its economic effects on industry and local governments (Bryner 1995). The Clinton White House resisted similar economic arguments when in 1997 it supported the EPA's recommendation to tighten air pollution standards for ozone and fine particulates.[7] Yet George W. Bush's administration leaned strongly the other way. It sought to give greater weight to economic effects of clean air policies and thus pull back from Clinton administration initiatives, particularly for older industrial facilities such as coal-burning power plants (Vig 2016).[8] As the example of the Clean Power Plan in the chapter's opening illustrates, the Obama administration was closer to Bill Clinton's presidency in its actions. In contrast, the Trump administration almost certainly will favor a quite different approach, one that is likely to reflect the positions endorsed by Republicans and reflected in the party's 2016 platform on environmental protection issues.[9]

Federal air pollution control policy dates back to the original and modest Clean Air Act of 1963, which provided for federal support for air pollution research as well as assistance to the states for developing their own pollution control agencies. Prior to the 1963 Act, federal action was limited to a small research program in the Public Health Service authorized in 1955. The 1970 amendments to the CAA followed several incremental adjustments in federal policy, including the 1965 Motor Vehicle Air Pollution Control Act and a 1965 amendment to the CAA that began the federal program for setting emissions standards for new motor vehicles. A 1967 Air Quality Act provided funds to the states to plan for air pollution control, required them to establish air quality control regions (i.e., geographic areas with shared air quality problems), and directed the federal government to study health effects of air pollution to assist the states in their control strategies.

Congress adopted the radically different 1970 CAA both in response to sharply increased public concern about the environment, as discussed in Chapter 4, and because it saw little progress in cleaning the air under the previous statutes. The states as well as the federal government had been slow in responding to worsening air quality problems, states were reluctant to use the powers they were given, and the automobile industry displayed little commitment to pollution control. With near unanimity, Congress approved a far stronger Act despite intense industry pressure to weaken it. It also did so in the face of significant doubts about both available technology and governmental capacity to implement the law (Bryner 1995; Jones 1975).

The new policy mandated National Ambient Air Quality Standards (NAAQS), which were to be set by the EPA and be uniform across the country, with enforcement shared by the federal and state governments. As discussed in Chapter 2, these standards deal with permissible concentrations of chemicals in the air. The primary standards were to protect human health, and secondary standards, where necessary, were aimed at protecting buildings, forests, water, crops, and similar nonhealth values. The EPA was to set the NAAQS at levels that would "provide an adequate margin of safety" to protect the public from "any known or anticipated adverse effects" associated with six major, or criteria, pollutants: sulfur dioxide, nitrogen dioxide, lead, ozone, carbon monoxide, and particulate matter. The standard for lead was added in 1977 and revised in 2008. A standard for hydrocarbons issued by the EPA under the 1970 Act was eliminated in 1978 as unnecessary.

The Act also required that an "ample margin of safety" be set for toxic or hazardous air pollutants such as arsenic, chromium, hydrogen chloride, zinc, pesticides, and radioactive substances. Congress assumed that a safe level of air pollution existed and standards could be set accordingly for air toxics as well as the criteria pollutants. The Act has been interpreted as requiring the setting of the crucially important NAAQS without regard to the costs of attainment (P. Portney 1990). If control technologies were not available to meet these standards, Congress expected them to be developed by fixed deadlines. The goal was to reduce air pollution to acceptable levels.

The 1970 CAA and subsequent amendments also set national emissions standards for mobile sources of air pollution: cars, trucks, and buses. Congress explicitly called for a 90 percent reduction in hydrocarbon and carbon monoxide emissions from the levels of 1970, to be achieved by the 1975 model year, and a 90 percent reduction in the level of nitrogen oxides by the 1976 model year. Yet it gave the EPA the authority to waive the deadlines, which it did several times. Similarly, the Act set tough emissions standards for stationary sources such as refineries, chemical companies, and other industrial facilities. New sources of pollution were to be held to New Source Performance Standards to be set industry by industry and enforced by the states. The standards were to be based on use of state-of-the-art control technologies (best available technology [BAT]), with at least some recognition that economic costs and energy use should be taken into account. Existing sources (e.g., older industrial facilities) were held to lower standards set by the states, a decision that became highly controversial by the 2000s.

To deal with existing sources of air pollution, each state was to prepare a State Implementation Plan (SIP) that would detail how it would meet EPA standards and guidelines. States have the primary responsibility for implementing those sections of the Act dealing with stationary sources; the EPA retains authority for mobile sources. The 1970 Act called for all areas of the nation to be in compliance with the national air standards by 1975, a date later extended repeatedly. The EPA could reject an SIP if it could not be expected to bring the state into compliance, and the agency could impose sanctions on those states, such as banning construction of large new sources of air pollution, including power plants and refineries, or cutting off highly valued federal highway and sewer funds.[10]

The 1977 Amendments In the 1977 amendments to the CAA, Congress backtracked in some respects from its early uncompromising position, such as on the dates by which compliance was to be achieved. Yet it left the major goals of the law intact and even strengthened the Act on requirements for nonattainment areas and provisions for prevention of significant deterioration (PSD) in those areas already cleaner than the national standards.

Congress established three classes of clean areas. In Class I (national parks and similar areas), air quality would be protected against any deterioration. In Class II, the Act specified the amount of additional pollution that would be permitted. Finally, in Class III, air pollution was allowed to continue until it reached the level set by national standards. Congress further provided for protection and enhancement of visibility in national parks and wilderness areas affected by haze and smog. A new and controversial provision in the 1977 amendments called for the use of so-called scrubbers to remove sulfur dioxide emission from new fossil-fuel-burning power plants whether those plants used low- or high-sulfur coal. The action was widely understood to be an effort to protect the high-sulfur coal industry (Ackerman and Hassler 1981).

Substantial progress in meeting policy goals was made during the 1970s, and the results were evident in cleaner air in most U.S. cities. Nevertheless, unhealthy levels of air pollution continued, and control of toxic air pollutants called for in the 1970 Act proved difficult to achieve. Newer problems, such as acid rain and the contribution of greenhouse gas emissions to climate change, demanded attention. At the same time, criticism mounted over the EPA's implementation of the CAA, particularly its inconsistent, inflexible, and costly regulations and inadequate guidelines for state action. Technical obstacles to meeting the Act's goals and deadlines also became apparent. Conflicts over reformulation of the Act were so great that Congress was unable to fashion a compromise acceptable to all parties until 1990.

The 1990 Amendments The 1990 amendments to the CAA further extended the Act's reach to control of the precursors of acid rain (sulfur dioxide and nitrogen oxides) emitted primarily by coal-burning power plants and to chlorofluorocarbons (CFCs) that damage the ozone layer. Among the most innovative provisions in Title IV of the 1990 amendments was the use of a new emissions trading program for reducing sulfur dioxide emissions that later became a model for the proposed cap-and-trade component of climate change policy. Title II of the amendments called for further reductions (of 35 to 60 percent) in automobile tailpipe emissions between 1994 and 1996, and mandated development of cleaner fuels for use in selected areas of the nation. Oxygen-containing additives were to be used in fuels in communities with high levels of carbon monoxide (chiefly in the winter, when carbon monoxide is more of a problem). Reformulated, or cleaner, gasoline was to be used in cities with severe ozone problems. The reformulated fuels require more refining and cost slightly more. They burn more thoroughly and evaporate more slowly, and contain much lower concentrations of toxic compounds such as toluene and benzene. These fuels also have oxygen-containing additives.

Because residents of many metropolitan areas are still forced to breathe polluted air, Title I of the Act set out an elaborate and exacting multitiered plan intended to bring all urban areas into compliance with national air quality standards within 3 to 20 years, depending on the severity of their air pollution. The amendments invited private lawsuits to compel compliance with those deadlines.

Unhappy with the EPA's dismal progress in regulating hazardous air pollutants, Congress departed sharply from the 1970 Act. It required the agency to set emission limits for all major industrial sources of hazardous or toxic air pollutants (e.g., chemical companies, refineries, and steel plants). These rules were intended to reduce emissions by as much as 90 percent by the year 2003 through technology-based standards. Title III listed 189 specific toxic chemicals that were to be regulated as hazardous air pollutants. Within eight years of setting emission limits for industrial operations, the agency was required to set new health-based standards for those chemicals determined to be carcinogens representing a risk of one cancer case in 1 million exposed individuals.

In Title V of the Act, Congress established a new permit program to facilitate enforcement of the Act. Major stationary sources of air pollution are now required to have EPA-issued operating permits that specify allowable emissions and control measures that must be used (Bryner 1995).

As attention has shifted from Congress to the intricacies of the EPA's rule-making and state implementation efforts, controversy over the 1990 CAA Amendments has continued. The broad scope and demanding requirements of the 1990 Act guarantee that conflict is not likely to fade anytime soon.[11]

Proposed Reforms Recent years have brought many proposals to change the CAA in incremental ways, through both legislation action and administrative rules. For example, the Bush administration in 2002 proposed a Clear Skies Initiative, backed by business groups, that would have used market incentives to control emissions of mercury, nitrogen dioxide, and sulfur dioxide from power plants. The administration argued that the new approach would cut emissions faster and more cheaply than conventional regulatory approaches.[12] Environmentalists and other opponents disagreed, asserting that the current CAA could achieve better results and more quickly if properly implemented. Bush was unsuccessful in Congress, which voted narrowly and along largely partisan lines in 2005 to defeat the proposal; Democrats and environmentalists argued strongly against it.

The Bush administration then sought to make similar changes through administrative rules over which it had more control. Here too the president was largely unsuccessful. His Clean Air Interstate Rule (CAIR) issued in 2005 set new standards for conventional air pollution (sulfur dioxide and nitrogen dioxide) in 28 eastern states, and another rule dealt with mercury emissions from power plants. Both rules raised current standards, but not to the level favored by EPA scientists. Eventually they were overturned by the federal courts, with CAIR reinstated in late 2008 as an interim measure (Vig 2016).[13] The Obama administration struggled as well with CAIR. It revised the Bush rule, seeking additional cuts in sulfur dioxide and nitrogen dioxide from power plants, but was sued by the industry and lost in federal court in 2012. The EPA continued to work on the challenge while the Bush rule remained in place, and in January 2015 proposed a Cross-State Air Pollution Rule to replace CAIR.[14]

Environmentalists, among many other critics, were even more strongly opposed to a related Bush initiative to ease the CAA's new source review (NSR) requirements. Long a point of contention, the NSR standards were intended to force older coal-fired power plants, oil refineries, smelters and steel mills, pulp and paper mills, and other industrial facilities to install new emissions controls when their plants undergo certain major renovations rather than mere "routine maintenance, repair, and replacement." Many facilities attempted to modernize their equipment but avoided the added expense of pollution control by describing their work as maintenance only. Those plants faced aggressive enforcement of the NSR rules under the Clinton administration. New Bush administration rules adopted in 2003 allowed plants to undertake extensive changes without invoking the NSR standards as long as the total cost of modernizing the production facility was below a specified level. EPA officials argued that the older plants and factories needed the flexibility that the Bush rules would provide. Yet as one press account put it, the new rules "triggered a storm of criticism from environmentalists, Democrats, and some Republicans," as well as dozens of lawsuits.[15]

In more recent years, three key actions under the CAA have generated controversy and a flurry of congressional initiatives to change the Act. One of these is the long-standing effort to reduce emissions of mercury and air toxics from coal-fired power plants and other industrial sources. The Obama administration issued new standards that were widely criticized by industry and its supporters in Congress, but they were upheld by the Supreme Court in 2016. The second was yet another increase in the national standard for ozone, which lowered the allowed level to 70 parts per billion from the previous standard of 75 parts per billion; it fell short of what environmentalists and public health experts had hoped to see while also displeasing industry. The third, as noted at the chapter's opening, is the administration's Clean Power Plan to limit greenhouse gas emissions.[16]

The Clean Water Act

The Federal Water Pollution Control Act Amendments of 1972, now known as the Clean Water Act (CWA), is the major federal policy regulating surface water quality. As was the case with the Clean Air Act, the CWA dramatically altered the original and very limited Water Pollution Control Act (1948), which emphasized research, investigations, and surveys of water problems.[17] Under the 1948 Act, there was no federal authority to establish water quality standards or to restrict discharge of pollutants. Amendments adopted in 1956 also failed to establish any meaningful control over discharge of pollutants. The 1965 Water Quality Act went much further by requiring states to establish water quality standards for interstate bodies of water and implementation plans to achieve those standards, and by providing for federal oversight of the process. Yet the 1965 law was widely viewed as administratively and politically unworkable and ineffective, in part because of significant variation among the states in their economic resources, bureaucratic expertise, and degree of commitment to water quality goals.

The 1972 CWA was intended to correct these deficiencies by setting a national policy for water pollution control. It established deadlines for elimination of the discharge of pollutants into navigable waters by 1985, and stated that all waters were to be "fishable and swimmable" by 1983. It also encouraged technological innovation and areawide planning for attainment of water quality (Freeman 1990). The 1972 Act was itself revised and strengthened in 1977 and again in 1987 without fundamentally altering the goals or means to achieve them. Congress, however, postponed several deadlines for compliance and established new provisions for toxic water pollutants, the discharge of which in "toxic amounts" was to be prohibited. Throughout the 1990s Congress was deeply divided over how to revise the Act, and the conflict continued in the 2000s and 2010s.[18]

The goals of the 1972 Act may have been admirable, but they proved to be wildly unrealistic. The tasks were of a staggering magnitude, industry actively opposed the Act's objectives and frequently challenged the EPA in court, technology proved to be costly, and planning for control of nonpoint sources (i.e., those with no specific point of origin) was inadequately funded and difficult to establish. Thus deadlines were postponed and achievement of goals suffered.

For example, in 1992 the International Joint Commission reported that the United States had yet to eliminate completely the discharge of any persistent toxic chemical. The achievement of fishable and swimmable waters is supposed to mean, as stated in the 1977 Act, that the water quality provides for "the protection and propagation of a balanced population of shellfish, fish, and wildlife" as well as recreation in and on the water. As noted in Chapter 2, the EPA reported in 2016 that 55 percent of rivers and streams and 75 percent of lakes and ponds assessed failed to meet those standards. Nevertheless, as the first sentence of the CWA states, it aspires to "restore and maintain the chemical, physical, and biological integrity of the nation's waters." Elaborate efforts are under way to move toward those challenging objectives, and signs of progress are evident.

Much like the Clean Air Act, the CWA gives primary responsibility for implementation to the states, as long as they follow federal standards and guidelines. Dischargers into navigable waterways must meet water quality standards and effluent limits, and they operate under a permit that specifies the terms of allowable discharge and control technologies to be used. The EPA has granted authority to most states to issue those permits, which operate under the National Pollutant Discharge Elimination System (NPDES). The NPDES applies to municipal wastewater treatment facilities as well as to industry. Compliance with the permits is determined by self-reported discharge data and on-site inspections by state personnel. Studies suggest, however, that underreporting and weak enforcement of the law are common (Hunter and Waterman 1996). For example, an environmental group in Los Angeles (joined by the EPA) sued the city for a "chronic, continuing, and unacceptable number" of spills from the sewage collection system into area waters in violation of the CWA. The EPA pursued similar cases in Atlanta, Baltimore, Miami, and New Orleans. In 2009 an exhaustive investigation by the *New York Times* found continuing problems of poor enforcement of the CWA by the states.[19] The CWA permits private citizens to file lawsuits against polluters to help enforce the law; any financial penalties are paid to the federal government. The U.S. Supreme Court upheld that provision of the law in early 2000 in *Friends of the Earth v. Laidlaw Environmental Services*.[20]

The states also establish Water Quality Criteria (WQC) that define the maximum concentrations of pollutants allowable in surface waters. In theory, the WQC concentrations would be set at levels posing no threat to individual organisms, populations, species, communities, and ecosystems (including humans). States do so using EPA guidelines that take into account the uses of a given body of water as defined by the states (e.g., fishing, boating, and waste disposal). The purpose is to prevent degradation that interferes with the designated uses. States may consider benefits and costs in establishing water quality standards.

Effluent limitations specify how much a given discharger, such as a manufacturing facility, is allowed to emit into the water and the specific treatment technologies that must be used to stay within such limits. The EPA has defined such effluent limitations for different categories of industry based on available treatment technologies. Economists and industry leaders have long objected that the requirements are irrational: "To put it simply, standards are set on the basis of what can be done with available technology, rather than what should be done to achieve ambient water quality standards, to balance benefits and costs, or to satisfy any other criteria" (Freeman 1990, 106). Critics also object to what they consider to be vague statutory language such as "best practical," "best available," and "reasonable costs," which grant enormous discretion to administrative agencies to interpret complex and varied scientific, engineering, and economic information. In response, defenders of the CWA argue that use of approaches that call for BAT is a major reason the nation has achieved the degree of progress it has under the Act.

A politically attractive feature of the CWA was federal funding to assist local communities to build modern municipal wastewater treatment facilities. The federal government initially assumed 75 percent of the capital costs, and for several years in the 1970s it subsidized such construction to the tune of $7 billion per year. Later called "water infrastructure" and "state and tribal assistance" grants, the percentage of federal assistance was reduced in the 1980s; in recent years it stood at about $3.0 billion per year. The 1987 revision of the CWA authorized creation of a state revolving loan fund program to help local governments build wastewater treatment facilities; the communities later repay the states. All 50 states have such funds. Between 1987 and 1996, Congress spent about $11 billion on the loan program as it phased out the earlier nationally funded construction grant program.

The discharge of toxic chemicals has proved much more difficult to regulate than conventional pollutants. Although bodies of water may assimilate a certain amount of biologically degradable waste products, the same cannot be said for toxic chemicals, such as PCBs, dioxins, mercury, lead, and other heavy metals, which often accumulate in toxic hot spots in river and lake sediments. By the late 1990s, a consensus was emerging that the best course of action was to identify and end the use of the most toxic, persistent, and bioaccumulative pollutants. For example, this position was a cornerstone of the EPA's Great Lakes Five-Year Strategy. The agency's

Great Lakes Water Quality Initiative called for the "virtual elimination" of discharges of persistent toxic substances throughout the Great Lakes Basin.

Unlike conventional, or "point," sources such as industry discharge pipes, nonpoint sources of water pollution such as agricultural runoff have proved to be exceptionally difficult to manage. The 1987 CWA amendments required the states to develop an EPA-approved plan for control of nonpoint sources such as urban stormwater runoff; cropland erosion; and runoff from construction sites, woodlands, pastures, and feedlots. Before implementation of the CWA, these sources constituted between 57 and 98 percent of total discharges of phosphorus, nitrogen, suspended solids, and biological oxygen demand in the nation's surface waters (Freeman 1990, 109). As discussed in Chapter 2, even by 2016 they remained responsible for the majority of stream pollution.

So far, most states have chosen voluntary approaches using "best management practices" to deal with nonpoint sources. In 1998, however, the Clinton administration proposed and Congress approved a new Clean Water Action Plan that provided $1.7 billion over five years to help state and local governments deal with nonpoint source water pollution. In addition, in 2000, the EPA approved a new rule under its Total Maximum Daily Load (TMDL) program that provided a framework for cooperation with the states "to finish the job of cleaning up America's polluted waterways." States were to regulate water pollution by focusing on the quality of a body of water as well as the actions of individual dischargers, and to promote cost-effective cleanup by ensuring that all sources of pollution are considered as cleanup plans are developed and approved.[21] The TMDL process has been subject to extensive litigation, but the agency continues to use its authority under the CWA to work with the states to achieve improved water quality.[22]

Conflicts continue over how best to deal with nonpoint sources. In 2015 the Obama administration announced a major new "Waters of the United States" rule, developed jointly by the EPA and the Army Corps of Engineers under the CWA. It was intended to bolster the federal government's authority over pollution of rivers, lakes, streams and wetlands that was put into question by several Supreme Court rulings. But the new rule was challenged by business interests such as farmers, real estate interests, golf course owners, fertilizer and pesticide makers, oil and gas developers, and Republican members of Congress. They argued that it was a federal overreach and would harm economic growth and infringe on their property rights.[23] The Trump administration announced in February 2017 that the EPA would begin the lengthy process of rewriting the rule to address those concerns.

The Safe Drinking Water Act

The 1974 Safe Drinking Water Act (SDWA) was designed to ensure the quality and safety of drinking water by specifying minimum public health standards for public water supplies. The Act authorized the EPA to set

National Primary Drinking Water Standards for chemical and microbiological contaminants for tap water. The Act also required regular monitoring of water supplies to ensure that pollutants stayed below safe levels.

The EPA made slow progress in setting standards. Only 22 standards for 18 substances had been set by the mid-1980s. In 1986 a Congress frustrated with both the EPA's pace of implementation and insufficient action by state and local governments strengthened the Act. Congress required the EPA to determine maximum contaminant levels for 83 specific chemicals by 1989 and set quality standards for them, set standards for another 25 contaminants by 1991, and set standards for 25 more every three years. Congress was highly prescriptive in detailing what contaminants would be regulated, how they would be treated, and the timetable for action. The standards were to be based on a contaminant's potential for causing illness and the financial capacity of medium- to large-size water systems to foot the bill for the purification technology.

States have the primary responsibility for enforcing those standards for the tens of thousands of public water systems in the United States. Water systems were to use the best available technology to remove contaminants and monitor for the presence of a host of chemicals. Even the EPA acknowledges that the states receive far less funding than needed to comply. The problems are especially severe for the thousands of small water systems that can ill afford the cost of expensive new water treatment technologies.

For those reasons, the nation's governors and mayors pressed Congress in the mid-1990s to ease regulatory red tape by focusing on tests for contamination and monitoring of only those chemicals posing the greatest risk to human health. The drinking water law symbolized a broader complaint about unfunded federal mandates that require states and localities to spend their scarce local funds on environmental programs over which they have no say. The SDWA also reflected concern over the high marginal costs of further improvements in environmental quality after the gains of the previous 20 years.

When the SDWA came up for reauthorization, the Safe Drinking Water Act Coalition, representing a dozen organizations of state and local officials, lobbied aggressively for reducing the regulatory burden on states. It sought the use of less expensive and slightly less effective technologies, less strict water quality standards when public health would not be endangered, and a new federal revolving loan fund to defray the cost for smaller water systems. Environmentalists were equally as determined to keep stringent public health protections in place.[24]

Groundwater contamination is of special concern for municipalities that rely on well water and for the nation's rural residents. As discussed in Chapter 2, aquifers may be contaminated by improper disposal of hazardous wastes and leaking underground storage tanks, and from agricultural runoff (e.g., nitrates and pesticides), among other sources. By 2000, for example, the EPA was urging the phaseout of the gasoline additive methyl tertiary butyl ether (MTBE) out of concern that it had already contaminated several thousand groundwater sites around the nation, and in early 2006 it urged Congress to drop the Clean Air Act requirement for using additives such as MTBE in gasoline. Groundwater historically has been governed chiefly by state and local governments. Yet it is affected by the SDWA, the CWA, and many other federal statutes, with no consistent standards or coordination of enforcement.

In 1996, Congress agreed to renew the SDWA. Both the House and the Senate voted overwhelmingly for the new law, which established a new, more flexible approach to regulating water contaminants based on their risk to public health; the Act also permitted the consideration of costs and benefits of proposed regulations. The 1996 law ended the previous requirement for setting standards for 25 additional contaminants every three years. Instead, every five years the EPA is to publish a list of unregulated contaminants found in drinking water and then use that list when it proposes to regulate a new contaminant. The Act also authorized federal support for state-administered loan and grant funds to help localities meet federal drinking water standards. States are allowed to transfer funds between the clean water and drinking water revolving funds. Under pressure from the environmental community, the Act also created a new right-to-know provision that requires community water systems to provide their customers with annual consumer confidence reports on the safety of local water supplies. Small water systems face reduced standards out of concern for the cost of compliance.[25]

As discussed in Chapter 2, the continuing challenges in providing safe drinking water to cities across the nation were made clear by the discovery of unsafe levels of lead discovered in Flint, Michigan's water in 2015. High lead levels were found in many other cities across the nation, and in many schools, prompting renewed concern about what else needs to be done to insure safe drinking water quality, not only for lead but for other chemicals as well, many of them unregulated. The problems are even greater for those who rely on well water.[26]

The Resource Conservation and Recovery Act

Although the federal government had dealt earlier with solid waste in the 1965 Solid Waste Disposal Act (SWDA), by the 1970s concern was shifting to hazardous waste. In 1976 Congress enacted the Resource Conservation and Recovery Act (RCRA) as amendments to the SWDA and to the 1970 Resource Recovery Act. RCRA (pronounced "rick rah") was to regulate existing hazardous waste disposal practices as well as promote the conservation and recovery of resources through comprehensive management of solid waste. Congress addressed the problem of abandoned hazardous waste sites in the 1980 Superfund legislation, discussed later.

RCRA required the EPA to develop criteria for the safe disposal of solid waste and the Commerce Department to promote waste recovery technologies and waste conservation. The EPA was to develop a cradle-to-grave system of regulation that would monitor and control the production, storage, transportation, and disposal of wastes considered hazardous, and it was to determine the appropriate technology for disposal of wastes.

The Act delegated to the EPA most of the tasks of identifying and characterizing such wastes (the agency counts more than 500 chemical compounds and mixtures) and determining whether they are hazardous. That judgment is to be based on explicit measures of toxicity, ignitability, corrosivity, and chemical reactivity. If a waste is positive by any one of these indicators, or is a "listed" hazardous waste, it is governed by RCRA's regulations (Dower 1990).

RCRA also established a paper trail for keeping track of the generation and transportation of hazardous wastes that was intended to eliminate so-called midnight or illegal dumping. Eventually, the EPA developed a national manifest system (the paperwork that accounts for transport of the waste) for that purpose. However, because most hazardous waste never leaves its site of generation, the manifest system governs only a small portion of the total. More important is that RCRA called for the EPA to set standards for the treatment, storage, and disposal of hazardous wastes that are "necessary to protect human health and the environment." As is the case for the air and water acts, the EPA over time delegated authority to most states to implement RCRA.

Initially, the EPA was exceedingly slow in implementing RCRA, in part because of the unexpected complexity of the tasks, lack of sufficient data, and staff and budget constraints. In addition, environmentalists, EPA technical staff, the chemical industry, and the White House (especially in the Reagan administration) battled frequently over the stringency of the regulations (S. Cohen 1984). The EPA took four years to issue the first major regulations and two additional years to issue final technical or performance standards for incinerators, landfills, and surface storage tanks that had to be met for licensed or permitted facilities. In the meantime, public concern had escalated because of publicity over horror stories involving disposal of hazardous waste at Love Canal, New York, and soil contaminated with dioxin-tainted waste oil at Times Beach, Missouri. EPA relations with Capitol Hill were severely strained in the early 1980s during Anne Burford's tumultuous reign as administrator, and the Reagan administration ultimately had no legislative proposal for renewal of RCRA that would allow the EPA to put forth its own vision of a workable policy.

As a result of these developments, Congress grew profoundly distrustful of the EPA's "slow and timid implementation of existing law," and it sharply limited administrative discretion in its 1984 rewrite of RCRA, officially called the Hazardous and Solid Waste Amendments (HSWA). The 1984 RCRA amendments rank among the most detailed and restrictive of environmental measures ever enacted, with 76 statutory deadlines, 8 of them with so-called hammer provisions that were to take effect if the EPA failed to act in time (Halley 1994). Congress uses this hammer language in environmental and other acts to impose a legislative regulation if an agency fails to adopt its own regulations by the stated deadline. Such provisions are intended to force agency compliance with the law, but they may also interfere with sound policy implementation, particularly when agency budgets are tight and much technical uncertainty surrounds the problems being addressed.

The 1984 Act sought to phase out disposal of most hazardous wastes in landfills by establishing demanding standards of safety and expand control to cover additional sources and wastes (particularly from small sources previously exempt). In addition it extended RCRA regulation to underground storage tanks (USTs) holding petroleum, pesticides, solvents, and gasoline, and moved much more quickly toward program goals by setting out a highly specific timetable for various mandated actions. The effect was to drive up dramatically the cost of hazardous waste disposal. Although economists question the economic logic of these provisions (Dower 1990), Congress helped bring about an outcome long favored by environmentalists: the internalization of environmental and health costs of improper disposal of wastes. If disposal of wastes is extraordinarily expensive, a powerful incentive to produce less waste exists, thus leading (eventually) to source reduction, recycling, and new treatment technologies, which the 1984 amendments ranked as far more desirable than land disposal. At least that is the idea. The effects can be seen in how many manufacturers today have adopted lifecycle analysis and green business plans to reduce, reuse, or recycle materials previously discarded as waste (Mazmanian and Kraft 2009; Press and Mazmanian 2016).

Congress struggled in the 1990s with reauthorization of RCRA without resolving continuing conflicts. Through 1992 the George H. W. Bush administration opposed revamping the Act, saying it was unnecessary. Members of Congress, however, heard warnings of impending solid waste crises because most of the nation's remaining landfills were to close over the next 15 years. Environmentalists pressed for higher levels of waste reduction and waste recovery through recycling, and tighter controls on waste incineration. Local governments worried about what to do with incinerator ash that may be classified as hazardous under a 1994 U.S. Supreme Court decision, and some states fought the solid waste industry over efforts to restrict interstate transport of solid wastes. As was often the case over the past two decades, environmental gridlock prevailed as each side fought for its preferred solutions, and no consensus emerged on a comprehensive revision of RCRA (Kraft 2016).

The Toxic Substances Control Act

After five years of development and debate, Congress enacted the Toxic Substances Control Act (TSCA) in 1976. The EPA was given comprehensive authority to identify, evaluate, and regulate risks associated with the full lifecycle of commercial chemicals, both those already in commerce as well as new ones in preparation. Yet tens of thousands of existing compounds were grandfathered in; no comprehensive testing for health and safety was required. TSCA (pronounced "toss kah") aspired to develop adequate data on the effect of chemical substances on health and the environment and to regulate those chemicals posing an "unreasonable risk of injury to health or the environment" without unduly burdening industry and impeding technological innovation.

The EPA was to produce an inventory of chemicals in commercial production, and it was given authority to require testing by industry where data are insufficient and the chemical may present an unacceptable risk. Exercise of that authority was made difficult and time-consuming, however. An Interagency Testing Committee, with representatives from eight federal agencies, was established to recommend candidates and priorities for chemical testing. Where data are adequate, the EPA may regulate the manufacture, processing, use, distribution, or disposal of the chemical. Options range from banning the chemical to labeling requirements, again with demanding, formal rule-making procedures required (Shapiro 1990).

Congress also granted to the EPA the authority to screen new chemicals. The agency must be notified 90 days before manufacture of a new chemical substance, when the manufacturer must supply any available test data to the agency in a Premanufacturing Notice. If the EPA determines that the chemical may pose an unreasonable risk to health or the environment, it may ban or limit manufacture until further information is provided. The requirements here are more easily met than for existing chemicals, and the EPA can act more quickly.

Although the meaning of "unreasonable risk" is not formally defined in the Act, Congress clearly intended some kind of balancing of the risks and the benefits to society of the chemicals in question (Shapiro 1990). TSCA was modified by amendments in 1986, by the Asbestos Hazard Emergency Response Act, and in 1992 by the Residential Lead-Based Paint Hazard Reduction Act. The asbestos legislation required the EPA to develop strategies for inspecting schools for asbestos-containing material and controlling the risk appropriately. The paint hazard legislation called for a variety of actions to reduce public exposure to lead from paint. Such actions include inspection and abatement of lead hazards in low-income housing, disclosure of the risks of lead-based paint prior to the sale of homes built before 1978, and development by the EPA of a training and certification program for lead abatement contractors.

As the case with the other major acts, the implementation of TSCA has not gone smoothly. The EPA encountered resistance from industry in getting the necessary information, had difficulty recruiting sufficient trained personnel for the regulatory tasks, and made very slow progress in achieving TSCA's objectives. The EPA's job was made more difficult than it otherwise might have been by forcing the agency to prove that a chemical was unsafe or posed an unreasonable risk. As a result of these stipulations in the law and the other constraints the agency faced, only a handful of chemicals out of the approximately 85,000 in use had been banned under TSCA. The agency could not even notify the public with information on chemical production and risk because TSCA prohibited the disclosure of confidential business information. In light of this poor record, the GAO called on Congress to revise the Act to give the EPA added authority to obtain such information and to shift more of the burden to industry to demonstrate the safety of chemicals in use; many critics agreed with that recommendation.[27]

After years of unsuccessful efforts to modernize and strengthen the Act, in 2016 Congress approved the Frank R. Lautenberg Chemical Safety for the 21st Century Act, a major revision of TSCA. The new Act was not as strong as some environmentalists preferred, but it did mandate that the EPA evaluate existing chemicals with a new risk-based safety standard, that it do so with clear and enforceable deadlines, with increased transparency for chemical information, and with assurances that the agency would have the budgetary resources to carry out its responsibilities for chemical safety. A list of the first ten chemicals to be studied was released in late 2016.[28]

The Federal Insecticide, Fungicide, and Rodenticide Act

Federal regulation of pesticides is much older than laws dealing with other chemical risks. It dates back to a 1910 Insecticide Act designed to protect consumers from fraudulent products. In 1947 Congress enacted the Federal Insecticide, Fungicide, and Rodenticide Act (FIFRA), authorizing a registration and labeling program, and it gave authority for its implementation to the Department of Agriculture. Concern focused chiefly on the efficacy of pesticides as agricultural chemicals. By the 1960s, following the publication of Rachel Carson's *Silent Spring*, public attention shifted to environmental consequences of pesticide use. Congress amended FIFRA (pronounced "fif rah") in 1964, 1972, and 1978, establishing a new regulatory framework. Jurisdiction over the Act was given to the EPA in 1970. A 1996 amendment discussed later pertains especially to pesticide levels in food.

FIFRA requires that pesticides used commercially within the United States be registered by the EPA. It sets as a criterion for registration that the pesticide not pose "any unreasonable risk to man or the environment, taking into account the economic, social, and environmental costs and benefits of the use" (Shapiro 1990). The law is less stringent than other environmental statutes of the 1970s, and critics assert that the government has given greater weight to economic arguments than to the effects on public health. The EPA is required to balance costs and benefits, with the burden of proof of harm placed on the government if the agency attempts to cancel or suspend registration of an existing pesticide. For a new pesticide, the burden lies on the manufacturer to demonstrate safety. Procedures under the law historically have been cumbersome, however, making regulatory action difficult.

These statutory provisions reflected the still considerable power of the pesticide lobby despite the many gains environmental, health, and farmworker groups have made against the long-influential agricultural subgovernment (Bosso 1987). Because of its origins in the agricultural policy community, FIFRA differs in many respects from other environmental laws. Indeed, environmentalists have referred to it as an "anachronistic statute" that is "riddled with loopholes and industry-oriented provisions." Although reauthorized in 1988 after years of political controversy and legislative stalemate, the Act reflected only modest changes, leading critics to dub it "FIFRA Lite."

The EPA is also required under the Food, Drug, and Cosmetic Act to establish maximum permissible concentrations of pesticides in or on both raw agricultural products (e.g., fresh fruits and vegetables) and processed foods. Those standards are then enforced by the Food and Drug Administration (FDA) and the Department of Agriculture. Until the 1996 amendments, the EPA was governed in part by the Delaney clause in the Act that prohibited any food additive shown to cause cancer in laboratory animals. Of the roughly 400 kinds of pesticides used on food crops, more than 70, including the most commonly used, cause cancer in laboratory animals. In a long-awaited 1993 report, the National Academy of Sciences indicated that children may be at special risk from exposure to trace levels of pesticides from foods as well as from lawn care products and household insect sprays. Representative Henry Waxman (D-Calif.), chair of the Health and the Environment subcommittee in the House, termed the report a "wake-up call to all of us" about the "unnecessary risk from pesticides in food."[29]

Most of the debate in the mid- to late 1990s over FIFRA concerned whether, and in what way, to modify the Delaney clause. To bring the law into conformity with practice and with contemporary views of the relatively minor risks to public health posed by minute pesticide residues in food, the Clinton administration proposed in 1993 a more realistic "negligible risk" standard. It would have allowed no more than one additional case of cancer for every 1 million people. The food and chemical industries supported such an easing of the Delaney policy, but many environmental groups opposed the action.

The impasse continued until 1996, at which point an agreement on pesticide policy emerged rapidly and unexpectedly. Court decisions required the EPA to act aggressively to enforce the Delaney clause barring trace amounts of chemicals in processed foods. The agency would have been forced to begin canceling the use of some common pesticides. Industry fear of such potential and costly EPA action set the stage for a remarkable agreement to support the Food Quality Protection Act of 1996. In addition, Republican lawmakers were eager to vote for an election-year environmental bill after having suffered politically throughout 1995 and 1996 in battles with the Clinton White House over environmental policies. The Act passed both the House and Senate without a single dissenting vote and in record time. It was hailed by both major parties as a key achievement of the otherwise conflict-ridden 104th Congress. The Act essentially reflected proposals made by the Clinton administration in 1994, although without much support at that time by the leading players in pesticide policy.[30]

The Food Quality Protection Act replaced the decades-old Delaney clause, requiring the EPA to use a new uniform "reasonable risk" approach to regulating pesticides used on food, fiber, and other crops. The EPA would set a tolerance level to ensure that people who eat both raw and processed foods face a "reasonable certainty of no harm." Such language is generally interpreted to mean no more than a 1-in-1-million lifetime chance exists that the chemical could cause cancer. The agency was required to review all tolerances within 10 years. The Act also required that special attention be given to the many different ways in which both children and adults are exposed to these chemicals, such as through drinking water, pest-control sprays used in the house, and garden products. Doing so is an enormous challenge given the state of scientific knowledge. Yet it also makes sense to assess all health risks, not just for cancer, and to consider the cumulative risks of exposure to multiple pesticide residues on food, not just a single chemical. The EPA was to take unusual precaution to protect children against such risks, establishing up to a tenfold margin of safety. State agencies generally cannot impose pesticide standards tighter than those of the federal government without petitioning the EPA for permission to do so, but states could refuse to follow an EPA action to relax a standard to below the 1-in-1-million risk level.

In addition to amending the Delaney clause, the new Act amended FIFRA with respect to the EPA's role in registration, or approval, of pesticides. The agency is to establish procedures to ensure that each pesticide registration is reviewed every 15 years. The law gives broader power to the EPA to suspend or change the use of a suspect pesticide immediately through an emergency order; it would have 90 days to follow through by issuing a formal notice of cancellation. The Act also establishes procedures to speed up EPA review of what are called "minor use pesticides" used on many fruits, vegetables, and specialty crops (as distinguished from those used on major crops such as wheat, corn, soybeans, cotton, and rice). Reviews are to take place within one year. Because the EPA has faced long delays in reviewing such registration applications, the Act authorizes the agency to collect additional fees from pesticide registrants to help avoid such delays. The 1996 law also mandates research, demonstration, and education programs to support integrated pest management and other alternatives to pesticide use.

The Comprehensive Environmental Response, Compensation, and Liability Act

Congress enacted the Comprehensive Environmental Response, Compensation, and Liability Act (CERCLA), better known as Superfund, in 1980 and revised it in 1986 with the Superfund Amendments and

Reauthorization Act (SARA). The Act is a partner to RCRA. Whereas RCRA deals with current hazardous waste generation and disposal, Superfund was directed primarily at the thousands of abandoned or uncontrolled hazardous waste sites. Little was known about the number, location, and risks associated with these sites, and existing law was thought to be insufficient to deal with the problem. With Superfund, Congress gave the EPA responsibility to respond to the problem by identifying, assessing, and cleaning up those sites. Where necessary, the EPA could use a special revolving fund (originally $1.6 billion), most of which was to be financed by a tax on manufacturers of petrochemical feedstocks and other organic chemicals and crude oil importers. The Act put both responsibility for the cleanup and financial liability on those who disposed of hazardous wastes at a site, a "polluter pays" policy.

Unhappy with the pace of cleanup and the Reagan administration's lax implementation of Superfund, in 1986, with SARA (pronounced "Sarah"), Congress authorized an additional $8.5 billion for the fund and mandated stringent cleanup standards using the best available technologies. SARA also established an entirely new Title III in the Act, also called the Emergency Planning and Community Right- to-Know Act (EPCRA). It provided for public release of information about chemicals made by, stored in, and released by local businesses, published each year as the Toxics Release Inventory. EPCRA also required the creation of state and local committees to plan for emergency chemical releases (Hadden 1989; Hamilton 2005; Kraft, Stephan, and Abel 2011).

Superfund Provisions and Controversies Superfund gives the EPA authority to identify the parties responsible for inactive or abandoned hazardous waste sites and to force cleanup. It may also cleanup sites itself and seek restitution from the responsible parties. Such actions are governed by complicated "strict, joint, and several liability" provisions of the Act that can be especially burdensome on minor contributing parties. The parties responsible may be sued as a group or individually for all the cleanup costs even if they are not fully at fault. Settlement of Superfund cases, however, often is based on an allocation of liability related to the amount of hazardous substances contributed by each party. The Act's retroactive liability provision also holds companies liable for wastes disposed of legally prior to 1980.

In addition, Superfund requires that sites be identified and ranked according to their priority for cleanup. The EPA and the states nominate sites for a National Priorities List (NPL), and the EPA uses a hazard-ranking system to measure the severity of risks at each site and thus set priorities for cleanup. The rankings do not reflect actual human or environmental exposures but rather potential health and environmental risks as judged by EPA project officers and technical consultants (Dower 1990; Mazmanian and Morell 1992, 31). Only sites listed on the NPL qualify for long-term cleanup under Superfund and for use of the federal dollars associated with the program.

The EPA has evaluated tens of thousands of sites (both government and privately owned) for possible inclusion on the NPL. These sites include pesticide plants, landfills, small industrial sites, rivers and harbors with contaminated sediments, and former nuclear weapons production facilities such as the Hanford Reservation in Washington state, where soil has been poisoned with chemical and radioactive wastes. Although critics often have pointed to the modest number of NPL sites that have been fully cleaned up at any given time (see Chapter 2), defenders of the program, including the EPA itself, have long offered a far more positive assessment (De Saillan 1993; Rahm 1998).

The full process—from identification and preliminary assessment of a site to hazard ranking, listing, remedial design, and remediation itself—is complex and time-consuming. It can take as long as 15 years (some state cleanups take only two or three years), which helps explain the relatively slow pace of actual cleanup. Groundwater cleanup can be especially difficult and costly. Other reasons for the limited progress have included extensive litigation among potentially responsible parties and insurance companies and the enormous difficulty in locating hazardous waste treatment and disposal sites because of community opposition (Hird 1994; Mazmanian and Morell 1992).

Controversy over the Superfund program has centered on the degree of cleanup needed for any given site (and hence the cost). Cleanup costs historically have averaged about $30 million per NPL site, but with wide variability of costs depending on the nature of the risks at the site and the cleanup standard used. In addition, beginning in 1995 Congress chose not to reauthorize the taxes needed to replenish CERCLA's (pronounced "serk la") trust fund. Chemical and oil industry representatives had long sought to end the taxes, which they viewed as unfair to them.

Proposed Reforms Since its reauthorization in 1986, Superfund has in many ways epitomized environmental policy gridlock. Despite the work of numerous special commissions and congressional committees over the years, agreement on reform of the widely criticized Superfund program has proved elusive.

Industry has complained that returning all sites to pristine or "greenfield" conditions is unnecessarily burdensome if such sites are intended for further industrial use, as many are. Business groups also have objected to being forced to clean up trace amounts of chemicals that pose little or no measurable health risk. In contrast, throughout much of the 1990s, environmentalists pressed for uniform standards for all sites nationwide and generally opposed the flexibility that industry sought in these standards. They were more favorably inclined toward industry's position, however, if local communities could be given a significant say in cleanup decisions. Grassroots groups associated with the environmental justice movement actively sought early citizen participation in these decisions to ensure that minority communities were ranked high in priority for cleanup actions.

Although agreement seemed close on most of the key issues, including the allocation of liability for cleanup costs among responsible parties, Congress was unable to renew the program. When the Republicans gained control of the House and Senate following the 1994 elections, polarization on Superfund renewal and most other environmental policies increased. Republicans proposed sweeping reforms of Superfund to reduce liability for the business community and to free responsible parties from litigation, but they failed to gain sufficient support for passage of a renewed law.

In the 1990s, the EPA itself agreed that the program's liability provisions needed to be revamped to reduce the burden on small businesses and to ensure that funds went to cleanup rather than litigation. Indeed, the agency instituted reforms of its own that "significantly changed how the Superfund program operates," making it a "fairer, more effective, and more efficient program," according to former EPA administrator Carol Browner.[31] EPA officials argued that overhauling the Act was no longer necessary and could even erode many of the improvements the agency instituted administratively. Partly as a result, Republicans scaled back their ambitious reform bill, and Democrats similarly began to focus on cleaning up some 500,000 so-called brownfields (contaminated areas) that could be used to bolster economic development in urban areas.

The EPA started to assist cities in redevelopment of such urban industrial land by removing thousands of such sites from possible inclusion under Superfund and by funding demonstration cleanup projects. States also began to adopt laws that eased the threat of liability and adjusted pollution standards for such sites.[32] In early 2002 President Bush signed a bipartisan brownfields bill that authorized $250 million per year for five years to help states clean up and redevelop such sites. The measure also limited the liability of some small businesses, and the EPA would be restrained from seeking additional cleanup of a site if the state certifies it to have been restored.[33]

The EPA under Bush also proposed reforms of the Toxics Release Inventory (TRI) program as one way to reduce the burden on industry in reporting each year on chemicals released to the environment. Despite opposition in Congress, among the public, and even by the EPA's Science Advisory Board, the new TRI Burden Reduction Rule took effect in January 2007. The 2009 TRI report seemed to indicate that it had only a modest effect, but objections continued in Congress, and it ended the rule in 2009 via a provision in that year's budget bill. The Obama EPA applauded the demise of the rule and pledged to "restore the rigorous reporting standards of this vital program" (Kraft, Stephan, and Abel 2011: ch. 7).[34]

In part because of limited federal resources and the rising demand for cleaning up contaminated sites around the nation, the Bush administration called for fundamental changes in the Superfund program. Passage of a broad Superfund reform bill, however, will depend on a shift in the political climate that can bring the various policy actors closer together on this highly contentious program. In the meantime, cleanup activities are proceeding across the nation, making reform of the program appear less urgent than in earlier years.

The Institutional Context of Policy Implementation

As the preceding discussion makes clear, these seven core statutes present the EPA with an astonishingly large and bewildering array of administrative tasks that are essential to meet congressional mandates for environmental protection. It would be truly remarkable if the agency could pull it all off, and especially if it could keep Congress and the multitude of constituency groups happy with the results. That the EPA shares responsibility for implementing these statutes, and about a dozen others, with the states is a mixed blessing that creates supervisory headaches even while it relieves the agency of some of the routine burdens of administration (Rabe 2016; Scheberle 2004).

Critics of regulatory policy often lump all agencies together. Yet they are a highly varied lot, and their individual characteristics must be considered to understand why they operate as they do. The EPA's success or failure in policy implementation is affected by most of the usual factors shaping administrative decision making and by some that are distinctive to the agency (Bryner 1987). Some of these are largely beyond the control of agency officials, such as the intractability of many environmental problems, changing economic conditions and technology, constrained budgetary resources, statutory specifications (e.g., sanctions and incentives provided for inducing compliance), and political judgments made by Congress and the White House. Others are influenced to at least some extent by agency behavior. The administrative and leadership skills of agency officials, for instance, significantly affect staff recruitment and expertise, internal organization and priorities, cooperation elicited from other federal agencies, and political support or opposition from the White House and Congress. Through their policy choices and public outreach efforts, EPA officials can also try to shape the public's attitudes toward environmental issues and the agency's legitimacy and competency in the eyes of important policy actors such as the environmental community, business, and state and local governments.

The EPA's Organization, Budget, and Staff

The EPA's organizational structure, budgetary resources, and staff characteristics are especially important for policy implementation. President Richard Nixon created the agency by executive order on December 2, 1970, following submission of a reorganization plan to Congress. The order transferred most (although not all) of the existing federal environmental programs to the EPA, which was established as an independent executive agency. Its administrator and other top officials are nominated by the president and confirmed by the Senate. Unlike comparable environmental ministries in other Western democracies, the EPA was not created with cabinet rank, and the agency's administrator is the only head of a regulatory agency reporting directly to the president. However, presidents have routinely granted the EPA administrator cabinet status. Proposals to convert the agency into a Department of the Environment, with cabinet status, have languished in Congress, a victim of persistent controversies over environmental policy.

For years, the physical location of the agency in a remote corner of southwest Washington, DC, in two converted apartment buildings had symbolized the EPA's uncertain status in the universe of federal agencies. In 1997, however, the EPA staff began moving into its impressive new headquarters in the palatial Ronald Reagan Building and International Trade Center in the center of the city, not far from the White House. If nothing else, the agency's new surroundings testify to its growing responsibilities and unquestioned importance.

Organizational Structure As shown in Figure 5.1, the EPA's organization reflects its media-specific responsibilities, with separate program offices for air and radiation; water; pesticides, toxic substances, and pollution prevention; and solid waste and emergency response. Each of these program offices has operated independently, even though many studies have recommended that pollution control efforts across the different media (air, water, and land) would be more effective if they were better integrated (Bryner and Duffy 2012; Davies and Mazurek 1998; National Academy of Public Administration 1995).

As discussed below, some of these organizational oddities can be traced to the EPA's origins in 1970 by the presidential order that somewhat awkwardly consolidated programs from agencies scattered across the federal government. Had Congress created the agency through passage of a so-called organic law, we might have seen more policy integration (Rosenbaum 2013a). There have been some modest efforts over time to achieve the same result. For example, the Clinton administration's Common Sense Initiative (CSI) and its other efforts to reinvent environmental regulation included encouragement of cross-media pollution control. The CSI was intended to work with selected industries (e.g., auto manufacturing or computers and electronics) through a consensus approach that engaged various stakeholders to look at all aspects of an industry's actions on a cross-media basis. The idea was to better coordinate rules and regulations, simplify the process, and reduce the cost of compliance. The EPA's formal structure and its administrative culture, however, have been significant obstacles in moving away from the old single-medium approach and conventional regulation (Coglianese and Allen 2004; Fiorino 2006, 2009; Kraft and Scheberle 1998; Rosenbaum 2013a). Time will tell if the agency is able to make the transition, but without congressional willingness to alter the basic statutes that have created the present EPA organizational structure, the change will be difficult.

Office of the Administrator	
Headquarters Offices	**Regional Offices Around the Nation**
Office of Administration and Resources Management	Region 1/Boston
Office of Air and Radiation	Region 2/New York
Office of Chemical Safety and Pollution Prevention	Region 3/Philadelphia
Office of the Chief Financial Officer	Region 4/Atlanta
Office of Enforcement and Compliance Assurance	Region 5/Chicago
Office of Environmental Information	Region 6/Dallas
Office of General Counsel	Region 7/Kansas City
Office of Inspector General	Region 8/Denver
Office of International and Tribal Affairs	Region 9/San Francisco
Office of Research and Development	Region 10/Seattle
Office of Land and Emergency Management	
Office of Water	

FIGURE 5.1 Organizational Structure of the U.S. Environmental Protection Agency

Source: U.S. EPA webpage: www.epa.gov/aboutepa/epa-organization-chart. Accessed January 9, 2017.

As is the case with many federal agencies, much of the EPA's routine policy implementation takes place in its 10 regional offices. Two-thirds of the agency's staff work in those offices or in other facilities outside of Washington, DC, such as scientific laboratories, where they work closely with state governments (Rabe 2016; Scheberle 2004). Rule-making and policy development, however, remain the responsibility of the headquarters staff.

Resources and Staff In its first full year in 1971, the EPA had a staff of about 5,700 and a total budget of $4.2 billion (P. Portney 2000). It has grown much larger over time, as have its responsibilities. It is now far and away the largest federal regulatory agency. In 2016 the staff stood at 15,376, down significantly from its peak of about 18,000 in the late 1990s. Its overall budget was at about $8.1 billion, down from a peak of $10.3 billion in 2010.[35] The agency's operating budget (the funds used to run agency programs) has been between $3 and $4 billion annually in recent years. In constant dollars, however, the agency's operating budget was nearly flat over the 36-year period of 1980 to 2016 despite the many new responsibilities given to it by Congress during that time (Conant and Balint 2016; Vig and Kraft 2016). After substantial declines in its resources during the Bush administration, the EPA enjoyed a substantial increase early in the Obama administration, only to fall victim to the broader concern about federal spending and see its budget fall back to its previous level by 2016. In early 2017, the Donald Trump administration signaled its intention to cut the EPA's budget and staff by up to 30 percent, but the final decision will be up to Congress. Whatever the future brings in the administration of President Donald Trump and thereafter, the historical budget picture tells us that for years the EPA has fallen well short of the resources needed to implement environmental protection policies successfully.

Not surprisingly, the EPA tends to recruit a staff strongly committed to its mission. Yet that staff comes with a diversity of professional training and problem-solving orientations that can breed conflict over implementation strategies (Landy, Roberts, and Thomas 1994). The staff consists predominantly of scientists and engineers who are assisted by a multitude of lawyers, economists, and policy analysts. By one count in the late 1990s, the agency employed some 4,000 scientists, 2,700 engineers, and more than 1,000 lawyers. Among its political appointees at the policymaking level in the agency, a background in law is the most common; most of the EPA administrators have held law degrees (Morgenstern 1999). With the notable exception of Anne Burford in the early 1980s, the EPA has attracted talented and respected administrators despite controversies over their policy decisions.

Science at the EPA As might be expected for an agency dealing with demanding technical problems, the EPA has developed a reputation for expertise even while the quality of its science often has been disparaged by its critics. The EPA also makes extensive use of outside scientists, especially through its Science Advisory Board (SAB), created by Congress in 1978. The SAB advises the agency as requested through a series of specialized committees; conducts an annual review of the scientific adequacy of EPA's research and development (R&D) work; and reviews the technical quality of proposed criteria documents, standards, and regulations.

Numerous studies in previous years found the agency to be inadequately staffed and its scientific work insufficient. They have also faulted the EPA for lacking a strategy for long-term environmental research essential to its mission (Carnegie Commission 1992, 1993; Powell 1999). Equally important is improving the capacity of EPA administrators to apply uncertain environmental science to policy decisions. Particularly during the

Bush administration, the use or nonuse of science in setting environmental quality standards became a prominent issue. As discussed in Chapter 1, President Obama promised to restore the role of science in environmental policy and to increase funding for scientific research (Ascher, Steelman, and Healy 2010; Keller 2009; Rosenbaum 2013a). Support for environmental research has recovered from its low point in the Reagan administration, but it remains a small portion of the federal R&D budget.[36]

Working with the States

Beyond its relation with other federal agencies, the EPA has developed an elaborate program, both formal and informal, to share environmental protection activities with the 50 states (Rabe 2016). Many of the states have program requirements that exceed the minimum federal standards, and states also operate many of their own programs that are separate from federally mandated activities. The states are also responsible for most of the enforcement actions taken under federal environmental laws for delegated programs.

When the states operate their programs under authority delegated to them by the EPA, they are supervised in part by the agency's Washington headquarters, but chiefly by the regional offices. Those offices keep in close contact with state officials and other environmental policy actors at the state and local levels. Among the most important of those local actors are citizen activists and environmental watchdog groups who monitor and review key implementation actions such as the issuance of air and water pollution permits and new regulations.

In some of the more environmentally progressive states, a kind of symbiotic relationship has developed between the state agency and citizen groups. Agency employees need the citizen groups to bring sufficient political pressure on sometimes reluctant state governments to push for more aggressive implementation. Citizen groups also turn to the state agencies (and the EPA itself) for financial assistance through various grant programs designed to promote public education and pollution prevention initiatives. Citizens may serve as well on local, regional, and state stakeholder advisory committees on which both the states and the EPA increasingly rely. In many states, business and industry groups may have the dominant influence in such decision-making processes.

In addition to the delegated programs, the federal government offers a variety of voluntary programs to the states, generally by making available funds to establish state programs to deal with particular environmental problems. The Indoor Radon Abatement Act, for example, encourages states to adopt radon programs and to inform the public about health risks related to radon. In a third type of action, states may be under direct federal mandates to establish a program; examples are a State Implementation Plan under the Clean Air Act and Wellhead Protection Programs under the Safe Drinking Water Act (Scheberle 1998).

As might be expected in such a system of intricate and politically delicate federal–state relations, the respective roles of the federal government and the states have varied significantly over time. During the 1980s states often complained about late issuance of regulations, inflexibility in the federal grant conditions and mandatory policy guidelines that wasted state resources, stifled initiative, and added unnecessary costs (Kraft, Clary, and Tobin 1988). Similar concerns were commonly voiced during the 1990s, 2000s, and 2010s, although generally relationships between the EPA and the states are much better today. Some experiments undertaken during the Clinton administration, such as the CSI noted earlier, Project XL, and the National Environmental Performance Partnership System (NEPPS), made some difference even if they fell short of the stated goal of finding "cleaner, cheaper, smarter" ways to reduce or prevent pollution in cooperation with the states (Durant, Fiorino, and O'Leary 2017; Fiorino 2006; Rabe 2016; Scheberle 2004, 2013).

Even if some of the recent efforts to improve federal–state relations and local environmental action have yet to prove themselves, there is reason to be optimistic about the future role of the states and also of local governments. Many states, such as California, Minnesota, Oregon, Washington, and New York, have demonstrated a strong commitment to environmental protection goals. As discussed in Chapter 3, hundreds of highly innovative state, local, and regional policy initiatives on pollution prevention, use of economic incentives, and public-disclosure mandates also testify to the potential for innovation at these levels of government (John 1994; Klyza and Sousa 2013; Mazmanian and Kraft 2009; Rabe 2016). At the same time, caution is warranted because some states and localities are likely to lack either the commitment to such environmental quality goals or the resources to put programs into effect. In addition there is the challenge of dealing with transboundary pollution (where pollutants move across state and national boundaries), the need to ensure that local economic and other interest groups do not exert undue pressure on state governments to weaken environmental protection, and the reality that states and localities will continue to depend on federal research and technical support that cannot be duplicated at the state level.

Political Support and Opposition

All the factors discussed here affect the EPA's ability to perform its many statutory tasks. Both political support for the agency and opposition to it are equally important. Over time, the EPA has benefited from strong support for environmental protection goals in Congress (most notably among Democrats), among the public at large, and among the well-organized environmental community. That support has allowed it to fend off critics and for the most part to prevent weakening of its statutory authority. Members of Congress consider the EPA, like other federal regulatory agencies, to be a creature of their own making, and they keep close watch over its operation. They also defend it from presidents critical of its mission, as they did during the 1980s, although they frequently engage in EPA bureau-bashing to score political points about burdensome regulations. Congress may grant or withhold administrative discretion to the EPA depending on the prevailing trust of the agency's leadership and confidence in the president. As it demonstrated with its reauthorization of RCRA in 1984 and with the Clean Air Act in 1990, Congress may choose to specify environmental standards and deadlines in great detail so as to compel the EPA to do what it wants (Bryner 1995; Halley 1994; Kraft 2013a, 2016).

One or both houses of Congress also can be highly critical of an EPA when distrust runs high. For example, in 2013 Republicans in the Senate tried to block President Obama's nomination of Gina McCarthy as his second EPA administrator as part of a larger effort to pressure the agency to release certain information used to support its regulatory activities. Her confirmation vote was held up for more than four months, the longest such delay in the agency's history.[37] In July 2013, a House Appropriations subcommittee voted to cut the EPA's budget by an astonishing 34 percent and eliminate all funding for greenhouse gas regulations that the Obama White House had announced a month earlier. The proposal, with virtually no chance of success, was yet another signal that House Republicans remained deeply dissatisfied with EPA's rule-making actions.[38]

By 2016, the EPA faced even sharper criticism from Congress and from Republican presidential candidates in what seemed to be an ever-escalating partisan division over the agency, including promises by critics such as Donald Trump to drastically cut its budget and responsibilities and shift many of its duties to the states. Trump's nominee to lead the agency, Scott Pruitt, Oklahoma's attorney general, a long-time critic of the EPA and a strong supporter of the fossil fuel industry, appeared to share such views.[39]

The critics of EPA decision making have not been without considerable political clout over the past several decades. Industry, state and local governments concerned about the cost of environmental protection, and conservative groups opposed to government regulation have found receptive ears in Congress among both Democrats and Republicans (Kamieniecki 2006; Kraft and Kamieniecki 2007). In addition, since the EPA's creation, presidents have taken a keen interest in its activities, and each has devised some mechanism that allows close White House supervision of the agency's regulatory program (Harris and Milkis 1996; Shanley 1992; Vig 2016).

The EPA has at best a mixed record of success, which reflects both the scope and complexity of the environmental problems it addresses and its organizational features. After a period of institutional growth and development in the 1970s, the agency suffered severe budget and personnel cuts in the early to mid-1980s, which took a toll on staff morale. Since then, the EPA has struggled to redefine its mission, improve its capabilities for risk assessment and environmental management, and cope with the enormously difficult tasks given to it by Congress.

Many students of environmental policy are convinced that the agency still has a long way to go to improve its performance (Davies and Mazurek 1998; Fiorino 2006, 2009; Klyza and Sousa 2013; Press 2015; Rosenbaum 2013a). If its responsibilities continue to exceed the resources provided to it, and if the agency and Congress are unable to institute much-needed reforms, it will likely disappoint the environmental community as well as the regulated parties. A review of environmental rule-making and enforcement helps illuminate some of the many challenges the agency faces in implementing environmental policy in the twenty-first century.

Setting Environmental Standards

Under the command-and-control, or direct regulation, approach that prevails in environmental policy today, implementation involves the setting and enforcing of environmental standards. The process involves a number of distinct scientific, analytic, and political tasks that cut across the different policy areas discussed earlier. These tasks include the determination of overall environmental policy goals and objectives; the setting of environmental quality criteria, quality standards, and emissions standards; and the enforcement of the standards through the various incentives and sanctions provided in the statutes. Table 5.2 summarizes these components of command-and-control regulation, which are discussed in detail later.

Environmental Goals and Objectives

Environmental policy goals and objectives are set by elected public officials, especially Congress, and reflect their conception of how environmental quality is to be reconciled with other social and economic values. Goals and objectives historically have been general rather than specific (e.g., "fishable and swimmable waters" under the CWA). They also have been highly ambitious, especially in light of available technologies and resources. They have emphasized important symbolic values and emotionally charged images (e.g., clean air, clean water, public health, safe drinking water) to maintain public support, even when the statutory language has embodied inevitable compromises over competing values and priorities. Congress grants authority to the EPA to fill in the details by providing for administrative discretion in developing rules and regulations (Bryner 1987, 1995; Furlong 2007; Kerwin and Furlong 2011; Rinfret and Furlong 2013). By the 1980s, however, as we saw earlier, Congress grew impatient with the EPA and set highly specific goals and objectives and tighter deadlines, often with hammer clauses meant greatly to reduce agency discretion. Nonetheless, Congress is rarely clear in establishing priorities among the environmental policy goals it sets for the EPA and other agencies. It seems content to say "do it all" even when it fails to allocate the funds necessary for the job (National Academy of Public Administration 1995, 2000). Of course, the goals and

TABLE 5.2 Steps involved in command-and-control environmental regulation

Steps in the process	Activities
Establish environmental goals and objectives	Sets general policy goals and objectives. Usually a legislative decision that balances environmental quality goals against social and economic considerations. Grants power to administrative agency to develop necessary rules and regulations.
Determine environmental quality criteria	Uses experimental and public health data as well as modeling exercises to establish the relationship between pollution and health or ecological effects. Essentially requires health and ecological risk assessments, largely technical decisions.
Set environmental quality standards	Determines the level of pollution that is acceptable in light of health and ecological effects and other considerations as allowed by law (such as economic costs). Quality standards reflect the maximum amount of pollution deemed to be socially tolerable. They are the result of an agency risk evaluation and reflect a policy judgment as well as technical analysis.
Set emissions standards	Sets a maximum amount of pollutants that individual sources such as power plants, manufacturing facilities, or automobiles, buses, and trucks are allowed to release without exceeding the capacity of the environment as identified in the quality standards. Such agency decisions reflect a judgment about environmental science, technology, public health, and, as permitted, economic effects of regulation.
Enforce the standards and other requirements	Uses the methods as specified in the pertinent statute to monitor compliance with environmental quality and emissions standards and to enforce legal requirements. Normally penalties or sanctions exist for noncompliance, and they are imposed through legal and administrative mechanisms spelled out in the law. Most compliance is voluntary or achieved through negotiation with the regulated parties.

objectives given to the EPA under specific statutes also reflect the often conflicting perspectives of environmentalists, their adversaries in industry, and a multiplicity of technical and scientific interests that weigh in on what the nation should do about a given environmental challenge, from air pollution and pesticides to toxic chemicals and drinking water. As discussed earlier, the EPA has no statutory charter or organic law that defines its mission and explicitly sets out its policy objectives and some sense of priority among them. That omission is a major liability, because the agency administers about a dozen major environmental statutes adopted at different times by different congressional committees for different reasons, but without any clear sense of priorities among those laws and what they call for the agency to do; an agency charter might have helped in that regard.[40]

The EPA also is not a comprehensive environmental agency, and it would not be even if it were made into a cabinet department. That is because significant environmental and natural resource responsibilities have been given to other agencies scattered across the executive branch, and the EPA cannot easily work with them in implementing its laws; for example, the EPA and the Department of Energy have clashed frequently over cleanup of contaminated federal facilities on the Superfund's NPL, among other issues. These deficiencies make the EPA more vulnerable than other agencies to short-term forces such as changes in public opinion, shifting legislative majorities, and varying presidential agendas. It also complicates the job of setting agency priorities and allocating scarce resources without congressional specifications about which program should take precedence.

Environmental Quality Criteria

Unlike the political process that sets broad environmental policy goals and objectives, environmental quality criteria lie chiefly in the scientific realm. They spell out what kinds of pollutants are associated with adverse health or environmental effects. In making such determinations, the EPA and other agencies such as the FDA and Occupational Safety and Health Administration (OSHA) draw from experimental and epidemiological studies using health data statistics as well as modeling exercises both from within and outside of government. Setting environmental criteria requires some kind of risk assessment to answer key questions. What is the relationship between pollution and health? For example, how do fine particulates emitted from power plants and other sources reach people, and what effects do they have when they do? How might hazardous waste sites release certain chemicals, and how might they affect public health? How do toxic chemicals in stream and lake sediments affect the functioning of ecosystems? At what level of contamination for chemicals such as PCBs or dioxin can we detect either human health or ecosystem effects, and is there a "safe" level that does not require intervention? Studies of such relationships eventually allow government agencies to set environmental protection criteria.

Health Risk Assessment Because these determinations set the stage for regulatory action, risk assessment has been at the center of disputes over environmental protection policy for over three decades. Scientific controversies abound over the most appropriate models, assumptions, and measurements even in areas in which there has been extensive experience with these methods, such as testing potential carcinogens (Andrews 2006b, 2016; Rushefsky 1986). No one approach to conducting assessments can completely resolve these arguments.

Health risk assessments normally involve a series of analytic procedures: identifying a given hazard, determining whether and how exposure to it can have adverse health effects, determining how many people (and which groups of people) are likely to be exposed to the substance, and describing the overall health risk, such as the increased chances of developing cancer or respiratory illness.[41] None of these activities is easy, and a good deal of uncertainty characterizes the whole process. At each step, myriad scientific and policy judgments are required to determine which methods to use and how to infer human health risk from limited epidemiological evidence or data drawn from animal exposures. The data gathering itself is complex, time-consuming, and expensive, and the potential for misinterpretation is always present.

A major EPA study of dioxin released in 1994 in draft form illustrated all these problems, and it has been extensively debated since then, much as has the EPA's study of the effects of secondhand smoke discussed in Chapter 2. In the case of dioxin, a family of persistent bioaccumulative toxic chemicals that share a similar chemical structure and toxicity, the EPA concluded that it leads to "worrisome" health problems. These problems included an increased likelihood of cancer, damage to reproductive functions, stunted fetal growth, and weakened immune systems, even at extremely low exposure levels. Based on those findings, the EPA was prepared to take steps to reduce exposure to the chemical. The dioxin risk assessment took three years to complete, involved about 100 scientists within and outside of government, and ran to some 2,000 pages.[42] In late 2000, after six years of scientific debate, reanalysis of the data, and redrafting of the conclusions, an outside group of scientists convened by the EPA's Science Advisory Board concluded that the massive report was "by and large a very fair and balanced description" of health risks.[43] Although not very visible to the public, such exhaustive analysis and extended regulatory decision making is by no means uncommon.

Risk assessments of this kind have tended to concentrate on individual pollutants and on cancer risks, but such an approach is not sufficient to detect health risks. Synergistic or interactive effects of multiple pollutants are also important, but they are hard to determine, as are long-term risks of exposure. Moreover, less adequate information is available about a host of health concerns other than cancer, such as the effects of environmental exposure on nervous systems, reproduction, and immune systems. Many have argued persuasively that new approaches are needed. A major study in 1997, for example, called for a more comprehensive effort to examine multiple contaminants and sources of exposure as well as the value perspectives of diverse stakeholders (Presidential/Congressional Commission on Risk Assessment and Risk Management 1997). The EPA does consider what it calls "aggregate and cumulative" exposure to toxic chemicals, and it has a range of tools and guidelines that it provides to community groups and others who seek such an assessment, particularly in regard to questions of environmental justice concerns.[44]

Ecological Risk Assessment   Much of the debate over risk assessment has focused on health risks. Increasingly, the concepts are being extended to ecological risks (U.S. EPA 1992b). Because knowledge of ecosystem functioning is even less well developed than knowledge of how pollutants affect public health, the nation needs to ensure that environmental science research can address such questions. Whether the issue is the effects of toxic chemicals on the nation's surface water quality, the effects of acid precipitation on aquatic ecosystems, or the probability of climate change related to the buildup of greenhouse gases, regulatory decisions depend critically on improving environmental science and bringing it to bear more effectively on policy decisions (Ascher, Steelman, and Healy 2010; Carnegie Commission 1993; Keller 2009).

Setting Quality Standards

After risk assessments permit at least tentative answers to the question of how pollutants affect health and the environment, the EPA and other agencies have to determine the tolerable level of contamination based on the defined criteria. These levels are called "environmental quality standards." Setting them involves not only risk assessment but risk evaluation. The latter is a policy judgment about how much risk is acceptable to society or to the particular community or groups at risk, including sensitive populations (such as children, pregnant women, or the elderly) and disadvantaged or minority groups. For example, what is the maximum level of ground-level ozone acceptable in light of its adverse health effects? What is the permissible level of lead or arsenic in drinking water? What level of pesticide residue on food is tolerable? For years, critics have urged the EPA and other agencies to distinguish clearly between the scientific basis of such choices and their policy judgments and to educate the public and policymakers on the issues. To illustrate how environmental quality criteria and standards are developed, Table 5.3 lists the major effects, primarily health effects, of the six major ambient air pollutants regulated under the Clean Air Act. Table 5.4 indicates the quality standards, the NAAQS, for the same six pollutants.

A revealing example of the mix of science and politics in environmental quality standards concerns the setting of drinking water quality standards for arsenic. The Clinton administration had proposed a new rule that would have set the acceptable level at 10 parts per billion beginning in 2006, an 80 percent reduction over prevailing U.S. standards but identical to the standards of the European Union and the World Health Organization. The mining industry and some municipalities had lobbied hard for a weaker

TABLE 5.3 Effects of ambient air pollutants regulated by the Clean Air Act

Pollutants	Effects
Carbon monoxide	Impairs the blood's ability to carry oxygen to the body's organs and tissues; can damage cardiovascular system, impair vision, reduce work capacity, and reduce learning ability.
Nitrogen dioxide	Can irritate the lungs and lower resistance to respiratory infections such as influenza. Long-term exposure can increase acute respiratory disease in children. Also a precursor to both ozone and acid precipitation.
Ozone	Repeated exposure can cause respiratory infection and lung inflammation, aggravate preexisting respiratory diseases such as asthma, and cause premature aging of the lungs. Short-term exposure may decrease lung function, cause eye irritation and nasal congestion, and reduce resistance to infection. May also damage trees and crops.
Lead	Accumulates in the blood, bones, and soft tissues and can adversely affect the kidneys, liver, nervous system, and other organs. Can cause seizures, mental retardation, and behavioral disorders. Most seriously affects fetuses and children; may be a factor in high blood pressure and heart disease in adults.
Particulate matter	May cause eye and throat irritation, bronchitis, lung damage, decreased lung function, and cancer. Such effects are more pronounced among sensitive groups, including children, the elderly, and those with cardiopulmonary disease such as asthma. Most serious health risks are related to fine particulates (PM-2.5). May also decrease visibility and cause soiling and materials damage.
Sulfur dioxide	Affects breathing and respiratory illness and may alter the defenses of the lungs and aggravate existing cardiovascular disease. Effects are greatest for asthmatics, children, and the elderly. Also a precursor of acid precipitation.

Source: U.S. Environmental Protection Agency, Office of Air and Radiation, *National Air Quality: Status and Trends through 2015*, and previous annual reports. Available at: www.epa.gov/air-trends.

TABLE 5.4 National ambient air quality standards in effect in 2016

Pollutant	Standard value	Standard type
Carbon monoxide (CO)		
8-hour average	9 ppm (10 mg/m³)	Primary
1-hour average	35 ppm (40 mg/m³)	Primary
Nitrogen dioxide (NO2)		
Annual mean	0.053 ppm (100 µg/m³)	Primary and secondary
Ozone (O₃)		
8-hour average	0.070 ppm	Primary and secondary
Lead (Pb)		
Quarterly average	0.15 µg/m³	Primary and secondary
Particulate matter less than 10 micrometers (PM-10)		
24-hour average	150 µg/m³	Primary and secondary
Particulate matter less than 2.5 micrometers (PM-2.5)		
Annual mean	15 µg/m³	Primary and secondary
24-hour average	35 µg/m³	Primary and secondary
Sulfur dioxide (SO₂)		
1-hour average	0.075 ppm	Primary
3-hour average	0.50 ppm	Secondary

Source: U.S. Environmental Protection Agency, Office of Air and Radiation: www.epa.gov/criteria-air-pollutants/naaqs-table (accessed October 5, 2016). The Clean Air Act established two kinds of air quality standards. Primary standards set limits designed to protect public health, which includes the health of sensitive populations such as asthmatics, children, and the elderly. Secondary standards set limits designed to protect public welfare, which includes protection against decreased visibility, damage to animals, crops, vegetation, and buildings. The table lists the National Ambient Air Quality Standards (NAAQS) set by the EPA for six principal pollutants, which are called criteria pollutants. The units of measure for the standards are parts per million (ppm) by volume, milligrams per cubic meter of air (mg/m3), and micrograms per cubic meter of air (µg/m3).

standard out of concern for the costs of compliance. In March 2001 the Bush EPA announced it would withdraw the Clinton rule on the grounds that it was not supported by scientific research; that decision was widely condemned as inappropriate, and it caused significant political harm to a Bush White House eager to demonstrate its environmental protection credentials. Six months later, a National Academy of Sciences panel, asked to update an earlier report on arsenic in drinking water, concluded that, if anything, the Clinton administration had underestimated the risk of cancer. The Bush EPA then decided to leave the Clinton standards in place (Andrews 2006b).

These crucial decisions about acceptable risk levels are never easy to make, even if some analytic tools are available to estimate the public's general risk preferences or tolerances or whether the public is able to participate directly in the process. Whatever the basis for decisions, the consequences are important. If environmental and health risks are exaggerated and if unnecessary or excessive regulations are imposed, the nation (or state or community) pays a price in added costs of compliance and possibly wasteful diversion of economic resources. If, however, risks are ignored or underestimated, we may fail to protect human health and environmental quality sufficiently, and as a result, severe or irreversible damage may occur.

As discussed earlier, risk-based priority-setting has become a kind of mantra in commentary on reform of environmental policy. The EPA's 1990 study *Reducing Risk* set the tone for this ongoing debate, which is now heard at the state level as well. The EPA has tried to help the states identify and respond to their most pressing environmental risks, recognizing that they lack the financial resources to do everything required by the welter of federal environmental statutes (Davies 1996). If the comparative-risk strategy is to work, methodologies for both human health and ecological risk assessments will need improvement, as will our capacity to evaluate scientific findings and to ensure they are integrated with policy judgments. Risk assessments alone cannot determine policy. They also should not replace careful judgment by scientists, regulators, and the public about proper levels of safety, trade-offs between risks and benefits, or priorities for regulatory efforts. They can, however, bring much-needed information to participants in those decisions.

Emissions Standards

Emissions standards follow from the environmental quality standards. They regulate what individual sources (e.g., factories, refineries, automobiles, and wastewater treatment plants) are allowed to emit into the air, water, or land without exceeding the overall capacity of the environment reflected in the quality standards. In most cases, decisions on air and water permits are made by state agencies using federal standards and guidelines. Such agency decisions reflect judgment about environmental science, public health, available emission control technologies, and, where permitted, economic repercussions of regulatory decisions.

Balancing Statutory Goals and Costs

The costs of environmental regulation are high enough that most of the decisions described here have become intensely controversial, whether the issue is automobile emissions standards or water quality criteria. Consider the following case.

In late March 2013, the EPA issued new standards for cars and gasoline to be phased in between 2017 and 2025. In developing the proposed rule, the EPA staff met with a variety of stakeholder groups. In this case, these included representatives from the automobile industry and the oil and gas industry, and also environmental, consumer, and public health organizations.

The new rules require oil refiners to remove additional sulfur from gasoline, and the agency also expected automobile manufacturers to install improved pollution control technologies that can work only with that reduction in sulfur, which otherwise could adversely affect the catalytic converters that remove pollutants from the car's exhaust. The car makers approved of the changes in part so that all 50 states would have the same requirements. The new rules essentially duplicated those already in effect in California, and also in Europe, Japan, and South Korea. Objections came from the oil refiners, who argued that the EPA's calculations of the costs were too low.

The EPA argued that the new rules would "significantly reduce harmful pollution, prevent thousands of premature deaths and illnesses, while also enabling efficiency improvements in the cars and trucks we drive." The agency said that it used a "proven systems approach that addresses vehicle and fuels as an integrated system," and thus would enable "the greatest pollution reduction at the lowest cost."

Specifically, the agency concluded that the new standards for reducing the level of sulfur in gasoline would "slash emissions of a range of harmful pollutants" and maintain "science-based national ambient air quality standards to protect public health" while also providing the flexibility to aid small refineries, including giving them additional time for compliance. The EPA said that the new rules would "prevent up to 2,400 premature deaths, 23,000 cases of respiratory ailments in children, 3,200 hospital admissions and asthma-related emergency room visits, and 1.8 million lost school days, work days and days when activities would be restricted due to pollution." The agency calculated that by the year 2030, when the rule would be fully implemented, these health-related benefits would be between $8 and $23 billion each year while the costs would be $3.4 billion per year.

In short, the benefits of the new rules would be about two to seven times the estimated costs if the EPA's estimates are correct. The oil industry, represented by the American Petroleum Institute and the American Fuel and

Petrochemical Manufacturers, believed the costs would have been much higher. As is typically the case in these kinds of complex regulatory processes, the EPA must receive and respond to public comments before it can finalize the rules, and both the auto industry and the oil refiners are likely to present data to reinforce their arguments. Public health and environmental groups will weigh in as well. Following the public comment period, the EPA will issue the final rules, which are subject to possible challenge in court.[45]

As this case illustrates, environmental protection can be costly, but estimates of the costs and benefits of environmental rules are not easy to make. EPA economists can and do estimate the costs of compliance with environmental regulations, and they typically find that benefits to public health exceed the costs to industry to comply with the rules. The annual reports from the Office of Information and Regulatory Affairs (OIRA) discussed later confirm these calculations. Industry groups typically cite high costs of compliance, and yet the measurement of such costs is not as simple and straightforward as industry or state and local governments often suggest. The cost of complying with environmental regulations depends on technological developments that cannot always be foreseen accurately. Moreover, annual costs may well decline over time as manufacturing and other industrial processes change. For obvious political reasons, industry tends to use estimates at the high end of the range to argue against additional regulations, whereas environmental groups and government agencies invariably use lower estimates.

Adopting and Enforcing Regulations

Implementing statutes requires more than setting environmental standards. Agency officials must interpret often vague statutory language and develop the means to achieve policy goals. That typically requires drafting guidelines and regulations that are legally binding. The 1990 Clean Air Act, for example, was more than 400 pages long and required the EPA to write hundreds of new regulations, 55 of them within two years of enactment. It is scarcely surprising that the EPA falls behind in meeting such expectations and is often compelled to act when environmentalists and others file suit in federal court. Such suits have an important drawback. Judicial decisions can force the agency to concentrate on the disputed issues to the detriment of other statutory provisions (Melnick 1983; O'Leary 1993).

Administrative Rule-Making

The federal Administrative Procedure Act, specifications in individual environmental statutes, and judicial rulings all have sought to make the exercise of administrative discretion transparent, or visible, and accountable to the public. In addition, agencies are not to engage in arbitrary and capricious actions. That is, they must base their decisions on the record or docket for any given issue and must stay within the guidelines for such decisions that are set out in the statutes or pertinent judicial rulings. Such stipulations, however, cannot guarantee well-designed or effective regulations, only adherence to the law. They also provide only minimal assurance of agency responsiveness to public preferences, because the administrative process cannot easily accommodate full and regular participation by environmental and citizen groups, nor by the general public. Whether at the federal or state level, it is not surprising that the access to administrative agencies afforded to competing interest groups and their influence on decision making is not equal. By any measure, industry groups have a major advantage over environmentalists, and particularly in Republican administrations that ideologically tend to be more probusiness than Democratic administrations, although this does not mean that business groups always win the policy battles (Furlong 2007; Kamieniecki 2006; Kraft and Kamieniecki 2007).

The administrative rule-making process is straightforward in its basic outline, even if its execution is not. When agencies such as the EPA determine that a rule is needed, they may publish an advance notice of proposed rulemaking in the *Federal Register* to signal their intent to consider a rule (although this is unusual). They assemble the requisite scientific, economic, and other data and then begin formulation of a draft rule or regulation. When a draft is ready, another published notice in the *Federal Register* invites public comment. The agency submits the draft rule to the White House Office of Management and Budget (OMB) for review and clearance, which at times has been done prior to public notice. In late 2002 the OMB announced that, as an element in the new "E-Government Initiatives" in the Bush administration, it would launch a centralized Web portal that would allow any citizen to view and submit comments on federal regulations (www.regulation.gov).

All presidents since Ronald Reagan's in the 1980s have relied on centralized White House oversight of agency rule-making as part of their broader effort to control the federal bureaucracy. EPA rules have been a major target of the reviews (National Academy of Public Administration 1987; Shanley 1992; Vig 2016). These reviews take place in the Office of Information and Regulatory Affairs (OIRA), which is part of the White House Office of Management and Budget. The procedures require that the EPA and other agencies conduct economic analyses that compare the benefits and costs of proposed regulations, such as the Clean Power Plan discussed at the chapter's opening.

Critics have long faulted these procedures in some administrations on many grounds, including closed decision making, poor documentation, bias in discussing issues with regulated interests, lack of technical expertise, and regulatory delays (Berry and Portney 1995; Cooper and West 1988; Eads and Fix 1984). Sometimes business and industry gained short-term regulatory relief as a consequence (Furlong 1995a; Vig 2016), but few laws were changed, and many of their deficiencies continue to this day.[46] If President Donald Trump is to reverse many of the Obama environmental initiatives, such as the Clean Power Plan, or change direction on EPA's many environmental regulations, his administration would likely do that through the OIRA review process, in addition to working with Congress to cut funding for implementing specific policies—for example, through commonly used appropriations riders (Kraft 2016). But there are many obstacles to changing established rules and regulations, so the process may well not be either as fast or as successful as the new administration anticipates.[47]

After consideration of public comments, data, studies, and other material submitted to the agency by interested parties, including any recommendations by OIRA, the agency publishes the final rule in the *Federal Register*, accompanied by agency responses to the major issues raised during the public participation stage (Bryner 1987; Furlong 1995b; Rinfret and Furlong 2013). A roughly analogous process exists for state agency rule-making.

The EPA and other agencies have to defend their work carefully, and they assemble the evidence in an elaborate rule-making docket. This includes agency planning documents and studies, legal memoranda, advisory committee reports, public comments, summaries of meetings and hearings, scientific and economic analyses, the proposed and final rules, and more. The entire rule-making process can easily take three or more years to complete, not counting the time needed for judicial or congressional review (Furlong 1995b; Kerwin and Furlong 2011).

These complicated processes are difficult to avoid, however, given the nation's dedication to due process and protection of individual rights. The high stakes involved in environmental policy compound the problem, as numerous parties seek to participate in and influence the administrative process. The larger and better-financed trade associations, industries, and other organizations employ an army of law firms and technical consultants to help them make their case (Haeder and Yackee 2015; Kamieniecki 2006). Although environmental and citizen groups are rarely as powerful as business interests (Furlong 1997), they often have significant opportunities to shape the outcome, especially at state and local levels (Duffy 2003; Kraft and Kamieniecki 2007; K. Portney 2013). Even at the federal level, however, the EPA has tried to encourage citizen participation in its decision making through a variety of innovative approaches (Beierle and Cayford 2002; Daley 2013).

Participants in rule-making bring with them diverse and conflicting perspectives on environmental problems (scientific, legal, administrative, economic, and political), which are inherently difficult to reconcile. Unfortunately, the adversarial U.S. political system encourages seemingly endless disputation among them, particularly where procedural delays benefit one or more parties. The disappointed losers have additional options, including suing the agency and making their case again in the federal courts.

Over the past several decades, EPA officials have asserted that some 80 percent of major EPA regulations have been contested in court because of their significance and economic impact. Others have disputed those figures, saying they are far too high. In recent years, the EPA has been sued about 100 times a year by environmental or business groups or the states. The result can be protracted legal proceedings, long delays in implementing the laws, and excessive costs.

These effects have motivated critics to seek "regulatory reform" measures in Congress that would further constrain the EPA's regulatory process by requiring additional economic and other studies to support proposed regulations (Andrews 2006b; Freeman 2006). Partly in response to congressional criticism, the Clinton administration in 1995 initiated its "regulatory reinvention" programs to foster a more cooperative, consensus-building approach to environmental regulation (Fiorino 2006). Similarly, EPA administrators have experimented over a longer period with a form of consensus-based rule-making called "regulatory negotiation" (Weber 1998, 1999). The idea is that the various stakeholders will come together and work cooperatively to negotiate and agree on regulatory changes in a way that will limit subsequent legal challenges. The record on such negotiations is mixed. One study of the EPA's use of negotiated rule-making, in fact, concluded that not only did it not save the agency any time, but it actually stimulated more, not less, litigation. The reasons for these outcomes seem to be that such negotiation added new sources of conflict and raised expectations about the benefits of participation in rule-making that could not be met (Bennear and Coglianese 2013; Coglianese 1997; see also O'Leary and Bingham 2003).

Enforcement and Compliance

Environmental policies mean little without monitoring of regulated parties and enforcement actions that can ensure a high level of compliance. Yet one of the acknowledged weaknesses of the command-and-control approach to environmental regulation is that such close monitoring of compliance is rare because of the difficulty of the task and the lack of sufficient resources (Davies and Mazurek 1998; Press 2015; Russell 1990). The sheer number of facilities that would need to be inspected is astonishing. It includes an estimated 40,000 stationary air sources, 90,000 facilities with water permits, over 425,000 hazardous wastes facilities, 400,000 underground injection wells, and 173,000 drinking water systems (U.S. EPA 1999).

Understandably, the EPA and the states rely heavily on self-monitoring by industry and other regulated parties, who then report their results to regulatory authorities. Despite the public impression to the contrary, visits and inspections of industrial facilities by regulatory officials are infrequent. The effect is further diminished by the common practice of announcing such inspections in advance (Russell 1990). The EPA's Office of Enforcement and

Compliance Assurance publishes an annual "accomplishments report" that highlights the record, although recent GAO studies have argued that much better and more accurate reporting of environmental enforcement is needed to judge how successful implementation has been (U.S. GAO 2008).

Perhaps as a consequence of the weak incentives this approach creates for complying with the law, studies have found high rates of violation of environmental standards. In 1998, for example, the EPA's own inspector general found widespread enforcement failures at the state and local levels for both air and water pollution control. Some wastewater treatment plants were operating with obsolete permits or none at all. In one state, half of the major air pollution sources were not inspected between 1990 and 1996, and in 1995 and 1996, the state stopped reporting significant violation of air quality regulations to the federal government. The report faulted both federal and state officials for falling short of goals.[48] Similarly, a GAO study in 1994 found that one in six of inspected major industrial and municipal sources were in significant violation of their permits (Freeman 2006). More recent surveys have found similar noncompliance rates, which vary considerably from one industrial sector to another.

Considerable variation in enforcement activity also exists across the 50 states, explainable in part by public perceptions of environmental problems, state economic conditions, and interest groups' strength (Hunter and Waterman 1996; Rabe 2016). Moreover, the aggressiveness of enforcement efforts may make a difference in achieving environmental quality goals (Ringquist 1993).[49]

If environmental regulation in practice often appears to be less strict than we might assume, it has not reduced the level of criticism. Industry and state and local governments have complained frequently about environmental regulations that they see as burdensome, costly, and inflexible. The critics often suggest that the effectiveness and efficiency of environmental policy could be improved through greater use of cooperation, negotiation, and financial incentives to promote achievement of environmental goals (Fiorino 2006; Sexton et al. 1999).

It is hard to say who is right. Surprisingly little empirical evidence speaks definitively to the question of which approach produces the best results. It may well be that collaborative and cooperative approaches work better than conventional regulation, at least for some kinds of environmental protection actions. At a minimum, their use can help bring the stakeholders together and review both the scientific evidence and policy alternatives (Kraft 2009; Lubell, Leach, and Sabatier 2009). Many environmentalists, however, remain skeptical of moving too far from the relative certainty of direct or conventional regulation.[50] Given this state of affairs, it would be useful for agencies to experiment with a variety of policy tools, old and new, and to evaluate programs carefully to see which strategies produce the best results (Bennear and Coglianese 2013; Coglianese 2012; Press 2015; Susskind and Schulman 2013).

Even when the laws appear to be coercive and invite adversarial relations between government and industry, the reality is that the enforcement process is fundamentally one of self-compliance and negotiation. Agencies at both the federal and state levels encourage compliance through informal means, using meetings, telephone conversations, letters, and other exchanges. Only when such efforts fail do more formal means of enforcement come into play. Agencies may then turn to an increasingly severe series of formal actions. These start with what are called Notices of Violation, where the agency indicates it has found a failure to comply with regulatory law. The agency may then proceed to an Administrative Order, where it stipulates action that must be taken by the party out of compliance (e.g., a state agency or an industrial facility). It may also list companies as ineligible for federal contracts, grants, and loans, as allowed by the statute. As a last resort, when all these actions fail to yield compliance, the EPA can move to civil and criminal prosecution with the aid of the Justice Department's Environment and Natural Resources division (Hunter and Waterman 1992, 1996; Ozymy and Jarrell 2015). Even here, however, most cases are settled out of court, clearly signaling that the EPA is reluctant to use the courts in routine enforcement actions (O'Leary 2016).

Box 5.1 summarizes notable cases in which the EPA has imposed substantial fines for egregious violations of environmental law. It is, of course, in the agency's interest that such cases be well publicized, as doing so sends a strong signal to industry that noncompliance not only may be costly but could harm a company's reputation with the public. As discussed in Chapter 3, most enforcement actions take place at the state level, with considerable variation from state to state. Data on enforcement activities, however, are not as complete or accurate as they should be, making comparisons among the states and assessments of their effectiveness very difficult.

▬▬▬ BOX 5.1 ENFORCING ENVIRONMENTAL LAW: ▬▬▬ UNUSUAL PENALTIES

Five cases illustrate both the scope of violations of environmental law and what enforcement efforts can achieve through use of fines and other penalties. For a full list of EPA civil cases and settlements from 1998 to present, with details on the cases, see one of the agency's key enforcement webpages: https://cfpub.epa.gov/enforcement/cases.

• In October 1998 diesel truck engine manufacturers agreed to pay $83 million in fines and spend $1 billion on environmental improvements to settle EPA accusations that they cheated on engine performance tests, resulting in far more pollution than legally allowed. It was the most expensive settlement ever for a clean air case and involved the world's leading manufacturers of such engines, including Mack Trucks Inc., Cummins Engine Co., and Caterpillar Inc.

- In 1999, the EPA reached a $20 million cleanup and penalty settlement with one of the nation's largest copper companies, Asarco. It had pretended for years that it was recycling metals in accordance with its permits, but in reality it was illegally burning hazardous waste to save the cost of proper disposal of the materials. EPA didn't disclose the details of the case until two grassroots environmental groups in El Paso, Texas, which were opposed to the continued operation of the smelter, sued the company and compelled release of the information.

- In January 2005 ConocoPhillips, the largest oil-refining company in the nation, settled with the federal Justice Department over violations of the Clean Air Act. The government said the settlement would lead to annual reductions of some 47,000 tons of dangerous emissions. The company was to pay civil fines of $4.5 million and invest a much larger sum, $525 million, in technological improvements at nine refineries in seven states to comply with the new source review sections of the federal Clean Air Act. It is to spend an additional $10 million on related environmental projects that also will lead to lowered emissions.

- In 2015, the Department of Justice announced that the British oil company BP would pay a record $20.8 billion to the U.S. government to cover damages caused by the *Deepwater Horizon* oil spill in the Gulf of Mexico in 2010. The agreement included a record $5.5 billion in Clean Water Act penalties. The final settlement resolves the many civil claims against BP and five Gulf states. Attorney General Loretta Lynch said it was "the largest settlement with a single entity in American history."

- In 2016, German automaker Volkswagen agreed to spend up to $14.7 billion to settle allegations that it cheated on emissions tests and deceived customers, with much of that money to compensate consumers who bought the vehicles. The company also agreed to spend $4.7 billion to mitigate pollution from the cars and to invest in green vehicle technology.

Conclusions

With all the criticism directed at it, we might be tempted to conclude that hardly anything is right with the present environmental regulatory regime and that only wholesale policy and management change would improve the situation. Such appraisals ignore important, if uneven, improvements in environmental quality over the past four decades that are directly and indirectly tied to environmental policies, including command-and-control policies (see Chapter 2). They also ignore major shifts now under way in industry and government such as pollution prevention, green technology development, and environmental research that arguably are related to federal environmental policy efforts over this time period and strong public support for them (Fiorino 2006; Press 2015; Press and Mazmanian 2016).

The problems with environmental policies and with the EPA are real enough, although not without solutions. Some of the blame for the present state of affairs surely lies with EPA and other federal officials who could have done a better job of managing their programs. Congress is equally, if not more, responsible, however, for the deficiencies of environmental protection policy. It has burdened the EPA with far more tasks than it can possibly handle with its budgetary resources. It also has deprived the agency of the discretion and tools it needs to set priorities among its varied programs and to spend money effectively and efficiently. In addition, the EPA has long received mixed signals about what it is expected to do from Capitol Hill, the White House, the courts, other federal agencies, state and local governments, environmentalists, and industry (Andrews 2016; Rosenbaum 2013a).

Thoughtful assessments of what might be done to improve environmental policy are not hard to come by (Bennear and Coglianese 2013; Davies and Mazurek 1998; Eisner 2007; Fiorino 2006, 2013; Kamieniecki and Kraft 2013); some of these are discussed in Chapter 7. Solutions depend on policymakers developing a broader and clearer understanding of environmental goals than we have seen to date. They also require the political will to pursue those goals with a diversity of strategies (e.g., regulation, market incentives, public education, information disclosure, and public–private partnerships) that can meet the varied expectations the nation has for environmental protection policy. Included here are not only policy effectiveness and efficiency, but also other values such as social equity and environmental justice. Dealing with a new generation of environmental problems, such as nonpoint pollution and urban sprawl, requires rethinking which policies will work best. Even the effective policies of the past must be judged by their suitability for the future. There is all the more reason today, then, to evaluate environmental programs more frequently and more rigorously to determine just how successful they are or can be. That goal in turn speaks to the need to improve the quality and dissemination of environmental data.

The most essential requirement is taking a far more comprehensive and integrated approach to environmental policy as well as concentrating on the long-term goal of sustainable development. A recent National Academy of Sciences report put the challenge well: "Environmental protection in the 21st century requires a new way of thinking about pollution and its drivers, scale, effects, and solutions" (Committee on Science for EPA's Future 2012). Among other things, this means trying to integrate the pursuit of environmental, economic, and social values at all levels of government. The public must be part of any dialogue toward these ends, from the community to the national and international levels. Admittedly, it is a challenge at a time of substantial cynicism toward government and the political process. Yet success in working toward sustainable communities across the United

States indicates a great potential for these innovative efforts (Mazmanian and Kraft 2009; K. Portney 2013). Effective public participation in these critical decisions requires that citizens become far better informed about the nature of environmental problems and risks, how they compare with one another, the costs of dealing with them, the trade-offs involved, and the policy choices we face as a nation.

Discussion Questions

1   Do the major environmental protection laws reviewed in this chapter need significant change? If so, what kinds of changes are most needed?
2   How good a job does the EPA do in implementing environmental protection laws? What factors are most important in shaping the way the EPA does its job? What actions could be taken to improve the EPA's implementation of the laws?
3   During the Bush administration the EPA was often criticized for being too supportive of the business community in the way it balanced the benefits of environmental protection and the costs imposed on society. Is this a fair criticism? Could the Obama administration be criticized for moving too far in the opposite direction, that is, for giving too little consideration to the economic impact of environmental regulations?
4   Decision making within administrative agencies such as the EPA and comparable state agencies is often subjected to intense lobbying, particularly by regulated parties. Would greater public participation in such decision making be desirable? If so, how would you encourage or facilitate such participation?
5   Most of the major federal environmental protection laws are administered largely by the states under federal supervision. Are the states doing a good job in handling their responsibilities? How would you determine that? Where would you go to find pertinent information on state activities?

Suggested Readings

Bryner, Gary C. 1995. *Blue Skies, Green Politics: The Clean Air Act of 1990 and Its Implementation*, 2nd edn. Washington, DC: CQ Press.

Davies, J. Clarence, and Jan Mazurek. 1998. *Pollution Control in the United States: Evaluating the System*. Washington, DC: Resources for the Future.

Eisner, Marc Allen. 2007. *Governing the Environment: The Transformation of Environmental Regulation*. Boulder, CO: Lynne Rienner.

Fiorino, Daniel J. 2006. *The New Environmental Regulation*. Cambridge, MA: MIT Press.

Klyza, Christopher McGrory, and David Sousa. 2013. *American Environmental Policy, 1990–2012: Beyond Gridlock*, updated and expanded edn. Cambridge, MA: MIT Press.

Portney, Paul R., and Robert N. Stavins, eds. 2000. *Public Policy for Environmental Protection*, 2nd edn. Washington, DC: Resources for the Future.

Notes

1 The estimates come from the comprehensive economic analysis done by the agency, and summarized at its webpage for the CPP: www.epa.gov/cleanpowerplan/fact-sheet-clean-power-plan-benefits.

2 See the EPA page on the CPP at: www.epa.gov/cleanpowerplan. The plan's details, its history, and the economic analyses are all available at the EPA website.

3 Coral Davenport, "Appeals Court Hears Challenge to Obama's Climate Change Rules," *New York Times*, September 27, 2016.

4 Ashley Parker and Coral Davenport, "Donald Trump's Energy Plan: More Fossil Fuels and Fewer Rules," *New York Times*, May 26, 2016; and Coral Davenport, "Climate Change Divide Bursts to Forefront in Presidential Campaign," *New York Times*, August 1, 2016. The partisan divide on a range of environmental and energy issues also can be seen in the party platforms, available at: www.presidency.ucsb.edu/platforms.php.

5 I focus in this chapter on these seven key acts. By any measure they are the most important ones dealing with pollution control. Others, though, also merit attention, such as the Pollution Prevention Act of 1990 and the Oil Pollution Act, also of 1990.

6 In the late 1990s, the U.S. EPA put the cost at $170 billion each year, which some analysts (e.g., P. Portney 1998) consider to be too high. There is no easy way to determine total societal costs of compliance, and the business sector and its supporters often overestimate these costs. It is particularly difficult to know if costs will continue at the same level over time, and it is equally difficult to put a dollar value on the benefits of environmental regulations.

7 John Cushman, "Clinton Sharply Tightens Air Pollution Regulations Despite Concern Over Costs," *New York Times*, June 26, 1997.

8 See also the comprehensive overview of the Bush administration EPA by Margaret Kriz, "Vanishing Act," *National Journal*, April 12, 2008.

9 Andrew C. Revkin, "Obama's Ambitious Global Warming Action Plan," *New York Times*, June 25, 2013; and Coral Davenport, "Donald Trump Could Put Climate Change on Course for 'Danger Zone,'" *New York Times*, November 10, 2016.

10 The far-reaching and innovative Southern California clean air plan resulted from precisely such a rejection. The formally submitted California SIP openly admitted that it would not bring the state into compliance with national standards. Local environmentalists sued the EPA, arguing that under the provisions of the Clean Air Act, it could not accept such a plan. A federal appeals court agreed. For the details, see Mazmanian (2009).

11 For more discussion of the Clean Air Act, see Bryner (1995) and Portney and Stavins (2000).

12 In proposing the Clear Skies initiative, the Bush White House chose a less stringent approach to air pollution reform than recommended by the EPA. The decision was one of many indications that the EPA was less influential in the Bush White House than it was in the Clinton administration. See Katharine Q. Seelye, "White House Rejected a Stricter E.P.A. Alternative to the Clear Skies Plan," *New York Times*, April 28, 2002.

13 Felicity Barringer, "2 Decisions Signal End of Bush Clean-Air Steps," *New York Times*, July 12, 2008; and "In Reversal, Court Allows a Bush Plan on Pollution," *New York Times*, December 24, 2008.

14 Juliet Eilperin, "Federal Appeals Court Strikes Down Obama Air Pollution Rule," *Washington Post*, August 21, 2012. The new Obama interstate air pollution rule is described in detail on the EPA's webpage for it: www3.epa.gov/crossstaterule/.

15 Matthew L. Wald, "E.P.A. Says It Will Change Rules Governing Industrial Pollution," *New York Times*, November 23, 2002; Juliet Eilperin, "New Rules Could Allow Power Plants to Pollute More," *Washington Post*, August 31, 2005; and Michael Janofsky, "Judges Overturn Bush Bid to Ease Pollution Rules," *New York Times*, March 18, 2006. Current NSR rules can be found at: www.epa.gov/nsr.

16 See Brady Dennis, "Supreme Court Rejects Case Challenging Key White House Air Pollution Regulation," *Washington Post*, June 13, 2016; Coral Davenport, "E.P.A. to Unveil New Limit for Smog-Causing Emissions," *New York Times*, October 1, 2015.

17 The history of federal water pollution control dates back to the Refuse Act of 1899, which was intended to prevent constraints on navigation. The Act prohibited the discharge or deposit of "any refuse matter" into "any navigable water" of the United States. The volume of waste products such as fiber and sawdust from papermills and sawmills was so great in some rivers and channels that it threatened to block navigation. Administered by the U.S. Army Corps of Engineers, the Refuse Act had little or no effect on most industrial and municipal water pollution (Freeman 1990).

18 For a recent review of the CWA, its early history, and current proposals for reform, see "Congress's Water Challenge," a special symposium in *Extensions* (A Journal of the Carl Albert Congressional Research and Studies Center), Summer 2016: 2–23. See also Milazzo (2006).

19 Barbara Whitaker, "Federal Judge Rules Los Angeles Violates Clean Water Laws," *New York Times*, December 24, 2002; and Charles Duhigg, "Clean Water Laws Neglected, at a Cost," *New York Times*, September 13, 2009.

20 There are similar citizen suit provisions in other environmental laws, most notably the Clean Air Act, the Resource Conservation and Recovery Act, and the Emergency Planning and Community Right-to-Know Act.

21 See Margaret Kriz, "Testing the Waters at the EPA," *National Journal*, April 22, 2000: 1286–1287. For an assessment of the Total Maximum Daily Load provisions of the Clean Water Act and the EPA rule, see Jim Boyd, "Unleashing the Clean Water Act: The Promise and Challenge of the TMDL Approach to Water Quality," *Resources* 139 (Spring 2000): 7–10, available at: www.rff.org.

22 See the EPA webpage on use of the TMDL process and ongoing litigation: www.epa.gov/tmdl.

23 Coral Davenport, "Obama Announces New Rule Limiting Water Pollution," *New York Times*, May 27, 2015.

24 Margaret Kriz, "Cleaner Than Clean?" *National Journal*, April 23, 1994: 946–949.

25 David Hosansky, "Drinking Water Bill Clears; Clinton Expected to Sign," *CQ Weekly Report*, August 3, 1996: 2179–2180; and Allan Freedman, "Provisions: Safe Drinking Water Act Amendments," *CQ Weekly Report*, September 14, 1996: 2622–2627.

26 Michael Wines and John Schwartz, "Unsafe Lead Levels in Tap Water Not Limited to Flint," *New York Times*, February 8, 2016; and Gina McCarthy, "Michigan Evaded the EPA on Flint. We Can't Let That Happen Elsewhere," *Washington Post*, March 14, 2016.

27 For example, see a GAO report, *Options for Enhancing the Effectiveness of the Toxic Substances Control Act* (Washington, D.C.: GAO, GAO-09-428T, 2009); a second report, *Observations on the Toxic Substances Control Act and EPA Implementation* (Washington, D.C.: GAO, GAO-13-696T, June 13, 2013), and the related earlier report *Comparison of U.S. and Recently Enacted European Union Approaches against the Risks of Toxic Chemicals* (Washington, D.C.: GAO, GAO-07-825, 2007). See the editorial "A Toothless Law on Toxic Chemicals," *New York Times*, April 18, 2013.

28 See Coral Davenport and Emmarie Huetteman, "Lawmakers Reach Deal to Expand Regulation of Toxic Chemicals," *New York Times*, May 19, 2016. For details about the new Act, see the EPA webpage on it: www.epa.gov/assessing-and-managing-chemicals-under-tsca/frank-r-lautenberg-chemical-safety-21st-century-act.

29 Laura Michaelis, "Calls for Pesticide Reform Linked to New Report," *CQ Weekly Report*, July 3, 1993: 1730.

30 Davis Hosansky, "Rewrite of Laws on Pesticides on Way to President's Desk," *CQ Weekly Report*, July 27: 2101–2104; and "Provisions: Pesticide, Food Safety Law," *CQ Weekly Report*, September 7, 1996: 2546–2550.

31 Brody Mullins, "Will Superfund Reform Be Dumped Again?" *National Journal*, October 30, 1999: 3139–3140.

32 John Holusha, "Cities Redeveloping Old Industrial Sites with EPA's Aid," *New York Times*, December 4, 1995.

33 The measure is the Small Business Liability Relief and Brownfields Revitalization Act, PL 107-118 (2002).

34 See Matthew L. Wald, "A Drop in Toxic Emissions and a Rise in PCB Disposal," *New York Times*, March 20, 2009.

35 These numbers come from the EPA webpage on budget and staffing: www.epa.gov/planandbudget/budget.

36 Details about the federal environmental research budgets can be found at the website for the National Council for Science and the Environment: www.ncseonline.org.

37 John M. Broder, "Republicans Block Vote on Nominee to Lead E.P.A.," *New York Times*, May 9, 2013.

38 See Jonathan Weisman, "House G.O.P. Sets New Offensive on Obama Goals," *New York Times*, July 23, 2013.

39 See Coral Davenport, "E.P.A. Faces Bigger Tasks, Smaller Budgets and Louder Critics," *New York Times*, March 18, 2016; and Coral Davenport and Eric

Lipton, "Trump Picks Scott Pruitt, Climate Change Denialist, to Lead E.P.A.," *New York Times*, December 7, 2016.

40 In addition to the seven statutes discussed in this chapter, the EPA is also charged with administration of the Pollution Prevention Act, the Ocean Dumping Act, the Oil Pollution Act, the Solid Waste Disposal Act, the Emergency Planning and Community Right-to-Know Act (part of Superfund), and parts of the National Environmental Policy Act and the Endangered Species Act, among others.

41 For a comprehensive review and assessment of how this process works, see the report of the Presidential/Congressional Commission on Risk Assessment and Risk Management (1997). The Commission's reports and other studies and commentary on risk are available at: www.riskworld.com.

42 Gary Lee, "A Potential Killer's Modus Operandi," *Washington Post National Weekly Edition*, June 20–26, 1995, 38; and Keith Schneider, "EPA Moves to Reduce Health Risks from Dioxin," *New York Times*, September 14, 1994.

43 See Jocelyn Kaiser, "Panel Backs EPA Dioxin Assessment," *Science* 290 (November 10, 2000): 1071. For a description of dioxins and furans, see the EPA webpage on the subject of toxic chemicals: www.epa.gov/chemicals-under-tsca.

44 Information about this kind of assessment can be found on the agency's webpage: www.epa.gov/expobox/exposure-assessment-tools-tiers-and-types-aggregate-and-cumulative.

45 All quotations in this description of the controversy are taken from U.S. EPA, "EPA Proposes Achievable Cleaner Fuels and Cars Standard, Slashing Air Pollution and Providing Extensive Health Benefits" (Washington, DC: U.S. EPA, news release, March 29, 2013). For additional perspectives on the controversy, see Washington Post Editorial Board, "New EPA Rules on Tailpipe Emissions Will Save Lives," *Washington Post*, March 31, 2013; and Joe Taschler, "EPA Draws Criticism for Proposing Stricter Fuel Pollutant Controls," *Milwaukee Journal-Sentinel*, March 29, 2013.

46 For example, the independent OMB Watch stated that under the Bush administration, OIRA was "increasingly using its regulatory review authority to weaken or block health, safety, and environmental standards."

47 See, for example, Henry Fountain and Erica Goodenov, "Trump Has Options for Undoing Obama's Climate Legacy," *New York Times*, November 25, 2016. See also William W. Buzbee, "Dismantling Climate Rules Isn't So Easy," *New York Times*, December 8, 2016.

48 John H. Cushman, "E.P.A. and States Found to Be Lax on Pollution Law," *New York Times*, June 7, 1998.

49 For one particularly egregious example of decades-long violation of chemical pollution laws, see Nathaniel Rich, "The Lawyer Who Became DuPont's Worst Nightmare," *New York Times Magazine*, January 6, 2016.

50 At least some evidence supports the environmentalist position. For instance, a comparative study of enforcement of effluent regulations for the pulp and paper industries in the United States and Canada found that cooperative approaches to regulation may be less effective than traditional "coercive" approaches (Harrison 1995).

CHAPTER 6

Energy and Natural Resource Policies

In September 2016, the level of carbon dioxide in the Earth's atmosphere permanently passed a critical juncture: 400 parts per million for a 24-hour average at the Mauna Loa observation post in Hawaii. Scientists at NASA also indicated that each of the first six months of 2016 set a record for the warmest months globally based on modern temperature records. By year's end, it was expected that 2016 would join 2015 and 2014 as among the hottest years on record. The ten hottest years all have been since 1998. These reports helped to further crystalize increasing concern around the world about climate change and the adverse consequences it is anticipated to have on the environment, natural resources, human health, and economic well-being.[1]

Most nations have not done as much as they could have to slow the pace of a changing climate that scientists attribute largely to human activities, and particularly to the burning of fossil fuels: coal, oil, and natural gas (DiMento and Doughman 2014; IPCC 2013; Selin and VanDeveer 2016). Yet in November 2016, the landmark Paris Agreement on climate change took effect after the requisite number of nations formally ratified it (see Chapter 8). President Barack Obama said this was "a turning point for our planet," and the U.N. Secretary-General, Ban Ki-moon, described international support for the agreement as a "testament for the urgency of action."[2] In addition, in October 2016, more than 170 countries reached a legally binding agreement to replace refrigerant chemicals (hydrofluorocarbons, or HFCs) strongly linked to climate change, with specific targets and timetables for reduction of their production and use; HFCs have 1,000 times the effect on warming of carbon dioxide.[3] Under President Obama, the United States also began taking significant actions to reduce emissions of greenhouse gases, particularly through the EPA's Clean Power Plan discussed in Chapter 5, higher federal fuel-economy standards, and a substantially greater investment in renewable energy production. The Trump administration and a Republican Congress are likely to challenge these new directions in U.S. policy in the coming years, but many of the initiatives on energy use and climate change both in government and in the private sector will continue nonetheless.[4]

These policy actions illustrate well the way in which the political dialogue over the nation's use of its energy and other natural resources has shifted significantly over the past several decades. Historically, broad public support existed for production of abundant and cheap energy from fossil fuels. Most of the policies were not very controversial and few objected to the nation's reliance on fossil fuels, although today the public wants energy resources to be both cheap and clean (Ansolabehere and Konisky 2014; Rosenbaum 2015; Smith 2002). Much the same was true for use of natural resources and conservation programs. As we saw in Chapter 4, broad public support existed for treasured national parks and most people supported preservation of threatened and irreplaceable forests and other lands, wilderness, and endangered species (especially for well-recognized species such as bald eagles). Yet, conflicts almost always arose over the specific means used to achieve such general goals and the ways in which competing social values were balanced at any given time and place, and they continue to do so today (Andrews 2006a; Hays 1987; Lowry 1994).

These kinds of conflicts have escalated in recent decades in part because the stakes, such as climate change, are now so high and the decisions so visible to many. For reasons discussed in previous chapters, more people today pay attention to the decisions and are prepared to fight over them. For example, should the nation move ahead on the Clean Power Plan that will greatly restrict the use of coal-fired power plants that release about 40 percent of the nation's greenhouse gases? There is an intense partisan divide today on the question, as there is on climate change itself.[5] Should the federal government open more public lands and offshore areas to drilling for oil and natural gas, including gas produced through hydraulic fracturing or fracking, or would doing so in some areas present too great a risk to the environment and public health (Weber, Bernell, and Boudet 2016)?

Similar questions arise over natural resources other than coal, oil, and natural gas. During the 1990s, Secretary of the Interior Bruce Babbitt sought to reverse 12 years of Republican rule that favored economic development over resource conservation. With the election of George W. Bush in 2000, the policy agenda abruptly changed again. Under Secretary of the Interior Gale A. Norton, who served through spring 2006, and then under her replacement, Dirk Kempthorne, the administration's actions were reminiscent of the prodevelopment Reagan administration. Under President Obama, priorities changed once more, even if to a lesser extent than many expected (Lowry 2006; Lubell and Segee 2013), and they are likely to shift again in the Trump administration, mostly likely to something resembling the Bush administration's preferences on use of natural resources for increased economic development.[6]

These disputes over energy and natural resources underscore the difficulty of making collective choices when conflicting social values are deeply held and winners and losers, such as coal, oil, and mining companies, or farmers dependent on irrigation water, can plainly see their fates. That is especially so when the political process is open to pressure from powerful interests eager to protect their share of the nation's economic pie and where the decisions may be of little interest to the general public. Scientific studies help resolve questions of fact, but they cannot substitute for political judgments about where the public interest lies. The chapter is divided into two parts, the first focusing on energy resources and policies and the second on other natural resources and conservation concerns that have long been the focus of governmental action.

The chapter seeks to:

- describe how these issues arise and are resolved in the two clusters of related environmental problems and policies: energy and natural resources;
- analyze the development and implementation of policies over time, and variation in priorities and emphases among presidential administrations; and
- build a capacity for critical appraisal of policy goals and means, emphasize the ways in which policies have been altered in response to shifting public preferences and interest group influence, and underscore the continuing need for policy evaluation and change to meet new demands that have arisen in the twenty-first century.

Energy Policy: Goals and Means

Energy policy is part environmental protection and part natural resource policy. The United States, however, has no comprehensive energy policy that compares to the extensive bureaucratic and regulatory machinery that governs environmental quality and natural resources. Rather, energy use is determined largely by the marketplace, with each major energy source shaped in part by an assortment of government subsidies and regulations adopted over decades and primarily for reasons that have little to do directly with the goals of energy policy as we think of them today.

Federal and state regulation of coal, natural gas, and oil, for example, historically has focused on prices and competition within each energy sector. It has served the interests of energy producers by stabilizing markets and ensuring profits, and it has tried to meet a larger public interest in ensuring reliable energy supplies at an affordable cost. Regulation of nuclear power differs from other energy policies because of its historic connection to national security.

From the late 1940s on, under the auspices of the Atomic Energy Acts of 1946 and 1954, federal agencies responsible for the civilian nuclear energy program shielded the technology from the marketplace—and from public scrutiny—to ensure rapid growth of its use. The Atomic Energy Commission (AEC) and its successor agencies, the Nuclear Regulatory Commission (NRC) and the DOE, vigorously promoted nuclear power as a critical component of the nation's mix of energy resources. Congress contributed to those goals by subsidizing nuclear energy through restrictions on liability set by the 1957 Price–Anderson Act (which limits the financial responsibility of plant owners to $10 billion in the event of an accident) and by provision of lavish R&D funds. All this was considered to be essential to create a new civilian nuclear power industry in light of the uncertainties and risks associated with it. Following the Three Mile Island nuclear accident in Pennsylvania in 1979, however, public opinion turned against building additional nuclear power plants. The Chernobyl nuclear plant disaster in Ukraine in 1986 further eroded public confidence in nuclear power even though that accident involved a faulty plant design not used in the United States. Similarly, the Fukushima Daiichi accident in Japan in 2011 highlighted additional concerns over plant design, the storage of nuclear waste, and the reliability of backup plans in cases of accidents.

To the extent that the nation had any discernible energy policy goal before the 1970s, it was to maintain a supply of abundant, cheap, and reliable energy, preferably from domestic sources, to support a growing economy and to ensure a reasonable profit for producers. Policymakers were convinced that a growing economy demanded ever-increasing energy supplies, and to meet that expected demand they relied largely on fossil fuels used at facilities such as coal-fired power plants and on the construction of nuclear power plants. Renewable energy sources at that time were a distinctly minor component in the overall system.

Since the 1970s, however, the nation's use of energy has been heavily influenced by newly adopted environmental policies and changing public attitudes. It is easy to see why. Exploration for energy sources and their extraction, transportation, refinement, and use can degrade the land, air, and water. The 1989 Exxon *Valdez* accident in Alaska, the 2010 BP *Deepwater Horizon* spill in the Gulf of Mexico, and thousands of lesser oil spills and accidents underscore the dangers of drilling for oil and moving it by ship, rail, or pipeline.[7] Mining for coal and hardrock mining for gold, silver, and copper can ravage the land and poison the waters around mines. There are more than 160,000 abandoned hardrock mining sites in the 12 Western states, and over 30,000 of them resulted in contaminated surface water and groundwater, with taxpayers left with paying for a multibillion cleanup (U.S. GAO 2011).

Similarly, drilling for oil, particularly in deep water offshore or in the Arctic, comes with risks of accidents and oil spills that can pollute the waters and harm marine life. Burning oil, coal, and natural gas and their by-products to generate energy and power the nation's cars, trucks, buses, and aircraft pollutes the air, causes acid rain, and leads to the buildup of damaging greenhouse gases. Use of nuclear power produces high-level waste products that must be isolated from the biosphere for tens of thousands of years.

Congress has adopted public policies to deal with all of these environmental effects resulting from energy production and use, from clean air and water laws to nuclear waste disposal, surface mining control, and oil spill prevention measures. By doing so, it slowly altered the production and use of energy in important, if sometimes unintended, ways.

The debate over energy policy today turns on what combination of energy resources best promotes the nation's long-term interest and whether and how federal, state, and local governments should encourage or discourage the development of particular energy resources—such as opening offshore lands to increased drilling for oil and gas or providing financial incentives to purchase fuel-efficient vehicles or install solar panels on homes. In general, governments have three basic strategies they can use for such purposes. They can try to increase energy supplies, decrease public demand for energy through conservation and efficiency measures, or alter the mix of fuels used through a variety of policy actions, such as regulation, public education, taxation, and the use of subsidies such as funding for R&D or provision of tax credits. The choices are never easy, and conflict among diverse parties (regional interests, energy producers, consumers, and environmentalists) is common (Hamilton 2013; Rosenbaum 2015).

Indirect Policy Impacts

Even without a comprehensive energy policy, federal, state, and local governments influence decision making on energy use in myriad ways. They do so through regulation of the by-products (e.g., air pollution), provision of services (e.g., building highways for motor vehicles), tax subsidies, and energy R&D assistance. The effects of such policies are rarely neutral, and the market is not truly free and competitive because of long-standing policy choices. For example, historically, policies have strongly favored mature and conventional energy sources such as oil, natural gas, coal, and nuclear power. They also have encouraged expansion of energy use rather than decrease in demand through improved energy efficiency and conservation.

Studies from the early 1990s indicated that U.S. taxpayers spent as much as $36 billion each year on federal energy subsidies, most of which favored fossil fuels and nuclear energy, although the DOE has long stated that the real subsidies were much lower (Koplow 1993). In 2005 a major assessment of the federal government's energy programs by the U.S. GAO estimated tax-related subsidies alone at $4.4 billion per year, with most of the benefits (about 88 percent) going to fossil fuel production (U.S. GAO 2005a). But by 2007, DOE data show that subsidies reached a new high of $16.7 billion, with renewable energy sources now topping the list, at least in part because of new and environmentally questionable subsidies for corn-based ethanol. The trend toward renewables continued through 2016, which drove some political conservatives and fossil fuel companies to protest that the pendulum had swung too far in that direction.[8]

Much the same historical favoritism toward fossil fuels can be seen internationally. The International Monetary Fund in 2015 estimated that if calculated properly to reflect the damage that use of fossil fuels causes to human health and the climate, energy subsidies amounted to $5.3 trillion a year, or 6.5 percent of global gross domestic product; it supported proposals to raise taxes on fossil fuels to reduce or eliminate such subsidies. Also in 2015, the International Energy Agency put the direct cost of fossil fuel subsidies (that is, not counting health and environmental effects) at a still impressive $550 billion per year globally, and it found that coal, oil, and natural gas received about four times what renewable energy did.[9]

By 2009, at the start of the Obama administration, greater sums yet were invested in energy development of all kinds, but with a new emphasis on clean energy sources, as part of the nation's economy recovery policies. These actions reflected both direct governmental spending and the kind of indirect spending or subsidies that we have long seen. Most of the direct investments in new energy technologies seem to have been successful despite some prominent failures, such as a major loan to the solar energy company Solyndra. The administration's critics frequently pointed to the few failures as evidence that government should not choose among energy sources or technologies. Yet the broader successes of the DOE's Loan Programs Office are well documented, and these include billions of dollars directed to advanced nuclear energy projects and advanced vehicles manufacturing in addition to wind and solar energy investments.[10]

Of course, many other federal and state programs indirectly subsidize the way we use energy, and they have done so for years. One example is government support for highway construction and maintenance and, until recently, comparable neglect of mass transportation systems such as passenger trains and urban light rail systems. While not directly an energy policy, strong spending on highways has encouraged use of motor vehicles and discouraged the use of rail and bus systems. It also has profoundly affected the design and growth of cities across the country, encouraging urban sprawl and making cities more energy-intensive than common elsewhere in the world in part because of their dependence on the automobile.

What difference do energy subsidies make for the way we use energy or the price that we pay for it? One example can be seen in the cost of gasoline. The *price* we pay at the pump, about $2.20 a gallon for regular gasoline in October 2016, is not the true *cost* of using the fuel. That price does not reflect the full expense of road construction and maintenance or the environmental and public health damage and other externalities related to access to the oil, transporting it around the world in supertankers, and ultimately burning its gasoline derivative in our cars, vans, sport utility vehicles (SUVs), and trucks (Parry 2002).

Whatever method is used to calculate the social cost of gasoline, the market price is all that drivers see. Over the past several decades that price was not sufficient to stimulate demand for fuel-efficient vehicles or to encourage increased public use of mass transit as an alternative to automobiles, and policymakers were loath to consider raising gasoline taxes. However, when gasoline prices rose sharply in the 2000s and 2010s, one pattern changed temporarily. There was a greater public demand for fuel-efficient cars, trucks, and SUVs, and auto makers responded to that demand with many new models. The new federal fuel efficiency rules will push auto makers in the same direction if they are maintained, even if U.S. gasoline prices remain as low as they were in 2016.

Shifting Energy Priorities

These varied and often obscure governmental energy programs and subsidies affect the availability and price of energy sources, and they have a perverse effect. Over time they have sanctioned and stimulated the use of environmentally risky energy sources while erecting barriers to sustainable sources. However, much has changed since 1990, and the nation is now in the midst of another round of major changes. Under both the George W. Bush and Bill Clinton administrations, policies and administrative priorities shifted enough that renewable energy sources, conservation, and improved efficiency began receiving new attention and support in both the public and private sectors. Bush's proposed national energy policy of 2001 (discussed later) also played a role, even though the proposal centered on increased use of fossil fuels. The Obama administration and Congress further altered the energy picture by spending historically large sums of money for energy-related measures as part of economic stimulus measures in 2009, with clean energy sources receiving a significant boost.

Environmentalists have long argued for an early and rapid shift away from fossil fuels and nuclear power and toward solar power, wind energy, geothermal sources, use of biomass, and other forms of renewable energy. They believe that such a transition is possible with well-designed public policies and the political leadership to get them enacted and implemented (Cooper 1999; Hunt and Sawin 2006; U.S. GAO 2005a). Others, particularly fossil fuel companies and utility executives, have disagreed and argued that such hopes for a renewable energy future are unrealistic. They see a smaller potential for solar, wind, biofuels, and other renewables, and limitations to how successful energy conservation can be. Thus they suggest a longer-term reliance on fossil fuels and a continuation or expansion of nuclear power.[11] The two major parties and their supporters have been similarly divided over the U.S. energy economy (Dunlap and McCright 2008; Dunlap, McCright, and Yarosh 2016; Guber and Bosso 2013a; Kraft 2013a). A brief examination of recent policy history indicates how these two different visions of a U.S. energy future have shaped policy choices.

The Energy Policy Cycle: 1973–1989

Over the last five decades, the United States has struggled with defining and setting national energy policy goals, with limited success. The early efforts, during the 1970s under Presidents Richard Nixon, Gerald Ford, and Jimmy Carter, were driven largely by concern for the security and stability of the energy supply in the wake of the 1973 oil price shock. In that year, the Organization of Petroleum Exporting Countries (OPEC) imposed an embargo on the sale of their oil, which led to a quadrupling of world oil prices and severe economic repercussions. In previous decades, little thought was given to energy conservation, and demand for energy grew dramatically. After 1973, with the reliability of oil supplies called into question, both the federal and state governments made greater efforts to encourage conservation and efficiency of use through a variety of taxation and regulatory actions. Such efforts included adoption in 1975 of the Energy Policy and Conservation Act. That Act established the Corporate Average Fuel Economy (CAFE) standards for motor vehicles, extended domestic oil price controls, and authorized the Strategic Petroleum Reserve to stockpile oil for future emergencies (Goodwin 1981; Marcus 1992).

Carter's National Energy Plan and Conservation Gains

Under the Carter administration, energy policy goals began shifting to provision of secure and clean energy sources, but reliance on market forces remained the preeminent policy approach. President Carter made his National Energy Plan, which he called the "moral equivalent of war," a top policy priority in 1977 and 1978. A small ad hoc energy task force working under the direction of James Schlesinger, Carter's secretary of energy, assembled the plan to meet a presidential deadline of April 1977. The group emphasized a strong governmental role rather than reliance on the private sector, and it looked more to conservation than to increasing domestic supplies for solutions to the energy crisis.

The plan drew little support on Capitol Hill. Congress objected to many of its provisions, and it also was lobbied heavily by oil- and natural gas-producing industries; utilities; automobile companies; and labor, consumer, and environmental groups, all of whom found something to dislike in the plan. As a result, Congress enacted some of Carter's proposals and rejected others without substituting an equally comprehensive energy policy (Kraft 1981).

In the end, Congress approved five key components, which collectively were called the National Energy Act of 1978. Among them was the Natural Gas Policy Act, which partially deregulated and altered natural gas pricing to make the fuel more competitive with other sources. Also in the package was the Public Utilities Regulatory Policy Act (PURPA), which helped create a market for small energy producers using unconventional sources such as solar and geothermal. Other provisions dealt with energy conservation, power plant and industrial fuel use, and energy taxes. Among other actions, Congress approved tax credits for home insulation, energy efficiency standards for home appliances, and taxes on so-called gas-guzzler cars. Environmental quality was a consideration at the time, but not the main concern. Indeed, Carter's plan aimed to *expand* use of coal because of its domestic abundance despite the environmental consequences of using such a notoriously dirty fuel. Yet Carter also greatly increased support for renewable energy sources.

In 1977 Congress established the DOE, which consolidated previously independent energy agencies into a cabinet department, with the NRC remaining an independent agency charged with overseeing nuclear safety. Despite its name, the DOE is not primarily an energy department. Most of its budget and staff are devoted to nuclear science and weapons concerns, including nuclear waste disposal and cleanup of former weapons production facilities. Its highly regarded laboratories, such as Argonne, Oak Ridge, Brookhaven, and Lawrence Livermore, pursue a diverse array of strategic science and technological objectives.

Despite these policy and institutional limitations, the United States (and other industrialized nations) made great strides in energy conservation in the 1970s and 1980s. Slower economic growth and a decline in older and inefficient heavy industries contributed to the energy savings. Consumer and industry demand for energy-efficient cars, buildings, lighting, motors, and appliances made a difference as well. American industry in the late 1980s used only 70 percent of the energy needed in 1973 to produce the same goods. Appliances in the early 1990s were about 75 percent more efficient than they were in the late 1970s. Passenger automobiles in 1991 averaged about 22 miles per gallon compared with only 14 miles per gallon in 1973 (U.S. DOE 1998).[12]

These gains were impressive, even if a growing population, a stronger economy, and Americans' penchant for larger vehicles, larger homes, and a wider variety of electrical appliances translated into increased energy use over time (U.S. DOE 1998). From today's perspective, it would be hard to call many of the energy policies of this era a great success because government programs remained complex, contradictory, and inefficient. Moreover, even with these improvements in energy efficiency, energy use per person in the United States has remained more than double that of Japan and most European nations.

Reagan's Nonpolicy on Energy

Many of the most innovative policies of the 1970s, including government support for conservation and development and use of alternative energy sources, did not last long. What remained in the early 1980s was cut back sharply during the Reagan administration. President Ronald Reagan strongly opposed a federal role on energy policy and favored reliance on the "free market." He sought (unsuccessfully) to dismantle the DOE, whose very existence symbolized federal intrusion into the energy marketplace. Some of his positions were broadly endorsed at the time because energy prices were declining.

In response to these conditions, Congress repealed tax breaks for installing energy-saving devices and approved Reagan's budget cuts that effectively ended conservation and renewable energy programs (Axelrod 1984; Rosenbaum 2015). Between 1980 and 1990, for example, solar and renewable energy research funding in the DOE declined by some 93 percent in constant dollars, and the department's energy conservation budget fell by 91 percent between 1981 and 1987.[13] All this was particularly striking because conservation of energy is one of the most effective ways to both reduce dependency on imported oil and lower environmental risks at a modest cost. It is a premier example of what analysts mean when they say smart policy involves picking the lowest hanging fruit on the energy tree— that is, getting a great return for a minimal effort.

The Reagan administration's energy budget also concealed inconsistencies in its ostensible reliance on free market forces. For example, support for nuclear programs was increased even while virtually every other program was cut back sharply, usually without much attention paid to evidence of program success or failure. Programs to prepare for oil emergencies suffered because Reagan did as little as possible to meet legislative targets for filling the Strategic Petroleum Reserve, leaving the nation vulnerable to oil price shocks. Reagan even ordered his staff to remove solar panels installed at the White House by President Carter, a symbol in conflict with the administration's energy policy agenda. One journalist described the essence of the Reagan strategy as "duck, defer, and deliberate" (Hogan 1984).

Energy Policy for the Twenty-First Century

Energy issues reappeared on the political agenda in the late 1980s as the nation's dependence on oil imports rose once again and concern began to mount about global climate change following the hot and dry summer of 1988. In 1970 the United States imported 23 percent of its oil. By 1991 the figure climbed to 45 percent and by 2008, to 58 percent. The reasons for increased reliance on imported oil are plain enough: a decline in domestic energy production, complacency among both the public and policymakers, and a sharp increase in use of motor vehicles and other transportation that is reliant on oil. Although domestic energy production is once again a priority, its decline over the previous several decades can be explained in part by the stringent requirements of new environmental laws, including the National Environmental Policy Act (NEPA) and the Clean Air Act. NEPA mandated arduous environmental impact statements that made clear the environmental consequences of energy extraction and use, whether the sources were oil, coal, or nuclear power. These effects prompted a debate that continues to this day over whether environmental goals are compatible with the level of energy production the nation has experienced in recent years. One can see this clearly in the ongoing argument over the environmental effects of rapidly increasing natural gas fracking.

As discussed in Chapter 2, the United States and other nations rely heavily on fossil fuels: coal, oil, and natural gas. More than 80 percent of the energy consumed in the United States and in most other nations in recent years has come from fossil fuels. Use of such fuels produces great quantities of carbon dioxide and thus contributes to the risk of climate change.

Reliance on oil imports to meet U.S. energy needs has proven to be a particularly risky strategy. Some two-thirds of the 19 million barrels of oil used in the United States each day goes to transportation: trucks, planes, buses, and automobiles. The oil imports needed to satisfy America's insatiable appetite have widened the U.S. trade deficit, contributed to inflation, and increased dependence on politically unstable regions of the world. Only in the early 2010s did the nation see a sharp decline in the percentage of oil that is imported, a reflection of increased domestic production as well as improved efficiency. By 2012, U.S. reliance on imported oil dropped to about 40 percent, and by 2015, it was down to about 24 percent, according to the DOE's Energy Information Administration; that was the lowest level since 1970. Most analysts expect dependency on imported oil to decline further over the next few years.

Despite important environmental, economic, and national security impacts of the nation's energy use, policymakers had been reluctant until recently to push the public to change its energy habits through either higher fuel efficiency standards (regulation) or significant increases in the gasoline tax (market incentives). Energy issues generally have continued to be low in salience for both the public and for policymakers, and the media have tended not to cover them extensively except during periods of energy crises or rapidly rising prices. These characteristics greatly constrained formulation of U.S. energy policy during the 1980s and 1990s, and even into the 2000s and 2010s. Actions taken during the presidential administrations of George H. W. Bush, Bill Clinton, and George W. Bush illustrate the prevailing politics of energy policy and the continuing challenges that advocates of stronger policy action are likely to face.

The Bush Administration's National Energy Strategy

In 1989, President George H.W. Bush directed his DOE to develop a National Energy Strategy (NES), which it prepared following extensive analysis within the department as well as nationwide public hearings. Bush defended the NES as an acceptable balance of energy production and conservation, whereas environmentalists argued that the plan tilted too much toward production, risking environmental damage in the process, and that it did little for energy conservation or mitigation of climate change. They successfully opposed opening the Arctic National Wildlife Refuge (ANWR, pronounced "ann waar") to oil and gas exploration, and they pressed hard, but without success, for big increases in the CAFE standards as an alternative to increasing oil supplies. Eventually, the wildlife refuge and the CAFE provisions were omitted from the final legislation to gain support from each side. Both issues would reappear when Bush's son, George W. Bush, sent his own energy policy proposals to Congress in 2001 (discussed later). As is usually the case with energy policy bills, in 1991 Congress was besieged by lobbyists, particularly from energy interests and automobile manufacturers, who sought to maintain their advantages under current policies.

The outcome of congressional decision making in the early 1990s was largely political gridlock. There was too little concern and consensus about energy policy among the public and no effective way to restrain the politics of self-interest of energy producers. Thus the final bill displeased environmentalists, and other key players acknowledged that it would be merely a foundation on which to build a more comprehensive energy policy in the future (Idelson 1992a). Nevertheless, the 1992 Energy Policy Act set out some important goals and established unusual incentives for achieving them. The 1992 Act, a massive measure running to some 1,300 pages, called for greater energy conservation and efficiency in electric appliances, buildings, lighting, plumbing, commercial and industrial motors, and heating and cooling systems. It also streamlined licensing requirements for nuclear power plants in the hope of jump-starting an ailing industry. In addition, it provided tax relief to independent oil and gas drillers to try to stimulate production (Idelson 1992b).

These were significant achievements, yet problems remained. The market forces that determine energy prices still did not adequately reflect either the environmental or national security costs of using energy. The 1992 Act did not raise the CAFE standards for motor vehicles, which was the top priority of environmental groups, nor did it do much to reduce the use of oil.

The Clinton Administration Tries Its Hand

These deficiencies of the 1992 Act were apparent when President Bill Clinton assumed office in January 1993. Environmental groups, still unhappy with the Act, urged the president to create a high-level energy task force to review conflicting studies and build political consensus for a more effective energy policy. Clinton's transition staff promised a series of actions to accelerate energy efficiency in buildings and appliances, government purchase of alternative-fuel vehicles and energy-efficient computers, and research support for conservation technologies and renewable energy sources. The president announced in his Earth Day address in April 1993 that he would issue executive orders promoting such actions where possible. One such order directed all federal agencies to achieve by 2010 a 35 percent improvement in energy efficiency and a 30 percent cut in greenhouse gas emissions.[14]

The BTU Tax and Gasoline President Clinton learned early in his administration that solving the nation's energy problems entailed overcoming severe political obstacles. As part of his deficit-reduction package announced in early 1993, for example, he had proposed a broad energy tax based on the heat output of fuel, or British thermal units (BTUs). He expected the tax to raise some $72 billion over five years while simultaneously reducing the use of fossil fuels, thus curbing pollution and reducing oil imports. The proposal bore some resemblance to the carbon tax (based on carbon dioxide emissions) that had long been advocated by environmentalists (Rabe 2017).

Despite these high hopes, however, Clinton's BTU tax was an instant political failure. It was greeted by a tidal wave of opposition on Capitol Hill, reflecting complaints from industry groups and others (farmers, energy-producing states, and states reliant on home heating oil) that the plan would cost them too much money, reduce their competitiveness, and put people out of work. The National Association of Manufacturers, the U.S. Chamber of Commerce, the Chemical Manufacturers Association (later renamed the American Chemistry Council), and the American Petroleum Institute, among others, worked actively to defeat the tax through sophisticated use of satellite feeds, talk radio, opinion polls, a blizzard of newspaper editorials, and mass mailings to citizens urging them to protest the tax. In the end, Congress agreed only to a 4.3 cent per gallon increase in the federal gas tax, despite the lowest market price for gasoline in a generation.[15]

Gas taxes in the United States remain well below those of other industrialized nations. In recent years, federal, state, and local taxes (state and local taxes vary widely) averaged about 48 cents per gallon, about 21 percent of the retail price of gasoline in 2016. In Europe, however, taxes have been up to 80 percent of the cost of gasoline paid at the pump, which explains why the cost of gasoline there (and in Japan and Canada) is about two to three times as much as it is in the United States. The politics of energy in recent years has dictated that only painless measures would be acceptable in the U.S. Congress and at the state and local level.

A similar reluctance to constrain the use of gasoline is evident in federal fuel economy standards. For six years beginning in 1995, a Republican Congress enacted legislation that blocked the Department of Transportation from reviewing or changing fuel economy standards for vehicles in an effort to prevent President Clinton from raising mileage standards. Congress made that decision even as the average fuel economy of U.S. vehicles dropped to its lowest level since 1980.[16] For the 2003 model cars and passenger trucks, the EPA reported an average of 20.8 miles per gallon, some 6 percent *below* the high point of 15 years earlier. Before Americans began buying so many SUVs, the average was 22.1. However, a number of recent actions are pushing the nation to higher fuel economy. Among these are tougher air pollution rules for automobiles; Bush administration approval in 2006 of a modest increase in fuel economy standards for SUVs, pickup trucks, and vans; action by Congress in 2007 to raise the CAFE standards; and especially the decision of the Obama administration to set new and much higher targets for vehicle fuel efficiency (see Chapter 5).

The Partnership for a New Generation of Vehicles The Clinton administration's Clean Car Initiative, later renamed the Partnership for a New Generation of Vehicles (PNGV), was expected to help achieve some of the same objectives as the rejected BTU tax and ultimately assist the nation in raising fuel economy. The PNGV called for the federal government to coordinate its R&D spending with the three largest U.S. automobile makers (Ford, General Motors, and DaimlerChrysler). Announced in 1993, the program was intended to produce a "supercar" that could get 80 miles per gallon with low pollutant emissions and without a loss in performance, passenger capacity, or safety. It enjoyed some success, and it may have moved some auto makers, particularly Honda and Toyota, to begin selling fuel-efficient hybrid vehicles in the U.S. market in 2000. However, the Bush administration in 2002 ended the PNGV program and substituted an initiative to develop hydrogen-based or fuel cell-powered vehicles, termed FreedomCAR (Freedom Cooperative Automotive Research). President Obama cut funding for that program in his first year in office and directed funding toward development of electric vehicles and other technologies.

Beyond the PNGV, the Clinton administration took other modest steps toward strengthening U.S. energy policy. It extended by 10 years a moratorium on offshore oil and gas drilling that began in the first Bush administration in 1990. It endorsed the Kyoto Protocol, which calls for reduction of U.S. greenhouse gas emissions. It also sharply increased spending on energy conservation and renewable energy resources, and in 1998 it consolidated various energy initiatives into a Comprehensive National Energy Strategy prepared by the DOE, which it transmitted to Congress (Cooper 1999).

Energy Policy under George W. Bush and Barack Obama

From the first days of President George W. Bush's administration, it was clear that new energy policy priorities would prevail. For example, the president decided to keep some Clinton administration energy efficiency rules for appliances but to oppose higher standards for new central air-conditioning systems. The rules were set to go into effect in February 2001 after years of development and negotiations with the affected industries.[17]

Controversies over the administration's energy policies did not let up over the next seven years. Most of the attention focused on Bush's national energy plan, which he announced in May 2001. Prepared by a task force chaired by Vice President Dick Cheney, the plan called for significant increases in the use of fossil fuels and nuclear energy as well as easing of environmental regulations that might inhibit new energy production. As discussed in Chapter 3, the Cheney task force consulted closely with major energy producers but not with environmental interests. Its recommendations to the president focused heavily on increasing energy supplies rather than reducing demand through conservation. Because of that strategy, it argued the nation needed to build 1,300 new power plants by 2020. Cheney himself dismissed the idea of conservation as a minor concern. It "may be a sign of personal virtue, but it is not a sufficient basis for a sound, comprehensive energy policy," he said.[18] His comment was at odds with studies by energy experts both within and outside of government. Scientists at national energy laboratories, for example, found that market-based, energy efficiency policies could reduce the nation's energy needs by fully a third through 2010.[19]

The Bush energy proposal initially did not fare well in Congress. The Republican House of Representatives approved it after what the press called "aggressive lobbying by the Bush administration, labor unions and the oil, gas and coal industries."[20] The House bill included generous tax and research benefits for the oil, natural gas, coal, and nuclear power industries, and it permitted oil and gas drilling in ANWR, a perennially contentious issue. Those same proposals, however, could not pass muster in the Senate, but environmentalists were not successful there either. In a replay of the 1991 energy debate, the Senate defeated efforts by environmentalist groups to increase auto fuel efficiency and also rejected Bush's proposal to drill in ANWR. Despite extended negotiations, neither side was prepared to compromise given the intense and conflicting views within the core constituencies of each political party.[21]

It is a telling comment about U.S. energy politics that members of Congress could not muster support for a national energy policy even in the aftermath of California's well-publicized struggle with an energy crisis, new concern over the integrity of the nation's electric power grid, and another war in the oil-rich Middle East.[22] In the hope of generating more support for his bill, the president tried to link it with national security concerns following the terrorist attacks of 2001, but he was largely unsuccessful in doing so (Cooper 2002). That relationship was more broadly endorsed several years later as a number of conservative organizations began warning about the nation's dependency on imported oil. Competing energy bills were debated repeatedly in Congress for the next four years with similar partisan divisions. Democrats favored increases in auto and truck fuel efficiency standards and they opposed drilling for oil in ANWR. Republicans were equally adamant that ANWR must be opened to energy development, but they opposed any increase in fuel efficiency standards (Guber and Bosso 2007; Kraft 2016). Intense lobbying by car manufacturers, labor unions, the oil and gas industry, and environmentalists continued.

The political dynamics of the energy debate changed in 2005 as gasoline and other fuel prices, and public discontent over them, rose. By summer 2005 Congress surprised many when it managed to resolve differences between the two political parties and approve the Energy Policy Act of 2005, the first major overhaul of U.S. energy policy since 1992. The bill passed with bipartisan support and President Bush signed the measure in August, saying it would spur new domestic production of oil and natural gas and encourage expansion of renewable sources of energy. The emphasis in the 1,700-page law, however, clearly was on expansion of conventional fossil fuel sources and nuclear power. It included no new requirements for improving fuel efficiency standards for automobiles and SUVs, it did not mandate any reduction in greenhouse gas emissions, and it imposed no new requirements on utilities to rely more on renewable power sources.

Consistent with the president's initial proposal, the law gave billions of dollars in federal tax credits and other subsidies to energy producers as an incentive to generate more energy. The granting of such benefits meant that the bill's estimated cost of $12.3 billion over 10 years was twice what the president had proposed in 2001. Critics were quick to say that the incentives were excessively generous ("spectacular giveaways" was one newspaper's summary) and unnecessary at a time when energy prices were reaching new highs. They also faulted Congress for including thousands of individual pork-barrel projects in the bill to ensure its passage.[23] The law called for expanded energy R&D, and, to the dismay of environmentalists, it included provisions to streamline the process for building new energy facilities (i.e., to reduce consideration of environmental impacts). In addition, the measure required utilities to modernize the nation's electricity grid to ensure reliable delivery of electric energy.

Some provisions of the new law, however, pleased environmentalists. There were new energy efficiency standards for federal office buildings, programs to encourage the states to foster energy conservation, and requirements for the federal government to purchase an increasing percentage of its electricity from renewable sources. There also were new tax deductions or credits for consumers who purchased renewable power systems for their homes or improved energy efficiency in their homes, or who bought hybrid vehicles; however, these were fairly modest and available for only a few years. There were more substantial provisions of this kind for commercial buildings. In addition, the law authorized billions of dollars for R&D intended to increase energy efficiency, diversify energy supplies, and reduce environmental impacts of energy use (Evans and Schatz 2005).

Late in 2007 Congress finally agreed on a modest energy package, the Energy Independence and Security Act of 2007. It set a new national fuel-economy standard of 35 miles per gallon by 2020, the first significant change in the CAFE standard since 1975 and a 40 percent increase over the prevailing average of 25 miles per gallon. The Act also sought to increase the supply of alternative fuel by setting a renewable fuel standard that required fuel producers to use at least 36 billion gallons of biofuels by 2022, including both corn-based ethanol and other sources. By 2016, the nation used about 14 billion gallons of ethanol and 2 billion gallons of biodiesel a year, and EPA mandated that for 2017 that this total include 4.3 billion gallons of advanced biofuels, a level that is still only half of congressional goals under the 2007 Act. Cellulosic biofuels made from non-corn feedstocks have long fallen short of the Act's specifications.[24] Other provisions of the bill sought to improve efficiency in lighting and appliances and to increase federal agency use of efficiency measures and renewable energy sources.

As gas prices soared to new highs in 2008, energy issues once again rose to some prominence across the nation, and increasingly they were linked to climate change. States continued a trend of approving new requirements for use of renewable energy (Betsill and Rabe 2009; Rabe 2004, 2016), and a climate change bill reached the floor of the U.S. Senate for the first time. As discussed in Chapter 4, the 2008 presidential election also gave new impetus to the search for national energy policy, with both John McCain and Barack Obama urging action on climate change, and leading corporations beginning to endorse the necessity of climate change policy.[25] However, the Republican Party continued to emphasize the need for increasing domestic oil and gas supplies (particularly for offshore drilling) and building additional nuclear power plants, while Democrats urged support for conservation, efficiency, and renewable energy and linked such a strategy to creation of green jobs; by fall of 2008, however, they too endorsed renewed offshore drilling with significant restraints to protect the environment. Former Vice President Al Gore even called in mid-2008 for a crash program to produce all electricity from carbon-free sources within ten years.[26]

These debates continued through 2009 in the midst of a severe recession, with the House narrowly approving a major climate change and energy bill in June that would impose mandatory caps on emission of greenhouse gases. The House bill ran to more than 1,400 pages and integrated the climate change components with a diversity of other energy measures, including the first national renewable energy target; spending on new energy projects; and subsidies for low-carbon agriculture, electric vehicle development, and clean coal research. However, the same kinds of regional and partisan divisions evident in earlier periods were evident in 2009 as well, with Democrats from the older industrial Midwest and agricultural states worried about the impact on their local economies even as the U.S. EPA pegged the cost of the bill for the average household at only about $80 to $111 a year by 2020. The Senate was less receptive to the bill, and President Obama was too preoccupied with economic recovery and health care policy concerns in 2010 to provide the leadership essential to win Senate approval.[27]

In another action, the Obama administration substantially altered energy policy in early 2009 by including about $80 billion in spending, tax incentives, and loan guarantees to promote energy efficiency, renewable energy sources, fuel-efficient cars, mass transit, and clean coal as part of the economic stimulus bill, the American Recovery and Reinvestment Act of 2009; $39 billion of that amount went to the DOE. By its size alone, the measure constituted the biggest energy bill in U.S. history. It provided money for research on capturing and storing carbon dioxide from coal-fired power plants, research on advanced car batteries, grants and loans to modernize the nation's electric power grid and increase its capacity to transmit power from renewable sources, and nearly $18 billion for mass transit, Amtrak, and high-speed rail. The administration also brokered an agreement with the auto industry to substantially increase vehicle fuel efficiency standards to a fleet average of 54.5 miles per gallon by 2025. At the same time, it continued many of the Bush administration's efforts to increase oil and gas drilling on public lands, moving the nation much closer to the goal of energy independence.[28]

However, the Obama administration ultimately rejected the Keystone XL pipeline that was intended to bring Canadian tar sands oil to the U.S., and it proposed the first national regulations of hydraulic fracking for oil and gas production on public lands (Weber, Bernell, and Boudet 2016). In December 2016, the Army Corps of Engineers announced that it would not grant a final easement for the controversial Dakota Access Pipeline, and indicated that an alternative route that did not directly affect tribal land and cultural resources would be preferable. The Trump administration, however, favored construction of both pipelines.[29]

With increasing partisan conflict in Congress, new energy and climate change proposals fared poorly after 2010, particularly in the Republican-controlled House. As noted in the chapter's opening, the Obama administration finally settled on a series of actions that the president could launch without approval by Congress. These included new EPA regulations on carbon dioxide emissions from existing power plants (the Clean Power Plan), a variety of spending initiatives to spur the development of new renewable energy technologies, and continued development of renewable energy resources on public lands. By many measures, these varied energy policy actions may well be one of the Obama administration's most notable legacies.[30] Some of these decisions may well be reversed in the Trump administration, which brings a quite different set of priorities to energy policy, although actions to change direction might well be tempered by the commitments already made by corporations and energy companies to renewable energy development, conservation, and efficiency. There also is considerable support across the political spectrum for continued investment in clean energy sources (Ansolabehere and Konisky 2014).[31]

State and Local Energy Initiatives

Some of the most promising energy policy initiatives, much like environmental protection actions, occur outside Washington, DC. State and local policymakers can more easily build consensus for innovations than is possible in the contentious arena of national politics, where partisan and ideological battles often make agreement difficult (Betsill and Rabe 2009; Rabe 2016, 2018). One example is Sacramento, California, where residents voted in 1989 to close their publicly owned but troubled Rancho Seco nuclear power plant that provided half of the local power. The Sacramento Municipal Utility District (SMUD) became a thriving laboratory for energy conservation and use of renewable fuels, and its programs are still active today. Indeed, in 2009 it started a new program to see if friendly competition among neighbors might spur even greater achievement in energy conservation, and it seems to be working.[32] Tight environmental restrictions throughout California have made conservation and efficiency highly attractive to utilities in the state that now find it difficult to build additional generating plants. This is one reason the state has emerged as a national leader in the use of solar power and other renewable sources of energy; by 2009 it had two-thirds of the entire nation's solar capacity, and it continued to push solar energy. The state has consistently funded solar energy through rebates and other financial incentives to encourage rooftop solar installations, with some communities, such as Berkeley, offering their own financial packages to spur use of solar power. Other states and cities are beginning to offer similar programs. Solar energy has been so widely adopted in both California and Arizona that utilities have pressed the state governments to reduce these financial incentives for fear of losing their customers.[33]

Another example of state-level innovation concerns home construction. The 1992 Energy Policy Act requires states to review their residential building codes to determine whether they need revisions to meet or exceed the Model Energy Code. But many cities and states rushed to approve even stronger codes for both homes and commercial buildings. California's energy-efficient building and appliance codes save the state an estimated $6 billion a year. So-called zero-energy homes can be built to be so efficient that they rely almost exclusively on solar power. Short of that, homes and businesses clearly can be far more energy-efficient than they have been. Austin, Texas, has one of the nation's strictest building codes and requires an energy inspection before a building may be occupied. Yet most cities and states have far weaker requirements even though few policy changes could do more in the long run to save energy and reduce greenhouse gas emissions.[34] Other examples of state and local policy innovations on energy and climate change abound. Box 6.1 summarizes some of the most notable of them that have been adopted in recent years.

■ BOX 6.1 STATE AND LOCAL ENERGY POLICY INITIATIVES ■

Although the federal government has struggled in recent years to overcome policy gridlock on energy issues, state and local governments have become increasingly active and creative in addressing energy issues, including their link to climate change.

• By 2012, 29 states with about 60 percent of the nation's population had enacted renewable energy portfolios that call for a certain percentage of the electricity used in the state to come from renewable sources. Many of the states continue to increase their goals for reliance on renewable energy, with

California and New York calling for 50 percent renewable use by 2030 (Rabe 2016).

- In 2002 California approved legislation that for the first time would compel automakers to limit emissions of carbon dioxide by building more fuel-efficient vehicles. In 2004 the California Air Resources Board (ARB) released its draft regulations. The California standards became the basis for new national fuel economy standards that the Obama administration announced in 2009 after negotiations with the auto industry.

- In 2000 the Seattle city council pledged to meet the city's future electricity needs through renewable energy and gains in energy efficiency. The city indicated that it would strive to have no net emissions that are linked to global climate change. In 2008, the city adopted a climate change action plan that is intended to help guide efforts to expand use of mass transit, bike lanes, green building standards, use of clean vehicles in the city fleet, and assistance to the business community in finding ways to cut energy costs and reduce carbon footprints.

- State policymakers in California adopted the nation's most ambitious and largest energy conservation program, with a strong focus on incentives for individuals to conserve energy. The California Energy Commission programs (www.energy.ca.gov) are among the most innovative and effective in the nation.

- The city of Lancaster, California, announced in 2013 that it now requires almost all new homes to be built with solar panels on the roof or be located within a subdivision that produces one kilowatt of solar energy per house. It persuaded one of the leading home building companies, KB Homes, to pursue this vision of a solar city, and by 2016 the city was on its way to being the first energy net-zero community in the nation by producing locally all of the energy that it consumes.

Natural Resources and Policy Change

Equally significant changes have been taking place in U.S. natural resources policy since the late 1980s. As noted earlier in the chapter, however, the emphasis can shift substantially from one presidential administration to the next. Despite the differing policy agendas of Interior Secretary Bruce Babbitt in the Clinton administration, his counterpart, Gale Norton, in the first six years of the Bush administration, and Ken Salazar and Sally Jewell in the Obama administration, over the past several decades an historic shift has taken place away from resource policies that favor economic development. These changes are also evident at state, local, and regional levels where governments, environmental groups, and the private sector have found common cause in promoting sustainable community initiatives and developing ecosystem-based management approaches that promise to overcome the often-fragmented and ineffective policy actions of the past (Koontz et al. 2004; Layzer 2008, 2013; Mazmanian and Kraft 2009; Sabatier et al. 2005; Thomas 2003).

Natural resource policy actions invite sharp conflict as different interests clash over how best to use the resources, evident in disputes over drilling for oil in ANWR and in offshore areas, increasing logging in national forests and on public lands in the West, and protecting habitats of threatened and endangered species. Yet they also signal the potential for a new era of cooperation as environmentalist groups and development interests try to find ways to reconcile environmental and economic goals. Even if many of the battles continue and the ultimate outcome remains uncertain, one thing is clear. Some of the most ineffective and inefficient natural resource policies of past decades have come under increasing attack (Lowry 2003, 2006; Lubell and Segee 2013). Slowly, what had been a laissez-faire stance on ecologically damaging activities and generous government subsidies for shortsighted and uneconomic resource extraction have been giving way to a new goal of sustainable development. The short-term conflicts get much attention in the press, but the more important story is the redefined resource agenda and new public values driving natural resource decision making, from the local to the international level.

Environmental Stewardship or Economic Development?

The United States is richly endowed with natural resources. Even though the federal government gave away much of its original land before the early twentieth-century conservation movement curtailed the practice, the public domain includes about 640 million acres, or 28 percent of the nation's total land area of 2.3 billion acres. About half of that is in Alaska, where some 62 percent of the state is federally owned, and much of the rest is in the spacious Western states; about 47 percent of the 11 coterminous Western states is federally owned (Congressional Research Service 2012). These public lands and waters include awe-inspiring mountain ranges, vast stretches of open desert and high plains, pristine forests, spectacular rivers and lakes, and the magnificent national parks, such as Yellowstone, Yosemite, Grand Teton, Glacier, and Grand Canyon. They also contain valuable timber, minerals, energy resources, and water vital to irrigated crops in the West.

Even submerged offshore lands are precious. According to a 2011 estimate by the Bureau of Ocean Energy Management in the Department of the Interior (one of two agencies that replaced the old Minerals Management Service), the federally governed 1.7 billion acres of land on the outer continental shelf (OCS) may contain nearly 90 billion barrels of undiscovered and technically recoverable oil and almost 400 trillion cubic feet of natural gas. In recent years, about 36 million acres of OCS land was leased for oil and gas production, accounting for about 7 percent of U.S. natural gas production and about 24 percent of oil production.[35] The energy industry strongly favors increased production on these lands, while environmentalists tend to resist expansion of offshore production. In December 2016, President Obama announced what he termed a "permanent ban" on offshore oil and gas drilling in a large portion of federally owned Arctic waters and along the Atlantic coast from Virginia to Maine. He did so with an unusually broad interpretation of his authority under the 1953 Outer Continental Shelf Lands Act. The Trump administration and the Republican Congress are likely to challenge the action.[36]

Congress has chosen to set aside some areas—the parks, wild rivers, wilderness areas, and national seashores—to protect them from almost all development. Most public lands are only partially protected. They are subject to long-standing, but intentionally vague, "multiple-use" doctrines that Congress intended to help balance competing national objectives of economic development and environmental preservation. Thus agency administrators are expected to protect and exploit resources simultaneously. They preserve public lands and waters for recreation and aesthetic enjoyment, and protect ecologically vital watersheds and fish and wildlife habitat. Yet they also try to ensure commercial development of the commodities on those lands, such as minerals and timber. Agency officials serve as stewards of the public domain, a job that involves refereeing the many disputes that arise among the multitude of interests competing for access to it.

Natural resource policies govern those decisions, most of which fall within the jurisdiction of the Interior Department and Agriculture Department. Each of the major policies, agencies, and public land systems is described later. Conflicts over these policies and the decisions the agencies have made to implement them have escalated dramatically since the late 1960s. Among the primary reasons for the new controversy are the rise of the environmental movement and public support for its goals, rapid population growth in the West where most of the public lands are located, and surging interest in recreation (such as mountain climbing, white-water rafting, and off-road vehicle use). Each of these social changes has created new demands on the public lands and the agencies that govern them. For example, those who want greater access to public lands for recreation may compete with commercial interests that seek to harvest the resources, such as minerals and timber. Ultimately, government agencies have to make choices about who gains access to public lands and who does not.

Added to these developments are what economists call structural economic shifts that have imperiled some commercial activities in the West, including extractive industries such as forestry and mining that have been in decline for some time. They also include traditional activities such as ranching, which depends on low-cost grazing on public lands, and farming; in the arid West, that means dependence on federally subsidized irrigation water.

Changes in these economic enterprises can severely threaten thousands of people in the West whose livelihoods depend on continued access to public lands and waters. Even with a robust national economy, such individuals, and the communities in which they live, suffer genuine harm. Deservedly or not, they often blame environmental policies and actions of the federal government for their dire situation (Brick and Cawley 1996; Switzer 1997; Tierney and Frasure 1998). The 2016 standoff between armed, antigovernment protesters and the federal government at a wildlife refuge in Eastern Oregon is a case in point. Such conflicts have occurred for decades, especially in the West, where much of the land is federally owned.[37]

As the "wise use" movement of the 1990s and the more recent disputes vividly demonstrate, crafting solutions that satisfy all these parties is always difficult, and sometimes seemingly impossible. The extent to which consensus can be built will test the nation's capacity to put the concepts of sustainable development and ecosystem-based management into practice. Success is likely to depend on generating credible and compelling scientific analyses of the environmental effects of resource use, and also on designing policies to mitigate unavoidable and adverse economic and social repercussions. Few people advocate having such crucial value choices made by a centralized and distant bureaucracy. Thus equally important to the goal of sustainable development is the creation of decision-making processes capable of fostering constructive policy dialogue and consensus-building among stakeholders at all levels of government, and especially in affected communities (Gerlak, Heikkila, and Lubell 2013; Mazmanian and Kraft 2009; Sabatier et al. 2005; Weber 2003).

The Environmentalist Challenge to Resource Development

Natural resources policy has a much longer history in the United States than either environmental protection or energy policy. As discussed in Chapter 4, policies designed to encourage settlement of the West transferred over 1 billion acres of federal domain land to the states and private parties before ended officially in 1976. Well before the environmental decade of the 1970s, the conservation movement instituted the first of a series of protectionist policies with the creation of national parks and monuments and the establishment of the National Park Service, Forest Service, Bureau of Reclamation, and other federal resource agencies. For most of the twentieth century, conflicts over protection and development of federal lands had been relatively muted and politically contained, in part because natural resource subgovernments, also discussed in Chapter 4, dominated the issues and promoted consensus on policy goals and means (Clarke and McCool 1996; Culhane 1981; McCool 1990). Scholars disagree about the extent of agency "capture" by regulated interests (such as the influence of mining and oil and gas companies in Interior Department agencies or of forest products companies in the Forest Service). Yet it would be fair to say that long-settled policies that governed mining, oil and gas development, logging, grazing, agriculture, and other uses of public lands and waters have rarely emerged as major political issues with the larger public. All that changed as the environmental movement gathered steam in the 1960s, when it scored its first policy successes in resource conservation.

Gains in Resource Protection and Political Access The Wilderness Act of 1964 created the National Wilderness Preservation System to set aside undeveloped areas of federal land where "the earth and its community of life are untrammeled by man." The Land and Water Conservation Fund Act of 1964 provided federal grants to the states for planning for, acquiring, and developing land and water areas for recreation. The fund also provides money to buy property for national parks, forests, and refuges managed by the federal government. In 1968 Congress established the National Wild and Scenic Rivers System to protect free-flowing rivers in their natural state.

In a fitting symbol of the dozens of environmental measures to follow, on its last day in session in December 1969, Congress enacted the National Environmental Policy Act (NEPA), and President Richard Nixon signed it into law on January 1, 1970. NEPA (pronounced "knee pah") requires the preparation of environmental impact statements (EISs) for all "major Federal actions significantly affecting the quality of the human environment" (Caldwell 1998). Of equal importance was the creation by NEPA and other statutes and judicial rulings of the 1970s of a major role for the public in environmental decision making, altering forever the political dynamics of natural resources policy (Dana and Fairfax 1980).

These new policies, and the political movements that inspired them, brought to the fore the previously latent conflicts in natural resources that are now so common. During the 1970s environmentalists gained access to the natural resource subgovernments, from the national to the local level. They became regular participants in agency decision making, and they gained powerful allies on Capitol Hill as natural resources committees and subcommittees began to reflect the public's strong support for resource preservation efforts. They also played an active role in the courts, using NEPA's environmental impact statement process to oppose many development projects that they viewed as environmentally damaging (Caldwell 1998; Wenner 1982).

Reaction in the West None of this change was good news for traditional resource constituencies, especially in the Western states. They saw their historic access to public lands and waters jeopardized by the new demands for preservation and recreation, and by a different set of policy actors who were unlikely to acquiesce to the old distributive formulas. In the early

1980s, and more recently under wise use and property rights banners, the user groups fought back, using rhetoric and political symbols equally as powerful as those offered by the environmental community (Brick and Cawley 1996; Cawley 1993; Davis 2001).

Environmentalists speak passionately about preserving nature, particularly wilderness areas, and they often base their arguments in environmental science and ecology. Ecosystem-based management, for example, has emerged as a powerful concept that derives in large part from recent advances in ecology, along with what is often called critical loads assessment and adaptive management (Bäckstrand 2017; Cortner and Moote 1999; Layzer 2008, 2013; Layzer and Schulman 2017). Ecologists also are likely to identify the varied and essential "services" that nature provides to humans, such as purification of air and water, prevention of flooding, and provision of food (Daily 1997). Yet equally important to many environmental groups and individuals are the strong aesthetic and moral values they hold about conservation of natural systems (Kellert 1996).

In contrast, user groups are much more likely to adopt a utilitarian or instrumental view of natural resources. They talk about both economic and commercial values and the preservation of local communities long dependent on public lands and waters. They refer as well to threats posed to the Western "way of life" and culture, and they remain skeptical about the science behind environmentalist assertions.[38] Some have been particularly critical of the ecosystem-based management approaches to which federal agencies have turned (Layzer 2013). For all these reasons, user groups evince a distinct preference for state and local control of public lands over federal dominance, and for private property rights over governmental regulation. They are convinced that decisions on natural resources will be more rational if they are made locally and if property owners are more fully in control of their own land (Tierney and Frasure 1998).

The major policies and programs continue to reflect the ambivalence the nation displays toward the use of natural resources. Strong public support exists for resource conservation and environmental preservation, but these issues typically fail to command the visibility needed to mobilize the public. The result is that consensus in Congress on these statutes is less than robust. Members of Congress also tend to be highly sensitive to the pleas of politically significant constituencies. Mining, logging, ranching, oil and gas, and agricultural interests lobby intensely to protect their benefits, and they are well represented on Capitol Hill. That is particularly so in the Senate, where sparsely settled Western states enjoy the same representation as the most populous states; no matter how small the population, each state has two senators.

These institutional and political characteristics help explain a good deal of the congressional opposition to the Clinton administration's highly visible proposals for reform of natural resource policies. Just as important, however, is the absence of public concern over issues such as mining, oil and gas drilling, logging, and grazing on public lands. Few people not directly affected by the policies are likely to think much about proposals for reform of the General Mining Law of 1872, appropriate fee structures for grazing cattle on federal land, or what constitutes a reasonable royalty payment for oil and gas extraction from leased public lands. The low salience of the issues weakens the reformers' ability to push their agenda, and contributes to the legislative gridlock that has characterized these policy conflicts in recent years.

Ironically, the West is being transformed politically by an enormous influx of so-called lifestyle refugees into states such as Arizona, Colorado, Idaho, Wyoming, Montana, Oregon, Washington, and Utah. The New West is overwhelmingly urban and suburban, and it has many of the fastest-growing states in the country. It is being built not on the extractive industries such as mining and forestry that dominated the West in decades past, but on communications, electronics and computer manufacturing, tourism, recreation, and retirees.[39] As one sign of the transformation, the number of metal miners in the United States fell by half between the early 1980s and late 1990s as more of the business shifted to other nations. The outdoor recreation industry, in contrast, now supports three times more jobs than the oil and gas sector, and outdoor enthusiasts spend nearly $650 billion a year, are responsible for over 6 million jobs, and generate $80 billion a year in federal, state, and local tax revenues.[40] These demographic and economic changes already have affected Congress as noted earlier, and they are likely to have a more significant effect on both local and national environmental politics and policies over time.

Natural Resource Policies and Agencies

Much like federal energy policy, natural resource policies are both simple and complex. They are simplest at the level of basic choices made about preservation or development of public resources or equity in the payment of user fees. They are most convoluted in the detailed and arcane rules and procedures governing program implementation. Debates over policy proposals similarly can be fairly straightforward or all but indecipherable to those outside the resource policy communities.

Table 6.1 offers a brief description of the major federal natural resource policies and lists their implementing agencies.[41] To understand the politics of natural resources policy requires us to pay at least some attention to the agencies themselves. Congress has granted the agencies great discretion to interpret and implement the statutes, which puts them at the center of political battles over protection versus economic exploitation of the public domain at a time of fundamental policy and administrative changes. The conflicts can be illustrated with a selective review of how the agencies are implementing the new resource policies.

TABLE 6.1 Major federal natural resource policies

Statute	Implementing agency	Key provisions and features
Multiple Use– Sustained Yield Act of 1960, PL 86-517	Interior Department: Forest Service	Defined multiple-use and sustained yield concepts for the Forest Service. Required that officials consider diverse values in managing forestlands, including protection of fish and wildlife. Made clear that the forests should be managed to "best meet the needs of the American people" and not necessarily to yield the highest dollar return.
Wilderness Act of 1964, PL 88-577	Agriculture Department; Interior Department	Established the National Wilderness Preservation System comprising federal lands designated as "wilderness areas," to remain "unimpaired for future use and enjoyment as wilderness." Authorized review of public lands for possible inclusion in the system.
Land and Water Conservation Fund Act of 1964, PL 88-578	Interior Department	Created the Land and Water Conservation Fund, which receives money from the sale of off-shore oil and gas leases in the outer continental shelf. Authorized appropriations from the fund for matching grants for state and local planning, acquisition, and development of land for recreation purposes and for acquisition of lands and waters for federal recreation areas.
Wild and Scenic Rivers Act of 1968, PL 90-542	Interior Department	Authorized protection of selected rivers with "outstandingly remarkable features," including scenic, biological, archaeological, or cultural value. Rivers may be designated as wild, scenic, or recreational.
National Environmental Policy Act of 1969, PL 91-190	All agencies; coordinated by the Council on Environmental Quality	Declared a national policy to "encourage productive and enjoyable harmony between man and his environment"; required environmental impact statements; created the Council on Environmental Quality.

TABLE 6.1 (*continued*)

Statute	Implementing agency	Key provisions and features
Marine Protection Research, and Sanctuaries Act of 1972 (Ocean Dumping Act), PL 92-532	U.S. Environmental Protection Agency	Authorized research and monitoring of long-range effects of pollution, overfishing, and other acts on ocean ecosystems. Regulated ocean dumping through an EPA permit system that allows disposal of waste materials only in designated areas.
Coastal Zone Management Act of 1972, PL 92-583	Office of Ocean and Coastal Resource Management	Authorized federal grants to states to develop coastal zone management plans under federal guidelines and to acquire and operate estuarine sanctuaries.
Marine Mammal Protection Act of 1972, PL 92-522	National Marine Fisheries Service	Established a moratorium on the taking of marine mammals and a ban on importation of marine mammals and products made from them, with certain exceptions. Created a federal responsibility for conservation of marine mammals.
Endangered Species Act of 1973, PL 93-205	Fish and Wildlife Service, National Marine Fisheries Service	Broadened federal authority to protect all "threatened" as well as "endangered" species; authorized grant program to assist the states; required coordination among all federal agencies.
Magnuson–Stevens Fishery Conservation and Management Act of 1976, Public Law 94-265	National Marine Fisheries Service, NOAA	Fosters long-term biological and economic sustainability of the nation's marine fisheries. Seeks to prevent overfishing, rebuild stocks, increase long-term economic and social benefits, and ensure a safe and sustainable supply of seafood.
Federal Land Policy and Management Act of 1976, PL 94-579	Bureau of Land Management	Gave Bureau of Land Management authority to manage public lands for long-term benefits; officially ended policy of disposing of public lands through privatization. Provided for use of national forests and grasslands for livestock grazing under a permit system.

TABLE 6.1 (*continued*)

Statute	Implementing agency	Key provisions and features
National Forest Management Act of 1976, PL 94-588	Forest Service	Extended and elaborated processes set out in the 1974 Forest and Rangeland Renewable Resources Planning Act. Gave statutory permanence to national forestlands and set new standards for their planning and management, including full public participation; provided new authority for management, harvesting, and selling of timber, and restricted timber use to protect soil and watersheds; limited clear-cutting.
Surface Mining Control and Reclamation Act of 1977, PL 95-87	Interior Department, Office of Surface Mining	Established environmental controls over surface mining of coal; limited mining on farmland, alluvial valleys, and slopes; required restoration of land to original contours.
Alaska National Interest Lands Conservation Act of 1980, PP 96-487	Interior Department; Agriculture Department	Protected 103 million acres of Alaskan land as national wilderness, forest, wildlife refuges, and parks, and other areas of special management and study.
Omnibus Public Lands Management Act of 2009, PL 111-11	Interior Department; Agriculture Department	Consolidated 164 public lands measures that protect 2 million acres of wilderness in nine states; establish new national trails and parks; and protect 1,100 miles of 86 new wild and scenic rivers in eight states. The most significant expansion of federal land conservation programs in 15 years.

Administration of public lands is assigned chiefly to four federal agencies. The Bureau of Land Management, the Fish and Wildlife Service, and the National Park Service are housed in the Interior Department. The Forest Service, often at odds with the Interior Department, has been in the Department of Agriculture since Gifford Pinchot had the nation's newly created forest reserves transferred there in 1905. Together, the four agencies control an estimated 609 million acres, or over 95 percent of the total public domain lands. The Department of Defense manages about 19 million acres, and the remaining lands are under the jurisdiction of numerous other agencies, including other Interior and Agriculture departmental agencies such as the Bureau of Reclamation, the Department of Energy, and the Tennessee Valley Authority. Other agencies are involved in scientific studies and monitoring of public lands that contribute to policymaking, such as the U.S. Geological Survey in the Interior Department and the Natural Resources Conservation Service, located in the Agriculture Department (U.S. GAO 1997b; Congressional Research Service 2012).[42]

As Clarke and McCool (1996) demonstrate, each agency has its distinctive origins, constituencies, characteristics, and decision-making style. Fish and Wildlife Service and National Park Service lands are governed by specialized missions, and for the most part are well protected from development. In contrast, Forest Service and Bureau of Land Management lands are subject to multiple-use doctrines that pose a greater risk of environmental degradation. These doctrines also require agency administrators to juggle competing interests and reconcile conflicting interpretations of the law, always under the watchful eye of Congress and the interest groups and industries that are affected. The two agencies, however, have markedly different histories and orientations (Dana and Fairfax 1980).

Managing the Nation's Forests

Forests occupy about a third of the U.S. land area, with the majority owned privately or by the states. The nation had been losing half a million acres of private forestland a year to urban expansion and agriculture, which contributed to ardent interest in those forestlands under federal control. However, the Department of Agriculture's National Resources Inventory found that total nonfederal forestland in the nation increased from 1982 to 2007, most of which appears to be in private timberland. The inventory also found an accelerating rate of loss of agricultural land as cities expand outward.[43] Even if the overall trend of lost forestland has changed, concern continues over the quality of the remaining land as well as fragmentation and other alterations of land that provides critical habitat to species.

The responsibility for managing the federal lands and the Forest Service itself reflect the era when both were born: Pinchot's progressive conservation movement in the early twentieth century. Its awkward blend of resource protection and use continues to this day. The Forest Service has a long tradition of professional forest management, although environmentalists often have faulted it for excessive devotion to the interests of the timber industry. They have been particularly critical of the service's approval of clear-cutting of forests and its insufficient protection of habitat and biological diversity (Culhane 1981; Lowry 2006).

At the instigation of the Forest Service and to respond to an increasing number of people seeking to enjoy the trails and streams of the national forests, Congress enacted a milestone statute in 1960, the Multiple Use–Sustained Yield Act. It defined multiple use as including outdoor recreation, fish and wildlife, and ranging as well as timber production, and the Act made clear that the forests should be managed to "best meet the needs of the American people" and "not necessarily [through] uses that will give the greatest dollar return." The Act set no priorities, and thus gave the Forest Service discretion to expand its preservation of forest resources.

The National Forest Management Act Environmentalist concern rose significantly as the Forest Service began implementing the National Forest Management Act (NFMA) of 1976 early in the Reagan administration. The NFMA amended the 1974 Forest and Rangeland Renewable Resources Planning Act, which had set timber production as a primary goal. The 1974 Act, however, also had established a general planning process that helped shift the Forest Service (and the Bureau of Land Management) away from what had been an overwhelming emphasis on timber production.

The 1976 Act extended this process and added further specifications. It required the Forest Service to prepare long-term comprehensive plans for the lands under its jurisdiction and to involve the public in its decision making through meetings and hearings. Thus the process made explicit the trade-offs between protecting the forest environment and allowing commercial development of it under the legal doctrines of sustained yield and multiple use.

Conflicts between forest preservation and development became especially acute as the Forest Service came under growing pressure in the mid-1980s to increase allowable timber harvest. It tried to resist such demands from political appointees in the Reagan administration out of concern that even the level of timber harvesting at that time was not sustainable. Such pressures on the Forest Service continued through the 1980s (Clarke and McCool 1996). Environmentalists and industry, or both, regularly contested the forest plans and the environmental impact statements that accompanied them. Environmentalists argued that the agency was deviating too much from its multiple-use mission and fostering instead "tree farming" in large areas of national forests. These challenges reached a peak in the George H. W. Bush administration, when environmentalists frequently filed administrative appeals to delay or block Forest Service timber sales.[44] Controversies continued throughout the 1990s over the extent of logging operations in the national forests and the sufficiency of the Forest Service's environmental assessments to document the consequences of timber sales.[45] Such disputes over forest plans notwithstanding, the new planning process under the 1976 law has been widely considered a model for natural resource management.

Changes in the U.S. Forest Service The Forest Service is a large agency, with more than 35,000 permanent employees, a budget of about $6 billion in fiscal 2017, and responsibility for over 193 million acres of public lands. In recent years, it has cut back sharply on sale of timber and on the revenues it has brought to the federal treasury. Critics have long asserted, however, that the revenue from timber sales is deceptive because the costs incurred by the government in providing access for timber harvesting (e.g., building and maintaining logging roads) has often exceeded the revenue. Hence concern is expressed over below-cost timber sales; even the Forest Service concedes that it loses money on sales of timber. For these and other reasons, particularly preservation of habitat, some environmental organizations (most notably the Sierra Club) have called for an end to all logging in national forests. Environmentalists say that the nation could save more than $1 billion per year by eliminating the subsidies for logging in the nation's forests.

The Forest Service also supervises grazing, use of water resources, and recreation on its lands, and it does so with a strong sense of mission and high professional standards. In their assessment of federal resource agencies, Clarke and McCool (1996) award the Forest Service one of two "bureaucratic superstar" ratings (the other goes to the U.S. Army Corps of Engineers) based on a reputation for bureaucratic power, professionalism, and political acumen.

Such accolades notwithstanding, like all natural resource agencies, the Forest Service in recent years has been undergoing major changes as it adjusts to new expectations for sustainable resource management and ecosystem protection. Studies by the National Research Council (1990), among others, have encouraged the service to incorporate elements of ecosystem-based management, for example, by placing greater emphasis on the ecological role of forests and their effects on climate change, educating the public on such issues, and financing Forest Service activities with greater reliance on fees from all users, from loggers and miners to campers and hikers. Such fees would reduce pressures to favor logging (Lowry 2006; O'Toole 1988).

The Clinton administration moved strongly in that direction under several chiefs of the service, including Jack Ward Thomas and Michael Dombeck.[46] Following through on an initiative by Dombeck to place a moratorium on construction of new logging roads in remote areas of national forests, President Clinton announced in October 1999 that he would use his executive authority to speed through permanent protection of some 40 million acres of federal forestland in six states. The proposal, termed "positively breathtaking" by a *New York Times* editorial, sought to create near-wilderness status for the land, prohibiting road building, logging, and mining. It was to add to the 34 million acres of the national forests already classified as wilderness areas. Conservationists applauded the move as a "grand slam," but the timber industry termed it an "extreme form of preservation." Western Republicans in Congress predictably were unhappy with the administration's proposal.[47]

Critics might be tempted to view these changes in the Forest Service and the legal protections for forestland as merely the policy preferences of the Clinton administration, but they also reflect recent developments in ecology and an improved understanding of ecosystem functioning. At about the same time the administration was proposing its new approaches to forestland (and other land), an independent 13-member scientific committee recommended that "ecological sustainability" become the principal goal in managing the national forests and grasslands, a position that Clinton's secretary of agriculture, Dan Glickman, endorsed as "a new planning framework for the management of our forests for the 21st century."[48]

In some respects, the new directions taken by the Forest Service in the 1990s also were a response to changing demographics and economics, especially in the West. Although timber cutting has declined by about two-thirds over the past decade, the number of recreational visitors has leaped by over 40 percent. As one journalist put it in 1999, "hikers, hunters, bikers, campers, and skiers increasingly dominate forest policy."[49]

The administration of George W. Bush was much less supportive of these new perspectives on how to use the national forests. The administration made clear that it favored substantial increases in logging more in line with the preferences of the timber industry, and it approved a series of measures intended to favor logging over preservation. For example, in 2004, after two years of dispute, the administration gave managers of the national forests more discretion in approving commercial activities such as logging, oil and gas drilling, and off-road vehicle use, and demanded less assessment of the environmental impacts when revising forest plans. The rules cut back as well on public participation in development of forest plans.[50] In addition, Bush succeeded in gaining congressional approval of the Healthy Forests Restoration Act of 2003, a law that permits increased logging in federal forests (defined as fuel reduction) as one way to limit the risk of wildfires (Jalonick 2004). The combination of the new forest rules and the new law will reduce the ability of environmental groups and others to challenge such actions, even though independent studies show that such challenges pose no barrier to fire prevention (U.S. GAO 2003).

The change demonstrated how effective the Bush administration was in portraying or framing a shift in forest policy as protection against wildfires and promotion of forest health; doing so makes it more politically attractive (Vaughn and Cortner 2004). Yet one real concern was the considerable cost to the Forest Service of fighting fires each year. In 1995, it spent 16 percent of its budget battling wildfires, and that rose to 52 percent by 2015. Barring changes, it expects to spend 67 percent of its budget on wildfires by 2025.[51] Rising temperatures and dry conditions in the forests are major factors in the rising number of fires and their intensity; both are linked to climate change.

The Bush administration did not always disappoint the environmental community. In late 2001 it approved a Clinton-era plan to protect old-growth woodlands in 11.5 million acres in the Sierra Nevada mountain range. The administration upheld a Forest Service decision that rejected appeals by loggers, ski resort owners, and off-road vehicle groups. As is often the case, the Forest Service plan took nine years and millions of dollars to create. It was part of the service's efforts to protect the endangered northern spotted owl. Environmentalists cheered the decision; logging interests expressed disappointment.[52]

The Obama administration moved cautiously in developing new policies, but it clearly reinforced the Clinton-era emphasis on collaborative ecosystem-based management and stakeholder involvement in agency decisions (Lubell and Segee 2013). Moreover, as noted earlier, Obama's interior secretaries, Ken Salazar and Sally Jewel, and the agriculture secretary, Tom Vilsack, brought to the Forest Service and other public lands agencies a quite different set of priorities from that of the Bush administration. In early 2012, for example, the administration finalized new guidelines for management of forest lands that focused on protection of watersheds and wildlife, and that require tougher scientific standards that are used when balancing conflicting demands from industry with those from environmental groups. The new forest-planning rules replaced previous versions that did not survive court challenges that have been mounted since 1982 in an effort to satisfy competing visions for use of the lands.[53]

Battles over Wilderness

The history of wilderness designation demonstrates many of the same conflicts of values over whether public lands should be set aside in a protected status or commercial development permitted. For many, they are economic decisions, incorporating a view of natural resources as commodities to be exploited. Others see the decisions primarily as involving moral choices in which they demand the greatest form of protection possible for the few wild places remaining in the nation. Government policymakers are obliged to follow legal dictates in their decision making, but they are regularly pulled in one of these two directions as they exercise the discretion given to them under the law.

As part of its review of land use in the 1970s, the Forest Service embarked on an ambitious effort to inventory roadless land within the national forest system for possible inclusion in the protected wilderness system. The first Roadless Area Review and Evaluation survey (RARE I) was completed in 1976. It elicited strong disapproval by environmental groups over inadequate environmental impact statements and insufficient public involvement in the process. The Carter administration completed a second survey, RARE II, in 1979. It recommended more wilderness areas but also sought to meet public demand for timber. More litigation by environmentalists and the states followed, again based on insufficient adherence to NEPA procedures.

The Reagan administration was far more skeptical about the value of wilderness preservation, and its actions reflected those beliefs. Interior Secretary James Watt provoked enormous controversy over proposals to open wilderness areas to mineral development, which the Wilderness Act allowed under some restrictions. After a 1982 court ruling that questioned RARE II's consistency with NEPA's environmental impact statement requirements, Reagan ordered a broad RARE III on *all* lands on which Congress had not yet acted. His administration strongly favored development over wilderness protection, and Watt went on to withdraw 1 million acres of potential wilderness from additional study and possible protection. Congress and wilderness advocates bitterly opposed those actions, and they cost the administration support for its other policy initiatives on natural resources (Leshy 1984).

The biggest congressional designation of wilderness areas had come just before the Reagan era, in 1980, with the creation of over 50 million acres of wilderness in Alaska. In 1990, after years of environmentalist pressure and resistance by Alaska, Congress withheld from logging more than 1 million acres of the Tongass National Forest in southeast Alaska. Nearly 300,000 acres were set aside as wilderness in this last major expanse of temperate rain forest in North America, and limited mining and road building are to be allowed on over 700,000 acres.

As noted earlier, the Clinton administration and environmentalists mounted a major campaign to put even more land into various states of protection, including wilderness designation. Clinton pressed hard for his Lands Legacy initiative, of which additional wilderness preservation was a part. The administration also provided over $1 billion per year for local, state, and federal agencies to preserve more open lands. Among other decisions, Clinton used the 1906 Antiquities Act to create a number of new national monuments, including the 1.9-million-acre Grand Staircase–Escalante National Monument in Utah's red-rock country.[54]

In the final days of his administration, Clinton issued a sweeping rule to protect roadless areas in the national forests from future road construction, intended to prevent development about 58 million acres of forests and open the way for wilderness designation. Legal challenges by industry and some states followed. By 2005 the Bush administration announced a new and complex procedure to replace the Clinton rules. The State Petitioning Rule would have given the governors of each state a choice about which national forest areas located within their states should remain roadless.

The new policy reflected the Bush administration's belief that such decisions should be made within each state to reflect local conditions and public preferences and to limit future litigation. Environmentalists said the Bush rule effectively would have repealed the Clinton-era wilderness protection plan and hand over the forests to the timber industry and other development interests; they went on to challenge it in federal court.[55] The Bush administration revised the rule in 2007 after the initial one was blocked by a federal judge for lacking sufficient environmental reviews under NEPA, but court challenges continued. In the case of the much-disputed Tongass National Forest in Alaska, the Bush administration removed roadless area protection to open up some 9 million acres to mining, road building, and logging, a move favored by Alaska's lawmakers and the timber industry. Yet, reflecting current market conditions for lumber, few timber companies rushed in to bid on the newly opened areas.

As court battles over the Clinton and Bush policies continued, Congress took a different tack on wilderness creation. With rare bipartisan cooperation, by 2008 it had assembled a massive public lands bill that included about 2 million acres of new wilderness area, mostly in the West. Longtime adversaries came together to seek common ground in protecting vast areas of federal land, recognizing that such areas can be an economic boon to many local communities that previously were dependent on extractive industries. President Bush also was eager to create a public lands legacy at the end of his administration, and supported the efforts. Congress finally approved the law early in the Obama administration as the Omnibus Public Lands Management Act of 2009.[56]

Like Clinton and most other presidents, Bush also used the Antiquities Act of 1906 to protect large areas of American-controlled Pacific Ocean islands, reefs, sea floor, and sea surface as marine national monuments, which would protect them from fishing, oil exploration, and other forms of commercial development. The action was widely praised by environmental groups and came to be called Bush's Blue Legacy.

After signing the 2009 Act, the Obama administration moved cautiously on proposing additions to wilderness areas, seeking to build sufficient public support to ward off critics who see such efforts as locking up public lands that may be used for oil and gas and other energy development. In late 2011, as part of the administration's America's Great Outdoors Initiative, the president called for 18 new wilderness and conservation area declarations in Western states, which would have to be approved by Congress. The Interior Department also identified over 100 high-priority conservation projects and was working with state and local groups to advance them. In 2015, the president proposed setting aside some 12 million acres in Alaska as wilderness. The proposal included 1.5 million acres of ANWR's coastal plain, nearly 6 million acres of the Brooks mountain range, and about 5 million acres of the Porcupine Plateau. Congressional Republicans promised to challenge the actions.[57] By late 2016, the president had used his authority under the Antiquities Act to establish 29 new monuments, far more than any other president. He also expanded other monuments, including an exceptionally large increase in marine monuments.[58]

Governing the Range

The Bureau of Land Management (BLM) has leaned even more heavily than the Forest Service toward the resource use end of the spectrum. The BLM governs more federal land (about 248 million acres) than any other agency, but it has suffered from a historic indifference to environmental values compared with the Forest Service. The BLM has a budget that is less than one-quarter that of the Forest Service (at $1.3 billion in fiscal 2017) and a staff of about 10,000. The bureau is also in charge of federal mineral leases on all public domain and outer continental shelf lands.

BLM Deficiencies and Needs Clarke and McCool classify the BLM as a "shooting star" agency that burned brightly for a short time but now faces a precarious future. It is a relatively new federal agency, formed in 1946 by executive actions merging Interior's General Land Office and the U.S. Grazing Service, two agencies with a reputation for inept land management. The BLM is widely viewed as weak politically and historically highly permissive toward its chief constituency groups, the mining industry and ranchers. Those characteristics have led scholars to term it a "captured" agency (Foss 1960; McConnell 1966).

As Paul Culhane (1981) observed, however, in more recent years the BLM has recruited professional staff with credentials in scientific land management and a commitment to progressive conservation comparable to those in the Forest Service. The difference between the two agencies lies in the political milieu in which they function. To meet new expectations for sustainable resource management on public lands, the BLM will need to gain more political independence from its traditional constituencies and build a broader base of public support.

The Federal Land Policy and Management Act Congress tried to stimulate such an organizational shift with passage of the Federal Land Policy and Management Act (FLPMA) of 1976, also known as the BLM Organic Act. FLPMA formally ended the 200-year-old policy of disposing of the public domain, repealed more than 2,000 antiquated public land laws, amended the 1934 Taylor Grazing Act, and mandated wilderness reviews for all roadless BLM lands with wilderness characteristics. More important, the Act established the bureau legislatively as an agency and gave it the authority to inventory and manage the public lands under its jurisdiction. Agency officials had sought the authorizing legislation to clarify its responsibilities and to give it the legal authority to apply tools of modern land management. The new legislation helped the BLM establish greater authority over the public lands under a broad multiple-use mandate that leaned toward environmental values and away from a position of grazing as dominant use.

FLPMA gave the BLM full multiple-use powers that matched those of the Forest Service. It defined multiple use in a way that should encourage environmental sustainability:

> Management of the public lands and their various resource values so that they are utilized in the combination that will best meet the present and future needs of the American people … a combination of balanced and diverse resource use that takes into account the long-term needs of future generations for renewable and nonrenewable resources, including, but not limited to, recreation, range, timber, minerals, watershed, wildlife and fish, and natural scenic, scientific and historical values.

As the case with most legislation, FLPMA represented a compromise needed to secure the approval of key interests (Dana and Fairfax 1980).

Much like its counterpart governing the nation's forests, FLPMA established a land use planning process for BLM lands that required extensive public participation and coordination with state and local governments as well as with Indian tribes. Here, too, Congress specifically chose to delegate authority for land use decisions to the agencies. The Act increased the authority of the BLM to regulate grazing, allowing the secretary of the interior to specify the terms and conditions of leases and permits, including reduction in the number of livestock on the lands. However, it maintained the grazing permit system, the local boards that supervise it, and the existing fee structure. All have been sharply criticized by study commissions and environmentalists for contributing to the degradation of public rangelands (Mangun and Henning 1999).

BLM Lands and the Sagebrush Rebellion

Since the passage of FLPMA, the BLM has been moving slowly toward the new goal of sustainable resource management. Indeed, the Sagebrush Rebellion of the late 1970s largely grew out of the frustration of Western ranchers, who were angry over the BLM's implementation of that law. Their reaction was stimulated by decisions concerning grazing fees and protection of wildlife, native plants, and predators (Cawley 1993; Clarke and McCool 1996). The ranchers tried to force the transfer of federal lands to state or private ownership, where they believed they could exert more control. In 1979 the Nevada legislature approved a bill demanding that the federal government turn over all BLM land in Nevada to the state, an action usually credited as the first shot fired in the rebellion. Eighty-two percent of Nevada is federally owned, with smaller, but still large, percentages common in the Western states (running from 28 to 68 percent).

The Reagan administration, and particularly James Watt's Interior Department, shared the rebels' political ideology and accommodated their demands to some extent (Culhane 1984). With the election of Bill Clinton, the same battles were joined once more under the new "wise use" label. BLM lands were at the center of two of the most controversial proposals on Interior Secretary Bruce Babbitt's resource agenda: raising grazing fees and reforming the long, outmoded 1872 mining law. The law has allowed hardrock mining on federal lands without any royalty payments (such payments are paid for mining on state lands), and it has had few requirements for restoration of the nearly 100,000 abandoned and contaminated mine sites on federal lands in the West (Riebsame 1996; U.S. GAO 2009).

Babbitt's efforts built on a trend plainly evident in Congress before the 1992 election. For years, members had been seeking revisions in public lands and water policy to respond to increasing demands for preservation and recreation. The shift toward preservation and away from unrestrained resource use could be seen in a diversity of measures in the early to mid-1990s, such as the Omnibus Water Act of 1992 and the California Desert Protection Act of 1994. The former revised Western water projects by instituting new pricing systems to encourage conservation and authorizing extensive wildlife and environmental protection, mitigation, and restoration programs; the latter designated some 7.5 million acres of wilderness on federal land within California. As discussed earlier, however, the Bush administration reversed some of these trends. It reflected a more traditional view of natural resource policy priorities that favored industry and economic development (Lowry 2006).[59]

As mentioned earlier in the chapter, some of the same disputes over federal management of western land under the BLM arose again in recent years, and sparked an intense and highly publicized confrontation at an Oregon wildlife refuge. The quieter push to return federal land to the states has received far less attention.[60]

Other Protected Lands and Agencies

Some of the public domain is spared the intensity of disputes that characterizes decisions over use of Forest Service and BLM lands. In these cases, Congress has specified by statute that they be secure from much or all development after a decision has been made to place the lands within a protected class. These lands are those governed largely by the National Park Service and the U.S. Fish and Wildlife Service (FWS). Box 6.2 lists the five major divisions of federal lands, one incorporating marine sanctuaries and estuaries, and one incorporating rangelands.

▓▓▓ BOX 6.2 PRIMARY FEDERAL LAND SYSTEMS ▓▓▓

National Park System

The first national park (Yellowstone) was created in 1872, and the National Park System (NPS) itself was established with passage of the National Park Service Act of 1916. The NPS had grown by 2016 to contain 413 sites, of which 58 were national parks, the crown jewels of the system; its annual budget is about $3 billion. Most of the parks are in Alaska and the West, but the National Park System also includes over 300 national monuments, battlefields, memorials, historic sites, recreational areas, scenic parkways and trails, wilderness areas, near-wilderness areas, seashores and lakeshores, and some 84 million acres of land. Most of the system's lands are closed to mining, timber harvesting, grazing, and other economic uses, but Congress grants exemptions on a case-by-case basis when it approves the parks.

National Wildlife Refuge System

The first national wildlife refuge was created in 1903, and the National Wildlife

Refuge System (NWRS) was formally established in 1966 by the National Wildlife Refuge System Administration Act. Today the NWRS is a sprawling and diverse system containing more than 560 refuges, 38 wetland management districts, and other protected areas covering about 150 million acres of land and water scattered over all 50 states. The system has the only federal lands specifically dedicated to wildlife preservation. Refuges are open to some commercial activities, including grazing, mining, and oil drilling.

National Forest System

The first national forests were created in 1891, and the National Forest System (NFS) was established in 1905 with the creation of the National Forest Service in the Department of Agriculture. The system now includes more than 193 million acres of land in 154 forests, largely in the West, Southeast, and Alaska. There are 50 national forests in 23 eastern states as well. The NFS is managed chiefly by the Forest Service, although some BLM lands are included in the system.

National Wilderness Preservation System

Created in 1964, the National Wilderness Preservation System (NWPS) consists of over 109 million acres of land, 56 million of which were added in Alaska in 1980 and most of the rest in the 11 Western states although there are wilderness areas in 44 states. The NWPS contains over 762 wilderness areas of widely varying size. NWPS lands are set aside forever as undeveloped, roadless areas, without permanent improvements or human habitation. Only officially designated wilderness areas are protected from commercial development. Wilderness areas are not entirely separate from the other systems; they are located in the national park system, national forest system, national wildlife refuge system, and on BLM lands.

National Wild and Scenic River System

Established in 1968, the river system in 2015 consisted of nearly 12,700 total miles in 208 rivers in 40 states and the Commonwealth of Puerto Rico in one of three designations: wild, scenic, or recreational. This is only 0.025 percent (one quarter of one percent) of the nation's rivers. These protected segments of rivers are to be in free-flowing condition—that is, unblocked by a dam—and to possess remarkable scenic, recreational, ecological, and other values. The shorelines of designated rivers are protected from federally permitted development.

National Marine Sanctuaries and National Estuarine Research Reserves

The National Marine Sanctuaries program was established by the Marine Protection, Research and Sanctuaries Act of 1972, and contains 14 sites and 170,000 square miles of unique marine and Great Lakes recreational, ecological, historical, research, educational, and esthetic resources, managed by the National Oceanic and Atmospheric

Administration (NOAA). The sanctuaries are, in effect, equivalent to national parks in a marine environment.

National Rangelands

Located chiefly in the western states and Alaska, rangelands consist of grasslands, prairie, deserts, and scrub forests. Much of the land is suitable for grazing of cattle, sheep, and other livestock. About 300 million acres of U.S. rangeland consists of federally owned lands, most of which are managed by the BLM and the rest by the Forest Service. Rangelands are the largest category of public domain lands.

Sources: Compiled from government agency and nonprofit organization webpages. A useful guide to these lands and their facilities can be found at the site for the National Parks Conservation Association: www.npca.org.

The National Park Service The National Park System is the most visible of the nation's public lands. The number of visitors continues to grow, and in recent years has been over 300 million. For the most popular national parks, such as Great Smoky Mountains, Grand Canyon, Olympic, Yosemite, Rocky Mountain, Yellowstone, and Grand Teton National Parks, the hordes of tourists are overwhelming the capacity of the parks to accommodate them properly. Demands have been increasing on the parks' water, roadways, and personnel, and maintenance has been deferred at many of the national park units because of chronically deficient budgets for the agency. The National Park Service (NPS) estimated in 1998 that it would cost over $5 billion to deal with the accumulated maintenance needs (roads, bridges, sewer systems, and outbuildings) at national parks, monuments, and wilderness areas. In more recent years that amount has risen to about $12 billion. In Yellowstone alone the backlog stood at over $600 million, but Congress has long refused to provide the funds.[61]

National Park System lands are closed to most economic uses, including mining, grazing, energy development, and timber harvesting, although such activities on adjacent land can seriously affect environmental quality within the parks (Freemuth 1991). These areas are managed by the NPS, an agency with about 20,000 employees (only a small number of them scientists) and a budget of about $3 billion in fiscal 2017. That budget has more than doubled since 1985, yet it remains insufficient.

Several studies have criticized the Park Service for insufficient training of employees and having inadequate capabilities for scientific research that can be used in support of its resource protection policies. William Lowry's (1994) analysis of the Park Service suggests that many of its problems can be traced to weakened political consensus and support for policy goals (especially long-term preservation of parklands). This has led to increased intervention by Congress and the White House to promote short-term and politically popular objectives. Congress approved some action in 1998 in a

National Parks Omnibus Management Act, which dealt primarily with the operation of concessions within the parks, development of a training program for Park Service employees, and creation of a new process for the service to recommend areas to be studied for possible inclusion in the park system. Yet it is clear that major efforts to reverse environmental damage and to restore the national parks to their former glory are needed in the next few decades, and some progress toward those goals is already evident (Lowry 2009).

Sharp conflict over the use of snowmobiles in Yellowstone and other national parks illustrates the ongoing challenge the Park Service faces today. This is particularly so with efforts to base management decisions more on environmental science than on service to constituency groups. After 10 years of studies and extensive public review, the Clinton administration proposed to exclude snowmobiles from nearly all national parks, monuments, and recreational areas because of the noise and pollution they generate and because of the effects on wildlife. The Park Service wanted to phase in the change over three years to ease the transition. The snowmobile industry and local outfitters, however, remained unhappy, and they persuaded the Bush administration to alter course. Despite continuing public support for the snowmobile ban, the administration sought to allow the vehicles to continue to be used, and environmentalists and others successfully challenged that decision in federal court. In contrast to the bitter conflict over the snowmobile case, the Bush administration decided to back an NPS plan by banning swamp buggies and other off-road vehicles in the Big Cypress preserve in Everglades National Park. Analysts argued that the difference lay in the stronger preference of the local community in Florida for the ban and in the power of the state's green voters.[62]

Wildlife Refuges Much like the National Park System lands, wilderness areas (primarily within the National Forest System but including some BLM lands) are given permanent protection against development, as discussed earlier. That is less true, however, for wildlife refuges (governed by the FWS). In addition to preserving habitats for a diversity of wildlife, these refuge lands are open to hunting, boating, grazing, mining, and oil and gas drilling, among other private uses. By law the refuges enjoy a degree of protection second only to that accorded to wilderness areas.

Environmentalists continue to argue for reducing those uses of wildlife refuges that are incompatible with the protection of wetlands, woodlands, deserts, and other fragile habitats. Supportive legislators have introduced such proposals in Congress. Under President George H. W. Bush's director of the FWS, John Turner, the agency began curtailing some incompatible uses of wildlife refuges. It also embarked on a comprehensive inventory of refuges to identify those uses that could pose a threat to wildlife.

In 1997 President Clinton signed the National Wildlife Refuge System Improvement Act (PL 105-57), which was intended to strengthen and improve the refuge system. The Act defines the dominant refuge goal as wildlife conservation, and provides for compatible wildlife-dependent recreation. It also establishes management guidelines for the FWS to make such compatibility determinations. Priority public uses of refuges include hunting, fishing, wildlife observation and photography, and environmental education and interpretation. The George W. Bush administration was more favorably inclined toward oil and gas production in the refuges. Most notably, as discussed earlier, it proposed to allow such drilling in ANWR in Alaska, and it indicated a priority for energy production on other public lands, including within some national parks. As noted earlier, President Obama proposed protecting 1.5 million acres of ANWR as wilderness to shield it from oil and gas production.

Environmental Impacts and Natural Resources Decision Making

Two of the most important environmental policies since the late 1960s merit special attention because of their wide application to public (and sometimes private) lands and their attempt to improve the way environmental science is used in natural resources decision making. They are the Endangered Species Act and the National Environmental Policy Act.

The Endangered Species Act

No other natural resource policy better captures the new environmental spirit since the late 1960s than the Endangered Species Act (ESA). It is one of the strongest federal environmental laws, and it symbolizes the nation's commitment to resource conservation goals. For that reason, the ESA has become a lightning rod for anti-environmental rhetoric and protest. The FWS, which implements the Act for land-based species (the National Marine Fisheries Service handles water-based species), has been a target of frequent congressional attention and intervention in recent years.

The goal of the 1973 Act, according to one leading study, was "clear and unambiguous—the recovery of all species threatened with extinction" (Tobin 1990, 27). A species could be classified as endangered if it faced the danger of extinction in all or a significant portion of its range. It could be listed as threatened if it was likely to become endangered within the "foreseeable future." Congress made the protective actions unqualified. All takings of such a species would be prohibited, whether on state, federal, or private land. Restrictions are less stringent, however, for plants than for animals; plants are not fully protected when they are on private land. In *TVA v. Hill* (1978), involving a tiny fish, the snail darter, the U.S. Supreme Court upheld the act's constitutionality and made clear that under the ESA, no federal action could jeopardize a species' existence, regardless of cost or consequences.

Congress modified the ESA several times after its initial enactment in attempts to mollify the critics. For example, in 1982 it authorized habitat conservation plans. It even created a cabinet-level Endangered Species Committee, dubbed the God Squad, with authority to grant exemptions to the law, which have been rare. As is often the case with environmental policies, the result is a set of complex and cumbersome procedures and decision rules: (1) determining whether a given species is either threatened or endangered and should be listed, (2) designating critical habitats to be protected, (3) enforcing regulations that govern activities directly affecting the species and their habitats, and (4) implementing "recovery plans" for the species.

To complicate matters, Congress has never provided sufficient funds for the FWS to implement the Act, and the agency has lacked the bureaucratic strength and resources necessary to fend off constituencies adversely affected by the ESA (Tobin 1990). The FWS has operated in recent years with nearly 9,000 employees and a budget of about $3 billion a year (in 2017).

Implementing the ESA: Achievements and Needs As stated in Chapter 2, in 2016 the FWS reported that more than more than 1,594 U.S. species of plants and animals were listed as threatened or endangered.[63] Until very recently, the FWS made relatively slow progress in designating critical habitats even for endangered species, and recovery of species on the list had been quite limited; only about 30 species have been officially declared to be "recovered." Moreover, many species became extinct while these bureaucratic processes dragged on, and many others are thought to be "conservation-reliant"; that is, they can survive only if they remain on the list. However, to judge from its own data (reviewed in Chapter 2), the agency appears to have made progress in recent years. It has also been particularly eager to publicize its success in protecting the "charismatic megafauna" such as the American bald eagle, California condors, Florida panthers, and whooping cranes. A surprisingly large percentage of the FWS's budget has been devoted to such species, in part because of public interest in them.

One of the most important changes in recent years is in the way the Act is implemented. Despite the intense publicity given to some conflicts over a particular species, and resulting lawsuits, the federal government, landowners, and other stakeholders increasingly have sought to promote a more cooperative approach to conserving habitat and the species that rely on it. The hope is that land conservation need not unduly prevent economic development. The Bush administration has called this approach "cooperative conservation," and others have termed it "collaborative decision making" or "sustainable development." One prominent example is a widely praised plan to conserve a large tract of biologically rich land near San Diego, California. Similar efforts helped build a broad coalition of supporters for a massive though tenuous federal–state project to restore the Florida Everglades and to protect the California Bay–Delta (Lowry 2006; Lubell and Segee 2013).

Even before the more cooperative approaches of recent decades, studies of the ESA found that it prevented relatively few development projects from going forward. That was because most developers agreed to make adjustments in their plans to avoid disrupting critical habitats, albeit at some economic cost.[64] Pertinent to these decisions is that section 7 of the Act requires that all federal agencies consult with the FWS or the National Marine Fisheries Service to ensure that their actions do not "jeopardize" a species or "destroy or adversely modify" critical habitat. Many opponents of the law have pointed specifically to this consultation process for blocking or slowing land use activities, although recent analysis of how this consultation works in practice finds little justification for the criticism (Malcom and Li 2015).

A greater problem with the ESA is that it was designed to focus on individual species rather than the ecosystems of which they are a part. That focus reflects the origin of the law in the early 1970s, which preceded contemporary perspectives on biodiversity conservation and ecosystem-based management. The need for a broader conception of species conservation is clear today. The northern spotted owl, for example, the object of ferocious battles over timber harvesting during the early 1990s, shares its habitat with over 1,400 other species dependent on old-growth forests; of those species, 40 were listed at the time as threatened or endangered. Yet, predictably, media coverage and political controversy focused on the owl, distorting public understanding of the real issues.

Slowly both the public and policymakers are coming to understand the larger purpose of biodiversity conservation, both within the United States and internationally. One of the best illustrations of this important change comes from a series of efforts being made in the Pacific Northwest to save wild species of salmon. Removal of dams in the Columbia River Basin clearly imposes a short-term cost, especially on local farmers. Yet elected officials and the public in the Northwest and elsewhere around the nation have come to recognize the necessity of species and habitat preservation (Lowry 2003; Lubell and Segee 2013). For example, in March 1999 the federal government announced that it would list nine types of salmon under the ESA, forcing new building restrictions and raising taxes across the Seattle area. Yet polls at the time indicated overwhelming public support in the region for taking whatever action was necessary to restore the salmon runs in the area, which had declined to a fraction of their historical levels.[65]

Assessing Biological Resources Actions like these listings cannot be taken without a great deal of scientific knowledge to identify species and ecosystem functions that are at risk. The ecosystem-based management approach now favored by biologists and ecologists thus suggests the need for a significantly improved database of knowledge not only for actions under the ESA but for more effective natural resources management in general. That goal was a major reason for creating a new National Biological

Service in the Department of the Interior, which was folded into the department's U.S. Geological Survey (USGS) in 1996. Initially renamed the Natural Resources Science Agency, the program was consolidated into a new Biological Resources Division of the USGS.

The USGS itself was established in 1879 and is now the nation's largest earth science research agency, with about 10,000 employees and a $1.2 billion budget. President Obama named Marcia McNutt as its director, the first woman to head the survey in its history. She also assumed a new position as science adviser to the secretary of the interior in a move that signaled a clear intention to give greater weight to science in agency decisions than was common under the Bush administration (Lowry 2006; Lubell and Segee 2013).

The new effort within the Biological Resources division of USGS was to consolidate scientific research in an effort to inventory and monitor all plant and animal species in the nation and their habitats. To do that, the division established a National Biological Information Infrastructure, an electronic gateway to biological data and information maintained by federal, state, and local government agencies; private sector organizations; and other partners around the United States and the world.[66] These efforts have been complemented by the work of private organizations to inventory the nation's biological resources, most notably the H. John Heinz III Center for Science, Economics and the Environment (2008).

Renewing the ESA and Resolving Conflicts The ESA has been the object of repeated studies and reform efforts over the past several decades. In one effort to appease opponents who repeatedly blocked renewal of the Act during the 1990s, the Clinton White House proposed a diversity of administrative changes intended to ensure that species recovery plans are "scientifically sound and sensitive to human needs." New scientific peer review processes were to be used, representation on planning bodies would be broadened, private landowners would be informed early in the process about allowable actions, and multispecies listings and recovery plans would receive emphasis. In later attempts to accommodate private landowners, the administration strongly encouraged the use of habitat conservation plans on private lands, which hold an estimated 80 percent of all protected species. Such plans are voluntary yet binding agreements in which a landowner adopts conservation measures in exchange for the right to develop the property and a guarantee of "no surprises" with respect to future governmental restrictions on the land's use.[67]

None of this satisfied the ESA's critics in Congress. Over the years, they have proposed a series of legislative changes that would give greater weight to the rights of property owners, provide additional incentives for their cooperation, and call for a higher standard of scientific evidence for demonstrating the status of species. As of 2016, no proposals had attracted sufficient support to win congressional approval. Government scientists have been skeptical of the calls for relying on "sound science," saying such data often do not exist and the requirements would merely benefit those who lose when a species is protected. Environmentalists also complained that the argument is merely a smoke screen for efforts to weaken the ESA. In 2001 the chair of the House Resources Committee captured well the general dilemma of trying to amend the ESA when such diverse expectations and interests collide: "We have not reauthorized it because no one could agree on how to reform and modernize the law. Everyone agrees there are problems with the Act, but no one can agree on how to fix them."[68]

Controversies continued during the Bush administration, which often found itself at odds with environmentalists over the Act and with FWS scientists. Even the Department of the Interior's inspector general found that one high-level Bush appointee, Julie MacDonald, had inappropriately altered the science used in more than a half dozen major rulings on the ESA; she resigned her position in 2007, just before a House inquiry was to start.[69] The administration did list the polar bear as a threatened species because of its disappearing ice habitat. Yet it also sought to minimize the effect of that listing on oil and gas exploration in the Arctic and to ensure that the bear's listing would not authorize using the ESA to regulate greenhouse gas emissions that seem to be the cause of the habitat loss. It reduced budgets and staffing in support of the ESA, and near the end of Bush's presidency sought a major change in ESA regulations, sharply reducing the need for federal agencies to seek independent scientific review of projects that could harm endangered species on federal land.

The Obama administration quickly put that ruling on hold and called for a full review of it. Nonetheless, it failed to move quickly to chart a new path for protection of endangered species—perhaps itself a sign of how difficult it is even for Democratic presidents to make much headway in this policy area (Lubell and Segee 2013).[70] However, following a 2011 court settlement of a lawsuit brought by conservation groups, the Fish and Wildlife Service committed to making final decisions by 2018 for all of the species under consideration for listing that have long been backlogged. As of 2016, that included about 550 species.[71]

International Efforts to Protect Species International agreements, specially the Convention on International Trade in Endangered Species (CITES), also play a role in protection of species. U.S. leadership led to approval of CITES (pronounced "cite teas"), which became effective in 1975. The agreement is overseen by the UN Environment Programme in cooperation with the nongovernmental International Union for the Conservation of Nature (IUCN) and the World Wildlife Fund (Caldwell 1996). Other private groups, such as the Nature Conservancy, contribute through negotiating land donations or outright purchase of habitats.

CITES is supposed to operate through a system of certificates and permits that restrict or prohibit international trade of species in different categories of protection (i.e., those threatened with extinction, those that may be threatened, or those whose exploitation should be prevented). Some 33,000 different species of plants and animals are regulated in this manner. As might be expected, it has been difficult to meet the treaty's ambitious objectives. In particular, it has not succeeded in ending a continuing international market in animal smuggling, especially in Southeast Asia. Japan has been a particular target of environmentalist protest, and African nations have regularly argued with decisions related to protection of the elephant (Vaughn 2004).[72]

The National Environmental Policy Act

Few people in 1969 anticipated the effects that the National Environmental Policy Act would have on decision making across the entire federal government. Yet since its adoption, this procedural policy has transformed expectations for the way government agencies should consider the effects of their actions on the environment. Its influence on land use decisions affecting natural resources has been particularly striking. NEPA's success owes much to the entrepreneurial use of the environmental impact statement process by environmentalists and administrative leaders to advance environmental values, both at the federal level and in parallel cases at state and local levels where similar impact assessments under "little NEPAs" are required (Bartlett 1989; Caldwell 1982, 1998). Some states, such as California and Washington, have been especially demanding in their requirements for impact statements for both state and private projects. Beyond its success in the United States, nearly 100 countries have adopted the environmental impact assessment provisions of NEPA, making it the most frequently copied U.S. statute.

NEPAs Goals and the EIS Process Even with later amendments, NEPA remains a brief statute at about six pages. Section 101(a) of the Act acknowledges the "profound impact of man's activity on the interrelations of all components of the natural environment" and the "critical importance of restoring and maintaining environmental quality to the overall welfare and development of man." The instrument for achieving those goals is the EIS process, which was to use "a systematic, interdisciplinary approach" to ensure the "integrated use of the natural and social sciences" in planning and decision making. As stated in Section 102(2)(c), EISs are to offer a detailed statement on the environmental impact of the proposed action, any adverse environmental effects that cannot be avoided, alternatives to the action contemplated, the relationship between "local short-term uses" of the environment and the "maintenance and enhancement of long-term productivity," and any "irreversible and irretrievable commitments of resources" that the proposed action would require.

In addition, the statute calls for wide consultation with federal agencies and publication of the EIS for public review. The intent was not to block development projects but to open and broaden the decision-making process. As was the case with protection of species under the ESA, few actions have been halted entirely. Instead, agencies follow one of two courses of action. The first is that they no longer even propose projects and programs that may have unacceptable impacts on the environment. The second is that when they do both propose and move ahead with projects and programs, they employ mitigation measures to eliminate or greatly reduce the environmental impacts.

Compliance and Policy Learning in the Bureaucracy During the 1970s and 1980s, federal agencies grew accustomed to NEPA requirements and to public involvement in their decision making. Some, like the much-criticized U.S. Army Corps of Engineers, dramatically altered their behavior in the process (Mazmanian and Nienaber 1979). Others, such as the DOE, made far less progress in adapting to the new norms of open and environmentally sensitive decision making. They serve as a reminder that statutes alone cannot bring about organizational change (Clary and Kraft 1989).

The Council on Environmental Quality (CEQ) has tried to help with the process of organizational adaptation. It is responsible under NEPA for supervising the EIS process, and it has worked closely with federal agencies through workshops and consultations to define their NEPA responsibilities. With a series of court rulings, CEQ regulations have also clarified the extent of the mandated EISs and the format to be used to enhance their utility. CEQ regulations distinguish environmental assessments (EAs) from EISs. The EAs are more limited in scope and more concise, and they are used when a project and its impacts do not require a full EIS under NEPA. Agencies also keep a Record of Decision (ROD), a public document that reflects the final decision, the rationale behind it, and commitments to monitoring and mitigation (Eccleston 1999).[73]

Administrative Challenges under NEPA As noted, the EIS process has been used frequently by environmental groups to contest actions of natural resource agencies, such as the Forest Service and the BLM. That pattern continued from the 1990s to the 2010s. About 400 to 500 draft, final, and supplemental EISs have been filed by all federal agencies in recent years, most prepared by the Forest Service, U.S. Army Corps of Engineers, Federal Highway Administration, Bureau of Land Management, and National Park Service. There are many more EAs than EISs prepared each year.

Unfortunately, many impact statements still fall short of the expectations for comprehensive and interdisciplinary assessments of likely environmental effects. Thus they disappoint those who have hoped the mandated administrative process would "make bureaucracies think" about the consequences of their actions. Some impacts have been ignored as unimportant, and others have proved hard to forecast accurately. The State Department's EIS on the proposed Keystone XL pipeline in 2013 is a case in point. The EPA sharply criticized the report as an inadequate review of the likely impacts of the pipeline, particularly on climate change.[74]

Obviously, limited knowledge of biological, geological, and other natural systems constrains anyone's ability to forecast all significant impacts on the environment of development projects. Thus improvement of EISs will require expanded knowledge of ecosystem functioning as well as of related natural and social systems. For many projects, policymakers of necessity have to make decisions under conditions of some uncertainty.[75]

Partly because of these deficiencies, court cases under NEPA continue. The most common complaint over the years has been that no EIS was prepared when one should have been or that the EIS or EA was inadequate. The most frequent plaintiffs by far in these cases have been environmental groups and individual or citizen groups, as has been the case since 1970.

Because NEPA has been used so effectively by environmentalists to challenge development projects, it has its share of critics. Responding to their concerns about delays in developments such as building a new dam or logging in federal forests, the Bush administration targeted NEPA for reform in ways that caused alarm among environmental groups. The administration asserted that environmentalists had abused NEPA by filing thousands of nuisance lawsuits that were intended to halt development. Therefore, as noted earlier in the discussion of U.S. forestland, it sought to streamline and speed up the NEPA process as it applied to highway and airport construction and logging of national forests, among other activities. It also sought a congressional exemption for certain agencies (particularly the Defense Department) from its requirements.[76] In addition, the administration tried to exempt most U.S.-controlled ocean waters from NEPA but lost that battle in federal court.

In 2002, the CEQ, under the Bush-appointed chair, James Connaughton, established an interagency NEPA Task Force to review the law's effects and recommend changes in its implementation. That action created further suspicion among environmental groups while receiving strong endorsements from conservatives and development interests.[77]

The new CEQ chair in the Obama administration, Nancy Sutley, took a different posture on NEPA. She argued that federal agencies should be able to find the flexibility to carry out NEPA reviews in a way that maintains the law's principles and goals without "undoing the whole thing." "A scalpel is probably better than a bulldozer to deal with NEPA," she said.[78] By 2010, the Obama CEQ proposed steps to modernize NEPA at its 40th anniversary, arguing that the new measures would assist federal agencies in meeting NEPA's goals while also enhancing public involvement, increasing transparency, and easing implementation. In a further expansion of NEPA's scope, in 2016 Obama's CEQ issued new guidance that requires all federal agencies to include climate change impacts in their environmental reviews, and to quantify those impacts where possible. The Natural Resources Defense Council called the new procedures a "game changer," and other environmental groups praised the move, which may be altered by the Trump administration.[79]

Conclusions

Much like environmental protection policy, criticisms of energy and natural resources policy are plentiful. They come in a variety of forms, as do the proposals for reform, and many of them were reviewed throughout the chapter. Some of the proposals are similar to those associated with environmental protection policy. For example, regulations should be more flexible to take into account local conditions, and stakeholders should be given sufficient opportunity to voice their concerns. Also similar, but with environmentalists making the case this time, is the proposal that market incentives be used to improve environmental protection, particularly that user fees be set at a level that discourages environmental degradation and fosters sustainability. Improved scientific knowledge and better integration of decision making across programs and agencies are common suggestions here as well, and they are crucial to developing sufficient institutional capacity for ecosystem management and sustainable development. Some of these issues are discussed in Chapter 7.

As repeated efforts to devise acceptable and legal solutions to the protection of old-growth forest ecosystems in the Pacific Northwest attest, natural resource policies also require the development of creative ways to involve the American public in policy decisions that affect their communities and livelihoods while maintaining adherence to professional norms of natural resource management. Some would dismiss such hopes as unrealistic. Yet experience in the Pacific Northwest and elsewhere suggests that the economic livelihood of rural communities can indeed be reconciled with resource conservation. It has been achieved through small-scale efforts to develop environmentally sound businesses and through the realization that the future economy of many communities depends more on maintenance of recreation and tourism opportunities than on traditional extractive industries. At this level, removed from the often bitter and ideological national debates over balancing the economy and the environment, new approaches seem to work (Mazmanian and Kraft 2009).

Many cases over the past few decades illustrate that development interests, environmentalists, and state and local officials can work together and resolve their differences (Johnson 1993; Koontz 2005; Layzer 2008, 2013; Lubell and Segee 2013; Wondolleck and Yaffee 2000). Local and regional ecological restoration efforts suggest similar possibilities. Examining the Chesapeake Bay Program, for instance, Knopman, Susman, and Landy (1999, 26) said that it "stands as a model of public–private partnerships, regional cooperation, and citizen engagement" and illustrated well the potential of such "civic environmentalism," although others have disagreed with that particular assessment (Ernst 2003, 2009). The authors point as well to the establishment of public land trusts across the nation; collaborative watershed councils in the Pacific Northwest; and similar local and regional environmental success stories involving collaboration among citizens, property owners, environmental action groups, and local, state, and federal agencies (see also Fairfax and Guenzler 2001; Sabatier et al. 2005; Weber 2003). Other studies find comparable achievements through ad hoc and voluntary processes that have helped foster consensus in the creation of habitat conservation plans under the federal Endangered Species Act, as well as build public support for restoration of degraded ecosystems, reclamation of contaminated mining sites in the West, smart-growth strategies in urban and suburban areas, and the redevelopment of contaminated urban land (Lubell and Segee 2013; Paehlke 2013a; K. Portney 2013, 2016).

These experiments in environmental mediation and collaborative decision making clearly are very promising, even if obstacles remain in applying them on a larger scale (Gerlak, Heikkila, and Lubell 2013). Such approaches may be particularly difficult to use when participants hold passionate and conflicting views about the values at stake, such as with protection of ecologically critical and esthetically treasured wilderness areas; access to valuable timber, energy, water, and mineral sources; and protection of property rights and jobs in economic hard times. Many people will see little reason to compromise on what they consider to be fundamental principles. One conclusion is that to make sustainable development a reality over the next several decades requires a search for new ways to make these critical choices about our collective environmental future. This need is as vital in the many arenas outside government that shape energy and natural resources as it is within government itself.

Discussion Questions

1   Why has it been so difficult for the federal government to adopt a comprehensive national energy policy? What might be done to increase public concern about energy issues and build support for energy policy?

2   The United States long had substantial subsidies for the development and use of fossil fuels and nuclear power, but not to the same extent for renewable energy sources, energy efficiency, and conservation. What explains the different treatment of these energy sources over time? Should the federal and state governments provide comparable subsidies to spur development of alternative sources of energy such as wind power and solar power, as many have done in recent years?

3   Most natural resource policies establish procedures for resolving conflicts between the objectives of economic development and conservation. What are the most promising ways to try to integrate these concerns and promote a transition to sustainable use of resources? For example, what kinds of decision-making processes could help resolve conflicts over issues such as the use of snowmobiles

in national parks, restrictions on timber harvesting or mining operations, or oil drilling in wildlife refuges?

4   Are the procedures established by the National Environmental Policy Act for conduct of environmental assessments and impact statements working well or not? Should those procedures be continued, or, as the Bush administration had proposed, should they be streamlined to permit faster action on economic development projects such as highway construction and logging operations?

5   The Endangered Species Act (ESA) has been faulted for giving too much weight to protection of threatened or endangered species and too little to the rights of property owners and others affected by decisions under the Act. Should the ESA be changed to respond to these criticisms? Is there a way to alter it to make it both more effective in protecting species and biological diversity and also more acceptable to the public and the constituencies affected by it?

Suggested Readings

Davis, Charles, ed. 2001. *Western Public Lands and Environmental Politics*, 2nd edn. Boulder, CO: Westview Press.

Klyza, Christopher M. 1996. *Who Controls Public Lands? Mining, Forestry, and Grazing Policies, 1870–1990*. Chapel Hill: University of North Carolina Press.

Layzer, Judith A. 2008. *Natural Experiments: Ecosystem-Based Management and the Environment*. Cambridge, MA: MIT Press.

Lowry, William R. 2009. *Repairing Paradise: The Restoration of Nature in America's National Parks*. Washington, DC: Brookings Institution Press.

Nie, Martin. 2008. *The Governance of Western Public Lands: Mapping Its Present and Future*. Lawrence: University Press of Kansas.

Sabatier, Paul, Will Focht, Mark Lubell, et al., eds. 2005. *Swimming Upstream: Collaborative Approaches to Watershed Management*. Cambridge, MA: MIT Press.

Notes

1   Henry Fountain, "Global Temperatures Are on Course for Another Record This Year," *New York Times*, July 2016. Rising public concern about climate change is documented regularly on by the Gallup poll. In a March 16, 2016 report, Gallup said that public concern was at an eight-year high.

2   Associated Press, "Paris Climate Agreement to Take Effect Nov. 4," *New York Times*, October 5, 2016.

3   Coral Davenport, "Nations, Fighting Powerful Refrigerant That Warms Planet, Reach Landmark Deal," *New York Times*, October 15, 2016.

4   Juliet Eilperin, Steven Mufson, and Philip Rucker, "The Oil and Gas Industry Is Quickly Amassing Power in Trump's Washington," *Washington Post*, December 14, 2016; Coral Davenport, "Donald Trump Could Put Climate Change on Course for 'Danger Zone,'" *New York Times,* November 10, 2016; and

Marianne Lavelle, "In Trump, U.S. Puts a Climate Denier in Its Highest Office and All Climate Change Action in Limbo," *Inside Climate News*, November 9, 2016.

5 See Brian Kennedy, "Clinton, Trump Supporters Worlds Apart on Views of Climate Change and Its Scientists," Pew Research Center, October 10, 2016. See also Dunlap, McCright, and Yarosh (2016), and Ashley Parker and Coral Davenport, "Donald Trump's Energy Plan: More Fossil Fuels and Fewer Rules," *New York Times*, May 26, 2016.

6 See Eilperin, Mufson, and Rucker, "The Oil and Gas Industry Is Quickly Amassing Power in Trump's Washington," and Jack Healy and Kirk Johnson, "Battles Lines Over Trump's Lands Policy Stretch Across 640 Million Acres," *New York Times*, November 19, 2016.

7 See, for example, Kirk Johnson, "Pacific Northwest Weighs Response to Risks Posed by Oil Trains," *New York Times*, July 31, 2016.

8 The DOE calculates only direct subsidies such as tax expenditures and research and development, not indirect subsidies such as highway construction. See, for example, "Direct Federal Financial Interventions and Subsidies in Energy in Fiscal Year 2013" (March 12, 2013), available at the agency's website: www. eia.doe.gov.

9 See a summary of the IMF report in Editorial Board, "The High Cost of Dirty Fuels," *New York Times*, May 21, 2015. On the IEA estimates, see Alex Morales, "Fossil Fuels with $550 Billion Subsidies Hurt Renewables," *Bloomberg Businessweek*, November 11, 2014. The numbers come from the IEA's World Energy Outlook of that year.

10 See, for example, a Brookings Institution review of these programs: Mark Muro and Jonathan Rothwell, "Why the U.S. Should Not Abandon Its Clean Energy Lending Programs," September 27, 2011, available at: www.brookings.edu. See also Justin Doom, "U.S. Expects $5 billion from Program that Funded Solyndra," *Bloomberg*, November 12, 2014, available at: bloomberg.com; Brian Eckhouse and Eric Roston, "Energy Loans," *Bloomberg Businessweek*, December 5–11, 2016; and Eric Lipton and Clifford Krauss, "A Gold Rush of Subsidies in the Search for Clean Energy," *New York Times*, November 11, 2011.

11 For energy industry views, see the website for the Edison Electric Institute: www. eei.org. Issues ranging from clean-air rules to climate change are covered at the site. See also the American Petroleum Institute at: www.api.org and the American Coal Council at: www.americancoalcouncil.org.

12 As noted in Chapter 2, one of the best sources for up-to-date statistics on energy use is DOE's Energy Information Administration: www.eia.doe.gov/. The site includes data on U.S. energy sources, historical patterns, and forecasts for future demand.

13 These figures reflect my own calculations of budgetary change in these periods, drawn from the annual federal budgets and adjusted for inflation.

14 White House press release, "The Greening of the White House: Saving Energy, Saving Money and Protecting Our Environment," December 2, 1999. On the same day, the White House announced new consumer incentives by major American corporations to help promote energy-efficient products. Among the companies were Best Buy, Home Depot, Maytag, Phillips Lighting, and Whirlpool.

15 Michael L. Wald, "After 20 Years, America's Foot Is Still on the Gas," *New York Times*, October 17, 1993; and Michael Wines, "Tax's Demise Illustrates First Rule of Lobbying: Work, Work, Work," *New York Times*, June 14, 1993.

16 Keith Bradsher, "With Sport Utility Vehicles More Popular, Overall Automobile Fuel Economy Continues to Fall," *New York Times*, October 5, 1999.

17 See Matthew L. Wald, "Clinton Energy-Saving Rules Are Getting a Second Look," *New York Times*, March 31, 2001. By November 2005 the DOE was also widely criticized for its failure to issue any new energy efficiency standards for household appliances. It has repeatedly missed congressional deadlines for water heaters, dryers, furnaces, and many other products. In the absence of DOE action, the states have become the real force behind improved appliance efficiency. See Ben Evans, "Calls for Conservation Are, So Far, Just Calls," *CQ Weekly*, November 7, 2005: 2968–2969.

18 Joseph Kahn, "Cheney Promotes Increasing Supply as Energy Policy," *New York Times*, May 1, 2001.

19 Joseph Kahn, "U.S. Scientists See Big Power Savings from Conservation," *New York Times*, May 6, 2001.

20 Chuck McCutcheon, "House Passage of Bush Energy Plan Sets Up Clash with Senate," *CQ Weekly*, August 4, 2001: 1915–1917.

21 See David E. Rosenbaum, "Senate Passes an Energy Bill Called Flawed by Both Sides," *New York Times*, April 26, 2002.

22 Rebecca Adams, "Not Even Rumblings of War Shake Loose an Energy Policy," *CQ Weekly*, October 5, 2002: 2570–2573.

23 Edmund L. Andrews, "Vague Law and Hard Lobbying Add Up to Billions for Big Oil," *New York Times*, March 27, 2006; and Michael Grunwald and Juliet Eilperin, "A Smorgasbord with Mostly Pork: Oil and Gas Firms Win Big in the New Energy Bill," *Washington Post* National Weekly Edition, August 8–14, 2006: 18.

24 Steven Mufson, "EPA Sets New Biofuel Targets. Troubled Program Could End up on Trump's Chopping Block," *Washington Post*, November 23, 2016. For details on the program, see Government Accountability Office, *Renewable Fuel Standard: Low Expected Production Volumes Make It Unlikely That Advanced Biofuels Can Meet Increasing Targets* (Washington, D.C.: GAO, GAO-17-108, November 28, 2016).

25 Margaret Kriz, "Hot Opportunities," *National Journal*, July 7, 2007, 14–33, and "Changed Climates," *National Journal*, February 7, 2009: 40–43; Julie Kosterlitz, "Breaking the Mold," *National Journal*, May 30, 2009: 24–27.

26 John Broder, "Gore Calls for Energy Shift to Avoid a Global Crisis," *New York Times*, July 18, 2008.

27 John M. Broder, "Geography Is Dividing Democrats over Energy," *New York Times*, January 27, 2009, and "House Backs Bill, 219-212, to Curb Global Warming," *New York Times*, June 27, 2009. For a detailed account of White House and Senate actions in 2010, see Ryan Lizza, "As the World Burns," *New Yorker*, October 11, 2010: 70–83.

28 See, for example, "Clifford Krauss and Eric Lipton, "U.S. Is Inching Toward Elusive Goal of Energy Independence," *New York Times*, March 22, 2012; and Jad Mouawad, "Fuel to Burn: Now What?" *New York Times*, April 10, 2012.

29 Jack Healy and Nicholas Fandos, "Protesters Gain Victory in Fight Over Dakota Access Oil Pipeline," *New York Times*, December 4, 2016.

30 See, for example, Diane Cardwell, "U.S. Revives Aid Program for Clean Energy," *New York Times*, September 19, 2013.

31 See, for example, Matthew Philips, "Clean Power Is Too Hot for Even Trump to Cool," *Bloomberg Businessweek*, November 16, 2016; David Victor, "What to Expect from Trump on Energy Policy," Brookings Institution, November 17, 2016; John Metcalfe and Laura Bliss, "How Cities Plan to Fight Climate Change in the Trump Years," *The Atlantic CityLab*, November 22, 2016; and The Economist, "Up in Smoke? What Will Happen If America's President-Elect Follows Through on Pledges to Tear up Environmental Laws," November 26, 2016, available at: www.economist.com. On bipartisan support for clean energy, see a survey done just after the election by the Conservative Energy Network, summarized in Thomas Content, "GOP Turns Attention to Clean Energy," *Milwaukee Journal Sentinel*, December 2, 2016.

32 See Leslie Kaufman, "Utilities Turn Their Customers Green, with Envy," *New York Times*, January 31, 2009.

33 Diane Cardwell, "On Rooftops, a Rival for Utilities," *New York Times*, July 26, 2013. See also Merrian C. Fuller, Stephen Compagni Portis, and Daniel M. Kammen, "Toward a Low-Carbon Economy: Municipal Financing for Energy Efficiency and Solar Power," *Environment*, 51(1) (January/February 2009): 22–32.

34 See Clifford Krauss, "Tightened Codes Bring a New Enforcer, the Energy Inspector," *New York Times*, July 18, 2009.

35 See Bureau of Ocean Energy Management, "Assessment of Undiscovered Technically Recoverable Oil and Gas Resources of the Nation's Outer Continental Shelf, 2011," available at the bureau's website: www.boem.gov/. See also the bureau's report "Oil and Gas Leasing on the Outer Continental Shelf," available on the same website.

36 Coral Davenport, "Obama Bans Drilling in Parts of the Atlantic and the Arctic," *New York Times*, December 20, 2016.

37 See Alan Feuer, "The Ideological Roots of the Oregon Standoff," *New York Times*, January 9, 2016; and Jack Healy and Kirk Johnson, "The Larger, but Quieter Than Bundy, Push to Take Over Federal Land," *New York Times*, January 10, 2016.

38 Timothy Egan, "Wingtip 'Cowboys' in Last Stand to Hold on to Low Grazing Fees," *New York Times*, October 29, 1993; and Margaret Kriz, "Quick Draw," *National Journal*, November 13, 1993: 2711–2716.

39 Timothy Egan, "Get Used to the New West, Land Managers Tell the Old West," *New York Times*, February 12, 1998.

40 James Brooke, "West Celebrates Mining's Past, but Not Its Future," *New York Times*, October 4, 1998; and Timothy Egan, "A Secretary to Match the Setting," *New York Times*, February 8, 2013. Egan's figures come from a recent study by the Outdoor Industry Association, "The Outdoor Recreation Economy," available at the organization's website: www.outdoorindustry.org.

41 For a fuller description of natural resources policy, see Mangun and Henning (1999) and Davis (2001); for a more historical assessment, see Andrews (2006a) and Christopher McGrory Klyza, *Who Controls Public Lands? Mining, Forestry, and Grazing Policies, 1870–1990* (Chapel Hill: University of North Carolina Press, 1996).

42　Federal authority to regulate land use comes from the Constitution, Article 4, Section 3, which gives Congress the "power to dispose of and make all needful rules and regulations respecting the territory or other property belonging to the United States."

43　Katharine Q. Seelye, "Suburban Sprawl and Government Turf," *CQ Weekly*, March 13, 2001: 586–590. The National Resources Inventory reports are available at: www.nrcs.usda.gov/technical/NRI/.

44　Keith Schneider, "Administration Tries to Limit Rule Used to Halt Logging of National Forests," *New York Times*, April 28, 1992.

45　John M. Cushman, "Audit Faults Forest Service on Logging Damage in U.S. Forests," *New York Times*, February 5, 1999.

46　Timothy Egan, "Sweeping Reversal of U.S. Land Policy Sought by Clinton," *New York Times*, February 24, 1993.

47　David E. Sanger and Sam Howe Verhovek, "Clinton Proposes Wider Protection for U.S. Forests," *New York Times*, October 14, 1999.

48　The committee's report was not without controversy. Some ecologists and foresters questioned whether sustainability is a clear enough concept to serve such a purpose, and others saw such a priority-setting exercise as an inherently political choice that ultimately must be made by Congress. See Charles C. Mann and Mark L. Plummer, "Calls for 'Sustainability' in Forests Sparks a Fire," *Science* 283 (March 26, 1999): 1996–1998.

49　James Brooke, "Environmentalists Battle Growth of Ski Resorts," *New York Times*, January 19, 1999.

50　Felicity Barringer, "Administration Overhauls Rules for U.S. Forests," *New York Times*, December 23, 2004; and "In Bush Policy Reversal, Reinstated Limits on Logging in Old Growth-Forests." For the earlier history of the rules, see Robert Pear, "Bush Plan Given More Discretion to Forest Managers on Logging," *New York Times*, November 28, 2002.

51　See U.S. Forest Service, "The Rising Cost of Wildfire Operations," August 4, 2015, available at: www.fs.fed.us.

52　See Barringer, "Bush Record," and Brinkley, "Out of Spotlight."

53　Juliet Eilperin, "Obama Administration Issues Major Rewrite of National Forest Rules," *Washington Post*, January 26, 2012.

54　Timothy Egan, "Putting Some Space between His Presidency and History," *New York Times*, January 16, 2000, "Week in Review"; and Margaret Kriz, "Call of the Wild," *National Journal*, October 23, 1999: 3038–3043.

55　Felicity Barringer, "Bush Administration Rolls Back Rule on Building Forest Roads," *New York Times*, May 6, 2005. For a broader assessment of differences in forest decision making at the state and federal level, see Tomas M. Koontz, *Federalism in the Forest: National Versus State Natural Resource Policy* (Washington, DC: Georgetown University Press, 2002). The tale of the Clinton and Bush actions on the roadless rules is recounted in Tom Turner's *Roadless Rules: The Struggle for the Last Wild Forests* (Washington, DC: Island Press, 2009).

56　Juliet Eilperin, "Keeping the Wilderness Untamed," *Washington Post* National Weekly Edition, June 23–July 6, 2008.

57　Juliet Eilperin, "Obama Administration to Propose New Wilderness Protections in Arctic Refuge—Alaska Republicans Declare War," *Washington Post*, January 26, 2015.

58 A summary of Obama's actions can be found in Douglas Brinkley, "Obama the Monument Maker," *New York Times*, August 27, 2016; and Juliet Eilperin and Brady Dennis, "With New Monuments in Nevada, Utah, Obama Adds to His Environmental Legacy," *Washington Post*, December 28, 2016. A full list of presidentially established national monuments under the Antiquities Act can be found at the website for the National Parks Conservation Association: www. npca.org/resources/2658-monuments-protected-under-the-antiquities-act.

59 See Joby Warrick and Juliet Eilperin, "Big Energy in the Wild West: The Bush Administration's Land-Use Decisions Favor Oil and Gas," *Washington Post* National Weekly Edition, October 4–10, 2004.

60 Feuer, "The Ideological Roots of the Oregon Standoff" and Healy and Johnson, "The Larger, but Quieter Than Bundy, Push to Take Over Federal Land."

61 Charles Pope, "National Parks, Private Funds: Trouble in Paradise?" *CQ Weekly*, October 31, 1998: 2938–2941; and Darryl Fears, "National Park Service Turns 100, and Some Sites Are Showing Their Age," *Washington Post*, August 24, 2016. The full National Park Service "deferred maintenance report can be found at: www.nps.gov/subjects/plandesignconstruct/defermain.htm.

62 Jim Robbins, "Judge Rejects Plan for More Snowmobiles at National Parks," *New York Times*, September 16, 2008; and Blaine Harden, "National and State Politics Help Safeguard a Swamp," *New York Times*, April 3, 2002.

63 A summary and more detailed accounts can be found at the website for the Fish and Wildlife Service: www.fws.gov/. The site also includes U.S. regulations pertaining to endangered species, habitat conservation plans, and similar information.

64 See Tobin (1990), Tom Kenworthy, "Federal Projects Are Not Endangered," *Washington Post* National Weekly Edition, March 9–15, 1992: 37, and World Wildlife Fund, "Old-Growth Forests, Ecosystem Management, and Option 9," *Conservation Issues*, 1 (May/June, 1994): 5–8. A recent press release reviews efforts to build on the agency's successes in this regard: "Fish and Wildlife Service, NOAA Propose Actions to Build on Successes of Endangered Species Act," May 18, 2015, at the agency's website: www.fws.gov.

65 Sam Howe Verhovek, "An Expensive Fish," *New York Times*, March 17, 1999.

66 The website for the new program is: www.nbii.gov/.

67 New York Times, "U.S. Issues New Rules on Protected Species," *New York Times*, June 15, 1994: 7; and John M. Cushman, "The Endangered Species Act Gets a Makeover," *New York Times*, June 2, 1998: 2. See also a U.S. GAO letter to Congress in December 2008 that recounts recent studies and recommendations, *Endangered Species Act: Many GAO Recommendations Have Been Implemented, but Some Issues Remain Unresolved* (Washington, D.C.: GAO, GAO-09-225R, 2009).

68 Cited in *Science and Environmental Policy Update*, the Ecological Society of America online newsletter, April 20, 2001. For an update on conflicts over the Act in Congress, see Felicity Barringer, "Endangered Species Act Faces Broad New Challenges," *New York Times*, June 26, 2005.

69 Felicity Barringer, "Interior Official Steps Down After Report of Rules Violation," *New York Times*, May 2, 2007. See also the U.S. GAO exhaustive study of the accusations, *U.S. Fish and Wildlife Service: Endangered Species Act Decision Making* (Washington, D.C.: GAO, GAO-08-688T, 2008).

70 Felicity Barringer, "Polar Bear Is Protected under Endangered Species Act," *New York Times*, May 15, 2008; and Cornelia Dean, "Bid to Undo Bush Memo on Threats to Species," *New York Times*, March 4, 2009.

71 Michael Wines, "Coming Soon: Long-Delayed Decisions on Endangered Species," *New York Times*, March 6, 2013; and Fish and Wildlife Service, "Improving ESA Implementation: Prioritizing the Service's Listing Work," July 2016, on the agency's website: www.fws.gov.

72 See Samuel K. Wasser, Bill Clark, and Cathy Laurie, "The Ivory Trail," *Scientific American*, July 2009: 68–76.

73 The Council on Environmental Quality maintains a NEPA Net, with the full text of the statute, current regulations and guidance documents, statistics regarding NEPA and its impacts, an overall evaluation of NEPA, and links to other websites: https://ceq.doe.gov/welcome.html. See also the EPA website for NEPA implementation: www.epa.gov/nepa.

74 See John M. Broder, "State Department Criticized by E.P.A. on Pipeline Report," *New York Times*, April 22, 2013.

75 For a review of NEPA's application and assessments of its effects on environmental decision making, see a symposium edited by Bartlett and Malone (1993), and a special issue of the journal *Environmental Practice* on NEPA (December 2003). See also Caldwell (1998).

76 See Michael Janofsky, "Pentagon Is Asking Congress to Loosen Environmental Laws," *New York Times*, May 11, 2005. For the military, the administration argued that NEPA and other environmental laws seriously interfere with military readiness and training. The military spends about $4 billion a year to comply with various environmental laws. The Pentagon argued that the money could be better spent for direct military preparedness.

77 The task force had its own webpage: http://ceq.hss.doe.gov/ntf/. For a discussion of the controversies raised by the Bush initiatives on NEPA, see an extensive article by Margaret Kriz: "Bush's Quiet Plan," *National Journal*, November 23, 2002: 3472–3479.

78 The statements are taken from "CEQ Chief Urges Agencies to Take Fresh Approach to NEPA," *Greenwire* news service, March 23, 2009. For an overview of the CEQ's activities, see its webpage: www.whitehouse.gov/administration/eop/ceq.

79 Chris Mooney, "From Now On, Every Government Agency Will Have to Consider Climate Change," *Washington Post*, August 2, 2016.

CHAPTER 7

Evaluating
Environmental Policy

Among the less prominent of President Barack Obama's nominees for executive office during his first term was one that gave environmentalists pause but was cheered by their opponents. Harvard law professor Cass R. Sunstein was selected to head the Office of Information and Regulatory Affairs (OIRA) within the powerful White House Office of Management and Budget (OMB). A senior staff member at the Competitive Enterprise Institute captured the relatively positive reaction by conservatives to Sunstein's appointment: "He is the best we could have hoped for from this Administration." The business community also was pleased with Sunstein's selection because OIRA plays a pivotal, if largely unseen, role in the world of federal regulation. The office oversees and can significantly affect the activities of all regulatory agencies, including the U.S. EPA. Under the George W. Bush administration, OIRA was vigilant in guarding against costly new regulations, including those dealing with the environment. Although Sunstein did not follow in the footsteps of his immediate predecessors at OIRA, John Graham and Susan Dudley, who were even more suspicious of environmental rules, like them he was committed to applying cost–benefit analysis to judge the acceptability of proposed new regulations (Morgenstern 2017).[1] Environmentalists have questioned whether the use of such economic analysis is appropriate in environmental policy decisions.

OIRA's role in the Obama administration provides an appropriate window into the varied challenges facing environmental and natural resource policies over the next several decades, both within the United States and worldwide. Donald Trump's administration has pledged to critically review major environmental regulations, particularly the Clean Power Plan of 2015, as well as to reform the EPA itself. As noted in Chapter 5, OIRA is likely to play at least as important a role today as it did during the Bush and Obama administrations.[2]

The previous chapters have examined key environmental problems and the major policy actions taken by government in response to them, as well as policy achievements and deficiencies. As we have seen, disagreements often arise over whether to continue present policies, such as the Clean Air Act or the Endangered Species Act, or change them in some significant ways, and even greater controversy surrounds the approval of new regulations under these decades-old laws, such as the Clean Power Plan. The promise of change can be seen in the success of many different kinds of policy alternatives, some minor and others far more consequential, adopted at the state and local levels as well as at the federal level. These include, for example, the use of market incentives for energy and water conservation and reduction in greenhouse gas emissions, the use of information disclosure to inform the public about risks of toxic chemicals, and provision of greater flexibility in the design and implementation of regulations (Durant, Fiorino, and O'Leary 2017; Eisner 2007; Fiorino 2006; Klyza and Sousa 2013). The success of such policy innovation is not automatic, but depends on how carefully the new policy is designed and carried out.

This chapter:

- builds on the previous discussions to make a case for evaluation of current environmental policies as well as assessment of the policy alternatives that are commonly suggested to complement or replace them;
- aids readers in understanding the need for such evaluations; the different ways in which evaluations of environmental, energy, and natural resources policy are conducted; and the varied interpretations that policy analysts, scholars, and policymakers bring to this activity; and
- helps readers develop a capacity to think critically and creatively about alternative policy proposals, and how to use different standards for such assessments, including effectiveness, efficiency, and fairness or equity.

Chapter 8 continues this focus by examining the third generation of environmental policy and the long-term goal of sustainable development, particularly at the international level.

Critiques of Environmental Policy

Concern over the effectiveness, efficiency, or equity of modern environmental policy is not new. It dates back at least to the late 1970s during the Carter administration, and it was a prominent feature of Ronald Reagan's presidency during the 1980s (Vig and Kraft 1984, 2016). The distinction today is that dissatisfaction with environmental and natural resource policies is far more widespread than it was in the past.

As we saw in Chapters 5 and 6, business and industry groups have long complained that the nation imposes excessive costs and other burdens on society through its environmental regulatory activities. A common argument is that government may overregulate in an effort to deal with relatively minor risks to public health and the environment, or it may set environmental standards at a level that cannot easily be justified by science or the economic costs of achieving those standards. In doing so, critics say, regulations can place unnecessary burdens on individual firms and the economy as a whole, harming economic growth or employment.

Similarly, state and local governments struggling to meet federal environmental mandates have demanded greater flexibility and increased federal funds to cope with their manifold responsibilities. And natural resource users such as ranchers, loggers, miners, farmers, and oil and gas companies fight to prevent what they view as precipitous and unwarranted loss of federal subsidies that have helped assure them of financial success. Workers in those industries and the communities in which they live often blame environmental policies (and environmentalists) for threatening their economic livelihood. The so-called war on coal is one of many arguments of this kind, even though coal mining and employment in that sector has been declining for many years for reasons that have little to do with environmental laws and regulations.[3]

Analysts at conservative and libertarian think tanks such as the Heritage Foundation, the Competitive Enterprise Institute, the Cato Institute, and the Heartland Institute tend to object in principle to regulation and natural resources decision making dominated by the federal government. As an alternative, they favor shifting environmental responsibilities to state and local levels and relying where possible on private markets (Anderson and Leal 2001; Greve and Smith 1992; Layzer 2012). They have been joined in many of these positions over time by supporters of the property rights and wise use movements, among others.[4]

Environmentalists are unhappy as well, although for very different reasons. They applaud the strong policies adopted since the 1960s, but they argue that too frequently environmental protection measures are weakened by legislative compromises when approved by Congress, or further compromised during implementation in executive agencies by public officials insufficiently committed to their goals or unwilling to fight with politically powerful entrenched interests. Environmentalists also believe that providing too much regulatory flexibility or self-regulation can encourage industry to evade the law and thus slow achievement of environmental goals (Schoenbrod 2005). In addition, they worry that some of the new approaches used in natural resources management, such as collaborative decision making, may tilt excessively toward economic development at the expense of ecosystem health. At least one major study released in 2016 confirms some of these fears. It found that U.S. environmental performance lagged well behind that of other leading industrialized nations, coming in at number 26 among 180 nations that were ranked.[5] Other comparisons also have found that U.S. environmental and energy policies were behind those of many other developed nations (Harrison and Sundstrom 2010; Vig and Faure 2004; Vogel 2012; Wiener et al. 2010).

Some of these criticisms have more merit than others, but all should be taken seriously. Since 1970 both government and industry have invested large sums of money in scientific research, technological development, and pollution control and abatement. Total federal spending on environmental and natural resource policies recently has been about $40 billion a year (Vig and Kraft 2016). As noted earlier, however, the private sector and state and local governments pay most of the costs of complying with federal environmental protection policies. That cost doubled between 1970 and 1995 (CEQ 1999) and is now thought to be over $200 billion per year, although the EPA has not issued a comprehensive estimate of such costs since the 1990s.

In the absence of an EPA accounting of full compliance costs, critics have suggested that the number is higher number in today's economy, but there is no reliable consensus on the actual amount. The great failing in trying to come up with such numbers is that they only make sense if compared to estimates of the benefits of regulation, which also are very high, and typically are far higher than the costs. Moreover, experience indicates that estimates of initial compliance costs often are higher than actual costs over time because of technological innovations and other changes that follow new regulations.[6] As shown in Chapter 6, there also are costs and burdens associated with energy and natural resource policies that may restrict economic development. It is reasonable to ask, therefore, as many critics do, what such policies and expenditures bring the public in return. Are the costs justifiable in light of the goals of environmental policies, their achievements, and thus the benefits created for society? Will they continue to be in the future?

The creation of economic costs and benefits and the efficiency of environmental regulations are not the only standards by which to judge environmental policies, although they are important (Olmstead 2016). Using other criteria, such as equity or environmental justice or the extent and impact of public participation, we often ask which policies and programs have proven to be the most successful and which the least—sometimes expressed as what works and what does not (Beardsley, Davies, and Hersh 1997; Bennear and Coglianese 2005; Fiorino 2006; Kamieniecki and Kraft 2013). We also want to know what other effects the policies have had, and what the implications are for redesigning environmental policies for the twenty-first century. That is, will newly redesigned policies promise more success and fewer adverse effects, and how much can we learn from policy experimentation and evaluation (Durant, Fiorino, and O'Leary 2017; Fiorino 2001)? Chapter 1 highlighted these kinds of questions in introducing a framework of environmental policy analysis.

Much of the debate today centers on whether the command-and-control regulation adopted during the first era of environmental policies in the 1970s should be changed in some way in light of today's challenges and concerns about the impacts of regulation. As discussed elsewhere in the text, we can think of this kind of criticism, prominent during the 1980s and 1990s, as the second generation of environmental policy, where efficiency-based reforms have been widely discussed (Mazmanian and Kraft 2009). For example, should the nation rely more on market incentives, provision of flexibility in implementation and enforcement, use of information disclosure, and increased devolution of responsibility to the states? Would doing so make environmental policy less costly, more acceptable to society, or more effective in achieving policy objectives? Equally significant is the broader task of formulating new environmental and resource policies that can steer the nation and world toward the long-term goal of sustainable development (Mazmanian and Nijaki 2013; Sachs 2015). The complex and formidable third generation of environmental problems, such as climate change, loss of biodiversity, and meeting the needs of a growing population, will thoroughly test our capacity to design, adopt, and implement such policies (see Chapter 8).

Environmental Policy Evaluation

There is no debate over the need to evaluate how well environmental policies are working, how efficient they are, or how equitably they distribute benefits to the population. Environmentalists, policymakers, public health experts, business leaders, and academic students of environmental policy all agree on this score. They also advance many different arguments for conducting and using such evaluations to improve environmental policies. One is that environmental policies can be costly, as we have seen, not only for government but also for industry and others who must comply with resulting regulations. Thus it is reasonable to ask if the policies are achieving their goals, and at an acceptable cost to society.

A second argument is that because of high and continuing federal deficits (made much worse after the severe recession of 2008–2009, which sharply increased government spending), government budgetary resources are likely to remain scarce. With limited money available, evaluations can help in making decisions about where best to invest those funds— that is, how to set priorities. Knowing what works and what does not is helpful, as is now widely recognized in debates over health care policy where evidence-based medicine is seen as essential to reduce rapidly rising costs.

A third argument is that many environmental and natural resource policies and programs are technically complex, making it difficult to determine just how well they are working, particularly in the short term. In such cases, formal or systematic evaluations can provide better answers than available in any other way. Such information might also provide some assurance to the public that the policies or programs are indeed on the right track.

Even if nearly everyone thinks that evaluations are a good idea, the reality is that assessments or evaluations come in many different forms. Some are more reliable and useful than others. For example, the U.S. GAO is noted for its rigorous assessment of environmental, energy, and natural resource programs, as are panels of the National Research Council. Similarly, some prominent think tanks, such as Resources for the Future, the Brookings Institution, and the National Academy of Public Administration (NAPA), have provided comprehensive and sound evaluations of government programs over the past two to three decades. Many of them also propose innovative ideas for policy reforms (Harrington, Morgenstern, and Sterner 2004; Kettl 2002; Morgenstern and Portney 2004; National Academy of Public Administration 1995, 2000).

Other evaluations, however, may not live up to the high standards set by these organizations. Congressional committees may conduct oversight hearings or initiate limited and sometimes politically motivated investigations of the EPA or other government agencies and issue reports and recommendations, but their depth and quality vary widely. Environmental groups such as the Sierra Club, Union of Concerned Scientists, or Natural Resources Defense Council issue their own critiques of government programs and offer alternatives, and business organizations do the same, but all are at least somewhat limited and may be biased.

The best of evaluation studies gather extensive scientific data and analyze the results objectively. Others, however, may more closely resemble partisan or ideological assessments of programs and agencies. Given the variable standards that are applied in such evaluations, policies and programs that some (e.g., conservative or business groups) judge to be failures are likely to be considered ringing successes by others (e.g., environmental groups). Because of these differences, evaluations and studies that recommend new directions in environmental policy need to be read critically and not simply accepted at face value.

What is the best way to determine whether environmental policies are working well and to consider whether policy alternatives would work better? In theory, evaluation of policies and programs is straightforward. One would specify a policy or program's goals and objectives. Appropriate measures would be developed, and pertinent data would be collected and analyzed to see if the goals and objectives are being met, and at a reasonable cost (Jones 1984; Weiss 1998). The findings then would be carefully considered by policymakers and others. In the end, policies and programs thought to be successful would be kept and those that are not living up to expectations would be changed in some manner in the hope that a revised approach would work better. These are the evaluation and policy change stages of the model of policymaking introduced in Chapter 3.

In reality, assessing environmental policy is much more complicated. It also can be a deeply political and highly partisan process. There are winners and losers in policy choices, and each side of a debate is likely to take an active interest in any efforts to evaluate policies and programs that affect them. Think about federal subsidies to agricultural, mining, timber, and energy industries and how important they are to the beneficiaries. Or consider how the trucking industry or coal-fired power plants would be affected by changes in the Clean Air Act or vehicle fuel efficiency standards, or how environmental groups would respond to proposals to eliminate or drastically reduce federal programs on energy efficiency, renewable energy research, or climate change. Supporters may shield some programs from critical assessment, whereas those that are politically vulnerable may have repeated evaluations thrust upon them by well-placed critics in Congress or the executive branch, or their equivalents at state and local levels or in the private sector.

None of these constraints diminishes the genuine need for serious environmental policy and program evaluations, as is the case in other areas of public policy (Knaap and Kim 1998; Kraft and Furlong 2018; Patton, Sawicki, and Clark 2016; Susskind and Schulman 2013). Their value lies in contributing to systematic, critical, and independent thinking in the policymaking process. In addition, the Government Performance and Results Act (GPRA) of 1993 requires that all existing programs be evaluated regularly and their performance or achievements be demonstrated. The Act encourages agencies to focus on results, service quality, and public satisfaction, and it requires both annual performance plans and annual performance reports.

What do we mean by such evaluations? Evaluation generally means appraising the merit of governmental processes and programs. The term "policy evaluation" usually refers to judging the worth or effects of public policies. It may include an assessment of policy goals or the means used to achieve them (such as regulation versus market incentives), an analysis of the process of implementation (such as federal–state relations in enforcement actions), or an appraisal of their effects (e.g., how much they cost and the value of the benefits they provide).

"Program evaluation" is a more specialized term. It means judging the success of programs that have already been approved and have been implemented and, especially, determining whether and how they affect the problems to which they are directed. Among other effects, analysts seek to learn how programs alter individual and corporate behavior (e.g., actions to comply with environmental laws), how they change the way decisions are made (such as encouraging public involvement or collaboration at the local level), and especially whether over time they improve environmental quality itself.

Most environmental evaluations understandably focus on what analysts call program *outcomes*, the actual effects of public policies on environmental conditions. These outcomes are distinguished from program *outputs*, which are agency decisions made under the law, such as the number of inspections made, administrative orders issued, or other enforcement actions taken. Even when done properly, however, looking at environmental outcomes such as air and water quality or improvements in ecosystem health generally is not sufficient. To get a fuller picture of how environmental programs are working and what might be changed to improve them requires an examination as well of how decisions are made and how well institutions are performing (Bartlett 1994; Baber and Bartlett 2005).

Program Outcomes

In outcomes evaluation, analysts compare measures of environmental quality outcomes with policy objectives. In effect, they are asking whether the air and water are cleaner, the drinking water safer, the hazardous waste sites cleaned up, and endangered species protected. Chapter 2 reviewed these kinds of data, and references throughout the text (particularly in the endnotes, tables, and boxes) indicate where the most current data can be found, such as at agency websites. However, evaluating environmental policies by using such indicators of public or ecological health is almost never as simple as imagined. Experts may disagree about which environmental indicators are most appropriate, the necessary data may not be available or sufficient, and there may be questions of how to interpret the data (Kraft, Stephan, and Abel 2011; Ringquist 1995).

Many questions also arise about how to conduct such evaluations, and thus both proponents and critics of environmental programs can use outcome measures to demonstrate either impressive policy achievements or serious shortcomings. As Chapter 2 indicated, much depends on the indicators that are chosen, the time period for which data are collected, and how the evidence is assessed. Given the politically divisive atmosphere in which evaluations are conducted, we can expect that some groups will purposely choose measures that lead to their preferred conclusions. Hence all evaluations, and especially those conducted by partisan organizations, should be read with keen attention to possible bias. The conclusions that are reached may have profound implications for agency management and program implementation, redirection of program priorities and spending, or decisions to change the policy itself. Thus it is important to get the evaluations right.

Examining Decision Making and Institutions

As important as policy outcomes such as clean air and water are, they are not everything. Many analysts also ask about whether there has been sufficient public participation, whether decisions are well grounded in science and economic analysis, whether a program (such as federal wilderness protection) is being implemented at the right level of government (federal or state), or whether an agency has sufficient resources and leadership to implement the policy successfully.

All of these questions suggest the need for a different kind of evaluation that focuses not only on environmental outcomes but on decision-making processes and on governmental institutions. Analysts sometimes refer to these as *process evaluations* and *institutional evaluations*. The first attempts to evaluate the merit of decision-making processes themselves, such as opportunities that are provided for public involvement (Bartlett 1990; Beierle and Cayford 2002; Daley 2013). Advocates of environmental justice, for instance, argue strongly for community participation in evaluation of hazardous or nuclear waste threats (Bullard 1994; Konisky 2015, 2016; Kraft 1996, 2000; Ringquist 2006). The second asks about the strengths and weaknesses of the institutions charged with implementing environmental policies. For example, does an agency have sufficient capacity (e.g., budgetary resources, staff, and leadership) to handle its policy responsibilities, or are the states able to take on additional duties if current federal powers are further devolved to them? How strongly does the agency enforce current law? Is the agency well managed, and does it develop good working relationships with key stakeholders so that it can be more successful? We have many evaluations of this kind as well, both for the United States and for other nations (Davies and Mazurek 1998; Durant, Fiorino, and O'Leary 2017; Harrison and Sundstrom 2010; Steinberg and VanDeveer 2012; Vig and Kraft 2016).

Signs of Progress

Using all three forms of evaluation gives a more complete and realistic picture than is possible by examining outcomes alone. In this section, we consider selective evidence on outcomes, decision making, and institutions. The discussion draws especially from the outcome measures presented in Chapter 2, and to a lesser extent in Chapters 5 and 6. That evidence suggests progress has been made in meeting environmental quality goals in some areas while falling short in others. As the earlier reviews indicated, no simple generalization can capture the full story across all environmental protection, energy, and natural resource policies. Yet a strong case can be made that conditions would likely be substantially worse today if the major environmental policies had not been in place.

Environmental Protection Policies

Such a conclusion is particularly valid for air and water pollution control, where enormous gains have been recorded since the early 1970s. Even better results might have been obtained in these and other areas had sufficient resources been provided to the EPA and state agencies, had the programs been better managed, had the federal government established better working relations with the states, and had less time been spent by all parties in lengthy and contentious administrative and legal proceedings.

Where additional improvement must be made—for example, in controlling toxic chemicals, cleaning up abandoned waste sites, and reducing hazardous air pollutants—these conclusions should inspire at least some confidence in the regulatory approaches that have been so widely disparaged since the early 1980s, particularly when they are combined with other approaches in the form of hybrid policies (Klyza and Sousa 2013; Kraft, Stephen, and Abel 2011). These results also should help suggest the kinds of policy and administrative changes that might improve the effectiveness and efficiency of environmental policies and yield better results in the future.

For example, hazardous waste remediation at both private sites and government facilities, such as former nuclear weapons plants and military installations, will tax the resolve and resources of government and industry for decades to come. For the very large number of sites needing cleanup, as noted in Chapter 1, the nation will spend hundreds of billions of dollars over the next 30 to 50 years in pursuit of that goal (Probst and Konisky 2001; Probst and Lowe 2000). The scope of these activities demands that programs be well designed and managed and that the funds be used efficiently. Yet evaluations by the GAO, the former Office of Technology Assessment, and independent analysts have long criticized remediation efforts on nearly all counts, from ineffective use of contractors to handle the cleanup tasks to insufficient provision for public involvement in decision making. Clearly, the nation can do a better job (Kraft 1994b).

Perhaps the greatest environmental policy success has been recorded in air pollution control. As discussed in Chapter 2, most of the key indicators show that emissions and concentrations of pollutants have declined impressively and that air quality has been improving nationwide. The latest reports on air quality from the EPA confirm the long-term trend despite continued population and economic growth and increased reliance on motor vehicles (U.S. EPA 2016). At least some of the improvement is clearly attributable to enforcement of the Clean Air Act. Such conclusions, however, do not mean that every air quality proposal or regulation is necessarily justified on economic grounds. Some can easily pass a benefit–cost comparison test whereas others will not. Federal and state regulators make these kinds of judgments as they adopt new standards and new regulations, and also as they issue and enforce air and water quality permits at the state level (Freeman 2006; Olmstead 2016; Pautz and Rinfret 2013).

State-level studies support this line of argument. Ringquist's comparison of the 50 states concluded that "strong air quality programs result in decreased levels of pollutant emissions" even when controlling for other variables such as the states' economy and politics. The stronger programs produce greater reductions in ambient air pollutants. Enforcement is a key factor. States that vigorously enforce controls on stationary sources have lower emissions. The most important variables in this study were consistency in enforcement and well-focused and well-supported administrative efforts (Ringquist 1993, 150–151). The states would be less effective in producing such outcomes without a powerful federal EPA to back them up as a so-called "gorilla in the closet" and thus spur enforcement actions that regulated parties will take seriously.

Some of these same conclusions apply to water pollution control. The nation's water quality has improved significantly since the 1960s (thanks to the Clean Water Act and the Safe Drinking Water Act). Progress here, however, has been much more uneven and slower in coming than in air quality. As highlighted in Chapter 2, there have been substantial reductions in discharge of pollutants from point sources and advances in drinking water quality, particularly in cities. However, as the lead contamination crises in many cities, including Flint, Michigan, demonstrated in 2015 and 2016, much more needs to be done to provide safe drinking water. In contrast, controlling nonpoint sources has enjoyed only minimal success and remains a major focus of current water quality program efforts. Of course, nonpoint sources are by definition much harder to identify and link to surface water pollution, and also not easily amenable to a regulatory approach. As discussed in Chapter 2, this is a major reason why further progress on water quality has stalled. Groundwater quality in many areas continues to deteriorate as well (U.S. EPA 2009). These conditions help explain Ringquist's (1993) findings that states with stronger and more comprehensive water quality programs experienced no greater improvement in stream quality over the time period he studied.

The picture is similarly mixed on toxic chemicals and cleanup of hazardous waste sites, as noted in Chapter 2. The EPA's annual Toxics Release Inventory shows important reductions in releases of toxic chemicals by major industrial sources, thanks to mandatory public disclosure of emissions data (Kraft, Stephan, and Abel 2011). Other pollution prevention programs, from the EPA's 33/50 effort to reduce releases of the most dangerous chemicals to the agency's Energy Star program, also have had significant, if uneven, success (Press and Mazmanian 2016). Even cleanup actions under Superfund arguably have accomplished far more than usually acknowledged, but the very high costs of cleanup of some sites have inhibited more aggressive action, and likely will continue to do so.

In these and other programs, deficiencies in the major environmental protection policies have hardly gone unnoticed. Dozens of studies by academics, research institutes, environmental groups, and business organizations have provided detailed criticism and recommendations for policy change. Many of these studies have been harshly critical of the command-and-control policies adopted in the 1970s as ineffective, inefficient, and overly intrusive, and they have recommended greater use of a diversity of new approaches. Such approaches range from public education and market incentives to greater decentralization of environmental responsibilities to states and communities (e.g., Davies and Mazurek 1998; Fiorino 2006; National Academy of Public Administration 1995, 2000; Portney and Stavins 2000; Press 2015; Sexton et al. 1999).

Particularly at the national level, policymakers have had at their disposal abundant critical analyses and proposals for policy change. Nonetheless, as indicated in Chapter 5, members of Congress have been unable to agree on how to rewrite most of the key statutes to address the concerns and recommendations from these studies. Hence the deficiencies in these programs remain, and both the EPA and the states have struggled to adopt at least some of the new policy recommendations through administrative means (Durant, Fiorino, and O'Leary 2017; Eisner 2007; Klyza and Sousa 2013; Vig and Kraft 2016).

Natural Resource Policies

Judging the success of natural resource policies is no easier than determining whether clean air and clean water policies are working. The kinds of measures often used here—acres of "protected lands" set aside in national parks and wilderness areas, the number of annual visitors to national parks, and the like—are useful but highly imperfect indicators of the policy goals of providing recreational opportunities, preserving esthetic values, and especially protecting the functioning of ecological systems. Other yardsticks can be used for the economic functions of natural resource policies such as ensuring the availability of sufficient rangeland, timber, minerals, water, and energy resources, or aiming for maximum sustainable yield of the resource. As discussed in Chapter 6, the concepts of ecosystem-based management, adaptive management, and critical loads increasingly have been recognized as one way to develop more useful indicators of success (Bäckstrand 2017; Layzer 2008, 2013; Layzer and Schulman 2017). Natural resource agencies such as the National Park Service, Forest Service, Bureau of Land Management, and Fish and Wildlife Service (FWS) report regularly on these activities. Such reports permit some modest assessment of important qualities of U.S. natural resources policy, its achievements and its shortcomings, even if they fall well short of a national ecosystem assessment.[7]

Yet if such results suggest impressive dedication to setting aside land in a protected status and meeting the recreational needs of the American public, there are some equally troublesome statistics in the government's reports. By most measures, for example, the nation continues to lose ecologically critical wetlands to development. Despite the encouraging signs of growth in acreage and visits to national parks, plenty of problems remain, from congestion and crime to air pollution from nearby power plants and threats from other developments.

In some respects, the Endangered Species Act (ESA) is typical of the halting progress and widely disparate assessments of resource policies. Although there have been impressive achievements in listing species and establishment of habitat conservation plans, as discussed in Chapter 2, the Act has saved only a modest number of species, and it is not preventing the loss of habitats and continued degradation of ecosystems, nor the extinction of many endangered species. Moreover, in a 2006 report, the GAO concluded that the success of the Act "is difficult to measure" because recovery plans indicate that species might not be recovered for up to 50 years. Hence the GAO concluded that "simply counting the number of extinct and recovered species periodically or over time" may not tell us much about the overall success of the recovery programs (U.S. GAO 2006). Part of the explanation for the Act's limited success to date lies in a chronic and severe shortfall in budgets and staff for doing the work mandated under the Act. The design of the ESA itself is also to blame, as is the tendency of the FWS to concentrate its limited resources on charismatic species that attract public support. Moreover, the ESA has run into furious political opposition because it exemplifies for many the threat that government regulation can pose to property rights and development projects. Such conflicts have impeded its success.

Data Assessment and Public Dialogue

Aside from such compilations of annual losses and gains in resource use, as the ESA example illustrates, policy conflicts continue over the core question of how to balance economic development and environmental preservation. These controversies exist despite much more frequent use by both government and the business community of the concept of sustainable development, which emphasizes the need to consider the interconnections between economic development and the environment. Whether the issue is oil and gas drilling or mining on public lands, grazing rights and fees, agriculture and water use, or preservation of old-growth forests, the choices today continue to pit environmentalists against resource industries and local communities.

As discussed in Chapter 6, however, many communities and regions have developed new approaches to resource management that bring together environmentalists, citizens, development interests, and public officials in ways that often promote consensus over local development and environmental issues (Gerlak, Heikkila, and Lubell 2013; Layzer 2008, 2013; Sabatier et al. 2005). These success stories speak to the potential for more widespread public dialogue over natural resources and environmental protection. Yet for such public involvement to succeed, better indicators of ecosystem functioning and health are needed.

In that regard, among the most striking omissions in efforts to evaluate environmental protection and natural resource programs are reliable measures of ecosystem health. Ecologists are not entirely in agreement on what it means to call an ecosystem healthy or sustainable, and controversy exists as well over the most appropriate ecological indicators to use. Yet there is little question that such measures of ecosystem functioning and health are essential if changes over time in national forests, rangelands, parks, wilderness areas, and other public and private lands are to be tracked (Bäckstrand 2017; O'Malley and Wing 2000). How do we know, for example, if local land use controls promote healthy rivers, lakes, and bays if we have no way to measure the health of water bodies and the organisms they contain? At a minimum there needs to be more regular monitoring of critical ecosystem functions and assessment of what the data mean. Unfortunately, that may be difficult to do, as budget cuts often hinder the collection of such data.[8]

The very idea of ecosystem-based management rests on the assumption that we can learn how ecosystems function and how they respond to changing stressors in the environment (Cortner and Moote 1999; Layzer 2008, 2013; Layzer and Schulman 2017). Similarly, the movement toward sustainable communities and regions is predicated on the belief that we can develop meaningful indicators of ecosystem functioning, say within watersheds. The pursuit of sustainable communities depends as well on the selection of appropriate and publicly acceptable measures of the communities' social and economic health, which in some ways is equally challenging (Mazmanian and Kraft 2009; K. Portney 2013).

Agencies, environmental groups, and scientists can help promote citizen involvement and collaborative decision making by assisting the public in understanding the data being produced and by facilitating discussion of what the information means. Such assistance and community dialogue are particularly crucial at local and regional levels, where citizens may be poorly equipped to assess environmental and other community problems and decide how best to deal with them. Scientists are often reluctant to play such an active role in public affairs, yet forecasts of dire environmental trends have prompted numerous pleas from prominent scientists for the scientific community to become far more engaged in precisely these kinds of activities (Ascher, Steelman, and Healy 2010; Lubchenco 1998).

Costs, Benefits, and Risks

The improvements in air and water quality since 1970, and other signs of progress in environmental and natural resources policy, are welcome news. Yet such findings fail to address some of the major criticisms directed at these policies, as noted in the chapter's opening. One of the most important is that environmental gains come at too high a cost—in money, jobs, property rights, freedom to choose—and that alternative approaches such as market incentives or providing greater flexibility to industry and state and local governments would allow for achievement of the same environmental quality at a lower cost to society (Freeman 1990, 2006; Keohane and Olmstead 2007; Olmstead 2013, 2016; Portney and Stavins 2000).

Economist Paul Portney has expressed the argument succinctly: "How then do we distinguish wise from unwise policy proposals? The answer is at once very simple and very complicated," he says. Portney notes that the wise or desirable regulations are those that "promise to produce positive effects (improved human health, ecosystem protection, aesthetic amenities)" that more than offset the negative effects. These typically are higher prices that affect consumers, possible plant closures, job losses, or reduced productivity. That is, Portney argues that "wise regulations are those that pass a kind of commonsense benefit–cost test." It is up to elected and appointed officials, as well as the public, to consider such factors when appraising the worth of any proposed regulation (1994, 22–23).

Economists typically express this perspective more rigorously. They might refer to "maximizing net benefits" as a policy goal, and they would define cost effectiveness in such decisions as "choosing the policy that can achieve a given environmental standard at least cost" (Olmstead 2016, 222). Some economists invoke the classic concept of Pareto optimality to define when such decisions are efficient, which is when the allocation of resources is such that it is impossible to make anyone better off without making someone else worse off. That is, it is said to be an economically efficient way to balance environmental benefits and costs. Done in this way, such analysis could assist in choosing the optimal environmental standards, or in selecting from among policy alternatives such as relying on regulation or providing market-based approaches to achieve the same goal.

To these kinds of assumptions, political scientists would add that such regulatory decisions invariably involve not just economics, but also pressures from industry and other organized interests to make decisions that benefit them, whether or not such decisions are in the larger public interest, or meet some textbook definition of economic efficiency. As Harold Lasswell (1958) noted decades ago, policy decisions are at heart about who gets what, when, and how. Contemporary analyses of environmental policy decisions about who wins and who loses reflect much the same perspective (Kamieniecki 2006; Kraft and Kamieniecki 2007; Layzer 2012; Vig and Kraft 2016).

Economic perspectives remain important even if we recognize the political character of decision making. According to Portney, for example, economic research has demonstrated that the nation can meet at least some environmental goals for perhaps as little as 50 percent of the annual cost of complying with federal environmental regulations. Even if the amount saved is well less than 50 percent, it could nevertheless be substantial. Such reductions can be achieved, Portney has argued, through an explicit (although qualitative and open) weighing of costs and benefits in the policy process—an approach that compensates for the limitations of quantitative cost–benefit analysis. Some stringent environmental regulations could easily survive such a test (e.g., removal of lead from gasoline and the phaseout of chlorofluorocarbons [CFCs] are two historical examples), whereas others might not (such as a significant decrease in current permissible ozone levels in cities).

These kinds of arguments for considering economic costs are hard to dismiss. Objections can certainly be raised to relying uncritically on formal cost–benefit analysis or risk assessment, and environmentalists and many others have done so for years (Swartzman, Liroff, and Croke 1982; Tong 1986). Critics generally point to important costs and benefits that may be omitted from such calculations and to ethical objections to representing human health, lives, and ecosystem functioning by somewhat arbitrary economic values or market considerations. In 2005, for example, the GAO identified four significant shortcomings in the EPA's economic analysis of its proposed options for controlling release of mercury, including a failure to estimate "the value of the health benefits directly related to decreased mercury emissions." The agency concluded that those weaknesses limited the usefulness of the analysis for policymakers (U.S. GAO 2005c).

Despite such examples of poor analysis, it is difficult to argue that costs and benefits of environmental policies should not be considered at all or should be given little weight. As Portney and many other critics have suggested, at a minimum society has to confront some inescapable trade-offs between environmental regulation and other forms of economic investment (see also Freeman 2006 and Olmstead 2016). Money spent on the environment is not available in the short run for other social purposes such as education, health care, infrastructure modernization, or job creation. Even the promise of sustainable development cannot entirely eliminate such choices, however much it might point to myriad ways to better reconcile environmental protection and economic growth and to the prospect of full compatibility of economic and ecological goals in the long run. It is hardly a surprise that we have competing economic analyses of how best to respond to climate change, where estimating costs and benefits over 100 years or more presents exceptional challenges, and where varying assumptions about suitable discount rates and the appropriate time horizon to use can lead to dramatically different conclusions (Nordhaus 2008; Stern 2007).

The trade-offs become starker as environmental management deals with marginal gains in environmental quality. That is, as we reduce pollutants to small residual amounts, the marginal dollar cost of each additional unit of improvement can rise sharply (Freeman 2006; Olmstead 2016; Tietenberg and Lewis 2016). The tendency of legislators to draft what economists call "absolutist" and unrealistic goals such as "zero discharge" or "lowest achievable emissions" does not take into account such marginal costs. Nor is public support for environmental protection informed by such economic thinking. With costs of environmental protection continuing to rise, the case for reconsidering such goals is compelling.

Comparing Risks and Setting Priorities

A variant of the argument for making greater use of cost–benefit analysis or its close cousin, cost-effectiveness analysis, as we saw earlier, is to use comparative risk assessment in which health and environmental risks are ranked to allow for the setting of policy priorities. The EPA has long argued, most famously in its 1987 study, *Unfinished Business*, for risk-based priority setting. Its 1990 study, *Reducing Risk* (1990b), made the case convincingly and reached a large audience of influential policymakers.

The agency's Science Advisory Board, which wrote the 1990 study, concluded that the EPA should target its environmental protection efforts, or set priorities, on the basis of opportunities for the greatest risk reduction, using "all the tools available to reduce risk" (such as public education and market incentives as well as regulation). Too often, the report noted, environmental statutes and agency decisions emphasize some risks of relatively little import while neglecting others of much greater magnitude. The report urged that more attention be given to ecological as well as to public health risks, improving the data and methodologies for risk assessment, emphasizing pollution prevention, and improving public understanding of environmental risks to assist in the national effort to redirect priorities.

Subsequent analyses of environmental protection policies have emphasized the same line of argument (Andrews 2006b; Davies 1996; National Academy of Public Administration 1995, 2000). This is the core question: If available resources are limited, how can they best be used to minimize public health risks and promote environmental quality? The premise here is that although environmental policies may reduce risks, some are far more efficient at doing so than others. Thus, depending on which programs are well funded and which regulations are aggressively enforced, governments and private parties can spend a great deal of money without a concomitant return in risk reduction. That is, the public's health and the quality of the environment may not be improved enough to justify the actions taken.

Some environmental protection efforts could easily withstand such a comparative risk test. Examples include regulating urban smog, fine particulates, and lead; instituting new efforts to deal with indoor air quality; and (up to a point, at least) limiting the buildup of greenhouse gases through reduction in use of fossil fuels. Other programs, such as cleanup of hazardous waste sites, would probably fail to measure up quite as well. Public acceptance of this approach is by no means guaranteed, given often sharp differences between public views of the risks posed and those of technical experts. A further impediment is the substantial decline of public confidence in both scientific experts and government, and the heightened level of partisanship over environmental policy in the 2010s. As argued in Chapter 5, credible risk rankings of this kind also depend on improved databases and use of better analytic methodologies for health and ecological risk assessments (Davies 1996).

Some efforts have been made to try this kind of comparative risk study at the state level, at the encouragement of the federal EPA. For example, in 1994 a report prepared for the California EPA was praised by scientists for its careful review of evidence on dozens of environmental hazards and the risks posed by each. The two-year study by 100 scientists was hailed especially for its careful explanation of methodologies, data sources, and assumptions behind the risk assessments. The report served as a model for other states as the federal EPA pressed them to identify and act on their most serious environmental risks.[9]

Controversies over Cost–Benefit Analysis and Risk Assessment

These thoughtful and constructive efforts to use more economic analysis and risk assessments should be clearly distinguished from proposals debated in Congress from the mid-1990s to today that would impose far more demanding requirements on the EPA and other agencies, even for fairly minor regulatory actions. Most of these measures were intended to slow the regulatory process and avert costs rather than to facilitate better understanding of the costs and risks (Andrews 2006b). By one count, proposals of this kind could have increased by 30-fold the number of regulatory analyses conducted each year, while providing little useful information to policymakers and the public (P. Portney 1995). The result might well have been "paralysis by analysis" as agencies struggled to meet highly prescriptive congressional demands for cost assessments and other activities that offered little hope of improving environmental policy. Congress chose not to approve most of these proposals (Kraft 2013a, 2016).[10]

Many environmentalists object on even more fundamental grounds to putting policy choices in economic terms. In some cases, they prefer that policy debate take place in moral rather than economic terms. Protection of biodiversity or promotion of ecosystem health, for example, might be grounded in environmental ethics that recognize the rights of other species and future generations (Paehlke 2000, 2013b). As Mark Sagoff (1988) put it, such a moral attitude "regards hazardous pollution and environmental degradation as evils society must eliminate if it is to live up to its ideals and aspirations" (pp. 195–196). Economic analysis, in contrast, tends to value the environment primarily in terms of its instrumental value to humans. From this perspective, balancing the benefits of social regulation against the costs seems to be merely a matter of "organized common sense" (Freeman 2006).

In considering the use of risk assessment and cost–benefit analysis, environmentalists question how objective the exercise will be. In particular, they tend to be skeptical that in this kind of economic calculus all the relevant costs and benefits can or will be measured and weighed fairly. This skepticism is a legitimate concern shared by many policy analysts (Anderson 2015; Kraft and Furlong 2018). For environmental policy, benefits typically are harder to estimate than costs. Benefits such as improved public health from reduced exposure to toxic air pollutants are difficult to document, and their value subject to considerable debate. In contrast, the costs imposed on industry may be easy to identify and easily measurable. In addition, analysts may heavily discount long-term benefits to public health and the environment because those benefits could come far in the future, and their future value has to be compared to the present value of the dollar (which is usually much lower).[11] These objections are less an indictment of the principle or professional practice of cost–benefit analysis than they are an expression of distrust in the way such analysis may be used by partisan advocates. They also reflect doubt that the political process will afford an open dialogue on the critical policy choices at stake—such as restrictions on mining operations, logging of forests, or removal of dams—to protect species and ecosystems.

Even the strongest advocates of cost–benefit analysis concede that the method is most appropriate when the requisite data are available and when its limitations are recognized both by those doing the analysis and those who use it in making decisions. As is the case with risk assessment, invariably critical choices must be made in specifying the most important costs and benefits to be considered, which can be measured and which cannot, the way in which intangible values such as human health are weighed, and how long-term benefits and costs are dealt with to make them comparable to present dollar values (Harrington, Morgenstern, and Nelson 1999; Tong 1986).

Above all else, cost–benefit analysis and risk assessment must be recognized as providing only one kind of information to consider in making environmental policy decisions. Such analysis should not necessarily determine the outcome when other important values are at stake. This is one of the reasons why a different approach is more common in Europe than in the United States. European nations employ an abundance of caution in regulating environmental risks, relying on the precautionary principle; in effect, they are saying if in doubt about the health risk, assume the worst and regulate it. In contrast, the United States generally follows an approach that balances risks against the cost of acting on them (Vogel 2012; Wiener et al. 2010).

The EPA itself, as discussed in Chapter 5, is required to justify its regulatory proposals with this kind of economic analysis, which is subject to review by the OMB, as discussed in the chapter's opening. Thus the agency engages in extensive analysis of its regulations, and that analysis becomes a key part of the political debate over new rules, such as those associated with the Clean Power Plan. Occasionally, the agency engages in an even more comprehensive analysis of the costs of its regulatory activities.[12] One example dealing with the costs and benefits of the Clean Air Act is given in Box 7.1 The OMB itself regularly publishes its estimates of the costs and benefits of federal regulatory programs, including those managed by the EPA, and these are available at the website for OIRA, along with a discussion of the methodology that the agencies use in making these estimates.[13]

■■■■ BOX 7.1 THE COSTS AND BENEFITS OF THE ■■■■ CLEAN AIR ACT

The Clean Air Act Amendments of 1990 require the EPA to conduct periodic studies (subject to external review) to assess the costs and benefits of the act's overall effects. The agency concluded in a 1997 study that the total monetized benefits realized between 1970 and 1990 were between $5.6 and $49.4 trillion, with a mean estimate of $22 trillion. The direct compliance expenditures were estimated to be $0.5 trillion ($523 billion). A large part of the benefits came from reducing two pollutants, lead and particulate matter. The study used an array of computer models to compare two scenarios. One was the actual environmental and economic conditions that have been observed. The second was built from a projection of conditions that would have prevailed without the federal, state, and local programs developed pursuant to the goals of Clean Air Acts of 1970 and 1977.

In a follow-up study released in November 1999 after six years of research, the EPA forecast that in the year 2010, the benefits of the Act would exceed its costs by four to one—that is, an estimated $110 billion for the benefits expected and $27 billion for the anticipated costs.

Finally, in the latest study, released in 2011 and containing estimates through 2020, the agency concluded that the "direct benefits to the American people ... vastly exceed compliance costs."

The benefits were estimated to be $2 trillion in 2020, or more than 30 times the estimated costs in the medium projection, and 90 times the costs in the high projection. Even in the low projection model, the benefits were three times the costs.

Does this kind of comparison of costs and benefits of the CAA seem valid? What objections might be raised? All three studies are available at the EPA's website. For a critique of the original study and its conclusions, see Krupnick (2002).

Environmentalists' Use of Economic Analysis

Despite a continuing discomfort with economic analysis, environmental groups for years have conducted their own studies as a counterpoint to government and industry arguments about the high cost of environmental actions. In 1994, for example, the Wilderness Society reported that recreation and tourism in national forests brought in more money than timber harvests. For the area studied (five states in the Southeast), the society put the value of harvested timber at $32 million a year and the economic benefits each year of recreation and tourism at $379 million. The report concluded that policies emphasizing timber production were "out of step with economic realities."[14] Environmentalists have used similar studies to support arguments for protecting old-growth forests in the Pacific Northwest, where the region's economy depends heavily on tourism.

Increasingly analysts and environmentalists report on the environmental costs of human activities that previously were given little thought, from raising beef to transporting a variety of foods over long distances. The carbon footprints of these activities are of special interest, and the findings are often striking. For example, half a gallon of orange juice can have a footprint of 3.75 pounds of CO_2, mostly from energy and fertilizer use in production, processing, and shipment. Each pound of beef produced through conventional methods today (not grass-fed) generates between 3.6 and 6.8 pounds of CO_2. Meat production as a whole is said to contribute between 14 and 22 percent of the 36 billion tons of CO_2-equivalent greenhouse gases the world releases each year.[15]

In an unusual three-year study focusing on the Chicago metropolitan area, the Forest Service found that planting thousands of trees would bring a net benefit of $38 million over 30 years by reducing costs of heating and cooling buildings and by absorbing air pollution. Just three strategically placed trees could save a Chicago homeowner $50 to $90 a year.[16] Studies of this kind led Chicago to initiate extensive rooftop gardens as part of a five-city pilot project assisted by the U.S. EPA's Urban Heat Island Project and the DOE; the city has since gone well beyond these initial measures with an aggressive program of urban greening. In a related move, the Los Angeles Department of Water and Power began a program in 2002 to give away 100,000 shade trees to its customers to help cool homes and reduce demand for electricity for air conditioners, as well as to remove air pollutants.

In a more extensive effort of this kind, in 2007 the New York City Parks Department measured the economic benefits of the city's hundreds of thousands of street trees using a program called Stratum that takes into account a tree's impact on property values, its absorption of CO_2, and its contribution to energy savings through provision of shade. The city concluded that street trees provided an annual net benefit (after accounting for the cost of planting and upkeep) of $122 million, or $5.60 in benefits for every dollar the city spent on trees.[17]

Environmental groups in the Great Lakes area made much of studies on the deceptively low price of the road salt used to melt snow and ice in winter. The EPA has put the damage to vehicles, highways, bridges, and related infrastructures at $5 billion a year. Hence local governments might find that buying "more expensive" substitutes for salt is actually cheaper when environmental impacts and other damages from salt are factored into the equation. In the early 1990s, one New York state agency estimated that winter road salt carried a *true* cost of $800 to $2,000 per ton (far higher than the alternatives) when one considers the effect on wetlands, freshwater supplies, and vegetation, among other environmental damage.[18]

Jobs, the Economy, and the Environment

Aside from objections to the inefficiency of some environmental regulations, a broader indictment has been made against environmental policy. Some scholars, public officials, and advocacy groups have implied that the nation must choose between two paths in fundamental conflict, suggested in the "economy versus the environment" debate of the 1990s. Conservative critics of environmental policy, for example, have argued that environmental regulation slows the rate of economic growth, costs jobs, and thereby unintentionally makes the population worse off.

As one example, Wildavsky (1988) asserted that by "searching for safety" and favoring governmental regulations that constrain economic investment and growth, environmentalists actually cause the population to be less safe. That is because fewer people can afford a lifestyle (e.g., diet, physical security, and access to health services) that historically has been associated with improved health and well-being. His argument hinges on the questionable assumptions that regulations deal with trivial risks to public and ecosystem health and that investment in environmental protection weakens the economy and individual prosperity enough to more than offset whatever additional safety environmental policies produce.

Employment, Business Costs, and Environmental Policy

Anecdotal evidence related to the economic impact of environmental policies is easy to come by, but not very helpful. The American Petroleum Institute put the blame on environmental restrictions for the loss of 400,000 oil production-related jobs in the 1980s (Bezdek 1993). Mining companies have claimed that legislation to reform the 1872 General Mining Law could cost 47,000 jobs in an industry that has already suffered a substantial loss of its jobs; the Bureau of Mines had a far lower estimate of only 1,110 lost jobs.[19]

Similarly, throughout his first term, President Obama's critics frequently charged that his environmental and energy regulatory proposals were "job killing," although little evidence supported such an assertion. Most regulations both create and cost jobs as businesses adapt to new agency requirements. For example, the BlueGreen Alliance, a partnership between labor unions and environmentalists, concluded in a 2013 study that the new fuel economy standards approved by the Obama administration would create up to 570,000 jobs by 2030, most of them in manufacturing of parts and assembly of the vehicles.[20]

One recent economic analysis found that the Obama Clean Power Plan was likely to create up to 273,000 jobs over the next several decades. The study concluded that job losses suffered at closed coal-fired power plants would be more than offset by investments in renewable energy and productivity gains across the economy as well as in gradual reductions in the price of electricity.[21] Similarly, researchers at Duke University found that while 49,000 jobs were lost in the coal industry from 2008 through 2012, some 175,000 jobs were created in the natural gas, solar, and wind industries.[22]

Critics may disagree with such economic analyses, but it is apparent that many policymakers are well aware of the need to improve the economy at the same time as the nation moves toward greater use of renewable energy and acts on climate change. Such ideas are, of course, central to the concept of sustainable development or sustainable growth, namely, that one can foster economic development while simultaneously protecting the environment and human health (Mazmanian and Kraft 2009; Sachs 2015; World Commission on Environment and Development 1987).

On the other side of this debate, the Institute for Energy Research, funded heavily by the fossil fuel industry and prominent in the climate denial movement, for years sought to end state efforts to require utilities to produce a certain percentage of their electricity from renewable energy resources (called renewable energy portfolios). Among other sources, the institute often relied on a discredited study that asserted more than two jobs were lost for every new renewable energy job that was created, when nearly the opposite was the case. Despite the study's faults, it became a prominent part of the debate in state legislatures and Washington.[23]

For those who find contradictory findings like these to be disconcerting, scholars increasingly have tried to sort through the real impacts of environmental and energy regulation to counter partisan assertions, and also to clarify precisely when regulation is needed and how it can be used in a way that meets the varied expectations we have for it. These essential analyses should help to inform what is often an ideological and unproductive debate over the role of regulation in today's economy, and particularly in environmental protection and energy policy (Coglianese 2016; Coglianese, Finkel, and Carrigan 2014).

Job losses clearly have occurred in specific industries, communities, and regions as a result of environmental mandates. Coal mining in Kentucky and West Virginia is one notable example, as is oil and gas exploration on public lands in the West. There may be fewer losses than initial estimates often suggest, although that is of little comfort to those who lose their jobs or to the businesses forced to close their doors. Fortunately, there is much that governments and the private sector can do to minimize adverse effects through job retraining efforts, financial incentives for workers to pursue new degrees and skills, subsidized loan programs, and similar actions. Successful implementation of environmental policies requires that policymakers think more seriously about using such approaches to avoid needless conflict over otherwise broadly endorsed environmental goals.[24]

At the national or macroeconomic level, environmental policies historically have only a small effect on the economy no matter what measure is used: inflation, productivity, or jobs (P. Portney 2000). At this level, economic analyses have found that environmental policies increase inflation and decrease productivity *only very slightly*. Those policies have also led to a net increase in employment (Peskin, Portney, and Kneese 1981; Tietenberg and Lewis 2016).[25] To explore that relationship, a team of economists from Resources for the Future studied four heavily polluting industries during the 1990s: pulp and paper, plastics, petroleum refining, and iron and steel. They found that increased environmental spending in these industries *did not* cause a significant reduction in industry-level employment (Morgenstern, Pizer, and Shih 1999; see also Morgenstern 2017).

It is also apparent that the costs of complying with environmental regulations, even when substantial, are far lower than many other costs of doing business, such as providing for employee health care insurance and maintaining competitive salaries. One study, for instance, put pollution control costs at only 1 percent of total company costs on average for manufacturing industries; the highest costs were found for basic chemical industries, where it was 3 percent (Eskeland and Harrison 2003). Yet often the environmental expenditures are singled out for criticism. Of course, as noted earlier, when compliance costs are higher than they need be because of inefficient rules and regulations, those requirements could be changed and greater flexibility provided to the business community. Much recent action by both the EPA and the states to reform environmental policies has been directed at precisely these ways of reducing compliance costs, and additional actions to reduce the impacts of environmental regulations are likely in the Trump administration.

Even when employment and other economic effects are larger than these numbers indicate, economist Paul Portney offers an important observation: "Counting jobs created or destroyed is simply a poor way to evaluate environmental policies" (1994, 22). A policy and the regulations it generates may cost jobs and still be judged desirable because it eliminates harmful pollution or protects valued resources. This does not make the loss of jobs any more acceptable, either to the communities in which they occur or to elected officials who represent those communities. Conversely, policies that generate jobs may be bad for the environment and public health. Policymakers should be able to design employment policies that do not produce such negative effects. It is for this reason that the Obama administration in 2009 emphasized the creation of "green jobs" as part of its economic recovery measures.[26]

These dilemmas speak to the need for sustainable development. Sustainability requires attention to what is environmentally sound and economically efficient, but also to what is socially and politically acceptable and just. The trick for policymakers is how to develop policies that can meet all of these expectations, particularly protecting the environment while creating jobs and spurring innovation that promises future gains in economic efficiency. Effective political leadership is one way to do that. Increasingly, labor unions also recognize that the old debate about jobs and the environment is unproductive. Many organizations, such as the BlueGreen Alliance (www.bluegreenalliance.org/) stress the need for sustainable jobs and environmental policies that protect the health of workers, their families, and the communities in which they live. Moreover, as discussed in Chapter 8, green businesses are proliferating in the United States and other nations, and major corporations increasingly recognize and support sustainability principles (Esty and Winston 2006; Press and Mazmanian 2016).

The same lesson can be seen in the U.S. environmental technology industry. Obama's first secretary of energy, Steven Chu, for example, was widely praised for support of "energy innovation hubs" that focused research and development on such critical topics as carbon capture and storage technologies, improved batteries for energy storage, smart grid improvements, and production of biofuels. Universities, national laboratories, and private industry were invited to work together to win substantial research awards as the government sought to stimulate what it called "game-changing" breakthroughs.

Beyond what the federal government does, such efforts have been evident for years. For example, green technologies have been among the preferred areas for venture capital in the Silicon Valley area of California (Flavin 2008).[27] In one striking illustration of the potential of such public investment, a study by economists at the University of California, Berkeley, in 2006 found that California's plan to sharply reduce its greenhouse gas emissions would create tens of thousands of jobs in the state and boost its economic output by some $60 billion by 2020. The state's gains are expected to come in part from its anticipated sales of greenhouse gas-reducing technologies.[28] Much the same argument has been advanced recently by supporters of higher fuel efficiency standards for vehicles—that is, that there are likely to be highly favorable economic and jobs impacts from the new rules.[29]

Seeking Common Ground: Toward Environmental Sustainability

Although some of these arguments about the positive economic effects of environmental policies are long on hope and short on empirical evidence, some studies lend support. Lax environmental standards seem to insulate inefficient and outmoded firms from the need to innovate and invest in new equipment. Such investments are likely to be essential to compete successfully in a twenty-first-century global economy (Bezdek 1993; Porter and van der Linde 1995). There may be some short-term economic advantages to weak environmental laws, as debates over the North American Free Trade Agreement (NAFTA) and other international trade issues have highlighted (Vogel 2006). Over the long run, however, policies that promote environmentally sound and efficient technologies and processes, not those that are environmentally degrading and wasteful, seem to offer the best hope, particularly if full cost accounting is used to assess environmental damages fairly (discussed later).

Some of the most compelling evidence of the relationship between the economy and environmental policy comes from analysis of state policy efforts. For example, Bowman and Tompkins (1993) carefully examined the relationship between state environmental policy commitment and economic growth and development. They acknowledged that such analysis is difficult because of the complex interrelationship of the variables, yet they concluded that "environmentalism is not invariably associated with restricted economic growth—indeed, if anything, most of the evidence ... favors the suggestion that it is at least *associated* with higher levels of economic growth." Another analysis of these relationships by Feiock and Stream (2001) examined change in economic performance of the 50 states between 1973 and 1991, and came to much the same conclusions (see also Meyer 1993). Similarly, in late 2016, a Brookings Institution analysis of decarbonization efforts and economic growth in the states from 2000 through 2014 found that 33 states both reduced their carbon emissions and enjoyed economic growth at the same time. In short, reducing greenhouse gas emissions did not harm the economy. The authors concluded that "President-elect Trump's assumption of an opposition between economic growth and environmental stewardship is false."[30]

Environmental Justice

Another critical aspect of pursuing sustainability, especially at the local level, is the need to consider environmental justice. Critics argue that social or community well-being must take into account inequalities among groups in the population, particularly the poor and minorities. The environmental justice movement has focused on the inequitable burden that is often placed on poor and minority communities that have rates of exposure to toxic chemicals and other pollutants that are higher than usual (Bryant and Mohai 1992; Konisky 2015).

A study by the EPA in 1992 confirmed a disproportionate impact on poor and minority groups (U.S. EPA 1992a), and many other studies since that time have reached similar conclusions (Ringquist 2006). The EPA urged an increased priority within the agency be given to equity issues and to targeting of high concentrations of risk in specific population subgroups, and the Clinton administration took actions to address those concerns. The agency established an Office of Environmental Justice (OEJ) to deal with environmental impacts on minority and low-income populations. The OEJ defines environmental justice as "the fair treatment and meaningful involvement of all people regardless of race, color, national origin, or income with respect to the development, implementation, and enforcement of environmental laws, regulations, and policies."[31]

On February 11, 1994, President Clinton issued Executive Order 12898, which called for all federal agencies to develop strategies for achieving environmental justice. The order also reinforced existing law by forbidding discrimination in all agency policies, programs, and activities on the basis of race, color, or national origin. This executive order is overseen by the OEJ, which has developed elaborate guidelines for its implementation and compliance. Each of the 10 EPA regional offices around the country has an environmental justice coordinator who is to facilitate this process.[32]

Since that time, interest in questions of environmental equity has grown both within and outside of government, even if further policy actions have been modest (Foreman 1998; Konisky 2015, 2016; Ringquist 2006). In part, the new visibility of these issues reflects successful grassroots organizing in poor and minority communities. It also signals a new willingness in established civil rights organizations to devote more attention to environmental health issues, and a determination in the national environmental organizations to incorporate environmental justice concerns (Bryant 1995). As more and better data are collected on exposure to hazardous and toxic chemicals and their health effects, the issues may gain more public attention.

There is increasing recognition as well that sustainable community actions must consider social aspects of development as well as economic and environmental issues (Paehlke 2013b; K. Portney 2013), and that in many communities environmental justice concerns continue to be given far less attention than they merit. No doubt they are more difficult to address, and poorly represented segments of a community may have less political and economic clout to advance their interests. The deficiency is sometimes recognized both at the community and state level when attention is focused on particular deficiencies or risks, such as the lead contamination of drinking water in Flint, Michigan, in 2015, and similar discoveries around the nation following the media's examination of the Flint case. These concerns suggest that much more attention needs to be given to enhancing community-based environmental management efforts, both on pollution and health issues and on the broader efforts to develop sustainability initiatives at the local and regional levels (Mazmanian and Kraft 2009).

Environmental justice concerns are important for another reason. More than any other recent development, concern over environmental equity forces policymakers to confront the ethical issues inherent in choosing environmental policy strategies. Whether the focus is on inequitable exposure to environmental pollution across population subgroups within the United States or other nations, or on the enormous economic and environmental inequities between poor and rich nations, the contrasts are remarkable. They make clear that policy decisions involve more than questions of environmental science and technology. They also go beyond consideration of aggregate national costs and benefits, which is the most common way to view the economic effects of environmental policies. The distribution of risks, costs, and benefits across the population, across nations, and across generations merits greater attention in evaluating environmental policy.

Reforming Environmental Regulation

As noted throughout the book, a persistent criticism of environmental policy is that it relies too heavily on centralized, technically driven, command-and-control regulation in which government sets environmental quality goals, the methods to achieve them, and deadlines, with penalties for noncompliance. Aside from the issue of costly inefficiencies addressed earlier, such regulation is often criticized as poorly conceived, cumbersome, time-consuming, arbitrary, and vulnerable to political interference (Davies and Mazurek 1998; Eisner 2007; Fiorino 2006, 2013). Hence, in recent years, economists and policy analysis have suggested a range of alternatives that may either substitute for direct regulation or supplement it (Freeman 2006; Portney and Stavins 2000; Press and Mazmanian 2016). The core question is what combination of policy strategies is the best to use in a given case, for example, integrating elements of regulation, market incentives, and information disclosure.

The Case for Policy Alternatives

There is little real argument today over the wisdom of using such alternatives to regulation as market-based incentives (such as carbon taxes), disclosure of information, public education, negotiation, voluntarism, stakeholder collaboration, and public–private partnerships. They are among the policy approaches that governments at all levels consider, and they have enjoyed wide use in recent years (Durant, Fiorino, and O'Leary 2017; Eisner 2007; Mazmanian and Kraft 2009). Many environmental problems simply cannot be addressed effectively with traditional regulatory tools alone, but incentives and educational efforts may be useful supplements. One example is nonpoint water pollution control that must deal with thousands of dispersed sources such as small farms. Another is indoor air quality, which affects people in millions of individual homes and commercial buildings. A third is individual consumer purchases, for which energy efficiency, recycling, or other environmental goals might be sought. The use of product labels and other forms of communication to inform consumers about their choices is common. "Green labeling" has been widely used in Europe and is slowly becoming more popular in the United States (Mastny 2004). Table 7.1 lists some of the most commonly considered policy approaches to deal with environmental and resource problems.

As appealing as some of the alternative approaches are, most come with uncertainties and limitations or disadvantages as well as advantages. Many questions come to mind. Are these alternatives, such as market incentives, likely to be as effective as regulation? Will they be cheaper or more easily implemented? Will they be more efficient in the use of society's fiscal resources? Will citizens be capable of using the information they are given to better achieve their goals, such as minimizing contact with toxic chemicals, reducing pesticide exposure through the food supply, or improving the quality of drinking water (Hadden 1986; Hamilton 2005; Kraft, Stephan, and Abel 2011)?

Unfortunately, there is little empirical evidence that answers such questions definitively. Few rigorous evaluations have been done for the conventional regulatory programs, and even fewer are available for the kinds of policy innovation under discussion (Bennear and Coglianese 2005, 2013; Davies and Mazurek 1998; Knaap and Kim 1998). What we do have is a plethora of innovative state and local actions that appear to have worked well (e.g., John and Mlay 1999; Knopman, Susman, and Landy 1999; Rabe 2004, 2016; Weber 2003). There have also been some experiments in regulatory flexibility and collaborative decision making at the federal level that offer a mixed picture (Bennear and Coglianese 2013; Coglianese 1997; Coglianese and Allen 2004; Koontz et al. 2004; Marcus, Geffen, and Sexton 2002). Similarly, case studies of collaborative decision making in water quality (Kraft 2009), use of market-based approaches in air quality (Mazmanian 2009), and use of ecosystem-based management (Layzer 2008, 2013; Rabe and Gaden 2009; Sabatier et al. 2005) indicate substantial potential for alternatives to command-and-control regulation. Yet they all suggest some major limitations to these new approaches as well. Examination of several of these approaches illuminates both their potential and their pitfalls.

TABLE 7.1   Policy alternative for environmental protection and natural resource management

Government action	Description and illustrations
Regulation	Establishment and enforcement of standards, with sanctions for noncompliance (environmental regulation under the Clean Air Act, Clean Water Act, and Superfund; energy efficiency requirements)
Tort law	Use of legal liability laws to provide relief to injured parties who have suffered a personal loss, for example, from pollution that affects their health or livelihood
Using market incentives	Imposition of taxes or charges or development of tradable permits that create incentives and disincentives for action (raising gasoline taxes to encourage fuel conservation; creating tradable permits for carbon dioxide emissions)
Education and communication	Provision of information to the public through formal programs or other actions (disclosure of toxic chemical releases, labels indicating auto fuel efficiency, formal environmental education programs)
Taxing and spending	Taxation of an activity at a level that encourages or discourages it (tax credits to encourage purchase of fuel-efficient vehicles, green taxes to discourage corporate pollution) or spending money on preferred programs (energy R&D support)
Purchasing goods and services	Purchase of products and services for government agencies (fuel-efficient fleet vehicles, recycled paper products, or products with low carbon emissions for federal or state governments)
Rationing	Limitation of access to scarce resources (permits for backpacking and limited campsites in national parks, restrictions on energy or water use during periods of scarcity, limits on fishing to encourage sustainable harvests)
Privatization and contracting out	Transfer of public services or property from government to the private sector (concessions at national parks, sale of federal property) or contracting out for services (DOE contracts for cleanup of former nuclear weapons production facilities)
Charging fees	Imposition of fees for government services (use of national, state, or county parks; fees charged for use of public lands for grazing, mining, timber harvesting; variable pricing for household waste)

TABLE 7.1 (*continued*)	
Government action	**Description and illustrations**
Use of subsidies	Provision of loans, direct payments, tax credits, and price supports (low fees for mineral and water rights, agricultural and irrigation subsidies, financial incentives to protect wetlands under the federal Wetlands Reserve Program)
Creation of public trusts	Placement of property in public trusts (local land conservation trusts, some components of the federal Wetlands Reserve Program)
Support of research and development	Conduct or support of research and development (support for environmental research at the EPA, NOAA, and NSF; energy research sponsored by the DOE)
Assessment for damages	Use of tort law to award damages to plaintiffs for harm suffered, or government imposition of damage assessments (private suits against corporations for damages; natural resource damage assessments under Superfund)
Self-regulation	Voluntary adoption of performance standards by industry or others (ISO 14000 environmental management system standards, chemical industry's Responsible Care program; state programs for environmental self-regulation)

Sources: The table draws from the author's own work, and reflects a common typology of possible public policy actions. See, for example, Anderson (2015), Kraft and Furlong (2018), and Patton, Sawicki, and Clark (2016).

The Promise of Market Incentives   The basic logic of market alternatives is clear enough. If, for example, we all drive a great deal and are thought to be wasting fuel, contributing to traffic congestion and pollution, and also to the buildup of carbon dioxide in the atmosphere, how might such behavior be discouraged? Various regulatory schemes might work, from setting high fuel economy standards for automobiles, vans, and SUVs to restricting use of private vehicles through carpooling and other means. Yet such actions would involve a level of bureaucratic intrusion that may be socially unacceptable and politically infeasible. Such standards also have not worked very well over the past two decades in reducing the use of motor vehicles and gasoline (Portney 2002). Some critics even argue that as vehicles become more fuel-efficient, we will all think it acceptable to drive even more, thus negating the achievements of fuel efficiency standards; this is often called the "efficiency dilemma" or "rebound dilemma."

A market alternative would be to raise gasoline taxes, or to adopt a carbon tax, to a level that is sufficient to achieve the same goals. Higher prices for gasoline would create incentives for all of us to drive less, seek more fuel-efficient vehicles, and rely more on mass transit or other means of transport. Over time, changing consumer preferences could build a market for efficient vehicles to which automobile manufacturers could respond. In theory, a market incentive such as this one can reduce the bureaucratic intrusiveness and costs associated with direct regulation. Regrettably, as noted earlier in the text, public resistance to higher fuel costs and timidity on the part of public officials makes imposition of such a gas tax (or a broader carbon tax) politically infeasible at this time. In principle, however, this kind of policy approach offers an alternative to regulation that is appealing on many grounds (Freeman 2006; Olmstead 2013, 2016; Rabe 2017; Rabe and Borick 2012; Tietenberg and Lewis 2016).

The popular "cash-for-clunkers" program of 2009, described in Chapter 1, vividly demonstrated the appeal of market incentives as people flooded into car dealerships to rid themselves of older and inefficient vehicles, particularly trucks and SUVs. However, the cost for each ton of carbon dioxide emissions saved was very high, more than ten times the cost of the climate change policy that was being considered by Congress at that time. Of course, the main purpose of the clunkers program was to sell more new cars and only secondarily to improve the environment.[33]

Similar cases have been made for imposition of so-called green taxes to discourage pollution. One Organisation for Economic Co-operation and Development (OECD) study in 2001 found that even though the large U.S. economy leads the world in pollution, it imposes the lowest green taxes as a percentage of gross domestic product (GDP) of any industrial nation. Thus there would seem to be plenty of opportunity to consider expanded use of green taxes in the United States, particularly when the economy is doing well and such taxes might be viewed less negatively. One widely recognized example is the tax credit available to buyers of electric vehicles and plug-in hybrids, which is designed to build a market for such vehicles while their costs remain fairly high. Another that has been much less visible, and also uncertain from year to year, is a tax credit for the wind power industry that many of its supporters view as critical to further development of the industry and the jobs that it creates.[34]

Both the EPA and the states have experimented since the 1970s with market incentives and other alternatives to regulation.[35] These innovations are encouraging, if still controversial and limited in actual use. In the Clean Air Act amendments of 1990, Congress authorized emissions trading to reduce precursors of acid rain. The idea is that some firms will find it relatively inexpensive to reduce emissions; for others, it will be costly. The latter can purchase permits or allowances from the former to release those emissions, creating an identical overall reduction in emissions but at a lower cost to the affected firms. Thus the market in sulfur dioxide permits has allowed more efficient (less costly) reduction in emissions while meeting the Act's acid rain goals, even if the program has not fully lived up to its promise. Others see considerable potential for use of market incentives, from encouraging smarter use of flood plains and protecting endangered species on private lands to energy conservation by citizens and corporations, control of greenhouse gas emissions in Europe, and control of sulfur dioxide emissions in countries such as China (Evans and Kruger 2007; Olmstead 2013, 2016; Shogren 2004; Tietenberg and Lewis 2006; Wang et al. 2004).

Even those analysts who have been among the strongest supporters of market-based environmental tools, however, recognize their limited achievements to date. For example, Hockenstein, Stavins, and Whitehead (1997) concluded in one early review of the experience that "market-based instruments have generally failed to meet the great expectations that we had had for them. As a result, they now lie only on the periphery of environmental policy" (p. 13). Other analysts have expressed concern that such market trading schemes, even if effective, may result in local toxic "hot spots" that could exacerbate problems of environmental injustice; poor and minority populations living close to the source of emissions could see their exposures increase (Solomon and Lee 2000). And a 2007 study of energy conservation by the McKinsey Global Institute concluded that market forces alone, even with much higher energy prices, would not be enough to bring about a major shift to energy-efficient technologies; government energy standards would also be necessary.[36] Supporters of market incentives have by no means given up. Rather, they argue that the next generation of these instruments must be better designed and managed to become a more central element in environmental policy.

Innovation by State and Local Governments John (1994) examined similar innovations at the state level. He showed how, through the use of non-regulatory tools and cooperative approaches, state governments reduced the use of agricultural chemicals in Iowa, helped devise a plan for restoring the Florida Everglades, and used demand-side management to conserve electricity in Colorado. Sometimes such programs work well and sometimes not. But proponents of them express great faith that they can be, as one set of authors put it, "at once more effective and flexible than current arrangements yet also more democratic." They based their assessment on cases as diverse as state use of Toxics Release Inventory data, restoration of the Chesapeake Bay in Maryland, and the development of habitat conservation plans in California (Karkkainen, Fung, and Sabel 2000, 690).

Parallel innovations in energy conservation have occurred, as discussed in Chapter 6. Utilities in the early 1990s offered discounts of 80 percent or more to customers buying energy-efficient compact fluorescent light bulbs. In the 2010s, many were doing the same thing either directly to their customers or through subsidized retail sales in stores such as Costco, only this time with far more efficient LED light bulbs. Why? It was cheaper for the utilities virtually to give away the new bulbs than to build the extra generating capacity they would need to meet consumer demand. The regulatory and financial hurdles of designing, getting approval for, and building additional plants made the light bulb offers attractive in comparison. Much the same is true of rebates offered by utilities to buyers of energy-efficient appliances such as refrigerators, washers, dryers, and central air-conditioning systems. Some cities that have strongly embraced sustainability initiatives, such as Seattle, Washington, and Portland, Oregon, have gone much further in encouraging energy conservation in homes and businesses and through solid support for public transportation, such as light rail lines (Paehlke 2013a; K. Portney 2009, 2013; Rabe 2016).

Assessing New Policy Approaches

As discussed earlier, some skepticism is warranted in appraising these new policy instruments, particularly when experience with them is limited. Just as environmentalists and policymakers favored regulatory policies in the 1970s and 1980s, the language of business schools dominated policy debate in the 1990s and 2000s. Policy analysts have urged that programs be more customer-driven, decentralized, and competitive, and that citizens, communities, and bureaucrats be empowered to take action in an entrepreneurial spirit. Mission-oriented problem-solving and flexibility were to replace fixed rules and procedures, and design and market incentives often have been favored over planning and regulation. Privatization and contracting out also have been touted as more effective than relying on government employees (Durant, Fiorino, and O'Leary 2017; Sexton et al. 1999). Self-regulation by industry through adoption of environmental management systems is cited as a tool that can improve environmental performance more effectively and efficiently than government regulation (Borck and Coglianese 2009; Coglianese and Nash 2001, 2002, 2006; Potoski and Prakash 2005; Prakash and Potoski 2006).[37]

Governments are often urged to support such actions, sometimes as an alternative to regulation and sometimes in conjunction with it. For instance, the EPA introduced a National Environmental Performance Track program, a voluntary public–private partnership that recognized and rewarded businesses and public facilities for exceptional environmental performance that exceeded regulatory requirements. Initiated by the Clinton administration, the program was strongly embraced by the Bush administration as a way to make environmental protection efforts less burdensome to the business community. It enrolled some of the most environmentally responsible companies in the nation and promised them fewer routine inspections; it also attempted to free them from some regulatory rules. Critics, however, faulted the program for being too soft on industries that continue to miss federal pollution standards, and for not attracting more support from the business community (Fiorino 2006). The Obama administration ended the program in 2009.

Many of these proposals are problematic, whereas others may be reasonable supplements or alternatives to current practice. Few, however, have been studied carefully. As argued earlier, policy analysis and program evaluation could help separate the promising approaches from the unworkable, and give policymakers some guidance as to which actions are most likely to pan out (Eisner 2007; Potoski and Prakash 2013; Press and Mazmanian 2016). For which environmental programs does decentralization make sense, and for which does a centralized, uniform national policy work best? To what extent can reliance on private lawsuits reduce the need for government regulation in, for example, oil-spill prevention? A brief review of several alternatives to regulation hints at the mixed picture they present.

Tort Law Before the expansion of environmental laws in the 1970s, legal recourse for environmental harm rested largely on common-law concepts such as personal injury and liability for damages. Those injured could ask the courts for compensation for the harm suffered (McSpadden 2000). Even though environmental policy now provides many other ways both to prevent such harm and to compensate those injured, tort law can supplement other measures. Torts refer to injuries to a person's body, financial situation, or other interest that are caused by another person's negligence or carelessness. Environmental lawyers have tried to use tort law to deal with exposure to toxic chemicals, lead paint, and a variety of other environmental harms.[38]

One illustration of the potential of using tort law comes from the 1989 Exxon *Valdez* oil spill cleanup and settlement. Exxon Mobil spent over $2 billion cleaning up Prince William Sound in Alaska, and $1.3 billion in civil and criminal penalties and settlements of claims filed by some 11,000 residents and businesses in the area. In August 1994, a federal jury ordered Exxon to pay $289 million in compensatory damages to over 10,000 Alaskan fishers who had filed a class action lawsuit. The biggest judgment by far was another jury decision in 1994 ordering the oil company to pay $5 billion in punitive damages to approximately 34,000 fishers, landowners, and other Alaskans.[39] The huge award, which Exxon Mobil appealed repeatedly over the years, was by far the largest civil judgment ever in a pollution case at that time.[40]

Perhaps the greatest limitation to using tort law to compensate for environmental damage, however, is that it does nothing to prevent the injury or loss. Even the extensive cleanup effort after the *Valdez* accident captured only 3 to 4 percent of the oil that was spilled, and the effects on marine life were profound. Similar arguments have been advanced over the 2010 BP *Deepwater Horizon* spill. It is also difficult to prove the existence of some kinds of environmental harm (e.g., health effects) and to show convincingly under rules of law that the harm is directly related to a specific company or practice. Those limitations were demonstrated well in Jonathan Harr's book *A Civil Action*, which was turned into a 1999 film. The story focused on a case involving eight families in Woburn, Massachusetts, who had children who died from leukemia. Their lawyers found it challenging and costly to show that illegally dumped toxic chemicals entered the community's water supply and were directly responsible for the children's deaths.

Contracting Out and Privatization The use of market incentives and tort law is still limited. These approaches may turn out to work far better in some instances than in others, but it is difficult to generalize about their promise. A few examples of contracting out and privatization suggest what needs to be examined.

Consider the tendency of some government agencies to rely heavily on outside contractors, which can be viewed as a form of privatization. The Bush administration announced in November 2002 that it was giving serious consideration to privatizing as many as half of the civilian jobs in the federal workforce, and Bush's secretary of the interior, Gale Norton, embraced the idea and planned to outsource thousands of Interior Department positions. The administration defended its actions as likely to save taxpayers' money by ensuring the lowest cost for many routine government duties.[41] Yet many analysts are skeptical about how well privatization and contracting out can meet such expectations (Raymond 2003; Savas 2000).

Some of the evidence to date gives cause for concern. Kettl, for example, reports that the EPA depended so much on contractors for its Superfund program in the 1990s that it turned to them for help in responding to congressional inquiries, analyzing legislation, and drafting regulations and standards. Contractors "drafted memos, international agreements, and congressional testimony for top EPA officials... . They even wrote the Superfund program's annual report to Congress" (Kettl 1993, 112). Cases such as this one led the GAO to be sharply critical of the EPA's lax supervision of contractors, which the GAO argued made the agency vulnerable to contractor waste, fraud, and abuse (U.S. GAO 1992). Much the same could be said for many DOE programs. The DOE is the world's largest civilian contracting agency, and in 1997 it earmarked more than 90 percent of its $17.5 billion budget for contracts. In 2002 the GAO estimated that about three-quarters of the DOE's budget was spent at some 30 major research, development, production, and environmental cleanup sites around the country, with most of the work being done by contractors. For years, however, government auditors pointed to severe weaknesses in the DOE's contracting practices, many of which continue today (U.S. GAO 1997a, 2002, 2005b).[42]

Each case for privatization or greater reliance on competitive markets must be assessed on its own terms. Markets and incentives may work well in some instances and not in others. There is no persuasive case for across-the-board reductions in government budgets and staff (as emphasized in the

1980s) and a switch to market mechanisms on the grounds that markets are inherently superior for allocation of public goods. One must also remember that markets must be structured in some fashion and also policed, and consumers must have access to the necessary information to make rational choices. These requirements imply a continued need for government bureaucracies and the courts to ensure sufficient consideration of the public interest in environmental protection.

New Directions in Energy and Natural Resources Policy

As several of these examples and the discussion in Chapter 6 illustrate, many of the same ideas prominent in discussions of environmental protection policy are proposed for reform of natural resources and energy policies. Critics of all stripes have long found fault with policies they consider outmoded, costly to the government, and environmentally destructive. These distributive or subsidy policies include extensive federal support of commercial nuclear energy from its inception in the 1950s, below-cost sales of timber by the Forest Service, and the U.S. Army Corps of Engineers' long-standing preference for building dams and levees as the chief way to control flooding. Other prominent examples are minimal grazing and mining fees for use of federal land in the West that have led to degradation of land and water supplies and lost revenue to government, and subsidies that encourage farming on flood-prone land by reimbursing crop losses when rivers overflow. Most of these policies have had strong support in Congress and powerful constituencies prepared to defend them, making their elimination politically difficult in any administration.

The political climate today, however, suggests that such inefficient and ineffective policies will continue to be examined critically and possibly eliminated (Lowry 2006; Lubell and Segee 2013). For example, a 2006 report from the Interior Department showed that the United States offers some of the most generous subsidies in the world to encourage companies to drill for oil in publicly owned offshore lands, yet the government has received very little in royalties in return. Moreover, the inducements to oil companies seem to be responsible for only a very slight increase in production.[43] Similar reports in recent years have found fault with federal subsidies for timber, mining, energy, and waste disposal, and subsidized irrigation for farmers, among others. One economic analysis in 2016 extended that argument to a failure to consider the social cost of carbon. It argues that 40 percent of all coal mined in the nation comes from federal lands, but that royalty rates and noncompetitive auction practices of the government fail to reflect the social costs of using that coal.[44]

The Appeal of User Fees

Among the most important natural resources policy reforms is the imposition of higher fees for those using public lands for private purposes. Additional fees, or reduced subsidies, bring more money to the federal treasury, although that is not the main reason for instituting the changes. The purposes are to eliminate or reduce inequitable subsidies to user groups, especially for programs that degrade the environment and deplete or waste natural resources, and to increase market efficiencies (Lowry 2006; Myers and Kent 2001; Roodman 1997).[45] By one estimate, the federal government spends approximately $17 billion a year to manage resources that produce less than $7 billion a year in revenues, and it also must cover the cost of repairing environmental damage. Those costs may be quite high. For example, analysts estimate more than 200,000 abandoned mines exist in the United States; the cost of cleanup could be more than $72 billion. Not all are as severely contaminated as the infamous Summitville mine in Colorado, but as noted in Chapter 6, tens of thousands of abandoned hardrock mines threaten both surface water and groundwater.[46]

In perhaps the most egregious case under the 1872 General Mining Law, Secretary of the Interior Bruce Babbitt was forced by a federal court ruling in May 1994 to sign a contract with a Canadian-based mining company, American Barrick Resources, for a mere $9,565. That contract gave the company the right to mine an estimated $10 billion worth of gold on public land without paying any royalties. There is no shortage of examples of comparable inequities in other areas of natural resource policies.

Aside from higher fees for commercial uses of public lands, many urge that fees for entering national parks should be raised as well. Given the enormous maintenance backlog at the parks, and opposition in Congress to appropriating more funds, should entrance fees be hiked? The National Park Service has been reluctant to raise the fees, and it often faces public resistance in doing so. Yet selectively higher fees could help to relieve congestion at the busiest parks while also raising much-needed funds for repairs.[47]

Privatization of Public Land and Private Land Conservation

Despite its poor reputation during the Reagan administration's efforts at environmental deregulation (Vig and Kraft 1984), proponents of the privatization of public lands continue to argue forcefully that private ownership of what are now public lands would likely increase efficiency in management and yield an optimal mix of goods and services for society. Advocates take this position in part because they believe that public bureaucracies have failed to manage natural resources efficiently and that agency employees have few direct incentives to do so. They believe that even noncommodity values such as wilderness and recreation can be better served in private markets (Anderson and Leal 2001; Raymond 2003; Yandle 1999).

Such a position may be compelling on the grounds that federal agencies have indeed not managed the public domain very well. Yet critics of privatization assert that although markets may be more efficient than public bureaucracies in managing commodities such as energy resources, minerals, and timber, they are not reliable mechanisms for determining collective values for parks, preservation of wildlife, and maintenance of critical ecosystem functions. Moreover, emphasis on efficiency alone tends to neglect other public values such as equity in access and assurance that land and other resources will be preserved for future generations (Lowry 2006).

Representing a different kind of private action that is gaining favor in environmental circles, since 1951 the Nature Conservancy has purchased ecologically sensitive land to preserve habitats and species. With the assistance of its more than 1 million members, the conservancy has helped protect more than 21 million acres of habitat in the United States and more than 103 million acres globally. It owns nearly 2 million acres in the United States and also holds more than 3 million acres in conservation easements in the country. The conservancy projects constitute the largest system of private nature sanctuaries in the world.[48] It also works with developers, industry, farmers, and local governments to encourage new approaches to resource management. Other environmental groups have pursued similar strategies. Nonprofit land trusts, for example, have been established around the nation to work toward conservation of ecologically sensitive land (Fairfax and Guenzler 2001). The lands acquired in this way often are turned over to government agencies to manage.

Even more striking is the effort by some wealthy individuals to buy tracts of land to set aside for conservation purposes, a pattern set years ago by the Rockefeller family, among others (Fairfax et al. 2005). No one seems to have done more in this regard recently than Cable News Network founder Ted Turner. In the late 1990s, Turner established a billion-dollar trust fund through the UN Foundation that focuses on programs dealing with children's health, environmental conservation, climate change, women's issues, and population growth. In addition, Turner acquired substantial land in South America and several large ranches in Montana, New Mexico, and Nebraska that are devoted to wildlife conservation—more than a dozen properties totally over 2 million acres in the United States alone. A rich American couple, Douglas Tompkins and his wife, Kristine McDivitt, bought more than 2,000 square miles of wilderness in southern Chile, an area larger than Rhode Island. They intention was to conserve most of the land and eventually donate it to the people of Chile.[49]

A variation on the use of privatization to conserve public land is the very successful Wetlands Reserve Program (WRP) established under the federal Farm Bill and administered by the Agriculture Department's Natural Resources Conservation Service. This voluntary program provides significant financial incentives for farmers to retire marginal lands for use in wetland restoration or conservation. It is a contractual conservation trust or easement of varying time duration; some are for 30 years and others are set up permanently. There is also a wetland restoration cost-sharing agreement available for a minimum of 10 years to reestablish degraded or lost wetland habitat. In addition to the WRP is a related Conservation Reserve Program that offers annual payments and cost sharing to establish long-term resource-conserving cover on environmentally sensitive land; the program provides an estimated 34 million acres of habitat for birds and other wildlife.[50]

Social Cost Accounting

An even more important step to take advantage of market forces is the adoption of economic accounting measures that reflect the depletion or degradation of natural resources and thus more accurately depict the country's standard of living and the sustainability of its consumption of resources. For instance, the CEQ reported during the early 1990s that agriculture, forestry, fisheries, and mining combined contributed more than $130 billion to the nation's economy. Yet such national income accounts almost never reflect the obvious loss that occurs when natural resources are exhausted or damaged. The subject of social cost accounting has been taken seriously by at least some public officials in the United States as well as globally (Hecht 1999). For example, in the 1990s, President Clinton directed the Bureau of Economic Analysis (BEA) in the Commerce Department to begin work on recalculating the U.S. GDP along greener lines.[51] Similarly, through its Design for the Environment Program, the EPA has worked with industry, academia, and the accounting profession to encourage a fuller and more accurate consideration of environmental costs. From the growing demand for carbon footprint analysis to the search for new ways to measure economic well-being, a clear trend has emerged (Talberth 2008). The United States, however, has not been among the world's leaders in advancing environmental accounting even as advocates for sustainability, such as the organizations Redefining Progress and Sustainable Measures, have proffered new ways to measure gains in societal well-being.[52]

Yet in 2009 the United States did advance the case for using the social costs of carbon emissions in regulatory decision making. A working group of officials from federal agencies developed an estimate of the cost that was about $36 per ton of carbon dioxide (an estimate that some would raise today and others would lower), and that calculation played a major role in the cost–benefit analyses agencies have used for some 100 regulations on energy efficiency, vehicle fuel economy standards, and the Clean Power Plan. Two of the developers of that measure defend it as "the linchpin of national climate policy," because without it there would be no quantifiable estimate of the benefits of taking action. The measure has been upheld in the courts, although future challenges in the Trump administration seem likely.[53]

Ecologists have broadened the dialogue over social cost accounting by highlighting the many free ecosystem services that nature provides to human society, which are rarely reflected in national accounting mechanisms (Daily and Ellison 2002; Kareiva et al. 2011; National Research Council 2004). A study published in *Science* in 2002, for instance, examined five stringently selected cases around the world in which intact ecosystems had been converted for logging, farming, or fishing. The researchers estimated the value of water filtration, carbon absorption, and other ecological services and found them to far outweigh the financial gain from development in all five cases. Indeed, they argued that putting money into nature conservation would yield a 100-to-1 payoff. Extrapolating from their five cases, they estimated that a global system of marine and terrestrial nature preserves would cost about $45 billion a year but yield $4.4 to $5.2 trillion in ecosystem services each year. The scientists thus concluded that such nature conservation presents a compelling economic argument (Balmford et al. 2002).

Government Purchasing Power

Another alternative to regulation is using the buying power of government to change existing markets. The federal government alone makes use of 500,000 buildings and buys more than $200 billion a year in goods and services. If added to purchases by state and local governments, the public sector accounts for about 18 percent of the nation's total economic output. That is big enough that some simple changes can produce remarkable effects on the economy and on emerging green markets. Equally impressive opportunities are available for nonprofit organizations and industry to use their substantial purchasing power to change the way products are manufactured and used. Many already are doing so (Mastny 2004).

A good example of using purchasing power involves computer equipment. Computers and related office equipment such as copiers and printers were among the fastest-growing energy users in commercial buildings (and colleges and universities) over the past several decades. After 1994 all federal agencies were required to buy energy-efficient computers when they replace equipment. By guaranteeing a market for energy-efficient machines, the policy allowed manufacturers to shift to new technology. That change involved the minor redesign of monitor, printer, and computer circuits, but yielded substantial energy savings.

A more contemporary example of the same kind of action is the EPA's decision in 2007 to ask all hotels and convention centers that bid for EPA business to respond to questions about their recycling programs, energy efficiency, and related matters. One of the directors of the agency's procurement program put the logic of this move clearly: "We can use our own purchasing power to influence behavior, and to strengthen the link to our mission of protecting health and the environment." The new rule came from the agency's Green Meetings Work Group, but the General Services

Administration, which sets such policies for the entire federal government, was urging all agencies to consult the EPA's checklist for such arrangements. The federal government in recent years has spent over $13 billion annually on travel.[54]

Ecosystem-Based Management

A more fundamental way to reform natural resource policies as well as pollution control efforts is through the use of ecosystem-based management. Historically, governments developed policies to deal with discrete elements of the environment such as forests, water, soil, and species, often through different federal agencies and without coordination among them. Since its founding in 1970, the EPA has dealt almost exclusively with public health and paid little attention to maintenance of ecosystem health. The agency also rarely has coordinated efforts across the separate media of land, water, and air.

These conventional approaches have contributed to ineffective and inefficient environmental policy.[55] They also have resulted in public policies that sometimes concentrate limited resources on small public health risks that bring few benefits at high cost while larger risks are ignored. The backlash against environmental policy in the 1990s—from industry, state and local governments, and the property rights and wise use movements—derived from these policy weaknesses as much as anything else.

The more comprehensive ecosystem-based management approach has gradually established a foothold (Cortner and Moote 1999; Layzer 2008, 2013). It reflects advances in ecological research that are beginning to build an understanding of ecosystem functioning. To some extent it also incorporates ideas of ecological rationality advanced by social scientists (e.g., Bartlett 1986). Rather than focus on individual rivers and localized cleanup efforts, for example, emphasis has shifted to entire watersheds and the diverse sources of environmental degradation that must be assessed and managed (Daily 1997). As mentioned in Chapter 1, for instance, in a path-breaking decision, New York City chose in 1997 to protect its large upstate watersheds rather than construct an expensive water treatment plant. The effort seems to have been successful, and may become a model for other cities (Platt, Barten, and Pfeffer 2000).

Those advocating for ecosystem-based management also generally endorse greater public participation or stakeholder involvement in the process, as discussed at the end of Chapter 6. There are both advantages and disadvantages to doing so, and a large academic literature has developed around the question of how best to design such public involvement processes so that they allow decisions to be made in a timely manner and incorporate both public values and management expertise effectively. Studies of watershed management in particular suggest how to balance sometimes competing concerns of this kind (Daley 2013; Gerlak, Heikkila, and Lubell 2013; Layzer 2008, 2013; Sabatier et al. 2005).

Similarly, instead of trying to save individual endangered species, the new goal is the preservation or restoration of ecosystems themselves. The Florida Everglades restoration project is a case in point. Among other results, the restoration of habitat in the Everglades may save 68 endangered and threatened species under the South Florida Multi-Species Recovery Plan, the largest such plan ever in the United States. The plan demonstrates the feasibility of an ecosystem rather than single-species approach to wildlife protection. An especially attractive feature of the plan is that it has been broadly embraced by diverse local stakeholders, from environmentalists to sugarcane growers, many of whom cooperated in the project's design. Yet, as sometimes happens, restoration plans can bog down during implementation, and in this case both costs and opposition have risen (Layzer 2008, 2013; U.S. GAO 2007). Rising sea levels and warming temperatures attributable to climate change also threaten the recovery plan.

New approaches to ecological risk assessment, critical loads, and adaptive management, although still in their infancy, promise to provide the necessary knowledge on which to base a broader, more holistic, and better-focused attack on environmental problems (Bäckstrand 2017; Layzer and Schulman 2017). Major flooding in the Midwest over the past several decades has reinforced concern that human actions such as draining and filling of wetlands, replacing the tallgrass prairies with plowed fields, and other changes to the land have increased the risk of catastrophic floods. Similar concerns were raised about loss of wetlands in Louisiana in 2005, which worsened the effects of Hurricane Katrina.[56]

Conclusions

Since their beginnings in the 1970s modern environmental and natural resource policies have become highly complex, and their reach has extended to every segment of the economy and every corner of the nation. Their costs and impacts on society are much debated. They are also at the center of many political controversies over the role of government in protecting public health and managing the nation's natural resources. Evaluating their successes and failures helps inform these debates, even if such studies cannot answer all questions or eliminate conflicts over the direction of environmental policy.

One of the best ways to ensure that new scientific knowledge and policy and program evaluations are brought to bear on policy choices is to design such studies into the policies themselves. The Montreal Protocol that governs international action to phase out ozone-depleting chemicals like CFCs offers one model for doing so. It integrates continuous assessment of changing environmental conditions with new policy actions. Congress has occasionally provided mechanisms of this kind for pollution control policies. In 1977 it created the National Commission on Air Quality and charged it with overseeing and evaluating the EPA's performance in implementing the Clean Air Act. The 1972 Clean Water Act created a National Commission on Water Quality to study technical, economic, social, and environmental questions related to achieving certain goals established by the policy. Its report guided Congress in revision of the act in 1977 (Freeman 1990).

Another imperative is rethinking the logic of policy design (Schneider and Ingram 1990, 1997). For a policy to work well, it must be based on an understanding not only of environmental conditions but also of the institutions and people who implement the policy and those who have to comply with the regulations and other directives it produces. Analysts and policymakers can, and should, do a better job in the future. Citizens can help by learning about how well policies are working, and by participating in decision making at all levels of government that affect the reform and redirection of environmental policy.

Discussion Questions

1   What is the best way to assess whether progress is being made with environmental protection or natural resource policies? For any particular program, how would you determine whether it has been successful or not?

2   Controversies continue over the use of cost–benefit analysis and risk assessment in environmental policy decisions. Are these methods helpful in deciding which policies and programs, or particular regulations, are acceptable or not? What else should be considered in making such a judgment?

3   Should environmental organizations try to support their recommended actions with economic analyses, as many have done in recent years? Are their arguments on behalf of environmental protection or resource conservation likely to be more persuasive if they do so? If not, what else should be the basis for their arguments?

4   Among the most widely discussed alternatives to command-and-control regulation is the use of market-based approaches or market incentives. Is their use a positive development or not? For what kinds of environmental or resource issues are market-based approaches most likely to be effective? For which are they least likely to be effective?

5   The imposition of higher user fees for access to public lands is often recommended as a way to reduce environmental degradation attributable to mining, ranching, agriculture, and timber harvesting. What are the advantages and disadvantages of raising such fees for those who use public lands for commercial purposes?

Suggested Readings

Dietz, Thomas, and Paul C. Stern, eds. 2003. *New Tools for Environmental Protection: Education, Information, and Voluntary Measures.* Washington, DC: National Academy Press.

Durant, Robert F., Daniel J. Fiorino, and Rosemary O'Leary, eds. 2017. *Environmental Governance Reconsidered: Challenges, Choices, and Opportunities*, 2nd edn. Cambridge, MA: MIT Press.

Eisner, Marc Allen. 2007. *Governing the Environment: The Transformation of Environmental Regulation.* Boulder, CO: Lynne Rienner.

Fiorino, Daniel J. 2006. *The New Environmental Regulation.* Cambridge, MA: MIT Press.

Mazmanian, Daniel A., and Michael E. Kraft, eds. 2009. *Toward Sustainable Communities: Transition and Transformations in Environmental Policy*, 2nd edn. Cambridge, MA: MIT Press.

Vig, Norman J., and Michael E. Kraft, eds. 2016. *Environmental Policy: New Directions for the Twenty-First Century*, 9th edn. Washington, DC: CQ Press/ Sage.

Notes

1 John Carey, "Greener, Yes, But Not at Any Price," *Bloomberg BusinessWeek*, March 9, 2009. Sunstein left the administration in 2012, and President Obama nominated Howard Shelanski, an economist and lawyer, for the post. Like Sunstein, he favored a balanced approach to regulation.

2 Henry Fountain and Erica Goode, "Trump Has Options for Undoing Obama's Climate Legacy," *New York Times*, November 25, 2016. Beyond OIRA, opponents of regulation in Congress seem likely to use a law from the 1990s, the Congressional Review Act, to overturn some of the Obama regulations approved in the last year of his presidency. See David Malakoff, "Republicans Ready a Regulatory Rollback," *Science* 354, November 25, 2016: 951.

3 See, for example, Clifford Krauss and Michael Corkery, "A Bleak Outlook for Trump's Promises to Bring Back Jobs for Coal Miners," *New York Times*, November 20, 2016; and Devashree Saha, "Five Charts That Show Why Trump Can't Deliver on His Coal Promises," Brookings Institution, December 6, 2016.

4 See Felicity Barringer and Michael Janofsky, "G.O.P. Plans to Give Environmental Rules a Free-Market Tilt," *New York Times*, November 8, 2004.

5 The 2016 study, issued jointly by Yale and Columbia, was the latest in a series of such rankings that date back to 2002. The report is available at: http://epi. yale.edu.

6 Ruth Greenspan Bell, "For EPA Regulations, Cost Predictions Are Overstated" (Washington, DC: World Resources Institute, November 17, 2010), available at the WRI website: www.wri.org. OIRA issues an annual report to Congress detailing its estimates of regulatory costs and benefits, and for environmental regulations the benefits typically exceed the costs, often by a large margin. The reports can be found at: www.whitehouse.gov/omb/inforeg_regpol_reports_ congress.

7 See, for example, Stephen T. Jackson et al., "Toward a National, Sustained U.S. Ecosystem Assessment," *Science* 354 (November 18, 2016): 838–839.

8 For example, John Schwartz, "Experts See Peril in Reduced Monitoring of Nation's Streams and Rivers," *New York Times*, April 11, 2006.

9 Richard Stone, "California Report Sets Standard for Comparing Risks," *Science* 266 (October 14, 1994): 214.

10 One measure that Congress was able to approve was the Small Business and Regulatory Enforcement Fairness Act of 1996 (PL 104-121). It allowed small businesses to seek legal redress when agencies such as the EPA or BLM failed to conduct an adequate study of the economic impacts of their regulations. See Allan Freedman, "GOP's Secret Weapon against Regulations: Finesse," *CQ Weekly*, September 5, 1998: 2314–2320.

11 Economists and analysts would respond by saying that economic methods for estimating environmental and resource values when there are no evident market values are fairly sophisticated and widely used. For a discussion of how benefits and other environmental values can be estimated and used in decision making, see Freeman (2006). For a contrasting perspective, see Sagoff (1988).

12 EPA maintains a National Center for Environmental Economics that conducts and oversees research of this kind. Other useful sites include the World Resources Institute (www.wri.org), Resources for the Future (www.rff.org), and the Commerce Department's Bureau of Economic Analysis (www.bea.gov/), which reports on pollution and abatement expenditures. See also Bell, "For EPA Regulations, Cost Predictions Are Overstated."

13 See the reports made to Congress at: www.whitehouse.gov/omb/rewrite/inforeg /regpol-reports_congress.html.

14 Ronald Smothers, "Group Urges Tough Limits on Logging," *New York Times*, May 27, 1994.

15 Nathan Fiala, "The Greenhouse Hamburger," *Scientific American*, February 2009: 72–75. The estimate for orange juice comes from Tropicana and was reported in the *New York Times*, January 22, 2009. Updates for estimates like this can easily be found today.

16 William K. Stevens, "Money Grow on Trees? No, But Study Finds Next Best Thing," *New York Times*, April 12, 1994.

17 David K. Randall, "Perhaps Only God Can Make a Tree, but Only People Could Put a Dollar Value on It," *New York Times*, April 18, 2007.

18 For a detailed economic assessment of the costs of highway salting, see Donald F. Vitaliano, "An Economic Assessment of the Social Costs of Highway Salting and the Efficiency of Substituting a New Deicing Material," *Journal of Policy Analysis and Management* 11 (1992): 397–418.

19 Catalina Camia, "Severity of Job Loss at Issue in Mining Law Overhaul," *CQ Weekly Report*, January 8, 1994: 18–20.

20 See Bruce Bartlett, "Misrepresentation, Regulations, and Jobs," *New York Times*, October 4, 2011; and Elizabeth Dwoskin and Mark Drajem, "Who's Afraid of a Little Regulation," *Bloomberg BusinessWeek*, February 13–19, 2012. The BlueGreen Alliance study is available at: www.bluegreenalliance.org/ news/latest/improving-vehicle-fuel-economy-to-create-570000-u-s-jobs.

21 The study by two economists at the University of Maryland was reported in John Cushman, "EPA's Clean Power Plan Will Create Quarter-Million Jobs," *Inside Climate News*, April 21, 2015.

22 Drew Haerer and Lincoln Pratson, "Employment Trends in the U.S. Electricity Sector, 2008–2012," *Energy Policy* 82 (July 2015): 85–98. For a comprehensive review of these kinds of cost predictions and forecasts of jobs lost and created, see Bell, "For EPA Regulations, Cost Predictions Are Overstated."

23 The report is discussed in Evan Halper, "Trump Brings Koch Network's Anti-Green-Energy Stance from the Fringe to the Center of Power," *Los Angeles Times*, December 5, 2016. The president of the Institute for Energy Research, Thomas Pyle, was named by Donald Trump to head the Department of Energy's transition team, suggesting that the Trump administration's DOE will have a radically different set of priorities than it did in the Obama's administration.

24 For example, see Coral Davenport, "U.S. Pledges to Ease Pain of Closing Coal Mines in Shift to Cleaner Energy," *New York Times*, January 15, 2016.

25 Estimates of economic impacts show a wide variance, depending on the methods and models used and on the economic indicators selected. Over the past decade, such studies indicate that the effect on inflation and productivity is probably between 0.1 and 0.4 of a percentage point. In one early accounting, the CEQ noted in its 1979 *Environmental Quality* report that the annual accruing benefits of all federal environmental programs were substantially greater than the total cost of compliance. It also found the effect of these programs on the economy to be marginal.

26 See Neil Munro, "A Paler Shade of Green," *National Journal*, August 1, 2009: 44–45; and Elizabeth Wasserman, "A Greener Path to Prosperity?" *CQ Weekly*, April 20, 2009: 923.

27 See also Laurie J. Flynn, "Silicon Valley Rebounds, Led by Green Technology," *New York Times*, January 29, 2007: C8; and Rebecca Adams, "The Promise of Eco-Technology," *CQ Weekly*, April 23, 2007: 11.

28 A detailed assessment of the environmental technology sector can be found in a 1998 study prepared for the Office of Technology Policy in the Commerce Department, *The U.S. Environmental Industry*, available at: www.ta.doc.gov/Reports/Environmental/env.pdf. The California greenhouse gas emissions report can be found at: http://calclimate.berkeley.edu/managing_GHGs_in_CA.html.

29 See Roger H. Bezdek, "Economic and Jobs Impacts of Enhanced Fuel Efficiency Standards for Light Duty Vehicles in the USA," *International Journal of Engineering and Innovative Technology* 4(7) (January 2015): 122–135.

30 Davashree Saha and Mark Muro, "Growth, Carbon, and Trump: States Are 'Decoupling' Economic Growth from Emissions Growth," Brookings Institution, December 8, 2016; and Vivek Wadhwa and Mark Muro, "Trump Says Energy Regulations Are Hurting Economic Growth. The Evidence Says Otherwise," *Washington Post*, December 21, 2016.

31 The quotation comes from the EPA website for the Office of Environmental Justice.

32 The Office of Environmental Justice website has a description of the executive order and provides links to the federal guidance documents for its implementation, in addition to other pertinent material: www.epa.gov/compliance/environmental justice/index.html.

33 See Jad Mouawad, "High Carbon Cost for 'Clunkers' Program," *New York Times*, August 14, 2009.

34 See Matthew L. Wald, "Developers of Wind Farms Run a Race against the Calendar," *New York Times*, September 20, 2012; and Congressional Budget

Office, "Federal Financial Support for the Development and Production of Fuels and Energy Technologies" (Washington, DC: CBO, March 2012).

35 The EPA began to make use of market incentives like this one in 1976. In addition to the offset and bubble policies for air pollution control, programs in which incentives were used included wetlands mitigation banking, the phaseout of lead in gasoline, an air toxics offsets program, scrappage of old cars ("cash for clunkers"), privatization of wastewater systems, and incentives for safer pesticides.

36 See Steve Lohn, "Energy Standards Needed, Report Says," *New York Times*, May 17, 2007.

37 See also a symposium on the subject of voluntary environmental programs in the *Policy Studies Journal* 36(1) (2008), edited by Jorge Rivera and Peter deLeon.

38 On lead paint litigation, see Pam Belluck, "Lead Paint Suits Echo Approach to Tobacco," *New York Times*, September 21, 2002.

39 Keith Schneider, "Exxon Is Ordered to Pay $5 Billion for Alaska Spill," *New York Times*, September 17, 1994.

40 Adam Liptak, "Damages Cut Against Exxon in Valdez Case," *New York Times*, June 26, 2008. On the appeals court decision, see Felicity Barringer, "Appeals Panel Cuts Award in Valdez Spill by Exxon," *New York Times*, December 23, 2006.

41 See Richard W. Stevenson, "Government Plan May Make Private up to 850,000 Jobs," *New York Times*, November 15, 2002; and Kerry Tremain, "Pink Slips in the Parks: The Bush Administration Privatizes Our Public Treasures," *Sierra* (September/October, 2003): 27–33, 52.

42 See Jo Thomas, "Suit Accuses Federal Contractors of Mishandling Cleanup at Nuclear Lab," *New York Times*, February 19, 2001. See also Joel Brinkley, "Energy Dept. Contractors Due for More Scrutiny," *New York Times*, November 24, 2002. According to this report, the DOE has acknowledged its failure to supervise contractors. Moreover, an internal DOE report concluded that the department's program to clean up nuclear weapons production facilities (handled almost entirely by contractors) has been fundamentally mismanaged since its founding, wasting much of the $60 billion spent.

43 Edmund L. Andrews, "Study Suggests Incentives on Oil Barely Help U.S.," *New York Times*, December 22, 2006.

44 Kenneth Gillingham et al., "Reforming the U.S. Coal Leasing Program," *Science* 354 (December 2, 2016): 1096–1098.

45 The GAO reported in 1994 that studies by agricultural economists suggest that higher water prices being instituted in Western water projects will increase irrigation efficiency and conservation, and thereby reduce environmental degradation attributable to irrigation as well as free up water currently used for irrigation for other purposes (U.S. GAO 1994).

46 Robert McClure and Andrew Schneider, "Shafting the West," *OnEarth* (Spring 2002): 33–36; Charles Pope, "Political Ground May Be Shifting under Mine Operators," *CQ Weekly*, September 11, 1999: 2111–2114; Jane Perlez and Kirk Johnson, "Behind Gold's Glitter: Torn Lands and Pointed Questions," *New York Times*, October 24, 2005.

47 See Margaret A. Walls, "Protecting Our National Parks: New Entrance Fees Can Help," *Resources*, Fall 2016: 21–25.

48 The Nature Conservancy's home page provides additional information on its activities: http://nature.org/.

49 See Krista West, "The Billionaire Conservationist," *Scientific American* (August 2002): 34–35; and Larry Rohter, "An American in Chile Finds Conservation a Hard Slog," *New York Times*, August 7, 2005. Tompkins passed away in late 2015. Plans and actions of the Tompkins Conservation organization can be found at its website: www.tompkinsconservation.org.

50 Descriptions of the programs and current statistics can be found at one of the USDA websites: www.ers.usda.gov/Features/farmbill/analysis/landretirement. htm.

51 By some accounts, these initiatives date back to proposals during the Ford administration. The Commerce Department began the new calculations in the last year of the George H. W. Bush administration.

52 Among the leading sites for such analysis and measures are: www.sustainable. org/ (Sustainable Communities Network); www.sustainablemeasures.com/ (for sustainability indicators); www.globalfootprint.org (Global Footprint Network); and www.rprogress.org/ (Redefining Progress).

53 Michael Greenstone and Cass R. Sunstein, "Donald Trump Should Know: This Is What Climate Change Costs Us," *New York Times*, December 15, 2016. See also David Malakoff, Robert F. Service, and Warren Cornwall, "Trump Team Targets Key Climate Metric," *Science* 354 (December 16, 2016): 1364–1365. The calculated cost of carbon depends heavily on the chosen discount rate to use in estimating long-term benefits and costs, as well as on whether such analysis should consider global effects of carbon or only U.S. impacts.

54 Claudia H. Deutsch, "Want E.P.A. Hotel and Convention Center Business? Be a Bit Greener," *New York Times*, April 18, 2007.

55 The Conservation Foundation, now part of the World Wildlife Fund, for years sponsored research and issued position papers on cross-media pollution control as part of its Options for a New Environmental Policy project. One element of that work was the development of a model environmental policy for the nation that incorporated these integrative principles. See National Commission on the Environment (1993).

56 Joel Achenbach, "An Act of Man? Waterlogged Iowans Blame Flood Damage on Development Wrought by Humans," *Washington Post* National Weekly Edition, June 23–July 6, 2008: 13.

CHAPTER 8

Environmental Policy and Politics for the Twenty-First Century

In a telling sign of the times, in 2008 King County, Washington (Seattle), instituted a new rule for building plans, public works projects, and land use. Would a particular development increase or decrease the region's greenhouse gas emissions? Said then county executive Ron Sims, "We are totally committed to reducing emissions, but it requires rethinking the way we do our activities." Where people previously based such decisions on quite different criteria, Sims noted that times have changed: "That way doesn't work in an age of global warming."[1] From cities in the vanguard of the sustainability movement, such as Seattle and Portland, Oregon, to colleges and universities across the nation, new approaches to construction, housing, transportation, food production, and energy use increasingly are being endorsed and put into action. Although these developments hardly signal a fundamental societal transformation in the United States or elsewhere in the world, they do point to the emergence of sustainability as a major concern domestically and internationally.

Previous chapters have described the development and implementation of U.S. environmental policies, their effects, and alternative policy strategies that might improve their performance. Any assessment of environmental policy and politics also must identify longer-term trends and emerging needs that could change the way we appraise environmental problems and the solutions that are called for. This chapter focuses on selected environmental issues both in the United States and globally that are likely to be among the most important in the decades ahead. They illustrate an evolving agenda for environmental policy that is centered on the achievement of sustainable development or sustainable growth and involves more global interaction than has prevailed since the modern environmental movement began in the late 1960s. These issues were first introduced in Chapter 1 as presenting a daunting array of challenges to policymaking in the early twenty-first century as Earth's population grows and aspirations for economic development around the world soar.

This final chapter begins with an overview of the third generation of environmental policy and politics, also introduced in Chapter 1, and compares it to the previous two generations that have dominated U.S. policy debate over nearly five decades. It then traces the new focus on sustainability that emerged in the late 1980s and has slowly gained support. Today, such concerns are most evident within the United States in the rise of the sustainable community movement and in efforts to deal with local and regional issues such as the consequences of urban sprawl and new actions to promote energy efficiency, public transportation, and environmental quality in urban areas (K. Portney 2013, 2016). They are also apparent in nascent efforts by many leading corporations to green their operations and embrace sustainability goals (Esty and Winston 2006; Hawken 2007; Press and Mazmanian 2016).

The chapter then turns to international environmental policy, which presents a different array of issues, institutions, and policy actions than discussed in earlier chapters. They have remained prominent as the world's nations struggled to respond to climate change and related developments while also trying to stimulate economic growth. Discussion here concentrates on the institutional and political factors that will affect the pursuit of sustainable development in the decades ahead through a diversity of international environmental agreements and national actions.

These two parts of the chapter share four key objectives:

- to promote understanding and analysis of environmental policy evolution since the late 1960s;
- to clarify new expectations for how cities, states, the federal government, and the private sector should make decisions about sustainable development or sustainable growth;
- to build capacity for evaluating policies and proposals for action at all levels of government as well as in the private sector;
- to improve understanding of the magnitude and complexity of global challenges and the extent to which governments, nongovernmental organizations, and the private sector are equipped to devise solutions.

Environmental Goals and Policy Choices: Domestic and Global

Given the controversial nature of environmental problems and policies, it is no surprise that we find diverse and conflicting perspectives among policymakers, analysts, and activists about what actions to take and the role that government should play. Some commentators, particularly conservatives, are technological optimists. They see a future of economic prosperity, continued advancement in technical prowess, and few environmental or resource problems that cannot be solved with human ingenuity and determination. Many of them also tend to express more confidence in free-market solutions than in government planning and regulation (Huber 2000; Lomborg 2001; Simon 1995).

In contrast, other observers and many environmental scientists are far less sanguine about our collective capacity to address environmental problems. They believe that without significant changes in human behavior and economic activity, the United States and the world face a perilous future. They characterized it as presenting multiple ecological and public health risks that threaten economic well-being, social equity, and world peace. Such observers often look to public policy initiatives domestically and internationally to try to reduce or eliminate those risks (Brown 2010; Meadows, Randers, and Meadows 2004; O'Neill 2009; Starke 2008; World Commission on Environment and Development 1987).

Such differences in estimates of human well-being and ecological health in the twenty-first century reflect at least one point of agreement: The future is not determined solely by demographic, technological, and environmental changes over which human beings have little control. It is influenced as well by our values and the way we think about and act toward the natural world. That is, to a large extent the human future will reflect what individuals and nations want it to be and the actions they take to realize their visions. Of necessity, government decisions will be among the most important of such critical social choices.

Nearly three decades ago, the late Stephen Schneider (1990), an environmental scientist and climate expert, argued that society might choose among three quite different courses of action: (1) relying on technological fixes or corrective measures with little change in human behavior and institutions; (2) adapting to changing environmental conditions without attempting to counteract them; and (3) trying to prevent the adverse changes from occurring in the first place by altering the practices that cause them.

Environmentalists almost always prefer preventive measures, which they believe are essential to avoid severe or irreversible consequences such as global climate change, and also a smarter choice economically as the cost of action in the future might be much higher than it is today. In contrast, technological optimists, and many others, view technological fixes and adaptation as realistic and less costly alternatives, particularly if substantial uncertainty exists about the severity of environmental risks.

Regardless of whether one is a technological optimist or what we might call an environmental realist, it is clear that citizens and policymakers make an explicit choice about their preferred policies. Such a choice is likely to be affected by their perceptions of the relative risks, costs, and benefits of government action, and they often disagree strongly about all three. Media commentators may offer sharply differing accounts of the severity of the problems, the extent of consensus among scientists, and the kinds of governmental and private actions thought to be necessary. Their television shows, talk radio programs, editorials, webpages, blogs, and tweets can be so suffused with ideological bias that clear public understanding of the issues is made difficult.

Environmental policies historically have been based on each of the three strategies that Schneider outlined, although often in ill-defined and awkward combinations that are hard to decipher as policymakers try to respond to varied political and economic interests. In recent years, however, there has been an increasing emphasis on prevention of environmental degradation and the risks it often presents for public health; climate change is a good example of this. Even as conflict continues over the policy choices that we face, much agreement exists on the broader environmental agenda for the twenty-first century despite the political polarization that is so evident in the United States today, particularly at the national level.

That agenda has been the object of extensive inquiry and debate in many different forums since 1990, including governmental agencies at the city and state level, environmental and other citizen organizations, corporations, committees of Congress, executive agencies, and international organizations and conferences. It was the central focus of the 1992 Earth Summit and at the preparatory meetings that preceded it. Agenda 21, endorsed at that meeting, offered a general blueprint, or plan of action, for global sustainable development and for the institutional and policy changes it requires (United Nations 1993). Considering or taking such actions will preoccupy the nations of the world over the next several decades and very likely for most of the twenty-first century. How the United States and other countries respond to those challenges and how swiftly they formulate and implement suitable environmental policies and other reforms will significantly affect the quality of life in both developed and less developed nations in the future (Axelrod and VanDeveer 2015; O'Neill 2009; Tobin 2016). The United States is slowly coming to terms with that reality in what is often called a third generation of environmental policy, but it is clear that neither citizens nor policymakers will abandon old ideas, policies, and practices easily.

Three Epochs of Environmental Policy and Politics

Previous chapters recounted the adoption of the first epoch or generation of U.S. environmental protection and resource policies from the 1960s and 1970s and the effects they have had over time. It is clear that they produced significant gains. Yet, as discussed in Chapter 7, these policies also have exhibited serious weaknesses, and often have fallen short in achieving their goals. In response to rising criticism from the late 1970s to the early twenty-first century, a second epoch of environmental policy ideas has been much discussed. The proposals have centered on reform of the statutes enacted in the previous decades more than their replacement, with emphasis on promotion of efficiency, flexibility, cooperation between government and industry, and the use of market incentives, voluntary pollution reduction, and other nonregulatory and less intrusive policy tools (Durant, Fiorino, and O'Leary 2017; Fiorino 2006; Eisner 2007).

A third epoch of environmental policy has been evolving since the late 1980s. It has not yet replaced the two earlier epochs. Rather, it has built on them and incorporated new ways of thinking about environmental problems, policy goals, and the best means for achieving them (Mazmanian and Kraft 2009). For example, there is likely to be more comprehensive and integrated analysis of the way in which human activities affect natural systems and, in turn, how human society depends on the healthy functioning of such systems, from the purification of air and water to pollination of agricultural crops and the stabilization of climate. A global as well as local, regional, or national perspective is also a key element in this new view of environmental policy.

The most distinctive characteristic of third-epoch policy discussions is an emphasis on sustainability, or the imperative over time to reconcile the demands of human society with the capability of natural systems to meet its needs. At the beginning of the Clinton administration, the independent and bipartisan National Commission on the Environment urged a national focus on sustainable development or sustainable growth to underscore the inextricable linkage of environmental and economic goals. It endorsed a series of policy and institutional changes to achieve them (National Commission on the Environment 1993). By the end of the 1990s, the National Research Council (1999) issued a similar report calling for a "common journey" toward sustainability.

The implications of a shift to sustainability are profound. They range from the redesign of industrial processes to the promotion of sustainable use of natural resources such as agricultural land and forestland, surface water and groundwater, and energy. Substantial changes in human behavior would be called for as well, whether encouraged through regulation, provision of economic incentives, or public education. The need for new kinds of knowledge and new methods of analysis to promote sustainability and help formulate public policies is equally important (Ehrenfeld 2008; Mazmanian and Kraft 2009; Parris 2003; Thiele 2016). Although the third generation of policy extends to global environmental problems and thus to international policy efforts, its advancement has perhaps been most noticeable at local and regional levels in the United States and other nations, where many communities have begun to take sustainability seriously, much like the case of King County, Washington, noted at the chapter's opening (Paehlke 2013a; K. Portney 2009, 2013, 2016).

It should be said that these three epochs in environmental policy are not completely separate, nor is their evolution over time linear. There is much back and forth as the ideas are proposed and debated, and adopted or rejected, at least temporarily. So elements of the first epoch persist in the major environmental statutes and the operation of the EPA even as reformist ideas of the second epoch are discussed and at least some of them adopted.

Similarly, components of sustainability are embraced widely at the state and local level, and in the business community, even if not at the national level. Moreover, the nature of sustainability and its desirability as a long-term goal continue to be subjects of considerable debate in some quarters. So we can see elements of incremental policymaking as well as the kind of punctuated equilibrium form of policy change that was discussed in Chapter 3.

Toward Sustainable Development?

The political process usually pushes policymakers toward preoccupation with short-term policy disputes and the tasks of reconciling diverse interests. Even when a general consensus exists on long-term goals such as sustainable development or sustainable growth, both citizens and policymakers find it difficult to get a firm fix on how that abstract concept affects short-term decisions on controversial public policies, from energy and water use to agricultural practices and transportation planning. It does not help that governments, like most other organizations, tend to be deficient in their capacity to forecast the future and plan sufficiently for it. Instead, ordinarily policymakers muddle through, making incremental adjustments as needed. This time-tested strategy may work well when the rate of change is slow enough to permit such adaptation. Higher rates of change are problematic for governments as well as other organizations, including corporations (Ophuls 2011; Ophuls and Boyan 1992). That is especially true when decision makers must act without sufficient knowledge of the scope of change; the probable impacts on the environment, economy, and society; and the effectiveness of alternative strategies of response.

The United States and other nations find themselves in precisely this predicament in the second decade of the twenty-first century. Forecasts of changing environmental conditions offer little basis for complacency. Yet they also come with enough uncertainty that disputes over the facts and the logic of competing policy strategies may prevent agreement and action. This is one reason that so many analysts believe that an enormous improvement is needed in our capacity to make reliable scientific forecasts and to integrate them effectively with decision making. Solid political skills in building public consensus on policy action are equally vital (Ascher, Steelman, and Healy 2010). The Clinton administration's initiatives on sustainable development in the 1990s hinted at what is needed, although ultimately they had only a modest impact on public policy. The current sustainable community initiatives, however, build on that heritage and offer much greater promise.

The President's Council on Sustainable Development

In June 1993 President Clinton created by Executive Order 12852 the President's Council on Sustainable Development (PCSD) to advise him on sustainability issues. The Council's staff made plain at the time that it was to work to develop "bold, new approaches to achieve economic, environmental, and equity goals."[2] As discussed earlier, from the Brundtland Commission report of 1987, *Our Common Future*, to the Earth Summit's Agenda 21, environmentalists have pressed government to make sustainable development the central guiding principle of environmental and economic policymaking. The PCSD helped set the foundation for such a change in perspective and demonstrate how society could link short-term policy decisions to long-term environmental goals. To guide its work, the Council even adopted the Brundtland Commission's definition of sustainable development discussed in Chapter 1.

Throughout the 1990s the Council functioned largely as an "envisioning" body to clarify the meaning and practical impact of sustainability. It brought together top corporate officials, leaders of environmental organizations, and administration officials, including members of the cabinet, to explore the connection between the environmental agenda and current policies. It also held hundreds of formal and informal meetings and hearings across the country during which its eight task forces gathered information about subjects such as population and consumption; eco-efficiency; sustainable agriculture; energy and transportation; and innovative local, state, and regional approaches. In early 1996 the Council released its main report, *Sustainable America: A New Consensus for Prosperity, Opportunity, and a Healthy Environment for the Future.*

Sustainable Development at State and Local Levels

The PCSD's activities during the 1990s reflected ongoing action by state and local governments in support of sustainable development, and also encouraged them to innovate in new ways. In cooperation with industry and environmental organizations, many of these governments have recognized the need to formulate strategies for sustainable development. Some of them have been doing so under the banner of the sustainable community movement or in the process of implementing new so-called smart growth initiatives that encourage or require local governments to develop long-term land use or growth management plans.

State and local governments are likely to play an especially crucial role in effective land use planning, a function historically handled at the local level. With encouragement and support from the federal government, states and localities can fashion land use planning policies that promise to protect environmentally sensitive areas such as wetlands and watersheds as well as biological diversity, encourage energy conservation and efficiency, sustain the productivity of agricultural land, select appropriate sites for locating industry and housing, and meet the many other environmental needs that fall within local jurisdictions. Public involvement in the formulation of such land use plans often helps ensure responsiveness to public needs and the requisite degree of public support for implementation of the plans (Knopman, Susman, and Landy 1999; K. Portney 2013, 2016).

Control of urban sprawl and setting aside land for conservation purposes have proven to be popular with voters in recent years, as discussed in Chapter 4. Many elected officials have endorsed both enthusiastically from the 1990s to the present. As a notable example, former governor of New Jersey James E. McGreevey pledged to reshape the image of his state dramatically as a bastion of spreading subdivisions and clogged highways. Soon after his inauguration in 2002, the governor established a Smart Growth Policy Council to fight a "war on sprawl" that would go far beyond the actions of his predecessor, Christine Todd Whitman.[3] Similarly, in 1999 Georgia established a new Regional Transportation Authority with the power to halt development of new shopping malls in overly congested areas if road transportation is insufficient. The authority also can plan and build rail or bus systems to try to reduce traffic congestion. Sprawl in the Atlanta metropolitan area led to the initiative.[4]

The willingness to raise local taxes to pay for open space preservation and to halt the spread of cities and suburbs into surrounding countryside is especially noteworthy. Voters' preferences are understandable. According to New Jersey's Garden State Preservation Trust, an organization set up to administer the state's new program, development can reach a point of diminishing or negative returns. That is, new residential or commercial development might cost more in additional public services than it generates in new property taxes. The American Farmland Trust argues that the pattern holds in most states in which suburban growth has become a big issue.[5] Sprawl is also a leading contributor to the loss of farmland, and it results in the loss of billions of gallons of water as rainfall is washed away from impervious surfaces such as roadways and parking lots rather than filtering into the soil to recharge aquifers.[6]

The sustainable community movement goes well beyond land use policies. Across the nation, many state and local governments have taken a strong interest not only in curbing urban sprawl and conserving open space but in restoring damaged ecosystems and adopting innovative policies on transportation, urban design, energy use, housing, and many related concerns (Mazmanian and Kraft 2009; Paehlke 2013a; Press 2002; Rose 2016). Often these kinds of decisions are made by using new and promising forms of collaborative decision making, or engagement of community stakeholders, that can foster local consensus on action. It is not always easy to foster such community collaboration, but some communities have done so successfully on specific projects and to further sustainability goals in general (Daley 2013; John and Mlay 1999; K. Portney 2016). Many such efforts continue to give minimal attention to social justice or equity concerns even if their other goals are admirable (Agyeman 2013; Agyeman, Bullard, and Evans 2003; Konisky 2015). Nonetheless, scholars who study such attempts at collaborative governance have identified many of the factors that promote success in such actions (e.g., Gerlak, Heikkila, and Lubell 2013).

According to political scientist Kent Portney, at least 49 of the largest 55 cities in the United States have "invested significant amounts of time, resources, and political capital in the development of initiatives to pursue varying levels of sustainability" (K. Portney 2013, xi). These include Portland, Seattle, San Jose, San Francisco, Denver, Phoenix, Chicago, Philadelphia, Boston, and New York City. Many smaller cities have done much the same, including Boulder, Colorado; Grand Rapids, Michigan; Santa Monica, California; and Chattanooga, Tennessee. Other cities are considering similar actions (see also K. Portney 2009 and 2016), and the EPA has long funded several small programs that are designed to promote such community sustainability efforts.[7] It is notable as well that over 1,000 U.S. cities have signed on to the U.S. Mayors Climate Protection Agreement, thus signaling widespread support for local action on climate change (www. usmayors.org/climateprotection/agreement.htm).

Despite much evidence on progress within cities and states, there is a long way to go. It will not be easy to stimulate and maintain sustainable development over time or to foster a change in society's values that is as essential to achievement of environmental sustainability as is public policy. It would be useful to know more about what kinds of initiatives work well and what kinds do not, which actions are likely to receive public and policymaker support and which are not, and what conditions encourage (or discourage) successful policies and programs (Kraft 2017a). The same questions apply to international efforts to encourage sustainable development, discussed later.

Business and the Environment

No matter how carefully designed and effective public policies might be, government activities are necessarily limited in their ability to change consumer behavior and industrial activities. Thus environmental sustainability depends as well on actions taken in the private sector, including those by business organizations. That realization both cheers and worries environmental activists.

Business and industry groups have often been active opponents of environmental policy, and pursuit of profit by private corporations and landowners is responsible for much of the abuse of natural resources in the United States and globally. Many leading business groups, including national and state chambers of commerce, continue their efforts to weaken federal and state environmental laws and regulations that they believe are too costly and burdensome—efforts in which they often are joined by conservative ideological groups with an inherent distrust of government regulation (Kamieniecki 2006; Kraft and Kamieniecki 2007; Layzer 2012). Nonetheless, some of the largest and best-known U.S. corporations have demonstrated a willingness to foster sustainable resource use, to support pollution prevention initiatives, and to develop and market green products, and technological innovations are helping to spur these changes (Fiorino 2006; Press and Mazmanian 2016). Adoption of Corporate Social Responsibility (CSR) standards for such actions is now widespread, and even many smaller companies support CSR principles.

Among those often named as embodying this corporate trend for much of the past decade are General Electric, S. C. Johnson, Johnson Controls, Duke Energy, DuPont, and Walmart, but many other companies are taking the challenge seriously. Other companies are eager to join these ranks and to embrace sustainability even more strongly. Google, for example, has a global network of 13 large data centers, each with hundreds of thousands of computers. It consumed 5.7 terawatt-hours of electricity in 2015, about the same as the entire city of San Francisco, but the company says that by 2017 all of its energy will be generated by wind and solar power. Microsoft says that it reached a level of 100 percent carbon neutrality in 2014, much through purchase of carbon offsets. However, by 2018 it is committed to generating half of its electric power from wind, solar, and hydroelectric sources.[8]

Symbolic of these kinds of efforts, the owners of one new building completed in Seattle in 2013 say it is the world's greenest office complex. The six-story, 50,000 square-foot Bullitt Center opened on Earth Day, April 22, and features both water and energy self-sufficiency. It has rooftop solar panels sufficient to meet all of the building's needs and composting toilets, and it collects rainwater for all of its water needs. The office space is said to be completely carbon-neutral and has been built to last 250 years. The building also has no on-site parking for cars, to discourage individuals from driving them, but it does reserve space for bicycles, and even offers rainwater-fed showers on each floor for its bicycle commuters. Other building features and current news about the structure can be found on its website: www.bullittcenter.org.[9]

This so-called greening of industry is evident in many other quarters, and it has been stimulated in part by federal, state, and local environmental policies, new technologies, and changing market conditions. Pollution prevention as a strategy proved to make good economic sense for many corporations. They saved money by reducing or eliminating the production of wastes and pollutants rather than by disposing of them or cleaning them up, and by reducing their energy use through better construction techniques and improved lighting, heating, and cooling of buildings. They use cleaner technologies, improved production processes, better controls and materials handling, and materials substitution. Corporate environmental management systems such as the chemical industry's Responsible Care program and the broader ISO 14001, a set of environmental standards established by the private International Organization for Standardization, have become increasingly common as well (Coglianese and Nash 2001; Potoski and Prakash 2005; Press and Mazmanian 2016). Federal actions such as publication of the annual Toxics Release Inventory also provide incentives for companies to minimize pollution and avoid public censure (Graham and Miller 2001; Hamilton 2005; Kraft, Stephan, and Abel 2011).

Such shifts in corporate behavior are most evident among progressive or socially conscious businesses where visionary CEOs such as the late Ray Anderson of Interface committed their corporations to achieving sustainability over time (Assadourian 2006; Esty and Winston 2006;

Hawken 1994).[10] Before he died in late 2011, Apple's Steve Jobs was actively involved in designing a new corporate headquarters in Cupertino, California, that he wanted to be a model of sustainability. The building is to generate all of its own electricity, with its roof holding 700,000 square feet of solar panels generating 8 megawatts of power; it is slated to open in 2017.[11] Among automobile manufacturers, Honda has long had a similar reputation. It is the only major auto manufacturer that did not join the industry trade association in the 1990s and 2000s in fighting tougher fuel efficiency and emissions standards, and its cars have regularly set new standards for environmental performance.[12] In documenting websites that cover these shifts in product design more than a decade ago, Parris (2006, 3) found the trend widespread: "Some of the world's largest companies are working to integrate principles of sustainable product design." One of the most striking is Walmart, often criticized in the past by consumer advocates and environmentalists for its practices. It announced in 2005 that it would pursue sweeping environmental goals, including a doubling of its trucks' fuel efficiency, minimization of packaging, and reduction of energy use in its stores. Even more important, it said it would demand similar changes among the thousands of companies that supply it with goods and services, and it seems to have stuck to these commitments since then.[13]

Environmentalists have cooperated with industry leaders in some cases to propose new models of "natural capitalism" that they hope will appeal to corporations willing to rethink the way they do business (Hawken, Lovins, and Lovins 1999). For many corporations, however, their initial efforts have been far more limited. Sometimes the actions appear to be little more than public relations gimmicks and symbolic gestures, as when auto manufacturers, mining companies, and oil companies run glossy ads in national magazines touting their environmental credentials. Environmentalists deride such corporate actions as "greenwashing," in which corporations highlight their positive contributions and ignore the environmental harm they cause. In other cases, corporations have made real and meaningful environmental progress that can be justified as economically beneficial, even in the short term.

Consumers can do much to motivate businesses to take environmental concerns seriously. They can exercise their collective financial power directly in the marketplace as well as through the vast sums they maintain in pension and other retirement accounts. In the last several years, some of the largest state pension funds have successfully pushed corporations in the direction of environmental sustainability. The case for more honest social accountability reporting by corporations received a big boost in the aftermath of scandals over failure of the Enron Corporation and indictment of its auditor, Arthur Andersen, and again in 2008 and 2009 in the aftermath of the financial disasters on Wall Street. Social reporting, including environmental audits, is now increasingly popular (Baue 2008).

Citizens and the Environment

As much as any other change in society, environmental sustainability depends on public attitudes, values, and behavior. Without a supportive public, governments are unlikely to enact and implement strong environmental policies that are perceived to constrain individuals' lifestyles, limit their rights, or raise their taxes. Nor will businesses market green products that are not otherwise economically defensible. An informed, environmentally committed, and active public provides the incentives that policymakers and the business community need to steer a course toward sustainability (Shabecoff 2000).

Helping the public become environmentally literate and participate effectively in decision-making processes, both public and private, is an essential part of any long-term environmental agenda. Recent trends in U.S. politics offer a sobering picture of the obstacles to citizen participation, but they also hint at the opportunities (Beierle and Cayford 2002; Daley 2013). For example, as discussed in Chapter 4, organized environmental groups do much to educate the public on the issues and to facilitate their participation in governmental processes. There also has been enormous growth in the number of nongovernmental organizations (NGOs) both within the United States and worldwide, and they exert considerable influence on media coverage of environmental problems and on public policy decisions (McCormick 2011; National Research Council 2001; O'Neill 2009, 2013).

One of the most encouraging trends is the rapid expansion of environmental information that is available to citizens, even if much of it is used far less than it might be. A vast quantity of data can be found on government agency websites, from the EPA and the DOE to the Fish and Wildlife Service, as well as on the sites managed by nonprofit organizations and corporations. Yet many people remain disengaged from government, public life, and the political process, so they are unlikely to seek out information about environmental policy developments or even to inquire about environmental problems in their own communities (Putnam 2000; Skocpol and Fiorina 1999). However, the situation is hardly hopeless. The successful transformation of many cities referred to earlier suggests what can be done to motivate people to take more interest in local environmental conditions and to work toward creating more sustainable communities (Mazmanian and Kraft 2009; Paehlke 2013a; K. Portney 2013, 2016).

International Environmental Policy and Politics

If progress toward sustainable development or sustainable growth has been slow and uneven within the United States, it has been even less impressive at the international level. This is despite its strong endorsement at the Earth Summit of 1992 and in countless documents, meetings, speeches, and promises since that time. Recent reviews point to more than 1,000 international legal instruments that focus on the environment in some fashion. Yet their implementation to date has been halting, and their effectiveness over time is by no means assured. Moreover, few rich nations have lived up to the commitments made at the Earth Summit to increase their economic development assistance to poor nations.

Not all the news is so disappointing. Some international environmental treaties, most notably the Montreal Protocol to protect the stratospheric ozone layer, have been highly successful. The Convention on International Trade in Endangered Species (CITES) discussed in Chapter 6 is another example of cooperative international action that has enjoyed considerable success. Under the right conditions, then, nations can join with one another to deal successfully with global environmental threats (O'Neill 2009, 2013, 2015; Downie 2015). This last section of the chapter turns to some of the most important developments in international environmental policy and the factors that are likely to affect pursuit of global sustainable development in the future.

Environmental Institutions and Policies

International environmental issues, much like their domestic counterparts, rose to prominence on government agendas during the 1960s and 1970s. As Lynton Caldwell noted so well, they presented nations with "new geophysical imperatives" with which most policymakers had no experience. That was because global environmental changes were "occurring on unprecedented scales" that were "not yet faced by modern society" (Caldwell 1990, 303). Without historical precedent, policymakers in the 1970s struggled to adapt conventional diplomatic approaches to the new problems. The search for new policy ideas and new political processes to build support for them continues today.

From Stockholm to Rio: 1972 to 1992 Symbolizing the emerging global concern for environmental problems at the time, the United Nations convened a Conference on the Human Environment in Stockholm in June 1972, attended by 113 nations. The conference theme of Only One Earth underscored the newly recognized importance of addressing global environmental problems through concerted international action. One outcome of this conference was establishment of the United Nations Environment Programme (UNEP) as a forum for discussing and studying international environmental issues, joining other specialized UN agencies such as the World Health Organization (WHO) and the Food and Agriculture Organization (FAO).

In recognition of the role of developing nations in international affairs, UNEP was located in Nairobi, Kenya, far from other UN agencies. It also initially suffered from a small operating budget and staff. Over time, however, both its budget and staff increased and it won respect and cooperation from established international agencies and NGOs such as the World Conservation Union and World Wildlife Fund. It also began to exercise influence on environmental policy (O'Neill 2015; Soroos 2011). Other international organizations, because of their size, experience, and prominence, have had greater effects on environmental and economic decisions, particularly on the direction of economic development. These include the World Bank, whose assets and influence dwarf those of UNEP. Table 8.1 lists these and other organizations whose websites provide invaluable information about international environmental policy.

TABLE 8.1　Selected international environmental policy websites

Organization	Special features and links	Web address
United Nations	Extensive links to UN organizations, conferences, and international activities.	www.un.org/en/
UN Environment Programme	Elaborate links to international environmental actions, scientific assessments, and key documents such as Agenda 21 and major environmental treaties.	www.unep.org
UN Development Programme	Links to activities and reports on economic development and environment.	www.undp.org
UN Population Fund	Funds population assistance programs worldwide, particularly family planning and reproductive health. Issues reports on population growth and its effects.	www.unfpa.org
UN Food and Agriculture Organization	One of the largest UN organizations, focusing on agriculture, forestry, fisheries, and rural development. Works to alleviate poverty and hunger worldwide.	www.fao.org
World Health Organization	A specialized UN organization focusing on health issues. Collects extensive data on the status of human health worldwide.	www.who.int/en/

TABLE 8.1 (*continued*)

Organization	Special features and links	Web address
Division for Sustainable Development	Established at the 1992 Earth Summit to follow up on recommended actions. Monitors implementation of international agreements.	https://sustainable development. un.org/about/dsd
World Bank	One of the largest sources of economic development assistance to developing nations.	www.worldbank. org
International Monetary Fund	One of the largest sources of international funding for economic development.	www.imf.org
Global Environment Facility	Assists developing nations in funding sustainable development goals in biodiversity loss, climate change, international waters, ozone-layer depletion, land degradation, and persistent organic pollutants.	www.gefweb.org
European Union	The regional governing federation for Europe, with extensive environmental rules that apply to member states.	https://europa.eu/ european-union/ index_en
Intergovernmental Panel on Climate Change (IPCC)	The United Nations-sponsored scientific assessment panel that studies global climate change.	www.ipcc.ch
World Trade Organization (WTO)	The leading organization that oversees and enforces international trade.	www.wto.org

On the 20th anniversary of the Stockholm conference, the world's nations convened in Rio de Janeiro for the United Nations Conference on Environment and Development (UNCED), better known as the Earth Summit. By 1992 there was a more palpable sense of urgency about global environmental problems such as climate change, degradation of agricultural land, water scarcity, loss of critical habitat, and threats to biological diversity, all of which were exacerbated by a growing human population. The conference organizers hoped that delegates would significantly strengthen international action and set a firm course toward sustainable development that could address the full range of environmental threats. These hopes were captured in the summit's slogan: Our Last Chance to Save the Earth.

Sustainable development provided the intellectual framework for the Rio conference, building on the Brundtland Commission report *Our Common Future* (World Commission on Environment and Development 1987). Most critically, that report and the summit itself defined environmental issues as integrally related to economic development. That is, environmental protection was seen as best achieved through the pursuit of sustainable development in decisions on agriculture, transportation, energy use, water development, and other sectors. Likewise, economic development that ignores environmental and resource constraints was thought unlikely to succeed over time.

As indicated at the beginning of Chapter 1, the Earth Summit was the largest international diplomatic conference ever held as of 1992, and its activities and recommendations were much anticipated and closely watched. Among its most important actions were approval of (1) a Rio Declaration on Environment and Development that set out 27 broad principles to guide future actions; (2) a nonbinding Agenda 21, a long-term plan of action for achieving conference goals of environmentally sound development; (3) a nonbinding statement on forest principles that recommended action by nations to assess the impact of forest loss and to minimize loss; and (4) two international agreements, a Framework Convention on Climate Change and a Convention on Biological Diversity, both of which were considered to be legally binding documents (United Nations 1993). The climate change convention sought to reduce greenhouse gas emissions to 1990 levels by 2000 and eventually stabilize them at a level that would prevent human-caused climate change; it has provided the basic structure of international agreements on climate change since that time. The biodiversity convention required signatory nations to develop an inventory of their plants and wildlife and to develop plans to protect endangered species. It also mandated that nations signing the treaty share research, profits, and technologies with the countries that supply the genetic resources. Both are addressed later in the chapter.

Agenda 21 is of obvious importance as the main plan of action to emerge from the meeting. Some critics fault it as an 800-page treatise that merely points to general goals of sustainable development, with no commitments from developed nations for specific actions or economic assistance to poor nations. On the other hand, some conservatives see it as a threat to the ideas of limited government and protection of individual rights, and they harbor deep suspicions about both the long-term goals and the particular governmental actions it inspires.[14] Yet as an official and broadly endorsed statement on the world's need for environmentally compatible economic development, the document both incorporates a new perspective on development and outlines a path for bold global action that reflects a broad public consensus (Sachs 2015).

UN Conferences on Sustainable Development Continue On the 10th and 20th anniversaries of the Earth Summit, the United Nations once again organized international conferences to follow-up on the commitments made in 1992. In 2002, delegates from more than 100 of the world's nations met in Johannesburg, South Africa, for the World Summit on Sustainable Development. Few observers of international environmental policy believed the Johannesburg conference would match Rio in setting new directions for economic development, and the meeting itself received less attention in the news media despite the presence of some 40,000 participants (Speth 2003). In June 2012, delegates assembled once more for what was called Rio+20, held in same city as the 1992 meeting. Much like the 2002 meeting, delegates faced an ambitious agenda and dealt with some of the most intractable issues related to sustainable development and world poverty. As the case in 2002, the conference received minimal media coverage despite the attendance of some 50,000 participants and 100 heads of state or government. The UN websites for each meeting convey well both the expansive agendas and the relatively modest achievements.[15]

Nonetheless, conference organizers in both cases saw considerable value in the meetings, as did at least some independent observers. The organizers believed that the conferences "reaffirmed sustainable development as a central element of the international agenda and gave new impetus to global action to fight poverty and protect the environment." They argued as well that "understanding of sustainable development was broadened and strengthened" by the summits, in particular "the important linkages between poverty, the environment and the use of natural resources."[16] Even the *New York Times* concluded that the 2002 meeting was "reasonably successful" because it offered a conceptual framework for integrating environmental protection and economic growth and produced a 65-page plan of implementation.[17] That plan was agreed to by more than 100 governments that pledged to work together to achieve environmental goals and to reduce world poverty. Few concrete plans emerged from the meeting, however, and under the Bush administration the United States campaigned against specific timetables and goals.[18]

The 2012 meeting adopted a theme of growth in a green economy, which was highlighted in a final document, *The Future We Want*. The *New York Times* summarized its perspective on the event in a headline that read: "Progress on the Sidelines as Rio Conference Ends." Greenpeace was harsher; it termed the meeting "a failure of epic proportions." The Pew Environment Group was slightly more generous in its appraisal. "It would be a mistake to call Rio a failure," it said, "but for a once-in-a-decade meeting with so much at stake, it was a far cry from a success."[19] President Obama chose not to attend the meeting, but his administration's representatives touted small-scale development programs that have been much praised as realistic and cost-effective steps toward alleviating global poverty, such as production of clean cookstoves and local energy projects. A fair conclusion would be that neither the far-reaching goals of Agenda 21 or the newer hopes expressed at Johannesburg and Rio to end global poverty are likely to be achieved either easily or soon (Tobin 2016).

Despite limited results, many who are working tirelessly on the issue of worldwide poverty are determined to push forward. The United Nations has continued to promote its goal of sharply reducing world poverty through its Millennium Development Goals, and development specialists such as Jeffrey Sachs, author of *The End of Poverty* (2005) and *The Age of Sustainable Development* (2015), have campaigned passionately to persuade policymakers to increase their commitment of funds for the effort. Some progress is evident, as seen in the declining proportion of households in developing nations that fall below the level of "extreme poverty." The United Nations' Human Development Report for 2015 indicates that this measure of poverty dropped from 47 percent in 1990 to 14 percent by 2015, although the rate varies considerably by region of the world. Sub-Saharan Africa continues to have one of the highest levels of extreme poverty: 41 percent.[20]

In 2015, the United Nations replaced the Millennium Development Goals, which were set to expire that year. The new goals are embodied in a 2030 Agenda for Sustainable Development. It calls on countries to achieve over the next 15 years 17 distinct goals that reflect "our shared vision of humanity and a social contract between the world's leaders and the people," according to UN Secretary-General Ban Ki-moon. The goals include an end to poverty and hunger; promotion of gender equity, quality education, and good health and well-being; the production of affordable and clean energy, as well as clean water and sanitation; responsible consumption and production; decent work and economic growth; sustainable communities and cities; and action on climate change. The website for the new agenda offers elaborate descriptions, pertinent information, and news for each of these goals.[21]

International Environmental Agreements In addition to prominent conferences at which international agreements are formulated, debated, and endorsed, environmental treaties emerge from discussions between two or more nations and through a variety of other meetings and forums for negotiations. Although, as noted earlier, environmental issues constitute a portion of perhaps a thousand international agreements, only about 230 agreements are predominantly environmental in character. UNEP considers over 40 of these to be "core environmental conventions" (Weiss and Jacobson 1999). Table 8.2 provides a select list of some of the most important of these along with their associated websites. Those sites offer a great deal of information about provisions of the agreements, actions taken, and progress made toward achievement of their goals.

Some environmental agreements focus on the establishment of regional, rather than international, institutions and policies. For instance, the European Union (EU) has moved to harmonize environmental regulations while also promoting freer trade among its member nations, and EU environmental standards are among the highest in the world (Vig and Faure 2004). Recently, for example, the EU has developed innovative and tough initiatives to deal with hazardous substances and electronic waste, and is

TABLE 8.2 Selected international environmental agreements

Agreement	Key goals and objectives	Date of adoption	Number of parties 2012	Website
UN Convention on the Law of the Sea (UNCLOS)	Establishes a framework to govern ocean use, designates 200-mile exclusive economic zones, and includes provisions on conservation of living marine resources, protection of marine populations, and protection of the oceans from pollution.	1982	164	www.un.org/Depts/los/index.htm
Convention on International Trade in Endangered Species of Wild Fauna and Flora (CITES)	Establishes a framework for protection of endangered species. Nations that agree to the Convention implement national laws to ensure that international trade in specimens of wild animals and plants does not threaten their survival.	1973	183	www.cites.org
Montreal Protocol on Substances That Deplete the Ozone Layer	Requires the gradual phaseout of CFCs, halons, and other chemicals damaging the stratospheric ozone layer that protects life on Earth from harmful ultraviolet radiation. The protocol has been modified several times to reflect new scientific knowledge. Fewer nations have ratified the amendments adopted after 1987.	1987	197	http://ozone.unep.org/

TABLE 8.2 (*continued*)

Agreement	Key goals and objectives	Date of adoption	Number of parties 2012	Website
Basel Convention on the Control of Transboundary Movement of Hazardous Wastes and Their Disposal	Restricts international export of hazardous wastes from industrial to developing nations, unless the latter agree to import them. A 1994 amendment bans all hazardous waste exports to developing nations for final disposal and recovery.	1989	185	www.basel.int
Convention on Biological Diversity (CBD)	Establishes a framework for the conservation of biodiversity, sustainable use of biological resources, and fair and equitable sharing of the benefits of using genetic resources. A biosafety protocol of 2000 deals with the effects of transporting genetically modified organisms across national boundaries.	1992	196	www.cbd.int
UN Framework Convention on Climate Change*	Establishes a framework for addressing the release of greenhouse gases. Requires industrialized nations to reduce emissions of carbon dioxide by a specified amount within a particular timeframe so as to meet the overall goal of stabilizing atmospheric concentration of gases that contribute to climate change.	1997	197	http://unfccc.int/2860.php

TABLE 8.2 (*continued*)

Agreement	Key goals and objectives	Date of adoption	Number of parties 2012	Website
Stockholm Convention on Persistent Organic Pollutants (POPs)	A global agreement to protect human health and the environment from persistent organic pollutants (POPs) such as dioxins and polychlorinated biphenyls (PCBs). Governments are to take measures to eliminate or reduce the release of POPs into the environment.	2001	180	www.pops.int

Note: * The Paris Agreement of 2015 is the latest of the climate change accords, and it took effect in November 2016. The Kyoto Protocol was set to expire in 2012, and new amendments were adopted in Doha, Qatar, in December of that year.

Sources: Hilary French and Lisa Mastny, "Controlling International Environmental Crime," in Linda Starke, ed., *State of the World 2001* (Washington, DC: Worldwatch Institute), 169–170; UN Environment Programme webpage (www.unep.org); and the webpages for the individual agreements.

setting a new standard for such actions (Axelrod and Schreurs 2015; Selin and VanDeveer 2006, 2015).

The North American Free Trade Agreement (NAFTA) is an example of a regional trade agreement that has some modest environmental components. A supplemental environmental agreement negotiated by the Clinton administration created a Commission for Environmental Cooperation that was to oversee NAFTA's operation and resolve some disputes that arose. The trade agreement seeks to prevent any of the three nations from using environmental regulations to gain an economic advantage, but it does not override international agreements such as the Montreal Protocol or CITES. Experience to date suggests that NAFTA has helped strengthen Mexico's environmental policies and standards, but progress has been limited by Mexico's economic difficulties in recent years (Esty 2015; Vogel 2006).

Environmental organizations were sharply divided over NAFTA's adoption, and they continue to voice concern over the agreement's potential to weaken U.S. environmental regulations. They express similar concerns about the effect of economic globalization on the environment, and they have frequently protested decisions of the World Trade Organization. Over time, freer trade among nations is more likely to aid rather than weaken environmental protection. As poor nations develop economically, they are more likely to favor stronger environmental standards (Vogel 2006). In the short term, however, conflicts are certain to arise with economic growth in Eastern Europe, Asia, Latin America, and Africa.

There is increasing recognition that global environmental politics involves more than what critics call the top–down approach to planetary management that we see in UN conferences and the major treaties that are listed in Table 8.2 (Speth 2002, 2004). Supplementing this conventional approach are diverse efforts to deal with environmental threats, including economic development and social changes that are better characterized as forms of bottom-up problem-solving. For instance, there has been much emphasis in recent years on management of critical natural resources by indigenous people, who have an obvious stake in the maintenance of productive forests, fisheries, and agricultural land. Some of these new perspectives were evident at the World Summit in 2002 and at the Rio+20 meeting in 2012, as discussion focused less on new international treaties and more on pragmatic solutions for fighting environmental degradation and global poverty, and including corporations and NGOs in future meetings.

Institutional Capacity for Global Sustainable Development

The large body of international law established since the late 1960s helps govern the global environment, and numerous international institutions in addition to UNEP have been established to assist in their implementation

(Caldwell 1996; Chasek, Downie, and Brown 2014; DeSombre 2006; O'Neill 2009; Soroos 2011). International conferences that focus broadly on the environment and development, such as the Earth Summit, and more specialized meetings focusing on food, population, water, human settlements, and climate, have defined the issues and spurred international agreements. Taken together, these activities have accomplished much, even if far less than their supporters had sought to achieve (Axelrod and VanDeveer 2015). Any assessment of additional requirements to protect the global environment and to assist nations in moving along a path of sustainable development, however, must be grounded in political realities that are less encouraging.

Institutions such as UNEP and the conference diplomacy that has characterized international environmental policy are necessarily limited in bringing about significant policy and institutional changes, particularly in the short term. UNEP, for example, has served primarily as a catalyst for environmental action by member states. International institutions such as the World Bank are well-staffed and powerful influences on the world's economic development. Yet as one striking example, the bank has a history of favoring large, environmentally destructive development projects such as coal-fired power plants and large dams to generate hydroelectric power. In recent years, it has promised more careful attention to the environmental impacts of its projects, but environmentalists remain skeptical of such pledges, and for good reason. Recent reports indicate that the bank's commitments were not matched by real changes in lending practices.[22]

However constrained global institutions such as UNEP and the World Bank have been in fostering sustainable development, environmentalists nonetheless remain hopeful that their capacity for future leadership can be enhanced. For instance, the World Summit in 2002 called for strengthening and streamlining the UN system's environmental agencies and programs and improving cooperation among the United Nations, the World Bank, the International Monetary Fund, and the World Trade Organization. It also sought to increase the availability of information on international issues and to promote greater involvement by NGO representatives. Perhaps not surprisingly, the summit delegates called on all nations to prepare and adopt national and local Agenda 21s, to ratify and implement environmental treaties, and to honor the funding pledges from Rio.

Many new concerns that have not been addressed to date are likely to arise in the coming years, including how best to protect natural resources in the Arctic, where development is likely to accelerate as a result of climate change. Nations already are eyeing oil and natural gas resources in the Arctic as areas long frozen in ice become more accessible. Yet much more scientific research is need on both natural systems and on social, cultural, and political aspects of the Arctic.[23]

Implementing International Environmental Policy Even with substantial improvement in global institutions, implementation of international agreements is likely to remain a stumbling block for a long time. Such agreements are invariably weaker than domestic environmental laws, and they apply unevenly to the world's nations. Only those nations signing the agreements are obliged to comply, and compliance is by no means automatic, any more than it is for domestic environmental policies. Moreover, no international institution has legal authority over nation states comparable to their own governments, and each nation continues to define its interest based on well-entrenched concepts of national sovereignty (Downie 2015; Faure and Lefevere 2015; Peel 2011; Young, King, and Schroeder 2008). Only slowly are nations beginning to "green" the idea of sovereignty as it applies to international relations (Litfin 1998). James Gustave Speth (2002) expressed the limitations well: "International environmental law is plagued by vague agreements, minimal requirements, lax enforcement, and underfunded support" (p. 20). The treaties, he observes, are mostly frameworks for action; by themselves they do not drive change. Moreover, the process of negotiation that leads to approval of the treaties provides considerable leverage to countries that seek to protect the status quo. Thus the United States weakened the Kyoto Protocol on climate change and later withdrew from it anyway.

That said, international treaties and agreements such as the Montreal Protocol and CITES, as noted, have had significant success. For those agreements that have been studied closely, it is apparent that implementation and compliance have been improving. In part that is attributable to increased public concern for the environment, enhanced media coverage of the issues, and pressure from both national and international NGOs, such as environmental groups (DeSombre 2002; Weiss and Jacobson 1999). Environmental NGOs have been proliferating in recent years and have become influential political actors in shaping both policy adoption and implementation. They have contributed as well to the development of a global civil society in which human concerns the world over can be debated and acted on (Kamieniecki 1993; McCormick 2011; National Research Council 2001; O'Neill 2009; Wapner 1996).

As a result in part of such NGO campaigns, new environmental agreements continue to be formulated and approved. In October 2013, for example, after more than a decade of public activism and negotiations, the Minamata Convention on Mercury was signed in Japan. It calls on signatory nations to take a range of actions to reduce mercury pollution, including emissions from coal-fired power plants; mercury pollution is linked to birth defects and brain damage, among other effects. The Obama administration approved the agreement by executive action in November 2013.[24]

In situations in which compliance with international agreements is insufficient, several strategies may help: so-called sunshine methods (e.g., national reporting, on-site monitoring by NGOs, and media access), provision of positive incentives (e.g., financial and technical assistance and training programs), and coercive measures (sanctions and penalties). In short, much like domestic policies, specific actions may be taken to improve compliance with international environmental policies (Weiss and Jacobson 1999).

As an illustration of compliance difficulties, between 2003 and 2005, the Bush administration sought "critical use exemptions" from the Ozone Secretariat of UNEP for the pesticide methyl bromide. Under provisions of the Montreal Protocol, the chemical was to be banned from use after 2005. The administration was trying to help farmers, golf course operators, and others who wanted to continue using the pesticide on the grounds that no acceptable substitutes were available. Environmentalists objected that granting of too many exemptions would undermine the treaty and threaten damage to the ozone layer. They pressured the White House to minimize the requests for exemptions under the treaty. Final decisions on such exemptions are made by an expert advisory panel to the Ozone Secretariat.[25]

Despite these kinds of challenges, the Montreal Protocol is widely viewed as the most effective environmental agreement ever adopted. Experience with its formulation and implementation suggests how other global environmental issues might be addressed. In his assessment of the protocol more than two decades ago, for instance, Richard Benedick (1991) concluded that a number of features might be equally appropriate for other environmental treaties. Among them are the following: (1) a need to have scientists play an unaccustomed but critical role in negotiations; (2) the possibility that governments may have to act in the face of scientific uncertainty (the so-called precautionary principle); (3) the necessity of educating and mobilizing public opinion to generate pressure on governments and private companies to act; (4) the desirability of a leading country taking preemptive environmental protection measures in advance of a global agreement to help build international support; (5) sufficient recognition in an agreement of economic inequalities among countries; (6) employment of market incentives to stimulate technological innovation; and (7) the involvement of citizen groups and industry in diplomatic efforts to formulate and adopt such treaties (see also DeSombre and Barkin 2011; Young, King, and Schroeder 2008). By 2016, agreement was reached on a new plan that modifies the Montreal Protocol yet again, this time to ban the use of hydrofluorocarbons (HFCs), a powerful greenhouse gas used in air conditioners and refrigerators. HFCs were developed to replace chlorofluorocarbons or CFCs that were harming the ozone layer, but unexpectedly, they worsened climate change, and so they too needed to be replaced.[26]

Political Commitment by Developed Nations This experience speaks to what is needed to achieve the demanding goals of the Earth Summit's Agenda 21 and the two follow-up conferences. In the early 1990s, the UNCED secretariat estimated that the cost of implementing Agenda 21 would be about $600 billion per year between 1993 and 2000. Developing nations were to provide most of those funds. The plan, however, called for the industrialized nations to contribute $125 billion a year beyond what they already provided under a variety of existing programs. The target aid level was 0.7 percent of GNP "as soon as possible." At the time, U.S. aid totaled about 0.2 percent of GNP, less in percentage terms than amounts contributed by 14 other nations.

The new spending, part of which was to be funneled through the Global Environment Facility (GEF), was roughly to double the levels of support then in existence. The GEF is an international financing mechanism originally established as a partnership involving the World Bank, the UN Development Programme, and UNEP to provide developing nations with the means to bypass polluting and wasteful technologies and move toward sustainable economic development. It was restructured after UNCED as a larger and better-financed agency to assist in implementing international conventions on ozone depletion, biodiversity, and climate change as well as provisions of Agenda 21 (Soroos 2011). Such "financial transfer institutions" are increasingly viewed as essential for environmental protection in developing nations, but they are also problematic and not always effective (Keohane and Levy 1996).

The financial pledges from developed nations were an essential component of Agenda 21 and necessary to help poor nations make progress toward the economic development and environmental protection goals of the Earth Summit. Yet most developed nations have fallen well short of those commitments, and the United States has been among the worst performers. In comparisons of economic aid contributed by developed countries, it has come in near the bottom of the list, at least when viewed as a percentage of the overall size of national economies. According to the Organisation for Economic Co-operation and Development, in 2015 the United States contributed 0.17 percent of its Gross National Income to developing nations, far below the target level of 0.7 percent. However, the actual dollar amount of development assistance was easily the highest in the world at about $31.08 billion a year, far above the amount contributed by the next largest contributor, the United Kingdom.[27]

In 1997, following a five-year review of Agenda 21's achievements, the United Nations concluded that global environmental conditions had worsened and that "overall trends remain unsustainable"; it urged more intensive action. In his comprehensive review of international action on Agenda 21, Bryner (1999) found that "relatively little changed during the first five years in the structure of the global community and its capacity to organize for sustainable development" (p. 183). His views were echoed by many others at that time. More than a decade after the Earth Summit, despite many initiatives by individual nations, international organizations, businesses, and NGOs to work toward sustainable development, progress had been modest at best, especially from the perspective of developing nations (Najam 2015).

In a 2002 review of events since Rio, UN Secretary-General Kofi Annan expressed similar disappointment that progress "has been slower than anticipated." Conservation measures, he argued, were "far from satisfactory," the environment is "still treated as an unwelcome guest" at discussions of finance and the world economy, and high-consumption lifestyles "continue to tax the Earth's natural life-support systems" (Annan 2002, 12). Annan was hopeful, however, that the Johannesburg summit would launch a major assault on global poverty that could pave the way for further progress on the environmental front. He looked especially to partnerships among governments, private businesses, nonprofit groups, scholars, and concerned citizens as the best way to bring about creative change. As noted earlier, the UN Millennium Development Goals are an expression of such hope.

By 2012, further progress remained elusive. In a report reviewing accomplishments under Agenda 21, the UN's Division for Sustainable Development drew a mixed conclusion. It noted that while Agenda 21 had "acquired considerable coverage" among nations, its implementation "remains far from universal or effective." Progress, it said had been "patchy," and most Agenda 21 outcomes "have still not been realized."[28] Agenda 21 set out such an expansive set of expectations that few would have imagined great progress would come in only 20 years. Moreover, the global economic turmoil after 2007 doubtless has limited actions in recent years. With economic growth robust in China, India, Brazil, and many other developing nations, the future may bring greater success.

U.S. Leadership on Global Environmental Issues For the current ensemble of international institutions, agreements, and agendas to succeed in reaching the goal of environmental sustainability, strong public support, governmental commitment, and especially political leadership will be needed within each nation. There are good reasons to be skeptical that all will be forthcoming in the near term. Within the fragmented U.S. political system, for example, leadership generally can come only from the White House. Yet it was largely absent under Ronald Reagan and George H. W. Bush, and it was much weaker under Bill Clinton than environmentalists had hoped to see.

The Clinton administration was supportive of the UNCED climate change and biodiversity agreements, and it took a strong stance on the need to reduce world population growth, as discussed later. Nonetheless, environmental groups criticized the administration for its lack of forceful leadership on climate change issues, and for its positions on expanding international trade that might pose a threat to U.S. environmental standards (Vogel 2006). They were even more critical of the ineffective leadership of Congress on international environmental issues during the 1990s, particularly its refusal to sign the biodiversity and climate change conventions (Paarlberg 1999).

Under President George W. Bush, the United States withdrew further from its previous position as a global environmental leader, most notably on climate change issues. The administration maintained that climate science was too inexact to warrant demanding and costly national policies and, as discussed later, withdrew from the Kyoto Protocol. Because of its decision to abandon its long-standing leadership role on the environment, allies in Europe and elsewhere openly dissented from the U.S. position (Vig and Faure 2004). President Obama sought to make commitment to climate change action a significant part of his presidential legacy, lending full U.S. support to the Paris Agreement (discussed later in the chapter). But President Donald Trump pledged to reverse course on climate change, even more forcefully than did the Bush administration. Almost certainly, U.S. global environmental leadership under Trump will be weaker than it was under Obama.

These disappointments notwithstanding, the goals and the processes that UNCED set in motion remain highly important. As UNCED organizer Maurice Strong observed, the 1992 meeting was a "launching pad," not a quick fix. The previously fuzzy concept of sustainable development was given a clearer form, and guiding principles and goals were set in place that will shape international economic and environmental decision making over the next several decades. The mutual dependency of environmental health and economic well-being was firmly established, and realization of such relationships set a new context for international politics and ethics in the twenty-first century.

What is needed over the next several decades is concerted action to build on the commitments made at Rio and Johannesburg. The choices are stark. The world will likely experience phenomenal economic growth over the next half century and more. That growth has a real potential to seriously erode environmental systems and make the world's people worse off in many ways. If the right choices are made, however, they can help to restore damaged ecosystems, protect public health, and promote widespread prosperity (Hawken 2007). As James Gustave Speth (2002) stated, there "is still world enough and time for this century to see the coming of a future more wondrous, intimate, and bountiful than our scenarios can imagine. But this world will not be won without a profound commitment to urgent action" (p. 24).[29]

Political Conflict and Global Environmental Policy

Despite general agreement on the goals of sustainable development, international environmental policy and politics will be characterized by considerable conflict in the decades ahead. As discussed earlier, third-generation global environmental issues are difficult to address given their scale, scope, cost, uncertainties, and the necessity of a level of cooperation among nations that is never easy to achieve. As evident in declining support for economic assistance for poor nations just described, political leadership by the developed nations has not always been forthcoming. The United

States in particular seems disinclined to play its historical leadership role on these issues. Commenting on climate change politics more than a decade ago, for example, Lamont Hempel noted that although "unquestionably a world leader in many aspects of environmental protection, the United States is increasingly viewed as the world's leading laggard when it comes to global warming issues" (2006, 288).

Conflicts over global environmental policy often reflect the distinctly different viewpoints of developed and developing nations (Agyeman 2013; Najam 2015; Sachs 2015). These were evident at the Earth Summit in 1992, and they continue to reflect the wide disparities in economic status between rich and poor nations. Simply put, developing nations put a high priority on economic development and often argue that rich nations should be doing considerably more to aid development in their nations to permit them to move toward global goals of sustainability.

A brief review of controversies that have surrounded three of the most important third-generation environmental issues helps illuminate both the potential and pitfalls of international environmental policy and politics as well as these continuing conflicts between rich and poor nations. The descriptions focus on the linkages between domestic politics (especially within the United States) and international policy (DeSombre 2000, 2015) and also underscore the difficulty of addressing complex global environmental problems. In all three cases, the evidence points toward substantial achievements over the past five decades in establishing long-term international environmental goals and public policies to help reach them. Yet, as Speth suggested in the statement cited above, if the world is to make significant progress toward sustainable development, a much greater commitment by both citizens and policymakers, in both developed and developing nations, will be needed in the future. Many scholars have echoed such an agenda, calling for far greater involvement of citizens in the policymaking process around the world, and development of innovative governance mechanisms to facilitate such participation (Baber and Bartlett 2015; Steinberg 2015; Steinberg and VanDeveer 2012).

Climate Change

Climate change is widely considered to be the most significant environmental problem of the twenty-first century. It is also a prime example of what scholars sometimes refer to as third-generation environmental issues. These are long-term challenges that are global in scale, often highly complex, and come with substantial scientific uncertainty, such as continuing questions over the magnitude, timing, and location of their effects (DiMento and Doughman 2014; IPCC 2013; National Climate Assessment 2014; National Research Council 2011). Political conflicts over how to respond to the risks of climate change often are anchored in the short-term costs of cutting back on use of fossil fuels and the presumed implications for economic development.

Political support for U.S. action on climate change has varied, depending on the party in power. Democratic administrations, such as Obama's, have been supportive, but Republican administrations, such as George W. Bush's and Donald Trump's, have tilted toward denial of the problem and weak support for global agreements on climate change. Aside from ideological differences between the parties, especially on expansion of governmental responsibilities and regulation, the issue has failed to arouse much public concern or sense of urgency. Climate change continues to be perplexing to many people, and it remains a low-salience issue, in part because warming to date has not been all that unpleasant for most people (Guber and Bosso 2013a; Nisbet 2016; Selin and VanDeveer 2016).[30] Minimal political support in the past and continued opposition to action on climate change also can be attributed to the influence of the fossil fuel, automobile, and other industries that might be adversely affected by policy action to curb emissions of greenhouse gases. The ongoing campaign of what the press calls climate deniers or climate skeptics plays a role as well (Dunlap 2013; Dunlap and McCright 2015).

The Framework Convention on Climate Change was agreed to by 150 nations at the 1992 Earth Summit, and by 197 countries by 2016. Following a series of international meetings culminating in Kyoto, Japan, in December 1997, delegates approved the Kyoto Protocol, which set out country-by-country targets for reduced emission of greenhouse gases. Of special importance for the United States, the agreement called for 39 industrialized nations to reduce their emissions about 5 percent below 1990 levels by 2012. As noted in Chapter 2, the U.S. target was 7 percent below its 1990 level, in effect a reduction of about 30 to 35 percent from emissions that would otherwise occur (Hempel 2006). The protocol applied to all major greenhouse gases, not just carbon dioxide. At a follow-up meeting in Buenos Aires in November 1998, the Clinton administration signed the agreement, but the U.S. Congress remained opposed, and Clinton never sent the treaty to the Senate for consideration, knowing that he could not hope to gain the two-thirds vote from that body that he needed.

The Clinton White House tried to make the U.S. position more palatable to industry and Congress by proposing extensive use of emissions trading with developing nations to meet the U.S. reduction targets. Indeed, most of the cost of the administration's planned cutbacks in U.S. emissions depended on the use of such market-based incentives. Environmentalists argued strongly that the United States could and should do better through an intensive program of energy conservation and research and development in support of alternative energy sources. Reflecting those views, more than half of the states and over 1,000 cities have promoted energy conservation and efficiency as well as uses of renewable energy sources out of concern for global climate change (Betsill and Rabe 2009; Rabe 2004, 2010, 2016; Rabe and Mundo 2007). As discussed in previous chapters, California and the states in the Northeast have been among the most innovative leaders in this regard as they have experimented with cap-and-trade programs and other policy strategies (Rabe 2017; Raymond 2016).

The distinctive weakness in the U.S. response to climate change has been at the national level. This was evident, for example, in the Bush administration. Bush adopted a far more skeptical stance on climate change than was prevalent throughout the 1990s. Most striking was his announcement in March 2001 that he would withdraw the United States from the Kyoto Protocol. The Bush administration also made clear that the United States would not be bound by the Kyoto Protocol or decisions made to implement it. The White House said that the agreement would harm the U.S. economy and create unacceptable inequities by exempting large developing nations (particularly China and India) from the treaty's requirements. In its place the administration called for additional scientific research and in 2002 urged U.S. companies to set voluntary targets for reduction in greenhouse gas emissions.[31]

As discussed in Chapter 6, at the same time the Bush administration made these decisions, it was proposing a U.S. national energy policy grounded largely in expanded use of fossil fuels, which would inevitably *increase*, not decrease, greenhouse gas emissions. Environmentalists denounced Bush's positions on both climate change and energy policy as unjustified, and they called for a strong national climate change policy that would reduce greenhouse gas emissions equal to or greater than called for under the Kyoto Protocol (Gardiner and Jacobson 2002; Hempel 2006; Selin and VanDeveer 2016; Victor 2004).[32]

Despite their pledges to adhere to the historic Kyoto agreement, however, other nations also exhibited reluctance to embrace a strong treaty, and over time many of the signatory nations fell short of their commitments (Giddens 2011; Harrison and Sundstrom 2010; Regan 2015; Selin and VanDeveer 2009, 2016). So while the U.S. stance under the Bush administration stands alone in some respects, the political reality is that it was difficult for other nations as well to maintain a strong commitment to action on climate change. The economic downturn after 2007 compounded the problem as the short-term costs of action loomed large.

A series of international climate change meetings in recent years to replace the Kyoto Protocol has demonstrated the continuing challenge of building political support for tough policies, but also great hope for the future as climate change science and forecasts improved and international cooperation on action increased. The scientific agreement has been evident in the periodic reports of the IPCC, which are exceptionally thorough and highly regarded. As discussed in Chapter 2, these reports are frequently cited by scientists and scientific organizations, environmental groups, government policymakers, officials in international organizations, business leaders, and others for their reliable assessment of climate. The scientific consensus is also made plain in the periodic U.S. National Climate Assessment reports, the latest of which is set for release in 2018.[33]

International policy on climate change reflects this scientific consensus, but also the perspectives and needs of diverse constituencies, including nation states, international nongovernmental organizations, and private-sector interests. As discussed previously, developed and developing nations often have taken distinctly different positions on the issues, reflecting their varied experience and needs. Discussions at a series of international conferences to update and eventually replace the Kyoto Protocol focused on how to resolve conflicts over climate change targets and timetables (how much to reduce greenhouse gas emissions and by when), which nations should take the lead, how to establish international cooperation on implementation programs, how to take deal with various actions (such as forest management) that can used to offset emissions, adaptation mechanisms, financing for climate change mitigation, and information-gathering and assessment, among other issues (Selin and VanDeveer 2016).

These discussions took place at a series of international meetings, or Conferences of the Parties (COP), in Bali (2007), Copenhagen (2009), Cancun (2010), Durban (2011), Doha (2012), Warsaw (2013), Lima (2014), Paris (2015), and Marrakesh (2016). Until the December 2015 meeting in Paris, critics often faulted the various agreements that were reached as relatively weak and unlikely to reduce greenhouse gas emissions sufficiently to remain below a rise of 2 degrees Celsius (3.6 degrees Fahrenheit) of warming above pre-industrial levels, the target strongly recommended by climate scientists. The Paris Agreement, however, was an exception.

That agreement for the first time reflected nearly universal support among the world's nations to mount ambitious actions to reduce greenhouse gas emissions and to adapt to likely effects of climate change in the future. There also is to be a higher level of support from rich nations to assist developing nation in making these efforts ($100 billion annually). All nations are to develop what are termed "nationally determined contributions" to emissions reduction, and regularly report on implementation efforts and the level of reduction reached. These plans are to be revisited and strengthened over time, in part because it is widely understood that currently expected actions under the agreement will get the world only about halfway to the desired emissions reduction targets.[34] The agreement also calls for a global stocktaking every five years to assess progress. While national efforts remain voluntary, there are reasons to be hopeful that progress will be greater than under previous agreements, particularly if the United States and other leading emitters follow through on their commitments. The 2016 Marrakesh meeting focused on how best to achieve these goals.[35]

On November 4, 2016, 119 of the 197 parties to the agreement formally ratified it, including the required 55 parties accounting for at least 55 percent of the total global greenhouse gas emissions; it took effect the following month. The Paris Agreement is not formally a treaty and therefore did not require Senate approval in the United States. It was sufficient for the Obama administration to accept it formally. As noted earlier, President Trump promised during the 2016 campaign to withdraw from the Paris Agreement, and it remains to be seen whether his administration will do so, and what the consequences of such an action will be.[36]

In terms of the U.S. response, by the late 2000s, the political climate began shifting, in part a result of increasing scientific and popular consensus on the imperative of action. The change was striking as leading corporations, cities, states, and formerly skeptical members of Congress began to press for solutions. The Senate itself passed a nonbinding resolution in 2005 saying that to combat climate change the United States must turn to mandatory restrictions on greenhouse gases, a repudiation of the Bush approach.[37] Even the intelligence agencies and the nation's military leaders began to worry about the impact of climate change on national security (Matthew 2013).[38] As a reflection of such social, economic, and political shifts, the U.S. House approved a national climate change policy in 2009, although the Senate did not go along, and the economic recession and election results in 2010 through 2016 made additional action by Congress unlikely. As discussed in Chapter 6, however, in 2013 President Obama announced a renewed effort to use his executive authority to advance U.S. national climate change policy, the major results of which were the Clean Power Plan and increased vehicle fuel efficiency standards.

Even without a formal national climate change policy, the United States has taken significant steps toward reducing its release of greenhouse gases, primarily through substitution of natural gas for coal in power plants and increasing reliance on renewable sources, particularly wind power. By some measures, the United States may even come close to meeting the target that President Obama set for the nation at the 2009 climate meeting in Copenhagen. This is a 17 percent reduction from 2005 levels by 2020.[39] Beyond the president's commitments to taking action domestically, he adopted a stance on international negotiations that contrasted sharply with the Bush administration (Kraft 2012).

Whatever the position the United States takes in the future on the Paris Agreement, the challenge of dealing with climate change is clearly enormous and will remain so for decades. Scientific confidence in the effects of climate change continues to grow, and new studies by the IPCC and others should help to build political consensus on the need to take action. Nonetheless, implementation of climate stabilization policies and programs in the years ahead will depend heavily on the capacity of the world's nations to maintain these agreements and to foster cooperation between industrialized nations and rapidly developing nations such as China and India. That surely will not be easy to do, although new research in political science and related disciplines may provide some answers for how best to design new institutions and procedures that can help (Keohane 2015).

By early 2017, China announced that it intends to spend more than $360 billion through 2020 to advance its use of renewable energy such as wind and solar, just as the U.S. government seemed likely to pull back from previous commitments under the Trump administration.[40] The next few years will tell us much about each nation's intentions and priorities in a time of rapidly changing technologies and lower costs for renewables.

Protection of Biological Diversity

Any program of sustainable development also must include policies to halt the loss of biological diversity, restore ecosystem health, and maintain the ecological functions essential to long-term environmental sustainability. Within the United States, controversies over the Endangered Species Act attest to the obstacles in formulating and implementing policies and programs to achieve such goals. International policy for protection of biodiversity is a relatively recent development that depends largely on efforts within individual nations to inventory and protect species and the habitats in which they live. Almost no one believes that these tasks will be achieved easily, in light of growing human demand for land and resources and short-term economic pressures—for instance, to harvest tropical forests or to extract valuable fossil fuels—that often drive out concern for long-term ecosystem preservation (Tobin 2016). The UN Millennium Ecosystem Assessment, a four-year $24 million study of threats to the world's ecosystems, confirmed such fears. It found that 60 percent of global ecosystems are being degraded or used in an unsustainable manner, and that 10 to 30 percent of mammal, bird, and amphibian species may be threatened with extinction as a result.[41]

The chief international policy for biodiversity protection is the UN Convention on Biological Diversity (CBD). After a decade of formulation, it was approved at the 1992 Earth Summit and took effect in late 1993. As of 2016, 196 nations had ratified the CBD and become parties to the agreement. The United States was not among them. The Clinton administration endorsed the CBD, but the Senate, whose approval is required under the U.S. Constitution, had reservations. Among them were the implications for intellectual property rights to biological and genetic resources—a source of conflict because most of the biodiversity resources are in developing nations but likely to be used most by industrialized nations. The Bush administration did not seek Senate approval for the treaty and the Senate took no further action on it. Supporters of the CBD had urged the Obama administration to endorse and support U.S. ratification, but the Senate took no action, consistent with its position since the treaty was proposed in 1993.

The CBD is designed to slow the loss of Earth's biodiversity through adoption of national policies to conserve species and their habitats and to promote public awareness of conservation and sustainable uses of biological diversity. The CBD also produces a periodic update on the state of biodiversity called *Global Biodiversity Outlook*.[42] Parties under the treaty maintain their sovereign rights over biological resources within their countries, but they also assume responsibility for biodiversity conservation and sustainable use of biological resources. The CBD framework provides for an international forum, a series of meetings that bring together public officials, NGOs, academics, and others to discuss issues and review progress. The Conference of Parties, consisting of those nations that have ratified the treaty, constitutes a governing body for the CBD. It is charged with reviewing progress, identifying priorities, and setting work plans for members. Activities taken by developing countries in support of the convention are eligible for support through the GEF, which pools money from donor nations. Despite its lack of formal approval of the treaty, the United States continues to send delegations of government officials and representatives of environmental and business groups to CBD meetings.

The CBD commits parties to "fair and equitable sharing of the benefits arising out of the utilization of genetic resources." As is often the case in policy implementation, however, concern focuses on the details of such arrangements. Developed nations also are to provide developing countries with "new and additional financial resources" to enable them to meet expectations under the treaty. As shown earlier, however, such economic assistance has fallen short of expectations. Consequently, developing nations have lacked the resources to meet the treaty's goals.

Experience with CITES offered some hope that international public concern could be aroused and nations persuaded to adopt conservation policies, even if some of the notable successes under CITES have not had the lasting effects many had hoped for. As many Asian nations have developed large middle classes, demand for products made from endangered wildlife has increased, thus undercutting the agreement's goals. Demand in China has been particularly strong and has had a major effect on wildlife. Perhaps as a sign of a reversal in these trends, in late 2016 China announced that it would ban all commerce in ivory by the end of 2017, which, if successful, would help to end the killing of elephants in Africa.[43] Ultimately, solutions to trade in wildlife lie in cultural changes in those nations that can reduce consumer demand for the products as well as governmental action of the kind that China took.

The CBD faces even greater obstacles because its goals are more directly related to human pressures on the environment. Human society today uses more than 40 percent of global plant production and an estimated 50 percent of the world's freshwater runoff. As the population increases and economic growth continues, the potential for adversely affecting biodiversity is enormous. A prominent example is the destruction of Indonesian rainforests at the rate of about 4 million acres a year, or an area the size of Connecticut. By one estimate, 80 percent of Indonesia's timber trade is illegal, but intensive logging continues because of the desperate need for employment and economic gain, rampant corruption among government and military officials who profit from the timber industry, and strong demand around the world for prized tropical hardwood. Much the same is true for many other developing nations as well (Tobin 2016).[44] It is not surprising that international agreements on trade become yet another vehicle for environmentalists to press for protection of wildlife, as was done for the Trans-Pacific Partnership agreement in 2015.[45]

Despite the obvious constraints on biodiversity conservation, some nations, including developing nations that often are considered to be too preoccupied with alleviation of poverty to exhibit any concern for environmental protection, have made remarkable progress. Two cases in point are Costa Rica and Bolivia, each of which has adopted innovative and highly successful policies and programs to conserve tropical biodiversity. These programs include establishment in Costa Rica of one of the best national park systems in the world and pioneering efforts in promotion of ecotourism and biodiversity prospecting. The nation also had a president who "made sustainable development the conceptual underpinning of his entire administration" (Steinberg 2001, 3). Bolivia created the world's first debt-for-nature swap in which a portion of national debt is exchanged for land to be set aside for conservation purposes. It also developed the world's largest forest-based climate change mitigation project, organized a national environmental endowment that serves as a model for nations in the region, and "established an effective, high-profile biodiversity conservation agency" (Steinberg 2001, 4).

Why are some nations so committed and successful in pursuit of biodiversity protection goals while others lag far behind? With the world's biodiversity conservation largely in the hands of individual nations, particularly developing countries, that is an important question. In his study of four decades of reform in Costa Rica and Bolivia, Paul Steinberg (2001) suggests that much depends on policy leadership within the nations. That is, biodiversity conservation does not come about solely because of decisions made by international organizations, efforts by scientists and other experts (what Peter Haas has called epistemic communities), media coverage, or public pressure. It is equally a result of domestic political activities that help build national commitment to conservation goals. Steinberg finds in particular that "bilateral activists," individual policy entrepreneurs who operate in both the domestic and international spheres, have been enormously influential. These activists include reformers within government as well as activists associated with NGOs. Given the many obstacles to success in global biodiversity conservation, the study's conclusions offer a hopeful perspective on how other nations might initiate comparable policies.

Population Growth and Economic Development

Stabilization of the human population is an essential component of sustainable development even if it is not discussed often in this context. Simply put, there can be no sustainability in a world with an ever-increasing number of people and a rising level of resource consumption. Both must be addressed. Developed nations generally have moved through what is called a demographic transition to a persistent low rate of population growth, with many either at zero growth or close to it. At the same time, however, most developed nations also have very high rates of consumption of energy and natural resources, and rely on advanced technologies that can have negative environmental impacts, such as extensive use of automobiles for transportation and heavy reliance on fossil fuels for energy needs. For example, as discussed in Chapter 2, people in rich nations consume an estimated 32 times the resources that many people in developing nations do. Thus arguably they have a far greater impact on the world's environment. Americans in particular stand out in this regard. With 4.4 percent of the world's population, we consume one-fifth of global energy production, and we stand near the top of the world's greenhouse gas emitters on a per capita basis (Selin and VanDeveer 2016; Tobin 2016). It is easy to understand, therefore, that global sustainable development requires adjustment in both developed and developing nations.

As expected, rates of population growth have slowed in recent decades, to a global average of about 1.2 percent per year by 2016 and an average for developing nations (excluding China) of 1.7 percent. Among the nations with the most impressive declines in growth rates are Bangladesh, Kenya, Mexico, South Korea, Thailand, Tunisia, and China. Many reasons account for the slower growth rates, including economic and social development in poor nations, the availability of family planning and other health care services, and improvement in the status of women. Yet, as discussed in Chapter 2, the current rate of growth nevertheless translates into an increase in the world's population of over 88 million people annually and projections for a global population of 9.9 billion by 2050, up from 7.4 billion in early 2017. Almost all of that growth will be in developing nations, accompanied by a continuing explosion in urban populations around the world; by 2008, for the first time more than half of the world's population lived in towns and cities, a notable historical marker. In part for that reason, cities around the world increasingly are pioneering new approaches to climate change and the challenge of sustainable development (Rose 2016).[46]

Population growth is likely to continue, although at a slowing pace, throughout the twenty-first century, with important consequences for achieving economic development and environmental protection goals—including climate change—and for reducing global poverty, a longtime goal of the United Nations (Cohen, J. 2011; Population Reference Bureau 2016; Sachs 2015; United Nations 2015). Indeed, one report in 2009 found that nearly all of the usual actions that Americans take to reduce their carbon footprint (such as driving fuel-efficient vehicles, making careful food choices, and reducing home energy use) can be overwhelmed by the long-term effects of their own reproductive choices on release of greenhouse gases (Murtaugh and Schlax 2009). That is, having three or four children, as opposed to one or two, can have effects that are all but ignored by most of us.

Despite its enormous effects on families, economic development, and the environment, population growth is perched precariously on the international political agenda. Like many other third-generation environmental issues (albeit an indirect environmental issue), the problem is global and long-term, and it is nearly invisible to the average person. It is also difficult to appreciate how personal decisions on family size or national action on population policies that promote family planning can affect a range of environmental and economic conditions over time. In addition, population policy has been highly controversial because of perceived conflicts with deeply held cultural and religious values.

Individual nations have long had international population policies that were intended to fund family planning programs abroad. In addition, many nations have their own national population policies, primarily based on making available voluntary family planning services (United Nations 2015). The United States and other nations also have sought to aid other countries as they grapple with the challenges of growing populations. U.S. population policy assistance programs began in the early 1960s under President Lyndon Johnson, and they received strong bipartisan backing for two decades. The United States was a recognized leader in fostering family planning around the world and for years was the largest donor to the United Nations Fund for Population Activities (UNFPA), later renamed the United Nations Population Fund (Kraft 1994a). Yet after a UN conference on population in Mexico City in 1984, strong partisan differences on population assistance emerged. The Reagan administration, for example, ended all U.S. contributions to the UNFPA, the major multilateral funding agency for international family planning programs, and the cutoff continued under President George H. W. Bush from 1989 to early 1993. Both administrations sought to appease important conservative constituencies who were concerned about China's tough population policy as well as about moral issues related to both family planning and abortion; in 2016, to help spur economic growth, China reversed its one-child-per-family policy that it had set in 1979. Presidents Reagan and Bush did maintain support for U.S. bilateral population assistance programs in which the nation directly supplies funds to other countries, largely to support family planning programs. Nevertheless, the shift in population policy under both presidents contributed significantly to the virtual disappearance of population issues on the national agenda.

As soon as he took office, President Bill Clinton reversed the so-called Mexico City policy of the Reagan and Bush administrations and reestablished support for the UN population program. He also boosted funding for the nation's bilateral family planning assistance programs. In 1993 the Clinton administration already had signaled it would reclaim the leadership position on world population issues that the United States held in the 1960s and 1970s. It did so at the 1994 International Conference on Population and Development (ICPD) in Cairo, where delegates debated a proposed action plan on global population stabilization. Despite some controversies over reproductive health care, delegates to the historic meeting approved a 20-year "program of action" that they believed could hold world population to below UN projections at the time of 7.5 billion by 2020 and 9.8 billion by the year 2050; as noted earlier, current projections for 2050 are no lower today.

Nations agreed on the need to triple the amount the world spends on population stabilization, and they expanded the concept of population policy well beyond traditional family planning programs. The action plan called for governments and donor nations to support education for girls to help promote gender equity, to provide women with a range of choices on family planning and health care issues, and to improve the status of women in developing nations to empower them to make decisions related to reproductive choice. By late 1999 at a "Cairo Plus Five" conference, however, such measures appeared to be falling well short of pressing world needs.[47]

The partisan differences on population policy continued when President George W. Bush took office in 2001. He reinstated the Mexico City policy that withholds U.S. funds from international family planning programs run by overseas NGOs, largely those that include abortion-related services, medical referrals, research, or public information campaigns (Cincotta and Crane 2001). In addition, the following year the president decided to end U.S. funding for the United Nations Population Fund despite pleas for such financial support from Secretary of State Colin Powell.[48] Under long-standing U.S. law, the UN program already is barred from using U.S. money in China or in support of abortion services. The Bush administration continued to withhold the UNFPA funds in subsequent years. By 2006, it also proposed large cuts in U.S. bilateral population assistance programs, and threatened to withdraw the United States from the landmark ICPD "program of action."[49] Leaders of developing nations and both European and UN officials who view reproductive health care programs as one of the most effective ways to help reduce global poverty expressed similar concerns.[50]

Shortly after taking office, President Obama, like Clinton before him, reversed the ban on UN family planning contribution. In a January 23, 2009, executive order, he left the current funding for these programs (administered by the U.S. Agency for International Development) at $461 million in fiscal 2009 (which rose to over $600 million by 2016), but significantly expanded the number of groups qualified to receive grants to manage such programs. Obama also called on Congress to restore funding to the United Nations Population Fund.[51] Within days of taking office, Donald Trump reinstated a long-standing Republican policy that prohibits the granting of U.S. foreign aid to any health providers in other nations who discuss the use of abortion as part of family planning purposes, the so-called "gag rule."[52]

Aside from the impressive differences these kind of programs can make for economic development in poor nations, many argue that developing nations need not follow the historic path that rich nations did in the nineteenth and twentieth centuries. In particular, economic development does not need to rely on energy-intensive and environmentally destructive technologies and practices of the kind that were so widely used in the United States and Europe. A different pattern of development is possible if richer nations and international institutions help to provide access to modern technologies (e.g., in energy production and manufacturing) through financial and technical assistance, loan forgiveness, and foreign investment, and if developing nations can improve their governance and reduce corruption. A more sustainable form of development can lead to slower rates of population growth, following the pattern seen for decades in rich nations.

Neither Republican nor Democratic administrations in the United States have taken seriously one of the most notable omissions in U.S. population policy: a failure to exhibit any concern for population growth in the United States itself and its implications for sustainable development at home and abroad. As noted in Chapter 2, the United States is growing as fast as or faster than any other industrialized nation, at an estimated 0.7 percent (or about 2.3 million people) a year, including immigration (Population Reference Bureau 2016). This is more than five times the rate that prevails in most western European nations.[53] A larger U.S. population can dramatically increase demand for homes, automobiles, and other consumer products, as well as the energy and natural resources their production and use require. It also raises serious questions of equity in use of the world's resources in light of the very high U.S. level of consumption per capita (Seager and Polansky 2016; Tobin 2016).

Conclusions

Environmental policy depends on advances on many fronts: scientific research, technological innovation, reengineering of industrial processes and improvements in corporate management, enhancement of governmental capacities for policymaking and implementation, a more widespread embrace of environmental values, and increases in public knowledge and involvement. The early twenty-first century is a time of profound and unpredictable changes in all of these areas of human activity. It is also a difficult period for those who place their hope in government and political processes. Many today disparage government and politics and thereby contribute to the prevailing public cynicism. The effects are to limit the collective power of citizens and to increase the influence of well-organized special interests that pursue political values often at odds with those held by the public. An invigorated democratic politics is essential to any strategy for creating a just and sustainable society, and policymakers and activists could seek ways to make the political system more open to public participation and also more responsive to public needs.

The short-term environmental policy agenda for the next several decades of the twenty-first century is clear and broadly supported. There also are signs of progress in achieving it despite continuing battles over environmental protection and natural resources policies in the United States and within international policy forums. Individuals will disagree over the interpretation of the latest data and studies and over the way policymakers should reconcile conflicting positions on the issues. Those who find that the direction, form, or pace of policy and institutional changes are deficient should consider entering the fray to fight for their views.

The longer-term agenda of sustainable development is less distinct, but it is becoming sharper as communities, businesses, and nations attempt to define its meaning and shift programs and priorities to promote it. The challenges here are more daunting and demand more commitment than has been evident in either government or corporate circles, or many nonprofit organizations, including colleges and universities. Citizens need to press government, business, and other organizations to do a better job. They can help by building coalitions for environmental sustainability; articulating the social, economic, and political changes necessary; and devoting themselves to their realization.

Discussion Questions

1   What does it mean for a city to take sustainability seriously? Which cities, or colleges and universities, have done the most to move toward sustainability and what accounts for their success? What keeps other cities, or colleges and universities, from doing more?

2   To what extent has U.S. industry begun to work toward sustainable development? Which companies stand out for their commitments and actions to date? Are these developments a form of greenwashing, or do they indicate a significant change to implement environmental goals? What would motivate companies to do more?

3   What is the potential for citizen involvement in environmental decision making, at any level of government? What might encourage a greater level of such "civic environmentalism"?

4   Dozens of international environmental institutions and policies have been launched in the past five decades. To what extent do you think they are working well? What else is needed to deal effectively with global environmental challenges over the next several decades?

5   Polls indicate that global environmental problems evince less concern among the American public than more immediate threats to their health or well-being. What might increase the salience of global environmental problems for the public?

6   Some international environmental treaties have been more successful than others. What factors seem to most significantly affect the success of international agreements such the Paris Agreement on climate change or the Convention on Biological Diversity?

350   Chapter 8

Suggested Readings

Axelrod, Regina S. and Stacy D. VanDeveer, eds. 2015. *The Global Environment: Institutions, Law, and Policy*, 4th edn. Washington, DC: CQ Press.

Chasek, Pamela S., David L. Downie, and Janet Welsh Brown. 2017. *Global Environmental Politics*, 7th edn. Boulder, CO: Westview Press.

Mazmanian, Daniel A., and Michael E. Kraft, eds. 2009. *Toward Sustainable Communities: Transition and Transformations in Environmental Policy*, 2nd edn. Cambridge, MA: MIT Press.

O'Neill, Kate. 2009. *The Environment and International Relations*. New York: Cambridge University Press.

Portney, Kent E. 2013. *Taking Sustainable Cities Seriously: Economic Development, the Environment, and Quality of Life in American Cities*, 2nd edn. Cambridge, MA: MIT Press.

Notes

1 Juliet Eilperin, "Thinking Globally, Acting Locally: Communities Consider Their Carbon Footprint in Their Planning and Development," *Washington Post National Weekly Edition*, May 12–18, 2008.

2 The quotation is taken from the archives of the PCSD: http://clinton4.nara.gov/PCSD/.

3 Andrew Jacobs, "New Jersey Governor Enlists Himself in 'War on Sprawl,' II," *New York Times*, January 2, 2003.

4 David Firestone, "Georgia Setting Up Tough Anti-Sprawl Agency," *New York Times*, March 25, 1999.

5 See John Maggs, "Local Taxes Make the Garden State Greener," *National Journal*, April 8, 2000: 1146–1147. Arguments of this kind are common in proposals of sustainable communities, and websites focusing on those issues cover other studies. See, for example, the American Farmland Trust (www.farmland.org), the Smart Growth Network (www.smartgrowth.org), the Sprawl Watch Clearinghouse (www.sprawlwatch.org), the Sustainable Communities Network (www.sustainable.org), and the Land Trust Alliance (www.lta.org).

6 For information on the loss of farmland and water, see a study released in late 2002 by American Rivers, the Natural Resources Defense Council, and Smart Growth America: *Paving Our Way to Water Shortages: How Sprawl Aggravates the Effects of Drought*, available at: www.americanrivers.org.

7 The U.S. EPA maintains an Office of Sustainable Communities (OSC) to assist those communities seeking to adopt sustainability programs. It is located within the Office of Policy, which in turn is part of the office of the EPA administrator. The OSC activities are described on the website: www2.epa.gov/aboutepa/about-office-policy-op#OSC.

8 Quentin Hardy, "Google Says It Will Run Entirely on Renewable Energy in 2017," *New York Times*, December 6, 2016.

9 Bryn Nelson, "A Building Not Just Green, but Practically Self-Sustaining," *New York Times*, April 2, 2013.

10 Interface's employees have been formally trained in the company's environmental principles, which were derived from The Natural Step, a Swedish organization

dedicated to helping corporations become more environmentally responsible while maintaining profitability. Several websites are dedicated to these kinds of actions: The Natural Step (www.naturalstep.org), the World Business Council for Sustainable Development (www.wbcsd.ch), and the Coalition for Environmentally Responsible Economies (www.ceres.org).

11 See also Apple's intention to be a green energy producer for others: Diane Cardwell, "Apple Becomes a Green Energy Supplier, with Itself as a Customer," *New York Times*, August 23, 2016.

12 See Danny Hakim, "Honda Takes Up Case in U.S. for Green Energy," *New York Times*, June 2, 2002.

13 See, for example, Michael Barbaro and Felicity Barringer, "Wal-Mart to Seek Savings on Energy," *New York Times*, October 25, 2005; and Stephanie Rosenbloom, "At Wal-Mart, Labeling to Reflect Green Intent," *New York Times*, July 16, 2009.

14 See, for example, the website for Agenda 21 Conspiracy: http://agenda21conspiracy.com/; and Josh Voorhees, "Conspiracy, In Theory: How Right-Wing Scaremongering about a U.N. Global Takeover Has Evolved into a Surprisingly Effective Political Strategy Across the Country," *Slate*, May 5, 2014.

15 For coverage of the 2012 meeting, see the general site for the UN sustainable development program: the "follow-up" site: http://sustainabledevelopment.un.org/.

16 The statements come from "Key Outcomes of the Summit."

17 Editorial in the *New York Times*, September 6, 2002.

18 For an overview of the meeting, see Rachel L. Swarms, "Broad Accord Reached at Global Environmental Meeting," *New York Times*, September 4, 2002; James Dao, "Protesters Interrupt Powell Speech as U.N. Talks End," *New York Times*, September 5, 2002; and Andrew C. Revkin, "Small World After All," *New York Times*, September 5, 2002.

19 Simon Romero and John M. Broder, "Progress on the Sidelines as Rio Conference Ends," *New York Times*, June 23, 2012.

20 See United Nations, *Human Development Report 2015: Work for Human Development* (New York: United Nations Development Program, 2015); see also Jeffrey D. Sachs, "The End of Poverty, Soon," *New York Times*, September 24, 2013. For an overview of efforts in the aftermath of Rio+20, see Derek Osborn, "Building on Rio+20 to Spur Action for Sustainable Development," *Environment*, 55(3) (May/June 2013): 3–13. See also Edward B. Barbier, "The Green Economy Post Rio+20," *Science* 338 (November 16, 2012): 887–888.

21 These are at: https://sustainabledevelopment.un.org/sdgs.

22 See Andrew C. Revkin, "World Bank Criticized on Environmental Efforts," *New York Times*, July 22, 2008; and Bruce Rich, *Foreclosing the Future: The World Bank and the Politics of Environmental Destruction* (Washington, DC: Island Press, 2013).

23 See, for example, Robert Harris, "The Arctic: Past or Prologue?" *Environment* 54 (September/October 2012): 3–13; and Clive Tesar, Marc-Andre Dubois, and Alexander Shestakov, "Toward Strategic, Coherent, Policy-Relevant Arctic Science," *Science* 353 (September 23, 2016): 1368–1370.

24 For a history of the convention's development, see Naomi Lubick and David Malakoff, "With Pact's Completion, the Real Work Begins," *Science* 341 (September 27, 2013): 1443–1445.

25 See Rebecca Adams, "Ozone vs. Food Supply, a Chemical Dilemma," *CQ Weekly*, September 5, 2005: 2291–2292.

26 See Coral Davenport, "A Sequel to the Paris Climate Accord Is Developing in Vienna," *New York Times*, July 24, 2016.

27 It should be said that U.S. foreign aid is not distributed evenly to developing nations, but rather reflects U.S. foreign policy priorities. In recent years, for example, the aid was concentrated in the Middle East, Afghanistan, and Pakistan, with lesser amounts going to Kenya, South Africa, Columbia, Nigeria, and Ethiopia. The OECD data can be found at: www.oecd.org/dac/development-aid-rises-again-in-2015-spending-on-refugees-doubles.htm.

28 United Nations Division for Sustainable Development "Review of Implementation of Agenda 21 and the Rio Principles" (New York: United Nations, January 2012): http://sustainabledevelopment.un.org/content/documents/641Synthesis_report_Web.pdf. The quotations are from p. 8 of the document.

29 There is no shortage of scientific assessments of the world's environmental ills and scenarios for the future. For a review of data sources for global environmental outlooks, see Thomas M. Parris, "A Crystal Ball for Sustainability," *Environment*, 44 (September 2002): 3–4. One of the most useful is UNEP's series of state of the environment reports, the latest of which, the *Global Environmental Outlook-5* report, was released in 2012 to coincide with the Rio+20 conference. It assesses the state of the global atmosphere, land, water and biodiversity, covers changes since 1987, and spells out priorities for action. The UN considered *GEO-5* to be the most comprehensive UN report on the environment at the time of its release. These reports are based on the work of hundreds of scientific experts and typically are reviewed by up to 1,000 others for accuracy. The *GEO-5* report and the earlier reports can be found at: www.unep.org/geo. Planning for a GEO-6 report is now well under way.

30 On public reaction to modest warming to date, see Patrick J. Egan and Megan Mullin, "Global Warming Feels Quite Pleasant," *New York Times*, April 21, 2016.

31 Andrew C. Revkin, "Bush Offers Plan for Voluntary Measures to Limit Gas Emissions," *New York Times*, February 15, 2002.

32 For an account of reactions to the Bush plan, see Andrew C. Revkin, "Bush Offers Plan for Voluntary Measures to Limit Gas Emissions," *New York Times*, February 15, 2002.

33 See a summary of the draft report in John H. Cushman, Jr., "On Climate Change, Obama Lays Down a Scientific Gauntlet for Trump Administration," *Inside Climate News*, December 23, 2016.

34 Justin Gillis and Coral Davenport, "Leaders Roll Up Sleeves on Climate, but Experts Say Plans Don't Pack a Wallop," *New York Times*, April 21, 2016; and John Schwartz, "Paris Climate Deal Is Too Weak to Meet Goals, Report Finds," *New York Times*, November 16, 2016.

35 The details of the Paris Agreement can be found its dedicated webpage: http://unfccc.int/2860.php, and actions at the Marrakesh meeting in Charles F. Kennel, Stephen Briggs, and David G. Victor, "Making Climate Science More Relevant," *Science* 354 (October 28, 2016): 421–422. On the U.S. commitment as of late

2016, see Jean Chemnick, "Obama Presses Ahead with Plans for Deep Emissions Cuts," *Climate Wire*, November 17, 2016.

36 See Coral Davenport, "Donald Trump Could Put Climate Change on Course for 'Danger Zone,'" *New York Times*, November 10, 2016.

37 Margaret Kriz, "Heating Up," *National Journal*, August 6, 2005: 2504–2508; and Bret Schulte, "Turning up the Heat: A Surprising Consensus Is Transforming the Complex Politics of Global Warming," *U.S. News and World Report*, April 10, 2006.

38 See John M. Broder, "Climate Change Report Outlines Perils for U.S. Military," *New York Times*, November 9, 2012. Reports on the national security implications of climate change have come in recent years from the National Academy of Sciences as well as from the National Intelligence Council, among other bodies.

39 See, for example, Juliet Eilperin, "U.S. Could Fall Short of 2020 Climate Goal, New Study Says, but Target Remains in Reach," *Washington Post*, February 6, 2013.

40 Michael Forsythe, "China Aims to Spend at Least $360 Billion on Renewable Energy by 2020," *New York Times*, January 5, 2017.

41 The study's findings can be found at the project website: www.millennium assessment.org.

42 The third edition of the biodiversity outlook was released in 2011 (*Global Biodiversity Outlook 3*), and a fourth edition of the report in 2014. These documents can be found at the CBD webpage: www.cbd.int/gbo/.

43 Edward Wong and Jeffrey Gettleman, "China Bans Its Ivory Trade, Moving Against Elephant Poaching," *New York Times*, December 30, 2016. See the CITES webpage for news on what has been a growing demand for ivory: https://cites.org/eng/China_ivory_workshop_release.

44 Raymond Bonner, "Indonesia's Forests Go under the Ax for Flooring," *New York Times*, September 13, 2002. For an assessment of the relationship between biodiversity conservation and poverty, see William M. Adams et al., "Biodiversity Conservation and the Eradication of Poverty," *Science* 306 (November 12, 2004): 1146–1149. For a comprehensive account of illegal timber harvesting across Asia, see Peter S. Goodman and Peter Finn, "A Corrupt Timber Trade: Forests Are Destroyed in China's Race to Feed the Wood-Processing Industry," *Washington Post National Weekly Edition*, April 9–15, 2007: 6–9.

45 Ron Nixon and Coral Davenport, "Environmentalists Praise Wildlife Measures in Trans-Pacific Trade Pact," *New York Times*, October 5, 2015.

46 See also Michael Kimmelman, "The Kind of Thinking Cities Need," *New York Times*, October 30, 2016; and Nicholas S. Wigginton et al., "Cities Are the Future," special symposium in *Science* 352 (May 20, 2016): 904–947.

47 See Alan Cowell, "U.N. Population Meeting Adopts Program of Action," *New York Times*, September 14, 1994; and Paul Lewis, "Population Control Measures to Aid Women Are Stumbling," *New York Times*, April 11, 1999. A fuller account can be found in the UN Population Fund's *The State of the World Population 1999: A Time for Choices*, released in October of that year.

48 Todd S. Purdum, "U.S. Blocks Money for Family Clinics Promoted by U.N.," *New York Times*, July 23, 2002.

49 Celia Dugger, "U.S. Cuts Funds for Family Planning Overseas, Stirring Opposition," *New York Times*, February 15, 2006.

50　James Dao, "U.S. May Abandon Support of U.N. Population Accord," *New York Times*, November 2, 2002.

51　See Peter Baker, "Obama Reverses Rule on U.S. Abortion Aid," *New York Times*, January 26, 2009; and Adriel Bettelheim, "Obama Reverses Bush Policies," *CQ Weekly Online*, January 26, 2009: 184–185.

52　Somini Sengupta, "Trump Revives Ban on Foreign Aid to Groups That Give Abortion Counseling," *New York Times*, January 23, 2017.

53　Population estimates and projections can be found at the Census Bureau site: www.census.gov/. One recent study suggests that the long-term decline in fertility rates in developed nations may be ending, which would please many policymakers who were concerned about the economic consequences of declining populations. Yet the environmental implications would be less favorable. See Rob Stein, "A Welcome Reversal," *Washington Post* National Weekly Edition, August 17–23, 2009.

REFERENCES

Ackerman, Bruce A., and William T. Hassler. 1981. *Clean Coal/Dirty Air*. New Haven, CT: Yale University Press.

Agyeman, Julian. 2013. *Introducing Just Sustainabilities: Policy, Planning, and Practice*. New York: Zed Books.

Agyeman, Julian, Robert D. Bullard, and Bob Evans, eds. 2003. *Just Sustainabilities: Development in an Uneven World*. Cambridge, MA: MIT Press.

Allard, Dean C. 1978. *Spencer Fullerton Baird and the U.S. Fish Commission*. New York: Arno Press.

Anderson, James E. 2015. *Public Policymaking: An Introduction*, 8th edn. Stamford, CT: Cengage Learning.

Anderson, Terry L., and Donald R. Leal. 2001. *Free Market Environmentalism*, rev. edn. New York: Palgrave Macmillan.

Andrews, Richard N. L. 2006a. *Managing the Environment, Managing Ourselves: A History of American Environmental Policy*, 2nd edn. New Haven, CT: Yale University Press.

——. 2006b. "Risk-Based Decision Making: Policy, Science, and Politics." In *Environmental Policy*, 6th edn, edited by Norman J. Vig and Michael E. Kraft, 215–238. Washington, DC: CQ Press.

——. 2013. "Environmental Politics and Policy in Historical Perspective." In *The Oxford Handbook of U.S. Environmental Policy*, edited by Sheldon Kamieniecki and Michael E. Kraft, 23–47. New York: Oxford University Press.

——. 2016. "The Environmental Protection Agency." In *Environmental Policy*, 9th edn, edited by Norman J. Vig and Michael E. Kraft, 151–170. Washington, DC: CQ Press

Annan, Kofi A. 2002. "Toward a Sustainable Future." *Environment* 44 (September): 10–15.

Ansolabehere, Stephen, and David M. Konisky. 2014. *Cheap and Clean: How Americans Think about Energy in the Age of Global Warming*. Cambridge, MA: MIT Press.

Ascher, William, Toddi Steelman, and Robert Healy. 2010. *Knowledge and Environmental Policy: Re-Imagining the Boundaries of Science and Politics*. Cambridge, MA: MIT Press.

Assadourian, Erik. 2006. "Transforming Corporations." In *State of the World 2006*, edited by Linda Starke, 171–190. New York: W. W. Norton.

Axelrod, Regina S. 1984. "Energy Policy: Changing the Rules of the Game." In *Environmental Policy in the 1980s*, edited by Norman J. Vig and Michael E. Kraft, 203–225. Washington, DC: CQ Press.

Axelrod, Regina S., and Miranda A. Schreurs. 2015. "Environmental Policy Making and Global Leadership in the European Union." In *The Global Environment: Institutions, Law, and Policy*, edited by Regina S. Axelrod and Stacy D. VanDeveer, 157–186. Washington, DC: CQ Press.

Axelrod, Regina S., and Stacy VanDeveer, eds. 2015. *The Global Environment: Institutions, Law, and Policy*, 4th edn. Washington, DC: CQ Press.

Baber, Walter F., and Robert V. Bartlett. 2005. *Deliberative Environmental Politics: Democracy and Ecological Rationality*. Cambridge, MA: MIT Press.

——. 2013. "Green Political Ideas and Environmental Policy." In *The Oxford Handbook of U.S. Environmental Policy*, edited by Sheldon Kamieniecki and Michael E. Kraft, 48–67. New York: Oxford University Press.

——. 2015. *Consensus and Global Environmental Governance: Deliberative Democracy in Nature's Regime*. Cambridge, MA: MIT Press.

Bäckstrand, Karin. 2017. "Critical Loads: Negotiating What Nature Can Withstand." In *Conceptual Innovation in Environmental Policy*, edited by James Meadowcroft and Daniel J. Fiorino. Cambridge, MA: MIT Press.

Balmford, Andrew, Aaron Bruner, Philip Cooper, Robert Costanza, Stephen Farber, Rhys E. Green, et al. 2002. "Economic Reasons for Conserving Wild Nature." *Science* 297: 950–953.

Bartlett, Robert V. 1986. "Ecological Rationality: Reason and Environmental Policy." *Environmental Ethics* 8 (Fall): 221–240.

——, ed. 1989. *Policy Through Impact Assessment: Institutionalized Analysis as a Policy Strategy*. New York: Greenwood Press.

——. 1990. "Comprehensive Environmental Decision Making: Can It Work?" In *Environmental Policy in the 1990s*, edited by Norman J. Vig and Michael E. Kraft, 1–23. Washington, DC: CQ Press.

——. 1994. "Evaluating Environmental Policy Success and Failure." In *Environmental Policy in the 1990s*, 2nd edn, edited by Norman J. Vig and Michael E. Kraft, 167–187. Washington, DC: CQ Press.

Bartlett, Robert V., and Charles R. Malone, eds. 1993. "Science and the National Environmental Policy Act." *The Environmental Professional* 15(1): 1–149.

Baue, Bill. 2008. "Investing for Sustainability." In *State of the World 2008*, edited by Linda Starke, 180–195. New York: W. W. Norton.

Baumgartner, Frank R., and Bryan D. Jones. 1993. *Agendas and Instability in American Politics*. Chicago, IL: University of Chicago Press.

——, eds. 2002. *Policy Dynamics*. Chicago, IL: University of Chicago Press.

Beardsley, Dan, Terry Davies, and Robert Hersh. 1997. "Improving Environmental Management: What Works, What Doesn't." *Environment* 39 (September): 6–9, 28–35.

Beierle, Thomas C., and Jerry Cayford. 2002. *Democracy in Practice: Public Participation in Environmental Decisions*. Washington, DC: RFF Press.

Below, Amy. 2013. "Parties, Campaigns, and Elections." In *The Oxford Handbook of U.S. Environmental Policy*, edited by Sheldon Kamieniecki and Michael E. Kraft, 525–553. New York: Oxford University Press.

Benedick, Richard E. 1991. *Ozone Diplomacy*. Cambridge, MA: Harvard University Press.

Bennear, Lori Snyder, and Cary Coglianese. 2005. "Measuring Progress: Program Evaluation of Environmental Policies." *Environment* 47 (March): 22–39.

——. 2013. "Flexible Approaches to Environmental Regulation." In *The Oxford Handbook of U.S. Environmental Policy*, edited by Sheldon Kamieniecki and Michael E. Kraft, 582–604. New York: Oxford University Press.

Berkes, Fikret. 1999. *Sacred Ecology: Traditional Ecological Knowledge and Resource Management*. Philadelphia, PA: Taylor & Francis.

Berry, Jeffrey M. 1977. *Lobbying for the People: The Political Behavior of Public Interest Groups.* Princeton, NJ: Princeton University Press.

Berry, Jeffrey M., and Kent E. Portney. 1995. "Centralizing Regulatory Control and Interest Group Access: The Quayle Council on Competitiveness." In *Interest Group Politics*, 4th edn, edited by Allan J. Cigler and Burdett A. Loomis, 319–347. Washington, DC: CQ Press.

Berry, Jeffrey M., and Clyde Wilcox. 2009. *The Interest Group Society*, 5th edn. New York: Longman.

Betsill, Michele M., and Barry G. Rabe. 2009. "Climate Change and Multilevel Governance: The Evolving State and Local Roles." In *Toward Sustainable Communities: Transformations and Transition in Environmental Policy*, 2nd edn, edited by Daniel A. Mazmanian and Michael E. Kraft, 201–225. Cambridge, MA: MIT Press.

Bezdek, Roger H. 1993. "Environment and Economy: What's the Bottom Line?" *Environment* 35 (September): 7–11, 25–32.

Birkland, Thomas A. 1997. *After Disaster: Agenda Setting, Public Policy, and Focusing Events.* Washington, DC: Georgetown University Press.

Borck, Jonathan C., and Cary Coglianese. 2009. "Voluntary Environmental Programs: Assessing Their Effectiveness." *Annual Review of Environment and Resources* 34: 305–324.

Bosso, Christopher J. 1987. *Pesticides and Politics: The Life Cycle of a Public Issue.* Pittsburgh, PA: University of Pittsburgh Press.

——. 1994. "After the Movement: Environmental Activism in the 1990s." In *Environmental Policy in the 1990s*, 2nd edn, edited by Norman J. Vig and Michael E. Kraft, 31–50. Washington, DC: CQ Press.

——. 2000. "Environmental Groups and the New Political Landscape." In *Environmental Policy*, 4th edn, edited by Norman J. Vig and Michael E. Kraft, 55–76. Washington, DC: CQ Press.

——. 2005. *Environment, Inc.: From Grassroots to Beltway.* Lawrence: University Press of Kansas.

Bosso, Christopher J., and Michael Thomas Collins. 2002. "Just Another Tool? How Environmental Groups Use the Internet." In *Interest Group Politics*, 6th edn, edited by Allan J. Cigler and Burdett A. Loomis, 95–114. Washington, DC: CQ Press.

Bosso, Christopher J., and Deborah Lynn Guber. 2006. "Maintaining Presence: Environmental Advocacy and the Permanent Campaign." In *Environmental Policy*, 6th edn, edited by Norman J. Vig and Michael E. Kraft, 78–99. Washington, DC: CQ Press.

Bowman, Ann O'M., and Mark E. Tompkins. 1993. "Environmental Protection and Economic Development: Can States Have It Both Ways?" Paper presented at the annual meeting of the American Political Science Association, Washington, DC, September 2–5.

Brick, Philip D., and R. McGreggor Cawley, eds. 1996. *A Wolf in the Garden: The Land Rights Movement and the New Environmental Debate.* Lanham, MD: Rowman and Littlefield.

Brooks, Karl Boyd. 2009. *Before Earth Day: The Origins of American Environmental Law, 1945–1970.* Lawrence: University Press of Kansas.

Brown, Lester R. 2010. *Plan B 4.0: Mobilizing to Save Civilization.* New York: W. W. Norton.

Browner, Carol M. 1993. "Environmental Tobacco Smoke: EPA's Report." *EPA Journal* 19 (October–December): 18–19.

Bryant, Bunyan, eds. 1995. *Environmental Justice: Issues, Politics, and Solutions.* Washington, DC: Island Press.

Bryant, Bunyan, and Paul Mohai, eds. 1992. *Race and the Incidence of Environmental Hazards: A Time for Discourse.* Boulder, CO: Westview Press.

Bryner, Gary C. 1987. *Bureaucratic Discretion: Law and Policy in Federal Regulatory Agencies.* New York: Pergamon Press.

——. 1995. *Blue Skies, Green Politics: The Clean Air Act of 1990 and Its Implementation,* 2nd edn. Washington, DC: CQ Press.

——. 1999. "Agenda 21: Myth or Reality?" In *The Global Environment,* edited by Norman J. Vig and Regina S. Axelrod, 157–189. Washington, DC: CQ Press.

Bryner, Gary C., and Robert J. Duffy. 2012. *Integrating Climate, Energy, and Air Pollution Policies.* Cambridge, MA: MIT Press.

Bullard, Robert D. 1994. "Overcoming Racism in Environmental Decisionmaking." *Environment* 36 (May): 10–20, 39–44.

Burger, Joanna, and Michael Gochfeld. 1998. "The Tragedy of the Commons: 30 Years Later." *Environment* 40 (December): 4–13, 26–27.

Caldwell, Lynton Keith. 1970. *Environment: A Challenge for Modern Society.* Garden City, NY: Doubleday.

——. 1982. *Science and the National Environmental Policy Act: Redirecting Policy Through Procedural Reform.* Tuscaloosa: University of Alabama Press.

——. 1990. "International Environmental Politics: America's Response to Global Imperatives." In *Environmental Policy in the 1990s,* edited by Norman J. Vig and Michael E. Kraft, 301–321. Washington, DC: CQ Press.

——. 1996. *International Environmental Policy: Emergence and Dimensions,* 3rd edn. Durham, NC: Duke University Press.

——. 1998. *The National Environmental Policy Act: An Agenda for the Future.* Bloomington: Indiana University Press.

Calvert, Jerry W. 1989. "Party Politics and Environmental Policy." In *Environmental Politics and Policy,* edited by James P. Lester, 158–178. Durham, NC: Duke University Press.

Cantrill, James G., and Christine L. Oravec, eds. 1996. *The Symbolic Earth: Discourse and Our Creation of the Environment.* Lexington: University Press of Kentucky.

Carnegie Commission. 1992. *Environmental Research and Development: Strengthening the Federal Infrastructure.* New York: Carnegie Commission on Science, Technology, and Government.

——. 1993. *Risk and the Environment: Improving Regulatory Decision Making.* New York: Carnegie Commission on Science, Technology, and Government.

Catton, William R., Jr., and Riley E. Dunlap. 1980. "A New Ecological Paradigm for Post-Exuberant Sociology." *American Behavioral Scientist* 24: 15–47.

Cawley, R. McGreggor. 1993. *Federal Land, Western Anger: The Sagebrush Rebellion and Environmental Politics.* Lawrence: University of Kansas Press.

Chasek, Pamela S., David L. Downie, and Janet Welsh Brown. 2014. *Global Environmental Politics,* 6th edn. Boulder, CO: Westview Press.

Chivian, Eric, Michael McCally, Howard Hu, and Andrew Haines, eds. 1993. *Critical Condition: Human Health and the Environment.* Cambridge, MA: MIT Press.

Cincotta, Richard P., and Barbara B. Crane. 2001. "The Mexico City Policy and U.S. Family Planning Assistance." *Science* 294 (October 19): 525–526.

Clarke, Jeanne Nienaber, and Daniel McCool. 1996. *Staking Out the Terrain: Power and Performance Among Natural Resource Agencies*, 2nd edn. Albany: State University of New York Press.

Clary, Bruce B., and Michael E. Kraft. 1989. "Environmental Assessment, Science, and Policy Failure: The Politics of Nuclear Waste Disposal." In *Policy Through Impact Assessment*, edited by Robert Bartlett, 37–50. New York: Greenwood Press.

Cobb, Clifford, Ted Halstead, and Jonathan Rowe. 1995. "If the GDP Is Up, Why Is America Down?" *The Atlantic Monthly*, October: 59–78.

Coglianese, Cary. 1997. "Assessing Consensus: The Promise and Performance of Negotiated Rulemaking." *Duke Law Journal* 46: 1255–1349.

—— ed. 2012. *Regulatory Breakdown: The Crisis of Confidence in U.S. Regulation.* Philadelphia: University of Pennsylvania Press.

—— ed. 2016. *Achieving Regulatory Excellence.* Washington, DC: Brookings Institution Press.

Coglianese, Cary, and Laurie K. Allen. 2004. "Does Consensus Make Common Sense? An Analysis of EPA's Common Sense Initiative." *Environment* 46 (January): 10–25.

Coglianese, Cary, and Lori S. Bennear. 2005. "Program Evaluation of Environmental Policies: Toward Evidence-Based Decision Making." In *Decision Making for the Environment: Social and Behavioral Science Research Priorities*, edited by Garry D. Brewer and Paul C. Stern, 246–273. Washington, DC: National Academy Press.

Coglianese, Cary, Adam M. Finkel, and Christopher Carrigan, eds. 2014. *Does Regulation Kill Jobs?* Philadelphia: University of Pennsylvania Press.

Coglianese, Cary, and Jennifer Nash. 2001. *Regulating from the Inside: Can Environmental Management Systems Achieve Policy Goals?* Washington, DC: RFF Press.

——. 2002. "Policy Options for Improving Environmental Management in the Private Sector." *Environment* 44 (November): 11–23.

——. 2006. *Leveraging the Private Sector: Management-Based Strategies for Improving Environmental Performance.* Washington, DC: RFF Press.

Cohen, Joel E. 1995. *How Many People Can the Earth Support?* New York: W. W. Norton.

——. 2011. "Seven Billion." *New York Times*, October 23.

Cohen, Richard E. 1995. *Washington at Work: Back Rooms and Clean Air*, 2nd edn. New York: Allyn & Bacon.

Cohen, Steven. 1984. "Defusing the Toxic Time Bomb: Federal Hazardous Waste Programs." In *Environmental Policy in the 1980s*, edited by Norman J. Vig and Michael E. Kraft, 273–291. Washington, DC: CQ Press.

Cohen, Steven, Sheldon Kamieniecki, and Matthew A. Cahn. 2005. *Strategic Planning in Environmental Regulation: A Policy Approach That Works.* Cambridge, MA: MIT Press.

Colborn, Theo, Dianne Dumanoski, and John Peterson Myers. 1996. *Our Stolen Future: Are We Threatening Our Fertility, Intelligence, and Survival?* New York: Dutton.

Cole, Leonard A. 1993. *Element of Risk: The Politics of Radon*. Washington, DC: AAAS Press.

Committee on Science for EPA's Future. 2012. *Science for Environmental Protection: The Road Ahead*. Washington, DC: National Academy of Sciences.

Conant, James K., and Peter J. Balint. 2016. *The Life Cycles of the Council on Environmental Quality and the Environmental Protection Agency: 1970–2035*. New York: Oxford University Press.

Congressional Research Service. 2012. *Federal Land Ownership: Overview and Data*. Washington, DC: Congressional Research Service, February 8.

Cooper, Joseph, and William F. West. 1988. "Presidential Power and Republican Government: The Theory and Practice of OMB Review of Agency Rules." *Journal of Politics* 50 (November): 864–895.

Cooper, Mary H. (and the staff of *CQ Weekly*). 1999. "Energy Politics: What Next?" *CQ Outlook*, Supplement to *CQ Weekly*, March 20: 1–30.

——. 2002. "Energy Security at Risk: How Vulnerable Is America's Energy System?" *CQ Outlook*, Supplement to *CQ Weekly*, February 23: 1–15.

Cortner, Hanna J., and Margaret A. Moote. 1999. *The Politics of Ecosystem Management*. Washington, DC: Island Press.

Costanza, Robert. 1991. *Ecological Economics: The Science and Management of Sustainability*. New York: Columbia University Press.

Costanza, Robert, Ralph d'Arge, Randolf de Groot, Stephen Farber, Monica Grasso, and Bruce Hannon. 1997. "The Value of the World's Ecosystem Services and Natural Capital." *Nature* 387 (May 15): 253–260.

Council on Environmental Quality (CEQ). 1980. *Public Opinion on Environmental Issues: Results of a National Public Opinion Survey*. Washington, DC: CEQ.

——. 1998. *Environmental Quality, Along the American River: The 1996 Report of the Council on Environmental Quality*. Washington, DC: CEQ.

——. 1999. *Environmental Quality: The 1997 Report of the Council on Environmental Quality*. Washington, DC: CEQ.

Coyle, Kevin. 2005. *Environmental Literacy in America*. Washington, DC: National Environmental Education and Training Foundation, September.

Cronon, William. 1983. *Changes in the Land: Indians, Colonists, and the Ecology of New England*. New York: Hill and Wang.

Crosette, Barbara. 1999. "Rethinking Population at a Global Milestone." *New York Times*, September 19: "Week in Review."

Culhane, Paul J. 1981. *Public Lands Politics: Interest Group Influence on the Forest Service and the Bureau of Land Management*. Baltimore, MD: Johns Hopkins University Press.

——. 1984. "Sagebrush Rebels in Office: Jim Watt's Land and Water Politics." In *Environmental Policy in the 1980s*, edited by Norman J. Vig and Michael E. Kraft, 293–317. Washington, DC: CQ Press.

Daily, Gretchen C. 1997. *Nature's Services: Societal Dependence on Natural Ecosystems*. Washington, DC: Island Press.

Daily, Gretchen C., and Katherine Ellison. 2002. *The New Economy of Nature: The Quest to Make Conservation Profitable*. Washington, DC: Island Press.

Daley, Dorothy M. 2007. "Citizen Groups and Scientific Decisionmaking: Does Public Participation Influence Environmental Outcomes?" *Journal of Policy Analysis and Management* 26(2): 349–368.

——. 2013. "Public Participation, Citizen Engagement, and Environmental Decision-Making." In *The Oxford Handbook of U.S. Environmental Policy*, edited by Sheldon Kamieniecki and Michael E. Kraft, 487–503. New York: Oxford University Press.

Dalton, Russell J. 2005. "The Greening of the Globe? Cross-National Levels of Environmental Group Membership." *Environmental Politics* 14(1) (August): 441–459.

Dana, Samuel Trask, and Sally K. Fairfax. 1980. *Forest and Range Policy: Its Development in the United States*, 2nd edn. New York: McGraw-Hill.

Daniels, David P., Jon A. Krosnick, Michael P. Tichy, and Trevor Tompson. 2013. "Public Opinion on Environmental Policy in the United States." In *The Oxford Handbook of U.S. Environmental Policy*, ed. Sheldon Kamieniecki and Michael E. Kraft, 461–486. New York: Oxford University Press.

Davidson, Roger H., J. Oleszek Walter, Frances E. Lee, and Eric Schickler. 2016. *Congress and Its Members*, 15th edn. Washington, DC: CQ Press.

Davies, J. Clarence, ed. 1996. *Comparing Environmental Risks: Tools for Setting Government Priorities*. Washington, DC: Resources for the Future.

Davies, J. Clarence, III, and Barbara S. Davies. 1975. *The Politics of Pollution*, 2nd edn. Indianapolis, IN: Bobbs-Merrill.

Davies, J. Clarence, and Jan Mazurek. 1998. *Pollution Control in the United States: Evaluating the System*. Washington, DC: Resources for the Future.

Davis, Charles, ed. 2001. *Western Public Lands and Environmental Politics*, 2nd edn. Boulder, CO: Westview Press.

Desai, Uday, ed. 2002. *Environmental Politics and Policy in Industrialized Countries*. Cambridge, MA: MIT Press.

De Saillan, Charles. 1993. "In Praise of Super-Fund." *Environment* 35 (October): 42–44.

DeSombre, Elizabeth R. 2000. *Domestic Sources of International Environmental Policy: Industry, Environmentalists, and U.S. Power*. Cambridge, MA: MIT Press.

——. 2002. *The Global Environment and World Politics*. New York: Continuum Books.

——. 2006. *Global Environmental Institutions*. London: Routledge.

——. 2015. "Domestic Sources of U.S. Unilateralism." In *The Global Environment*, 4th edn, edited by Regina S. Axelrod and Stacy D. VanDeveer, 133–156. Washington, DC: CQ Press.

DeSombre, Elizabeth R., and J. Samuel Barkin. 2011. *Fish*. Malden, MA: Polity Press.

Deudney, Daniel H., and Richard A. Matthew, eds. 1999. *Contested Grounds: Security and Conflict in the New Environmental Politics*. Albany, NY: State University of New York Press.

DiMento, Joseph F. C., and Pamela Doughman, eds. 2014. *Climate Change: What It Means for Us, Our Children, and Our Grandchildren*, 2nd edn. Cambridge, MA: MIT Press.

Dower, Roger. 1990. "Hazardous Wastes." In *Public Policies for Environmental Protection*, edited by Paul R. Portney, 151–194. Washington, DC: Resource for the Future.

Downie, David Leonard. 2015. "International Environmental Regimes and the Success of Global Ozone Policy." In *The Global Environment*, 4th edn, edited by Regina S. Axelrod and Stacy D. VanDeveer, 83–109. Washington, DC: CQ Press.

Downs, Anthony. 1972. "Up and Down with Ecology: The 'Issue-Attention Cycle.'" *The Public Interest* 28 (Summer): 38–50.

Dryzek, John S. 2005. *The Politics of the Earth: Environmental Discourses*, 2nd edn. New York: Oxford University Press.

Dryzek, John S., and James P. Lester. 1995. "Alternative Views of the Environmental Problematic." In *Environmental Politics and Policy*, 2nd edn, edited by James P. Lester, 328–346. Durham, NC: Duke University Press.

Duffy, Robert J. 1997. *Nuclear Politics in America: A History and Theory of Government Regulation*. Lawrence: University Press of Kansas.

——. 2003. *The Green Agenda in American Politics: New Strategies for the Twenty-First Century*. Lawrence: University of Kansas Press.

——. 2013. "Organized Interests and Environmental Policy." In *The Oxford Handbook of U.S. Environmental Policy*, edited by Sheldon Kamieniecki and Michael E. Kraft, 504–524. New York: Oxford University Press.

Dunlap, Riley E. 1987. "Polls, Pollution, and Politics Revisited: Public Opinion on the Environment in the Reagan Era." *Environment* 29 (July/August): 6–11, 32–37.

——. 1992. "Trends in Public Opinion Toward Environmental Issues: 1965–1990." In *American Environmentalism*, edited by Riley E. Dunlap and Angela G. Mertig, 89–116. Philadelphia, PA: Taylor & Francis.

——. 1995. "Public Opinion and Environmental Policy." In *Environmental Politics and Policy*, 2nd edn, edited by James P. Lester, 63–114. Durham, NC: Duke University Press.

——. 2013. "Climate Change Skepticism and Denial: An Introduction." *American Behavioral Scientist* 57(6): 691–698.

Dunlap, Riley E., George H. Gallup, Jr., and Alec M. Gallup. 1993. "Of Global Concern: Results of the Health of the Planet Survey." *Environment* 35: 7–15, 23–48.

Dunlap, Riley E., and Peter J. Jacques. 2013. "Manufacturing Uncertainty: Conservative Think Tanks and Climate Change Denial Books." Available at the Yale Forum on Climate Change and the Media: www.yaleclimatemediaforum. org.

Dunlap, Riley E., Michael E. Kraft, and Eugene A. Rosa, eds. 1993. *Public Reactions to Nuclear Waste: Citizens' Views of Repository Siting*. Durham, NC: Duke University Press.

Dunlap, Riley E., and Aaron M. McCright. 2008. "A Widening Gap: Republican and Democratic Views on Climate Change." *Environment* 50 (November/December): 26–35.

——. 2015. "Challenging Climate Change: The Denial Countermovement." In *Climate Change and Society: Sociological Perspectives*, edited by Riley E. Dunlap and R. J. Brule, 300–332. New York: Oxford University Press.

Dunlap, Riley E., Aaron M. McCright, and Jerrod H. Yarosh. 2016. "The Political Divide on Climate Change: Partisan Polarization Widens in the U.S." *Environment* 58(5) (September/October): 4–22.

Dunlap, Riley E., and Richard York. 2008. "The Globalization of Environmental Concern and the Limits of the Post-Materialist Values Explanation: Evidence from Four Cross-National Surveys." *Sociological Quarterly* 49(4): 879–883.

——. 2012. "The Globalization of Environmental Concern. In *Comparative Environmental Politics: Theory, Practice, and Prospects*, edited by Paul F. Steinberg and Stacy D. VanDeveer, 89–112. Cambridge, MA: MIT Press.

Durant, Robert F. 1992. *The Administrative Presidency Revisited: Public Lands, the BLM, and the Reagan Revolution*. Albany: State University of New York Press.

Durant, Robert F., Daniel J. Fiorino, and Rosemary O'Leary, eds. 2017. *Environmental Governance Reconsidered: Challenges, Choices, and Opportunities*, 2nd edn. Cambridge, MA: MIT Press.

Durning, Alan. 1992. *How Much Is Enough? The Consumer Society and the Future of the Earth*. New York: W. W. Norton.

Eads, George C., and Michael Fix. 1984. *Relief or Reform? Reagan's Regulatory Dilemma*. Washington, DC: Urban Institute.

Eccleston, Charles H. 1999. *The NEPA Planning Process: A Comprehensive Guide with Emphasis on Efficiency*. New York: John Wiley.

Edelman, Murray. 1964. *The Symbolic Uses of Politics*. Urbana: University of Illinois Press.

Ehrenfeld, John R. 2008. *Sustainability by Design: A Subversive Strategy for Transforming Our Consumer Culture*. New Haven, CT: Yale University Press.

Eisner, Marc Allen. 2007. *Governing the Environment: The Transformation of Environmental Regulation*. Boulder, CO: Lynne Rienner.

Eisner, Marc Allen, Jeff Worsham, and Evan J. Ringquist. 2006. *Contemporary Regulatory Policy*, 2nd edn. Boulder, CO: Lynne Rienner.

Ernst, Howard R. 2003. *Chesapeake Bay Blues: Science, Politics, and the Struggle to Save the Bay*. Lanham, MD: Rowman and Littlefield.

——. 2009. *Fight for the Bay: Why a Dark Green Environmental Awakening Is Needed to Save the Chesapeake Bay*. Lanham, MD: Rowman and Littlefield.

Erskine, Hazel. 1972. "The Polls: Pollution and Its Costs." *Public Opinion Quarterly* 36 (Spring): 120–135.

Eskeland, Gunnar A., and Ann E. Harrison. 2003. "Moving to Greener Pastures? Multinationals and the Pollution Haven Hypothesis." *Journal of Development Economics* 70 (February): 1–23.

Esty, Daniel C. 2015. "Free Trade and Environmental Protection." In *The Global Environment: Institutions, Law, and Policy*, 4th edn, edited by Regina S. Axelrod and Stacy D. VanDeveer, 330–349. Washington, DC: CQ Press.

Esty, Daniel C., and Andrew S. Winston. 2006. *Green to Gold: How Smart Companies Use Environmental Strategy to Innovate, Create Value, and Build Competitive Advantage*. New Haven, CT: Yale University Press.

Evans, Ben, and Joseph J. Schatz. 2005. "Details of Energy Policy Law." *CQ Weekly* 5 (September): 2337–2345.

Evans, David A., and Joseph A. Kruger. 2007. "Where Are the Sky's Limits? Lessons from Chicago's Cap-and-Trade Program." *Environment* 49(2) (March): 18–32.

Fairfax, Sally K., and Darla Guenzler. 2001. *Conservation Trusts*. Lawrence: University Press of Kansas.

Fairfax, Sally K., Lauren Gwin, Mary Ann King, Leigh Raymond, and Laura A. Watt. 2005. *Buying Nature: The Limits of Land Acquisition as a Conservation Strategy, 1780–2004*. Cambridge, MA: MIT Press.

Faure, Michael G., and Jürgen Lefevere. 2015. "Compliance with Global Environmental Policy: Climate Change and Ozone Layer Cases." In *The Global Environment: Institutions, Law, and Policy*, 4th edn, edited by Regina S. Axelrod and Stacy D. VanDeveer, 110–132. Washington, DC: CQ Press.

Feiock, Richard C., and Christopher Stream. 2001. "Environmental Protection Versus Economic Development: A False Tradeoff?" *Public Administration Review* 61(3) (May/June): 313–321.

Fiorino, Daniel J. 2001. "Environmental Policy as Learning: A New View of an Old Landscape." *Public Administration Review* 61(3) (May/June): 322–334.

———. 2006. *The New Environmental Regulation*. Cambridge, MA: MIT Press.

———. 2009. "Regulating for the Future: A New Approach for Environmental Governance." In *Toward Sustainable Communities: Transformations and Transition in Environmental Policy*, 2nd edn, edited by Daniel A. Mazmanian and Michael E. Kraft, 63–86. Cambridge, MA: MIT Press.

———. 2013. "Environmental Bureaucracies: The Environmental Protection Agency." In *The Oxford Handbook of U.S. Environmental Policy*, edited by Sheldon Kamieniecki and Michael E. Kraft, 329–354. New York: Oxford University Press.

Fischer, Frank. 1990. *Technocracy and the Politics of Expertise*. Newbury Park, CA: Sage.

Flavin, Christopher. 2008. "Building a Low-Carbon Economy." In *State of the World 2008*, edited by Linda Starke, 75–90. New York: W. W. Norton.

Flynn, James, James Chalmers, Doug Easterling, Roger Kasperson, Howard Kunreuther, C. K. Mertz, et al. 1995. *One Hundred Centuries of Solitude: Redirecting America's High-Level Nuclear Waste Policy*. Boulder, CO: Westview Press.

Foreman, Christopher H., Jr. 1998. *The Promise and Peril of Environmental Justice*. Washington, DC: Brookings Institution Press.

Foss, Philip O. 1960. *Politics and Grass*. Seattle: University of Washington Press.

Freeman, A. Myrick, III. 1990. "Water Pollution Policy." In *Public Policies for Environmental Protection*, edited by Paul R. Portney, 97–149. Washington, DC: Resources for the Future.

———. 2006. "Economics, Incentives, and Environmental Regulation." In *Environmental Policy*, 6th edn, edited by Norman J. Vig and Michael E. Kraft, 193–214. Washington, DC: CQ Press.

Freemuth, John C. 1991. *Islands under Siege: National Parks and the Politics of External Threats*. Lawrence: University of Kansas Press.

Freudenburg, William R., and Robert Gramling. 2010. *Blowout in the Gulf: The BP Oil Spill Disaster and the Future of Energy in America*. Cambridge, MA: MIT Press.

Friedman, Benjamin M. 2005. *The Moral Consequence of Economic Growth*. New York: Alfred A. Knopf.

Friedman, Thomas. 2006. *The World Is Flat: A Brief History of the Twenty-First Century*. New York: Farrar, Straus and Giroux.

———. 2008. *Hot, Flat, and Crowded: Why We Need a Green Revolution and How It Can Renew America*. New York: Farrar, Straus and Giroux.

Furlong, Scott R. 1995a. "The 1992 Regulatory Moratorium: Did It Make a Difference? *Public Administration Review* 55: 254–262.

——. 1995b. "Reinventing Regulatory Development at the Environmental Protection Agency." *Policy Studies Journal* 23 (Fall): 466–482.

——. 1997. "Interest Group Influence on Rulemaking." *Administration and Society* 29 (July): 325–347.

——. 2007. "Businesses and the Environment: Influencing Agency Policymaking." In *Business and Environmental Policy*, edited by Michael E. Kraft and Sheldon Kamieniecki, 155–184. Cambridge, MA: MIT Press.

Gaddie, Ronald Keith, and James L. Regens. 2000. *Regulating Wetlands Protection: Environmental Federalism and the States*. Albany: State University of New York Press.

Gallagher, Kelly Sims, and Joanna I. Lewis. 2016. "China's Quest for a Green Economy." In *Environmental Policy*, 9th edn, edited by Norman J. Vig and Michael E. Kraft, 333–356. Washington, DC: CQ Press.

Gardiner, David, and Lisa Jacobson. 2002. "Will Voluntary Programs Be Sufficient to Reduce U.S. Greenhouse Gas Emissions?" *Environment* 44 (October): 24–33.

Gerlak, Andrea K., Tanya Heikkila, and Mark Lubell. 2013. "The Promise and Performance of Collaborative Governance." In *The Oxford Handbook of U.S. Environmental Policy*, edited by Sheldon Kamieniecki and Michael E. Kraft, 413–436. New York: Oxford University Press.

Gibbs, W. Wayt. 2001. "On the Termination of Species." *Scientific American* 227 (November): 40–49.

Giddens, Anthony. 2011. *The Politics of Climate Change*, 2nd edn. Malden, MA: Polity Press.

Global Strategy Group. 2004. "The Environmental Deficit: Survey on American Attitudes on the Environment." New York: Global Strategy Group and Yale University School of Forestry and Environmental Studies, May. Available at: www.yale.edu/forestry/downloads/yale_ enviro_poll.pdf.

Gonzalez, George A. 2001. *Corporate Power and the Environment: The Political Economy of U.S. Environmental Policy*. Lanham, MD: Rowman and Littlefield.

Goodwin, Craufurd D., ed. 1981. *Energy Policy in Perspective*. Washington, DC: Brookings Institution Press.

Gould, Lewis L. 1999. *Lady Bird Johnson: Our Environmental First Lady*. Lawrence: University of Kansas Press.

Graham, Mary, and Catherine Miller. 2001. "Disclosure of Toxic Releases in the United States." *Environment* 43: 8–20.

Greve, Michael S., and Fred L. Smith, Jr., eds. 1992. *Environmental Politics: Public Costs, Private Rewards*. New York: Praeger.

Guber, Deborah Lynn. 2003. *The Grassroots of a Green Revolution: Polling America on the Environment*. Cambridge, MA: MIT Press.

Guber, Deborah Lynn, and Christopher J. Bosso. 2007. "Framing ANWR: Citizens, Consumers, and the Privileged Position of Business." In *Business and Environmental Policy*, edited by Michael E. Kraft and Sheldon Kamieniecki, 35–59. Cambridge, MA: MIT Press.

——. 2013a. "High Hopes and Bitter Disappointment': Public Discourse and the Limits of the Environmental Movement in Climate Change Politics." In *Environmental Policy*, 8th edn, edited by Norman J. Vig and Michael E. Kraft, 54–82. Washington, DC: CQ Press.

——. 2013b. "Issue Framing, Agenda Setting, and Environmental Discourse." In *The Oxford Handbook of U.S. Environmental Policy*, edited by Sheldon

Kamieniecki and Michael E. Kraft, 437–460. New York: Oxford University Press.

Hadden, Susan G. 1986. *Read the Label: Reducing Risk by Providing Information.* Boulder, CO: Westview Press.

———. 1989. *A Citizen's Right to Know: Risk Communication and Public Policy.* Boulder, CO: Westview Press.

———. 1991. "Public Perception of Hazardous Waste." *Risk Analysis* 11(1): 47–57.

Haeder, Simon F., and Susan Webb Yackee. 2015. "Influence and the Administrative Process: Lobbying the U.S. President's Office of Management and Budget." *American Political Science Review* 109(3): 507–522.

Hall, Bob, and Mary Lee Kerr. 1991. *1991–92 Green Index: A State-by-State Guide to the Nation's Environmental Health.* Washington, DC: Island Press.

Halley, Alexis A. 1994. "Hazardous Waste Disposal: The Double-Edged Sword of the RCRA Land-Ban Hammers." In *Who Makes Public Policy? The Struggle for Control between Congress and the Executive*, edited by Robert S. Gilmour and Alexis A. Halley, 85–126. Chatham, NJ: Chatham House.

Hamilton, James T. 2005. *Regulation Through Revelation: The Origins, Politics, and Impacts of the Toxics Inventory Release Program.* New York: Cambridge University Press.

Hamilton, Michael S. 2013. *Energy Policy Analysis: A Conceptual Framework.* Armonk, NY: M. E. Sharpe.

Hardin, Garrett. 1968. "The Tragedy of the Commons." *Science* 162 (December 13): 1243–1248.

Harrington, Winston, Richard D. Morgenstern, and Peter Nelson. 1999. "Predicting the Costs of Environmental Regulations: How Accurate Are Regulators Estimates?" *Environment* 41 (September): 10–14, 40–44.

Harrington, Winston, Richard D. Morgenstern, and Thomas Sterner, eds. 2004. *Choosing Environmental Policy: Comparing Instruments and Outcomes in the United States and Europe.* Washington, DC: RFF Press.

Harris, Richard A., and Sidney M. Milkis. 1996. *The Politics of Regulatory Change: A Tale of Two Agencies*, 2nd edn. New York: Oxford University Press.

Harrison, Kathryn. 1995. "Is Cooperation the Answer? Canadian Environmental Enforcement in Comparative Context." *Journal of Policy Analysis and Management* 14 (Spring): 221–244.

Harrison, Kathryn, and Lisa McIntosh Sundstrom, eds. 2010. *Global Commons and Domestic Interests: The Comparative Politics of Climate Change.* Cambridge, MA: MIT Press.

Hawken, Paul. 1994. *The Ecology of Commerce: A Declaration of Sustainability.* New York: Harper Business.

———. 2007. *Blessed Unrest: How the Largest Social Movement in History Is Restoring Grace, Justice, and Beauty to the World.* New York: Penguin Books.

Hawken, Paul, Amory B. Lovins, and L. Hunter Lovins. 1999. *Natural Capitalism: Creating the Next Industrial Revolution.* New York: Little, Brown.

Hays, Samuel P. 1959. *Conservation and the Gospel of Efficiency.* Cambridge: Cambridge University Press.

———. 1987. *Beauty, Health, and Permanence: Environmental Politics in the United States, 1955–1985.* New York: Cambridge University Press.

———. 2000. *A History of Environmental Politics Since 1945.* Pittsburgh, PA: University of Pittsburgh Press.

Heald, Seth. 2016. "The Pope's Climate Message in the United States: Moral Arguments and Moral Disengagement." *Environment* 58(3): 4–13.

Heberlein, Thomas A. 2012. *Navigating Environmental Attitudes.* New York: Oxford University Press.

Hecht, Joy E. 1999. "Environmental Accounting: Where We Are Now, Where We Are Heading." *Resources* 135 (Spring): 14–17.

Hempel, Lamont C. 2006. "Climate Policy on the Installment Plan." In *Environmental Policy*, 6th edn, edited by Norman J. Vig and Michael E. Kraft, 288–310. Washington, DC: CQ Press.

———. 2009. "Conceptual and Analytical Challenges in Building Sustainable Communities." In *Toward Sustainable Communities*, 2nd edn, edited by Daniel A. Mazmanian and Michael E. Kraft, 33–62. Cambridge, MA: MIT Press.

———. 2013. "Evolving Concepts of Sustainability in Environmental Policy." In *The Oxford Handbook of U.S. Environmental Policy*, edited by Sheldon Kamieniecki and Michael E. Kraft, 67–92. New York: Oxford University Press.

Hird, John A. 1994. *Superfund: The Political Economy of Risk.* Baltimore, MD: Johns Hopkins University Press.

H. John Heinz III Center for Science, Economics and the Environment (Heinz Center). 2008. *The State of the Nation's Ecosystems: Measuring the Land, Waters, and Living Resources of the United States*, 2nd edn. Washington, DC: Island Press.

Hockenstein, B. Jeremy, Robert N. Stavins, and Bradley W. Whitehead. 1997. "Crafting the Next Generation of Market-Based Environmental Tools." *Environment* 39 (May): 13–20, 30–33.

Hogan, William H. 1984. "Energy Policy." In *Natural Resources and the Environment*, edited by Paul R. Portney. Washington, DC: Resources for the Future.

Huber, Peter. 2000. *Hard Green: Saving the Environment from the Environmentalists (A Conservative Manifesto).* New York: Basic Books.

Hunt, Suzanne, C., and Janet L. Sawin (with Peter Stair). 2006. "Cultivating Renewable Alternatives to Oil." In *State of the World 2006*, edited by Linda Starke. New York: W. W. Norton.

Hunter, Susan, and Richard W. Waterman. 1992. "Determining an Agency's Regulatory Style: How Does the EPA Water Office Enforce the Law?" *Western Political Quarterly* 45: 403–417.

———. 1996. *Enforcing the Law: The Case of the Clean Water Acts.* Armonk, NY: M. E. Sharpe.

Idelson, Holly. 1992a. "After Two-Year Odyssey, Energy Strategy Clears." *Congressional Quarterly Weekly Report* (October): 3141–3146.

———. 1992b. "National Energy Strategy Provisions." *Congressional Quarterly Weekly Report* (November): 3722–3730.

Inglehart, Ronald. 1990. *Culture Shift in Advanced Industrial Society.* Princeton, NJ: Princeton University Press.

Ingram, Helen M., and Dean E. Mann. 1983. "Environmental Protection Policy." In *Encyclopedia of Policy Studies*, edited by Stuart S. Nagel, 687–724. New York: Marcel Dekker.

Ingram, Helen M., and Steven Rathgeb Smith, eds. 1993. *Public Policy for Democracy.* Washington, DC: Brookings Institution Press.

Intergovernmental Panel on Climate Change (IPCC). 2007. *Synthesis Report. Contribution of Working Groups I, II and III to the Fourth Assessment Report of the Intergovernmental Panel on Climate Change.* [Core writing team: R. K. Pachauri and A. Reisinger (eds)] IPCC, Geneva. 104 pp. Available at: www.ipcc.ch.

——. 2013. *Climate Change 2013: The Physical Science Basis. Summary for Policymakers. Working Group I Contribution to the IPCC Fifth Assessment Report.* [T. F. Stocker, D. Qin, G. K. Plattner, M. Tignor, S. K. Allen, J. Boschung, A. Nauels, Y. Xia, V. Bex, and P. M. Midgley (eds)], September 27. Available at: www.ipcc.ch.

International Energy Agency. 2016. *Energy and Air Pollution: World Energy Outlook Special Report.* Paris: International Energy Agency.

Jalonick, Mary Clare. 2004. "Healthy Forests Initiative Provisions." *CQ Weekly* (January): 246–47.

Jamieson, Kathleen Hall, and Joseph N. Cappella. 2010. *Echo Chamber: Rush Limbaugh and the Conservative Media Establishment.* New York: Oxford University Press.

John, DeWitt. 1994. *Civic Environmentalism: Alternatives to Regulation in States and Communities.* Washington, DC: CQ Press.

——. 2004. "Civic Environmentalism." In *Environmental Governance Reconsidered,* edited by Robert F. Durant, Daniel J. Fiorino, and Rosemary O'Leary, 219–254. Cambridge, MA: MIT Press.

John, De Witt, and Marian Mlay. 1999. "Community-Based Environmental Protection: Encouraging Civic Environmentalism." In *Better Environmental Decisions,* edited by Ken Sexton, Alfred A. Marcus, K. William Easter, and Timothy D. Burkhardt, 353–376. Washington, DC: Island Press.

Johnson, Kirk. 1993. "Reconciling Rural Communities and Resource Conservation." *Environment* 35 (November): 16–20, 27–33.

Jones, Charles O. 1975. *Clean Air: The Policies and Politics of Pollution Control.* Pittsburgh, PA: University of Pittsburgh Press.

——. 1984. *An Introduction to the Study of Public Policy,* 3rd edn. Monterey, CA: Brooks/Cole.

Kamieniecki, Sheldon, ed. 1993. *Environmental Politics in the International Arena: Movements, Parties, Organizations, and Policy.* Albany: State University of New York Press.

——. 1995. "Political Parties and Environmental Policy." In *Environmental Politics and Policy,* edited by James P. Lester, 146–167. Durham, NC: Duke University Press.

——. 2006. *Corporate America and Environmental Policy: How Often Does Business Get Its Way?* Stanford, CA: Stanford University Press.

Kamieniecki, Sheldon, and Michael E. Kraft, eds. 2013. *The Oxford Handbook of U.S. Environmental Policy.* New York: Oxford University Press.

Kareiva, Peter, Heather Tallis, Taylor H. Ricketts, Gretchen C. Daily, and Stephen Polasky, eds. 2011. *Natural Capital: Theory and Practice of Mapping Ecosystem Services.* New York: Oxford University Press.

Karkkainen, Bradley C., Archon Fung, and Charles Sabel. 2000. "After Backyard Environmentalism: Toward a Performance-Based Regime of Environmental Regulation." *American Behavioral Scientist* 44: 690–709.

Kates, Robert W., William C. Clark, Robert Corell, J. Michael Hall, Carlo C. Jaeger, and Ian Lowe. 2001. "Sustainability Science." *Science* 292 (April): 641–642.

Kawachi, Ichiro, Graham A. Colditz, Frank E. Speizer, JoAnn E. Manson, Meir J. Stampfer, Walter C. Willett, et al. 1997. "A Prospective Study of Passive Smoking and Coronary Heart Disease." *Circulation* 95: 2374–2379.

Keller, Ann Campbell. 2009. *Science in Environmental Policy: The Politics of Objective Advice*. Cambridge, MA: MIT Press.

Kellert, Stephen R. 1996. *The Value of Life: Biological Diversity and Human Society*. Washington, DC: Island Press.

Kempton, Willett, James S. Boster, and Jennifer A. Hartley. 1996. *Environmental Values in American Culture*. Cambridge, MA: MIT Press.

Kent, Mary M., and Mark Mather. 2002. "What Drives U.S. Population Growth?" *Population Bulletin* 57 (December): 1–40.

Keohane, Nathaniel O., and Sheila M. Olmstead. 2007. *Markets and the Environment*. Washington, DC: Island Press.

Keohane, Robert O. 2015. "The Global Politics of Climate Change: Challenge for Political Science." *PS: Political Science and Politics*, January: 19–26.

Keohane, Robert O., and Marc A. Levy, eds. 1996. *Institutions for Environmental Aid: Pitfalls and Promise*. Cambridge, MA: MIT Press.

Kerwin, Cornelius M., and Scott R. Furlong. 2011. *Rulemaking: How Government Agencies Write Law and Make Policy*, 4th edn. Washington, DC: CQ Press.

Kettl, Donald F. 1993. *Sharing Power: Public Governance and Private Markets*. Washington, DC: Brookings Institution Press.

———. 2002. *Environmental Governance: A Report on the Next Generation of Environmental Policy*. Washington, DC: Brookings Institution Press.

Kingdon, John W. 1995. *Agendas, Alternatives, and Public Policies*, 2nd edn. New York: Longman.

Klyza, Christopher McGrory. 1996. *Who Controls Public Lands? Mining, Forestry, and Grazing Policies, 1870–1990*. Chapel Hill: University of North Carolina Press.

Klyza, Christopher McGrory, and David Sousa. 2013. *American Environmental Policy: Beyond Gridlock*, updated and expanded edition. Cambridge, MA: MIT Press.

Knaap, Gerrit J., and Tschangho John Kim, eds. 1998. *Environmental Program Evaluation: A Primer*. Champaign: University of Illinois Press.

Knopman, Debra S., Megan M. Susman, and Marc K. Landy. 1999. "Civic Environmentalism: Tackling Tough Land-Use Problems with Innovative Governance." *Environment* 41 (December): 24–32.

Keohane, Robert O. 2015. "The Global Politics of Climate Change: Challenge for Political Science." *PS: Political Science and Politics*, January: 19–26.

Konisky, David M., ed. 2015. *Failed Promises: Evaluating the Federal Government's Response to Environmental Justice*. Cambridge, MA: MIT Press.

———. 2016. "Environmental Justice Delayed: Failed Promises, Hope for the Future," *Environment* 58, 2 (March/April): 4–15.

Konisky, David M., and Neal D. Woods. 2012. "Measuring State Environmental Policy." *Review of Policy Research* 29, 4: 544–569.

———. 2016. "Environmental Policy, Federalism, and the Obama Presidency." *Publius: The Journal of Federalism* 46, 3: 366–391.

Koontz, Tomas M. 2002. *Federalism in the Forest: National Versus State Natural Resource Policy*. Washington, DC: Georgetown University Press.

Koontz, Tomas M. 2005. "We Finished the Plan, So Now What? Impacts of Collaborative Stakeholder Participation on Land Use Policy." *Policy Studies Journal* 33: 459–481.

Koontz, Tomas M., Toddi A. Steelman, JoAnn Car-min, Katrina Smith Korfmacher, Cassandra Moseley, and Craig W. Thomas. 2004. *Collaborative Environmental Management: What Roles for Government?* Washington, DC: RFF Press.

Koplow, Douglas N. 1993. *Federal Energy Subsidies: Energy, Environmental, and Fiscal Impacts.* Lexington, MA: Alliance to Save Energy.

Kraft, Michael E. 1981. "Congress and National Energy Policy: Assessing the Policy Process." In *Environment, Energy, Public Policy*, edited by Regina S. Axelrod, 37–59. Lexington, MA: Lexington Books.

——. 1984. "A New Environmental Policy Agenda: The 1980 Presidential Campaign and Its Aftermath." In *Environmental Policy in the 1980s*, edited by Norman J. Vig and Michael E. Kraft, 29–50. Washington, DC: CQ Press.

——. 1994a. "Population Policy." In *Encyclopedia of Policy Studies*, 2nd edn, edited by Stuart S. Nagel, 617–645. New York: Marcel Dekker.

——. 1994b. "Searching for Policy Success: Reinventing the Politics of Site Remediation." *The Environmental Professional* 16 (September): 245–253.

——. 1995. "Congress and Environmental Policy." In *Environmental Politics and Policy*, 2nd edn, edited by James P. Lester, 168–205. Durham, NC: Duke University Press.

——. 1996. "Democratic Dialogue and Acceptable Risks: The Politics of High-Level Nuclear Waste Disposal in the United States." In *Hazardous Waste Siting and Democratic Choice*, edited by Don Munton, 108–141. Washington, DC: Georgetown University Press.

——. 2000. "Policy Design and the Acceptability of Environmental Risks: Nuclear Waste Disposal in Canada and the United States." *Policy Studies Journal* 28(1): 206–218.

——. 2009. "Cleaning Wisconsin's Waters: From Command and Control to Collaborative Decision Making." In *Toward Sustainable Communities*, 2nd edn, edited by Daniel A. Mazmanian and Michael E. Kraft, 115–140. Cambridge, MA: MIT Press.

——. 2012. "U.S. Global Environmental Policy in the Post-Bush Era." In *U.S. Foreign Policy Today: American Renewal?* edited by Steven W. Hook and James M. Scott, 217–235. Washington, DC: CQ Press.

——. 2013a. "Congress and Environmental Policy." In *The Oxford Handbook of U.S. Environmental Policy*, edited by Sheldon Kamieniecki and Michael E. Kraft, 280–305. New York: Oxford University Press.

——. 2013b. "Nuclear Power and the Challenge of High-Level Waste Disposal in the United States." *Polity* 45(2): 265–280.

——. 2016. "Environmental Policy in Congress." In *Environmental Policy*, 9th edn, edited by Norman J. Vig and Michael E. Kraft, 103–127. Washington, DC: CQ Press.

——. 2017a. "Sustainability and Sustainable Cities." In *Environmental Governance Reconsidered: Challenges, Choices, and Opportunities*, 2nd edn, edited by Robert F. Durant, Daniel J. Fiorino, and Rosemary O'Leary. Cambridge, MA: MIT Press.

——. 2017b. "Environmental Risk: New Approaches Needed to Address Twenty-First Century Challenges." In *Conceptual Innovation in Environmental Policy*, edited by James M. Meadowcroft and Daniel J. Fiorino. Cambridge, MA: MIT Press.

Kraft, Michael E., Bruce B. Clary, and Richard J. Tobin. 1988. "The Impact of New Federalism on State Environmental Policy: The Great Lakes States." In *The Midwest Response to the New Federalism*, edited by Peter Eisinger and William Gormley, 204–233. Madison: University of Wisconsin Press.

Kraft, Michael E., and Scott R. Furlong. 2018. *Public Policy: Politics, Analysis, and Alternatives*, 6th edn. Washington, DC: CQ Press.

Kraft, Michael E., and Sheldon Kamieniecki, eds. 2007. *Business and Environmental Policy: Corporate Interests in the American Political System*. Cambridge, MA: MIT Press.

Kraft, Michael E., and Denise Scheberle. 1998. "Environmental Federalism at Decade's End: New Approaches and Strategies." *Publius: The Journal of Federalism* 28 (Winter): 131–146.

Kraft, Michael E., Mark Stephan, and Troy D. Abel. 2011. *Coming Clean: Information Disclosure and Environmental Performance*. Cambridge, MA: MIT Press.

Krupnick, Alan J. 2002. "Does the Clean Air Act Measure Up?" *Resources* 147: 2–3.

Lacey, Michael J., ed. 1989. *Government and Environmental Politics: Essays on Historical Developments Since World War II*. Baltimore, MD: Johns Hopkins University Press.

Ladd, Everett Carll, and Karlyn H. Bowman. 1995. *Attitudes Toward the Environment: Twenty-Five Years after Earth Day*. Washington, DC: American Enterprise Institute.

Landy, Marc K., Marc J. Roberts, and Stephen R. Thomas. 1994. *The Environmental Protection Agency: Asking the Wrong Questions*, 2nd edn. New York: Oxford University Press.

Layzer, Judith A. 2007. "Deep Freeze: How Business Has Shaped the Legislative Debate on Climate Change." In *Business and Environmental Policy: Corporate Interests in the American Political System*, edited by Michael E. Kraft and Sheldon Kamieniecki, 93–125. Cambridge, MA: MIT Press.

——. 2008. *Natural Experiments: Ecosystem-Based Management and the Environment*. Cambridge, MA: MIT Press.

——. 2012. *Open for Business: Conservatives' Opposition to Environmental Regulation*. Cambridge, MA: MIT Press.

——. 2013. "Ecosystem-Based Management and Restoration." In *The Oxford Handbook of U.S. Environmental Policy*, edited by Sheldon Kamieniecki and Michael E. Kraft, 605–630. New York: Oxford University Press.

Layzer, Judith A., and Alexis Schulman. 2017. "Adaptive Management: Popular but Difficult to Implement." In *Conceptual Innovation in Environmental Policy*, edited by James Meadowcroft and Daniel J. Fiorino. Cambridge, MA: MIT Press.

Lazarus, Richard J. 2004. *The Making of Environmental Law*. Chicago: University of Chicago Press.

Leiserowitz, Anthony A., and Lisa O. Fernandez. 2008. "Toward a New Consciousness: Values to Sustain Human and Natural Communities." *Environment* 50(5) (September/October): 62–69.

Leiserowitz, Anthony A., Edward Maibach, and Connie Roser-Renouf. 2009. *Climate Change in the American Mind: Americans' Climate Change Beliefs,*

Attitudes, Policy Preferences, and Actions. New Haven, CT: Yale Project on Climate Change. Available at: http://environment.yale.edu/.

Leiserowitz, Anthony, Edward Maibach, Connie Roser-Renouf, Geoff Feinberg, and Seth Rosenthal. 2015. *Climate Change in the American Mind.* New Haven, CT: Yale Project on Climate Change. Available at: http://environment.yale.edu/.

Leiserowitz, Anthony, Nicholas Smith, and Jennifer Marlon. 2010. *Americans' Knowledge of Climate Change.* New Haven, CT: Yale Project on Climate Change. Available at: http://environment.yale.edu/.

Leopold, Aldo. 1970. *A Sand County Almanac.* New York: Oxford University Press. Expanded edn, with additional essays from *Round River.* 1949. Reprint: New York: Ballantine Books (page references are to reprint edition).

Leshy, John D. 1984. "Natural Resource Policy." In *Natural Resources and the Environment,* edited by Paul R. Portney, 13–46. Washington, DC: Resources for the Future.

Lester, James P., ed. 1995. *Environmental Politics and Policy: Theories and Evidence,* 2nd edn. Durham, NC: Duke University Press.

Lewis, Martin W. 1994. *Green Delusions: An Environmentalist Critique of Radical Environmentalism.* Durham, NC: Duke University Press.

Lichter, S. Robert, and Stanley Rothman. 1999. *Environmental Cancer: A Political Disease?* New Haven, CT: Yale University Press.

Lindblom, Charles E., and Edward J. Woodhouse. 1993. *The Policy-Making Process,* 3rd edn. Englewood Cliffs, NJ: Prentice Hall.

Litfin, Karen T., ed. 1998. *The Greening of Sovereignty in World Politics.* Cambridge, MA: MIT Press.

Lomborg, Bjørn. 2001. *The Skeptical Environmentalist: Measuring the Real State of the World.* New York: Cambridge University Press.

Lowi, Theodore J. 1979. *The End of Liberalism,* 2nd edn. New York: W. W. Norton.

Lowry, William R. 1992. *The Dimensions of Federalism: State Governments and Pollution Control Policies.* Durham, NC: Duke University Press.

——. 1994. *The Capacity for Wonder: Preserving National Parks.* Washington, DC: Brookings Institution Press.

——. 2003. *Dam Politics: Restoring America's Rivers.* Washington, DC: Georgetown University Press.

——. 2006. "A Return to Traditional Priorities in Natural Resource Policies." In *Environmental Policy,* 6th edn, edited by Norman J. Vig and Michael E. Kraft, 311–332. Washington, DC: CQ Press.

——. 2009. *Repairing Paradise: The Restoration of Nature in America's National Parks.* Washington, DC: Brookings Institution Press.

Lubchenco, Jane. 1998. "Entering the Century of the Environment: A New Social Contract for Science." *Science* 279 (January 23): 491–497.

Lubell, Mark, William D. Leach, and Paul A. Sabatier. 2009. "Collaborative Watershed Partnerships in the Epoch of Sustainability." In *Toward Sustainable Communities,* 2nd edn, edited by Daniel A. Mazmanian and Michael E. Kraft, 255–288. Cambridge, MA: MIT Press.

Lubell, Mark, and Brian Segee. 2013. "Conflict and Cooperation in Natural Resource Management." In *Environmental Policy,* 8th edn, edited by Norman J. Vig and Michael E. Kraft, 185–205. Washington, DC: CQ Press.

MacNeill, Jim, Pieter Winsemius, and Taizo Yakushiji. 1991. *Beyond Interdependence: The Meshing of the World's Economy and the Earth's Ecology.* New York: Oxford University Press.

Malcom Jacob W., and Ya-Wei Li. 2015. "Data Contradict Common Perceptions about a Controversial Provision of the U.S. Endangered Species Act." *Proceedings of the National Academy of Sciences* 112(52): 15844–15849.

Mangun, William R., and Daniel H. Henning. 1999. *Managing the Environmental Crisis: Incorporating Competing Values in Natural Resource Administration,* 2nd edn. Durham, NC: Duke University Press.

Mann, Dean E. 1986. "Democratic Politics and Environmental Policy." In *Controversies in Environmental Policy,* edited by Sheldon Kamieniecki, Robert O'Brien, and Michael Clarke, 3–34. Albany: State University of New York Press.

Mann, Thomas E., and Norman J. Ornstein. 2012. *It's Even Worse Than It Looks: How the American Constitutional System Collided with the New Politics of Extremism.* New York: Basic Books.

Marcus, Alfred A. 1992. *Controversial Issues in Energy Policy.* Newbury Park, CA: Sage.

Marcus, Alfred A., Donald A. Geffen, and Ken Sexton. 2002. *Reinventing Environmental Regulation: Lessons from Project XL.* Washington, DC: RFF Press.

Mastny, Lisa. 2004. "Purchasing for People and the Planet." In *State of the World 2004,* edited by Linda Starke. Washington, DC: Worldwatch Institute.

Matthew, Richard A. 2013. "Environmental Security." In *Environmental Policy,* 8th edn, edited by Norman J. Vig and Michael E. Kraft, 344–367. Washington, DC: CQ Press.

Mazmanian, Daniel A. 2009. "Los Angeles' Clean Air Saga: Spanning the Three Epochs." In *Toward Sustainable Communities,* 2nd edn, edited by Daniel A. Mazmanian and Michael E. Kraft, 89–113. Cambridge, MA: MIT Press.

Mazmanian, Daniel A., and Michael E. Kraft, eds. 2009. *Toward Sustainable Communities: Transition and Transformations in Environmental Policy,* 2nd edn. Cambridge, MA: MIT Press.

Mazmanian, Daniel, and David Morell. 1992. *Beyond Superfailure: America's Toxics Policy for the 1990s.* Boulder, CO: Westview Press.

Mazmanian, Daniel A., and Jeanne Nienaber. 1979. *Can Organizations Change? Environmental Protection, Citizen Participation, and the Corps of Engineers.* Washington, DC: Brookings Institution Press.

Mazmanian, Daniel A., and Laurie Kay Nijaki. 2013. "Sustainable Development and Governance." In *The Oxford Handbook of U.S. Environmental Policy,* edited by Sheldon Kamieniecki and Michael E. Kraft, 184–206. New York: Oxford University Press.

Mazmanian, Daniel A., and Paul A. Sabatier. 1983. *Implementation and Public Policy.* Glenview, IL: Scott Foresman.

McConnell, Grant. 1966. *Private Power and American Democracy.* New York: Knopf.

McCool, Daniel. 1990. "Subgovernments as Determinants of Political Viability." *Political Science Quarterly* 105 (Summer): 269–293.

McCormick, John. 1989. *Reclaiming Paradise: The Global Environmental Movement.* Bloomington: Indiana University Press.

———. 2011. "The Role of Environmental NGOs in International Regimes." In *The Global Environment*, 3rd edn, edited by Regina S. Axelrod, Stacy D. VanDeveer, and David L. Downie, 92–110. Washington, DC: CQ Press.

McCright, Aaron M., Chenyang Xiao, and Riley E. Dunlap. 2014. "Political Polarization on Support for Government Spending on Environmental Protection in the USA, 1974–2012." *Social Science Research* 48: 251–260.

McSpadden, Lettie M. 2000. "Environmental Policy in the Courts." In *Environmental Policy*, 4th edn, edited by Norman J. Vig and Michael E. Kraft, 145–164. Washington, DC: CQ Press.

Meadowcroft, James. 2004. "Deliberative Democracy." In *Environmental Governance Reconsidered*, edited by Robert F. Durant, Daniel J. Fiorino, and Rosemary O'Leary, 183–217. Cambridge, MA: MIT Press.

Meadowcroft, James, and Daniel J. Fiorino, eds. 2017. *Conceptual Innovations in Environmental Policy*. Cambridge, MA: MIT Press.

Meadows, Donella H. 2008. *Thinking in Systems: A Primer*. White River Junction, VT: Chelsea Green.

Meadows, Donella, Jørgen Randers, and Dennis Meadows. 2004. *Limits to Growth: The 30-Year Update*. White River Junction, VT: Chelsea Green.

Melnick, R. Shep. 1983. *Regulation and the Courts: The Case of the Clean Air Act*. Washington, DC: Brookings Institution Press.

Meyer, Stephen M. 1993. *Environmentalism and Economic Prosperity*. Cambridge, MA: MIT Department of Political Science.

Milazzo, Paul Charles. 2006. *Unlikely Environmentalists: Congress and Clean Water, 1945–1972*. Lawrence: University Press of Kansas.

Milbrath, Lester W. 1984. *Environmentalists: Vanguard for a New Society*. Albany: State University of New York Press.

———. 1989. *Envisioning a Sustainable Society: Learning Our Way out*. Albany: State University of New York Press.

Miller, Kenton R., Walter V. Reid, and Charles Barber. 1991. "Deforestation and Species Loss: Responding to the Crisis." In *Preserving the Global Environment*, edited by Jessica Tuchman Mathews, 78–111. New York: W.W. Norton.

Mitchell, Robert Cameron. 1984. "Public Opinion and Environmental Politics in the 1970s and 1980s." In *Environmental Policy in the 1980s*, edited by Norman J. Vig and Michael E. Kraft, 51–74. Washington, DC: CQ Press.

———. 1989. "From Conservation to Environmental Movement: The Development of the Modern Environmental Lobbies." In *Government and Environmental Politics*, edited by Michael Lacey, 81–113. Baltimore, MD: Johns Hopkins University Press.

———. 1990. "Public Opinion and the Green Lobby: Poised for the 1990s." In *Environmental Policy in the 1990s*, edited by Norman J. Vig and Michael E. Kraft, 81–99. Washington, DC: CQ Press.

Mitchell, Robert Cameron, Angela G. Mertig, and Riley E. Dunlap. 1992. "Twenty Years of Environmental Mobilization: Trends among National Environmental Organizations." In *American Environmentalism*, edited by Riley E. Dunlap and Angela G. Mertig, 11–26. Philadelphia, PA: Taylor & Francis.

Moe, Terry M. 1980. *The Organization of Interests: Incentives and the Internal Dynamics of Political Interest Groups*. Chicago, IL: University of Chicago Press.

Morgenstern, Richard D. 1999. "An Historical Perspective on Regulatory Decision Making: The Role of Economic Analysis." In *Better Environmental Decisions*, edited by Ken Sexton, Alfred A. Marcus, K. William Easter, and Timothy D. Burkhardt, 113–132. Washington, DC: Island Press.

——. 2017. "Retrospective Analysis." In *Conceptual Innovation in Environmental Policy*, edited by James M. Meadowcroft and Daniel J. Fiorino. Cambridge, MA: MIT Press.

Morgenstern, Richard D., William A. Pizer, and Jhih-Shyang Shih. 1999. "Jobs Versus the Environment: Is There a Trade-off?" Washington, DC: Resources for the Future.

Morgenstern, Richard D., and Paul R. Portney, eds. 2004. *New Approaches on Energy and the Environment: Policy Advice for the President*. Washington, DC: RFF Press.

Munton, Don, ed. 1996. *Hazardous Waste Siting and Democratic Choice*. Washington, DC: Georgetown University Press.

Murtaugh, Paul A., and Michael G. Schlax. 2009. "Reproduction and the Carbon Legacy of Individuals." *Global Environmental Change: Human and Policy Dimensions* 19(1) (February): 14–20.

Myers, Norman. 1997. "The World's Forests and Their Ecosystem Services." In *Nature's Services*, edited by Gretchen C. Daily, 215–235. Washington, DC: Island Press.

Myers, Norman, and Jennifer Kent. 2001. *Perverse Subsidies: How Misused Tax Dollars Harm the Environment and the Economy*. Washington, DC: Island Press.

Najam, Adil. 2015. "The View from the South: Developing Countries in Global Environmental Politics." In *The Global Environment: Institutions, Law, and Policy*, 4th edn, edited by Regina S. Axelrod and Stacy D. VanDeveer, 213–233. Washington, DC: CQ Press.

Nash, Roderick Frazier. 1990. *American Environmentalism: Readings in Conservation History*, 3rd edn. New York: McGraw-Hill.

National Academy of Public Administration. 1987. *Presidential Management of Rulemaking in Regulatory Agencies*. Washington, DC: National Academy of Public Administration.

——. 1995. *Setting Priorities, Getting Results: A New Direction for EPA*. Washington, DC: National Academy of Public Administration.

——. 2000. *Environment.gov: Transforming Environmental Protection for the 21st Century*. Washington, DC: National Academy of Public Administration.

National Acid Precipitation Assessment Program. 1990. *Background on Acidic Deposition and the National Acid Precipitation Assessment Program and Assessment Highlights*. Washington, DC: NAPAP.

National Climate Assessment. 2014. *2014 National Climate Assessment*. Washington, DC: U.S. Global Change Research Program. Available at: http://nca2014.globalchange.gov/.

National Commission on the Environment. 1993. *Choosing a Sustainable Future: The Report of the National Commission on the Environment*. Washington, DC: Island Press.

National Research Council. 1990. *Forestry Research: A Mandate for Change*. Washington, DC: National Academy Press.

——. 1996. *Understanding Risk: Informing Decisions in a Democratic Society*. Washington, DC: National Academy Press.

——. 1999. *Our Common Journey: A Transition toward Sustainability*. Washington, DC: National Academy Press.

——. 2001. *The Role of Environmental NGOs: Russian Challenges, American Lessons*. Washington, DC: National Academy Press.

——. 2004. *Valuing Ecosystem Services: Toward Better Environmental Decision-Making*. Washington, DC: National Academies Press.

——. 2009. *Advice on the Department of Energy's Cleanup Technology Roadmap: Gaps and Bridges*. Washington, DC: National Academies Press.

——. 2011. *America's Climate Choices*. Washington, DC: National Academies Press.

Nelson, Gaylord (with Susan Campbell and Paul Wozniak). 2002. *Beyond Earth Day: Fulfilling the Promise*. Madison: University of Wisconsin Press.

Nisbet, Matthew C. 2009. "Communicating Climate Change: Why Frames Matter for Public Engagement." *Environment* 51(2) (March/April): 12–23.

——. 2011. "Climate Shift: Clear Vision for the Next Decade of Public Debate." Available at: http://climateshiftproject.org.

——. 2016. "Environmental Advocacy in the Obama Years: Assessing New Strategies for Political Change." In *Environmental Policy*, 9th edn, edited by Norman J. Vig and Michael E. Kraft, 58–78. Washington, DC: CQ Press.

Nordhaus, Richard. 2008. *A Question of Balance: Weighing the Options on Global Warming Policies*. New Haven, CT: Yale University Press.

O'Leary, Rosemary. 1993. *Environmental Change: Federal Courts and the EPA*. Philadelphia, PA: Temple University Press.

——. 2016. "Environmental Policy in the Courts." In *Environmental Policy*, 9th edn, edited by Norman J. Vig and Michael E. Kraft, 128–150. Washington, DC: CQ Press.

O'Leary, Rosemary, and Lisa B. Bingham, eds. 2003. *The Promise and Performance of Environmental Conflict Resolution*. Washington, DC: RFF Press.

Olmstead, Sheila M. 2013. "The Role of Market Incentives in Environmental Policy." In *The Oxford Handbook of U.S. Environmental Policy*, edited by Sheldon Kamieniecki and Michael E. Kraft, 553–581. New York: Oxford University Press.

——. 2016. "Applying Market Principles to Environmental Policy." In *Environmental Policy*, 9th edn, edited by Norman J. Vig and Michael E. Kraft, 215–238. Washington, DC: CQ Press.

Olson, Mancur. 1971. *The Logic of Collective Action*. Cambridge, MA: Harvard University Press.

O'Malley, Robin, and Kate Wing. 2000. "Forging a New Tool for Ecosystem Reporting." *Environment* 42 (April): 21–31.

O'Neill, Kate. 2009. *The Environment and International Relations*. New York: Cambridge University Press.

——. 2013. "Global Environmental Policy Making." In *The Oxford Handbook of U.S. Environmental Policy*, edited by Sheldon Kamieniecki and Michael E. Kraft, 230–258. New York: Oxford University Press.

——. 2015. "Architects, Agitators, and Entrepreneurs: International and Nongovernmental Organizations in Global Environmental Politics." In *The Global Environment: Institutions, Law, and Policy*, 4th edn, edited by Regina S. Axelrod and Stacy D. VanDeveer, 26–52. Washington, DC: CQ Press.

Ophuls, William. 2011. *Plato's Revenge: Politics in the Age of Ecology*. Cambridge, MA: MIT Press.

Ophuls, William, and A. Stephen Boyan, Jr. 1992. *Ecology and the Politics of Scarcity Revisited*. New York: W. H. Freeman.

Oreskes, Naomi, and Eric M. Conway. 2010. *Merchants of Doubt*. New York: Bloomsbury Press.

Ostrom, Elinor. 1990. *Governing the Commons: The Evolution of Institutions for Collective Action*. New York: Cambridge University Press.

——. 1999. "Coping with Tragedies of the Commons." In *Annual Review of Political Science*, vol. 2, edited by Nelson W. Polsby, 493–535. Palo Alto, CA: Annual Reviews.

——. 2007. "Institutional Rational Choice: An Assessment of the Institutional Analysis and Development Framework." In *Theories of the Policy Process*, 2nd edn, edited by Paul A. Sabatier, 21–64. Boulder, CO: Westview Press.

——. 2008. "The Challenge of Common-Pool Resources." *Environment* 50(4): 8–20.

Ostrom, Elinor, Thomas Dietz, Nives Dolšak, Paul C. Stern, Susan Stonich, and Elke U. Weber, eds. 2002. *The Drama of the Commons*. Washington, DC: National Academy Press.

O'Toole, Randall. 1988. *Reforming the Forest Service*. Washington, DC: Island Press.

Ott, Wayne R., and John W. Roberts. 1998. "Everyday Exposure to Toxic Pollutants." *Scientific American* 224 (February): 86–91.

Ozymy, Joshua, and Melissa Jarrell. 2015. "Wielding the Green Stick: Criminal Enforcement at the EPA under the Bush and Obama Administrations." *Environmental Politics* 24(1): 38–56.

Paarlberg, Robert L. 1999. "Lapsed Leadership: U.S. International Environmental Policy Since Rio." In *The Global Environment*, edited by Norman J. Vig and Regina S. Axelrod, 236–255. Washington, DC: CQ Press.

Paehlke, Robert C. 1989. *Environmentalism and the Future of Progressive Politics*. New Haven, CT: Yale University Press.

—— 2000. "Environmental Values and Public Policy." In *Environmental Policy*, 4th edn, edited by Norman J. Vig and Michael E. Kraft, 77–97. Washington, DC: CQ Press.

——. 2013a. "Ethical Challenges in Environmental Policy." In *The Oxford Handbook of U.S. Environmental Policy*, edited by Sheldon Kamieniecki and Michael E. Kraft, 93–113. New York: Oxford University Press.

——. 2013b. "Sustainable Development and Urban Life in North America." In *Environmental Policy*, 8th edn, edited by Norman J. Vig and Michael E. Kraft, 255–276. Washington, DC: CQ Press.

Parris, Thomas M. 2003. "Toward a Sustainability Transition: The International Consensus." *Environment* 45 (January/February): 13–22.

——. 2006. "Internet Resources for Sustainable Product Design." *Environment* 4(8) (March): 3.

Parry, Ian W. H. 2002. "Is Gasoline Under-Taxed in the United States?" *Resources* 148 (Summer): 28–33.

Patton, Carl V., David S. Sawicki, and Jennifer J. Clark. 2016. *Basic Methods of Policy Analysis and Planning*, 3rd edn. New York: Routledge.

Pautz, Michelle C., and Sara R. Rinfret. 2013. *The Lilliputians of Environmental Regulation: The Perspective of State Regulators*. New York: Routledge.

Peel, Jacqueline. 2011. "Environmental Protection in the Twenty-First Century: The Role of International Law." In *The Global Environment*, 3rd edn, edited by Regina S. Axelrod, Stacy D. VanDeveer, and David Leonard Downie, 48–69. Washington, DC: CQ Press.

Persily, Nathaniel, ed. 2015. *Solutions to Political Polarization in America*. New York: Oxford University Press.

Peskin, Henry M., Paul R. Portney, and Allen V. Kneese, eds. 1981. *Environmental Regulation and the U.S. Economy*. Baltimore, MD: Johns Hopkins University Press.

Platt, Rutherford H., Paul K. Barten, and Max J. Pfeffer. 2000. "A Full, Clean Glass? Managing New York City's Watersheds." *Environment* 42 (June): 6–20.

Poole, Keith T., and Howard Rosenthal. 2007. *Ideology and Congress*. Piscataway, NJ: Transaction.

Population Reference Bureau. 2016. *2016 World Population Data Sheet*. Washington, DC: Population Reference Bureau, September. Available at: www.prb.org.

Porter, Michael E., and Claas van der Linde. 1995. "Green and Competitive: Ending the Stalemate." *Harvard Business Review* 73 (September/October): 120–134.

Portney, Kent E. 2009. "Sustainability in American Cities: A Comprehensive Look at What Cities Are Doing and Why." In *Toward Sustainable Communities: Transition and Transformations in Environmental Policy*, edited by Daniel A. Mazmanian and Michael E. Kraft, 227–254. Cambridge, MA: MIT Press.

——. 2013. *Taking Sustainable Cities Seriously: Economic Development, the Environment, and Quality of Life in American Cities*, 2nd edn. Cambridge, MA: MIT Press.

——. 2015. *Sustainability*. Cambridge, MA: MIT Press.

——. 2016. "Taking Sustainable Cities Seriously: What Cities Are Doing." In *Environmental Policy*, 9th edn, edited by Norman J. Vig and Michael E. Kraft, 265–285. Washington, DC: CQ Press.

Portney, Paul R. 1990. "Air Pollution Policy." In *Public Policies for Environmental Protection*, edited by Paul R. Portney, 27–96. Washington, DC: Resources for the Future.

——. 1994. "Does Environmental Policy Conflict with Economic Growth?" *Resources* 115 (Spring): 21–23.

——. 1995. "Beware of the Killer Clauses inside the GOP's Contract." *Washington Post*, National Weekly Edition, January 23–29, 21.

——. 1998. "Counting the Costs: The Growing Role of Economics in Environmental Decisionmaking." *Environment* 40 (March): 14–18, 36–38.

——. 2000. "EPA and the Evolution of Federal Regulation." In *Public Policies for Environmental Protection*, 2nd edn, edited by Paul R. Portney and Robert N. Stavins, 11–30. Washington, DC: RFF Press.

——. 2002. "Penny-Wise and Pound-Fuelish? New Car Mileage Standards in the United States." *Resources* 147 (Spring): 10–15.

Portney, Paul R., and Robert N. Stavins, eds. 2000. *Public Policy for Environmental Protection*, 2nd edn. Washington, DC: Resources for the Future.

Postel, Sandra. 1988. "Controlling Toxic Chemicals." In *State of the World 1988*, edited by Linda Starke, 118–136. New York: W. W. Norton.

Potoski, Matthew, and Aseem Prakash. 2005. "Covenants with Weak Swords: ISO 14001 and Facilities' Environmental Performance." *Journal of Policy Analysis and Management* 24: 745–769.

——. 2013. "Do Voluntary Programs Reduce Pollution? Examining ISO 14001's Effectiveness Across Countries." *Policy Studies Journal* 41(2): 273–294.

Powell, Mark R. 1999. *Science at EPA: Information in the Regulatory Process*. Washington, DC: Resources for the Future.

Prakash, Aseem, and Matthew Potoski. 2006. *The Voluntary Environmentalists: Green Clubs, ISO 14001, and Voluntary Environmental Regulations*. New York: Cambridge University Press.

Pralle, Sarah B. 2006. *Branching Out, Digging In: Environmental Advocacy and Agenda Setting*. Washington, DC: Georgetown University Press.

Presidential/Congressional Commission on Risk Assessment and Risk Management. 1997. *Risk Assessment and Risk Management in Regulatory Decision-Making*, Final Report, vol. 2. Washington, DC: Commission Offices. (The report and other studies and commentary on risk are available at: www.riskworld.com.)

President's Council on Sustainable Development. 1996. *Sustainable America: A New Consensus for Prosperity, Opportunity, and a Healthy Environment for the Future*. Washington, DC: U.S. Government Printing Office.

Press, Daniel. 1994. *Democratic Dilemmas in the Age of Ecology: Trees and Toxics in the American West*. Durham, NC: Duke University Press.

——. 2002. *Saving Open Space: The Politics of Local Preservation in California*. Berkeley: University of California Press.

——. 2015. *American Environmental Policy: The Failures of Compliance, Abatement and Mitigation*. Northhampton, MA: Edward Elgar.

Press, Daniel, and Daniel A. Mazmanian. 2016. "Toward Sustainable Production: Finding Workable Strategies for Government and Industry." In *Environmental Policy*, 9th edn, edited by Norman J. Vig and Michael E. Kraft, 239–264. Washington, DC: CQ Press.

Press, Daniel, and Nicole Nakagawa. 2009. "Local Open-Space Preservation in the United States." In *Toward Sustainable Communities*, 2nd edn, edited by Daniel A. Mazmanian and Michael E. Kraft, 141–167. Cambridge, MA: MIT Press.

Princen, Thomas, Michael Maniates, and Ken Conca, eds. 2002. *Confronting Consumption*. Cambridge, MA: MIT Press.

Probst, Katherine N., and David M. Konisky (with Robert Hersh, Michael B. Batz, and Katherine D. Walker). 2001. *Superfund's Future: What Will It Cost?* Washington, DC: RFF Press.

Probst, Katherine N., and Adam I. Lowe. 2000. *Cleaning Up the Nuclear Weapons Complex: Does Anybody Care?* Washington, DC: Resources for the Future.

Probst, Katherine N., and Michael H. McGovern. 1998. *Long-Term Stewardship and the Nuclear Weapons Complex: The Challenge Ahead*. Washington, DC: Resources for the Future.

Putnam, Robert D. 2000. *Bowling Alone: The Collapse and Revival of American Community*. New York: Simon & Schuster.

Rabe, Barry G. 2004. *Greenhouse and Statehouse: The Emerging Politics of American Climate Change*. Washington, DC: Brookings Institution Press.

——. 2007. "Environmental Policy and the Bush Era: The Collision Between the Administrative Presidency and State Experimentation." *Publius: The Journal of Federalism* 37(3): 413–431.

——, ed. 2010. *Greenhouse Governance: Addressing Climate Change in America.* Washington, DC: Brookings Institution Press.

——. 2016. "Racing to the Top, the Bottom or the Middle of the Pack? The Evolving State Government Role in Environmental Protection." In *Environmental Policy*, 9th edn, edited by Norman J. Vig and Michael E. Kraft, 33–57. Washington, DC: CQ Press.

——. in press. *The Politics of Carbon Pricing.* Cambridge, MA: MIT Press.

Rabe, Barry G., and Christopher P. Borick. 2012. "Carbon Taxation and Policy Labeling: Experience from American States and Canadian Provinces." *Review of Policy Research* 29(3): 358–382.

Rabe, Barry G., and Marc Gaden. 2009. "Sustainability in a Regional Context: The Case of the Great Lakes Basin." In *Toward Sustainable Communities*, 2nd edn, edited by Daniel A. Mazmanian and Michael E. Kraft, 289–314. Cambridge, MA: MIT Press.

Rabe, Barry G., and Philip A. Mundo. 2007. "Business Influence in State-Level Environmental Policy." In *Business and Environmental Policy: Corporate Interests in the American Political System*, edited by Michael E. Kraft and Sheldon Kamieniecki, 265–297. Cambridge, MA: MIT Press.

Rahm, Dianne. 1998. "Controversial Cleanup: Superfund and the Implementation of U.S. Hazardous Waste Policy." *Policy Studies Journal* 26 (Winter): 719–734.

Raymond, Leigh. 2003. *Private Rights in Public Resources: Equity and Property Allocation in Market-Based Environmental Policy.* Washington, DC: RFF Press.

—— 2016. *Reclaiming the Atmospheric Commons: The Regional Greenhouse Gas Initiative and a New Model of Emissions Trading.* Cambridge, MA: MIT Press.

Regan, Patrick M. 2015. *The Politics of Global Climate Change.* New York: Routledge.

Reid, Walter V. 1997. "Strategies for Conserving Biodiversity." *Environment* 39 (September): 16–20, 39–43.

Renner, Michael. 2000. "Creating Jobs, Preserving the Environment." In *State of the World 2000*, edited by Lester R. Brown, Christopher Flavin, and Hilary French. Washington, DC: Worldwatch Institute.

Repetto, Robert, ed. 2006. *Punctuated Equilibrium and the Dynamics of U.S. Environmental Policy.* New Haven, CT: Yale University Press.

Riebsame, William. 1996. "Ending the Range Wars?" *Environment* 38 (May): 4–9, 27–29.

Rinfret, Sara R., and Scott R. Furlong. 2013. "Defining Environmental Rule Making." In *The Oxford Handbook of U.S. Environmental Policy*, edited by Sheldon Kamieniecki and Michael E. Kraft, 372–393. New York: Oxford University Press.

Ringquist, Evan J. 1993. *Environmental Protection at the State Level: Politics and Progress in Controlling Pollution.* Armonk, NY: M. E. Sharpe.

——. 1995. "Evaluating Environmental Policy Outcomes." In *Environmental Politics and Policy*, 2nd edn, edited by James P. Lester, 303–327. Durham, NC: Duke University Press.

——. 2006. "Environmental Justice: Normative Concerns, Empirical Evidence, and Government Action." In *Environmental Policy*, 6th edn, edited by Norman J. Vig and Michael E. Kraft, 239–263. Washington, DC: CQ Press.

Ringquist, Evan J., and Carl Dasse. 2004. "Lies, Damned Lies, and Campaign Promises? Environmental Legislation in the 105th Congress." *Social Science Quarterly* 85 (June): 400–419.

Ringquist, Evan J., Milena I. Neshkova, and Joseph Aamidor. 2013. "Campaign Promises, Democratic Governance, and Environmental Policy in the U.S. Congress." *Policy Studies Journal* 41(2): 365–387.

Roodman, David Malin. 1997. *Getting the Signals Right: Tax Reform to Protect the Environment and the Economy*. Washington, DC: Worldwatch Institute.

Rose, Jonathan F. P. 2016. *The Well-Tempered City: What Modern Science, Ancient Civilizations, and Human Nature Teach Us About the Future of Urban Life*. New York: Harper Wave.

Rosenbaum, Walter A. 2013a. "Capacity for Governance: Innovation and the Challenge of the Third Era." In *The Oxford Handbook of U.S. Environmental Policy*, edited by Sheldon Kamieniecki and Michael E. Kraft. New York: Oxford University Press.

——. 2013b. "Science, Politics, and Policy at the EPA." In *Environmental Policy*, 8th edn, edited by Norman J. Vig and Michael E. Kraft, 158–184. Washington, DC: CQ Press.

——. 2015. *American Energy: The Politics of 21st Century Policy*. Washington, DC: CQ Press.

Rothenberg, Lawrence S. 2002. *Environmental Choices: Policy Responses to Green Demands*. Washington, DC: CQ Press.

Rushefsky, Mark. 1986. *Making Cancer Policy*. Albany: State University of New York Press.

Russell, Clifford S. 1990. "Monitoring and Enforcement." In *Public Policies for Environmental Protection*, edited by Paul R. Portney, 243–274. Washington, DC: Resources for the Future.

Russell, Milton, E., William Colglazier, and Bruce E. Tonn. 1992. "The U.S. Hazardous Waste Legacy." *Environment* 34: 12–15, 34–39.

Sabatier, Paul A. 2007. *Theories of the Policy Process*, 2nd edn. Boulder, CO: Westview Press.

Sabatier, Paul A., Will Focht, Mark Lubell, Zev Trachtenberg, Arnold Vedlitz, and Marty Matlock, eds. 2005. *Swimming Upstream: Collaborative Approaches to Watershed Management*. Cambridge, MA: MIT Press.

Sachs, Jeffrey D. 2005. *The End of Poverty: Economic Possibilities for Our Time*. New York: Penguin Press.

——. 2015. *The Age of Sustainable Development*. New York: Oxford University Press.

Sagoff, Mark. 1988. *The Economy of the Earth*. Cambridge: Cambridge University Press.

Samet, Jonathan M., and John D. Spengler, eds. 1991. *Indoor Air Pollution: A Health Perspective*. Baltimore, MD: Johns Hopkins University Press.

Savas, E. S. 2000. *Privatization and Public–Private Partnerships*. London: Chatham House.

Schaefer, Mark, D. James Baker, John H. Gibbons, Charles G. Groat, Donald Kennedy, Charles F. Kennel, and David Rejeski. 2008. "An Earth Systems Science Agency." *Science* 321 (July 4): 44–45.

Schattschneider, E. E. 1960. *The Semi-Sovereign People: A Realist's View of Democracy in America*. New York: Holt, Rinehart and Winston.

Scheberle, Denise. 1998. "Partners in Policymaking: Forging Effective Federal-State Relations." *Environment* 40 (December): 14–20, 28–30.

———. 2004. *Federalism and Environmental Policy: Trust and the Politics of Implementation*, 2nd edn. Washington, DC: Georgetown University Press.

———. 2013. "Environmental Federalism and the Role of State and Local Governments." In *The Oxford Handbook of U.S. Environmental Policy*, edited by Sheldon Kamieniecki and Michael E. Kraft, 394–412. New York: Oxford University Press.

Schlozman, Kay Lehman, and John T. Tierney. 1986. *Organized Interests and American Democracy*. New York: Harper and Row.

Schneider, Anne L., and Helen Ingram. 1990. "Policy Design: Elements, Premises, and Strategies." In *Policy Theory and Policy Evaluation*, edited by Stuart S. Nagel, 77–102. Westport, CT: Greenwood Press.

———. 1997. *Policy Design for Democracy*. Lawrence: University of Kansas Press.

Schneider, Stephen H. 1990. "The Changing Climate." In *Managing Planet Earth*, edited by *Scientific American*, 25–36. New York: W. H. Freeman.

Schoenbrod, David. 2005. *Saving Our Environment from Washington: How Congress Grabs Power, Shirks Responsibility, and Shortchanges the People*. New Haven, CT: Yale University Press.

Sclove, Richard E. 1995. *Democracy and Technology*. New York: Guilford Press.

Seager, John, and Lee S. Polansky, eds. 2016. *The Good Crisis: How Population Stabilization Can Foster a Healthy U.S. Economy*. Washington, DC: Population Connection.

Selin, Henrik, and Stacy D. VanDeveer. 2006. "Raising Global Standards: Hazardous Substances and E-Waste Management in the European Union." *Environment* 48 (December): 7–18.

———. eds. 2009. *Changing Climates in North American Politics: Institutions, Policymaking and Multilevel Governance*. Cambridge, MA: MIT Press.

———. 2015. "Broader, Deeper and Greener: European Union Environmental Politics, Policies, and Outcomes." *Annual Review of Environment and Resources* 40: 309–335.

———. 2016. "Global Climate Change Governance: The Long Road to Paris." In *Environmental Policy*, 9th edn, edited by Norman J. Vig and Michael E. Kraft, 288–310. Washington, DC: CQ Press.

Sexton, Ken. 1999. "Setting Environmental Priorities: Is Comparative Risk Assessment the Answer?" In *Better Environmental Decisions*, edited by Ken Sexton, Alfred A. Marcus, K. William Easter, and Timothy D. Burkhardt, 195–219. Washington, DC: Island Press.

Sexton, Ken, Alfred A. Marcus, K. William Easter, and Timothy D. Burkhardt, eds. 1999. *Better Environmental Decisions: Strategies for Governments, Businesses, and Communities*. Washington, DC: Island Press.

Shabecoff, Philip. 1993. *A Fierce Green Fire: The American Environmental Movement*. New York: Hill and Wang.

———. 2000. *Earth Rising: American Environmentalism in the 21st Century*. Washington, DC: Island Press.

Shaiko, Ronald G. 1999. *Voices and Echoes for the Environment: Public Interest Representation in the 1990s and Beyond*. New York: Columbia University Press.

Shanley, Robert A. 1992. *Presidential Influence and Environmental Policy*. Westport, CT: Greenwood Press.

Shapiro, Michael. 1990. "Toxic Substances Policy." In *Public Policies for Environmental Protection*, edited by Paul R. Portney, 195–241. Washington, DC: Resources for the Future.

Shipan, Charles R., and William R. Lowry. 2001. "Environmental Policy and Party Divergence in Congress." *Political Research Quarterly* 54 (June): 245–263.

Shogren, Jason F., eds. 2004. *Species at Risk: Using Economic Incentives to Shelter Endangered Species on Private Lands*. Austin: University of Texas Press.

Shrader-Frechette, K. S. 1991. *Risk and Rationality: Philosophical Foundations for Populist Reforms*. Berkeley: University of California Press.

——. 1993. *Burying Uncertainty: Risk and the Case against Geological Disposal of Nuclear Waste*. Berkeley: University of California Press.

Shulman, Seth. 2006. *Undermining Science: Suppression and Distortion in the Bush Administration*. Berkeley, CA: University of California Press.

Sigman, Hilary. 2000. "Hazardous Waste and Toxic Substance Policies." In *Public Policies for Environmental Protection*, 2nd edn, edited by Paul R. Portney and Robert N. Stavins, 215–259. Washington, DC: RFF Press.

Simon, Julian L. 1995. *The State of Humanity*. Oxford: Basil Blackwell.

Sinclair, Barbara. 2017. *Unorthodox Lawmaking: New Legislative Processes in the U.S. Congress*, 5th edn. Washington, DC: CQ Press.

Skocpol, Theda. 2013. "Naming the Problem: What It Will Take to Counter Extremism and Engage Americans in the Fight against Global Warming." Prepared for a Symposium on the Politics of America's Fight Against Global Warming, Harvard University.

Skocpol, Theda, and Morris P. Fiorina, eds. 1999. *Civic Engagement in American Democracy*. Washington, DC: Brookings Institution Press.

Slovic, Paul. 1987. "Perception of Risk." *Science* 236: 280–285.

——. 1993. "Perceived Risk, Trust, and Democracy." *Risk Analysis* 13: 675–682.

Smardon, Richard, and Brenda Nordenstam. 1998. "Adirondacks and Beyond: Understanding Air Quality and Ecosystem Relationships." *Environmental Science and Policy* (special issue) 1(3): 139–267.

Smil, Vaclav. 2003. *Energy at the Crossroads: Global Perspectives and Uncertainties*. Cambridge, MA: MIT Press.

——. 2013. *Harvesting the Biosphere: What We Have Taken from Nature*. Cambridge, MA: MIT Press.

Smith, Eric R. A. N. 2002. *Energy, the Environment, and Public Opinion*. Lanham, MD: Rowman and Littlefield.

Solomon, Barry D., and Russell Lee. 2000. "Emissions Trading Systems and Environmental Justice." *Environment* 42 (October): 32–45.

Soroos, Marvin. 2011. "Global Institutions and the Environment: An Evolutionary Perspective." In *The Global Environment*, 3rd edn, edited by Regina S. Axelrod, Stacy D. VanDeveer, and David L. Downie, 24–47. Washington, DC: CQ Press.

Speth, James Gustave. 2002. "A New Green Regime: Attacking the Root Causes of Global Environmental Deterioration." *Environment* 44 (September): 16–25.

——. 2003. "Perspectives on the Johannesburg Summit." *Environment* 45 (January/February): 24–29.

——. 2004. *Red Sky at Morning: America and the Crisis of the Global Environment*. New Haven, CT: Yale University Press.

——. 2008. *The Bridge at the Edge of the World: Capitalism, the Environment, and Crossing from Crisis to Sustainability*. New Haven, CT: Yale University Press.

Starke, Linda, ed. 2008. *State of the World 2008: Innovations for a Sustainable Economy*. New York: W. W. Norton.

——. 2012. *State of the World 2012: Moving Toward Sustainable Prosperity*. Washington, DC: Island Press.

Steinberg, Paul F. 2001. *Environmental Leadership in Developing Countries: Transnational Relations and Biodiversity Policy in Costa Rica and Bolivia*. Cambridge, MA: MIT Press.

——. 2015. *Who Rules the Earth? How Social Rules Shape Our Planet and Our Lives*. New York: Oxford University Press.

Steinberg, Paul F., and Stacy D. VanDeveer, eds. 2012. *Comparative Environmental Politics: Theory, Practice, and Prospects*. Cambridge, MA: MIT Press.

Stern, Nicholas. 2007. *The Economic of Climate Change: The Stern Review*. Cambridge: Cambridge University Press.

Stone, Deborah. 2012. *Policy Paradox: The Art of Political Decision Making*, 3rd edn. New York: W. W. Norton.

Susskind, Lawrence, and Alexis Schulman. 2013. "Environmental Policy Evaluation and the Prospects of Public Learning." In *The Oxford Handbook of U.S. Environmental Policy*, edited by Sheldon Kamienicki and Michael E. Kraft, 677–692. New York: Oxford University Press.

Swartzman, Daniel, Richard A. Liroff, and Kevin G. Croke, eds. 1982. *Cost–Benefit Analysis and Environmental Regulations: Politics, Ethics, and Methods*. Washington, DC: Conservation Foundation.

Switzer, Jacqueline Vaughn. 1997. *Green Backlash: The History and Politics of Environmental Opposition in the U.S.* Boulder, CO: Lynne Rienner.

Talberth, John. 2008. "A New Bottom Line for Progress." In *State of the World 2008*, edited by Linda Starke, 18–31. New York: W. W. Norton.

Terborgh, John. 1999. *Requiem for Nature*. Washington, DC: Island Press.

Thiele, Leslie Paul. 2016. *Sustainability*. Malden, MA: Polity Press.

Thomas, Craig W. 2003. *Bureaucratic Landscapes: Interagency Cooperation and the Preservation of Biodiversity*. Cambridge, MA: MIT Press.

Tierney, John, and William Frasure. 1998. "Culture Wars on the Frontier: Interests, Values, and Policy Narratives in Public Lands Politics." In *Interest Group Politics*, 5th edn, edited by Allan J. Cigler and Burdett A. Loomis, 303–325. Washington, DC: CQ Press.

Tietenberg, Tom, and Lynne Lewis. 2006. *Emissions Trading: Principles and Practices*, 2nd edn. Washington, DC: RFF Press.

——. 2016. *Environmental and Natural Resources Economics*, 10th edn. New York: Routledge.

Tilman, David. 1997. "Biodiversity and Ecosystem Functioning." In *Nature's Services*, edited by Gretchen C. Daily, 93–112. Washington, DC: Island Press.

Tobin, Richard J. 1990. *The Expendable Future: U.S. Politics and the Protection of Biological Diversity*. Durham, NC: Duke University Press.

——. 2016. "Environment, Population, and the Developing World." In *Environmental Policy*, 9th edn, edited by Norman J. Vig and Michael E. Kraft, 311–332. Washington, DC: CQ Press.

Tong, Rosemarie. 1986. *Ethics in Policy Analysis*. Englewood Cliffs, NJ: Prentice Hall.

United Nations. 1993. *Agenda 21: The United Nations Programme of Action from Rio*. New York: United Nations.

——. 2013. *World Population Policies 2011*. New York: United Nations.

——. 2015. *Shelter from the Storm: State of the World Population 2015*. New York: United Nations Population Fund. Available at: www.unfpa.org/

U.S. Department of Energy (U.S. DOE). 1998. *Energy in the United States: A Brief History and Current Trends*. Washington, DC: U.S. DOE, Energy Information Administration.

U.S. Environmental Protection Agency (U.S. EPA). 1987. *Unfinished Business: A Comparative Assessment of Environmental Problems*. Washington, DC: U.S. EPA, Office of Policy, Planning, and Evaluation.

——. 1990a. *Environmental Investments: The Cost of a Clean Environment. Report of the Administrator of the Environmental Protection Agency to the Congress of the United States*. Washington, DC: U.S. EPA.

——. 1990b. *Reducing Risk: Setting Priorities and Strategies for Environmental Protection*. Washington, DC: U.S. EPA, Science Advisory Board.

——. 1992a. *Environmental Equity: Reducing Risk for All Communities*, 2 vols. Washington, DC: U.S. EPA, Office of Policy, Planning, and Evaluation.

——. 1992b. *Framework for Ecological Risk Assessment*. Washington, DC: U.S. EPA, Office of Research and Development.

——. 1999. *Enforcement and Compliance Assurance FY98 Accomplishments Report*. Office of Enforcement and Compliance Assurance. Washington, DC: U.S. EPA, June.

——. 2002. *National Water Quality Inventory: 2000 Report to Congress*. Washington, DC: U.S. EPA, Office of Water Quality, August.

——. 2006. *Drinking Water and Health: What You Need to Know*. Washington, DC: U.S. EPA. Retrieved January 27, 2006 at: www.epa.gov/safewater/dwhealth. html.

——. 2009. *National Water Quality Inventory: 2004 Report to Congress*. Washington, DC: U.S. EPA, Office of Water Quality, January. Available at: www.epa.gov/owow/305b/2004 report/.

——. 2016. *Our Nation's Air: Status and Trends Through 2015*. Washington, DC: U.S. EPA, Office of Air Quality Standards and Planning, February. Retrieved September 12, 2016 at: https://gispub.epa.gov/air/trendsreport/2016/.

U.S. Fish and Wildlife Service. 2012. *Report to Congress on the Recovery of Threatened and Endangered Species: Fiscal Years 2009–2010*. Washington, DC: Fish and Wildlife Service, January.

U.S. Government Accountability Office (U.S. GAO). 1992. *Environmental Protection Issues, Transition Series*. Washington, DC: U.S. Government Printing Office.

——. 1994. *Water Subsidies: Impact of Higher Irrigation Rates on Central Valley Project Farmers*. Washington, DC: U.S. GAO.

——. 1997a. *Department of Energy: Contract Reform Is Progressing, But Full Implementation Will Take Years*. Washington, DC: U.S. GAO.

——. 1997b. *Land Management Agencies: Major Activities at Selected Units Are Not Common Across Agencies*. Washington, DC: U.S. GAO.

——. 2002. *DOE Contractor Management: Opportunities to Promote Initiatives That Could Reduce Support-Related Costs*. Washington, DC: U.S. GAO, GAO-02-1000.

——. 2003. *Forest Service: Information on Appeals and Litigation Involving Fuels Reduction Activities*. Washington, DC: U.S. GAO, GAO-04-52.

——. 2005a. *National Energy Policy: Inventory of Major Federal Energy Programs and Status of Policy Recommendations.* Washington, DC: U.S. GAO, GAO-05-379.

——. 2005b. *Nuclear Waste: Better Performance Reporting Needed to Assess DOE's Ability to Achieve the Goals of the Accelerated Cleanup Program.* Washington, DC: U.S. GAO, GAO-05-764.

——. 2005c. *Observations on EPA's Cost-Benefit-Analysis of Its Mercury Control Options.* Washington, DC: GAO, GAO-05-252.

——. 2006. *Endangered Species: Time and Costs Required to Recover Species Are Largely Unknown.* Washington, DC: U.S. GAO, GAO-06-463R.

——. 2007. *Restoration Is Moving Forward but Is Facing Significant Delays, Implementation Challenges, and Rising Costs.* Washington, DC: U.S. GAO, GAO-07-520.

——. 2008. *Environmental Enforcement: EPA Needs to Improve the Accuracy and Transparency of Measures Used to Report on Program Effectiveness.* Washington, DC: U.S. GAO, GAO-08-111R.

——. 2009. *Information on State Royalties and the Number of Abandoned Mine Sites and Hazards.* Washington, DC: U.S. GAO, GAO-09-854T.

——. 2011. *Information on the Number of Hardrock Mines, Cost of Cleanup, and Value of Financial Assurances.* Washington, DC: U.S. GAO, GAO-11-834T.

U.S. National Intelligence Council. 2012. *Global Trends 2030: Alternative Worlds.* Washington, DC: National Intelligence Council.

U.S. Office of Technology Assessment. 1988. *Are We Cleaning up? 10 Superfund Case Studies.* Washington, DC: U.S. Government Printing Office.

——. 1991. *Complex Cleanup: The Environmental Legacy of Nuclear Weapons Production, Summary, OTA-0-485.* Washington, DC: U.S. Government Printing Office.

Vaughn, Jacqueline. 2004. *Environmental Politics: Domestic and Global Dimensions,* 4th edn. New York: Thomson Wadsworth.

Vaughn, Jacqueline, and Hanna Cortner. 2004. "Using Parallel Strategies to Promote Change: Forest Policymaking under George W. Bush." *Review of Policy Research* 21: 767–782.

Victor, David G. 2004. *The Collapse of the Kyoto Protocol and the Struggle to Slow Global Warming.* Princeton, NJ: Princeton University Press.

Vig, Norman J. 1994. "Presidential Leadership and the Environment: From Reagan and Bush to Clinton." In *Environmental Policy in the 1990s,* 2nd edn, edited by Norman J. Vig and Michael E. Kraft, 71–95. Washington, DC: CQ Press.

——. 2013. "The American Presidency and Environmental Policy." In *The Oxford Handbook of U.S. Environmental Policy,* edited by Sheldon Kamieniecki and Michael E. Kraft, 306–328. New York: Oxford University Press.

——. 2016. "Presidential Powers and Environmental Policy." In *Environmental Policy,* 8th edn, edited by Norman J. Vig and Michael E. Kraft, 84–108. Washington, DC: CQ Press.

Vig, Norman J., and Michael G. Faure, eds. 2004. *Green Giants? Environmental Policies of the United States and the European Union.* Cambridge, MA: MIT Press.

Vig, Norman J., and Michael E. Kraft, eds. 1984. *Environmental Policy in the 1980s: Reagan's New Agenda.* Washington, DC: CQ Press.

———. 2016. *Environmental Policy: New Directions for the Twenty-First Century*, 8th edn. Washington, DC: CQ Press.

Vogel, David. 2006. "International Trade and Environmental Regulation." In *Environmental Policy*, 6th edn, edited by Norman J. Vig and Michael E. Kraft, 354–373. Washington, DC: CQ Press.

———. 2012. *The Politics of Precaution: Regulating Health, Safety, and Environmental Risks in Europe and the United States*. Princeton, NJ: Princeton University Press.

Wackernagel, Mathis, and William Rees. 1996. *Our Ecological Footprint: Reducing Human Impact on the Earth*. Gabriola Island, BC, Canada: New Society.

Wang, Jinnan, Jintian Yang, Chazhong Ge, Dong Cao, and Jeremy Schreifels. 2004. "Controlling Sulfur Dioxide in China: Will Emissions Trading Work?" *Environment* 46 (June): 28–38.

Wapner, Paul. 1996. *Environmental Activism and World Civic Politics*. Albany: State University of New York Press.

Wargo, John. 1998. *Our Children's Toxic Legacy: How Science and Law Fail to Protect Us from Pesticides*, 2nd edn. New Haven, CT: Yale University Press.

Weber, Edward P. 1998. "Successful Collaboration: Negotiating Effective Regulations." *Environment* 40 (November): 10–15, 32–37.

———. 1999. *Pluralism by the Rules: Conflict and Cooperation in Environmental Regulation*. Washington, DC: Georgetown University Press.

———. 2003. *Bringing Society Back in: Grassroots Ecosystem Management, Accountability, and Sustainable Communities*. Cambridge, MA: MIT Press.

Weber, Edward P., David Bernell, and Hilary S. Boudet. 2016. "Energy Policy: Fracking, Renewables, and the Keystone XL Pipeline." In *Environmental Policy*, 9th edn, edited by Norman J. Vig and Michael E. Kraft, 172–193. Washington, DC: CQ Press/Sage.

Weimer, David L., and Aidan R. Vining. 2016. *Policy Analysis: Concepts and Practice*, 6th edn. New York: Routledge.

Weiss, Carol H. 1998. *Evaluation: Methods for Studying Programs and Policies*, 2nd edn. Upper Saddle River, NJ: Prentice Hall.

Weiss, Edith Brown, and Harold K. Jacobson. 1999. "Getting Countries to Comply with International Agreements." *Environment* 41 (July/August): 16–20, 37–45.

Wengert, Norman. 1994. "Land Use Policy." In *Encyclopedia of Policy Studies*, 2nd edn, edited by Stuart S. Nagel, 645–666. New York: Marcel Dekker.

Wenner, Lettie M. 1982. *The Environmental Decade in Court*. Bloomington: Indiana University Press.

Whitaker, John C. 1976. *Striking a Balance: Environment and Natural Resources Policy in the Nixon–Ford Years*. Washington, DC: American Enterprise Institute.

Whitford, Andrew B., and Karen Wong. 2009. "Political and Social Foundations for Environmental Sustainability." *Political Research Quarterly* 62(1) (March): 190–204.

Wiener, Jonathan B., Michael D. Rogers, James K. Hammitt, and Peter H. Sand, eds. 2010. *The Reality of Precaution: Comparing Risk Regulation in the United States and Europe*. Washington, DC: RFF Press.

Wildavsky, Aaron. 1988. *Searching for Safety*. New Brunswick, NJ: Transaction Books.

Wilson, Edward O. 1990. "Threats to Biodiversity." In *Managing Planet Earth*, edited by *Scientific American*, 49–59. New York: W. H. Freeman.

Wilson, James Q. 1980. "The Politics of Regulation." In *The Politics of Regulation*, edited by James Q. Wilson, 357–394. New York: Basic Books.

Wondolleck, Julia M., and Steven L. Yaffee. 2000. *Making Collaboration Work: Lessons from Innovation in Natural Resource Management*. Washington, DC: Island Press.

World Commission on Environment and Development. 1987. *Our Common Future*. New York: Oxford University Press.

Yaffee, Steven Lewis. 1994. *The Wisdom of the Spotted Owl: Policy Lessons for a New Century*. Washington, DC: Island Press.

Yandle, Bruce. 1999. *The Market Meets the Environment: Economic Analysis of Environmental Policy*. Lanham, MD: Rowman and Littlefield.

Young, Oran R., Leslie A. King, and Heike Schroeder, eds. 2008. *Institutions and Environmental Change: Principle Findings, Applications, and Research Frontiers*. Cambridge, MA: MIT Press.

INDEX

Locators in **bold** refer to tables and those in *italics* to figures.